Oxford Primary Dictionary

for East Africa

OXFORD
UNIVERSITY PRESS

OXFORD
UNIVERSITY PRESS

Great Clarendon Street, Oxford OX2 6DP

Oxford University Press is a department of the University of Oxford.
It furthers the University's objective of excellence in research, scholarship,
and education by publishing worldwide in

Oxford New York

Auckland Bangkok Buenos Aires Cape Town Chennai
Dar es Salaam Delhi Hong Kong Istanbul Karachi Kolkata
Kuala Lumpur Madrid Melbourne Mexico City Mumbai
Nairobi São Paulo Shanghai Taipei Tokyo Toronto

OXFORD and OXFORD ENGLISH are registered trademarks of
Oxford University Press in the UK and in certain other countries

© Oxford University Press 1999

Database right Oxford University Press (maker)

First published 1999
Tenth impression 2004

ISBN 0 19 431389 1

This dictionary includes some words which have or are asserted to have proprietary status as trademarks or
otherwise. Their inclusion does not imply that they have acquired for legal purposes a non-proprietary or
general significance nor any other judgement concerning their legal status In cases where the editorial staff
have some evidence that a word has proprietary status this is indicated in the entry for that word but no
judgement concerning the legal status of such words is made or implied thereby

Acknowledgements
Editorial team
Editor: Angela Crawley   Phonetics Editor: Michael Ashby
        James Greenan

Assistant Editor: Felicity Brooks   Compilers: Evadne Adrian-Vallance
                                                      Alice Deignan, Gary Dexter
                                                      Fiona MacKenzie

Consultants
Leah Kariuki, John Muitung'u (Kenya Institute of Education)
Febronia Mlekwa (Tanzania Institute of Education)
Gertrude Namu, Muriuki Njeru (OUP Kenya)
Gichema Wanjohi (Teachers' Service Commission, Nairobi)

Designers
Herb Bowes, Phil Hall

Illustrators
Anna Brookes, Martin Cox, Angelika Elsebach, Gay Galsworthy, Hardlines, Margaret Heath,
Richard Lewington, Vanessa Luff, Coral Mula, Oxford Illustrators, Martin Shovel, Harry Venning,
Margaret Wellbank, Michael Woods

We would like to thank the large team who made the production of this dictionary possible once the text was complete. Thanks
are also due to all the teachers and students who contributed comments and advice at various stages throughout the project

...ture and processing by Oxford University Press

Contents

A GUIDE TO THE DICTIONARY

Finding words and phrases

Words with the **same spelling** have different numbers.

Related words are given below the main word.

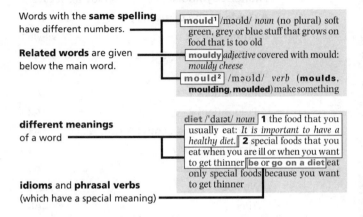

mould¹ /məʊld/ *noun* (no plural) soft green, grey or blue stuff that grows on food that is too old

mouldy *adjective* covered with mould: *mouldy cheese*

mould² /məʊld/ *verb* (**moulds, moulding, moulded**) make something

different meanings of a word

diet /'daɪət/ *noun* **1** the food that you usually eat: *It is important to have a healthy diet.* **2** special foods that you eat when you are ill or when you want to get thinner **be** or **go on a diet** eat only special foods because you want to get thinner

idioms and **phrasal verbs** (which have a special meaning)

Grammar

the **part of speech** (for example *noun*, *verb* or *adjective*)

the **forms of a verb**. We show the *he/she* form, the *-ing* form, the *past tense* (and the *past participle* at irregular verbs).

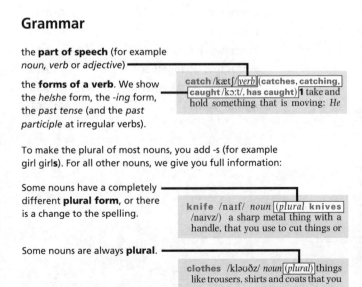

catch /kætʃ/ *verb* (**catches, catching, caught** /kɔːt/, **has caught**) **1** take and hold something that is moving: *He*

To make the plural of most nouns, you add -s (for example girl girl**s**). For all other nouns, we give you full information:

Some nouns have a completely different **plural form**, or there is a change to the spelling.

knife /naɪf/ *noun* (*plural* **knives** /naɪvz/) a sharp metal thing with a handle, that you use to cut things or

Some nouns are always **plural**.

clothes /kləʊðz/ *noun* (*plural*) things like trousers, shirts and coats that you

Sometimes a noun has **no plural** form and it cannot be used with *a* or *an*.

> **advice** /əd'vaɪs/ *noun* (no plural) words that you say to help somebody

a note giving information about **grammar**

> ✪ Be careful! You cannot say 'an advice'. You can say 'some advice' or 'a piece of advice': *I need some advice.* ○ *Let me give you a piece of advice.*

Comparative and **superlative** forms are given, unless they are formed with *more* and *most*.

> **funny** /'fʌni/ *adjective* (funnier, funniest) **1** a person or thing that is funny makes you laugh or smile

Understanding and using words

meaning

Example sentences help you to understand a word and show you how it is used.

pronunciation and **stress**

> **bus** /bʌs/ *noun* (plural buses) a thing like a big car, that carries a lot of people: *We went to town by bus.* ○ *Where do you get off the bus?*
> **bus-stop** /'bʌs stɒp/ *noun* a place where buses stop and people get on

related words

> **elephant** /'elɪfənt/ *noun* a very big wild animal from Africa or Asia, with a long nose (called a **trunk**) that hangs

The **opposites** of many words are given.

> **short** /ʃɔːt/ *adjective* (shorter, shortest) **1** very little from one end to the other: ○ *Her hair is very short.* ○ *We live a short distance from the beach.*
> ✪ opposite: long

vocabulary notes giving related words

> **lion** /laɪən/ *noun* a wild animal like a big cat with yellow fur. Lions live in Africa and parts of Asia.
> ✪ A female lion is called a **lioness** and a young lion is called a **cub**.

Some words are used only in special situations and there may be a word that is used more often, especially in speech.

> **purchase** /'pɜːtʃəs/ *verb* (purchases, purchasing, purchased /'pɜːtʃəst/) buy something: *The company has purchased three new shops.* ✪ **Buy** is the word that we usually use.

☛ tells you about a note or picture on a different page, or about a related word that you should look at.

Understanding and using words

DICTIONARY QUIZ

This quiz shows how the **Oxford Primary Dictionary for East Africa** can help you. You will find the answers to all these questions in the dictionary.

---

1 What metal do we get from **bauxite**?

2 What kind of animal is a **pupa**?

Meanings
The dictionary explains the meanings of words in simple language. The example sentences also help you to understand words and use them correctly. For more about this, look at page A16.

---

3 What is a young **goat** called?

4 What is the opposite of **wide**?

5 *I bought this book in the library.*
In this sentence, the word **library** is wrong. What is the right word?

Vocabulary
There are many notes (shown by ✪) that give useful extra vocabulary or show the differences between words.

The dictionary has a lot of pictures that help you understand words and that give extra vocabulary. As well as the pictures in the main part of the dictionary, there are special pages in the middle of the dictionary that have pictures showing things like The Human Body and Shapes and Sizes.

6 What is the name of the thick part of a **tree**, that grows up from the ground?

7 What is the name of this shape?

8 Is the word **lung** a noun, a verb or an adjective?

Grammar
You can check if a new word is a noun, a verb, an adjective, etc by looking in the dictionary.

9 Is it correct to say: Can you give me some **informations**?

The dictionary tells you about nouns. For example, it gives irregular and difficult noun plurals and tells you if a word cannot be used in the plural.

10 What is the past tense of the verb **break**?

The important verb forms are listed for each verb, and there is a list of irregular verbs with their past tenses and past participles on page 361.

11 What is the -ing form of the verb **hit**?

Spelling
You can use the dictionary to check how to spell a word, and it also shows small changes in the spelling of other forms of the word, for example the plurals of nouns and the -ing forms of verbs.

12 How do you spell the plural of **party**?

13 Do the words **peace** and **piece** have the same sound?

Pronunciation
The dictionary gives the pronunciation of words, and inside the front cover you will find help with reading the symbols.

14 How do you _say_ this **date**: 4 July 2010?

Extra information
The special pages in the middle also give useful information on topics like Dates, Numbers and Time.

a /ə/, /eɪ/ *article* **1** one or any: *Would you like a drink?* ○ *A dog has four legs.* ○ *He's a teacher.* **2** each, or for each: *She phones her mother three times a week.* ○ *These sweets cost 50 shillings a packet.*

> **a or an?**
>
> Before a word which starts with the sound of a, e, i, o or u, you use **an**, not **a**. Be careful! It is the sound that is important, not the spelling:
>
> | | |
> |---|---|
> | *a* box | *an* apple |
> | *a* singer | *an* hour |
> | *a* university | *an* MP |

abandon /ə'bændən/ *verb* (**abandons**, **abandoning**, **abandoned** /ə'bændənd/) **1** leave somebody or something completely: *He abandoned his car in the deep mud.* **2** stop doing something before it is finished: *When the storm started, we abandoned our game.*

abbey /'æbi/ *noun* (*plural* **abbeys**) a building where religious men or women (called **monks** and **nuns**) live or lived

abbreviate /ə'bri:vieɪt/ *verb* (**abbreviates**, **abbreviating**, **abbreviated**) make a word shorter by not saying or writing some of the letters: *The word 'telephone' is often abbreviated to 'phone'.*

abbreviation /ə,bri:vi'eɪʃn/ *noun* a short form of a word: *TV is an abbreviation for 'television'.*

ability /ə'bɪləti/ *noun* (*plural* **abilities**) the power and knowledge to do something: *She has the ability to pass the exam, but she must work harder.*

able /'eɪbl/ *adjective* **be able to** have the power and knowledge to do something: *Will you be able to come to the party?* ○ *Is Simon able to swim?* ☞ Look at **can**.

aboard /ə'bɔːd/ *adverb, preposition* on or onto a ship, train, bus or an aeroplane: *Are all the passengers aboard the ship?* ○ *We went aboard the plane.*

abolish /ə'bɒlɪʃ/ *verb* (**abolishes**, **abolishing**, **abolished** /ə'bɒlɪʃt/) stop or end something by law: *The Americans abolished slavery in 1863.*

abolition /,æbə'lɪʃn/ *noun* (no plural) *the abolition of hunting*

about /ə'baʊt/ *preposition, adverb* **1** a little more or less than; a little before or after: *She's about 50 years old.* ○ *I arrived at about two o'clock.* **2** of; on the subject of: *a book about cats* ○ *We talked about the problem.* ○ *What are you thinking about?* **3** in or to different places or in different directions: *The children were running about in the road.* ○ *There were books lying about on the floor.* **4** almost: *Dinner is about ready.* **5** in a place; here: *Is your mother about? I want to speak to her.* **be about to** be going to do something very soon: *The film is about to start.*

above /ə'bʌv/ *preposition, adverb* **1** in or to a higher place; higher than somebody or something: *I looked up at the sky above.* ○ *The office is above a shop.* ○ *There is a sign on the wall above the door.* ☞ picture on page A1. **2** more than a number or price: *children aged ten and above* **above all** more than any other thing; what is most important: *He's handsome and intelligent and, above all, he's kind!*

abroad /ə'brɔːd/ *adverb* in or to another country: *Would you like to go abroad to work?* ○ *She lives abroad.*

absence /'æbsəns/ *noun* (no plural) a time when a person or thing is not there: *I am doing Julie's job in her absence.*

absent /'æbsənt/ *adjective* not there; away: *He was absent from work yesterday because he was ill.*

absolute /'æbsəluːt/ *adjective* complete: *I've never played chess before. I'm an absolute beginner.*

absolutely *adverb* completely: *You're absolutely right.*

absorb /əbˈsɔːb/ *verb* (**absorbs**, **absorbing**, **absorbed** /əbˈsɔːbd/) take in something like liquid or heat, and hold it: *The dry ground absorbed all the rain.*

abstract /ˈæbstrækt/ *adjective* **1** about an idea, not a real thing: *abstract thought* **2** not like a real thing: *an abstract painting*

absurd /əbˈsɜːd/ *adjective* so silly that it makes you laugh: *You look absurd in that hat!* ○ *Don't be absurd! Of course I don't want to marry him!*

abuse /əˈbjuːz/ *verb* (**abuses**, **abusing**, **abused** /əˈbjuːzd/) **1** use something in a wrong or bad way: *The manager often abuses her power.* **2** be cruel or unkind to somebody: *The children were abused by their father.* **3** say rude things to somebody

abuse /əˈbjuːs/ *noun* (no plural) **1** using something in a wrong or bad way: *drug abuse* **2** being cruel or unkind to somebody: *child abuse* **3** rude words: *The driver shouted abuse at me.*

acacia /əˈkeɪʃə/ *noun* a kind of tree that grows in hot places, with small leaves and often with a flat top

accent /ˈæksent/ *noun* **1** the way a person from a certain place or country speaks a language: *She speaks English with an American accent.* **2** saying one word or part of a word more strongly than another: *In the word 'because', the accent is on the second part of the word.*

accept /əkˈsept/ *verb* (**accepts**, **accepting**, **accepted**) **1** say 'yes' when somebody asks you to have or do something: *I accepted the invitation to his party.* ○ *Please accept this present.* **2** believe that something is true: *She can't accept that her son is dead.*

acceptable /əkˈseptəbl/ *adjective* allowed by most people; good enough: *It's not acceptable to make so many mistakes.*

access /ˈækses/ *noun* (no plural) a way to go into a place or to use something: *The flying doctor visits villages that have no access to a hospital.* ○ *Do you have access to a computer at school?*

accident /ˈæksɪdənt/ *noun* something that happens by chance: *I had an accident when I was driving to work – my* car *hit a tree.* ○ *I'm sorry I broke your watch – it was an accident.* **by accident** by chance; not because you have planned it: *I took Jane's book by accident. I thought it was mine.*

accidental /ˌæksɪˈdentl/ *adjective* If something is accidental, it happens by chance: *accidental death*

accidentally /ˌæksɪˈdentəli/ *adverb*: *He accidentally broke the window.*

accommodation /əˌkɒməˈdeɪʃn/ *noun* (no plural) a place to stay or live: *It's difficult to find cheap accommodation in Mombasa.*

accompany /əˈkʌmpəni/ *verb* (**accompanies**, **accompanying**, **accompanied** /əˈkʌmpənid/) **1** go with somebody to a place: *Two teachers accompanied the class on their walk.* **2** happen at the same time as something else: *Thunder is usually accompanied by lightning.* **3** play music while somebody sings or plays another instrument: *You sing and I'll accompany you on the guitar.*

accord /əˈkɔːd/ *noun* (no plural) **of your own accord** because you want to, not because somebody has asked you: *She left the job of her own accord.*

according to /əˈkɔːdɪŋ tə/ *preposition* as somebody or something says: *According to Mike, this film is really good.* ○ *It's going to rain today, according to the newspaper.*

account /əˈkaʊnt/ *noun* **1** words that somebody says or writes about something that happened: *He gave the police an account of the car accident.* **2** an amount of money that you keep in a bank: *I paid the money into my bank account.* **3** **accounts** (plural) lists of all the money that a person or business receives and pays: *Who keeps (= does) the accounts for your business?* **on no account**, **not on any account** not for any reason: *On no account must you open this door.* **take account of something**, **take something into account** remember something when you are thinking about other things: *John is always last, but you must take his age into account – he is much younger than the other children.*

accountant /əˈkaʊntənt/ *noun* a

person whose job is to make lists of all the money that people or businesses receive and pay: *Susan is an account-ant.*

accurate /'ækjərət/ *adjective* exactly right; with no mistakes: *He gave an accurate description of the thief.* ✪ opposite: **inaccurate**

accurately *adverb*: *The map was accurately drawn.*

accuse /ə'kju:z/ *verb* (**accuses, accusing, accused** /ə'kju:zd/) say that somebody has done something wrong: *The police accused the woman of stealing.* ○ *He was accused of murder.*

accusation /,ækju'zeɪʃn/ *noun*: *The accusations were not true.*

ace /eɪs/ *noun* a playing-card which has only one shape on it: *the ace of hearts*

ache /eɪk/ *verb* (**aches, aching, ached** /eɪkt/) give you pain: *My legs ached after the long walk.*

ache *noun* a pain that lasts for a long time: *I've got a headache.* ○ *She's got toothache.* ○ *stomach-ache* ○ *earache*

achieve /ə'tʃi:v/ *verb* (**achieves, achieving, achieved** /ə'tʃi:vd/) do or finish something well after trying hard: *He worked hard and achieved his aim of becoming a doctor.*

achievement /ə'tʃi:vmənt/ *noun* something that somebody has done after trying hard: *Winning an Olympic gold medal was his greatest achievement.*

acid /'æsɪd/ *noun* a liquid that can burn things

acid rain /,æsɪd 'reɪn/ *noun* (no plural) rain that has chemicals in it from factories, for example. It can damage trees, rivers and buildings.

acknowledge /ək'nɒlɪdʒ/ *verb* (**acknowledges, acknowledging, acknowledged** /ək'nɒlɪdʒd/) **1** agree that something is true: *He acknowledged that he had made a mistake.* **2** say or write that you have received something: *She never acknowledged my letter.*

acquaintance /ə'kweɪntəns/ *noun* a person that you know a little

acquire /ə'kwaɪə(r)/ *verb* (**acquires,** **acquiring, acquired** /ə'kwaɪəd/) get or buy something: *He acquired some French from listening to the radio.*

acre /'eɪkə(r)/ *noun* a measure of land (= 0·405 of a hectare): *a farm of 40 acres*

acrobat /'ækrəbæt/ *noun* a person who does difficult movements of the body, for example in a **circus**

across /ə'krɒs/ *adverb, preposition* **1** from one side to the other side of something: *We walked across the field.* ☛ picture on page A2. **2** on the other side of something: *There is a bank across the road.* **3** from side to side: *The river is two kilometres across.*

act¹ /ækt/ *verb* (**acts, acting, acted**) **1** do something, or behave in a certain way: *Doctors acted quickly to save the boy's life after the accident.* ○ *Stop acting like a child!* **2** pretend to be somebody else in a play, film or television programme **act as something** do the job of another person, usually for a short time: *He acted as manager while his boss was ill.*

act² /ækt/ *noun* **1** something that you do: *an act of kindness* **2** one part of a play: *This play has five acts.* **3** a law that a government makes **in the act of** while doing something wrong: *I caught him in the act of stealing the money.*

acting /'æktɪŋ/ *noun* (no plural) being in plays or films: *Have you ever done any acting?*

action /'ækʃn/ *noun* **1** (no plural) doing things: *Now is the time for action!* ○ *I like films with a lot of action in them.* **2** (*plural* **actions**) something that you do: *The little girl copied her mother's actions.* **in action** doing something; working: *We watched the machine in action.*

active /'æktɪv/ *adjective* If you are active, you are always busy and able to do a lot of things: *My grandmother is 75 but she's still very active.* **in the active** where the person or thing doing the action is the subject of a sentence or verb: *In the sentence 'A girl broke the window', the verb is in the active.* ✪ opposite: **passive**

activity /æk'tɪvəti/ *noun* **1** (no plural) a lot of things happening and people doing things: *On the day of the festival there was a lot of activity in the streets.* **2** (*plural* **activities**) something that you do: *Fishing is one of his favourite activities.*

actor /'æktə(r)/ *noun* a person who acts in plays, films or television programmes

actress /'æktrəs/ *noun* (*plural* **actresses**) a woman who acts in plays, films or television programmes

actual /'æktʃuəl/ *adjective* that really happened; real: *We thought the bus would cost about 300 shillings, but the actual fare was much more.*

actually /'æktʃuəli/ *adverb* **1** really; in fact: *We thought it was going to rain, but actually it was sunny all day.* **2** a word that you use to disagree politely or when you say something new: *'Let's go by bus.' 'Actually, I think it would be quicker to go by train.'* ○ *I don't agree. I thought the film was very good, actually.*

AD /ˌeɪ 'diː/ *'AD'* in a date shows that it was after Christ was born: *AD 1066* ☞ Look at **BC**.

ad /æd/ *short for* **advertisement**

adapt /ə'dæpt/ *verb* (**adapts**, **adapting**, **adapted**) **1** change the way that you do things because you are in a new situation: *He has adapted very well to being at a new school.* **2** change something so that you can use it in a different way: *The car was adapted for use as a taxi.*

add /æd/ *verb* (**adds**, **adding**, **added**) **1** put something with something else: *Mix the flour with the milk and then add the eggs.* ○ *Add your name to the list.* **2** put numbers together: *If you add 2 and 5 together, you get 7.* ☼ opposite: **subtract** **3** say something more: *'Go away – and don't come back again,' she added.*

addict /'ædɪkt/ *noun* a person who cannot stop wanting something that is very bad for him/her: *a drug addict*

addicted /ə'dɪktɪd/ *adjective* not able to stop wanting something that is bad for you: *He is addicted to heroin.*

addition /ə'dɪʃn/ *noun* **1** (no plural) putting numbers together: *We learnt addition and subtraction at primary school.* **2** (*plural* **additions**) a thing or person that you add to other things or people: *They have a new addition to their family* (= a new baby). **in addition** also: *She plays the guitar, and in addition she writes her own songs.* **in addition to something** as well as: *He speaks five languages in addition to English.*

address /ə'dres/ *noun* (*plural* **addresses**) the number of the house and the name of the street and town where somebody lives or works: *Their address is 18 Mashundu Road, Nairobi.* ○ *Are you still living at that address?* ☞ picture on page A13

address *verb* (**addresses**, **addressing**, **addressed** /ə'drest/) write on a letter or parcel the name and address of the person you are sending it to: *The letter was addressed to James Odenda.*

adequate /'ædɪkwət/ *adjective* enough for what you need: *They are very poor and do not have adequate food or clothing.* ☼ opposite: **inadequate**

adjective /'ædʒɪktɪv/ *noun* a word that you use with a noun, that tells you more about it: *In the sentence 'This soup is hot', 'hot' is an adjective.*

adjust /ə'dʒʌst/ *verb* (**adjusts**, **adjusting**, **adjusted**) make a small change to something, to make it better: *You can adjust the height of this chair.*

administration /ədˌmɪnɪ'streɪʃn/ *noun* (no plural) controlling or managing something, for example a business, an office or a school

admiral /'ædmərəl/ *noun* a very important officer in the navy

admire /əd'maɪə(r)/ *verb* (**admires**, **admiring**, **admired** /əd'maɪəd/) think or say that somebody or something is very good: *I really admire you for doing such a difficult job.* ○ *They were admiring the view from the top of the hill.*

admiration /ˌædmə'reɪʃn/ *noun* (no plural) *I have great admiration for her work.*

admission /əd'mɪʃn/ *noun* (no plural) **1** letting somebody go into a place: *There is no admission to the park after 8 p.m.* **2** the money that you pay to go into a place: *Admission to the stadium is 750 shillings.*

admit /əd'mɪt/ *verb* (**admits**, **admitting**, **admitted**) **1** say that you have done something wrong: *He admitted stealing the money.* ○ *I admit that I made a mistake.* ✪ opposite: **deny 2** let somebody or something go into a place: *This ticket admits one person to the museum.*

adopt /ə'dɒpt/ *verb* (**adopts**, **adopting**, **adopted**) take the child of another person into your family to become your own child: *They adopted Stephen after his parents died.*

adore /ə'dɔː(r)/ *verb* (**adores**, **adoring**, **adored** /ə'dɔːd/) love somebody or something very much: *She adores her grandchildren.*

adult /'ædʌlt/ *noun* a person or an animal that has grown to the full size; not a child: *Adults as well as children will enjoy this film.*
adult *adjective*: *an adult ticket*

advance /əd'vɑːns/ *noun* (no plural) **in advance** before something happens: *We paid for the tickets in advance.*

advanced /əd'vɑːnst/ *adjective* of or for somebody who is already good at something; difficult: *an advanced English class*

advantage /əd'vɑːntɪdʒ/ *noun* something that helps you or that is useful: *When you're travelling in West Africa, it's a great advantage if you speak French.* ○ *One advantage of solar power is that it's cheap.* ✪ opposite: **disadvantage**. **take advantage of something** use something to help yourself: *Buy now and take advantage of these special prices!*

adventure /əd'ventʃə(r)/ *noun* something exciting that you do or that happens to you: *She wrote a book about her adventures as a journalist.*

adventurous /əd'ventʃərəs/ *adjective* An adventurous person likes to do exciting, dangerous things.

adverb /'ædvɜːb/ *noun* a word that tells you how, when or where something happens: *In the sentence 'Please speak slowly','slowly' is an adverb.*

advertise /'ædvətaɪz/ *verb* (**advertises**, **advertising**, **advertised** /'ædvətaɪzd/) give people information on posters, in newspapers, on television, etc about jobs, things to buy or events to go to: *That drink is advertised on the radio.* ○ *We sold our car by advertising it in the newspaper.*

advertisement /əd'vɜːtɪsmənt/ *noun* information on a poster, in a newspaper or on television that tells you about a job, something to buy or an event to go to: *I saw an advertisement for a cheap pick-up in the newspaper.* ✪ The short form is **advert** /'ædvɜːt/ or **ad**.

advertising /'ædvətaɪzɪŋ/ *noun* (no plural) telling people about things to buy: *He works in advertising.* ○ *The magazine gets a lot of money from advertising.*

advice /əd'vaɪs/ *noun* (no plural) words that you say to help somebody decide what to do: *He will give you advice about where to go.* **take somebody's advice** do what somebody says you should do: *I took the doctor's advice and stayed in bed.* ✪ Be careful! You cannot say 'an advice'. You can say 'some advice' or 'a piece of advice': *I need some advice.* ○ *Let me give you a piece of advice.*

advise /əd'vaɪz/ *verb* (**advises**, **advising**, **advised** /əd'vaɪzd/) tell somebody what you think they should do: *The doctor advised him to stop smoking.*

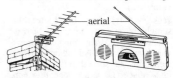

aerial /'eəriəl/ *noun* a wire that receives radio or television signals

aeroplane

aeroplane /'eərəpleɪn/ *noun* a machine that has wings and can fly ✪ An aeroplane (or **plane**) **lands** and **takes off** at an **airport**.

aerosol /ˈeərəsɒl/ *noun* a can with liquid in it. You press a button to make the liquid come out in a lot of very small drops.

affair /əˈfeə(r)/ *noun* **1** something that happens; an event: *The wedding was a very quiet affair.* **2** something that you need to do or think about; business: *Don't worry about that — it's not your affair.* ○ *foreign affairs*

affect /əˈfekt/ *verb* (**affects**, **affecting**, **affected**) make something different: *Smoking can affect your health.*

affection /əˈfekʃn/ *noun* (no plural) the feeling of loving or liking somebody: *She has great affection for her aunt.*

affectionate /əˈfekʃənət/ *adjective* that feels or shows love: *She gave him an affectionate kiss.*

affectionately *adverb*: *He smiled at his son affectionately.*

afford /əˈfɔːd/ *verb* (**affords**, **affording**, **afforded**) **can afford something** If you can afford something, you have enough money to pay for it: *I can't afford to buy a motorbike.*

afraid /əˈfreɪd/ *adjective* If you are afraid of something, it makes you feel fear: *Some people are afraid of snakes.* ○ *I was afraid to open the door.* **I'm afraid...** a polite way of saying that you are sorry: *I'm afraid I've lost your key.* ○ *I'm afraid that I can't come to your party.*

after[1] /ˈɑːftə(r)/ *preposition* **1** later than somebody or something: *Jane arrived after dinner.* ○ *After doing my homework, I went out.* **2** behind or following somebody or something: *Ten comes after nine.* ○ *Close the door after you.* **3** trying to get or catch somebody or something: *The police officer ran after her.* **after all 1** when you thought something different would happen: *I was worried about the exam, but it wasn't difficult after all.* **2** do not forget: *She doesn't understand. After all, she's only two.*

after[2] /ˈɑːftə(r)/ *conjunction, adverb* at a time later than somebody or something: *We arrived after the meeting had started.* ○ *Jane left at ten o'clock and I left soon after.*

afternoon /ˌɑːftəˈnuːn/ *noun* the part of a day between midday and the evening: *We had lunch and in the afternoon we went for a walk.* ○ *I saw Jane this afternoon.* ○ *Yesterday afternoon I went shopping.* ○ *I'll see you on Monday afternoon.*

afterwards /ˈɑːftəwədz/ *adverb* later: *We had dinner and went out to see a film afterwards.*

again /əˈgen/ *adverb* **1** one more time; once more: *Could you say that again, please?* ○ *I will never see him again.* **2** in the way that somebody or something was before: *You'll soon feel well again.* **again and again** many times: *I've told you again and again not to do that!*

against /əˈgenst/ *preposition* **1** on the other side in a game, fight, etc: *They played against a football team from another village.* **2** If you are against something, you do not like it: *Many people are against the plan.* **3** next to and touching somebody or something: *Put the cupboard against the wall.* ☛ picture on page A1. **4** to stop something: *Have you had an injection against the disease?*

age /eɪdʒ/ *noun* **1** (*plural* **ages**) the amount of time that somebody or something has been in the world: *She is seven years of age.* ○ *I started work at the age of 16.* ✪ When you want to ask about somebody's age, you usually say 'How old are you?' **2** (no plural) being old: *Her hair was grey with age.* **3** (*plural* **ages**) a certain time in history: *the Stone Age* (= when people used stone tools) **4** **ages** (plural) a very long time: *We waited ages for a bus.* ○ *She's lived here for ages.*

aged /eɪdʒd/ *adjective* at the age of: *They have two children, aged three and five.*

agency /ˈeɪdʒənsi/ *noun* (*plural* **agencies**) the work or office of somebody who does business for others: *A travel agency arranges travel for people.*

agent /ˈeɪdʒənt/ *noun* a person who does business for another person or for a company: *An actor's agent tries to find work for actors and actresses.* ○ *a travel agent*

age-set /ˈeɪdʒ set/ *noun* in some societies, a group of boys who are about the same age

aggressive /əˈgresɪv/ *adjective* If you are aggressive, you are ready to argue or fight: *He often gets aggressive after drinking alcohol.*

ago /əˈgəʊ/ *adverb* before now; in the past: *His wife died five years ago.* ○ *I learned to drive a long time ago.* **long ago** a very long time in the past: *Long ago there were no cars or aeroplanes.*

agony /ˈægəni/ *noun* (*plural* **agonies**) very great pain: *He screamed in agony.*

agree /əˈgriː/ *verb* (**agrees**, **agreeing**, **agreed** /əˈgriːd/) **1** have the same idea as another person about something: *Martin thinks we should sell our car but I don't agree.* ○ *I agree with you.* ✪ opposite: **disagree 2** say 'yes' when somebody asks you to do something: *Ann agreed to give me the money.* **3** decide something with another person: *We agreed to meet on March 3rd.* ○ *Eva and I agreed on a plan.*

agreement /əˈgriːmənt/ *noun* **1** (*plural* **agreements**) a plan or decision that two or more people or countries have made together: *There is a trade agreement between the two countries* (= they have agreed to buy things from and sell things to each other). **2** (no plural) having the same ideas as somebody or something: *We talked about which film we wanted to see, but there was not much agreement.* ✪ opposite: **disagreement**

agriculture /ˈægrɪkʌltʃə(r)/ *noun* (no plural) keeping animals and growing plants for food; farming

  agricultural /ˌægrɪˈkʌltʃərəl/ *adjective*: *agricultural workers*

ahead /əˈhed/ *adverb* **1** in front of somebody or something: *We could see a light ahead of us.* **2** into the future: *We must look ahead and make a plan.* **3** doing better than other people: *Grace is ahead of the other students in her class.* **go ahead** do something that you want to do; start to do something: *'Can I borrow your bicycle?' 'Yes, go ahead.'*

aid /eɪd/ *noun* (no plural) help, or something that gives help: *He walks with the aid of a stick.* ○ *The government sent aid to the victims of the earthquake.* ○ *a hearing aid* (= a small thing that you

put in your ear so you can hear better) **in aid of somebody** or **something** to get money for somebody or something: *There was a concert in aid of the new hospital.*

AIDS /eɪdz/ *noun* (no plural) a serious illness that stops the body protecting itself against diseases: *He contracted AIDS last year.*

aim[1] /eɪm/ *verb* (**aims**, **aiming**, **aimed** /eɪmd/) **1** point something, for example a gun, at somebody or something that you want to hit: *The farmer aimed his gun at the lion and fired.* **2** want or plan to do something: *He's aiming to leave at nine o'clock.* **3** plan something for a certain person or group: *This book is aimed at teenagers.*

  aim *noun* something that you want and plan to do: *Lucy's aim is to find a good job.*

air /eə(r)/ *noun* (no plural) **1** what you take in through your nose and mouth when you breathe **2** the space around and above things: *He threw the ball up in the air.* **by air** in an aircraft: *It's more expensive to travel by air than by train.* **on the air** on the radio or on television: *The programme will go on the air next month.*

air-conditioning /ˈeə kənˌdɪʃnɪŋ/ *noun* (no plural) a way of keeping the air in a building dry and not too hot

  air-conditioned /ˈeə kənˌdɪʃnd/ *adjective* with air-conditioning: *an air-conditioned office*

aircraft /ˈeəkrɑːft/ *noun* (*plural* **aircraft**) a machine that can fly, for example an aeroplane or a helicopter

air force /ˈeə fɔːs/ *noun* the aircraft that a country uses for fighting, and the people who fly them

air-hostess /ˈeə həʊstəs/ *noun* (*plural* **air-hostesses**) a woman whose job is to look after people on an aeroplane: *Alison is an air-hostess.*

airline /ˈeəlaɪn/ *noun* a company with aeroplanes that carry people or goods: *Lufthansa is a German airline.*

airmail /ˈeəmeɪl/ *noun* (no plural) a way of sending letters and parcels by aeroplane: *an airmail letter*

airport /ˈeəpɔːt/ *noun* a place where people get on and off aeroplanes, with buildings where passengers can wait: *I'll meet you at the airport.*

airstrip /ˈeəstrɪp/ *noun* a piece of land where aeroplanes can take off and land

aisle /aɪl/ *noun* a way between lines of seats, for example in a church or theatre

alarm[1] /əˈlɑːm/ *noun* **1** (no plural) a sudden feeling of fear: *He heard a noise, and jumped out of bed in alarm.* **2** (*plural* **alarms**) something that tells you about danger, for example by making a loud noise: *When the thieves broke the window, the alarm went off.* **3** an alarm clock

alarm[2] /əˈlɑːm/ *verb* (**alarms**, **alarming**, **alarmed** /əˈlɑːmd/) make somebody or something suddenly feel afraid or worried: *The noise alarmed the bird and it flew away.* ○ *She was alarmed to hear that Peter was ill.*

alarm clock /əˈlɑːm klɒk/ *noun* a clock that makes a noise to wake you up

alarm clock

album /ˈælbəm/ *noun* **1** a cassette, compact disc or record with about 50 minutes of music on it: *Have you heard this album?* ☛ Look at **single**. **2** a book with empty pages where you can put photographs or stamps, for example: *a photograph album*

alcohol /ˈælkəhɒl/ *noun* (no plural) **1** the liquid in drinks, for example wine, beer or whisky, that can make people feel drunk **2** drinks like wine, beer or whisky

alcoholic /ˌælkəˈhɒlɪk/ *adjective*: *an alcoholic drink*

ale /eɪl/ *noun* (no plural) beer ✪ **Beer** is the word that we usually use.

alert[1] /əˈlɜːt/ *adjective* awake and ready to do things: *A good driver is always alert.*

alert[2] /əˈlɜːt/ *noun* a warning of danger: *a malaria alert*

alien /ˈeɪliən/ *noun* a person or an animal that comes from another planet in space

alight /əˈlaɪt/ *adjective* on fire; burning: *A fire started in the kitchen and soon the whole house was alight.* **set something alight** make something start to burn: *The petrol was set alight by a cigarette.*

alike /əˈlaɪk/ *adjective* almost the same; not different: *The two sisters are very alike.*

alike *adverb* in the same way: *The twins always dress alike* (= wear the same clothes).

alive /əˈlaɪv/ *adjective* living; not dead: *Are your grandparents alive?*

all[1] /ɔːl/ *adjective, pronoun* **1** every one of a group: *All cats are animals but not all animals are cats.* ○ *I invited thirty people to the party, but not all of them came.* ○ *Are you all listening?* **2** every part of something; the whole of something: *She's eaten all the bread.* ○ *It rained all day.*

all[2] /ɔːl/ *adverb* completely: *She lives all alone.* ○ *He was dressed all in black.* **all along** from the beginning: *I knew all along that she was lying.*

alley /ˈæli/ *noun* (*plural* **alleys**) a narrow path between two buildings

alliance /əˈlaɪəns/ *noun* an agreement between countries or people to work together and help each other

alligator /ˈælɪɡeɪtə(r)/ *noun* a big long animal with sharp teeth. Alligators live in and near rivers.

allow /əˈlaʊ/ *verb* (**allows**, **allowing**, **allowed** /əˈlaʊd/) say that somebody can have or do something: *My parents allow me to stay out late at weekends.* ○ *Smoking is not allowed in most cinemas.* ○ *You're not allowed to park your car here.*

all right /ˌɔːl ˈraɪt/ *adjective* **1** good or good enough: *Is everything all right?* **2** well; not hurt: *I was ill, but I'm all right now.* **3** yes, I agree: *'Let's go home now.' 'All right.'*

ally /ˈælaɪ/ *noun* (*plural* **allies**) a person or country that agrees to help another person or country, for example in a war

almost /ˈɔːlməʊst/ *adverb* nearly; not quite: *It's almost three o'clock.* ○ *I almost fell into the river!*

alone /əˈləʊn/ *adverb* **1** without any

other person: *I don't like being alone in the house.* ○ *My grandmother lives alone.* **2** only: *You alone can help me.*

along[1] /ə'lɒŋ/ *preposition* **1** from one end of something towards the other end: *We walked along the road.* ☞ picture on page A2 **2** in a line next to something long: *There are trees along the river bank.*

along[2] /ə'lɒŋ/ *adverb* **1** forward: *He drove along very slowly.* **2** with me, you, etc: *We're going to the cinema. Why don't you come along too?*

alongside /ə'lɒŋsaɪd/ *preposition* next to something: *Put your bike alongside mine.*

aloud /ə'laʊd/ *adverb* speaking so that other people can hear: *I read the story aloud to my sister.*

alphabet /'ælfəbet/ *noun* all the letters of a language: *The English alphabet starts with A and ends with Z.*

alphabetical /ˌælfə'betɪkl/ *adjective* in the order of the alphabet: *Put these words in alphabetical order* (= with words beginning with A first, then B, then C, etc).

already /ɔːl'redi/ *adverb* before now or before then: *'Would you like something to eat.' 'No, thank you — I've already eaten.'* ○ *We ran to the station but the train had already left.*

already and **yet**

Yet means the same as **already**, but you only use it in negative sentences and in questions:

*I have finished this book **already**.*
*I haven't finished this book **yet**.*
*Have you finished this book **yet**?*

alright /ˌɔːl'raɪt/ = **all right**

also /'ɔːlsəʊ/ *adverb* as well; too: *She's the fastest runner in the school and she's also very clever.*

alter /'ɔːltə(r)/ *verb* (**alters**, **altering**, **altered** /'ɔːltəd/) **1** become different; change **2** make something different; change something: *These trousers are too long — I'm going to alter them* (= make them shorter by sewing).

alteration /ˌɔːltə'reɪʃn/ *noun* a small change

alternate /ɔːl'tɜːnət/ *adjective* first one and then the other: *I do the cooking on alternate days* (= Monday I do it, Tuesday I don't, Wednesday I do, Thursday I don't, etc).

alternative[1] /ɔːl'tɜːnətɪv/ *adjective* different; other: *The main road is closed so we'll have to use an alternative route.*

alternative[2] /ɔːl'tɜːnətɪv/ *noun* a thing that you can choose instead of another thing: *We could go by train — the alternative is to take two buses.*

although /ɔːl'ðəʊ/ *conjunction* **1** in spite of something; though: *Although she was ill, she went to work.* ○ *I bought the shoes although they were expensive.* **2** but: *I think he's from Tunisia, although I'm not sure.*

altogether /ˌɔːltə'geðə(r)/ *adverb* **1** counting everything or everybody: *Chris gave me £3 and Simon gave me £4, so I've got £7 altogether.* **2** completely: *I don't altogether agree with you.*

aluminium /ˌæljə'mɪniəm/ *noun* (no plural) a light metal

aluminum /ə'luːmɪnəm/ *American English for* **aluminium**

always /'ɔːlweɪz/ *adverb* **1** at all times; every time: *I have always lived in this town.* ○ *The bus is always late.* **2** for ever: *I will always remember that day.* **3** again and again: *My sister is always borrowing my clothes!*

a.m. /ˌeɪ 'em/ You use 'am' after a time to show that it is between midnight and midday: *I start work at 9 am.* ✪ We use **pm** for times between midday and midnight.

am *form of* **be**

amateur /'æmətə(r)/ *noun* a person who does something because he/she enjoys it, but does not get money for it

amateur *adjective*: *an amateur photographer* ☞ Look at **professional**.

amaze /ə'meɪz/ *verb* (**amazes**, **amazing**, **amazed** /ə'meɪzd/) make somebody very surprised: *Omar amazed me by remembering my birthday.*

amazed *adjective* If you are amazed, you are very surprised: *I was amazed to see John — I thought he was in hospital.*

amazement /ə'meɪzmənt/ *noun* (no

plural) great surprise: *She looked at me in amazement.*

amazing *adjective* If something is amazing, it surprises you very much: *She told us an amazing story.*

amazingly *adverb*: *Rose plays the violin amazingly well.*

ambassador /æm'bæsədə(r)/ *noun* an important person who goes to another country and works there for the government of his/her own country: *the Ugandan Ambassador to Britain* ✪ An ambassador works in an **embassy**.

ambition /æm'bɪʃn/ *noun* **1** (no plural) a very strong wish to do well: *Agatha is intelligent, but she has no ambition.* **2** something that you want to do: *My ambition is to become a doctor.*

ambitious /æm'bɪʃəs/ *adjective* A person who is ambitious wants to do well.

ambulance /'æmbjələns/ *noun* a special vehicle that takes people who are ill or hurt to hospital

ammunition /ˌæmjə'nɪʃn/ *noun* (no plural) things that you throw or fire from a gun to hurt or damage people or things: *The plane was carrying ammunition to the soldiers.*

among /ə'mʌŋ/, **amongst** /ə'mʌŋst/ *preposition* **1** in the middle of: *The house stands among the trees.* ☞ picture on page A1 **2** for or by more than two things or people: *He divided the money amongst his six children.*

---

among or **between**?

We use **among** and **amongst** when we are talking about more than two people or things. If there are only two people or things, we use **between**:

Sarah and I divided the cake between us.

I was standing between Alice and Kathy.

---

amount[1] /ə'maʊnt/ *noun* how much there is of something: *He spent a large amount of money.*

amount[2] /ə'maʊnt/ *verb* (**amounts**, **amounting**, **amounted**) **amount to something** make a certain amount

when you put everything together: *The cost of the repairs amounted to 10 000 shillings.*

amp /æmp/ *noun* a measure of electricity

amplifier /'æmplɪfaɪə(r)/ *noun* an electrical machine that makes sounds louder

amuse /ə'mjuːz/ *verb* (**amuses**, **amusing**, **amused** /ə'mjuːzd/) **1** make somebody smile or laugh: *Karim's joke did not amuse his mother.* **2** keep somebody happy and busy: *We played games to amuse ourselves on the long journey.*

amusement /ə'mjuːzmənt/ *noun* (no plural) the feeling that you have when you think something is funny: *We watched in amusement as the dog chased its tail.*

amusing /ə'mjuːzɪŋ/ *adjective* Something that is amusing makes you smile or laugh: *an amusing story*

an /ən/, /æn/ *article* **1** one or any: *I ate an apple.* **2** each, or for each: *The car was going at 100 kilometres an hour.* ☞ Note at **a**.

anaesthetic /ˌænəs'θetɪk/ *noun* something that a doctor gives you so that you will not feel pain in an **operation**

ancestor /'ænsestə(r)/ *noun* Your ancestors are the people in your family who lived a long time before you: *My ancestors came from West Africa.*

anchor /'æŋkə(r)/ *noun* a heavy metal thing that you drop into the water from a boat to stop the boat moving away

ancient /'eɪnʃənt/ *adjective* very old; from a time long ago: *ancient buildings*

and /ənd/, /ænd/ *conjunction* a word that joins words or parts of sentences together: *day and night* ○ *They sang and danced all evening.* ○ *The cat was black and white.*

angel /'eɪndʒl/ *noun* a messenger that comes from God. In pictures, angels usually have wings.

anger /'æŋgə(r)/ *noun* (no plural) the strong feeling that you have when you are not pleased about something: *He was filled with anger when he saw the boy trying to steal his car.*

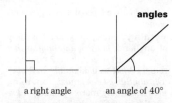

angles

a right angle   an angle of 40°

angle /ˈæŋgl/ *noun* the space where two lines that meet: *an angle of 40°*

angry /ˈæŋgri/ *adjective* (**angrier, angriest**) If you are angry, you feel or show anger: *My father was angry with me when I got home late.*

angrily /ˈæŋgrəli/ *adverb*: *'Somebody has taken my book!' she shouted angrily.*

animal /ˈænɪml/ *noun* **1** any living thing that is not a plant **2** any living thing that is not a bird, fish, insect, reptile or human: *Cats, sheep and rats are animals.*

ankle /ˈæŋkl/ *noun* the part of your leg where it joins your foot ☛ picture on page A4

anniversary /ˌænɪˈvɜːsəri/ *noun* (*plural* **anniversaries**) a day when you remember something special that happened on the same day in another year: *Today is their 25th wedding anniversary.*

announce /əˈnaʊns/ *verb* (**announces, announcing, announced** /əˈnaʊnst/) tell a lot of people about something important: *The teacher announced the winner of the competition.* ○ *She announced that she was going to have a baby.*

announcement /əˈnaʊnsmənt/ *noun* telling people about something: *I have an important announcement to make.*

announcer /əˈnaʊnsə(r)/ *noun* a person whose job is to tell us about programmes on radio or television

annoy /əˈnɔɪ/ *verb* (**annoys, annoying, annoyed** /əˈnɔɪd/) make somebody a little angry: *My brother annoys me when he leaves his clothes all over the floor.*

annoyance /əˈnɔɪəns/ *noun* (no plural) the feeling of being a little angry: *She could not hide her annoyance when I arrived late.*

annoyed *adjective* a little angry: *I was*

annoyed when he forgot to phone me. ○ *My dad is annoyed with me.*

annoying *adjective* If a person or thing is annoying, he/she/it makes you a little angry: *It's annoying when people don't listen to you.*

annual /ˈænjuəl/ *adjective* **1** that happens or comes once every year: *There is an annual meeting in June.* **2** for one year: *What is your annual income?* (= How much money do you get for one year's work?)

annually /ˈænjuəli/ *adverb*: *The company makes 50 000 cars annually.*

anonymous /əˈnɒnɪməs/ *adjective* **1** If a person is anonymous, other people do not know his/her name: *An anonymous caller told the police about the bomb.* **2** If something is anonymous, you do not know who did, gave or made it: *She received an anonymous letter.*

another /əˈnʌðə(r)/ *adjective, pronoun* **1** one more thing or person: *Would you like another drink?* ○ *I like these cakes — can I have another one?* **2** a different thing or person: *I can't see you tomorrow — can we meet another day?* ○ *I've read this book. Do you have another?*

answer¹ /ˈɑːnsə(r)/ *verb* (**answers, answering, answered** /ˈɑːnsəd/) **1** say or write something when somebody has asked a question: *I asked him if he was hungry but he didn't answer.* ○ *I couldn't answer all the exam questions.* **2** write a letter to somebody who has written to you: *She didn't answer my letter.* **answer the door** open the door when somebody knocks or rings: *Can you answer the door, please?* **answer the telephone** pick up the telephone when it rings, and speak

answer² /ˈɑːnsə(r)/ *noun* **1** something that you say or write when you answer somebody: *I asked Lucy a question but she didn't give me an answer.* ○ *Have you had an answer to your letter?* **2** a way of stopping a problem: *If you are tired, the answer is to go to bed early!*

answerphone /ˈɑːnsəfəʊn/, **answering machine** /ˈɑːnsərɪŋ məʃiːn/ *noun* a machine that answers the telephone for you and keeps messages so that you can listen to them later: *I left a message* *on the answerphone.*

ant /ænt/ *noun* a very small insect that lives in big groups

antelope /ˈæntɪləʊp/ *noun* a wild animal with horns and long thin legs, that can run fast

anthrax /ˈænθræks/ *noun* (no plural) a serious illness of cattle, sheep and sometimes humans. Anthrax harms the lungs and skin.

anti- /ˈænti/ *prefix*
anti- at the beginning of a word often means 'against':
an anti-smoking campaign

anticipate /ænˈtɪsɪpeɪt/ *verb* (**anticipates**, **anticipating**, **anticipated**) think that something will happen and be ready for it: *We didn't anticipate so many problems.*

anticlockwise /ˌæntɪˈklɒkwaɪz/ *adjective, adverb* When something moves anticlockwise, it moves in the opposite direction to the hands of a clock.

antique /ænˈtiːk/ *noun* an old thing that is worth a lot of money: *These chairs are antiques.*
antique *adjective*: *an antique vase*

anxiety /æŋˈzaɪəti/ *noun* (*plural* **anxieties**) a feeling of worry and fear

anxious /ˈæŋkʃəs/ *adjective* **1** worried and afraid: *She's anxious because her daughter hasn't arrived yet.* **2** If you are anxious to do something, you want to do it very much: *My family are anxious to meet you.*
anxiously *adverb*: *We waited very anxiously.*

any /ˈeni/ *adjective, pronoun* **1** a word that you use in questions and after 'not' and 'if'; some: *Have you got any money?* ○ *I don't speak any French.* ○ *She asked if I had any milk.* ○ *He needed medicine but there wasn't any.* **2** no special one: *Come any day next week.* ○ *Take any book you want.*
any *adverb* a little: *I can't walk any faster.*

anybody /ˈenibɒdi/, **anyone** /ˈeniwʌn/ *pronoun* **1** any person: *There wasn't anybody there.* ○ *Did you see anyone you know?* **2** no special person:

Anybody (= all people) *can play this game.*

anything /ˈeniθɪŋ/ *pronoun* **1** a thing of any kind: *Is there anything in that box?* ○ *I can't see anything.* **2** no special thing: *'What would you like to drink?' 'Oh, anything. I don't mind.'* **anything else** something more: *'Would you like anything else?' asked the waitress.* **anything like** the same as somebody or something in any way: *She isn't anything like her sister.*

anyway /ˈeniweɪ/, **anyhow** /ˈenihaʊ/ *adverb* **1** a word that you use when you give a second reason for something: *I don't want to see the film and anyhow I haven't got any money.* **2** no matter what is true; however: *It was very expensive but she bought it anyway.* **3** a word that you use when you start to talk about something different: *That's what John said. Anyway, how are you?*

anywhere /ˈeniweə(r)/ *adverb* **1** at, in or to any place: *Are you going anywhere nice?* ○ *I can't find my pen anywhere.* **2** no special place: *'Where shall I sit?' 'Oh, anywhere – it doesn't matter.'*

apart /əˈpɑːt/ *adverb* **1** away from the others; away from each other: *The two houses are 500 metres apart.* ○ *My mother and father live apart now.* **2** into parts: *He took my radio apart to repair it.* **apart from somebody** or **something** if you do not count somebody or something: *There were ten people in the room, apart from me.* ○ *I like all vegetables apart from carrots.*

apartment /əˈpɑːtmənt/ *American English for* **flat**

ape /eɪp/ *noun* an animal like a big monkey with no tail: *Gorillas and chimpanzees are apes.*

apologize /əˈpɒlədʒaɪz/ *verb* (**apologizes**, **apologizing**, **apologized** /əˈpɒlədʒaɪzd/) say that you are sorry about something that you have done: *I apologized to John for losing his book.*

apology /əˈpɒlədʒi/ *noun* (*plural* **apologies**) words that you say or write to show that you are sorry about something you have done: *Please accept my apologies.*

apostrophe /əˈpɒstrəfi/ *noun* the sign (') that you use in writing. You use it to show that you have left a letter out of a word, for example in 'I'm' (I am). You also use it to show that something belongs to somebody or something, for example in 'the boy's leg'.

appalling /əˈpɔːlɪŋ/ *adjective* very bad; terrible: *appalling cruelty*

apparent /əˈpærənt/ *adjective* easy to see or understand; clear: *It was apparent that she didn't like him.*

apparently *adverb* **1** You use 'apparently' to talk about what another person said, when you do not know if it is true: *Apparently, she has a big house and three cars.* **2** it seems: *He went to school today, so he's apparently feeling better.*

appeal[1] /əˈpiːl/ *verb* (**appeals, appealing, appealed** /əˈpiːld/) ask in a serious way for something that you want very much: *They appealed for food and clothing.* **appeal to somebody** please or interest somebody: *Living in a big city doesn't appeal to me.*

appeal[2] /əˈpiːl/ *noun* asking for something in a serious way: *They made an appeal for help.*

appear /əˈpɪə(r)/ *verb* (**appears, appearing, appeared** /əˈpɪəd/) **1** come and be seen: *The sun suddenly appeared from behind a cloud.* ○ *We waited for an hour but he didn't appear.* **2** seem: *It appears that I was wrong.*

appearance /əˈpɪərəns/ *noun* **1** the coming of somebody or something; when somebody or something is seen: *William's appearance at the meeting surprised everybody.* **2** what somebody or something looks like: *Her new glasses change her appearance.*

appetite /ˈæpɪtaɪt/ *noun* the feeling that you want to eat: *Swimming always gives me an appetite* (= makes me hungry).

applaud /əˈplɔːd/ *verb* (**applauds, applauding, applauded**) make a noise by hitting your hands together to show that you like something: *We all applauded loudly at the end of the song.*

applause /əˈplɔːz/ *noun* (no plural) when a lot of people hit their hands

together to show that they like something: *loud applause*

apple

apple /ˈæpl/ *noun* a hard round fruit

appliance /əˈplaɪəns/ *noun* a useful machine for doing something in the house: *Washing-machines and irons are electrical appliances.*

applicant /ˈæplɪkənt/ *noun* a person who asks for a job or a place at a university, for example: *There were six applicants for the job.*

application /ˌæplɪˈkeɪʃn/ *noun* writing to ask for something, for example a job

application form /ˌæplɪˈkeɪʃn fɔːm/ *noun* a special piece of paper that you write on when you are trying to get something, for example a job

apply /əˈplaɪ/ *verb* (**applies, applying, applied** /əˈplaɪd/) **1** write to ask for something: *Daniel has applied for a place at university.* **2** be about or be important to somebody or something: *This notice applies to all children over the age of twelve.*

appoint /əˈpɔɪnt/ *verb* (**appoints, appointing, appointed**) choose somebody for a job: *The bank has appointed a new manager.*

appointment /əˈpɔɪntmənt/ *noun* a time that you have fixed to meet somebody: *I've got an appointment with the doctor at ten o'clock.* ○ *You can telephone to make an appointment.*

appreciate /əˈpriːʃieɪt/ *verb* (**appreciates, appreciating, appreciated**) **1** understand and enjoy something: *Van Gogh's paintings were only appreciated after his death.* **2** understand something: *I appreciate your problem, but I can't help you.* **3** be pleased about something that somebody has done for you: *Thank you for your help. I appreciate it.*

appreciation /əˌpriːʃiˈeɪʃn/ *noun* (no plural) *We gave her some flowers to show our appreciation for her hard work.*

apprentice /əˈprentɪs/ *noun* a young person who is learning to do a job

approach[1] /əˈprəʊtʃ/ verb (approaches, approaching, approached /əˈprəʊtʃt/) come near or nearer to somebody or something: *When you approach the village, you will see a big house on your right.* ○ *I was approached by an old lady.* ○ *The exams were approaching.*

approach[2] /əˈprəʊtʃ/ noun **1** (no plural) coming near or nearer to somebody or something: *the approach of the rainy season* **2** (plural **approaches**) a way of doing something: *This is a new approach to treating Aids.*

appropriate /əˈprəʊpriət/ adjective right for that time, place or person; suitable: *Teaching would be an appropriate job for a lively girl like Joan.* ✪ opposite: **inappropriate**

approval /əˈpruːvl/ noun (no plural) showing or saying that somebody or something is good or right: *Vicky's parents gave the marriage their approval.*

approve /əˈpruːv/ verb (approves, approving, approved /əˈpruːvd/) think or say that something or somebody is good or right: *My parents don't approve of my friends.* ○ *She doesn't approve of smoking.* ✪ opposite: **disapprove**

approximate /əˈprɒksɪmət/ adjective almost correct but not exact: *The approximate time of arrival is three o'clock.*

approximately adverb about; not exactly: *I live approximately two kilometres from the station.*

apricot /ˈeɪprɪkɒt/ noun a small soft yellow fruit

April /ˈeɪprəl/ noun the fourth month of the year

apron /ˈeɪprən/ noun a thing that you wear over the front of your clothes to keep them clean, for example when you are cooking

arch /ɑːtʃ/ noun (plural **arches**) a part of a bridge, building or wall that is in the shape of a half circle

archaeology /ˌɑːkiˈɒlədʒi/ noun (no plural) the study of very old things like buildings and objects that are found in the ground

archbishop /ˌɑːtʃˈbɪʃəp/ noun a very important priest in the Christian church: *the Archbishop of Nairobi*

architect /ˈɑːkɪtekt/ noun a person whose job is to plan buildings

architecture /ˈɑːkɪtektʃə(r)/ noun (no plural) **1** planning and making buildings **2** the shape of buildings: *Do you like modern architecture?*

are form of **be**

area /ˈeəriə/ noun **1** a part of a town, country or the world: *Do you live in this area?* ○ *the desert areas of North Africa* **2** the size of a flat place. If a room is three metres wide and four metres long, it has an area of twelve square metres. **3** a space that you use for something special: *a warm-up area for athletes.*

aren't /ɑːnt/ = are not

argue /ˈɑːgjuː/ verb (argues, arguing, argued /ˈɑːgjuːd/) **1** say angrily to somebody because you do not agree: *My parents often argue about money.* ○ *I often argue with my brother.* **2** say why you think something is right or wrong: *Eriya argued that it would be unfair to report the boy to the police.*

argument /ˈɑːgjəmənt/ noun an angry talk between people with different ideas: *They had an argument about what kind of vehicle to buy.* ○ *I had an argument with my father.*

arithmetic /əˈrɪθmətɪk/ noun (no plural) working with numbers to find an answer

arm /ɑːm/ noun the part of your body from your shoulder to your hand: *Put your arms in the air.* ○ *He was carrying a book under his arm.* ☛ picture on page A4.

arm in arm with your arm holding another person's arm: *The two friends walked arm in arm.*

armchair

/ˈɑːmtʃeə(r)/ noun a soft chair with parts where you can put your arms: *She was asleep in an armchair.*

armed /ɑːmd/ adjective with a weapon, for example a gun: *an armed robber* ○

Are the police armed in your country?

the armed forces /ðɪ ˌɑːmd ˈfɔːsɪz/ *noun* the army, air force and navy

armour /ˈɑːmə(r)/ *noun* (no plural) metal clothes that men wore long ago to cover their bodies when they were fighting: *a suit of armour*

arms /ɑːmz/ *noun* (plural) guns, bombs and other weapons for fighting

army /ˈɑːmi/ *noun* (*plural* **armies**) a large group of soldiers who fight on land in a war: *He joined the army when he was 17.* ○ *the Egyptian Army*

around /əˈraʊnd/ *preposition, adverb* **1** in or to different places or in different directions: *We walked around for an hour looking for the street.* ○ *The children were running around the house.* ○ *Her clothes were lying around the room.* **2** on or to all sides of something, often in a circle: *We sat around the table.* ○ *He ran around the track.* ○ *There is a fence around the farm.* **3** in the opposite direction or in another direction: *Turn around and go back the way you came.* **4** a little more or less than; a little before or after: *We met at around seven o'clock.* **5** in a place; near here: *Is there a bank around here?* ○ *Is Angela around? I want to speak to her.*

arrange /əˈreɪndʒ/ *verb* (**arranges**, **arranging**, **arranged** /əˈreɪndʒd/) **1** make a plan for the future: *I have arranged to meet Ken at six o'clock.* ○ *We arranged a big party for Mr Dando's birthday.* **2** put things in a certain order or place: *Arrange the chairs in a circle.*

arrangement /əˈreɪndʒmənt/ *noun* **1** something that you plan or agree for the future: *They are making the arrangements for their wedding.* **2** a group of things put together so that they look nice: *a flower arrangement*

arrest /əˈrest/ *verb* (**arrests**, **arresting**, **arrested**) When the police arrest somebody, they make that person a prisoner because they think that he/she has done something wrong: *The thief was arrested yesterday.*

arrest *noun* arresting somebody: *The police made five arrests.* **be under arrest** be a prisoner of the police

arrival /əˈraɪvl/ *noun* coming to a place: *My brother met me at the airport on my arrival.* ☛ Look at **departure**.

arrive /əˈraɪv/ *verb* (**arrives**, **arriving**, **arrived** /əˈraɪvd/) **1** come to a place: *What time will we arrive in Dar es Salaam?* ○ *Has my letter arrived?* **2** come or happen: *The rainy season arrived early.*

arrogant /ˈærəgənt/ *adjective* A person who is arrogant thinks that he/she is better or more important than other people.

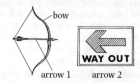

arrow 1   arrow 2

arrow /ˈærəʊ/ *noun* **1** a long thin piece of wood or metal with a point at one end. You shoot an arrow from a **bow**. **2** a sign in the shape of an arrow, that shows where something is or where you should go

arrowroot /ˈærəruːt/ *noun* (no plural) a plant with roots that we can eat or make into flour

art /ɑːt/ *noun* **1** (no plural) making beautiful things, like paintings and drawings **2** (no plural) beautiful things like paintings and drawings that somebody has made: *modern art* **3** **the arts** (plural) things like films, plays and literature: *How much money does the government spend on the arts?*

article /ˈɑːtɪkl/ *noun* **1** a piece of writing in a newspaper or magazine: *Did you read the article about tourism in yesterday's newspaper?* **2** a thing: *Many of the articles in the shop are half-price.* ○ *articles of clothing* (= things like skirts, socks and shirts) **3** The words 'a', 'an' and 'the' are called articles.

artificial /ˌɑːtɪˈfɪʃl/ *adjective* made by people; not natural: *an artificial leg*

artisan /ˌɑːtɪˈzæn/ *noun* a worker who is good at making things: *jua kali artisans*

artist /ˈɑːtɪst/ *noun* a person who

paints or draws pictures: *Yoweri is a good artist.*

artistic /ɑːˈtɪstɪk/ *adjective* good at painting, drawing or making beautiful things: *He's very artistic.*

as /əz/, /æz/ *conjunction, preposition* **1** while; at the same time that something is happening: *As I was going out, the telephone rang.* **2** because: *She didn't go to school as she was ill.* **3** in the same way; like: *Please do as I tell you!* **4** in the job of: *She works as a secretary for a big company.* **as ... as** words that you use to compare people or things; the same amount: *Paul is as tall as his father.* ○ *I don't work as hard as you.*

ash /æʃ/ *noun* (no plural) the grey stuff that you see after something has burned: *cigarette ash*

ashamed /əˈʃeɪmd/ *adjective* sorry and unhappy about something that you have done, or unhappy because you are not as good as other people in some way: *I was ashamed about lying to my parents.* ○ *She was ashamed of her son's behaviour.*

ashore /əˈʃɔː(r)/ *adverb* onto the land: *We left the boat and went ashore.*

ashtray /ˈæʃtreɪ/ *noun* a small dish for cigarette ash and the ends of cigarettes

aside /əˈsaɪd/ *adverb* on or to one side; away: *He put the letter aside while he did his homework.*

ask /ɑːsk/ *verb* (**asks**, **asking**, **asked** /ɑːskt/) **1** try to get an answer by using a question: *I asked him what the time was.* ○ *'What's your name?' she asked.* ○ *Meg asked the teacher a question.* ○ *I asked if I could go home early.* **2** say that you would like somebody to do something for you: *I asked Sara to help me cook.* **3** invite somebody: *Shariff has asked me to a party on Saturday.* **ask for somebody** say that you want to speak to somebody: *Phone this number and ask for Mrs Emoto.* **ask for something** say that you want somebody to give you something: *He asked his parents for a bicycle.*

askari /əsˈkɑːri/ *noun* an East African soldier or police officer, guard, etc

asleep /əˈsliːp/ *adjective* sleeping: *The*

baby is asleep in bed. ✪ opposite: **awake**. **fall asleep** start sleeping: *He fell asleep under a tree.*

aspect /ˈæspekt/ *noun* one part of a problem, idea, etc: *Spelling is one of the most difficult aspects of learning English.*

aspirin /ˈæsprɪn/ *noun* a medicine that stops pain: *I took two aspirins* (= two tablets of aspirin) *for my headache.*

assassinate /əˈsæsɪneɪt/ *verb* (**assassinates**, **assassinating**, **assassinated**) kill an important or famous person: *President Sadat was assassinated in 1981.*

assassination /ə,sæsɪˈneɪʃn/ *noun* killing an important or famous person

assault /əˈsɔːlt/ *verb* (**assaults**, **assaulting**, **assaulted**) suddenly start fighting or hurting somebody: *He assaulted a policeman.*

assault *noun*: *an assault on an old lady*

assembly /əˈsembli/ *noun* (*plural* **assemblies**) a meeting of a big group of people for a special reason: *Our school assembly* (= a meeting of all the students and teachers in the school) *is at 9.30 in the morning.*

assist /əˈsɪst/ *verb* (**assists**, **assisting**, **assisted**) help somebody: *The driver assisted her with her suitcases.*

assistance /əˈsɪstəns/ *noun* (no plural) help: *The agency offers assistance in finding a job.* ✪ **Help** is the word that we usually use.

assistant /əˈsɪstənt/ *noun* a person who helps: *Ms Njoro is not here today. Would you like to speak to her assistant?* ➥ Look also at **shop assistant**.

associate /əˈsəʊʃieɪt/ *verb* (**associates**, **associating**, **associated**) put two ideas together in your mind: *We usually associate Egypt with desert and pyramids.*

association /ə,səʊsiˈeɪʃn/ *noun* a group of people who join or work together for a special reason: *the Primary Teachers Association*

assume /əˈsjuːm/ *verb* (**assumes**, **assuming**, **assumed** /əˈsjuːmd/) think that something is true when you are not completely sure: *Rose is not here today, so I assume that she is ill.*

assure /əˈʃʊə(r)/ *verb* (**assures, assuring, assured** /əˈʃʊəd/) tell somebody what is true or certain so that they feel less worried: *I assure you that the dog isn't dangerous.*

astonish /əˈstɒnɪʃ/ *verb* (**astonishes, astonishing, astonished** /əˈstɒnɪʃt/) surprise somebody very much: *The news astonished everyone.*

astonished *adjective* If you are astonished, you are very surprised: *I was astonished when I heard that Winnie was getting married.*

astonishing *adjective* If something is astonishing, it surprises you very much: *astonishing news*

astonishment /əˈstɒnɪʃmənt/ *noun* (no plural) great surprise: *He looked at me in astonishment when I told him the news.*

astronaut /ˈæstrənɔːt/ *noun* a person who travels in a spaceship

astronomy /əˈstrɒnəmi/ *noun* (no plural) the study of the sun, moon, planets and stars

astronomer /əˈstrɒnəmə(r)/ *noun* a person who studies or knows a lot about astronomy

at /ət/, /æt/ *preposition* **1** a word that shows where somebody or something is: *They are at school.* ○ *Jane is at home.* ○ *The answer is at the back of the book.* **2** a word that shows when: *I go to bed at eleven o'clock.* ○ *At night you can see the stars.* ☛ Look at page A9. **3** towards somebody or something: *Look at the picture.* ○ *I smiled at her.* ○ *Somebody threw an egg at the President.* **4** a word that shows what somebody is doing or what is happening: *The two countries are at war.* **5** a word that shows how much, how fast, etc: *I bought two pencils at 10 shillings each.* **6** a word that shows how well somebody or something does something: *I'm not very good at maths.* **7** because of something: *We laughed at his jokes.*

ate *form of* eat

athlete /ˈæθliːt/ *noun* a person who is good at sports like running, jumping or throwing: *Athletes from all over the world go to the Olympic Games.*

athletics /æθˈletɪks/ *noun* (plural) sports like running, jumping or throwing

atlas /ˈætləs/ *noun* (*plural* **atlases**) a book of maps: *an atlas of the world*

atmosphere /ˈætməsfɪə(r)/ *noun* **1** (no plural) all the gases around the earth **2** (no plural) the air in a place: *a cool atmosphere* **3** (*plural* **atmospheres**) the feeling that places or people give you: *The atmosphere in the office was very friendly.*

atom /ˈætəm/ *noun* one of the very small things that everything is made of: *A molecule of water is made up of two atoms of hydrogen and one of oxygen.*

atomic /əˈtɒmɪk/ *adjective* **1** of or about atoms: *atomic physics* **2** using the great power that is made by breaking atoms: *an atomic bomb* ○ *atomic energy*

attach /əˈtætʃ/ *verb* (**attaches, attaching, attached** /əˈtætʃt/) join or fix one thing to another thing: *I attached the photo to the letter.* **be attached to somebody** or **something** like somebody or something very much: *He's very attached to you.*

attack /əˈtæk/ *verb* (**attacks, attacking, attacked** /əˈtækt/) start fighting or hurting somebody or something: *The army attacked the town.* ○ *The old man was attacked and his money was stolen.*

attack *noun* **1** trying to hurt somebody or something: *There was an attack on the President.* **2** a time when you are ill: *an attack of flu*

attempt /əˈtempt/ *verb* (**attempts, attempting, attempted**) try to do something: *He attempted to swim across the river.* ✪ **Try** is the word that we usually use.

attempt *noun*: *She made no attempt to help me.*

attend /əˈtend/ *verb* (**attends, attending, attended**) go to or be at a place where something is happening: *Did you attend the meeting?*

attention /əˈtenʃn/ *noun* (no plural) looking or listening carefully and with interest: *Can I have your attention, please?* (= please listen to me) **pay attention** look or listen carefully:

Please pay attention to what I'm saying.

attitude /'ætɪtjuːd/ *noun* the way you think or feel about something: *What's your attitude to marriage?*

attorney /ə'tɜːni/ *American English for* **lawyer**

attract /ə'trækt/ *verb* (**attracts**, **attracting**, **attracted**) **1** make somebody or something come nearer: *Magnets attract metal.* ○ *The birds were attracted by the smell of fish.* **2** make somebody like somebody or something: *He was attracted to her.*

attraction /ə'trækʃn/ *noun* **1** (*plural* **attractions**) something that people like and feel interested in: *Tanzania has a lot of tourist attractions, like Mount Kilimanjaro and the Serengeti National Park.* **2** (no plural) liking somebody or something very much; being liked very much: *I can't understand his attraction to her.*

attractive /ə'træktɪv/ *adjective* **1** A person who is attractive is nice to look at: *He's very attractive.* **2** Something that is attractive pleases you or interests you: *That's an attractive idea.* ○ opposite: **unattractive**

auction /'ɔːkʃn/ *noun* a sale where each thing is sold to the person who will give the most money for it

auction *verb* (**auctions**, **auctioning**, **auctioned** /'ɔːkʃnd/) sell something at an auction

audience /'ɔːdiəns/ *noun* all the people who are watching or listening to a film, play, concert or the television

August /'ɔːgəst/ *noun* the eighth month of the year

aunt /ɑːnt/ *noun* the sister of your mother or father, or the wife of your uncle ➡ picture on page A3

auntie /'ɑːnti/ *noun* aunt

authentic /ɔː'θentɪk/ *adjective* real and true: *He says that the painting is by a famous artist, but I don't believe that it's authentic.*

author /'ɔːθə(r)/ *noun* a person who writes books or stories: *Who is your favourite author?*

authority /ɔː'θɒrəti/ *noun* **1** (no plural) the power to tell people what they must do: *The police have the authority to stop*

cars. **2** (*plural* **authorities**) a group of people that tell other people what they must do: *the city authorities*

autobiography /ˌɔːtəbaɪ'ɒgrəfi/ *noun* (*plural* **autobiographies**) a book that a person has written about his/her life

autograph /'ɔːtəgrɑːf/ *noun* a famous person's name, that he/she has written: *He asked the singer for her autograph.*

automatic /ˌɔːtə'mætɪk/ *adjective* **1** If a machine is automatic, it can work by itself, without people controlling it: *an automatic washing-machine* **2** that you do without thinking: *Breathing is automatic.*

automatically /ˌɔːtə'mætɪkli/ *adverb*: *The security door closes automatically.*

automobile /'ɔːtəməbiːl/ *American English for* **car**

autumn /'ɔːtəm/ *noun* in cool countries, the part of the year between summer and winter: *In autumn, the leaves begin to fall from the trees.*

available /ə'veɪləbl/ *adjective* ready for you to use, have or see: *I'm sorry – the doctor is not available this afternoon.*

avenue /'ævənjuː/ *noun* a wide road or street: *The shop is in Nile Avenue.*

average /'ævərɪdʒ/ *noun* **1** (*plural* **averages**) a word that you use when you work with numbers: *The average of 2, 3 and 7 is 4* ($2 + 3 + 7 = 12$, and $12 \div 3 = 4$). **2** (no plural) what is ordinary or usual: *Soita's work at school is above average* (= better than the average).

average *adjective*: *The average age of the students is 19.*

avocado /ˌævə'kɑːdəʊ/ *noun* a soft green fruit with a hard skin and a large seed

avoid /ə'vɔɪd/ *verb* (**avoids**, **avoiding**, **avoided**) **1** stay away or go away from somebody or something: *We crossed the road to avoid the big dog.* **2** stop something from happening; try not to do something: *You should avoid wasting water.*

awake /ə'weɪk/ *adjective* not sleeping: *The children are still awake.* ○ opposite: **asleep**

award /ə'wɔːd/ *noun* a prize or money

that you give to somebody who has done something very well: *The company won a national award.*

award *verb* (**awards**, **awarding**, **awarded**) give a prize or money to somebody: *He was awarded first prize in the writing competition.*

aware /əˈweə(r)/ *adjective* If you are aware of something, you know about it: *I was aware that somebody was watching me.* ○ *He's not aware of the problem.* ✪ opposite: **unaware**

away /əˈweɪ/ *adverb* **1** to or in another place: *She ran away.* ○ *He put his books away.* **2** from a place: *The sea is two kilometres away.* **3** not here: *Awino is away from school today because she is*

ill. **4** in the future: *The holiday is only three weeks away.*

awful /ˈɔːfl/ *adjective* very bad: *The pain was awful.*

awfully /ˈɔːfli/ *adverb* very: *It was awfully hot.* ○ *I'm awfully sorry!*

awkward /ˈɔːkwəd/ *adjective* **1** difficult to do or use, for example: *This big box will be awkward to carry.* **2** not comfortable: *I felt awkward at the party because I didn't know anybody.* **3** difficult to please: *My son is very awkward. He never likes the food I give him.* **4** not able to move your body in an easy way: *He's very awkward when he dances.*

axe /æks/ *noun* a tool for cutting wood: *He chopped down the tree with an axe.*

Bb

baboon /bəˈbuːn/ *noun* a large monkey with big teeth

baby /ˈbeɪbi/ *noun* (*plural* **babies**) a very young child: *She's going to have a baby.*

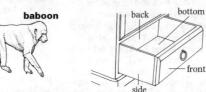

baboon

babysit /ˈbeɪbɪsɪt/ *verb* (**babysits**, **babysitting**, **babysat** /ˈbeɪbɪsæt/, **has babysat**) look after a child for a short time when the parents are not there

bachelor /ˈbætʃələ(r)/ *noun* **1** a man who has never married **2** a person who has finished studying at a university or college and who has a first **degree**: *a Bachelor of Science*

back[1] /bæk/ *noun* **1** the part that is behind or farthest from the front: *The answers are at the back of the book.* ○ *Write your address on the back of the cheque.* ○ *We sat at the back of the bus.* **2** the part of a person or an animal between the neck and the bottom: *He lay on his back and looked up at the sky.* ➥ picture on page A4

back to front with the back part in front **behind somebody's back** when somebody is not there, so that he/she does not know about it: *Don't talk about Daisy behind her back.*

back[2] /bæk/ *adjective* away from the front: *the back door*

back[3] /bæk/ *adverb* **1** away from the front: *I looked back to see if she was coming.* **2** in or to the place where somebody or something was before: *I'll be back* (= I will return) *at six o'clock.* ○ *Give the book back to me when you've read it.* ○ *We walked to the lake and back.* **3** as a way of returning or answering something: *He paid me the money back.* ○ *I wrote her a letter, but she didn't write back.* ○ *I was out when* *she phoned, so I phoned her back.* **back and forth** first one way and then the other, many times: *She travels back and forth between Nairobi and Kisumu.*

back⁴ /bæk/ *verb* (**backs**, **backing**, **backed** /bækt/) **1** move backwards or make something move backwards: *She backed the car into a parking space.* **2** say that you think that somebody or something is right or the best: *They're backing their school team.* **back away** move away backwards: *Ngatu backed away from the big dog.* **back out** not do something that you promised or agreed to do: *Kamal backed out of the game, so we only had ten players.*

backbone /ˈbækbəʊn/ *noun* the line of bones down the back of your body

background /ˈbækɡraʊnd/ *noun* the things at the back in a picture: *This is a photo of my house with the mountains in the background.* ✪ opposite: **foreground**

backstroke /ˈbækstrəʊk/ *noun* (no plural) a way of swimming on your back

backward /ˈbækwəd/ *adjective* towards the back: *a backward step*

backwards /ˈbækwədz/, **backward** /ˈbækwəd/ *adverb* **1** away from the front; towards the back: *He fell backwards and hit the back of his head.* **2** with the back or the end first: *If you say the alphabet backwards, you start with 'Z'.* **backwards and forwards** first one way and then the other way, many times: *The dog ran backwards and forwards.*

bacon /ˈbeɪkən/ *noun* (no plural) thin pieces of meat from a pig, that is prepared using salt or smoke ➡ Note at **pig**

bacteria /bækˈtɪərɪə/ *noun* (plural) very small things that live in air, water, earth, plants and animals. Some bacteria can make us ill.

bad /bæd/ *adjective* (**worse**, **worst**) **1** not good or nice: *The weather was very bad.* ○ *He's had some bad news – his uncle has died.* ○ *a bad smell* **2** serious: *She had a bad accident.* **3** not done or made well: *bad driving* **4** not able to work or do something well: *My eye-*

sight is bad. ○ *He's a bad teacher.* **5** too old to eat; not fresh: *bad eggs* **bad at something** If you are bad at something, you cannot do it well: *I'm very bad at sports.* **bad for you** If something is bad for you, it can make you ill: *Smoking is bad for you.* **go bad** become too old to eat: *This fish has gone bad.* **not bad** quite good: *'What was the film like?' 'Not bad.'* **too bad** words that you use to say that you cannot change something: *'I want to go out.' 'Too bad – you can't!'*

badge /bædʒ/ *noun* a small thing made of metal, plastic or cloth that you wear on your clothes. A badge can show that you belong to a school or club, for example, or it can have words or a picture on it: *Nyaboke sewed a badge on her guide's uniform.*

badly /ˈbædli/ *adverb* (**worse**, **worst**) **1** in a bad way; not well: *She played badly.* ○ *These clothes are badly made.* **2** very much: *He was badly hurt in the accident.* ○ *I badly need a holiday.*

badminton /ˈbædmɪntən/ *noun* (no plural) a game for two or four players who try to hit a kind of light ball with feathers on it (called a **shuttlecock**) over a high net, using **rackets**: *Do you want to play badminton?*

bad-tempered /ˌbæd ˈtempəd/ *adjective* often angry: *He's bad-tempered in the mornings.*

bag /bæɡ/ *noun* a thing made of cloth, paper, leather, etc. for holding and carrying things: *He put a spare shirt in his bag.* ○ *a plastic shopping bag* ➡ Look also at **carrier bag** and **handbag** and at the picture at **container**.

baggy /ˈbæɡi/ *adjective* If clothes are baggy, they are big and loose: *He was wearing baggy trousers.*

bake /beɪk/ *verb* (**bakes**, **baking**, **baked** /beɪkt/) cook food in an oven

baker /ˈbeɪkə(r)/ *noun* a person who makes and sells bread and cakes ✪ A shop that sells bread and cakes is called a **baker's** or a **bakery**.

balance¹ /ˈbæləns/ *verb* (**balances**, **balancing**, **balanced** /ˈbælənst/) make yourself or something stay without falling to one side or the other:

He balanced the bag on his head. ○ *She balanced on one leg.*

balance[2] /ˈbæləns/ *noun* **1** (no plural) when two sides are the same, so that something will not fall **2** (no plural) when two things are the same, so that one is not bigger or more important, for example: *You need a balance between work and play.* ✪ opposite: **imbalance 3** (*plural* **balances**) how much money you have or must pay after you have spent or paid some: *The machine costs 100 000 shillings. You can pay 10 000 now and the balance (= 90 000) over six months.*

keep your balance stay steady without falling: *He tried to keep his balance on the ice.* **lose your balance** become unsteady; fall: *She lost her balance and fell off her bike.*

balcony /ˈbælkəni/ *noun* (*plural* **balconies**) a small place on the outside wall of a building, above the ground, where you can stand or sit

bald /bɔːld/ *adjective* with no hair or not much hair: *My dad is going* (= becoming) *bald.* ☞ picture at **hair**

ball /bɔːl/ *noun* **1** a round thing that you use in games and sports: *Throw the ball to me.* ○ *a football* ○ *a tennis-ball* **2** any round thing: *a ball of string* ☞ picture on page A15

ballet /ˈbæleɪ/ *noun* a kind of dancing that tells a story with music but no words: *I went to see a ballet.* ○ *Do you like ballet?*

ballet dancer /ˈbæleɪ dɑːnsə(r)/ *noun* a person who dances in ballets

balloon /bəˈluːn/ *noun* **1** a small thing like a bag made of coloured rubber. You fill it with air or gas to make it big and round: *We are going to hang balloons around the room for the party.* **2** a very big bag that you fill with gas or air so that it can fly. People ride in a basket under it: *I would like to go up in a balloon.*

ballot /ˈbælət/ *noun* when people choose somebody or something by writing secretly on a piece of paper: *We held a ballot to choose a new chairman.*

ball-point /ˈbɔːl pɔɪnt/ *noun* a pen that has a very small ball at the end

ban /bæn/ *verb* (**bans**, **banning**, **banned** /bænd/) say that something must stop or must not happen: *The film was banned* (= people were not allowed to see it).

ban *noun: The council has imposed a ban on alcohol.*

banana /bəˈnɑːnə/ *noun* a long fruit with yellow or green skin

banana

band /bænd/ *noun* **1** a group of people who play music together: *a rock band* ○ *a jazz band* **2** a thin flat piece of material that you put around something: *I put a rubber band round the letters to keep them together.* ○ *The hat had a red band round it.*

bandage /ˈbændɪdʒ/ *noun* a long piece of white cloth that you put around a part of the body that is hurt

bandage *verb* (**bandages**, **bandaging**, **bandaged** /ˈbændɪdʒd/) put a bandage around a part of the body: *The doctor bandaged my foot.*

bandit /ˈbændɪt/ *noun* a person who attacks and robs people who are travelling: *They were killed by bandits in the mountains.*

bang[1] /bæŋ/ *noun* **1** a sudden very loud noise: *He shut the door with a bang.* **2** hitting somebody or something hard; being hit hard: *He fell and got a bang on the head.*

bang[2] /bæŋ/ *verb* (**bangs**, **banging**, **banged** /bæŋd/) make a loud noise by hitting something hard or by closing something: *He banged his head on the ceiling.* ○ *Don't bang the door!*

bank /bæŋk/ *noun* **1** a place that keeps money safe for people: *I've got 50 000 shillings in the bank.*

✪ If you have a bank **account**, you can **save** money, **pay** money **in** (or **deposit** it), or **draw** it **out** (or **withdraw** it). At a bank, you can also **exchange** the money of one country for the money of another. If you want to **borrow** money, a bank may **lend** it to you.

2 the land along the side of a river: *I climbed out of the boat onto the bank.*

banknote /ˈbæŋknəʊt/ *noun* a piece of paper money: *These are Egyptian banknotes.*

bankrupt /ˈbæŋkrʌpt/ *adjective* not able to pay the money that you should pay to people: *His business went* (= became) *bankrupt.*

banner /ˈbænə(r)/ *noun* a long piece of cloth with words on it. People carry banners to show what they think: *The banner said 'Stop the war'.*

baobab /ˈbeɪəbæb/ *noun* a kind of tree with a very thick trunk

baptize /bæpˈtaɪz/ *verb* (**baptizes**, **baptizing**, **baptized** /bæpˈtaɪzd/) put water on somebody or put somebody in water, and give them a name, to show that they belong to the Christian Church

baptism /ˈbæptɪzm/ *noun* a special time when somebody is baptized

bar[1] /bɑː(r)/ *noun* **1** a place where people can buy and have drinks and sometimes food: *There's a bar in the hotel.* ○ *a coffee bar* **2** a long table where you buy drinks in a bar or pub **3** a long piece of metal: *an iron bar* **4** a piece of something hard: *a bar of soap* ○ *a bar of gold* ☞ picture on page A15

bar[2] /bɑː(r)/ *verb* (**bars**, **barring**, **barred** /bɑːd/) put something across a place so that people cannot pass: *A line of police barred the road.*

barbecue /ˈbɑːbɪkjuː/ *noun* a party where you cook food on a fire outside: *We had a barbecue on the beach.*

barbed wire /ˌbɑːbd ˈwaɪə(r)/ *noun* (no plural) wire with a lot of sharp points on it. Some fences are made of barbed wire.

barber /ˈbɑːbə(r)/ *noun* a person whose job is to cut men's hair: *I went to the barber's* (= the barber's shop) *to have my hair cut.*

bare /beə(r)/ *adjective* **1** with no clothes or anything else covering it: *He had bare feet* (= he wasn't wearing shoes or socks). ○ *The walls were bare* (= with no pictures on them). **2** empty: *Everybody was buying the cheap coffee, and soon the shelves were bare.*

barefoot /ˈbeəfʊt/ *adjective, adverb* with no shoes or socks on your feet: *The children ran barefoot down the beach and into the sea.*

barely /ˈbeəli/ *adverb* almost not; only just: *She barely ate anything.*

bargain[1] /ˈbɑːgən/ *noun* something that is cheaper than usual: *This book was a bargain – it only cost 100 shillings.*

bargain[2] /ˈbɑːgən/ *verb* (**bargains**, **bargaining**, **bargained** /ˈbɑːgənd/) talk with somebody about the right price for something: *I think she'll sell the car for less if you bargain with her.*

barge /bɑːdʒ/ *noun* a long boat with a flat bottom for carrying things or people on rivers or canals

bark[1] /bɑːk/ *noun* (no plural) the stuff that covers the outside of a tree

bark[2] /bɑːk/ *noun* the short loud noise that a dog makes

bark *verb* (**barks**, **barking**, **barked** /bɑːkt/) make this noise: *The dog always barks at people it doesn't know.*

barley /ˈbɑːli/ *noun* (no plural) a plant that we use for food and for making beer and some other drinks

barman /ˈbɑːmən/ *noun* (plural **barmen** /ˈbɑːmən/) a man who sells drinks in a bar

barn /bɑːn/ *noun* a large building on a farm where you keep crops or animals

barometer /bəˈrɒmɪtə(r)/ *noun* an instrument that helps us to know what the weather will be like

barracks /ˈbærəks/ *noun* (plural) a building or group of buildings where soldiers live: *an army barracks*

barrel /ˈbærəl/ *noun* **1** a big container for liquids, with round sides and flat ends: *a barrel of oil* **2** the long metal part of a gun that a bullet goes through

barricade /ˌbærɪˈkeɪd/ *noun* a wall of things that people build quickly to stop other people going somewhere: *There was a barricade of lorries across the road.*

barricade *verb* (**barricades**, **barricading**, **barricaded**) stop people going somewhere by building a barricade: *He barricaded the door to keep the police out.*

barrier /ˈbæriə(r)/ *noun* a fence or gate that stops you going somewhere: *The car crashed into the safety barrier at the side of the road.*

barrow /ˈbærəʊ/ *noun* a small cart that you can push or pull

base[1] /beɪs/ *noun* **1** the bottom part of something; the part that something stands on: *The basket has a flat base.* **2** the place that you start from and go back to: *She travels all over the country but Nairobi is her base* (= the place where she lives). ○ *an army base*

base[2] /beɪs/ *verb* (**bases**, **basing**, **based** /beɪst/) **base something on something** make something, using another thing as an important part: *The film is based on a true story.*

baseball /ˈbeɪsbɔːl/ *noun* **1** (no plural) a game for two teams of nine players who try to hit a ball with a **bat** on a large field: *We played baseball in the park.* **2** (*plural* **baseballs**) a ball for playing this game

basement /ˈbeɪsmənt/ *noun* the part of a building that is under the ground

bases *plural of* **basis**

bash /bæʃ/ *verb* (**bashes**, **bashing**, **bashed** /bæʃt/) hit somebody or something very hard: *I fell and bashed my knee.*

basic /ˈbeɪsɪk/ *adjective* most important and necessary; simple: *A person's basic needs are food, clothes and a place to live.*

basically /ˈbeɪsɪkli/ *adverb* mostly; mainly: *Basically I like her, but I don't always agree with what she says.*

basin /ˈbeɪsn/ *noun* a round bowl for cooking or mixing food ☞ Look also at **wash-basin**.

basis /ˈbeɪsɪs/ *noun* (*plural* **bases** /ˈbeɪsiːz/) the most important part or idea, from which something grows: *Her notes formed the basis of a book.*

basket /ˈbɑːskɪt/ *noun* a container made of thin sticks or thin pieces of plastic or metal, that you use for holding or carrying things: *a shopping basket* ☞ Look also at **waste-paper basket**.

basket

basketball /ˈbɑːskɪtbɔːl/ *noun* **1** (no plural) a game for two teams of five players who try to throw a ball into a high net **2** (*plural* **basketballs**) a ball for playing this game

basketball

bass /beɪs/ *adjective* with a deep sound: *She plays the bass guitar.* ○ *a bass drum*

bat /bæt/ *noun* **1** an animal like a mouse with wings. Bats come out and fly at night. **2** a piece of wood for hitting the ball in a game like cricket or table tennis: *a baseball bat*

bat

batch /bætʃ/ *noun* (*plural* **batches**) a group of things: *She made a batch of cakes.*

bath /bɑːθ/ *noun* (*plural* **baths** /bɑːðz/) **1** a large thing that you fill with water and sit in to wash your body **2** washing your body in a bath: *I had a bath this morning.*

bathe /beɪð/ *verb* (**bathes**, **bathing**, **bathed** /beɪðd/) **1** wash a part of your body carefully: *He bathed the cut on his finger.* **2** swim in the sea or in a lake or river: *On hot days we often bathe in the lake.* ✪ It is more usual to say **go swimming**.

bathroom /ˈbɑːθruːm/ *noun* a room where you can wash and have a bath or shower

battery /ˈbætri/ *noun* (*plural* **batteries**) a thing that gives electricity. You put batteries inside things like torches and radios to make them work: *The car needs a new battery.*

battery

battle /ˈbætl/ *noun* **1** a fight between

armies in a war **2** trying very hard to do something difficult: *a battle against the illness*

battle *verb* (**battles**, **battling**, **battled** /'bætld/) try very hard to do something difficult: *The doctors battled to save her life.*

bauxite /'bɔːkseɪt/ *noun* (no plural) a kind of clay from which we get aluminium

bay /beɪ/ *noun* (*plural* **bays**) a place where the land goes inwards and the sea fills the space: *There was a ship in the bay.*

bazaar /bə'zɑː(r)/ *noun* a market in Asia or Africa

BC /ˌbiː'siː/ 'BC' in a date shows it was before Christ was born. ☞ Look at **AD**.

be /bi/, /biː/ *verb* **1** a word that you use when you name or describe somebody or something: *I'm* (= I am) *Ben.* ○ *Grass is green.* ○ *Are you hot?* ○ *Fred is a doctor.* ○ *Where were you yesterday?* ○ *It is six o'clock.* **2** happen: *Her birthday was in May.* **3** a word that you use with another verb: *'What are you doing?' 'I am reading.'* **4** a word that you use with part of another verb to show that something happens to somebody or something: *A lot of tea is grown in East Africa.* ○ *The airport was built in 1970.* **5** a word that shows that something must or will happen: *A new factory is to be built in Konza.*

beach /biːtʃ/ *noun* (*plural* **beaches**) a piece of land next to the sea that is covered with sand or stones: *a sandy beach*

bead /biːd/ *noun* a small ball of wood, glass or plastic with a hole in the middle. Beads are put on a string to make a necklace.

beak /biːk/ *noun* the hard pointed part of a bird's mouth ☞ picture at **bird**

beam /biːm/ *noun* **1** a long heavy piece of wood that holds up a roof or ceiling **2** a line of light: *the beams of a car's headlights*

bean /biːn/ *noun* the long thin part of some plants, or the seeds inside it, that we use as food: *green beans* ○ *coffee beans*

bean

bear[1] /beə(r)/ *noun* a big wild animal with thick fur ☞ Look also at **teddy bear**.

bear[2] /beə(r)/ *verb* (**bears**, **bearing**, **bore** /bɔː(r)/, **has borne** /bɔːn/) **1** have pain or problems without complaining: *The pain was difficult to bear.* **2** hold somebody or something up so that they do not fall: *The ice is too thin to bear your weight.* **can't bear something** hate something: *I can't bear this music.* ○ *He can't bear having nothing to do.*

---

be

present tense

		short forms	negative short forms
I	**am** /æm/	I**'m**	I**'m** not
you	**are** /ɑː(r)/	you**'re**	you **aren't**
he/she/it	**is** /ɪz/	he**'s**/she**'s**/it**'s**	he/she/it **isn't**
we	**are**	we**'re**	we **aren't**
you	**are**	you**'re**	you **aren't**
they	**are**	they**'re**	they **aren't**

past tense

I	**was** /wɒz/		*present participle* **being**
you	**were** /wɜː(r)/		*past participle* **been**
he/she/it	**was**		
we	**were**		
you	**were**		
they	**were**		

beard /bɪəd/ *noun* the hair on a man's chin and cheeks: *He has got a beard.*

beast /biːst/ *noun* a big animal ✪ **Animal** is the word that we usually use.

beat[1] /biːt/ *noun* a sound that comes again and again: *We heard the beat of the drums.* ○ *Can you feel her heartbeat?*

beat[2] /biːt/ *verb* (**beats**, **beating**, **beat**, **has beaten** /ˈbiːtn/) **1** win a fight or game against a person or group of people: *Daniel always beats me at wrestling* ○ *Our team was beaten.* **2** hit somebody or something very hard many times: *She beats her dog with a stick.* ○ *The rain was beating on the roof.* **3** make the same sound or movement many times: *His heart was beating fast.*

beautiful /ˈbjuːtəfl/ *adjective* very nice to see, hear or smell; lovely: *Those flowers are beautiful.* ○ *What a beautiful song!* ○ *a beautiful woman*

✪ When we talk about people, we usually use **beautiful** and **pretty** for women and girls, and **handsome** and **good-looking** for men and boys.

beauty /ˈbjuːti/ *noun* (no plural) being beautiful: *the beauty of the mountains*

because /bɪˈkɒz/ *conjunction* for the reason that: *He was angry because I was late.* **because of something** as a result of something: *We stayed at home because of the rain.*

become /bɪˈkʌm/ *verb* (**becomes**, **becoming**, **became** /bɪˈkeɪm/, **has become**) grow or change and begin to be something: *She became a doctor in 1982.* ○ *The weather is becoming cooler.* **become of somebody** or **something** happen to somebody or something: *What became of David? I haven't seen him for years.*

bed /bed/ *noun* **1** a thing that you sleep on: *I was tired, so I went to bed.* ○ *The children are in bed.* **2** the bottom of a river or the sea **make the bed** put the covers on a bed so that it is tidy and ready for somebody to sleep in it

bedclothes /ˈbedkləʊðz/ *noun* (plural) all the covers (for example **sheets** or blankets) that you put on a bed

bedroom /ˈbedruːm/ *noun* a room where you sleep

bee /biː/ *noun* a small insect that flies and makes honey: *The bee stung me on the arm.*

bee keeping /ˈbiː kiːpɪŋ/ *noun* (no plural) farming bees for their honey and wax

beef /biːf/ *noun* (no plural) meat from a cow: *roast beef* ☞ Note at **cow**.

beehive /ˈbiːhaɪv/ *noun* a box where bees live

been 1 *form of* **be 2** *form of* **go**[1] **have been to** have gone to a place and come back: *Have you ever been to Lake Victoria?* ☞ Note at **go**.

beer /bɪə(r)/ *noun* **1** (no plural) an alcoholic drink made from grain **2** (*plural* **beers**) a glass, bottle or can of beer: *Three beers, please.*

beetle /ˈbiːtl/ *noun* an insect with hard wings and a shiny body

before[1] /bɪˈfɔː(r)/ *preposition* **1** earlier than somebody or something: *He arrived before me.* ○ *I lived in Mombasa before coming to Nairobi.* **2** in front of somebody or something: *B comes before C in the alphabet.*

before[2] /bɪˈfɔː(r)/ *adverb* at an earlier time; in the past: *I've never met them before.* ○ *I've seen that man before.*

before[3] /bɪˈfɔː(r)/ *conjunction* earlier than the time that: *I said goodbye before I left.*

beforehand /bɪˈfɔːhænd/ *adverb* at an earlier time than something: *Tell me beforehand if you are going to be late.*

beg /beg/ *verb* (**begs**, **begging**, **begged** /begd/) **1** ask for money or food because you are very poor: *There was an old man begging in the street.* **2** ask somebody for something in a very strong way: *She begged me to stay with her.* ○ *He begged for help.* **I beg your pardon 1** I am sorry: *'You've taken my seat.' 'Oh, I beg your pardon.'* **2** What did you say?

beggar /ˈbegə(r)/ *noun* a person who asks other people for money or food

begin /bɪˈgɪn/ *verb* (**begins**, **beginning**, **began** /bɪˈgæn/, **has begun**

/bɪˈgʌn/) start to do something or start to happen: *The film begins at 7.30.* ○ *I'm beginning to feel cold.* ○ *The name John begins with a 'J'.* **to begin with** at first; at the beginning: *To begin with he was afraid of the water, but he soon learned to swim.*

beginner /bɪˈgɪnə(r)/ *noun* a person who is starting to do or learn something

beginning /bɪˈgɪnɪŋ/ *noun* the time or place where something starts; the first part of something: *I didn't see the beginning of the film.*

begun *form of* **begin**

behalf /bɪˈhɑːf/ *noun* **on behalf of somebody**, **on somebody's behalf** for somebody; in the place of somebody: *Mr Kairu is away, so I am writing to you on his behalf.*

behave /bɪˈheɪv/ *verb* (**behaves**, **behaving**, **behaved** /bɪˈheɪvd/) do and say things in a certain way when you are with other people: *They behaved very kindly towards me.* ○ *How can you teach a child to behave well?* **behave yourself** be good; do and say the right things: *Did the children behave themselves?*

behaviour /bɪˈheɪvjə(r)/ *noun* (no plural) the way you are; the way that you do and say things when you are with other people: *The teacher was pleased with the children's good behaviour.*

behind /bɪˈhaɪnd/ *preposition, adverb* **1** at or to the back of somebody or something: *I hid behind the wall.* ○ *I went in front and Mohamed followed behind.* ☞ picture on page A1. **2** slower or less good than somebody or something; slower or less good than you should be: *She is behind with her work because she is often ill.* **3** in the place where you were before: *I got off the bus but left my suitcase behind* (= on the bus).

being[1] *form of* **be**

being[2] /ˈbiːɪŋ/ *noun* a person or living thing: *a being from another planet*

belief /bɪˈliːf/ *noun* a sure feeling that something is true or real: *his belief in God*

believe /bɪˈliːv/ *verb* (**believes**,

believing, **believed** /bɪˈliːvd/) feel sure that something is true or right; feel sure that what somebody says is true: *She says she didn't take the money. Do you believe her?* ○ Long ago, people believed that the earth was flat. **believe in somebody** or **something** feel sure that somebody or something is real: *Do you believe in ghosts?*

bell /bel/ *noun* a metal thing that makes a sound when something hits or touches it: *The church bells were ringing.* ○ *I rang the bell and he answered the door.*

bell

belly /ˈbeli/ *noun* (*plural* **bellies**) the part of your body between your chest and your legs; your stomach

belong /bɪˈlɒŋ/ *verb* (**belongs**, **belonging**, **belonged** /bɪˈlɒŋd/) have its right or usual place: *That chair belongs in my room.* **belong to somebody** be somebody's: *'Who does this pen belong to?' 'It belongs to me.'* **belong to something** be in a group, club, etc: *He belongs to the school football club.*

belongings /bɪˈlɒŋɪŋz/ *noun* (plural) the things that you own: *They lost all their belongings in the fire.*

below /bɪˈləʊ/ *preposition, adverb* **1** in or to a lower place than somebody or something: *From the hill we could see the village below.* ○ *Your mouth is below your nose.* ○ *Do not write below this line.* ☞ picture on page A1. **2** less than a number or price: *The temperature was below zero.*

belt /belt/ *noun* a long piece of cloth or leather that you wear around the middle of your body ☞ picture at **suit**. Look also at **safety-belt** and **seatbelt**.

bench

bench /bentʃ/ *noun* (*plural* **benches**) **1** a long seat made of wood or metal, usually outside **2** a long table where somebody, for example a carpenter, works

bend[1] /bend/ *verb* (**bends**, **bending**, **bent** /bent/, **has bent**) become curved; make something that was straight into a curved shape: *Bend your legs!* ○ *She couldn't bend the metal bar.* **bend down**, **bend over** move your body forward and down: *She bent down to put on her shoes.*

bend[2] /bend/ *noun* a part of a road or river that is not straight: *Drive slowly – there's a bend in the road.*

beneath /bɪˈniːθ/ *preposition, adverb* in or to a lower place than somebody or something: *From the tower, they looked down on the city beneath.* **❂ Under** and **below** are the words that we usually use.

benefit /ˈbenɪfɪt/ *verb* (**benefits**, **benefiting**, **benefited**) be good or helpful in some way: *The new railway line will benefit several towns.* **benefit from something** get something good or useful from something: *She will benefit from a rest.*

benefit *noun* something that is good or helpful: *What are the benefits of learning another language?* ○ *I did it for your benefit* (= to help you).

bent *form of* bend[1]

berry /ˈberi/ *noun* (*plural* **berries**) a small soft fruit with seeds in it: *a strawberry* ○ *a blackberry* ○ *raspberries*

beside /bɪˈsaɪd/ *preposition* at the side of somebody or something; next to somebody or something: *Come and sit beside me.* ☞ picture on page A1

besides[1] /bɪˈsaɪdz/ *preposition* as well as somebody or something; if you do not count somebody or something: *There were four people in the room, besides me and Ayanga.*

besides[2] /bɪˈsaɪdz/ *adverb* also: *I don't like this shirt. Besides, it's too expensive.*

best[1] /best/ *adjective* (**good**, **better**, **best**) most good: *This is the best stew I have ever eaten!* ○ *Alando is my best friend.*

best[2] /best/ *adverb* **1** most well: *I work best in the morning.* **2** more than all others; most: *Which picture do you like best?*

best[3] /best/ *noun* (no plural) the most good person or thing: *Nazir and Hassan are good at running but Joshua is the best.* **all the best** words that you use when you say goodbye to somebody, to wish them success **do your best** do all that you can: *I don't know if I can finish the work today, but I'll do my best.*

bet /bet/ *verb* (**bets**, **betting**, **bet** or **betted**, **has bet** or **has betted**) say what you think will happen. If you are right, you win money, but if you are wrong, you lose money: *I bet you 10 shillings that our team will win.* **I bet** I am sure: *I bet it will rain tomorrow.* ○ *I bet you can't climb that tree.*

bet *noun: I lost the bet.*

betray /bɪˈtreɪ/ *verb* (**betrays**, **betraying**, **betrayed** /bɪˈtreɪd/) do something that harms somebody who was your friend: *The guards betrayed the King and let the enemy into the castle.*

better /ˈbetə(r)/ *adjective* (**good**, **better**, **best**) **1** more good: *This book is better than that one.* **2** less ill: *I was ill yesterday, but I feel better now.*

better *adverb* more well: *You speak French better than I do.* **better off** happier, richer, etc: *You look ill – you would be better off in bed.* ○ *I'm better off now that I've got a new job.* **had better** ought to; should: *You'd better go now if you want to catch the train.*

between /bɪˈtwiːn/ *preposition* **1** in the space in the middle of two things or people: *The letter B comes between A and C.* ○ *I sat between Faizal and Brenda.* ☞ picture on page A1. **2** to and from two places: *The boat sails between Zanzibar and Dar es Salaam.* **3** more than one thing but less than another thing: *The children are all between three and five years old.* **4** after one time and before the next time: *I'll meet you between 4.00 and 4.30.* **5** for or by two or more people or things: *We shared the food between us* (= each of us had some food). **6** a word that you use when you compare two people or things: *What is the difference between the two vehicles?* ☞ Note at **among**. **in between** in the middle of two things, people, times, etc: *I found my shoe in between two rocks.*

beware /bɪ'weə(r)/ *verb* **beware of somebody** or **something** be careful because somebody or something is dangerous: *Beware of the dog!* (words written on a sign)

bewildered /bɪ'wɪldəd/ *adjective* If you are bewildered, you do not understand something or you do not know what to do: *He was bewildered by all the noises of the big city.*

beyond /bɪ'jɒnd/ *preposition, adverb* on the other side of something; further than something: *The road continues beyond Eldoret.* ○ *We could see the lake and the mountains beyond.*

bib /bɪb/ *noun* a piece of cloth or plastic that a baby wears under its chin when it is eating

Bible /'baɪbl/ *noun* the holy book of the Christian and Jewish religions

handlebars **bicycle**
saddle
tyre
pedal
chain

bicycle /'baɪsɪk(ə)l/ *noun* a machine with two wheels. You sit on a bicycle and move your legs to make the wheels turn: *Can you ride a bicycle?* ✪ The short form of 'bicycle' is **bike**. **Cycle** means to travel by bicycle.

bid /bɪd/ *verb* (**bids, bidding, bid, has bid**) offer some money because you want to buy something: *He bid a lot of money for the oxen, but it was not enough.*

bid *noun* an offer of money for something that you want to buy: *He made a bid of 800 000 shillings for the piece of land.*

big /bɪg/ *adjective* (**bigger, biggest**) **1** not small; large: *Mombasa is a big city.* ○ *This shirt is too big for me.* ○ *How big is your flat?* ➡ picture on page A10. **2** great or important: *a big problem* **3** older: *Haika is my big sister.*

bike /baɪk/ *noun* a bicycle or a motorcycle

bilharzia /bɪl'hɑːtsɪə/ *noun* (no plural) a serious illness that you get from dirty water

bill /bɪl/ *noun* a piece of paper that shows how much money you must pay for something: *We have to pay our electricity bill.*

billion /'bɪlɪən/ *number* 1 000 000 000; one thousand million: *five billion shillings* ○ *There are billions of people in the world.*

bin /bɪn/ *noun* **1** a thing that you put rubbish in: *I threw the empty bag in the bin.* ➡ Look also at **dustbin**. **2** a thing with a lid that you keep things in: *a bread bin*

bind /baɪnd/ *verb* (**binds, binding, bound** /baʊnd/, **has bound**) tie string or rope round something to hold it firmly: *They bound the prisoner's arms and legs together.*

binoculars /bɪ'nɒkjələz/ *noun* (plural) special glasses that you use to see things that are far away

biography /baɪ'ɒgrəfi/ *noun* (plural **biographies**) the story of a person's life, that another person writes: *Have you read the biography of Nelson Mandela?*

biology /baɪ'ɒlədʒi/ *noun* (no plural) the study of the life of animals and plants: *Biology is my favourite subject at school.*

biologist /baɪ'ɒlədʒɪst/ *noun* a person who studies or knows a lot about biology

wing **bird**
beak

bird /bɜːd/ *noun* an animal with feathers and wings: *Ostriches and vultures are birds.*

✪ Most birds can **fly** and **sing**. They build **nests** and **lay eggs**.

bird of prey /ˌbɜːd əv 'preɪ/ *noun* a bird that catches and eats small birds and animals: *Eagles are birds of prey.*

Biro /'baɪərəʊ/ *noun* (plural **Biros**) a

pen that has a very small ball at the end ✪ **Biro** is a trade mark.

birth /bɜːθ/ *noun* the time when a baby comes out of its mother; being born: *the birth of a baby* ○ *What's your date of birth?* (= the date when you were born) **give birth** have a baby: *My sister gave birth to her second child last week.*

birthday /ˈbɜːθdeɪ/ *noun* (*plural* **birthdays**) the day each year that is the same as the date when you were born: *My birthday is on January 2nd.* ○ *a birthday present* ✪ When it is a person's birthday, we say **Happy Birthday!** or **Many happy returns!**

biscuit /ˈbɪskɪt/ *noun* a kind of small thin dry cake: *a packet of biscuits* ○ *a chocolate biscuit*

bishop /ˈbɪʃəp/ *noun* an important priest in the Christian church, who looks after all the churches in a large area

bit /bɪt/ *noun* a small piece or amount of something: *Would you like a bit of cake?* ○ *Some bits of the film were very funny.* **a bit 1** a little: *You look a bit tired.* **2** a short time: *Let's wait a bit.* **a bit of a** rather a: *It's a bit of a long way to the station.* **bit by bit** slowly or a little at a time: *Bit by bit, I started to feel better.* **come to bits**, **fall to bits** break into small pieces: *The cake fell to bits when I tried to cut it.*

bite¹ /baɪt/ *verb* (**bites**, **biting**, **bit** /bɪt/, **has bitten** /ˈbɪtn/) **1** cut something with your teeth: *That dog bit my leg!* **2** If an insect or snake bites you, it hurts you by pushing a small sharp part into your skin: *My brother was bitten by a snake.*

bite² /baɪt/ *noun* **1** a piece of food that you can put in your mouth: *He took a bite of the potato* **2** a painful place on your skin made by an insect or dog, for example: *a mosquito bite*

bitter¹ /ˈbɪtə(r)/ *adjective* **1** with a sharp unpleasant taste, like very strong coffee; not sweet **2** angry and sad about something that has happened: *He felt very bitter about losing his job.* **3** very cold: *a bitter wind*

black /blæk/ *adjective* (**blacker**, **black-**

est) **1** with the colour of the sky at night: *a black dog* **2** with dark skin: *Nelson Mandela was the first black president of South Africa.* **3** without milk: *black coffee*

black *noun* **1** the colour of the sky at night: *She was dressed in black.* **2** a person with dark skin **black and white** with the colours black, white and grey only: *We watched a black and white film on TV.*

blackberry /ˈblækbəri/ *noun* (*plural* **blackberries**) a small soft black fruit that grows on a bush

blackbird /ˈblækbɜːd/ *noun* a bird with black feathers

blackboard /ˈblækbɔːd/ *noun* a dark board that a teacher writes on with chalk: *Look at the blackboard.*

blackcurrant /ˌblækˈkʌrənt/ *noun* a small round black fruit that grows on a bush

blackmail /ˈblækmeɪl/ *noun* (no plural) saying that you will tell something bad about somebody if they do not give you money or do something for you

blade /bleɪd/ *noun* **1** the flat sharp part of a knife, sword or another thing that cuts **2** a long thin leaf of grass or wheat: *a blade of grass*

blame /bleɪm/ *verb* (**blames**, **blaming**, **blamed** /bleɪmd/) say that a certain person or thing made something bad happen: *The other driver blamed me for the accident.*

blame *noun* (no plural) **take the blame** say that you are the person who did something wrong: *Eve took the blame for the mistake.*

blank /blæŋk/ *adjective* **1** with no writing, pictures or anything else on it: *a blank piece of paper* **2** If your face is blank, it shows no feelings or understanding: *I asked her a question, but she just gave me a blank look.*

blanket /ˈblæŋkɪt/ *noun* a thick cover that you put on a bed

blast¹ /blɑːst/ *noun* **1** when a bomb explodes: *Two people were killed in the blast.* **2** a sudden movement of air: *a blast of cold air* **3** a loud sound made by a musical instrument like a trumpet

blast-off /ˈblɑːst ɒf/ *noun* the time when a spacecraft leaves the ground

blast² /blɑːst/ *verb* (**blasts**, **blasting**, **blasted**) make a hole in something with an explosion: *They blasted through the mountain to make a tunnel.*

blast furnace /ˈblɑːst fɜːnɪs/ *noun* a machine like a large stove for getting metal from ore

blaze /bleɪz/ *noun* a large strong fire: *The firemen put out the blaze.*

blaze *verb* (**blazes**, **blazing**, **blazed** /bleɪzd/) burn strongly and brightly: *a blazing fire*

blazer /ˈbleɪzə(r)/ *noun* a jacket. Blazers sometimes show which school or club you belong to.

bleak /bliːk/ *adjective* (**bleaker**, **bleakest**) cold and grey: *It was bleak on top of the mountain.*

bleed /bliːd/ *verb* (**bleeds**, **bleeding**, **bled** /bled/, **has bled**) lose blood: *I have cut my hand and it's bleeding.*

blend /blend/ *verb* (**blends**, **blending**, **blended**) 1 mix: *Blend the sugar and the butter together.* 2 look or sound good together: *These colours blend very well.*

blend *noun* a mixture of things: *This is a blend of two different kinds of coffee.*

bless /bles/ *verb* (**blesses**, **blessing**, **blessed** /blest/) ask for God's help for somebody or something: *The priest blessed the young couple.* **Bless you!** words that you say to somebody when they sneeze

blew *form of* **blow¹**

blind¹ /blaɪnd/ *adjective* not able to see: *The blind man had a dog to help him.* ○ *My grandfather is going* (= becoming) *blind.*

the blind *noun* (plural) people who are blind

blindness /ˈblaɪndnəs/ *noun* (no plural) being blind

blind² /blaɪnd/ *noun* a piece of cloth or other material that you pull down to cover a window

blind

blindfold /ˈblaɪndfəʊld/ *noun* a piece of cloth that you put over somebody's eyes so that they cannot see

blindfold *verb* (**blindfolds**, **blindfolding**, **blindfolded**) put a piece of cloth over somebody's eyes so that they cannot see

blink /blɪŋk/ *verb* (**blinks**, **blinking**, **blinked** /blɪŋkt/) shut and open your eyes very quickly

blister /ˈblɪstə(r)/ *noun* a small painful place on your skin, that is full of liquid. Rubbing or burning can cause blisters: *My new shoes gave me blisters.*

blob /blɒb/ *noun* a small piece of a thick liquid: *There are blobs of paint on the floor.*

block¹ /blɒk/ *noun* 1 a big heavy piece of something, with flat sides: *a block of wood* ○ *The bridge is made of concrete blocks.* 2 a big building with a lot of offices or flats inside: *an office block* ○ *a block of flats* 3 a group of buildings with streets all round it: *We drove round the block looking for the hotel.* 4 a thing that stops somebody or something from moving forward: *The police have put road blocks around the town.*

block² /blɒk/ *verb* (**blocks**, **blocking**, **blocked** /blɒkt/) stop somebody or something from moving forward: *A fallen tree blocked the road.*

blond /blɒnd/ *adjective* with light-coloured hair: *He's got blond hair.* ○ The spelling **blonde** is used for women: *She is tall and blonde.*

blonde *noun* a woman who has blond hair

blood /blʌd/ *noun* (no plural) the red liquid inside your body

bloody /ˈblʌdi/ *adjective* (**bloodier**, **bloodiest**) 1 covered with blood: *a bloody nose* 2 with a lot of killing: *It was a bloody war.*

bloom /bluːm/ *verb* (**blooms**, **blooming**, **bloomed** /bluːmd/) have flowers: *The orange trees are blooming.*

blossom /ˈblɒsəm/ *noun* (no plural) the flowers on a tree or bush: *orange blossom*

blossom *verb* (**blossoms**, **blossoming**, **blossomed** /ˈblɒsəmd/) have flowers: *The orange trees are blossoming.*

blouse /blaʊz/ *noun* a piece of clothing

like a shirt that a woman or girl wears on the top part of her body

blow[1] /bləʊ/ *verb* (**blows**, **blowing**, **blew** /bluː/, **has blown** /bləʊn/) **1** When air or wind blows, it moves: *The wind was blowing from the sea.* **2** move something through the air: *The wind blew my hat off.* **3** send air out from your mouth **4** send air out from your mouth into a musical instrument, for example, to make a noise: *The referee blew his whistle.* **blow up 1** explode; make something explode, for example with a bomb: *The plane blew up.* ○ *They blew up the station.* **2** fill something with air: *I blew up the tyre on my bicycle.*

blow[2] /bləʊ/ *noun* **1** hitting somebody or something hard; being hit hard: *He felt a blow on the back of his head and he fell.* **2** something that happens suddenly and that makes you very unhappy: *Her father's death was a terrible blow to her.*

blue /bluː/ *adjective* (**bluer**, **bluest**) with the colour of a clear sky on a sunny day: *He wore a bright blue shirt.* ○ *dark-blue*

blue *noun*: *She was dressed in blue.*

blunt /blʌnt/ *adjective* **1** with an edge or point that is not sharp: *This pencil is blunt.* **2** If you are blunt, you say what you think in a way that is not polite: *She was very blunt and told me that she didn't like my plan.*

blur /blɜː(r)/ *verb* (**blurs**, **blurring**, **blurred** /blɜːd/) make something less clear: *If you move while you are taking the photo, it will be blurred.*

blush /blʌʃ/ *verb* (**blushes**, **blushing**, **blushed** /blʌʃt/) If you blush, your face suddenly becomes red because you are shy, for example: *She blushed when he looked at her.*

boar /bɔː(r)/ *noun* **1** a male pig **2** a wild pig

board[1] /bɔːd/ *noun* **1** a long thin flat piece of wood: *I nailed a board across the broken window.* ○ *floorboards* **2** a flat piece of wood, for example, that you use for a special purpose: *There is a list of names on the notice-board.* ○ *a chessboard* ○ *an ironing-board* ☞ Look also at **blackboard**. **3** a group of people who have a special job, for example controlling a company: *the board of directors* **on board** on a ship or an aeroplane: *How many passengers are on board?*

board[2] /bɔːd/ *verb* (**boards**, **boarding**, **boarded**) get on a ship, bus, train or an aeroplane: *We boarded the plane at Kenyatta Airport.* ○ *Flight BA 193 to London is now boarding* (= is ready for passengers to get on).

boarding card /ˈbɔːdɪŋ kɑːd/ *noun* a card that you must show when you get on an aeroplane or a ship

boarding-school /ˈbɔːdɪŋ skuːl/ *noun* a school where the pupils live

boast /bəʊst/ *verb* (**boasts**, **boasting**, **boasted**) talk in a way that shows you are too proud of something that you have or something that you can do: *He boasted that he was the fastest runner in the school.*

boats

boat /bəʊt/ *noun* a small ship for travelling on water: *a fishing boat* ○ *We travelled by boat.*

body /ˈbɒdi/ *noun* (*plural* **bodies**) **1** all of a person or an animal, but not the mind: *Arms, legs, hands and feet are all parts of the body.* ○ *the human body* **2** all of a person or animal, but not the legs, arms or head **3** a dead person: *The police found a body in the river.*

bodyguard /ˈbɒdigɑːd/ *noun* a person or group of people whose job is to keep an important person safe: *The President's bodyguards all carry guns.*

boil /bɔɪl/ *verb* (**boils**, **boiling**, **boiled** /bɔɪld/) **1** When a liquid boils, it becomes very hot and makes steam and bubbles: *Water boils at 100° C.* **2** heat a liquid until it boils: *I boiled some water for the pasta.* **3** cook something in very hot water: *Boil the potatoes until they are soft.* ○ *boiled bananas* **boil over** boil and flow over the sides of a pan: *Don't let the stew boil over.*

boiler /ˈbɔɪlə(r)/ *noun* a big metal container that heats water for a building

boiling /ˈbɔɪlɪŋ/ *adjective* very hot: *I'm boiling.*

bold /bəʊld/ *adjective* (**bolder**, **boldest**) brave and not afraid: *It was very bold of you to ask for more money.*
boldly *adverb*: *He boldly said that he disagreed.*

bolt /bəʊlt/ *noun* **1** a piece of metal that you move across to lock a door **2** a thick metal pin that you use with another piece of metal (called a **nut**) to fix things together
bolt *verb* (**bolts**, **bolting**, **bolted**) lock a door by putting a bolt across it

bomb /bɒm/ *noun* a thing that explodes and hurts or damages people or things: *Aircraft dropped bombs on the city.* ○ *A bomb went off* (= exploded) *at the station.*
bomb *verb* (**bombs**, **bombing**, **bombed** /bɒmd/) attack people or a place with bombs: *The city was bombed in the war.*

bone /bəʊn/ *noun* one of the hard white parts inside the body of a person or an animal: *She broke a bone in her foot.* ○ *This fish has a lot of bones in it.*

bonfire /ˈbɒnfaɪə(r)/ *noun* a big fire that you make outside

bonnet /ˈbɒnɪt/ *noun* the front part of a car that covers the engine ☞ picture at **car**

book¹ /bʊk/ *noun* a thing that you read or write in, that has a lot of pieces of paper joined together inside a cover: *I'm reading a book by Meja Mwangi.* ○ *an exercise book*

book² /bʊk/ *verb* (**books**, **booking**, **booked** /bʊkt/) ask somebody to keep something for you so that you can use it later: *We've booked a room for the meeting.* ○ *The hotel is fully booked* (= all the rooms are full). **book in** tell the person at the desk in a hotel that you have arrived

bookcase /ˈbʊk keɪs/ *noun* a piece of furniture that you put books in

booking /ˈbʊkɪŋ/ *noun* asking somebody to keep something for you so that you can use it later: *When did you make your booking?*

booking-office /ˈbʊkɪŋ ɒfɪs/ *noun* a place where you buy tickets

booklet /ˈbʊklət/ *noun* a small thin book

bookshop /ˈbʊkʃɒp/ *noun* a shop that sells books

boom /buːm/ *verb* (**booms**, **booming**, **boomed** /buːmd/) make a loud deep sound: *We heard the guns booming in the distance.*

boots

boot /buːt/ *noun* **1** a shoe that covers your foot and ankle and sometimes part of your leg **2** the part of a car where you can put bags and boxes, usually at the back ☞ picture at **car**

border /ˈbɔːdə(r)/ *noun* **1** a line between two countries: *You need a passport to cross the border.* **2** a line along the edge of something: *white material with a blue border*

bore¹ *form of* **bear**²

bore² /bɔː(r)/ *verb* (**bores**, **boring**, **bored** /bɔːd/) If something bores you, it makes you feel tired because it is not interesting: *He bores everyone with his complaining.*

bored *adjective* not interested; unhappy because you have nothing interesting to do: *I get bored on long bus journeys.* ○ *I'm bored with studying.*

boredom /ˈæp;bɔːdəm/ *noun* (no plural) being bored

boring *adjective* not interesting: *That lesson was boring!*

bore³ /bɔː(r)/ *verb* (**bores**, **boring**, **bored** /bɔːd/) make a hole by pushing a tool into something: *They bored a deep hole in the ground to find water.*

born /bɔːn/ *adjective* **be born** start your life: *I was born in 1990.* ○ *Where were you born?*

borne *form of* **bear**²

book

bookcase

borrow or lend?

She is **lending** her son some money.

He is **borrowing** some money from his mother.

borrow /ˈbɒrəʊ/ *verb* (**borrows**, **borrowing**, **borrowed** /ˈbɒrəʊd/) take and use something that you will give back after a short time: *I borrowed some books from the library.* ○ *He borrowed 100 shillings from his father.*

boss /bɒs/ *noun* (*plural* **bosses**) a person who controls a place where people work and tells people what they must do: *I asked my boss for the morning off.*

bossy /ˈbɒsi/ *adjective* (**bossier**, **bossiest**) A bossy person likes to tell other people what to do: *My sister is very bossy.*

both /bəʊθ/ *adjective, pronoun* the two; not only one but also the other: *Hold it in both hands.* ○ *Both her brothers are doctors.* ○ *Both of us like swimming.* ○ *We both like swimming.*

both *adverb* **both... and** not only... but also: *Both Swahili and English are official languages in Tanzania.*

bother /ˈbɒðə(r)/ *verb* (**bothers**, **bothering**, **bothered** /ˈbɒðəd/) **1** do something that gives you extra work or that takes extra time: *Don't bother to wash the dishes – I'll do it later.* **2** worry somebody; stop somebody from doing something, for example thinking, working or sleeping: *Don't bother me now – I'm busy!* ○ *Is this music bothering you?* ○ *I'm sorry to bother you, but could you open the door for me?*

bother *noun* (no plural) trouble or difficulty: *'Thanks for your help!' 'It was no bother.'*

bothered *adjective* worried **can't be bothered** If you can't be bothered to do something, you do not want to do it

because it is too much work: *I can't be bothered to do my homework now.*

bottle /ˈbɒtl/ *noun*
a tall round glass or plastic container for liquids, with a thin part at the top: *a beer bottle* ○ *They drank two bottles of water.*

bottle

bottom /ˈbɒtəm/ *noun* **1** the lowest part of something: *They live at the bottom of the hill.* ○ *The book was at the bottom of my bag.* ○ *Look at the picture at the bottom of the page.* ✪ opposite: **top** ☛ picture at **back**. **2** the last part of something; the end: *The bank is at the bottom of the road.* ✪ opposite: **top** **3** the part of your body that you sit on: *She fell on her bottom.* ☛ picture on page A4

bottom *adjective* lowest: *Put the book on the bottom shelf.* ✪ opposite: **top**

bought *form of* **buy**

boulder /ˈbəʊldə(r)/ *noun* a very big rock

bounce

bounce /baʊns/ *verb* (**bounces**, **bouncing**, **bounced** /ˈbaʊnst/) **1** When a ball bounces, it moves away quickly after it hits something hard: *The ball bounced off the wall.* **2** make a ball do this: *The boy was bouncing a ball.* **3** jump up and down a lot: *The children were bouncing up and down to the music.*

bound[1] *form of* **bind**

bound[2] /baʊnd/ *adjective* **bound to** certain to do something: *She works very hard, so she is bound to pass the exam.*

bound[3] /baʊnd/ *adjective* **bound for** going to a place: *This ship is bound for Egypt.*

bound[4] /baʊnd/ *verb* (**bounds**, **bounding**, **bounded**) jump, or run with small jumps: *The gazelle bounded away.*

boundary /ˈbaʊndri/ *noun* (*plural* **boundaries**) a line between two places: *This fence is the boundary between the two farms.*

bouquet /buˈkeɪ/ *noun* a group of flowers that you give or get as a present

bow[1] /baʊ/ *verb* (**bows, bowing, bowed** /baʊd/) bend your head or body forward to show respect: *The actors bowed at the end of the play.*

bow *noun:* *He gave a bow and left the room.*

bow[2] /bəʊ/ *noun* a kind of knot with two round parts, that you use when you are tying shoes, etc

bow

bow[3] /bəʊ/ *noun* **1** a curved piece of wood with a string between its two ends. You use a bow to send **arrows** through the air. ☞ picture at **arrow 2** a long thin piece of wood with strong strings along it. You use it to play a **violin** or another musical instrument that has strings.

bowl[1] /bəʊl/ *noun* a deep round dish or container: *a sugar bowl* ○ *a bowl of soup*

bowl

bowl[2] /bəʊl/ *verb* (**bowls, bowling, bowled** /bəʊld/) throw a ball so that somebody can hit it in a game of cricket

box[1] /bɒks/ *noun* (*plural* **boxes**) a container with straight sides. A box often has a lid: *Put the books in a cardboard box.* ○ *a box of oranges* ○ *a box of matches* ☞ picture at **container**

box[2] /bɒks/ *verb* (**boxes, boxing, boxed** /bɒkst/) fight with your hands, wearing thick gloves, as a sport

boxer *noun* a person who boxes as a sport: *Muhammad Ali was a famous boxer.*

boxing *noun* (no plural) the sport of fighting with your hands, wearing thick gloves

box office /ˈbɒks ɒfɪs/ *noun* a place where you buy tickets in a theatre or cinema

boy /bɔɪ/ *noun* (*plural* **boys**) a male child; a young man

boyfriend /ˈbɔɪfrend/ *noun* a boy or man who is somebody's special friend: *She has had a lot of boyfriends.*

Boy Scout /ˌbɔɪ ˈskaʊt/ *noun* a member of a special club for boys

bra /brɑː/ *noun* (*plural* **bras**) a thing that a woman wears under her other clothes to cover and support her breasts

bracelet

bracelet /ˈbreɪslət/ *noun* a pretty piece of metal, wood or plastic that you wear around your arm

brackets /ˈbrækɪts/ *noun* (plural) marks like these ( ) that you use in writing: *(This sentence is written in brackets.)*

brain /breɪn/ *noun* the part inside the head of a person or an animal that thinks and feels: *The brain controls the rest of the body.*

brake /breɪk/ *noun* a thing that you move to make a car, bicycle, etc go slower or stop: *I put my foot on the brake.*

brake *verb* (**brakes, braking, braked** /breɪkt/) use a brake: *A child ran into the road and the driver braked suddenly.*

branch /brɑːntʃ/ *noun* (*plural* **branches**) **1** one of the parts of a tree that grow out from the **trunk** ☞ picture at **tree. 2** an office or a shop that is part of a big company: *This bank has branches all over the country.*

brand /brænd/ *noun* the name of a thing you buy that a certain company makes: *'Pepsi' is a famous brand of soft drink.*

brand-new /ˌbrænd ˈnjuː/ *adjective* completely new: *a brand-new car*

brass /brɑːs/ *noun* (no plural) a yellow metal

brave /breɪv/ *adjective* (**braver, bravest**) ready to do dangerous or difficult things without fear: *It was brave of her to go into the burning building.*

bravely *adverb: He fought bravely in the war.*

bravery /'breɪvəri/ *noun* (no plural) being brave

bread /bred/ *noun* (no plural) food made from flour and baked in an oven: *I bought a loaf of bread.*

breadth /bredθ/ *noun* how far it is from one side of something to the other ✪ The adjective is **broad**.

break[1] /breɪk/ *verb* (**breaks**, **breaking**, **broke** /brəʊk/, **has broken** /'brəʊkən/) **1** make something go into smaller pieces by dropping it or hitting it, for example: *He broke the window.* ○ *She has broken her arm.* **2** go into smaller pieces by falling or hitting, for example: *I dropped the cup and it broke.* **3** stop working; damage a machine so that it stops working: *The radio is broken.* ○ *You've broken my pen.* **break down 1** If a machine or car breaks down, it stops working: *We were late because our car broke down.* **2** If a person breaks down, he/she starts to cry: *He broke down when he heard the bad news.* **break in, break into something** go into a place by breaking a door or window so that you can steal something: *Thieves broke into the building. They broke in through a window.* **break off** take away a piece of something by breaking it: *He broke off a piece of bread and ate it.* **break out 1** start suddenly: *A fire broke out last night.* **2** get free from a place like a prison: *Four prisoners broke out of the jail last night.* **break up** start the school holidays: *We break up in two weeks.* **break up with somebody** stop being with somebody, for example a husband or wife, boyfriend or girl-friend: *Cherop broke up with her boy-friend last week.*

break[2] /breɪk/ *noun* **1** a short time when you stop doing something: *We worked all day without a break.* **2** a place where something opens or has broken: *The sun shone through a break in the clouds.*

breakdown /'breɪkdaʊn/ *noun* a time when a machine, car, etc stops work-ing: *We (= our car) had a breakdown on the way.*

breakfast /'brekfəst/ *noun* the first meal of the day: *I had breakfast at seven*

o'clock this morning.

breast /brest/ *noun* **1** one of the two soft round parts of a woman's body that can give milk **2** the front part of a bird's body

breast-stroke /'brest strəʊk/ *noun* (no plural) a way of swimming on your front

breath /breθ/ *noun* taking in or letting out air through your nose and mouth: *Take a deep breath.* **hold your breath** stop breathing for a short time **out of breath** breathing very quickly: *She was out of breath after climbing the stairs.*

breathe /briːð/ *verb* (**breathes**, **breathing**, **breathed** /briːðd/) take in and let out air through your nose and mouth: *The doctor told me to breathe in and then breathe out again slowly.*

breathless /'breθləs/ *adjective* If you are breathless, you are breathing quickly or with difficulty.

breed[1] /briːd/ *verb* (**breeds**, **breeding**, **bred** /bred/, **has bred**) **1** make young animals: *Birds breed in the spring.* **2** keep animals to make young ones: *They breed rabbits on their farm.*

breed[2] /briːd/ *noun* a kind of animal: *There are many different breeds of cattle.*

breeze /briːz/ *noun* a light wind

brewery /'bruːəri/ *noun* (plural **brew-eries**) a place where beer is made

bribe /braɪb/ *noun* money or a present that you give to somebody to make them do something

bribe *verb* (**bribes**, **bribing**, **bribed** /braɪbd/) give a bribe to somebody: *The prisoner bribed the guard to let him go free.*

brick /brɪk/ *noun* a small block made of hard clay, with two long sides and two short sides. Bricks are used for build-ing: *a brick wall*

bricklayer /'brɪkleɪə(r)/ *noun* a person whose job is to build things with bricks

bride /braɪd/ *noun* a woman on the day of her wedding

bridegroom /'braɪdgruːm/ *noun* a man on the day of his wedding

bridesmaid /'braɪdzmeɪd/ *noun* a girl or woman who helps a bride at her wedding

bridge

bridge /brɪdʒ/ *noun* a thing that is built over a road, railway or river so that people, trains or cars can cross it: *We walked over the bridge.*

brief /briːf/ *adjective* (**briefer**, **briefest**) short or quick: *a brief telephone call* **in brief** in a few words: *Here is the news in brief.* (words said on a radio or television programme)

briefly *adverb*: *We stopped work briefly for a drink.*

briefcase /ˈbriːfkeɪs/ *noun* a flat case for carrying papers in

briefcase

bright /braɪt/ *adjective* (**brighter**, **brightest**)
1 with a lot of light: *It was a bright sunny day.* ○ *That lamp is very bright.* **2** with a strong colour: *a bright-yellow shirt* **3** clever: *She is the brightest child in the class.*

brightly *adverb*: *brightly coloured clothes*
brightness /ˈbraɪtnəs/ *noun* (no plural) *the brightness of the sun*

brighten /ˈbraɪtn/, **brighten up** *verb* (**brightens**, **brightening**, **brightened** /ˈbraɪtnd/) become brighter or happier; make something brighter: *These flowers will brighten the room up.* ○ *Her face brightened when she heard the good news.*

brilliant /ˈbrɪliənt/ *adjective* **1** with a lot of light; very bright: *brilliant sunshine* **2** very intelligent: *a brilliant student* **3** very good; excellent: *The film was brilliant!*

brilliance /ˈbrɪliəns/ *noun* (no plural) *the brilliance of the light*

brilliantly *adverb*: *She played brilliantly.*

brim /brɪm/ *noun* **1** the edge around the top of something like a cup, bowl or glass **2** the wide part around the bottom of a hat

bring /brɪŋ/ *verb* (**brings**, **bringing**, **brought** /brɔːt/, **has brought**)
1 come to a place with somebody or something: *Can you bring me a glass of water?* ○ *Bring your brother with you next time you come.* **2** make something happen: *Money doesn't always bring happiness.* **bring back 1** return something: *I have brought back the book you lent me.* **2** make you remember something: *These old photographs bring back a lot of happy memories.* **bring somebody up** look after a child until he/she is grown up: *He was brought up by his aunt after his parents died.* **bring something up 1** be sick, so that food comes up from your stomach and out of your mouth **2** start to talk about something: *Can you bring up this problem at the next meeting?*

bristle /ˈbrɪsl/ *noun* a short thick hair like the hair on a brush

brittle /ˈbrɪtl/ *adjective* Something that is brittle is hard but breaks easily: *This glass is very brittle.*

broad /brɔːd/ *adjective* (**broader**, **broadest**) large from one side to the other; wide: *a broad river* ✪ The noun is **breadth**. ✪ opposite: **narrow**

broadcast /ˈbrɔːdkɑːst/ *verb* (**broadcasts**, **broadcasting**, **broadcast**, **has broadcast**) send out sound or pictures by radio or television: *The BBC broadcasts the news at 9 p.m.*

broadcast *noun* something that is sent out by radio or television: *a news broadcast*

broadcaster *noun* a person whose job is to talk on radio or television

broke, **broken** *forms of* **break**[1]

broken /ˈbrəʊkən/ *adjective* in pieces or not working: *a broken window* ○ *'What's the time?' 'I don't know – my watch is broken.'*

bronze /brɒnz/ *noun* (no plural) a brown metal made from copper and tin: *a bronze medal*

brooch /brəʊtʃ/ *noun* (*plural* **brooches**) a pretty thing with a pin at the back that you wear on your clothes

broom /bruːm/ *noun* a brush with a long handle that you use for sweeping

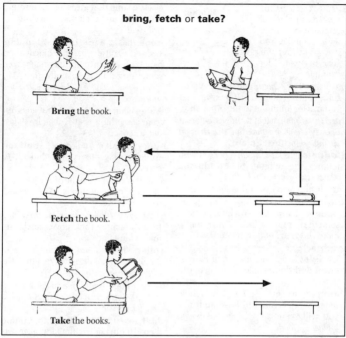

bring, fetch or **take?**

Bring the book.

Fetch the book.

Take the books.

brother /'brʌðə(r)/ *noun* Your brother is a man or boy who has the same parents as you: *My younger brother is called Hassan.* ○ *Njue and Cheka are brothers.*

brother-in-law /'brʌðər ɪn lɔː/ *noun* (*plural* **brothers-in-law**) **1** the brother of your wife or husband **2** the husband of your sister

brought *form of* **bring**

brow /braʊ/ *noun* the part of your face above your eyes

brown /braʊn/ *adjective* (**browner**, **brownest**) with the colour of coffee: *brown eyes*

brown *noun* the colour of coffee

bruise /bruːz/ *noun* a dark mark on your skin that comes after something hits it

bruise *verb* (**bruises**, **bruising**, **bruised** /bruːzd/) *He fell and bruised his leg.*

brush /brʌʃ/ *noun* (*plural* **brushes**) a

brushes

thing that you use for sweeping, cleaning, painting, etc: *She swept the sand out of the door with a brush.*
☛ Look also at **paintbrush** and **toothbrush**.

brush *verb* (**brushes**, **brushing**, **brushed** /brʌʃt/) use a brush to do something: *I brush my teeth twice a day.*

brutal /'bruːtl/ *adjective* very cruel: *a brutal murder*

brutally /'bruːtəli/ *adverb*: *She was brutally attacked.*

bubble /'bʌbl/ *noun* a small ball of air or gas inside a liquid: *We knew there were fish in the water because we could see bubbles on the surface.*

bubble *verb* (**bubbles**, **bubbling**, **bubbled** /'bʌbld/) make a lot of bubbles: *When water boils, it bubbles.*

bucket /ˈbʌkɪt/ *noun* a round metal or plastic container with a handle. You use a bucket for carrying water, for example

bucket

buckle /ˈbʌkl/ *noun* a metal or plastic thing on the end of a belt or strap that you use for joining it to the other end

bud /bʌd/ *noun* a leaf or flower before it opens: *There are buds on the trees in spring.* ☞ picture at **plant**

Buddhist /ˈbʊdɪst/ *noun* a person who follows the religion of **Buddhism**, which was started in India by Buddha
Buddhist *adjective*: *a Buddhist temple*

budge /bʌdʒ/ *verb* (**budges**, **budging**, **budged** /bʌdʒd/) move a little or make something move a little: *I'm trying to move this rock but it won't budge.*

budgerigar /ˈbʌdʒərɪɡɑː(r)/, **budgie** /ˈbʌdʒi/ *noun* a small blue or green bird that people often keep as a pet

budget /ˈbʌdʒɪt/ *noun* a plan of how much money you will have and how you will spend it: *We have a weekly budget for food.*
budget *verb* (**budgets**, **budgeting**, **budgeted**) plan how much money you will have and how you will spend it: *I am budgeting very carefully because I want to buy a television.*

buffalo /ˈbʌfələʊ/ *noun* (*plural* **buffalo** or **buffaloes**) a large wild cow with long horns

bug /bʌɡ/ *noun* **1** a small insect **2** an illness that is not serious: *I've caught a bug.*

build /bɪld/ *verb* (**builds**, **building**, **built** /bɪlt/, **has built**) make something by putting parts together: *He built a wall in front of the house.* ○ *The bridge is built of stone.*

builder /ˈbɪldə(r)/ *noun* a person whose job is to make buildings

building society /ˈbɪldɪŋ səsaɪəti/ *noun* (*plural* **building societies**) a kind of bank that lends you money when you want to buy a house or flat

built *form of* **build**

bulb /bʌlb/ *noun* **1** the glass part of an electric lamp that gives light **2** a round thing that some plants grow from: *a tulip bulb*

bulge /bʌldʒ/ *verb* (**bulges**, **bulging**, **bulged** /bʌldʒd/) become bigger than usual; go out in a round shape from something that is usually flat: *My stomach is bulging – I have eaten too much.*
bulge *noun* a round part that goes out from something that is usually flat: *a bulge in the wall*

bulky /ˈbʌlki/ *adjective* (**bulkier**, **bulkiest**) big, heavy and difficult to carry

bull /bʊl/ *noun* the male of the cow and of some other animals ☻ Note and picture at **cow**.

bulldozer /ˈbʊldəʊzə(r)/ *noun* a big heavy machine that moves earth and makes land flat

bullet /ˈbʊlɪt/ *noun* a small piece of metal that shoots out of a gun: *The bullet hit him in the leg.*

bully /ˈbʊli/ *noun* (*plural* **bullies**) a person who hurts or frightens a weaker person
bully *verb* (**bullies**, **bullying**, **bullied** /ˈbʊlid/) hurt or frighten a weaker person: *She was bullied by the older girls at school.*

bum /bʌm/ *noun* the part of your body that you sit on ☻ Be careful! Some people think this word is quite rude. **Bottom** is the more usual word.

bump¹ /bʌmp/ *verb* (**bumps**, **bumping**, **bumped** /bʌmpt/) **1** hit somebody or something when you are moving: *She bumped into a chair.* **2** hit a part of your body against something hard: *I bumped my head on the low ceiling.*
bump into somebody meet somebody by chance: *I bumped into Kadima today.*

bump² /bʌmp/ *noun* **1** when something hits another thing; the sound that this makes: *He fell and hit the ground with a bump.* **2** a small round fat place on your body where you have hit it: *I've got a bump on my head.* **3** a small part on something flat that is higher than the rest: *The car hit a bump in the road.*

bumper /'bʌmpə(r)/ *noun* a bar on the front and back of a car, lorry, etc. It helps to protect the car if it hits something.

bumpy /'bʌmpi/ *adjective* (**bumpier**, **bumpiest**) **1** with a lot of bumps: *a bumpy road* **2** that shakes you: *We had a very bumpy journey in an old bus.*

bunch /bʌntʃ/ *noun* (*plural* **bunches**) a group of things that grow together or that you tie or hold together: *a bunch of bananas* ○ *a bunch of keys* ☞ picture on page A15

bundle /'bʌndl/ *noun* a group of things that you tie or wrap together: *a bundle of old newspapers* ☞ picture on page A15

bungalow /'bʌŋgələʊ/ *noun* a house that has only one floor, with no upstairs rooms

bunk /bʌŋk/ *noun* a narrow bed that is fixed to a wall, on a ship or train, for example

buoy /bɔɪ/ *noun* (*plural* **buoys**) a thing that floats in the sea to show ships where there are dangerous places

burger /'bɜːgə(r)/ *noun* meat cut into very small pieces and made into a flat round shape, that you cook and eat between two pieces of bread

burglar /'bɜːglə(r)/ *noun* a person who goes into a building to steal things

burglary /'bɜːgləri/ *noun* (*plural* **burglaries**) going into a house to steal things: *There were two burglaries in this street last week.*

burgle /'bɜːgl/ *verb* (**burgles**, **burgling**, **burgled** /'bɜːgld/) go into a building to steal things: *Our house was burgled.*

burial /'beriəl/ *noun* the time when a dead body is put in the ground ✪ The verb is **bury**.

buried, **buries** *forms of* **bury**

burn¹ /bɜːn/ *verb* (**burns**, **burning**, **burnt** /bɜːnt/ or **burned** /bɜːnd/, **has burnt** or **has burned**) **1** make flames and heat; be on fire: *Paper burns easily.* ○ *She escaped from the burning building.* **2** harm or destroy somebody or something with fire or heat: *I burnt my fingers on a match.* ○ *We burned the wood on the fire.* **burn down** burn, or make a building burn, until there is nothing

left: *Their house burnt down.*

burn² /bɜːn/ *noun* a place on your body where fire or heat has hurt it: *I've got a burn on my arm from the cooker.*

burp /bɜːp/ *verb* (**burps**, **burping**, **burped** /bɜːpt/) make a noise from your mouth when air suddenly comes up from your stomach: *He burped loudly after he had finished eating.*

burp *noun*: *I heard a loud burp.*

burrow /'bʌrəʊ/ *noun* a hole in the ground where some animals, for example rabbits, live

burst¹ /bɜːst/ *verb* (**bursts**, **bursting**, **burst**, **has burst**) **1** break open suddenly because there is too much inside; make something break open suddenly: *The bag was so full that it burst.* ○ *The pipe burst.* **2** go or come suddenly: *Nazir burst into the room.* **burst into something** start doing something suddenly: *He read the letter and burst into tears* (= started to cry). ○ *The car burst into flames* (= started to burn). **burst out laughing** suddenly start to laugh: *When she saw my hat, she burst out laughing.*

burst² /bɜːst/ *noun* something that happens suddenly and quickly: *a burst of activity*

bury /'beri/ *verb* (**buries**, **burying**, **buried** /'berid/, **has buried**) **1** put a dead body in the ground ✪ The noun is **burial**. **2** put something in the ground or under something: *The dog buried a bone then dug it up again.*

bus /bʌs/ *noun* (*plural* **buses**) a thing like a big car, that carries a lot of people: *We went to Nakuru on the bus/by bus.* ○ *Where do you get off the bus?*

bus-stop /'bʌs stɒp/ *noun* a place where buses stop and people get on and off

bush /bʊʃ/ *noun* **1 the bush** (no plural) wild country that is not used for farming or building **2** (*plural* **bushes**) a plant like a small tree with a lot of branches: *a cotton bush*

business /'bɪznəs/ *noun* **1** (no plural) buying and selling things: *I want to go into business when I leave school.* ○ *Business is not very good this year.* **2** (*plural* **businesses**) a place where people sell or make things, for example a shop or factory **it's none of your business, mind your own business** words that you use when you do not want to tell somebody about something that is private: *'Where are you going?' 'Mind your own business!'* **on business** because of your work: *Mrs Gitau is in Uganda on business.*

businessman /'bɪznəsmən/ *noun* (*plural* **businessmen**) a man who works in an office and whose job is about buying and selling things

businesswoman /'bɪznəswʊmən/ *noun* (*plural* **businesswomen**) a woman who works in an office and whose job is about buying and selling things

busy /'bɪzi/ *adjective* (**busier, busiest**) **1** with a lot of things that you must do; working or not free: *Mr Ochom can't see you now – he's busy.* **2** with a lot of things happening: *I had a busy morning.* ○ *The roads are busier than usual today.*

busily /'bɪzɪli/ *adverb*: *He was busily writing a letter.*

but[1] /bət/, /bʌt/ *conjunction* a word that you use to show something different: *My sister speaks French but I don't.* ○ *He worked hard but he didn't pass the exam.* ○ *The teacher is strict but fair.*

but[2] /bət/, /bʌt/ *preposition* except: *She does nothing but study.*

butcher /'bʊtʃə(r)/ *noun* a person who cuts and sells meat ✿ A shop that sells meat is called a **butcher's.**

butter /'bʌtə(r)/ *noun* (no plural) soft yellow food that is made from milk. You put it on bread or use it in cooking.

butterfly /'bʌtəflaɪ/ *noun*

butterfly

(*plural* **butterflies**) an insect with big coloured wings

button /'bʌtn/ *noun* **1** a small round thing on clothes. You push it through a small hole (a **buttonhole**) to hold clothes together. **2** a small thing on a machine, that you push: *Press this button to ring the bell.*

button
buttonhole

buy /baɪ/ *verb* (**buys, buying, bought** /bɔːt/, **has bought**) give money to get something: *I bought a new watch.* ○ *He bought the car from a friend.* ☞ Look at **sell.**

buzz /bʌz/ *verb* (**buzzes, buzzing, buzzed** /bʌzd/) make a sound like bees **buzz** *noun* (*plural* **buzzes**) *the buzz of insects.*

by[1] /baɪ/ *preposition* **1** very near: *The telephone is by the door.* ○ *They live by the sea.* **2** from one side of somebody or something to the other; past: *He walked by me without speaking.* **3** not later than: *I must finish this work by six o'clock.* **4** a word that shows who or what did something: *Who is the book by?* (= Who wrote it?) ○ *She was caught by the police.* **5** using something: *I go to work by train.* ○ *He paid by cheque.* **6** a word that shows how: *You operate the machine by turning the handle.* **7** a word that shows how you measure something: *We buy material by the metre.* **8** a word that shows which part: *She took me by the hand.*

by[2] /baɪ/ *adverb* past: *She ran by without saying hello.*

bye /baɪ/, **bye-bye** /ˌbaɪ 'baɪ/ goodbye

Cc

C *short way of writing* **Celsius**, *short way of writing* **centigrade**

cab /kæb/ *noun* **1** *another word for* **taxi 2** the part of a lorry, train or bus where the driver sits

cabbage /'kæbɪdʒ/ *noun* a large round vegetable with thick green leaves

cabin /'kæbɪn/ *noun* **1** a small bedroom on a ship **2** a part of an aircraft: *the passengers in the first-class cabin* **3** a small simple house made of wood: *a log cabin at the edge of the lake*

cabinet /'kæbɪnət/ *noun* (*plural* **cabinets**) a piece of furniture that you can keep things in: *a bathroom cabinet* ○ *a filing cabinet* (= one that you use in an office to keep files in)

cable /'keɪbl/ *noun* **1** a wire that carries electricity or messages **2** a very strong thick rope or wire

cable television /ˌkeɪbl 'telɪvɪʒn/ *noun* (no plural) a way of sending pictures and sound along wires

cactus /'kæktəs/ *noun* (*plural* **cactuses** or **cacti** /'kæktaɪ/) a plant with a lot of sharp points that grows in hot dry places

café /'kæfeɪ/ *noun* a place where you can have a drink and something to eat

cage /keɪdʒ/

cage

noun a place with bars round it where animals or birds are kept so that they cannot escape

cake /keɪk/ *noun*

sweet food that you make from flour, eggs, sugar and butter and bake in the oven: *a chocolate cake* ○ *Would you like a piece of cake?*

calabash /'kæləbæʃ/ *noun* (*plural* **calabashes**) a container that is made from the hard, dried skin of a large fruit (a **gourd**)

calculate /'kælkjuleɪt/ *verb* (**calculates**, **calculating**, **calculated**) find the answer by using mathematics: *Can you calculate how much the groceries will cost?*

calculator /'kælkjuleɪtə(r)/ *noun* an electronic instrument that adds, subtracts, multiplies and divides

calendar /'kæləndə(r)/ *noun* a list of the days, weeks and months of one year: *Look at the calendar and tell me what day of the week December 2nd is this year.*

calf[1] /kɑ:f/ *noun* (*plural* **calves** /kɑ:vz/) a young cow ☯ Note and picture at **cow**.

calf[2] /kɑ:f/ *noun* the back of your leg, below your knee ☞ picture on page A4

call[1] /kɔ:l/ *noun* **1** a loud cry or shout: *a call for help* **2** using the telephone: *I had a call from Winnie.* ○ *I haven't got time to talk now – I'll give you a call later.* **3** a short visit to somebody: *We paid a call on Mrs Lugadya.*

call[2] /kɔ:l/ *verb* (**calls**, **calling**, **called** /kɔ:ld/) **1** speak loudly and clearly so that somebody who is far away can hear you: *'Breakfast is ready,' she called.* ○ *She called out the names of the winners.* **2** ask somebody to come: *Somebody call the police!* **3** give a name to somebody or something: *They called the baby Fatuma.* **4** telephone somebody: *I'll call you later.* ○ *Who's calling, please?* **be called** have as a name: *'What is your teacher called?' 'She's called Mrs Mtenga.'* **call somebody back** telephone somebody again: *I can't talk now – I'll call you back later.* **call for somebody** go to somebody's house on your way to a place so that they can come with you: *Marion usually calls for me in the morning and we walk to school together.* **call in** make a short visit: *I'll call in to see you this evening.* **call off** say that something that you have planned will not happen: *We called off the race because it was raining.*

call-box /'kɔ:l bɒks/ *noun* (*plural* **call-boxes**) a kind of small building in the street or in a public place that has a telephone in it

calm¹ /kɑːm/ *adjective* (**calmer**, **calmest**) **1** quiet, and not excited or afraid: *Try to keep calm — there's no danger.* **2** without much wind: *calm weather* **3** without big waves: *calm sea*

calmly *adverb*: *He spoke calmly about the accident.*

calm² /kɑːm/ *verb* (**calms**, **calming**, **calmed** /kɑːmd/) **calm down** become less afraid or excited; make somebody less afraid or excited: *Calm down and tell me what happened.*

calorie /ˈkæləri/ *noun* Food that has a lot of calories in it can make you fat.

calves *plural of* **calf**

came *form of* **come**

camel /ˈkæml/ *noun* a large animal with one or two round parts (called **humps**) on its back. Camels carry people and things in the desert.

camera /ˈkæmərə/ *noun* a thing that you use for taking photographs or moving pictures: *I need a new film for my camera.*

camp /kæmp/ *noun* a place where people live in tents for a short time

camp *verb* (**camps**, **camping**, **camped** /kæmpt/) live in a tent for a short time: *Some Girl Guides were camping on the hill.* ✪ It is more usual to say **go camping** when you mean that you are living in a tent on holiday: *We went camping by the lake.*

camping *noun* (no plural) living in a tent for a short time: *Camping isn't much fun when it rains.*

camp-site /ˈkæmp saɪt/ *noun* a place where you can camp

campaign /kæmˈpeɪn/ *noun* a plan to get a special result: *a campaign to stop people smoking*

can¹ /kən/, /kæn/ *modal verb* **1** be able to; be strong enough, clever enough, etc: *She can speak three languages.* ○ *Can you play draughts?* **2** be allowed to: *You can go now.* ○ *Can I have some more porridge, please?* ○ *The doctor says she can't go back to school yet.* **3** a word that you use when you ask somebody to do something: *Can you tell me the time, please?* **4** be possible or likely: *It can be very cold in the mountains at night.* **5** a word that you use with verbs

like *'see'*, *'hear'*, *'smell'* and *'taste'*: *I can smell something burning.* ○ *'What's that noise?'* *'I can't hear anything.'*

> ✪ The negative form of *'can'* is **cannot** /ˈkænɒt/ or the short form **can't** /kɑːnt/:
> *She can't swim.*
> The past tense of *'can'* is **could**. You use **be able to**, not **can**, to make the future and perfect tenses:
> *I* **can** *see it.*
> *You* **will be able to** *see it if you stand on this chair.*
> ☞ Look at the note on page 195 to find out more about **modal verbs**.

can² /kæn/ *noun* **1** a container used for carrying liquid: *an oilcan* **2** a metal container for food or drink that keeps it fresh: *a can of beer* ☛ picture at **container**

canal /kəˈnæl/ *noun* a path that is made through the land and filled with water so that boats can travel on it: *the Suez Canal*

canary /kəˈneəri/ *noun* (*plural* **canaries**) a small yellow bird

cancel /ˈkænsl/ *verb* (**cancels**, **cancelling**, **cancelled** /ˈkænsld/) say that something that you have planned will not happen: *The singer was ill, so the concert was cancelled.*

cancellation /ˌkænsəˈleɪʃn/ *noun*: *the cancellation of the President's visit*

cancer /ˈkænsə(r)/ *noun* a very dangerous illness that makes some **cells** (very small parts in the body) grow too fast: *Smoking can cause cancer.*

candidate /ˈkændɪdət/ *noun* **1** a person who wants to be chosen for something: *When the director leaves, there will be a lot of candidates for her job.* **2** a person who takes an examination

candle /ˈkændl/ *noun* a long round piece of wax with a string in the middle that burns to give light

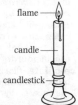

flame

candle

candlestick

candlestick /ˈkændlstɪk/ *noun* a thing that holds a candle

cane /keɪn/ *noun* the hollow stem of some plants: *sugar cane*

canned /kænd/ *adjective* in a can: *canned drinks*

cannot /ˈkænɒt/ = can not

canoe /kəˈnuː/ *noun* a light narrow boat that you use on rivers. You move it through the water with a piece of wood (called a **paddle**). ✪ When you talk about using a canoe, you often say **go canoeing**: *We went canoeing on the river.*

can't /kɑːnt/ = can not

canteen /kænˈtiːn/ *noun* the place where people eat when they are at school or work

canvas /ˈkænvəs/ *noun* (no plural) strong heavy cloth. Tents and sails are often made of canvas, and it is also used for painting pictures on.

cap /kæp/ *noun* **1** a soft hat: *a baseball cap* **2** a thing that covers the top of a bottle or tube: *Put the cap back on the bottle.*

cap

capable /ˈkeɪpəbl/ *adjective* **1** able to do something: *You are capable of passing the exam if you work harder.* **2** able to do things well: *a capable student* ✪ opposite: **incapable**

capacity /kəˈpæsəti/ *noun* (*plural* **capacities**) how much a container can hold: *a tank with a capacity of 1 000 litres*

cape /keɪp/ *noun* **1** a piece of clothing like a coat without sleeves **2** a high part of the land that goes out into the sea: *Cape Horn*

capital /ˈkæpɪtl/ *noun* **1** the most important city in a country, where the government is: *Addis Ababa is the capital of Ethiopia.* **2** (*also* **capital letter**) a big letter of the alphabet: *A, B and C are capitals, a, b and c are small letters.* ○ *Names of people and places begin with a capital letter.*

capsize /kæpˈsaɪz/ *verb* (**capsizes**, **capsizing**, **capsized** /kæpˈsaɪzd/) turn over in the water: *During the storm, the boat capsized.*

captain /ˈkæptɪn/ *noun* **1** the person who is in charge of a ship or an aircraft: *The captain sent a message by radio for help.* **2** the leader of a group of people: *He's the captain of the school football team.*

caption /ˈkæpʃn/ *noun* the words above or below a picture in a book or newspaper that tell you about it

captive /ˈkæptɪv/ *noun* a person who is not free; a prisoner

captivity /kæpˈtɪvəti/ *noun* (no plural) **in captivity** kept in a place that you cannot leave: *Wild animals are often unhappy in captivity* (= in a zoo, for example).

capture /ˈkæptʃə(r)/ *verb* (**captures**, **capturing**, **captured** /ˈkæptʃəd/) catch somebody and keep them somewhere so that they cannot leave: *The police captured the robbers.*

capture *noun* (no plural) *the capture of the escaped prisoners*

car /kɑː(r)/ *noun* a vehicle with four wheels, usually with enough space for four or five people: *She travels to work by car.*

car park /ˈkɑː pɑːk/ *noun* a piece of land or a building where you can put your car for a time

carbon /ˈkɑːbən/ *noun* (no plural) the

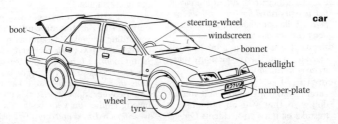

car

boot — steering-wheel — windscreen — bonnet — headlight — number-plate — wheel — tyre

chemical that coal and diamonds are made of and that is in all living things

card /kɑːd/ *noun* **1** a piece of thick stiff paper with writing or pictures on it: *We send Christmas cards, birthday cards and postcards to our friends.* ☛ Look also at **credit card** and **phonecard. 2** a playing-card; one of a set of 52 cards called a **pack of cards** that you use to play games. A pack has four groups of thirteen cards: **hearts**, **clubs**, **diamonds** and **spades**: *Let's have a game of cards.* ○ *They often play cards in the evening.*

cardboard /ˈkɑːdbɔːd/ *noun* (no plural) very thick paper that is used for making boxes, etc

cardigan /ˈkɑːdɪgən/ *noun* a knitted woollen jacket

cardinal /ˈkɑːdɪnl/ *noun* an important priest in the Roman Catholic church

care[1] /keə(r)/ *noun* (no plural) thinking about what you are doing so that you do not make a mistake or break something: *Wash these glasses with care!* **care of somebody** ☛ Look at **c/o**. **take care** be careful: *Take care when you cross the road.* **take care of somebody** or **something** look after somebody or something; do what is necessary: *Kageha is taking care of her sister's baby today.* ○ *I'll take care of the shopping if you do the cleaning.*

care[2] /keə(r)/ *verb* (**cares**, **caring**, **cared** /keəd/) think that it is important: *The only thing he cares about is money.* ○ *I don't care who wins — I'm not interested in football.* ✪ You use expressions like **I don't care**, **who cares?** and **I couldn't care less** when you feel a little angry and want to be rude. **care for somebody** or **something 1** do the things for somebody that they need: *After the accident, her parents cared for her until she was better.* **2** like somebody or something: *I don't care for classical music.*

career /kəˈrɪə(r)/ *noun* a job that you learn to do and then do for many years: *a career in teaching*

careful /ˈkeəfl/ *adjective* If you are careful, you think about what you are doing so that you do not make a mistake or have an accident: *Careful!*

The plate is very hot. ○ *Be careful with those glasses.*

carefully /ˈkeəfəli/ *adverb*: *Please listen carefully.*

careless /ˈkeələs/ *adjective* If you are careless, you do not think enough about what you are doing, so that you make mistakes: *Careless drivers can cause accidents.*

carelessly *adverb*: *She carelessly threw her coat on the floor.*

carelessness /ˈkeələsnəs/ *noun* (no plural) being careless

caretaker /ˈkeəteɪkə(r)/ *noun* a person whose job is to look after a large building like a school or a block of flats

cargo /ˈkɑːgəʊ/ *noun* (*plural* **cargoes**) the things that a ship or an aeroplane carries: *a cargo of wheat*

carnation /kɑːˈneɪʃn/ *noun* a pink, white or red flower with a nice smell

carpenter /ˈkɑːpəntə(r)/ *noun* a person who makes things from wood

carpentry /ˈkɑːpəntri/ *noun* (no plural) making things from wood

carpet /ˈkɑːpɪt/ *noun* a soft covering for a floor that is often made of wool

carriage /ˈkærɪdʒ/ *noun* one of the parts of a train where people sit: *The carriages at the back of the train were empty.*

carried *form of* **carry**

carrier bag /ˈkæriə bæg/, **carrier** *noun* a large bag made from plastic or paper that you use for carrying shopping

carrot

carrot /ˈkærət/ *noun* a long thin orange vegetable

carry /ˈkæri/ *verb* (**carries**, **carrying**, **carried** /ˈkærid/, **has carried**) **1** hold something and take it to another place or keep it with you: *He carried the suit to my room.* ○ *I can't carry this box — it's too heavy.* ○ *Do the police carry guns in your country?* ✪ Be careful! You use **wear**, not **carry**, to talk about having clothes on your body: *She is wearing a red dress and carrying a black* bag. **2** move people or things: *Special fast trains carry people to the city centre.*

carry on continue doing something: *Carry on with your work.* ○ *If you carry on to the end of this road, you'll see the post office on the right.* **carry out** do or finish what you have planned: *The swimming-pool was closed while they carried out the repairs.*

cart /kɑːt/ *noun* a wooden vehicle with two or four wheels that a horse usually pulls

carton /ˈkɑːtn/ *noun* a container made of cardboard or plastic: *a carton of milk* ☛ picture at **container**

cartoon /kɑːˈtuːn/ *noun* **1** a funny drawing, for example in a newspaper **2** a television or cinema film made with drawings, not pictures of real people and places: *a Mickey Mouse cartoon*

carve /kɑːv/ *verb* (**carves**, **carving**, **carved** /kɑːvd/) **1** cut wood or stone to make a picture or shape: *Her father carved a little horse for her out of wood.* **2** cut meat into thin pieces after you have cooked it

case /keɪs/ *noun* **1** a container like a box for keeping something in: *Put the camera back in its case.* ☛ Look also at **briefcase** and **suitcase. 2** an example of something: *There were four cases of this disease in the school last month.* **3** something that happens or something that is true: *'My bicycle's broken.' 'Well, in that case you'll have to walk.'* **4** a question that people in a court of law must decide about: *a divorce case* **5** a problem that the police must find an answer to: *a murder case*

in any case words that you use when you give a second reason for something: *I don't want to see the film, and in any case I'm too busy.* **in case** because something might happen: *Take some money in case you need it.*

cash¹ /kæʃ/ *noun* (no plural) money in coins and notes: *How would you like to pay: cash or cheque?*

cash desk /ˈkæʃ desk/ *noun* the place in a shop where you pay

cash² /kæʃ/ *verb* (**cashes**, **cashing**, **cashed** /kæʃt/) give a cheque and get money for it: *I'd like to cash a cheque, please.*

cash crop /ˈkæʃ krɒp/ *noun* plants that you grow to sell, not to use yourself

cashew /ˈkæʃuː/, **cashew nut** *noun* a curved nut that you can cook and eat

cashier /kæˈʃɪə(r)/ *noun* the person who gives or takes money in a bank

cassava /kəˈsɑːvə/ *noun* (no plural) a plant with fat roots, or the flour that we make from these roots

cassette /kəˈset/ *noun* a plastic box with special tape inside for storing and playing sound, music or moving pictures: *a video cassette* ○ *Put on* (= play) *your new cassette.*

cassette player /kəˈset pleɪə(r)/ **cassette recorder** /kəˈset rɪˌkɔːdə(r)/ *noun* a machine that can put (**record**) sound or music on tape and play it again later

castle /ˈkɑːsl/ *noun* a large old building that was built to keep people safe from their enemies

casual /ˈkæʒuəl/ *adjective* **1** showing that you are not worried about something; relaxed: *She gave us a casual wave as she passed.* **2** not for serious or important times: *You should not wear casual clothes to a job interview.*

casually /ˈkæʒuəli/ *adverb*

casualty /ˈkæʒuəlti/ *noun* (*plural* **casualties**) a person who is hurt or killed in an accident or a war

casualty department /ˈkæʒuəlti dɪpɑːtmənt/, **casualty** *noun* the place in a hospital where doctors help people who have been hurt in an accident

cat /kæt/ *noun* **1** an animal that people keep in their house to catch mice and rats ✪ A young cat is called a **kitten. 2** the name of a group of large wild animals. Tigers and lions are cats.

catch /kætʃ/ *verb* (**catches**, **catching**, **caught** /kɔːt/, **has caught**) **1** take and hold something that is moving: *He threw the ball to me and I caught it.* **2** find and hold somebody or something: *They caught a fish in the river.* ○ *The man ran so fast that the police couldn't catch him.* **3** see somebody when they are doing something wrong: *They caught the thief stealing the money.* **4** be early enough for a bus, train, etc that is going to leave: *You should run if you want to catch the bus.* ✪ opposite: **miss 5** get an illness: *She caught a cold.* **6** let something be held tightly: *I caught my fingers in the door.* **catch fire** start to burn: *The house caught fire.* **catch up** do something quickly so that you are not behind others: *If you miss a lesson, you can do some work at home to catch up.* ○ *Quick! Run after the others and catch them up.*

caterpillar /ˈkætəpɪlə(r)/ *noun* a thing like a long hairy worm that will become a butterfly or moth

cathedral /kəˈθiːdrəl/ *noun* a big important church

Catholic /ˈkæθəlɪk/ = **Roman Catholic**

cattle /ˈkætl/ *noun* (plural) cows and bulls: *a herd of cattle*

caught *form of* **catch**

cauliflower /ˈkɒlɪflaʊə(r)/ *noun* a large vegetable with green leaves outside and a hard white part in the middle

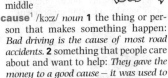

cauliflower

cause[1] /kɔːz/ *noun* **1** the thing or person that makes something happen: *Bad driving is the cause of most road accidents.* **2** something that people care about and want to help: *They gave the money to a good cause – it was used to build a new hospital.*

cause[2] /kɔːz/ *verb* (**causes, causing, caused** /kɔːzd/) be the reason why something happens: *Who caused the accident?* ○ *The fire was caused by a cigarette.*

caution /ˈkɔːʃn/ *noun* (no plural) great care: *Caution! Wet floor.*

cautious /ˈkɔːʃəs/ *adjective* careful because there may be danger

cautiously *adverb*: *Cautiously, he pushed open the door and looked into the room.*

cave /keɪv/ *noun* a large hole in the side of a mountain or under the ground: *Thousands of years ago, people lived in caves.*

CD /ˌsiː ˈdiː/ *short for* **compact disc**

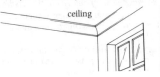

ceiling

ceiling /ˈsiːlɪŋ/ *noun* the part of a room over your head

celebrate /ˈseləbreɪt/ *verb* (**celebrates, celebrating, celebrated**) enjoy yourself because you have a special reason to be happy: *If you pass your exams, we'll have a party to celebrate.*

celebration /ˌseləˈbreɪʃn/ *noun* a time when you enjoy yourself because you have a special reason to be happy: *birthday celebrations*

cell /sel/ *noun* **1** a small room where a prisoner lives **2** the smallest living part of any plant or animal

cellar /ˈselə(r)/ *noun* a room in the part of a building that is under the ground: *a wine cellar*

Celsius /ˈselsiəs/ *noun* (no plural) a way of measuring temperature. Water freezes at 0°Celsius and boils at 100°Celsius. ✪ The short way of writing 'Celsius' is **C**: *52° C*

cement /sɪˈment/ *noun* (no plural) grey powder that becomes hard like stone when you mix it with water and leave it to dry. Cement is used in building.

cemetery /ˈsemətri/ *noun* (plural **cemeteries**) an area of ground where dead people are put under the earth

cent /sent/ *noun* money that people use in some countries. There are 100 cents in a **shilling**: *a fifty-cent coin* ○ *Can you lend me fifty cents?*

centigrade /ˈsentɪɡreɪd/ *another word for* **Celsius**

centilitre /ˈsentɪliːtə(r)/ *noun* a

measure of liquid. There are 100 centilitres in a **litre**. ✪ The short way of writing 'centilitre' is **cl**: *250 cl*

centimetre /ˈsentɪmiːtə(r)/ *noun* a measure of length. There are 100 centimetres in a **metre**. ✪ The short way of writing 'centimetre' is **cm**: *98 cm*

centipede /ˈsentɪpiːd/a long, thin animal with many legs

central /ˈsentrəl/ *adjective* in the middle part: *central Nairobi*

centre /ˈsentə(r)/ *noun* **1** the part in the middle: *the city centre* ○ *The flower has a yellow centre with white petals.* **2** a place where people come to do something special: *a shopping centre* ○ *They're building a big training centre in our town.*

century /ˈsentʃəri/ *noun* (*plural* **centuries**) **1** 100 years **2** a time of 100 years, that we use in dates: *We are living at the beginning of the twenty-first century.*

cereal /ˈsɪəriəl/ *noun* (*plural* **cereals**) a plant that farmers grow so that we can eat the seed: *Wheat and oats are cereals.*

ceremony /ˈserəməni/ *noun* (*plural* **ceremonies**) a time when you do something special and important: *the opening ceremony of the Olympic Games* ○ *a wedding ceremony*

certain[1] /ˈsɜːtn/ *adjective* without any doubt; sure: *I am certain that I have seen her before.* ○ *It's not certain that they will come.* **for certain** without any doubt: *I don't know for certain where she is.* **make certain** check something so that you are sure about it: *Please make certain that the window is closed before you leave.*

certain[2] /ˈsɜːtn/ *adjective* one or some that can be named: *It's cheaper to telephone at certain times of the day.* ○ *Do you want the work to be finished by a certain date?*

certainly /ˈsɜːtnli/ *adverb* **1** without any doubt: *She is certainly the best swimmer in the team.* **2** yes: 'Will you open the door for me, please?' 'Certainly.' **certainly not** no: 'Can I borrow your bicycle?' 'Certainly not!'

certificate /səˈtɪfɪkət/ *noun* an important piece of paper that shows that

something is true: *Your birth certificate shows when and where you were born.*

chain /tʃeɪn/ *noun* metal rings that are joined together: *Round her neck she wore a gold chain.* ○ *My bicycle chain is broken.* ☛ picture at **bicycle**

chain

chain *verb* (**chains**, **chaining**, **chained** /tʃeɪnd/) attach somebody or something to a place with a chain: *The dog was chained to the fence.*

chair /tʃeə(r)/ *noun* **1** a piece of furniture with four legs, a seat and a back that one person can sit on: *a table and four chairs* **2** a person who controls a meeting ✪ You can also say **chairman** /ˈtʃeəmən/, **chairwoman** /ˈtʃeə-wʊmən/ or **chairperson** /ˈtʃeəpɜːsn/.

chalk /tʃɔːk/ *noun* (no plural) **1** soft white rock: *The cliffs are made of chalk.* **2** a piece of this rock that you use for writing on a **blackboard**

challenge /ˈtʃælɪndʒ/ *verb* (**challenges**, **challenging**, **challenged** /ˈtʃælɪndʒd/) ask somebody to play a game with you or fight with you to see who wins: *The boxer challenged the world champion to a fight.*

challenge *noun* a new or difficult thing that makes you try hard: *Climbing the mountain will be a real challenge.*

chameleon /kəˈmiːliən/ *noun* a lizard with a long tongue and large eyes. Chameleons can change colour.

champion /ˈtʃæmpiən/ *noun* a person who is the best at a sport or game: *a chess champion* ○ *the world champion*

championship /ˈtʃæmpiənʃɪp/ *noun* a competition to find the champion: *Our team won the championship this year.*

chance /tʃɑːns/ *noun* **1** (*plural* **chances**) a time when you can do something: *It was their last chance to escape.* ○ *I haven't had a chance to write to Jane today. I'll do it tomorrow.* **2** (*plural* **chances**) a possibility that something may happen: *He has a good chance of passing the exam because he has worked hard.* **3** (no plural) something that happens that you cannot control; luck **by chance** not because you have planned it: *We met by chance at the station.* **take a chance** do something when it is possible that something bad may happen because of it

change[1] /tʃeɪndʒ/ *verb* (**changes**, **changing**, **changed** /tʃeɪndʒd/) **1** become different: *She has changed a lot since the last time I saw her – she looks much older.* ○ *Water changes into ice when it gets very cold.* **2** make something different: *Esther changes her hairstyle often.* **3** put or take something in place of another thing: *My new watch didn't work, so I took it back to the shop and changed it.* ○ *I went to the bank to change my US dollars into Kenyan shillings.* ○ *Can you change a 500 shilling note please? I need some 10 shilling coins.* **4** put on different clothes: *I must change before I go out.* ✪ You can also say **get changed**: *I must get changed before I go out.* **6** get off a train or bus and get on another one: *I have to change trains at Nairobi.*

change[2] /tʃeɪndʒ/ *noun* **1** (no plural) money that you get when you have paid too much: *I gave the shop assistant ten shillings. The sweets cost two shillings, so he gave me eight shillings change.* **2** (no plural) small pieces of money; coins: *I haven't got any change.* **3** (*plural* **changes**) a thing that is different now: *The new government has made a lot of changes.* **for a change** because you want something different: *I usually have tea in the morning, but today I had coffee for a change.*

channel /ˈtʃænl/ *noun* **1** a narrow place where water can go: *We dug a channel from the river to the field.* **2** one of the things you can choose on television: *Which channel are you watching?*

chapati /tʃəˈpɑːti/ *noun* a kind of flat bread

chapel /ˈtʃæpl/ *noun* a room or a small church where Christians go to pray

chapter /ˈtʃæptə(r)/ *noun* one of the parts of a book: *You start reading a book at the beginning of Chapter 1.*

character /ˈkærəktə(r)/ *noun* **1** (no plural) the way a person or thing is: *He has a strong character.* ○ *The new factory will change the character of the*

village. **2** (*plural* **characters**) a person in a play, book or film: *The main character in the novel is a twelve-year-old boy.*

charcoal /ˈtʃɑːkəʊl/ *noun* (no plural) black stuff that we make by burning wood. You use charcoal as a fuel or for drawing.

charge[1] /tʃɑːdʒ/ *verb* (**charges**, **charging**, **charged** /tʃɑːdʒd/) **1** ask somebody to pay a certain price for something: *The driver charged me 100 shillings for the ride.* **2** say that somebody has done something wrong: *The police have charged him with murder.* **3** move quickly and with a lot of force: *The bull charged.* ○ *The children charged into the room.*

charge[2] /tʃɑːdʒ/ *noun* **1** the money that you must pay for something: *There is an extra charge if you travel at night.* **2** a statement that somebody has done something wrong: *a charge of murder* **be in charge of somebody** or **something** look after or control somebody or something: *Tim is in charge of his baby brother while his mother is out.* ○ *The headmaster is in charge of the school.*

charity /ˈtʃærəti/ *noun* **1** (*plural* **charities**) a group of people who collect money to help people who need it: *The Red Cross is a charity.* **2** (no plural) being kind and helping other people

charm /tʃɑːm/ *noun* **1** (no plural) being able to make people like you: *Ann has a lot of charm.* **2** (*plural* **charms**) a small thing that you wear because you think it will bring good luck: *She wears a necklace with a lucky charm on it.*

charm *verb* (**charms**, **charming**, **charmed** /tʃɑːmd/) make somebody like you: *The baby charmed everybody with her smile.*

charming /ˈtʃɑːmɪŋ/ *adjective* lovely; beautiful: *a charming smile*

chart /tʃɑːt/ *noun* **1** a drawing that gives information about something: *a temperature chart* **2** a map of the sea that sailors use

chase /tʃeɪs/ *verb* (**chases**, **chasing**, **chased** /tʃeɪst/) run behind somebody or something and try to catch them: *We saw a cheetah chasing an antelope.* ○ *The police chased after the thief but he escaped.*

49 **chemistry**

chase *noun*: In that film there is an exciting car chase.

chat /tʃæt/ *noun* a friendly talk: *Let's have a chat about it later.*

chat *verb* (chats, chatting, chatted) talk in a friendly way

chatter /ˈtʃætə(r)/ *verb* (chatters, chattering, chattered /ˈtʃætəd/) talk quickly about things that are not very important: *Stop chattering and finish your work.*

cheap /tʃiːp/ *adjective* (cheaper, cheapest) Something that is cheap does not cost a lot of money: *Buses are cheaper than trains.* ○ *That restaurant is very good and quite cheap.* ✪ opposite: **expensive** or **dear**

cheat /tʃiːt/ *verb* (cheats, cheating, cheated) do something that is not honest or fair: *She cheated in the exam – she copied her friend's work.*

cheat *noun* a person who cheats

check¹ /tʃek/ *verb* (checks, checking, checked /tʃekt/) look at something to see that it is right, good, safe, etc: *When I checked the address I realized that I was in the wrong street.* ○ *At the garage the man checked the oil and water.* ○ *Check that all the windows are closed before you leave.* **check in** tell the person at the desk in a hotel or an airport that you have arrived: *I have to check in an hour before my flight.* **check out** pay your bill at a hotel and leave

check² /tʃek/ *noun* a look to see that everything is right, good, safe, etc: *Have a quick check to see that you haven't forgotten anything.*

check³ /tʃek/ *adjective* a pattern of squares

checked

checked /tʃekt/ *adjective* with a pattern of squares: *a checked shirt*

—check

checkout /ˈtʃekaʊt/ *noun* one of the places in a supermarket where you pay for the things you are buying

check-up /ˈtʃek ʌp/ *noun* an examination by a doctor to see if you are well

cheek /tʃiːk/ *noun* **1** (*plural* cheeks) one of the two round parts of your face under your eyes ☞ picture on page A4

2 (no plural) doing something without caring that it will make other people angry or unhappy: *What a cheek! Somebody has taken my seat!*

cheeky /ˈtʃiːki/ *adjective* (cheekier, cheekiest) not polite: *Don't be so cheeky!* ○ *She was punished for being cheeky to a teacher.*

cheer¹ /tʃɪə(r)/ *verb* (cheers, cheering, cheered /tʃɪəd/) shout to show that you are pleased: *The crowd cheered loudly when the President arrived.* **cheer up** make somebody happier; become happier: *We gave Beatrice some flowers to cheer her up.* ○ *Cheer up! You will feel better soon.*

cheer² /tʃɪə(r)/ *noun* a shout that shows that you are pleased: *The crowd gave a loud cheer as the singer came onto the stage.* **three cheers for … Hip, hip, hurray!** words that you shout when somebody has done something good: *Three cheers for the winner! Hip, hip, hurray!*

cheerful /ˈtʃɪəfl/ *adjective* happy: *a cheerful smile* ○ *You don't look very cheerful today. What's the matter?*

cheers /tʃɪəz/ a word that you say to somebody when you have a drink together ✪ People sometimes say **cheers** instead of **thank you** or **goodbye**.

cheese /tʃiːz/ *noun* yellow or white food made from milk

cheeseburger /ˈtʃiːzbɜːɡə(r)/ *noun* a hamburger with cheese in it

chef /ʃef/ *noun* a person who cooks the food in a restaurant

chemical¹ /ˈkemɪkl/ *noun* a solid or liquid substance that is used in chemistry or is made by chemistry

chemical² /ˈkemɪkl/ *adjective* of chemistry or used in chemistry: *a chemical experiment*

chemist /ˈkemɪst/ *noun* **1** a person who makes and sells medicines ✪ The shop where a chemist works is called a **chemist's**. It sells things like soap and perfume as well as medicines. **2** a person who studies chemistry or who makes chemicals

chemistry /ˈkemɪstri/ *noun* (no plural)

the science that studies gases, liquids and solids to find out what they are and what they do

cheque — signature

chicken

cock   chick   hen

cheque /tʃek/ *noun* a piece of paper from a bank that you can write on and use to pay for things: *I gave him a cheque for 5 000 shillings.* ○ *Can I pay by cheque?*

cheque-book /'tʃek bʊk/ *noun* a book of cheques

cherry /'tʃeri/ *noun* (*plural* **cherries**) a small round red or black fruit

cherry

chess /tʃes/ *noun* (no plural) a game that two people play with pieces called **chessmen** on a board that has black and white squares on it (called a **chessboard**)

chest[1] /tʃest/ *noun* the front part of your body below your shoulders and above your waist ☞ picture on page A4

chest[2] /tʃest/ *noun* a large strong box with a lid

chest of drawers /ˌtʃest əv 'drɔːz/ *noun* (*plural* **chests of drawers**) a piece of furniture like a box with parts that you can pull out (**drawers**). A chest of drawers is usually used for keeping clothes in.

chew /tʃuː/ *verb* (**chews**, **chewing**, **chewed** /tʃuːd/) use your teeth to make food soft

chewing-gum /'tʃuːm ɡʌm/ *noun* (no plural) sweet stuff that you can chew for a long time

chick /tʃɪk/ *noun* a young bird, especially a young chicken: *a hen with her chicks*

chicken /'tʃɪkɪn/ *noun* **1** (*plural* **chickens**) a bird that people keep on farms for its eggs and meat

❂ A female chicken is called a **hen** and a male chicken is called a **cock**. A young chicken is a **chick**.

2 (no plural) meat from a chicken: *roast chicken*

chickenpox /'tʃɪkɪnpɒks/ *noun* (no plural) an illness, especially of children. When you have chickenpox you feel very hot and get spots on your skin that itch.

chief[1] /tʃiːf/ *adjective* most important: *Bad driving is one of the chief causes of road accidents.*

chiefly *adverb* mostly; mainly: *The rain fell chiefly in the north of the country.*

chief[2] /tʃiːf/ *noun* the leader or ruler of a group of people: *the chief of a tribe*

child /tʃaɪld/ *noun* (*plural* **children** /'tʃɪldrən/) **1** a boy or girl: *There are 30 children in the class.* **2** a daughter or son: *One of her children got married last year.* ☞ picture on page A3

childhood /'tʃaɪldhʊd/ *noun* (no plural) the time when you are a child: *She had a happy childhood.*

childish /'tʃaɪldɪʃ/ *adjective* like a child, or for children: *childish games*

chilli /'tʃɪli/ *noun* a dried red pepper that tastes very hot

chilly /'tʃɪli/ *adjective* (**chillier**, **chilliest**) cold: *a chilly night*

chime /tʃaɪm/ *verb* (**chimes**, **chiming**, **chimed** /tʃaɪmd/) make the sound that a bell makes: *The clock chimed midnight.*

chimney /'tʃɪmni/ *noun* (*plural* **chimneys**) a large pipe over a fire that lets smoke go outside into the air ☞ picture at **house**

chimpanzee /ˌtʃɪmpæn'ziː/ *noun* an animal like a monkey with dark hair and no tail

chimpanzee

chin /tʃɪn/ *noun* the part of your face below your mouth ☞ picture on page A4

china /ˈtʃaɪnə/ *noun* (no plural) a hard white material made from earth, or things like plates and cups that are made from this: *a china cup*

chip[1] /tʃɪp/ *noun* **1** a small piece of wood, stone, china, etc that has broken off a larger piece **2** a piece of potato cooked in oil: *We had chicken and chips for lunch.* **3** a microchip; a very small thing inside a computer, for example, that makes it work **4** *American English for* **crisp**[2]

chip[2] /tʃɪp/ *verb* (**chips**, **chipping**, **chipped** /tʃɪpt/) break a small piece from something: *I chipped a cup.*

chirp /tʃɜːp/ *noun* the short high sound that a small bird makes

chirp *verb* (**chirps**, **chirping**, **chirped** /tʃɜːpt/) make this sound

chocolate /ˈtʃɒklət/ *noun* **1** (no plural) dark brown sweet food that is made from cocoa **2** (*plural* **chocolates**) a sweet made of chocolate

choice /tʃɔɪs/ *noun* **1** deciding which one; choosing: *You made the right choice.* ○ *We have no choice. We must go immediately.* **2** the number of things that you can choose: *There is a big choice of vegetables in the market.*

choir /ˈkwaɪə(r)/ *noun* a big group of people who sing together: *a school choir* ○ *the church choir*

choke /tʃəʊk/ *verb* (**chokes**, **choking**, **choked** /tʃəʊkt/) not be able to breathe because something is in your throat

cholera /ˈkɒlərə/ *noun* (no plural) a dangerous illness that makes you have bad diarrhoea and vomiting. You can get cholera from dirty food and water.

choose /tʃuːz/ *verb* (**chooses**, **choosing**, **chose** /tʃəʊz/, **has chosen** /ˈtʃəʊzn/) take the thing or person that you like best: *Maria chose a yellow and blue kanga.*

chop[1] /tʃɒp/ *verb* (**chops**, **chopping**, **chopped** /tʃɒpt/) cut something with a knife or an axe: *We chopped some wood for the fire.* ○ *Chop the meat up into small pieces.*

chop[2] /tʃɒp/ *noun* a thick slice of meat with a piece of bone in it: *a mutton chop*

chorus /ˈkɔːrəs/ *noun* (*plural* **choruses**) a part of a song that you repeat

christen /ˈkrɪsn/ *verb* (**christens**, **christening**, **christened** /ˈkrɪsnd/) give a first name to a baby and make him/her a member of the Christian church in a special ceremony

christening /ˈkrɪsnɪŋ/ *noun* the ceremony when a baby is christened

Christian /ˈkrɪstʃən/ *noun* a person who believes in Jesus Christ and what he taught

Christian *adjective*: *the Christian church*

Christian name /ˈkrɪstʃən neɪm/ *noun* a person's first name: *Her surname is Musamba and her Christian name is Sarah.* ☞ Note at **name**.

Christianity /ˌkrɪstiˈænəti/ *noun* (no plural) the religion that follows what Jesus Christ taught

Christmas /ˈkrɪsməs/ *noun* the special time when Christians remember the birth of Christ: *Merry Christmas!*

church /tʃɜːtʃ/ *noun* (*plural* **churches**) a building where Christians go to pray: *They go to church every Sunday.*

churchyard /ˈtʃɜːtʃjɑːd/ *noun* a piece of land around a church

cigar /sɪˈɡɑː(r)/ *noun* a roll of tobacco leaves that you can smoke

cigarette /ˌsɪɡəˈret/ *noun* small pieces of tobacco in a tube of paper that you can smoke

cinema /ˈsɪnəmə/ *noun* a place where you go to see a film: *Let's go to the cinema tonight.*

circle /ˈsɜːkl/ *noun* a round shape: *There are 360 degrees in a circle.* ☞ picture on page A5

circular /ˈsɜːkjələ(r)/ *adjective* with the shape of a circle; round: *A wheel is circular.*

circulate /ˈsɜːkjəleɪt/ *verb* (**circulates**, **circulating**, **circulated**) move round: *Blood circulates in our bodies.*

circumference /səˈkʌmfərəns/ *noun* the distance around a circle ☞ picture on page A5

circumstances /ˈsɜːkəmstənsɪz/ *noun* (plural) the facts that are true when something happens. **in** or **under the circumstances** because things are as they are: *My father was ill, so under the*

circumstances I decided to stay at home.
under no circumstances not at all;
never: *Under no circumstances should
you go out alone at night.*

citizen /ˈsɪtɪzn/ *noun* a person who
belongs to a country or a town: *a
Kenyan citizen.*

city (*plural* **cities**)/ˈsɪti/ *noun* a big and
important town: *the city of Kampala*
○ *the city centre*

civil /ˈsɪvl/ *adjective* of the people of a
country: *civil rights*

the Civil Service /ˌsɪvl ˈsɜːvɪs/ *noun*
(no plural) the people who work for the
government

civil war /ˌsɪvl ˈwɔː(r)/ *noun* a war
between groups of people in one
country

civilian /səˈvɪliən/ *noun* a person who
is not a soldier

civilization /ˌsɪvəlaɪˈzeɪʃn/ *noun* the
way people live together in a certain
place at a certain time: *ancient
civilizations*

cl *short way of writing* **centilitre**

claim /kleɪm/ *verb* (**claims**, **claiming**,
claimed /kleɪmd/) **1** ask for something
because it is yours: *If nobody claims the
camera you found, you can have it.* **2** say
that something is true: *Muanga claims
that he did the work without help.*

claim *noun:* *The workers are making a
claim for better pay.*

clan /klæn/ *noun* a group of people
who all have the same ancestors

clang /klæŋ/ *noun* the loud sound that
metal makes when you hit it with
something: *The iron gates shut with a
clang.*

clap /klæp/ *verb* (**claps**, **clapping**,
clapped /klæpt/) hit your hands
together to make a noise, usually to
show that you like something: *At the
end of the concert the audience clapped
loudly.*

clap *noun* the sound that you make
when you hit your hands together

clash /klæʃ/ *verb* (**clashes**, **clashing**,
clashed /klæʃt/) **1** fight or argue:
*Police clashed with football fans outside
the stadium last Saturday.* **2** be at the
same time: *The match clashed with my
swimming lesson, so I couldn't watch it.*

3 If colours clash, they do not look nice
together: *Your tie clashes with your shirt!*

class /klɑːs/ *noun* (*plural* **classes**) **1** a
group of children or students who
learn together: *The whole class passed
the exam.* ○ *There is a new girl in my
class.* **2** the time when you learn something with a teacher: *Classes begin at
nine o'clock.* ○ *You mustn't eat in class.*
3 a group of people or things that are
the same in some way: *There are many
different classes of animals.* **4** how good,
comfortable, etc something is: *It costs
more to travel first class.*

classroom /ˈklɑːsruːm/ *noun* a room
where you have lessons in a school

classic /ˈklæsɪk/ *noun* a book that is so
good that people read it for many years
after it was written

classical /ˈklæsɪkl/ *adjective* **1** in a
style that people have used for a long
time because they think it is good:
classical music **2** of ancient Greece or
Rome: *classical Greek*

clatter /ˈklætə(r)/ *noun* (no plural) a
loud noise that hard things make when
they hit each other: *the clatter of
cooking pots*

clause /klɔːz/ *noun* a part of a sentence
that has a verb in it

claw /klɔː/ *noun* one of the hard
pointed parts on the feet of some animals and birds: *Cats have sharp claws.*

clay /kleɪ/ *noun* (no plural) a kind of
heavy earth that becomes hard when it
is dry. Clay is used to make things like
pots and tiles.

clean[1] /kliːn/ *adjective* (**cleaner**,
cleanest) not dirty: *clean clothes*
○ *clean air* ☞ picture on page A11

clean[2] /kliːn/ *verb* (**cleans**, **cleaning**,
cleaned /kliːnd/) take away the dirt or
marks from something; make something clean: *Sam helped his mother to
clean the kitchen.* ○ *Don't forget to clean
your teeth before you go to bed.*

clean *noun* (no plural) *The car needs a
clean.*

clear[1] /klɪə(r)/ *adjective* (**clearer**,
clearest) **1** easy to see, hear or understand: *She spoke in a loud clear voice.* ○
This photograph is very clear. ○ *It's
clear that Jane is not happy.* **2** that you
can see through: *clear glass* **3** with

nothing in the way; empty: *The roads were very clear.* **4** bright; without clouds: *a clear day*

clear² /klɪə(r)/ *verb* (**clears**, **clearing**, **cleared** /klɪəd/) **1** take things away from a place because you do not need them there: *They cleared the rocks from the path.* ○ *When you have finished your meal, clear the table.* **2** become clear: *It rained in the morning, but in the afternoon the sky cleared.* **clear off** go away: *He got angry and told them to clear off.* **clear out** take everything out of a cupboard, room, etc so that you can clean it and make it tidy **clear up** make a place clean and tidy: *She helped me to clear up after the party.*

clearly /ˈklɪəli/ *adverb* **1** in a way that is easy to see, hear or understand: *Please speak louder – I can't hear you very clearly.* ○ *The notes explain very clearly what you have to do.* **2** without any doubt: *She is clearly very intelligent.*

clerk /klɑːk/ *noun* a person in an office or bank who does things like writing letters

clever /ˈklevə(r)/ *adjective* (**cleverer**, **cleverest**) able to learn, understand or do something quickly and well: *a clever student*

cleverly *adverb*: *The book is cleverly written.*

click /klɪk/ *noun* a short sharp sound: *I heard a click as someone switched the light on.*

click *verb* (**clicks**, **clicking**, **clicked** /klɪkt/) make this sound: *clicking cameras*

client /ˈklaɪənt/ *noun* a person who pays another person, for example a lawyer or an accountant, for help or advice

cliff

cliff /klɪf/ *noun* the high steep side of a hill by the sea

climate /ˈklaɪmət/ *noun* the sort of weather that a place has: *Coffee will not grow in a cold climate.*

climb /klaɪm/ *verb* (**climbs**, **climbing**, **climbed** /klaɪmd/) **1** go up or down, walking or using your hands and feet: *The cat climbed to the top of the tree.* ○ *They climbed the mountain.* **2** move to or from a place when it is not easy to do it: *The children climbed through a hole in the fence.* **3** move to a higher place: *The road climbs steeply.*

climb *noun* (no plural) *It was a long climb from the village to the top of the mountain.*

climber /ˈklaɪmə(r)/ *noun* a person who goes up and down mountains or rocks as a sport

cling /klɪŋ/ *verb* (**clings**, **clinging**, **clung** /klʌŋ/, **has clung**) hold or stick tightly to somebody or something: *The small child was crying and clinging to her mother.* ○ *His wet clothes clung to his body.*

clinic /ˈklɪnɪk/ *noun* a place where you can go to get special help from a doctor

clip /klɪp/ *noun* a small piece of metal or plastic for holding things together: *a paper-clip*

clip *verb* (**clips**, **clipping**, **clipped** /klɪpt/) join something to another thing with a clip: *I clipped the photo to the letter.*

cloak /kləʊk/ *noun* a very loose coat that has no sleeves

cloakroom /ˈkləʊkruːm/ *noun* **1** a place in a building where you can leave your coat or bag **2** a toilet in a public building

clock /klɒk/ *noun* a thing that shows you what time it is. It stands in a room or hangs on a wall: *an alarm clock* ✪ A thing that shows the time and that you wear on your wrist is called a **watch**.

> ✪ You say that a clock or watch is **fast** if it shows a time that is later than the real time. You say that it is **slow** if it shows a time that is earlier than the real time.

clockwise /ˈklɒkwaɪz/ *adjective*, *adverb* in the direction that the hands of a clock move: *Turn the handle clockwise.* ✪ opposite: **anticlockwise**

close¹ /kləʊs/ *adjective*, *adverb* (**closer**,

closest) **1** near: *We live close to the river.* ○ *You're too close to the fire.* **2** If people are close, they like or love each other very much: *I'm very close to my sister.* ○ *Jama and I are close friends.* **3** with only a very small difference: *'Did David win the race?' 'No, but it was very close.'* **4** careful: *Keep a close watch on the children.* **close together** with not much space between them: *The photographer asked us to stand closer together.*

closely *adverb* in a close way: *We watched her closely.* ○ *Salim entered, closely followed by Mike.*

close[2] /kləʊz/ *verb* (**closes**, **closing**, **closed** /kləʊzd/) **1** shut: *Please close the window.* ○ *Close your eyes!* ○ *The door closed quietly.* **2** stop being open, so that people cannot go there: *The banks close at 2 pm.* ✪ opposite: **open**.

close down shut and stop working; make something shut and stop working: *The shop closed down when the owner died.*

closed *adjective* not open; shut: *The shops are closed on Sundays.* ☞ picture on page A11

cloth /klɒθ/ *noun* **1** (no plural) material that is made of wool, cotton, etc and that we use for making clothes and other things ✪ **Material** is the word that we usually use. **2** a piece of cloth that you use for a special job: *a tablecloth* (= for covering a table) ○ *Wipe the floor with a cloth.*

clothes /kləʊðz/ *noun* (plural) things like trousers, shirts and coats that you wear to cover your body: *She was wearing new clothes.* ○ *Take off those wet clothes.*

clothing /ˈkləʊðɪŋ/ *noun* (no plural) clothes: *skirts, trousers and other pieces of clothing*

cloud /klaʊd/ *noun* **1** a white or grey shape in the sky that is made of small drops of water: *Look at those dark clouds. It's going to rain.* **2** dust or smoke that looks like a cloud: *clouds of smoke*

cloudy *adjective* (**cloudier**, **cloudiest**) with a lot of clouds: *a cloudy sky*

clove /kləʊv/ *noun* the dried young flower (**bud**) of a kind of tree. Cloves have a strong taste and you use them in cooking.

clown /klaʊn/ *noun* a person in a circus who wears funny clothes and makes people laugh

club[1] /klʌb/ *noun* a group of people who do something together, or the place where they meet: *I belong to the football club.* ☞ Look also at **nightclub**.

club *verb* (**clubs**, **clubbing**, **clubbed** /klʌbd/) **club together** give money so that a group of people can buy something: *We all clubbed together to buy Miriam and Miheso a wedding present.*

club[2] /klʌb/ *noun* **1** a heavy stick with a thick end **2** **clubs** (plural) the playing-cards that have the shape ♣ on them: *the three of clubs*

clue /kluː/ *noun* something that helps to find the answer to a problem, or to know the truth: *The police have found a clue that may help them to catch the murderer.* **not have a clue** not know something, or not know how to do something: *'What's his name?' 'I haven't a clue.'*

clumsy /ˈklʌmzi/ *adjective* (**clumsier**, **clumsiest**) If you are clumsy, you often drop things or do things badly because you do not move in an easy or careful way: *I'm so clumsy! I've just broken a glass.*

clumsily /ˈklʌmzəli/ *adverb*: *He clumsily knocked the cup off the table.*

clung *form of* **cling**

clutch /klʌtʃ/ *verb* (**clutches**, **clutching**, **clutched** /klʌtʃt/) hold something tightly: *The child clutched his mother's hand.*

cm *short way of writing* **centimetre**

Co /kəʊ/ *short for* **company** 1

c/o You use **c/o** (short for **care of**) when you are writing to somebody who is staying at another person's house: *Miss Harriet Gombe, c/o Mrs Marion Malaba*

coach[2] /kəʊtʃ/ *noun* (plural **coaches**) a person who teaches a sport: *a football coach*

coach *verb* (**coaches**, **coaching**, **coached** /kəʊtʃt/) teach somebody:

She is coaching the Kenyan team for the Olympics.

coal /kəʊl/ *noun* (no plural) hard black stuff that comes from under the ground and gives heat when you burn it

coarse /kɔːs/ *adjective* (**coarser**, **coarsest**) made of thick pieces so that it is not smooth: *coarse sand* ○ *coarse material*

coast /kəʊst/ *noun* the part of the land that is next to the sea: *Their village is near the coast.* ○ *Zanzibar is off the east coast of Africa.*

coastguard /ˈkəʊstɡɑːd/ *noun* a person whose job is to watch the sea and ships and help people who are in danger

coastline /ˈkəʊstlaɪn/ *noun* the edge of the land next to the sea: *a rocky coast*

coat /kəʊt/ *noun* **1** a piece of clothing that you wear over your other clothes when you go outside in cold weather or rain: *Put your coat on – it's cold today.* **2** the hair or fur that covers an animal: *A zebra has a striped coat.*

coat *verb* (**coats**, **coating**, **coated**) put a thin covering of something over another thing: *Their shoes were coated with mud.*

coat-hanger /ˈkəʊt hæŋə(r)/ *noun* a piece of wood, metal or plastic with a hook. You use it for hanging clothes on.

coat-hanger

cobra /ˈkəʊbrə/ *noun* a danger-ous snake that can make its neck big like a hood

cobra

cobweb /ˈkɒbweb/ *noun* a net that a spider makes to catch insects

cock /kɒk/ *noun* **1** a male bird **2** a male chicken

cockpit /ˈkɒkpɪt/ *noun* the part of a plane where the pilot sits

cockroach /ˈkɒkrəʊtʃ/ *noun* (*plural* **cockroaches**) a large, brown insect that often lives inside buildings

cocoa /ˈkəʊkəʊ/ *noun* (no plural) **1** a brown powder from the beans of a tree, that is used to make chocolate **2** a drink made from this powder

coconut /ˈkəʊkənʌt/ *noun* a very large brown nut that grows on trees. Coconuts are hard and hairy on the outside, and they have sweet white food and liquid inside.

cod /kɒd/ *noun* (*plural* **cod**) a fish that lives in the sea and that you can eat

code /kəʊd/ *noun* **1** a way of writing secret messages, using letters, numbers or special signs: *The list of names was written in code.* **2** a group of numbers or letters that helps you find something: *What's the code* (= the telephone number) *for Paris?* **3** a set of rules for a group of people: *the Highway Code* (= rules for people who are driving on the road)

coffee /ˈkɒfi/ *noun* **1** (no plural) brown powder made from the beans of a tree that grows in hot countries. You use it for making a drink. **2** (no plural) a drink of hot water mixed with this powder: *Would you like coffee or tea?* ○ *a cup of coffee* **3** (*plural* **coffees**) a cup of this drink: *Two coffees, please.* ✪ **White** coffee has milk in it and **black** coffee has no milk.

coffee-table /ˈkɒfi teɪbl/ *noun* a small low table

coffin /ˈkɒfɪn/ *noun* a box that you put a dead person's body in

coil /kɔɪl/ *noun* a long piece of rope or wire that goes round in circles: *a coil of rope*

coil *verb* (**coils**, **coiling**, **coiled** /kɔɪld/) make something into a lot of circles that are joined together: *The snake coiled itself round a branch.*

coin /kɔɪn/ *noun* a round piece of money made of metal: *a pound coin*

coincidence /kəʊˈɪnsɪdəns/ *noun* when things happen at the same time or in the same place by chance: *What a coincidence! I was thinking about you when you phoned!*

cola /ˈkəʊlə/ *noun* **1** (no plural) a sweet brown drink with bubbles in it **2** (*plural* **colas**) a glass, bottle or can of cola

cold[1] /kəʊld/ *adjective* (**colder**, **coldest**) **1** not hot or warm; with a low temperature. Ice and snow are cold: *Put your coat on — it's cold outside.* ○ *I'm cold. Will you put the heater on?* ○ *hot and cold water* ☞ picture on page A11 **2** not friendly or kind: *a cold person*

coldly *adverb* in an unfriendly way: *She looked at me coldly.*

cold² /kəʊld/ *noun* **1** (no plural) cold weather: *Don't go out in the cold.* **2** (*plural* **colds**) an illness that makes you sneeze and cough: *I've got a cold.* **catch a cold** become ill with a cold

collapse /kə'læps/ *verb* (**collapses**, **collapsing**, **collapsed** /kə'læpst/) fall down suddenly: *The building collapsed in the earthquake.* ○ *She collapsed in the street and she was taken to hospital.*

collapse *noun*: *the collapse of the bridge*

collar /'kɒlə(r)/ *noun* **1** the part of your clothes that goes round your neck **2** a band that you put round the neck of a dog or cat

collar

colleague /'kɒliːg/ *noun* a person who works with you

collect /kə'lekt/ *verb* (**collect**, **collecting**, **collected**) **1** take things from different people or places and put them together: *The waiter collected the dirty glasses.* **2** bring together things that are the same in some way, to study or enjoy them: *My friend collects stamps.* **3** go and bring somebody or something from a place: *She went to collect the parcel from the post office.*

collection /kə'lekʃn/ *noun* a group of things that somebody has brought together: *The museum has a large collection of traditional carvings.* ○ *a stamp collection*

collector /kə'lektə(r)/ *noun* a person who collects things as a hobby or as a job: *a stamp collector* ○ *a ticket collector at a railway station*

college /'kɒlɪdʒ/ *noun* a place where people go to study more difficult subjects after they have left school: *She's going to college next year.* ○ *My brother is at college.*

collide /kə'laɪd/ *verb* (**collides**, **colliding**, **collided**) move towards each other and hit each other: *The two trucks collided.* ○ *The pick-up collided with a bus.*

collision /kə'lɪʒn/ *noun* when things or people collide: *The driver of the car was killed in the collision.*

colon /'kəʊlən/ *noun* a mark (:) that you use in writing, for example before a list

colonel /'kɜːnl/ *noun* an officer in the army

colony /'kɒləni/ *noun* (*plural* **colonies**) a country that is ruled by another country: *Kenya was once a British colony.*

colour /'kʌlə(r)/ *noun* Red, blue, yellow and green are all colours: *'What colour are your new shoes?' 'Black.'*

✪ Some words that we use to talk about colours are **light**, **pale**, **dark**, **deep** and **bright**.

colour *verb* (**colours**, **colouring**, **coloured** /'kʌləd/) put colours on something: *The children coloured their pictures with crayons.*

coloured /'kʌləd/ *adjective* with a colour: *She was wearing a brightly coloured jumper.* ○ *coloured paper*

colourful /'kʌləfl/ *adjective* with a lot of bright colours: *a colourful dress*

column /'kɒləm/ *noun* **1** a tall piece of stone that is part of a building **2** a long thin piece of writing on one side or part of a page: *Each page of this dictionary has two columns.*

comb /kəʊm/ *noun* a flat piece of metal or plastic with a line of thin parts like teeth. You use it to make your hair tidy.
comb

comb *verb* (**combs**, **combing**, **combed** /kəʊmd/) make your hair tidy with a comb: *Have you combed your hair?*

combination /ˌkɒmbɪ'neɪʃn/ *noun* two or more things mixed together: *The building is a combination of new and old styles.*

combine /kəm'baɪn/ *verb* (**combined**, **combining**, **combined**

/kəm'baɪnd/) join or mix together: *The two schools combined and moved to a larger building.*

come /kʌm/ *verb* (**comes, coming, came** /keɪm/, **has come**) **1** move towards the person who is speaking or the place that you are talking about: *Come here, please.* ○ *The dog came when I called him.* ○ *I'm sorry, but I can't come to the party.* **2** arrive: *If you go along that road, you will come to the river.* ○ *A letter came for you this morning.* **3** be or happen: *June comes after May.* **4** go with the person who is speaking: *I'm going to a party tonight. Do you want to come?* **come across something** find something when you are not looking for it: *I came across these old photos yesterday.* **come apart** break into pieces: *These old shoes are coming apart.* **come back** return: *I'm going to my friend's house now and I'm coming back this evening.* **come from 1** be made from something: *Wool comes from sheep.* **2** The place that you come from is where you were born or where you live: *I come from Mombasa.* ○ *Where do you come from?* **come on!, come along!** words that you use for telling somebody to hurry or to try harder: *Come on! We'll be late!* **come out** appear: *The rain stopped and the sun came out.* ○ *This book came out in 1994.* **how come ...?** why or how...?: *How come you're here so early?* **to come** in the future: *I'll be very busy in the months to come.*

comedian /kə'mi:diən/ *noun* a person whose job is to make people laugh

comedy /'kɒmədi/ *noun* (*plural* **comedies**) a funny play or film

comfort /'kʌmfət/ *noun* **1** (no plural) having everything your body needs; being without pain or problems: *They have enough money to live in comfort.* **2** (*plural* **comforts**) a person or thing that helps you or makes life better: *Her children were a comfort to her when she was ill.*

comfort *verb* (**comforts, comforting, comforted**) make somebody feel less unhappy or worried: *A mother was comforting her crying child.*

comfortable /'kʌmftəbl/ *adjective*

1 nice to sit in, to be in, or to wear: *This is a very comfortable bed.* ○ *comfortable shoes* **2** with no pain or worry: *Sit down and make yourself comfortable.* ✪ opposite: **uncomfortable**

comfortably /'kʌmftəbli/ *adverb*: *He sat down comfortably in the armchair.*

comic[1] /'kɒmɪk/, **comical** /'kɒmɪkl/ *adjective* funny

comic[2] /'kɒmɪk/ *noun* a magazine for children, with pictures that tell a story

comma /'kɒmə/ *noun* (*plural* **commas**) a mark ( ) that you use in writing to make a short stop in a sentence

command /kə'mɑːnd/ *noun* **1** (*plural* **commands**) words that tell you that you must do something: *The soldiers must obey their general's commands.* **2** (no plural) the power to tell people what to do: *Who is in command of this ship?*

command *verb* (**commands, commanding, commanded**) tell somebody that they must do something: *He commanded us to leave immediately.* ✪ **Order** is the word that we usually use.

comment /'kɒment/ *noun* words that you say about something to show what you think: *She made some interesting comments about the film.*

comment *verb* (**comments, commenting, commented**) say what you think about something: *A lot of people at school commented on my new watch.*

commentary /'kɒməntri/ *noun* (*plural* **commentaries**) words that somebody says about something that is happening: *We listened to the radio commentary on the football match.*

commentator /'kɒmənteɪtə(r)/ *noun* a person who gives a commentary on radio or television

commerce /'kɒmɜːs/ *noun* (no plural) the work of buying and selling things

commercial /kə'mɜːʃl/ *adjective* for or about buying and selling things: *a commercial vehicle*

commercial *noun* a short film on television or radio that helps to sell something

commissioner /kə'mɪʃənə(r)/ *noun* an important person who works for the government: *the Provincial Commis-*

sioner ○ *the District Commissioner*

commit /kə'mɪt/ *verb* (**commits**, **committing**, **committed**) do something bad: *This man has committed a very serious crime.*

committee /kə'mɪti/ *noun* a group of people that other people choose to plan or organize something: *The members of the club choose a new committee every year.*

common[1] /'kɒmən/ *adjective* (**commoner**, **commonest**) **1** that you often see or that often happens: *Mohammed is a common name in many countries.* **2** that everybody in a group does or has: *People in East Africa have Swahili as a common language.* **have something in common** be like somebody in a certain way, or have the same interests as somebody: *Paul and I are good friends. We have a lot in common.*

common sense /ˌkɒmən 'sens/ *noun* (no plural) the ability to do the right thing and not make stupid mistakes, because of what you know about the world: *Jane's got no common sense. She left her money on the table and it was stolen.*

communal /kə'mju:nəl/ *adjective* If something is communal, all the members of a group can use it.

communicate /kə'mju:nɪkeɪt/ *verb* (**communicates**, **communicating**, **communicated**) talk or write to somebody: *The pilots communicate with the airport by radio.*

communication /kəˌmju:nɪ'keɪʃn/ *noun* **1** (no plural) talking or writing to somebody: *Communication is difficult when two people don't speak the same language.* **2 communications** (plural) ways of sending information or moving from one place to another: *There are good communications with the islands.*

community /kə'mju:nəti/ *noun* (*plural* **communities**) **1** the people who live in a place: *Life in a small farming community is very different from life in a big city.* **2** a group of people who join together, for example because they have the same interests or religion: *the Chinese community in Britain*

commute /kə'mju:t/ *verb* (**commutes**, **commuting**, **commuted**) travel a long way from home to work every day: *She lives in the country and commutes to Nairobi.*

commuter *noun* a person who commutes

compact disc /ˌkɒmpækt 'dɪsk/ *noun* a small round piece of plastic, like a record. You play it on a special machine called a **compact disc player**. ✪ The short form is **CD**.

compact disc

companion /kəm'pænɪən/ *noun* a person who is with another person

company /'kʌmpəni/ *noun* **1** (*plural* **companies**) a group of people who work to make or sell things: *an advertising company* **2** (no plural) being with other people: *She lives alone so she likes company at weekends.* **keep somebody company** be or go with somebody: *Please stay and keep me company for a while.*

comparative /kəm'pærətɪv/ *noun* in the form of an adjective or adverb that shows more of something: *The comparative of 'bad' is 'worse'.*

comparative *adjective*: *'Longer' is the comparative form of 'long'.*

compare /kəm'peə(r)/ *verb* (**compares**, **comparing**, **compared** /kəm'peəd/) think about or look at people or things together so that you can see how they are different: *We compared prices in Nairobi and Mombasa and found that Mombasa was cheaper.* ○ *Compare your answers with those at the back of the book.*

compared *adjective* if you compare somebody or something: *Musa is quite small, compared with his friends.*

comparison /kəm'pærɪsn/ *noun* seeing or understanding how things are different or the same: *We made a comparison of prices in three different towns.* **in** or **by comparison with somebody or something** if you see or think about somebody or something together with another person or thing: *Uganda is a small country compared to Sudan.*

compartment /kəm'pɑːtmənt/ *noun*

1 a small room in a train **2** a separate part inside a box or bag: *The suitcase had a secret compartment at the back.*

compass /ˈkʌmpəs/ *noun* (*plural* **compasses**) a thing with a needle that always shows where north is

compete /kəmˈpiːt/ *verb* (**competes**, **competing**, **competed**) try to win a race or competition: *Teams from many countries compete in the World Cup.*

competition /ˌkɒmpəˈtɪʃn/ *noun* **1** (*plural* **competitions**) a game or test that people try to win: *I entered the painting competition and won first prize.* **2** (no plural) trying to win or be best: *We were in competition with a team from another school.*

competitor /kəmˈpetɪtə(r)/ *noun* a person who is trying to win a competition

complain /kəmˈpleɪn/ *verb* (**complains**, **complaining**, **complained** /kəmˈpleɪnd/) say that you do not like something; say that you are unhappy or angry about something: *Sarah complained that she was too tired to walk any further.* ○ *She was complaining about the weather.*

complaint /kəmˈpleɪnt/ *noun* saying that you do not like something: *We made a complaint to the hotel manager about the dirty rooms.*

complete[1] /kəmˈpliːt/ *adjective* **1** with none of its parts missing: *I've got a complete set of teeth.* ✪ opposite: **incomplete** **2** finished: *The work is complete.* **3** in every way; total: *Their visit was a complete surprise.*

complete[2] /kəmˈpliːt/ *verb* (**completes**, **completing**, **completed**) finish doing or making something: *She was at university for two years but she did not complete her studies.* ○ *When will the new building be completed?*

completely /kəmˈpliːtli/ *adverb* totally; in every way: *The money has disappeared completely.* ○ *I completely forgot that it was your birthday!*

complex[1] /ˈkɒmpleks/ *adjective* difficult to understand because it has a lot of different parts: *a complex problem*

complex[2] /ˈkɒmpleks/ *noun* (*plural* **complexes**) a group of buildings: *a sports complex*

complicated /ˈkɒmplɪkeɪtɪd/ *adjective* difficult to understand because it has a lot of different parts: *I can't explain how to play the game. It's too complicated.*

compliment /ˈkɒmplɪmənt/ *noun* **pay somebody a compliment** say something nice about somebody: *I know she likes me because she's always paying me compliments.*

compliment *verb* (**compliments**, **complimenting**, **complimented**) say something nice about somebody: *They complimented Nelima on her cooking.*

compose /kəmˈpəʊz/ *verb* (**composes**, **composing**, **composed** /kəmˈpəʊzd/) write something, especially music: *Mr Mugambi has composed a school song.* **be composed of something** be made of something; have something as parts: *Water is composed of oxygen and hydrogen.*

composer /kəmˈpəʊzə(r)/ *noun* a person who writes music: *Mozart was the greatest composer of his day.*

composition /ˌkɒmpəˈzɪʃn/ *noun* a piece of writing or music

compound /ˈkɒmpaʊnd/ *noun* **1** something that is made of two or more parts: *Salt is a chemical compound.* **2** a word that is made from other words: *'Fingernail' and 'waiting-room' are compounds.*

comprehension /ˌkɒmprɪˈhenʃn/ *noun* (no plural) understanding something that you hear or read: *a test in listening comprehension*

compromise /ˈkɒmprəmaɪz/ *noun* an agreement with another person or group, when you both do part of what the other person or group wants: *After long talks, the workers and management reached a compromise.*

compulsory /kəmˈpʌlsəri/ *adjective* If something is compulsory, you must do it: *It's compulsory to study English at my school, but joining the English club is optional.*

computer /kəmˈpjuːtə(r)/ *noun* a machine that stores information and finds answers very quickly

computer

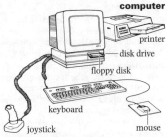

printer

disk drive

floppy disk

keyboard

joystick

mouse

computer program /kəmˈpjuːtə prəʊgræm/ *noun* information that tells a computer what to do

computer programmer /kəmˌpjuːtə ˈprəʊgræmə(r)/ *noun* a person who writes computer programs

computing *noun* (no plural) using computers to do work: *She is studying computing at college.*

conceal /kənˈsiːl/ *verb* (**conceals, concealing, concealed** /kənˈsiːld/) hide something: *They concealed the bomb in a suitcase.* ✪ **Hide** is the word that we usually use.

conceited /kənˈsiːtɪd/ *adjective* too proud of yourself and what you can do

concentrate /ˈkɒnsntreɪt/ *verb* (**concentrates, concentrating, concentrated**) think about what you are doing and not about anything else: *Stop looking out of the window and concentrate on your work!*

concentration /ˌkɒnsnˈtreɪʃn/ *noun* (no plural) *Concentration is very difficult when there's so much noise.*

concern[1] /kənˈsɜːn/ *verb* (**concerns, concerning, concerned** /kənˈsɜːnd/) **1** be important or interesting to somebody: *This notice concerns all passengers travelling to Kampala.* **2** worry somebody: *It concerns me that she is always late.* **3** be about something: *The story concerns a young boy and his parents.*

concerned *adjective* worried: *They are very concerned about their son's illness.*

concern[2] /kənˈsɜːn/ *noun* **1** (no plural) worry: *There is a lot of concern about this problem.* **2** (*plural* **concerns**) something that is important or interesting to somebody: *Her problems*

are not my concern.

concerning /kənˈsɜːnɪŋ/ *preposition* about: *Thank you for your letter concerning the date of the next meeting …*

concert /ˈkɒnsət/ *noun* music played for a lot of people: *a school concert*

conclusion /kənˈkluːʒn/ *noun* what you believe or decide after thinking carefully: *We came to the conclusion* (= we decided) *that you were right.*

concrete /ˈkɒnkriːt/ *noun* (no plural) hard grey material used for building things: *a concrete path*

condemn /kənˈdem/ *verb* (**condemns, condemning, condemned** /kənˈdemd/) **1** say that somebody must be punished in a certain way: *The murderer was condemned to death.* **2** say strongly that somebody or something is bad or wrong: *Many people condemned the council's decision.*

condition /kənˈdɪʃn/ *noun* **1** (no plural) how a person, animal or thing is: *The car was cheap and in good condition, so I bought it.* **2** (*plural* **conditions**) something that must happen before another thing can happen: *One of the conditions of the job is that you agree to work on Saturdays.* **3 conditions** (plural) how things are around you: *The prisoners lived in terrible conditions.* **on condition that** only if: *You can watch the football match on condition that you do your homework first.*

conduct /kənˈdʌkt/ *verb* (**conducts, conducting, conducted**) **1** stand in front of a group of musicians and control what they do: *Mr Mukasa conducted the school band.* **2** show somebody where to go: *She conducted us on a tour of the factory.*

conductor /kənˈdʌktə(r)/ *noun* **1** a person who stands in front of a group of musicians and controls what they do **2** a person who sells tickets on a bus **3** *American English for* **guard**[2] 2

cone /kəʊn/ *noun*
1 a shape with one flat round end and one pointed end ☛ picture on page A5 **2** the hard fruit of a

cone

pine or fir tree: *a pine cone*

conference /'kɒnfərəns/ *noun* a time when many people meet to talk about a special thing: *an international conference*

confess /kən'fes/ *verb* (**confesses**, **confessing**, **confessed** /kən'fest/) say that you have done something wrong: *She confessed that she had stolen the money.* ○ *He confessed to the crime.*

confession /kən'feʃn/ *noun* something that you confess: *She made a confession to the police.*

confidence /'kɒnfɪdəns/ *noun* (no plural) the feeling that you can do something well: *She answered the questions with confidence.* **have confidence in somebody** feel sure that somebody will do something well: *I'm sure you'll pass the exam. I have great confidence in you.* **in confidence** If somebody tells you something in confidence, it is a secret.

confident /'kɒnfɪdənt/ *adjective* sure that you can do something well, or that something will happen: *I'm confident that our team will win.*

confirm /kən'fɜːm/ *verb* (**confirms**, **confirming**, **confirmed** /kən'fɜːmd/) say that something is true or that something will happen: *The police confirmed that the dead man was murdered.*

conflict /'kɒnflɪkt/ *noun* a fight or an argument

confuse /kən'fjuːz/ *verb* (**confuses**, **confusing**, **confused** /kən'fjuːzd/) **1** mix somebody's ideas, so that they cannot think clearly or understand: *They confused me by asking so many questions.* **2** think that one thing or person is another thing or person: *Don't confuse the word 'weather' with 'whether'.*

confused *adjective* not able to think clearly: *I got confused and took the wrong books to school.*

confusing *adjective* difficult to understand: *This map is very confusing.*

confusion /kən'fjuːʒn/ *noun* (no plural) being confused: *He didn't speak any English and he looked at me in confusion when I asked him a question.*

congratulate /kən'grætʃuleɪt/ *verb*

(**congratulates**, **congratulating**, **congratulated**) tell somebody that you are pleased about something that they have done: *I congratulated Sue on passing her exam.*

congratulations /kən,grætʃu'leɪʃnz/ *noun* (plural) a word that shows you are pleased about something that somebody has done: *Congratulations on your new job!*

congress /'kɒŋgres/ *noun* (plural **congresses**) a meeting of many people to talk about important things: *He gave a speech at an international teachers' congress.*

conjunction /kən'dʒʌŋkʃn/ *noun* a word that joins other words or parts of a sentence: *'And', 'or' and 'but' are conjunctions.*

connect /kə'nekt/ *verb* (**connects**, **connecting**, **connected**) join one thing to another thing: *This wire connects the light to the switch.* ○ *The two cities are connected by a railway.*

connection /kə'nekʃn/ *noun* **1** the way that one thing is joined to another: *We had a bad connection on the phone so I couldn't hear him very well.* ○ *Is there a connection between violence and alcohol?* **2** a train, plane or bus that leaves a place soon after another arrives, so that people can change from one to the other: *The bus was late, so I missed my connection.* **in connection with something** about something: *The police want to talk to him in connection with the robbery.*

conscience /'kɒnʃəns/ *noun* the feeling inside you about what is right and wrong **have a clear conscience** feel that you have done nothing wrong **have a guilty conscience** feel that you have done something wrong

conscious /'kɒnʃəs/ *adjective* **1** awake and able to think: *The patient was conscious during the operation.* ✪ *opposite:* **unconscious 2** If you are conscious of something, you know about it: *I was conscious that somebody was watching me.*

consciousness /'kɒnʃəsnəs/ *noun* (no plural) **lose consciousness** stop being conscious: *As she fell, she hit her head and lost consciousness.*

consent /kən'sent/ *noun* (no plural) agreeing to let somebody do something: *Her parents gave their consent to the marriage.*

consequence /'kɒnsɪkwəns/ *noun* what happens because of something: *As a consequence of the recent landslides, 400 people have no homes.* ○ *The mistake had terrible consequences.*

consequently /'kɒnsɪkwəntli/ *adverb* because of that; therefore: *He didn't do any work, and consequently failed the exam.*

conservation /ˌkɒnsə'veɪʃn/ *noun* (no plural) taking good care of the world and its trees, lakes, plants, and animals: *the conservation of the rain forests*

consider /kən'sɪdə(r)/ *verb* (**considers**, **considering**, **considered** /kən'sɪdəd/) **1** think carefully about something: *I'm considering going to work with my uncle.* ○ *We must consider what to do next.* **2** think that something is true: *I consider her to be a good teacher.* **3** think about the feelings of other people when you do something: *He spent all his money on a car without considering what his family thought.*

considerable /kən'sɪdərəbl/ *adjective* great or large: *The car cost a considerable amount of money.*

considerably /kən'sɪdərəbli/ *adverb*: *Uganda is considerably smaller than Ethiopia.*

considerate /kən'sɪdərət/ *adjective* A person who is considerate is kind, and thinks and cares about other people: *Please be more considerate and don't play loud music late at night.* ✪ opposite: **inconsiderate**

consideration /kənˌsɪdə'reɪʃn/ *noun* (no plural) **1** thinking carefully about something: *After a lot of consideration, I decided not to accept the job.* **2** being kind, and caring about other people's feelings: *He shows no consideration for anybody else.* **take something into consideration** think carefully about something when you are deciding: *You must take the quality of the soil into consideration when deciding what crops to plant.*

consist /kən'sɪst/ *verb* (**consists**, **consisting**, **consisted**) **consist of something** be made of something; have as parts: *Water consists of hydrogen and oxygen.*

consistent /kən'sɪstənt/ *adjective* always the same: *His work isn't very consistent — sometimes it's good and sometimes it's terrible!* ✪ opposite: **inconsistent**

consonant /'kɒnsənənt/ *noun* any letter of the alphabet that is not *a, e, i, o* or *u* , or the sound that you make when you say it ☞ Look at **vowel**.

constant /'kɒnstənt/ *adjective* Something that is constant happens all the time: *the constant noise of traffic*

constantly *adverb*: *She talked constantly all evening.*

constituency /kən'stɪtjuənsi/ *noun* (*plural* **constituencies**) a town or an area that chooses one **Member of Parliament** (a person in the government)

constitution /ˌkɒnstɪ'tjuːʃn/ *noun* the laws of a country: *the Kenyan constitution*

construct /kən'strʌkt/ *verb* (**constructs**, **constructing**, **constructed**) build something: *The bridge was constructed out of stone.* ✪ **Build** is the word that we usually use.

construction /kən'strʌkʃn/ *noun* **1** (no plural) building something: *the construction of a new railway* **2** (*plural* **constructions**) something that people have built

consult /kən'sʌlt/ *verb* (**consults**, **consulting**, **consulted**) ask somebody or look in a book when you want to know something: *If the pain doesn't go away, you should consult a doctor.*

consume /kən'sjuːm/ *verb* (**consumes**, **consuming**, **consumed** /kən'sjuːmd/) eat, drink or use something: *This car consumes a lot of petrol.*

consumption /kən'sʌmpʃn/ *noun* (no plural) eating, drinking or using something: *This car has a high petrol consumption* (= it uses a lot of petrol).

contact[1] /'kɒntækt/ *noun* (no plural) meeting, talking to or writing to somebody: *Until Rita started work at the airport, she didn't have much contact*

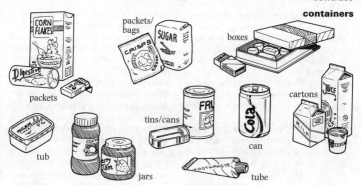

containers

packets/bags

boxes

packets

tins/cans

cartons

tub

jars

can

tube

---

with people from other countries. ○ *Are you still in contact with your old friends from school?* ○ *Doctors come into contact with (= meet) a lot of people.*

contact[2] /ˈkɒntækt/ *verb* (**contacts, contacting, contacted**) telephone or write to somebody, or go to see them: *If you see this man, please contact the police.*

contact lens /ˈkɒntækt lenz/ *noun* (*plural* **contact lenses**) a small round piece of plastic or glass that you wear in your eye so that you can see better

contain /kənˈteɪn/ *verb* (**contains, containing, contained** /kənˈteɪnd/) have something inside it: *This box contains pens and pencils.* ○ *Chocolate contains a lot of sugar.*

container /kənˈteɪnə(r)/ *noun* a thing that you can put other things in. Boxes, bottles, bags and jars are all containers.

content /kənˈtent/ *adjective* happy with what you have: *She is not content with the money she has – she wants more.*

contented *adjective* happy: *a contented smile* ✪ opposite: **discontented**

contents /ˈkɒntents/ *noun* (plural) what is inside something: *I poured the contents of the bottle into a bowl.* ○ *The contents page of a book tells you what is in it.*

contest /ˈkɒntest/ *noun* a game or competition that people try to win: *a boxing contest*

contestant /kənˈtestənt/ *noun* a

person who tries to win a contest: *There are six contestants in the race.*

context /ˈkɒntekst/ *noun* the words that come before and after another word or a sentence: *You can often understand the meaning of a word by looking at its context.*

continent /ˈkɒntɪnənt/ *noun* one of the seven big pieces of land in the world, for example Africa, Asia or Europe

continental /ˌkɒntɪˈnentl/ *adjective*

continual /kənˈtɪnjuəl/ *adjective* that happens often: *We have had continual problems with this machine.*

continually /kənˈtɪnjuəli/ *adverb*: *He is continually late for work.*

continue /kənˈtɪnjuː/ (**continues, continuing, continued** /kənˈtɪnjuːd/) **1** not stop happening or doing something: *We continued working until five o'clock.* ○ *The rain continued all afternoon.* **2** start again after stopping: *Let's have lunch now and continue the meeting this afternoon.* **3** go further: *We continued along the path until we came to the river.*

continuous /kənˈtɪnjuəs/ *adjective* Something that is continuous goes on and does not stop: *a continuous line* ○ *a continuous noise*

continuously *adverb*: *It rained continuously for five hours.*

contract /ˈkɒntrækt/ *noun* a piece of paper that says that somebody agrees to do something: *The company has signed a contract to build the new road.*

contradict /ˌkɒntrə'dɪkt/ *verb* (**contradicts**, **contradicting**, **contradicted**) say that something is wrong or not true: *'This is my book, not yours!' he shouted, and nobody dared to contradict him.*

contrary[1] /'kɒntrəri/ *noun* (no plural) **on the contrary** the opposite is true: *'You look ill, Ben.' 'On the contrary, I feel fine!'*

contrary[2] /'kɒntrəri/ *adjective* **contrary to something** very different from something; opposite to something: *He didn't stay in bed, contrary to the doctor's orders.*

contrast /kən'trɑːst/ *verb* (**contrasts**, **contrasting**, **contrasted**) look at or think about two or more things together and see the differences between them: *The book contrasts life today with life 100 years ago.*

contrast /'kɒntrɑːst/ *noun* a difference between things that you can see clearly: *There is a big contrast between the weather in Tanzania and in Egypt.*

contribute /kən'trɪbjuːt/ *verb* (**contributes**, **contributing**, **contributed**) give something when other people are giving too: *We contributed 100 shillings each to the fund.*

contribution /ˌkɒntrɪ'bjuːʃn/ *noun* something that you give when other people are giving too: *We are sending contributions of food and clothing to people in poor countries.*

control[1] /kən'trəʊl/ *noun* **1** (no plural) the power to make people or things do what you want: *As head of the company, he has control over how much workers are paid.* ○ *A teacher must be in control of the class.* **2 controls** (plural) the parts of a machine that you press or move to make it work: *the controls of an aeroplane.* **lose control** not be able to make people or things do what you want: *The driver lost control and the bus went into the river.* **out of control** If something is out of control, you cannot stop it or make it do what you want: *The truck went out of control and crashed.* **under control** If something is under control, it is doing what you want it to do: *The fire is under control.*

control[2] /kən'trəʊl/ *verb* (**controls**, **controlling**, **controlled** /kən'trəʊld/) make people or things do what you want: *He couldn't control his feelings and started to cry.* ○ *This switch controls the speed.*

controller *noun* a person who controls something: *an air traffic controller*

convenience /kən'viːniəns/ *noun* (no plural) being easy to use; making things easy: *For convenience, the books are kept in alphabetical order.*

convenient /kən'viːniənt/ *adjective* **1** easy to use or go to: *The bus stop is very convenient – it's outside my house.* **2** easy for somebody or something; suitable: *Let's meet on Friday. What's the most convenient time for you?* ✪ opposite: **inconvenient**

conveniently *adverb*: *We live conveniently close to the school.*

convent /'kɒnvənt/ *noun* a place where religious women, called **nuns**, live, work and pray

conversation /ˌkɒnvə'seɪʃn/ *noun* a talk: *She had a long conversation with her friend.*

conversion /kən'vɜːʃn/ *noun* changing something into another thing: *the conversion of the sun's heat to electricity*

convert /kən'vɜːt/ *verb* (**converts**, **converting**, **converted**) change into another thing: *They converted the offices into a school.*

convict /kən'vɪkt/ *verb* (**convicts**, **convicting**, **convicted**) decide in a court of law that somebody has done something wrong: *She was convicted of murder and sent to prison.*

convince /kən'vɪns/ *verb* (**convinces**, **convincing**, **convinced** /kən'vɪnst/) make somebody believe something: *I couldn't convince him that I was right.*

convinced *adjective* certain: *I'm convinced that I have seen her somewhere before.*

cook[1] /kʊk/ *verb* (**cooks**, **cooking**, **cooked** /kʊkt/) make food ready to eat by heating it: *My father cooked the dinner.* ○ *I am learning to cook.*

✪ There are many words for ways of cooking food. Look at **bake**, **boil**, **fry**, **grill**, **roast**, **stew** and **toast**.

cooking *noun* (no plural) **1** making food ready to eat: *Who does the cooking in your family?* **2** what you cook: *Italian cooking*

cook[2] /kʊk/ *noun* a person who cooks: *She works as a cook in a big hotel.* ○ *He is a good cook.*

cooker /ˈkʊkə(r)/ *noun* a thing that you use in a kitchen for cooking food. It has an **oven** for cooking food inside it and places for heating pans on the top: *an electric cooker*

cookery /ˈkʊkəri/ *noun* (no plural) making food ready to eat, often as a subject that you can study: *cookery lessons*

cool[1] /kuːl/ *adjective* (**cooler**, **coolest**) **1** a little cold; not warm: *cool water* ○ *I'd like a cool drink.* **2** calm; not excited

cool[2] /kuːl/ *verb* (**cools**, **cooling**, **cooled** /kuːld/) make something less hot; become less hot: *We let the food cool a little before we could eat it.* **cool down 1** become less hot: *We swam in the river to cool down after our long walk.* **2** become less excited or angry

cooperate /kəʊˈɒpəreɪt/ *verb* (**cooperates**, **cooperating**, **cooperated**) work together with someone else in a helpful way: *The two companies are cooperating with each other.*

cooperation /kəʊˌɒpəˈreɪʃn/ *noun* (no plural) help: *Thank you for your cooperation.*

cooperative /kəʊˈɒpərətɪv/ *adjective* happy to help: *The police asked her a lot of questions and she was very cooperative.*

cope /kəʊp/ *verb* (**copes**, **coping**, **coped** /kəʊpt/) **cope with somebody** or **something** do something well although it is difficult: *She has four young children. I don't know how she copes with them!*

copied *form of* **copy**[2]

copies 1 *plural of* **copy**[1] **2** *form of* **copy**[2]

copper /ˈkɒpə(r)/ *noun* (no plural) a metal with a colour between brown and red: *copper wire*

copy[1] /ˈkɒpi/ *noun* (*plural* **copies**) **1** a thing that is made to look exactly like another thing: *This is a copy of a* famous painting. ○ *The secretary made two copies of the letter.* **2** one book or newspaper: *Two million copies of the newspaper are sold every day.*

copy[2] /ˈkɒpi/ *verb* (**copies**, **copying**, **copied** /ˈkɒpid/, **has copied**) **1** write or draw something so that it is exactly the same as another thing: *The teacher asked us to copy the list of words into our books.* **2** try to look or do the same as another person: *Tom always copies what his brother does.*

cord /kɔːd/ *noun* strong thick string

core /kɔː(r)/ *noun* the middle part of some kinds of fruit, where the seeds are: *an apple core*

cork /kɔːk/ *noun* **1** (no plural) light strong stuff that comes from the outside of a special tree **2** (*plural* **corks**) a piece of cork that you put in a bottle to close it

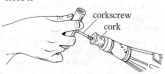
corkscrew
cork

corkscrew /ˈkɔːkskruː/ *noun* a thing that you use for taking corks out of bottles

corn /kɔːn/ *noun* (no plural) the seeds of plants like wheat or oats

The lamp is in the **corner**.

The bank is on the **corner**.

corner /ˈkɔːnə(r)/ *noun* a place where two lines, walls or roads meet

corporation /ˌkɔːpəˈreɪʃn/ *noun* a big company: *the Kenya Broadcasting Corporation*

corpse /kɔ:ps/ *noun* the body of a dead person

correct[1] /kəˈrekt/ *adjective* right or true; with no mistakes: *All your answers were correct.* ○ *What is the correct time, please?* ✪ opposite: **incorrect**

correctly *adverb*: *Have I spelt your name correctly?*

correct[2] /kəˈrekt/ *verb* (**corrects**, **correcting**, **corrected**) show where the mistakes are in something and make it right: *The class did the exercises and the teacher corrected them.* ○ *Please correct me if I make a mistake.*

correction /kəˈrekʃn/ *noun* the right word or answer that is put in the place of what was wrong: *When the teacher gave my homework back to me it was full of corrections.*

correspond /ˌkɒrəˈspɒnd/ *verb* (**corresponds**, **corresponding**, **corresponded**) be the same, or almost the same: *Does the name on the envelope correspond with the name inside the letter?*

correspondence /ˌkɒrəˈspɒndəns/ *noun* (no plural) writing letters; the letters that somebody writes or receives: *Her secretary reads all her correspondence.*

corridor /ˈkɒrɪdɔ:(r)/ *noun* a long narrow part inside a building with rooms on each side of it

cosmetics /kɒzˈmetɪks/ *noun* (plural) special powders or creams that you use on your face or hair to make yourself more beautiful

cost[1] /kɒst/ *noun* **1** the money that you must pay to have something: *The cost of the repairs was very high.* **2** what you lose or give to have another thing: *He saved the child at the cost of his own life.*

at all costs no matter what you must do to make it happen: *We must win at all costs.*

cost[2] /kɒst/ *verb* (**costs**, **costing**, **cost**, **has cost**) **1** have the price of: *This shirt cost 100 shillings.* ○ *How much did the book cost?* **2** make you lose something: *One mistake cost him his job.*

costly /ˈkɒstli/ *adjective* (**costlier**, **costliest**) expensive: *The repairs will be very costly.*

costume /ˈkɒstju:m/ *noun* the special clothes that people wear in a country or at a certain time: *The actors wore beautiful costumes.* ○ *traditional tribal costume* ☞ Look also at **swimming-costume**.

cosy /ˈkəʊzi/ *adjective* (**cosier**, **cosiest**) warm and comfortable: *a cosy room*

cot /kɒt/ *noun* a baby's bed with high sides

cotton /ˈkɒtn/ *noun* (no plural) cloth or thread that is made from the soft white stuff on the seeds of a special plant: *a cotton shirt* ○ *a reel of cotton* ☞ picture at **sew**

cotton wool /ˌkɒtn ˈwʊl/ *noun* (no plural) soft light stuff made from cotton: *The nurse cleaned the cut with cotton wool.*

couch /kaʊtʃ/ *noun* (*plural* **couches**) a long seat that you can sit or lie on

cough /kɒf/ *verb* (**coughs**, **coughing**, **coughed** /kɒft/) send air out of your throat with a sudden loud noise: *The smoke made me cough.*

cough *noun*: *He gave a little cough before he started to speak.* ○ *I've got a bad cough.*

could /kʊd/ *modal verb* **1** the word for 'can' in the past: *He could run very fast when he was young.* ○ *I could hear the birds singing.* **2** a word that shows what will perhaps happen or what is possible: *It could rain tomorrow.* ○ *I don't know where Fatuma is. She could be in the kitchen.* **3** a word that you use to ask something in a polite way: *Could you open the door?* ○ *Could I have another drink, please?*

✪ The negative form of 'could' is **could not** or the short form **couldn't** /ˈkʊdnt/: *It was dark and I couldn't see anything.* ☞ Look at the note on page 195 to find out more about **modal verbs**.

council /ˈkaʊnsl/ *noun* a group of people who are chosen to work together and to make rules and decide things: *The city council is planning to build a new road.*

councillor /ˈkaʊnsələ(r)/ *noun* a

member of a council

count¹ /kaʊnt/ *verb* (**counts**, **counting**, **counted**) **1** say numbers one after the other in the right order: *The children are learning to count from one to ten.* **2** look at people or things to see how many there are: *I have counted the chairs – there are 32.* **3** include somebody or something: *There are five people in my family, counting me.* **4** be important: *He said that my ideas don't count because I'm only a child!* **count on somebody** feel sure that somebody will do something for you: *Can I count on you to help me?*

count² /kaʊnt/ *noun* a time when you count things: *After an election there is a count of all the votes.* **keep count of something** know how many there are of something: *Try to keep count of the number of tickets you sell.* **lose count of something** not know how many there are of something

counter /ˈkaʊntə(r)/ *noun* **1** a long high table in a shop, bank or bar, that is between the people who work there and the people who want to buy things: *I put my money on the counter.* **2** a small round thing that you use when you play some games

countless /ˈkaʊntləs/ *adjective* very many: *I have tried to telephone him countless times.*

country /ˈkʌntri/ *noun* **1** (*plural* **countries**) an area of land with its own people and government: *Uganda, Tanzania and Kenya are countries.* **2 the country** (no plural) land that is not in a town: *Do you live in the town or the country?*

couple /ˈkʌpl/ *noun* two people who are married: *A young couple live next door.* **a couple of 1** two: *I invited a couple of friends to lunch.* **2** a few: *I'll be back in a couple of minutes.*

courage /ˈkʌrɪdʒ/ *noun* (no plural) not being afraid, or not showing that you are afraid when you do something dangerous or difficult: *She showed great courage when she went into the burning building to save the child.*

courageous /kəˈreɪdʒəs/ *adjective* brave: *a courageous young man*

course /kɔːs/ *noun* **1** a set of lessons on a certain subject: *He's taking a course in computer programming.* **2** the direction that something moves in: *We followed the course of the river.* **3** one part of a meal: *a three-course meal* ○ *I had chicken for the main course.* **4** a piece of ground for some kinds of sport: *a golf-course* ○ *a racecourse* **5** the time when something is happening: *During the course of the evening I began to feel more and more ill.* **change course** start to go in a different direction: *The plane had to change course because of the storm.* **of course** certainly: *Of course I'll help you.* ○ *'Can I borrow your pen?' 'Of course you can.'* ○ *'Are you angry with me?' 'Of course not!'*

court /kɔːt/ *noun* **1** (*also* **court of law**) a place where people (a **judge** or **jury**) decide if a person has done something wrong, and what the punishment will be: *The man will appear in court tomorrow.* **2** a piece of ground where you can play a certain sport: *a tennis-court*

courtyard /ˈkɔːtjɑːd/ *noun* an open space without a roof, inside a building or between buildings

cousin /ˈkʌzn/ *noun* the child of your aunt or uncle

cover¹ /ˈkʌvə(r)/ *verb* (**covers**, **covering**, **covered** /ˈkʌvəd/) put one thing over another thing to hide it or to keep it safe or warm: *Cover the floor with a newspaper before you start painting.* ○ *She covered her head with a scarf.* **be covered with** or **in something** have something all over yourself or itself: *The floor was covered in mud.*

cover² /ˈkʌvə(r)/ *noun* **1** a thing that you put over another thing, for example to keep it safe: *The computer has a plastic cover.* **2** the outside part of a book or magazine: *The book had a picture of a footballer on the cover.*

covering /ˈkʌvərɪŋ/ *noun* something that covers another thing: *There was a thick covering of dust on the floor.*

cow /kaʊ/ *noun* a big female farm animal that gives milk

> ✪ The male is called a **bull** and a young cow is called a **calf**. Meat from a cow is called **beef** and meat from a calf is called **veal**.

coward /ˈkaʊəd/ *noun* a person who is afraid when there is danger or a problem

cowpea /ˈkaʊˌpiː/ (*also* **black-eyed bean**) /ˌblæk aɪd ˈbiːn/a kind of bean that is white with a black spot

crab /kræb/ *noun*
an animal that lives in and near the sea. It has a hard shell and big claws.

crack¹ /kræk/ *noun* **1** a thin line on something where it is nearly broken: *There's a crack in this glass.* **2** a sudden loud noise: *a crack of thunder*

crack² /kræk/ *verb* (**cracks**, **cracking**, **cracked** /krækt/) break, but not into pieces: *The glass will crack if you pour boiling water into it.* ○ *This cup is cracked.*

crackle /ˈkrækl/ *verb* (**crackles**, **crackling**, **crackled** /ˈkrækld/) make a lot of short sharp sounds: *Dry wood crackles when you burn it.*

cradle /ˈkreɪdl/ *noun* a small bed for a baby

craft /krɑːft/ *noun* a job in which you make things carefully and cleverly with your hands: *Pottery and weaving are crafts.*

craftsman /ˈkrɑːftsmən/ *noun* (*plural* **craftsmen** /ˈkrɑːftsmən/) a man who is good at making things

cram /kræm/ *verb* (**crams**, **cramming**, **crammed** /kræmd/) push too many people or things into something: *She crammed her clothes into a bag.*

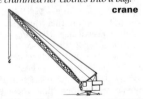
crane

crane /kreɪn/ *noun* a big machine with a long part for lifting heavy things

crash¹ /kræʃ/ *noun* (*plural* **crashes**) **1** an accident when something that is moving hits another thing: *He was killed in a car crash.* ○ *a plane crash* **2** a loud noise when something falls or hits another thing: *I heard a crash as the tree fell.*

crash² /kræʃ/ *verb* (**crashes**, **crashing**, **crashed** /kræʃt/) **1** have an accident; hit something: *The bus crashed into a tree.* **2** make something hit another thing: *My uncle crashed his car.* **3** fall or hit something with a loud noise: *A tree crashed through the window.*

crash-helmet /ˈkræʃ helmɪt/ *noun* a hard hat that you wear to keep your head safe: *Motor cyclists must wear crash-helmets in Britain.*

crate /kreɪt/ *noun* a big box for carrying bottles or other things

crawl /krɔːl/ *verb* (**crawls**, **crawling**, **crawled** /krɔːld/) **1** move slowly on your hands and knees: *Babies crawl before they can walk.* **2** move slowly with the body close to the ground: *An insect crawled across the floor.*

crawl *noun* (no plural) a way of swimming on your front

crayon /ˈkreɪən/ *noun* a soft thick coloured pencil: *The children were drawing pictures with crayons.*

crazy /ˈkreɪzi/ *adjective* (**crazier**, **craziest**) mad or very stupid: *You must be crazy to ride a bike at night with no lights.* **crazy about somebody** or **something** If you are crazy about somebody or something, you like them very much: *She's crazy about football.* ○ *He's crazy about her.* **go crazy** become very angry or excited: *My mum will go crazy if I get home late.*

creak /kriːk/ *verb* (**creaks**, **creaking**, **creaked** /kriːkt/) make a noise like a door that needs oil, or like an old wooden floor when you walk on it
creak *noun*: *The door opened with a creak.*

cream¹ /kriːm/ *noun* **1** (no plural) the thick liquid on the top of milk **2** (*plural* **creams**) a thick liquid that you put on your skin

cream² /kriːm/ *adjective* with a colour between white and yellow: *She was wearing a cream dress.*

creamery /ˈkriːməri/ *noun* (*plural* **creameries**) a place where we make milk into butter and cheese

creamy /ˈkriːmi/ *adjective* **1** with

cream in it: *a creamy sauce* **2** like cream: *a creamy colour*

crease /kriːs/ *verb* (**creases**, **creasing**, **creased** /kriːst/) **1** make untidy lines in paper or cloth by not being careful with it: *Don't sit on my jacket – you'll crease it.* **2** become full of untidy lines: *This shirt creases easily.*

crease *noun* a line in paper or cloth made by folding or pressing: *You need to iron this shirt – it's full of creases.*

create /kriˈeɪt/ *verb* (**creates**, **creating**, **created**) make something new: *Do you believe that God created the world?* ○ *The company has created a new kind of engine.*

creation /kriˈeɪʃn/ *noun* **1** (no plural) making something new: *the creation of the world* **2** (*plural* **creations**) a new thing that somebody has made: *Mickey Mouse was the creation of Walt Disney.*

creative /kriˈeɪtɪv/ *adjective* A person who is creative has a lot of new ideas or is good at making new things: *She's a very good painter – she's so creative.*

creator /kriˈeɪtə(r)/ *noun* a person who makes something new: *Walt Disney was the creator of Mickey Mouse.*

creature /ˈkriːtʃə(r)/ *noun* any living thing that is not a plant: *birds, fish and other creatures* ○ *This story is about creatures from another planet.*

credit[1] /ˈkredɪt/ *noun* (no plural) buying something and paying for it later: *I bought the pick-up on credit over two years.*

credit card /ˈkredɪt kɑːd/ *noun* a plastic card from a bank that you can use to buy something and pay for it later: *Can I pay by credit card?*

credit[2] /ˈkredɪt/ *noun* (no plural) saying that somebody or something is good: *I did all the work but John got all the credit for it!*

creep /kriːp/ *verb* (**creeps**, **creeping**, **crept** /krept/, **has crept**) move quietly and carefully so that nobody hears or sees you; move along close to the ground: *The cat crept towards the bird.* ○ *I crept into the room where the children were sleeping.*

crescent /ˈkreznt/ *noun* the shape of the moon when it is less than half a circle

crew /kruː/ *noun* all the people who work on a ship or an aeroplane

cricket[1] /ˈkrɪkɪt/ *noun* a small brown insect that makes a loud noise

cricket[2] /ˈkrɪkɪt/ *noun* (no plural) a game for two teams of eleven players who try to hit a small hard ball with a **bat** on a large field: *We watched a cricket match.*

cricketer *noun* a person who plays cricket

cried *form of* **cry**[1]

cries 1 *form of* **cry**[1] **2** *plural of* **cry**[2]

crime /kraɪm/ *noun* something that somebody does that is against the law: *Murder and robbery are serious crimes.*

criminal[1] /ˈkrɪmɪnl/ *noun* a person who does something that is against the law

criminal[2] /ˈkrɪmɪnl/ *adjective* **1** against the law: *Stealing is a criminal act.* **2** of crime: *She is studying criminal law.*

crimson /ˈkrɪmzn/ *adjective* with a dark red colour, like blood

cripple /ˈkrɪpl/ *verb* (**cripples**, **crippling**, **crippled** /ˈkrɪpld/) hurt your legs or back badly so that you cannot walk: *She was crippled in an accident.*

crisis /ˈkraɪsɪs/ *noun* (*plural* **crises** /ˈkraɪsiːz/) a time when something very dangerous or serious happens: *a political crisis*

crisp[1] /krɪsp/ *adjective* (**crisper**, **crispest**) **1** hard and dry: *The bread stayed in the oven too long and went crisp.* **2** fresh and not soft: *crisp apples*

crisp[2] /krɪsp/ *noun* a very thin piece of potato cooked in hot oil: *a packet of crisps*

critic /ˈkrɪtɪk/ *noun* **1** a person who says that somebody or something is wrong or bad: *critics of the government* **2** a person who writes about a book, film or play and says if he/she likes it or not: *The critics liked his new film.*

critical /ˈkrɪtɪkl/ *adjective* **1** If you are critical of somebody or something, you say that they are wrong or bad: *They were very critical of my work.* **2** very serious or dangerous: *a critical illness*

critically *adverb*: *She's critically ill.*

criticize /ˈkrɪtɪsaɪz/ *verb* (**criticizes, criticizing, criticized** /ˈkrɪtɪsaɪzd/) say that somebody or something is wrong or bad: *He criticizes everything I do!*

criticism /ˈkrɪtɪsɪzəm/ *noun* what you think is bad about somebody or something: *I listened to all their criticisms of my plan.*

croak /krəʊk/ *noun* the noise that a frog makes

croak *verb* (**croaks, croaking, croaked** /krəʊkt/) make a noise like a frog makes

crockery /ˈkrɒkəri/ *noun* (no plural) plates, cups and dishes

crocodile /ˈkrɒkədaɪl/ *noun* a big long animal with sharp teeth and a strong tail. Crocodiles live in rivers: *A crocodile is a reptile.*

crooked /ˈkrʊkɪd/ *adjective* not straight: *She has crooked teeth.*

crop /krɒp/ *noun* all the plants of one kind that a farmer grows at the same time: *There was a good crop of potatoes last year.* ○ *Rain is good for the crops.*

crop rotation /ˈkrɒp rəʊteɪʃn/ *noun* (no plural) growing a different crop on a piece of land each year so that the soil stays healthy

cross¹ /krɒs/ *noun* (*plural* **crosses**) **1** a mark like + or X: *The cross on the map shows where I live.* **2** something with the shape + or X: *She wears a cross around her neck.*

cross² /krɒs/ *verb* (**crosses, crossing, crossed** /krɒst/) **1** go from one side of something to the other: *Be careful when you cross the road.* **2** put one thing over another thing: *She sat down and crossed her legs.* **cross out** draw a line through a word or words, for example because you have made a mistake: *I crossed the word out and wrote it again.*

cross³ /krɒs/ *adjective* angry: *I was cross with her because she was late.*

crossing /ˈkrɒsɪŋ/ *noun* a place where cars must stop for people to cross the road

crossroads /ˈkrɒsrəʊdz/ *noun* (*plural* **crossroads**) a place where two roads

cross each other

crossword puzzle /ˈkrɒswɜːd pʌzl/, **crossword** *noun* a game on paper where you write words in squares

crossword
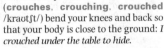

crouch /kraʊtʃ/ *verb* (**crouches, crouching, crouched** /kraʊtʃt/) bend your knees and back so that your body is close to the ground: *I crouched under the table to hide.*

crow¹ /krəʊ/ *noun* a black or mostly black bird that makes a loud noise

crow² /krəʊ/ *verb* (**crows, crowing, crowed** /krəʊd/) make a loud noise like a male chicken (a **cock**) makes early in the morning

crowd /kraʊd/ *noun* a lot of people together: *There was a large crowd at the football match.*

crowd *verb* (**crowds, crowding, crowded**) come together in a big group: *The journalists crowded round the Prime Minister.*

crowded *adjective* full of people: *The streets were very crowded.* ○ *a crowded bus*

crown /kraʊn/ *noun* a special thing that a king or queen wears on his or her head at important times

crown *verb* (**crowns, crowning, crowned** /kraʊnd/) put a crown on the head of a new king or queen: *Elizabeth II was crowned in 1952.*

crucial /ˈkruːʃl/ *adjective* very important: *a crucial moment*

cruel /ˈkruːəl/ *adjective* (**crueller, cruellest**) A person who is cruel is unkind and likes to hurt other people or animals: *He is cruel to his children.*

cruelly /ˈkruːəli/ *adverb* in a cruel way: *He was cruelly treated when he was a child.*

cruelty /ˈkruːəlti/ *noun* (no plural) being cruel

crumb /krʌm/ *noun* a very small piece of bread, cake or biscuit

crumble /ˈkrʌmbl/ *verb* (**crumbles, crumbling, crumbled** /ˈkrʌmbld/) break into very small pieces: *The old stone walls are crumbling.*

crunch /krʌntʃ/ *verb* (**crunches**, **crunching**, **crunched** /krʌntʃt/) **1** make a loud noise when you eat something that is hard: *The dog was crunching a bone.* **2** make a noise like this when you press it hard: *The pebbles crunched under our feet as we walked.*

crush /krʌʃ/ *verb* (**crushes**, **crushing**, **crushed** /krʌʃt/) press something very hard so that you break or damage it: *She sat on the egg and crushed it.*

crust /krʌst/ *noun* the hard part on the outside of bread

crusty *adjective* with a hard crust: *crusty bread*

crutch /krʌtʃ/ *noun* (*plural* **crutches**) a long stick that you put under your arm to help you walk when you have hurt your leg: *He broke his leg and now he's on crutches* (= he walks using crutches).

cry[1] /kraɪ/ *verb* (**cries**, **crying**, **cried** /kraɪd/, **has cried**) **1** have drops of water falling from your eyes, usually because you are unhappy: *The baby cries a lot.* **2** shout or make a loud noise: *'Help!' he cried.* ○ *She cried out in pain.*

cry[2] /kraɪ/ *noun* (*plural* **cries**) a loud noise that you make to show pain, fear or excitement, for example: *We heard her cries and ran to help.* ○ *the cry of a bird*

crystal /ˈkrɪstl/ *noun* **1** a kind of rock that looks like glass **2** a shape that some chemicals make when they are solid: *salt crystals*

cub /kʌb/ *noun* a young lion, bear, wolf, fox or tiger

cube /kjuːb/ *noun* a shape like a box with six square sides all the same size: *an ice-cube* ☞ picture on page A5

cubic /ˈkjuːbɪk/ *adjective*: *a cubic metre* (= a space like a cube that is one metre long on each side)

cucumber /ˈkjuːkʌmbə(r)/ *noun* a long vegetable with a green skin

cucumber

cuddle /ˈkʌdl/ *verb* (**cuddles**, **cuddling**, **cuddled** /ˈkʌdld/) hold somebody or something in your arms to show love: *He cuddled his baby.*

cuddle *noun* give somebody a cuddle cuddle somebody: *I gave her a cuddle.*

cuff /kʌf/ *noun* the end part of a sleeve, near your hand

cultivate /ˈkʌltɪveɪt/ *verb* (**cultivates**, **cultivating**, **cultivated**) **1** use land for growing plants: *Only a small area of the island was cultivated.* **2** keep and care for plants

cultivation /ˌkʌltɪˈveɪʃn/ *noun* (no plural) *cultivation of the land*

cultural /ˈkʌltʃərəl/ *adjective* **1** about the art, ideas and way of life of a group of people: *There are many cultural differences between Tanzania and Britain.* **2** about things like art, music or theatre

culture /ˈkʌltʃə(r)/ *noun* the art, ideas and way of life of a group of people: *She taught us about the culture of the Maasai.*

cunning /ˈkʌnɪŋ/ *adjective* clever; good at making people believe something that is not true: *Their plan was quite cunning.*

cup /kʌp/ *noun*
1 a small round container with a handle, that you can drink from: *a*

cup

saucer

cup and saucer **2** a large metal thing like a cup, that you get for winning in a sport

cupboard /ˈkʌbəd/ *noun* a piece of furniture with shelves and doors, where you keep things like clothes or food

cure[1] /kjʊə(r)/ *verb* (**cures**, **curing**, **cured** /kjʊəd/) **1** make an ill person well again: *The doctors can't cure her.* **2** make an illness go away: *Can this disease be cured?*

cure[2] /kjʊə(r)/ *noun* something that makes an illness go away: *a cure for cancer*

curiosity /ˌkjʊəriˈɒsəti/ *noun* (no plural) wanting to know about things: *I was full of curiosity about her letter.*

curious /ˈkjʊəriəs/ *adjective* **1** If you are curious, you want to know about something: *I am curious to know where she found the money.* **2** strange or unusual: *a curious noise*

curiously *adverb:* '*Where are you going?' she asked curiously.*

curl[1] /kɜːl/ *noun* a piece of hair in a round shape

curly *adjective* (**curlier**, **curliest**) with a lot of curls: *He's got curly hair.* ☞ picture at **hair**

curl[2] /kɜːl/ *verb* (**curls**, **curling**, **curled** /kɜːld/) bend into a round or curved shape: *The leaves were brown and curled.* **curl up** put your arms, legs and head close to your body: *The cat curled up and went to sleep.*

currency /ˈkʌrənsi/ *noun* (*plural* **currencies**) the money that a country uses: *The currency of Ethiopia is the birr.*

current[1] /ˈkʌrənt/ *adjective* Something that is current is happening or used now: *current fashions*

currently *adverb* now: *We are currently living in Narok.*

current[2] /ˈkʌrənt/ *noun* **1** air or water that is moving: *It is dangerous to swim here because of the strong current.* **2** electricity that is going through a wire

curry /ˈkʌri/ *noun* (*plural* **curries**) meat or vegetables cooked with spices. You often eat curry with rice.

curse /kɜːs/ *noun* words that wish for something bad to happen to somebody: *People say that there is a curse on this house.*

curtain /ˈkɜːtn/ *noun* a piece of cloth that you use to cover a window

curve /kɜːv/ *noun* a line that is not straight; a bend

curve *verb* (**curves**, **curving**, **curved** /kɜːvd/) make a round shape; bend: *The road curves to the right.*

curved *adjective:* a curved line

curtain

curve

cushion /ˈkʊʃn/ *noun* a bag filled with something soft. You put it on a chair and sit on it or rest your body against it.

custom /ˈkʌstəm/ *noun* something that a group of people usually do: *It is a custom in Japan to leave your shoes outside a house.*

customer /ˈkʌstəmə(r)/ *noun* a person who buys things from a shop

customs /ˈkʌstəmz/ *noun* (plural) the place at an airport or a port where you must show what you have brought with you from another country: *a customs officer*

cut[1] /kʌt/ *verb* (**cuts**, **cutting**, **cut**, **has cut**) **1** break or make a hole in something with a knife or scissors, for example: *I cut the string and opened the parcel.* ○ *I cut the mango in half* (= into two parts). ○ *She cut her finger on some broken glass.* **2** take one piece from something bigger: *Can you cut me a piece of that meat, please?* **3** make something shorter with a knife or scissors, for example: *Have you had your hair cut?* **be cut off** be kept alone, away from other people: *Our village was cut off by the floods.* **cut down 1** use, do or buy less of something: *The doctor told me to cut down on smoking.* **2** cut something so that it falls down: *We cut down the old tree.* **cut off** stop something: *The workmen cut off the electricity.* **cut out** take something from the place where it was by using scissors, etc: *I cut the picture out of the newspaper.* **cut up** break something into pieces with a knife or scissors, for example

cut[2] /kʌt/ *noun* a place where something has been cut: *I have a cut on my leg.*

cute /kjuːt/ *adjective* (**cuter**, **cutest**) pretty: *What a cute little baby!*

cutlery /ˈkʌtləri/ *noun* (no plural) knives, forks and spoons

cycle /ˈsaɪkl/ *noun* a bicycle: *a cycle shop*

cycle *verb* (**cycles**, **cycling**, **cycled** /ˈsaɪkld/) ride a bicycle: *I cycle to school every day.*

cylinder /ˈsɪlɪndə(r)/ *noun* a long

round shape, like a tube or a tin of food
☛ picture on page A5

dab /dæb/ verb (**dabs**, **dabbing**, **dabbed** /dæbd/) touch something lightly and quickly: She dabbed the cut with cotton wool.

dad /dæd/ noun father: Hello, Dad. ○ This is my dad.

daddy /'dædi/ noun (plural **daddies**) a word for 'father' that children use

daft /dɑːft/ adjective (**dafter**, **daftest**) silly; stupid: I think you're daft to work for nothing! ○ Don't be daft!

dagger /'dægə(r)/ noun a short pointed knife that people use as a weapon

daily /'deɪli/ adjective, adverb that happens or comes every day or once a day: There are daily flights between London and Nairobi. ○ a daily newspaper ○ The museum is open daily from 9 a.m. to 6 p.m.

dainty /'deɪnti/ adjective (**daintier**, **daintiest**) small and pretty: a dainty little girl

dairy /'deəri/ noun (plural **dairies**) a place where milk is kept or where food like butter and cheese is made

dala-dala /'dælə dælə/ noun (in Tanzania) a small bus

dam /dæm/ noun a wall that is built across a river to hold the water back

damage /'dæmɪdʒ/ verb (**damages**, **damaging**, **damaged** /'dæmɪdʒd/) break or harm something: The house was badly damaged by fire.

damage noun (no plural) He had an accident, but he didn't do any damage to his car.

damn /dæm/ a rude word that people sometimes use when they are angry: Damn! I've lost my key!

damp /dæmp/ adjective (**damper**, **dampest**) a little wet: a cold damp house

cylindrical /sɪ'lɪndrɪkl/ adjective with this shape

Dd

dance¹ /dɑːns/ verb (**dances**, **dancing**, **danced** /dɑːnst/) move your body to music: Denge dances well. ○ I danced with her all night.

dancer noun a person who dances: I'm not a very good dancer.

dancing noun (no plural) moving to music: The dancing went on all night.

dance² /dɑːns/ noun **1** movements that you do to music **2** a party where people dance: My parents are going to a dance tonight.

danger /'deɪndʒə(r)/ noun **1** (no plural) the possibility that something bad may happen: You may be in danger if you travel alone late at night. **2** (plural **dangers**) a person or thing that may bring harm or trouble: Smoking is a danger to health.

dangerous /'deɪndʒərəs/ adjective A person or thing that is dangerous may hurt you: It's dangerous to drive a car at night without any lights. ○ a dangerous illness

dangerously adverb: She drives dangerously.

dare /deə(r)/ verb (**dares**, **daring**, **dared** /deəd/) **1** be brave enough to do something: I daren't tell Fatima that I've lost her book. ○ I didn't dare ask for more money. **2** ask somebody to do something dangerous or silly to see if they are brave enough: I dare you to jump off that wall! **don't you dare** words that you use for telling somebody very strongly not to do something: Don't you dare read my letters! **how dare you** words that show you are very angry about something that somebody has done: How dare you speak to me like that!

daring /'deərɪŋ/ adjective not afraid to do dangerous things

dark[1] /dɑːk/ *adjective* (**darker**, **darkest**) **1** with no light, or not much light: *It was so dark that I couldn't see anything.* ○ *It gets dark very early in the winter.* ✪ opposite: **light 2** A dark colour is nearer to black than to white: *a dark-green skirt* ○ *He's got dark-brown eyes.* ✪ opposite: **light** or **pale 3** A person who is dark has brown or black hair or skin: *a thin, dark woman* ✪ opposite: **fair**

dark[2] /dɑːk/ *noun* (no plural) where there is no light: *Cats can see in the dark.* ○ *Are you afraid of the dark?* **after dark** after the sun goes down: *Don't go out alone after dark.* **before dark** before the sun goes down: *Make sure you get home before dark.*

darkness /'dɑːknəs/ *noun* (no plural) where there is no light **in darkness** with no light: *The whole house was in darkness.*

darling /'dɑːlɪŋ/ *noun* a name that you call somebody that you love: *Are you all right, darling?*

dart /dɑːt/ *verb* (**darts**, **darting**, **darted**) move quickly and suddenly: *He darted across the road.*

dash[1] /dæʃ/ *verb* (**dashes**, **dashing**, **dashed** /dæʃt/) run quickly: *I dashed into a shop when it started to rain.* ○ *I must dash – I'm late for work.*

dash[2] /dæʃ/ *noun* (*plural* **dashes**) **1** a mark (–) that you use in writing **2** a sudden short run: *The robber made a dash for the door.*

data /'deɪtə/ *noun* (plural) facts or information: *We are studying the data that we have collected.*

date[1] /deɪt/ *noun* the number of the day, the month and sometimes the year: *'What's the date today?' 'The first of February.'* ○ *Today's date is 11 September 1998.* ○ *What is your date of birth?* **out of date 1** not modern: *The machinery they use is completely out of date.* **2** too old, so that you cannot use it: *This ticket is out of date.* **up to date 1** modern **2** with the newest information: *Is this list of names up to date?*

date[2] /deɪt/ *noun* a small sweet brown fruit

daughter /'dɔːtə(r)/ *noun* a girl or woman who is somebody's child: *They have two daughters and a son.* ○ *My oldest daughter is a doctor.*

daughter-in-law /'dɔːtər ɪn lɔː/ *noun* (*plural* **daughters-in-law**) the wife of your son

dawn /dɔːn/ *noun* the time when the sun comes up

day /deɪ/ *noun* (*plural* **days**) **1** a time of 24 hours from midnight to the next midnight: *There are seven days in a week.* ○ *I went to Masaka for a few days.* ○ *'What day is it today?' 'Tuesday.'* **2** the time when it is light outside: *Most people work during the day and sleep at night.* **3** a time in the past: *In my grandparents' day, not many people had cars.* **one day 1** on a certain day in the past: *One day, a letter arrived.* ✪ We often use **one day** at the beginning of a story. **2** at some time in the future: *I hope to visit Canada one day.* **some day** at some time in the future: *Some day I'll be rich and famous.* **the day after tomorrow** not tomorrow, but the next day **the day before yesterday** not yesterday, but the day before **the other day** a few days ago: *I went to Kisumu the other day.* **these days** now: *A lot of people work with computers these days.*

daylight /'deɪlaɪt/ *noun* (no plural) the light from the sun during the day: *These colours look different in daylight.*

day off /ˌdeɪ 'ɒf/ *noun* (*plural* **days off**) a day when you do not go to work or school

daytime /'deɪtaɪm/ *noun* (no plural) the time when it is day and not night: *I prefer to study in the daytime and go out in the evening.*

dazzle /'dæzl/ *verb* (**dazzles**, **dazzling**, **dazzled** /'dæzld/) If a light dazzles you, it shines brightly in your eyes so that you cannot see for a short time: *I was dazzled by the car's lights.*

dead[1] /ded/ *adjective* **1** not living: *All my grandparents are dead.* ○ *Throw away those dead flowers.* **2** very quiet: *This town is dead: everywhere is closed after ten o'clock at night.* **a dead end** a street that is only open at one end

the dead *noun* (plural) dead people

dead[2] /ded/ *adverb* completely or very: *I'm dead tired.*

deadline /'dedlam/ *noun* a day or time before which you must do something: *The deadline for finishing this essay is next Tuesday.*

deadly /'dedli/ *adjective* (**deadlier**, **deadliest**) Something that is deadly may kill people or other living things: *a deadly weapon*

deadly *adverb* extremely: *I'm deadly serious.*

deaf /def/ *adjective* not able to hear

the deaf *noun* (plural) people who are deaf

deafen /'defn/ *verb* (**deafens**, **deafening**, **deafened** /'defnd/) make a very loud noise so that somebody cannot hear well: *We were deafened by the sound of a plane flying over our heads.*

deafness /'defnas/ *noun* (no plural) being deaf

deal[1] /di:l/ *noun* an agreement, usually about buying, selling or working: *Let's make a deal – I'll help you today if you help me tomorrow.*

deal[2] /di:l/ *noun* **a good deal** or **a great deal** a lot; much: *He's visited a great deal of the country.* ○ *We ate a great deal.*

deal[3] /di:l/ *verb* (**deals**, **dealing**, **dealt** /delt/, **has dealt**) **deal in something** buy and sell something in business: *We deal in insurance.* **deal out** give something to each person: *I dealt out the cards for the next game.* **deal with somebody** or **something 1** look after something and do what is necessary: *I am too busy to deal with this problem now.* **2** tell about something: *The first chapter of the book deals with letter-writing.*

dealer *noun* a person who buys and sells things: *drug dealers*

dear /dɪə(r)/ *adjective* (**dearer**, **dearest**) **1** a word that you use before a person's name at the beginning of a letter: *Dear Mr Banjo, ...* ○ *Dear Sir or Madam, ...* **2** that you love very much: *She was a dear friend.* **3** that costs a lot of money; expensive: *Those radios are too dear.* ✪ opposite: **cheap**

death /deθ/ *noun* when a life finishes: *He became manager of the company after his father's death.* ○ *There are thousands of deaths in car accidents every year.*

deathly (**deathlier**, **deathliest**) *adjective* like death: *There was a deathly silence.*

debate /dɪ'beɪt/ *noun* a public meeting where people talk about something important

debate *verb* (**debates**, **debating**, **debated**) *Parliament is debating the new law.*

debt /det/ *noun* money that you must pay back to somebody: *The company has borrowed a lot of money and it still has debts.* **in debt** If you are in debt, you must pay money to somebody.

decay /dɪ'keɪ/ *verb* (**decays**, **decaying**, **decayed** /dɪ'keɪd/) become bad or fall to pieces: *If you don't clean your teeth, they will decay.*

decay *noun* (no plural) *tooth decay*

deceive /dɪ'si:v/ *verb* (**deceives**, **deceiving**, **deceived** /dɪ'si:vd/) make somebody believe something that is not true: *Mueni's boyfriend deceived her – he didn't tell her he was already married.* ○ *He deceived me into thinking he was a police officer.*

December /dɪ'sembə(r)/ *noun* the twelfth month of the year

decent /'di:snt/ *adjective* **1** good enough; right: *You can't wear jeans for a job interview – you should buy some decent clothes.* **2** honest and good: *decent people*

decide /dɪ'saɪd/ *verb* (**decides**, **deciding**, **decided**) choose something after thinking: *I can't decide what colour to paint my room.* ○ *I've decided to look for a new job.* ○ *She decided that she didn't want to come.*

decimal /'desɪml/ *noun* a part of a number, written after a dot (called a **decimal point**), for example 0.75 ✪ We say '0.75' as 'zero point seven five'.

decision /dɪ'sɪʒn/ *noun* choosing something after thinking; deciding: *I must make a decision about what I'm going to do when I leave school.*

deck /dek/ *noun* the floor of a ship

declare /dɪˈkleə(r)/ *verb* (**declares**, **declaring**, **declared** /dɪˈkleəd/) **1** say very clearly what you think or what you will do, often to a lot of people: *He declared that he was not a thief.* ○ *The government has declared war on smugglers.* **2** In an airport or port you declare things that you have bought in another country so that you can pay tax on them: *Have you anything to declare?*

declaration /ˌdekləˈreɪʃn/ *noun*: *a declaration of independence*

decorate /ˈdekəreɪt/ *verb* (**decorates**, **decorating**, **decorated**) make something look nicer by adding beautiful things to it or by painting it: *We decorated the room with flowers.* ○ *The hotel is closed because they're decorating the rooms.*

decorations /ˌdekəˈreɪʃnz/ *noun* (plural) beautiful things that you add to something to make it look nicer

decrease /dɪˈkriːs/ *verb* (**decreases**, **decreasing**, **decreased** /dɪˈkriːst/) become smaller or less; make something smaller or less: *The number of people in the village has decreased from 200 to 100.*

decrease /ˈdiːkriːs/ *noun*: *There was a decrease in the number of people living in the village.* ✪ opposite: **increase**

deep /diːp/ *adjective* (**deeper**, **deepest**) **1** Something that is deep goes down a long way: *Be careful: the water is very deep.* ○ *There were deep cuts in his face.* ✪ opposite: **shallow** ☛ picture on page A10 **2** You use 'deep' to say or ask how far something is from the top to the bottom: *The hole was about six metres deep and three metres wide.* ✪ The noun is **depth**. **3** A deep colour is strong and dark: *She has deep-blue eyes.* ✪ opposite: **pale** or **light 4** A deep sound is low and strong: *He has a deep voice.* **5** Deep feelings are very strong: *deep sadness* **6** If you are in a deep sleep, it is difficult for somebody to wake you up: *She was in such a deep sleep that she didn't hear me calling her.*

deeply *adverb* strongly or completely: *He is sleeping very deeply.*

defeat /dɪˈfiːt/ *verb* (**defeats**, **defeat-** **ing**, **defeated**) win a fight or game against a person or group of people: *France defeated Brazil in the final.* ✪ **Beat** is the word that we usually use

defeat *noun* losing a game, fight or war

defence /dɪˈfens/ *noun* fighting against people who attack, or keeping away dangerous people or things: *They fought the war in defence of their country.*

defend /dɪˈfend/ *verb* (**defends**, **defending**, **defended**) **1** fight to keep away people or things that attack: *They defended the city against the enemy.* **2** say that somebody has not done something wrong: *My sister defended me when my father said I was lazy.* ○ *He had a lawyer to defend him in court.* **3** try to stop another person or team scoring goals or points in a game

defied, **defies** *forms of* defy

define /dɪˈfaɪn/ *verb* (**defines**, **defining**, **defined** /dɪˈfaɪnd/) say what a word means: *How do you define 'rich'?*

definite /ˈdefɪnət/ *adjective* sure; certain: *I want a definite answer, 'yes' or 'no'.* ○ *They might be able to find you a job but it's not definite.*

definitely *adverb* certainly: *I am definitely going to the match this evening – I have already bought my ticket.*

definition /ˌdefɪˈnɪʃn/ *noun* a group of words that tell you what another word means

defy /dɪˈfaɪ/ *verb* (**defies**, **defying**, **defied** /dɪˈfaɪd/, **has defied**) If you defy somebody or something, you do something that they say you should not do: *She defied her parents and stayed out all night.*

degree /dɪˈgriː/ *noun* **1** a measurement of temperature: *Water boils at 100 degrees Celsius (100° C).* **2** a measurement of angles: *There are 90 degrees (90°) in a right angle.* **3** Universities and colleges give degrees to students who have completed special courses there: *She has a degree in Mathematics.*

delay[1] /dɪˈleɪ/ *noun* (plural **delays**) a time when somebody or something is late: *There was a long delay at the airport.* **without delay** immediately: *You must pay the money without delay.*

delay[2] /dɪ'leɪ/ *verb* (**delays**, **delaying**, **delayed** /dɪ'leɪd/) **1** make somebody or something late: *My train was delayed for two hours because of the bad weather.* **2** not do something until a later time: *I delayed my holiday because I was ill.*

deliberate /dɪ'lɪbərət/ *adjective* that you want and plan to do, and do not do by mistake: *'Do you think it was an accident?' 'No, I'm sure it was deliberate.'*

deliberately *adverb*: *The police think that somebody started the fire deliberately.*

delicate /'delɪkət/ *adjective* **1** If something is delicate, you can break or damage it very easily: *This old book is very delicate.* **2** pretty and fine; not strong: *delicate colours like pale pink and pale blue* ○ *She had long, delicate fingers.*

delicious /dɪ'lɪʃəs/ *adjective* very good to eat: *This soup is delicious.*

delight[1] /dɪ'laɪt/ *verb* (**delights**, **delighting**, **delighted**) make somebody very pleased or happy

delighted *adjective* very pleased or happy: *I'm delighted to meet you.*

delight[2] /dɪ'laɪt/ *noun* (no plural) great happiness

delightful /dɪ'laɪtfl/ *adjective* very nice; lovely

deliver /dɪ'lɪvə(r)/ *verb* (**delivers**, **delivering**, **delivered** /dɪ'lɪvəd/) take something to the place where it must go: *The postman delivered two large parcels to the office.*

delivery /dɪ'lɪvəri/ *noun* (*plural* **deliveries**) *We are waiting for a delivery of bread.*

demand[1] /dɪ'mɑːnd/ *verb* (**demands**, **demanding**, **demanded**) say strongly that you must have something: *The workers are demanding more money.* ○ *She demanded to see the manager.*

demand[2] /dɪ'mɑːnd/ *noun* saying strongly that you must have something **in demand** wanted by a lot of people: *I'm in demand today – I've had eight telephone calls!*

democracy /dɪ'mɒkrəsi/ *noun* (*plural* **democracies**) **1** a system of government where the people choose their leader (by **voting**) **2** a country with a government that the people choose: *Kenya is a democracy.*

democrat /'deməkræt/ *noun* **1** a person who wants democracy **2** **Democrat** a person in the Democratic Party in the USA ☞ Look at **Republican**.

democratic /ˌdemə'krætɪk/ *adjective* If a country, etc is democratic, all the people in it can choose its leaders or decide about the way it is organized.

demolish /dɪ'mɒlɪʃ/ *verb* (**demolishes**, **demolishing**, **demolished** /dɪ'mɒlɪʃt/) break a building so that it falls down: *They demolished six houses and built a supermarket in their place.*

demonstrate /'demənstreɪt/ *verb* (**demonstrates**, **demonstrating**, **demonstrated**) **1** show something clearly: *He demonstrated how to operate the machine.* **2** walk or stand in public with a group of people to show that you have strong feelings about something: *Thousands of people demonstrated against the war.*

demonstration /ˌdemən'streɪʃn/ *noun* **1** a group of people walking or standing together in public to show that they have strong feelings about something: *There were demonstrations in the streets of the capital today.* **2** showing how to do something, or how something works: *He gave us a cookery demonstration.*

den /den/ *noun* the place where a wild animal lives

denied, **denies** *forms of* **deny**

denim /'denɪm/ *noun* (no plural) strong cotton material that is used for making jeans and other clothes. Denim is often blue: *a denim jacket*

dense /dens/ *adjective* **1** with a lot of things or people close together: *dense forests* **2** thick and difficult to see through: *dense smoke*

dent /dent/ *noun* a hollow place in something flat that comes when you hit it or press it hard: *There's a big dent in the side of my car.*

dent *verb* (**dents**, **denting**, **dented**) hit something and make a hollow place in it: *I dropped the tin and dented it.*

dentist /'dentɪst/ *noun* a person whose

job is to look after your teeth ✪ When we talk about visiting the dentist, we say **go to the dentist's**: *I've got toothache so I'm going to the dentist's.* ☞ Note at **tooth**.

deny /dɪˈnaɪ/ *verb* (**denies**, **denying**, **denied** /dɪˈnaɪd/, **has denied**) say that something is not true: *He denied that he had stolen the car.* ○ *They denied breaking the window.* ✪ opposite: **admit**

depart /dɪˈpɑːt/ *verb* (**departs**, **departing**, **departed**) leave a place: *The Nairobi train will depart in 5 minutes.* ✪ **Leave** is the word that we usually use.

department /dɪˈpɑːtmənt/ *noun* one of the parts of a university, school, government, shop, big company, etc: *The book department is on the second floor.* ○ *Professor Mulindwa is the head of the English department.*

department store /dɪˈpɑːtmənt stɔː(r)/ *noun* a big shop that sells a lot of different things

departure /dɪˈpɑːtʃə(r)/ *noun* leaving a place: *A board inside the airport shows arrivals and departures.*

depend /dɪˈpend/ *verb* (**depends**, **depending**, **depended**) **depend on somebody** or **something 1** need somebody or something: *She still depends on her parents for money because she hasn't got a job.* **2** trust somebody; feel sure that somebody or something will do what you want: *I know I can depend on my friends to help me.* **it depends**, **that depends** words that you use to show that something is not certain: *'Do you want to go for a swim tomorrow?' 'It depends on how much homework we have.'* ○ *'Can you lend me some money?' 'That depends. How much do you want?'*

dependent /dɪˈpendənt/ *adjective* If you are dependent on somebody or something, you need them: *A baby is completely dependent on its parents.*

deposit /dɪˈpɒzɪt/ *noun* **1** money that you pay to show that you want something and that you will pay the rest later: *I paid a deposit on a holiday.* **2** money that you pay into a bank

3 extra money that you pay when you rent something. You get it back if you do not damage or lose what you have rented.

deposit *verb* (**deposits**, **depositing**, **deposited**) put something somewhere to keep it safe: *The money was deposited in the bank.*

depress /dɪˈpres/ *verb* (**depresses**, **depressing**, **depressed** /dɪˈprest/) make somebody feel unhappy: *Seeing sick children really depresses me.*

depressed *adjective* If you are depressed, you are very unhappy: *He's been very depressed since he lost his job.*

depressing *adjective* Something that is depressing makes you very unhappy: *The stories in the newspaper are always so depressing.*

depression /dɪˈpreʃn/ *noun* (no plural) a feeling of unhappiness

depth /depθ/ *noun* how deep something is; how far it is from the top of something to the bottom: *What is the depth of the swimming-pool?* ○ *The hole was 2m in depth.*

deputy /ˈdepjəti/ *noun* (*plural* **deputies**) the person in a company, school, etc, who does the work of the leader when he/she is not there: *a deputy headmaster*

derivative /dɪˈrɪvətɪv/ *noun* a word that is made from another word: *'Sadness' is a derivative of 'sad'.*

descend /dɪˈsend/ *verb* (**descends**, **descending**, **descended**) go down: *The plane started to descend.* ✪ It is more usual to say **go down**.

descendant /dɪˈsendənt/ *noun* Your descendants are your children, grandchildren and everybody in your family who lives after you: *Queen Elizabeth II is a descendant of Queen Victoria.*

descent /dɪˈsent/ *noun* going down: *The plane began its descent to Munich airport.*

describe /dɪˈskraɪb/ *verb* (**describes**, **describing**, **described** /dɪˈskraɪbd/) say what somebody or something is like or what happened: *Can you describe the man you saw?* ○ *She described the accident to the police.*

description /dɪ'skrɪpʃn/ *noun* words that tell what somebody or something is like or what happened: *I have given the police a description of the thief.*

desert[1] /'dezət/ *noun* a large area of land that is usually covered with sand. Deserts are very dry and not many plants can grow there: *the Sahara Desert*

desert island /ˌdezət 'aɪlənd/ *noun* an island where nobody lives, in a hot part of the world

desert[2] /dɪ'zɜːt/ *verb* (**deserts**, **deserting**, **deserted**) leave a person or place when it is wrong to go: *He deserted his wife and children.*

deserted /dɪ'zɜːtɪd/ *adjective* empty, because all the people have left: *At night the streets are deserted.*

deserve /dɪ'zɜːv/ *verb* (**deserves**, **deserving**, **deserved** /dɪ'zɜːvd/) be good or bad enough to have something: *You have worked very hard and you deserve a rest.* ○ *They stole money from old people, so they deserve to go to prison.*

design[1] /dɪ'zaɪn/ *verb* (**designs**, **designing**, **designed** /dɪ'zaɪnd/) draw a plan that shows how to make something: *This new stove was designed to use very little fuel.*

design[2] /dɪ'zaɪn/ *noun* **1** a drawing that shows how to make something: *Have you seen the designs for the new houses?* **2** lines, shapes and colours on something: *His shirt has a design of blue and green squares on it.*

designer /dɪ'zaɪnə(r)/ *noun* a person whose job is to make drawings that show how something will be made: *a fashion designer*

desire /dɪ'zaɪə(r)/ *noun* a feeling of wanting something very much: *a desire for peace*

desk

desk /desk/ *noun* **1** a table with drawers, where you sit to write or work **2** a table or place in a building where somebody gives information, etc: *Ask at the information desk.*

despair /dɪ'speə(r)/ *noun* (no plural) a feeling of not having hope: *He was in despair because he had no money and nowhere to live.*

desperate /'despərət/ *adjective* **1** If you are desperate, you have no hope and you are ready to do anything to get what you want: *She is so desperate for a job that she will work anywhere.* **2** very serious: *The injured man was in desperate need of a doctor.*

desperately *adverb*: *He is desperately unhappy.*

desperation /ˌdespə'reɪʃn/ *noun* (no plural) the feeling of having no hope, that makes you do anything to get what you want: *In desperation, she sold her ring to get money for food.*

despise /dɪ'spaɪz/ *verb* (**despises**, **despising**, **despised** /dɪ'spaɪzd/) hate somebody or something very much: *I despise people who tell lies.*

despite /dɪ'spaɪt/ *preposition* although something is true; not noticing or not caring about something: *We decided to go out despite the bad weather.*

dessert /dɪ'zɜːt/ *noun* something sweet that you eat at the end of a meal: *We had ice-cream for dessert.*

dessertspoon /dɪ'zɜːtspuːn/ *noun* a spoon that you use for eating desserts

destination /ˌdestɪ'neɪʃn/ *noun* the place where somebody or something is going: *They were very tired when they finally reached their destination.*

destroy /dɪ'strɔɪ/ *verb* (**destroys**, **destroying**, **destroyed** /dɪ'strɔɪd/) break something completely so that you cannot use it again or so that it is gone: *The house was destroyed by fire.*

destruction /dɪ'strʌkʃn/ *noun* (no plural) breaking something completely so that you cannot use it again or so that it is gone: *the destruction of the crops by insects*

detached /dɪ'tætʃt/ *adjective* A detached house stands alone and is not joined to any other house.

detail /'diːteɪl/ *noun* **1** one of the very small parts that make the whole of something: *Tell me quickly what happened – I don't need to know all the details.* **2 details** (plural) information about something: *For more details, please telephone this number.* **in detail** with all the small parts: *Tell me about your plan in detail.*

detective /dɪ'tektɪv/ *noun* a person whose job is to find out who did a crime. Detectives are usually police officers: *Detectives are interviewing two men about the killing.*

detergent /dɪ'tɜ:dʒənt/ *noun* a powder or liquid that you use for washing things

determination /dɪ,tɜ:mɪ'neɪʃn/ *noun* (no plural) being certain that you want to do something: *She has shown great determination to succeed.*

determined /dɪ'tɜ:mɪnd/ *adjective* very certain that you want do something: *She is determined to win the match.*

detest /dɪ'test/ *verb* (**detests, detesting, detested**) hate somebody or something very much: *I detest spiders.*

detour /'di:tʊə(r)/ *noun* a longer way to a place when you cannot go by the usual way: *The bridge was closed so we had to make a detour.*

develop /dɪ'veləp/ *verb* (**develops, developing, developed** /dɪ'veləpt/) **1** become bigger or more complete; make something bigger or more complete: *Children develop into adults.* **2** begin to have something: *She developed the disease at the age of 27.* **3** When a photograph is developed, special chemicals are used on the film so that you can see the picture.

development /dɪ'veləpmənt/ *noun* **1** (no plural) becoming bigger or more complete; growing: *We studied the development of babies in their first year of life.* **2** (*plural* **developments**) something new that happens: *There are new developments in science almost every day.*

device /dɪ'vaɪs/ *noun* a tool or machine that you use for doing a special job: *a device for opening tins*

devil /'devl/ *noun* **1 the Devil** (no plural) the most powerful evil spirit, in the Christian religion **2** an evil being or

spirit

devote /dɪ'vəʊt/ *verb* (**devotes, devoting, devoted**) give a lot of time or energy to something: *She devoted her life to helping the poor.*

devoted *adjective* If you are devoted to somebody or something, you love them very much: *John is devoted to his wife and children.*

dew /dju:/ *noun* (no plural) small drops of water that form on plants and grass in the night: *In the morning, the grass was wet with dew.*

diagonal /daɪ'ægənl/ *adjective* If you draw a diagonal line from one corner of a square to another, you make two triangles. ☛ picture on page A5

diagram /'daɪəgræm/ *noun* a picture that explains something: *This diagram shows all the parts of an engine.*

dial /'daɪəl/ *noun* a circle with numbers or letters on it. Some telephones and clocks have dials.

dial *verb* (**dials, dialling, dialled** /'daɪəld/) make a telephone call by moving a dial or pushing buttons: *You have dialled the wrong number.*

dialogue /'daɪəlɒg/ *noun* words that people say to each other in a book, play or film

diameter /daɪ'æmɪtə(r)/ *noun* a straight line across a circle, through the centre ☛ picture on page A5

diamond /'daɪəmənd/ *noun* **1** a hard stone that looks like clear glass and is very expensive: *South Africa is famous for its diamond mines.* ○ *a diamond necklace* **2** the shape ♦ **3 diamonds** (plural) the playing-cards that have red shapes like diamonds on them: *the eight of diamonds*

diarrhoea /,daɪə'rɪə/ *noun* an illness that makes you pass waste material (**faeces**) from your body very often and in a more liquid form than usual

diary /'daɪəri/ *noun* (*plural* **diaries**) **1** a book where you write what you are going to do: *I'll look in my diary to see if I'm free tomorrow.* **2** a book where you write what you have done each day **keep a diary** write in a diary every day

dice /daɪs/ *noun* (*plural* **dice**) a small piece of wood or plastic with spots on the sides for playing games: *Throw the dice.*

dice

dictate /dɪkˈteɪt/ *verb* (**dictates, dictating, dictated**) **1** say words so that another person can write them: *She dictated a letter to her secretary.* **2** tell somebody that they must do something: *You can't dictate to me where I should go.*

dictation /dɪkˈteɪʃn/ *noun* words that you say so that another person can write them: *We had a dictation in English today* (= a test when we wrote what the teacher said).

dictator /dɪkˈteɪtə(r)/ *noun* a person who has complete control of a country

dictionary /ˈdɪkʃənri/ *noun* (*plural* **dictionaries**) a book that gives words from A to Z and explains what each word means

did *form of* **do**

didn't /ˈdɪdnt/ = **did not**

die /daɪ/ *verb* (**dies, dying, died** /daɪd/, **has died**) stop living: *People, animals and plants die if they don't have water.* **die down** slowly become less strong: *The storm died down.* **die of something** stop living because of an illness: *She died of a heart attack.*

diesel /ˈdiːzl/ *noun* **1** (*plural* **diesels**), (*also* **diesel engine**) an engine in buses, trains and some cars that uses oil, not petrol **2** oil that is used in diesel engines

diet /ˈdaɪət/ *noun* **1** the food that you usually eat: *It is important to have a healthy diet.* **2** special foods that you eat when you are ill or when you want to get thinner **be** or **go on a diet** eat only special foods because you want to get thinner

difference /ˈdɪfrəns/ *noun* the way that one thing is not the same as another thing: *There is a big difference between the female mosquito and the male.* ○ *What's the difference in price between these two bikes?* **make a difference** change something: *Your help has made a big difference – I under-*stand the work much better now. **make no difference** not change anything; not be important: *It makes no difference which train you catch – the price of the ticket is the same.* **tell the difference** see how one thing or person is different from another thing or person: *Sarah looks exactly like her sister – I can't tell the difference (between them).*

different /ˈdɪfrənt/ *adjective* **1** not the same: *These two shoes are different sizes!* ○ *Cricket is different from baseball.* **2** many and not the same: *They grow 15 different sorts of fruit.*

differently *adverb*: *He's very quiet at home but he behaves differently at school.*

difficult /ˈdɪfɪkəlt/ *adjective* **1** not easy to do or understand: *a difficult problem* ○ *The exam was very difficult.* ○ *It's difficult to learn a new language.* ✪ opposite: **easy 2** A person who is difficult is not easy to please or will not do what you want: *She's a very difficult child.*

difficulty /ˈdɪfɪkəlti/ *noun* (*plural* **difficulties**) a problem; something that is not easy to do or understand: *I have difficulty understanding his accent.* **with difficulty** not easily: *My grandfather walks with difficulty now.*

dig /dɪg/ *verb* (**digs, digging, dug** /dʌg/, **has dug**) move earth and make a hole in the ground: *You need to dig the garden before you plant the seeds.* ○ *They dug a tunnel* through the mountain for the new railway. **dig up** take something from the ground by digging: *They dug up some old coins in their field.*

dig

spade

digest /daɪˈdʒest/ *verb* (**digests, digesting, digested**) change food in your stomach so that your body can use it

digestion /daɪˈdʒestʃən/ *noun* (no plural) changing food in your stomach so that your body can use it

dignified /ˈdɪgnɪfaɪd/ *adjective* calm,

quiet and serious: *a dignified old lady*

dilute /darˈljuːt/ *verb* (**dilutes**, **diluting**, **diluted**) add water to another liquid: *You need to dilute this paint before you use it.*

dim /dɪm/ *adjective* (**dimmer**, **dimmest**) not bright or clear: *The light was so dim that we couldn't see anything.*

dimly *adverb*: *The room was dimly lit.*

dinghy /ˈdɪŋi/ *noun* (*plural* **dinghies**) a small boat

dining-room /ˈdaɪnɪŋ ruːm/ *noun* a room where people eat

dinner /ˈdɪnə(r)/ *noun* the largest meal of the day. You have dinner in the evening, or sometimes in the middle of the day: *What time do you usually have dinner?* ○ *What's for dinner?*

dinosaur
/ˈdaɪnəsɔː(r)/ *noun* a big wild animal that lived a very long time ago

dinosaur

dip /dɪp/ *verb* (**dips**, **dipping**, **dipped** /dɪpt/) put something into a liquid for a short time and then take it out again: *Dip your hand in the water to see how hot it is.*

diploma /dɪˈpləʊmə/ *noun* a piece of paper that shows you have passed an examination or finished special studies: *a teaching diploma*

diplomat /ˈdɪpləmæt/ *noun* a person whose job is to speak and do things for his/her country in another country

diplomatic /ˌdɪpləˈmætɪk/ *adjective*: *diplomatic talks*

direct¹ /dəˈrekt/ *adjective, adverb* **1** as straight as possible, without turning or stopping: *Which is the most direct way to the town centre from here?* ○ *You can fly direct from Nairobi to London.* ○ *The 6.45 train goes direct to Kampala.* **2** from one person or thing to another person or thing with nobody or nothing between them: *You should keep this plant out of direct sunlight.* ☛ Look at **indirect**.

direct² /dəˈrekt/ *verb* (**directs**, **directing**, **directed**) **1** tell somebody how to

get to a place: *The policeman directed us to the passport office.* **2** tell or show somebody how to do something; control somebody or something: *He has directed many plays at the National Theatre.*

direction /dəˈrekʃn/ *noun* where a person or thing is going or looking: *They got lost because they went in the wrong direction.*

directions /dəˈrekʃnz/ *noun* (plural) words that tell you how to get to a place or how to do something: *I couldn't find the school so I asked a woman for directions.* ○ *I didn't read the directions on the packet before I took the medicine.*

directly /dəˈrektli/ *adverb* **1** exactly; in a direct way: *The teacher was looking directly at me.* ○ *The post office is directly opposite the bank.* **2** very soon: *They left directly after breakfast.*

director /dəˈrektə(r)/ *noun* **1** a person who controls a business or a group of people **2** a person who controls a film or play, for example by telling the actors what to do

dirt /dɜːt/ *noun* (no plural) stuff that is not clean, for example mud or dust: *The children came into the house covered in dirt.*

---

dis- *prefix*

You can add **dis-** to the beginning of some words to give them the opposite meaning, for example:

disagree = not agree

dishonest = not honest

---

dirty /ˈdɜːti/ *adjective* (**dirtier**, **dirtiest**) not clean: *Your hands are dirty – go and wash them!* ☛ picture on page A11

disabled /dɪsˈeɪbld/ *adjective* not able to use a part of your body well: *Peter is disabled – he injured his legs in an accident.*

the disabled *noun* (plural) people who are disabled

disadvantage /ˌdɪsədˈvɑːntɪdʒ/ *noun* a problem that makes something difficult or less good: *One of the disadvantages of living by a main road is the noise.*

disagree /ˌdɪsəˈɡriː/ *verb* (**disagrees**, **disagreeing**, **disagreed** /ˌdɪsəˈɡriːd/) say that another person's idea is wrong; not agree: *I said it was a good film, but Francis disagreed with me.* ○ *My sister and I disagree about everything!*

disagreement /ˌdɪsəˈgriːmənt/ *noun* a talk between people with different ideas; an argument: *My parents sometimes have disagreements about money.*

disappear /ˌdɪsəˈpɪə(r)/ *verb* (**disappears, disappearing, disappeared** /ˌdɪsəˈpɪəd/) If a person or thing disappears, they go away so people cannot see them: *The sun disappeared behind the clouds.* ○ *The police are looking for a woman who disappeared on Sunday.*

disappearance /ˌdɪsəˈpɪərəns/ *noun*: *Everybody was worried about the child's disappearance.*

disappoint /ˌdɪsəˈpɔɪnt/ *verb* (**disappoints, disappointing, disappointed**) make you sad because what you wanted did not happen: *I'm sorry to disappoint you, but I can't come to your party.*

disappointed *adjective* If you are disappointed, you feel sad because what you wanted did not happen: *Urapoa was disappointed when she didn't win the prize.*

disappointing *adjective* If something is disappointing, it makes you feel sad because it is not as good as you hoped: *disappointing exam results*

disappointment /ˌdɪsəˈpɔɪntmənt/ *noun* **1** (no plural) a feeling of sadness because what you wanted did not happen: *She couldn't hide her disappointment when she lost the match.* **2** (plural **disappointments**) something that makes you sad because it is not what you hoped: *Sarah's party was a disappointment – only four people came.*

disapprove /ˌdɪsəˈpruːv/ *verb* (**disapproves, disapproving, disapproved** /ˌdɪsəˈpruːvd/) think that somebody or something is bad: *Joe's parents disapproved of his new girlfriend.*

disaster /dɪˈzɑːstə(r)/ *noun* **1** something very bad that happens and that may hurt a lot of people: *Floods and earthquakes are disasters.* **2** something that is very bad: *The match was a disaster! Our team lost 10-0!*

disastrous /dɪˈzɑːstrəs/ *adjective* very bad; that causes great trouble: *The heavy rain brought disastrous floods.*

disc /dɪsk/ *noun* a round flat thing ☛ Look also at **floppy disk** and **hard disk**.

discipline /ˈdɪsəplɪn/ *noun* (no plural) teaching you to control yourself and follow rules: *Children learn discipline at school.*

discipline *verb* (**disciplines, disciplining, disciplined** /ˈdɪsəplɪnd/): *You must discipline yourself to work harder.*

disc jockey /ˈdɪsk dʒɒki/ *noun* a person who plays records on the radio or at discos or nightclubs ☼ The short form is **DJ**.

disco /ˈdɪskəʊ/ *noun* (plural **discos**) a place where people dance and listen to pop music

disconnect /ˌdɪskəˈnekt/ *verb* (**disconnects, disconnecting, disconnected**) stop electricity, gas, etc: *Your 'phone will be disconnected if you don't pay the bill.*

discount /ˈdɪskaʊnt/ *noun* money that somebody takes away from the price of something to make it cheaper: *The company is offering a 50% discount on travel this week.*

discourage /dɪsˈkʌrɪdʒ/ *verb* (**discourages, discouraging, discouraged** /dɪsˈkʌrɪdʒd/) make somebody not want to do something: *Jane's parents tried to discourage her from leaving school.* ☼ opposite: **encourage**

discover /dɪˈskʌvə(r)/ *verb* (**discovers, discovering, discovered** /dɪˈskʌvəd/) find or learn something for the first time: *Who discovered the smallpox vaccine?* ○ *I was in the shop when I discovered that I did not have any money.*

discovery /dɪˈskʌvəri/ *noun* (plural **discoveries**) finding or learning something for the first time: *Scientists have made an important new discovery.*

discriminate /dɪˈskrɪmɪneɪt/ *verb* (**discriminates, discriminating, discriminated**) treat one person or a group in a different way to others: *This company discriminates against women – it pays them less than men for doing the same work.*

discrimination /dɪˌskrɪmɪˈneɪʃn/ noun (no plural) *religious discrimination* (= treating somebody in an unfair way because their religion is not the same as yours)

discuss /dɪˈskʌs/ verb (**discusses, discussing, discussed** /dɪˈskʌst/) talk about something: *I discussed the problem with my parents.*
discussion /dɪˈskʌʃn/ noun: *We had an interesting discussion about politics.*

disease /dɪˈziːz/ noun an illness: *Cholera and malaria are diseases.*

disgrace /dɪsˈɡreɪs/ noun (no plural) when other people stop thinking well of you, because you have done something bad: *He's in disgrace because he stole money from his brother.*
disgraceful /dɪsˈɡreɪsfl/ adjective Something that is disgraceful is very bad and makes you feel shame: *The way the football fans behaved was disgraceful.*

disguise /dɪsˈɡaɪz/ verb (**disguises, disguising, disguised** /dɪsˈɡaɪzd/) make somebody or something different so that people will not know who or what they are: *They disguised themselves as guards and escaped from the prison.*
disguise noun things that you wear so that people do not know who you are: *We went to the party in disguise.*

disgust /dɪsˈɡʌst/ noun (no plural) a strong feeling of not liking something: *They covered their faces in disgust when they smelt the dead elephant.*
disgust verb (**disgusts, disgusting, disgusted**) make somebody have a strong feeling of not liking something
disgusted adjective If you are disgusted, you have a strong feeling of not liking something: *I was disgusted to find a rat in the house.*
disgusting adjective very bad: *What a disgusting smell!*

dish /dɪʃ/ noun (plural **dishes**) **1** a container for food. You can use a dish to cook food in an oven, or to put food on the table. **2** a part of a meal: *We had a fish dish and a vegetable dish.* **3** the **dishes** (plural) all the plates, bowls, cups, etc that you must wash after a meal: *I'll wash the dishes.*

dishonest /dɪsˈɒnɪst/ adjective A person who is dishonest says things that are not true, or steals or cheats.

disinfectant /ˌdɪsɪnˈfektənt/ noun a liquid that you use for cleaning something very well: *The hospital smelt strongly of disinfectant.*

disk /dɪsk/ noun a flat thing that stores information for computers: *a floppy disk ○ a hard disk*
disk drive /ˈdɪsk draɪv/ noun the part of a computer where you can put **floppy disks** ☛ picture at **computer**

dislike /dɪsˈlaɪk/ verb (**dislikes, disliking, disliked** /dɪsˈlaɪkt/) not like somebody or something: *I dislike getting up early.*
dislike noun a feeling of not liking somebody or something: *I have a strong dislike of snakes.*

dismal /ˈdɪzməl/ adjective that makes you feel sad; not bright: *dark, dismal buildings*

dismay /dɪsˈmeɪ/ noun (no plural) a strong feeling of surprise and worry: *John looked at me in dismay when I told him about the accident.*
dismayed /dɪsˈmeɪd/ adjective: *I was dismayed to find that somebody had stolen my bike.*

dismiss /dɪsˈmɪs/ verb (**dismisses, dismissing, dismissed** /dɪsˈmɪst/) **1** make somebody leave their job: *He was dismissed for stealing money from the company.* ✪ **Sack** and **fire** are the words that we usually use. **2** allow somebody to leave a place: *The lesson finished and the teacher dismissed the class.*

disobey /ˌdɪsəˈbeɪ/ verb (**disobeys, disobeying, disobeyed** /ˌdɪsəˈbeɪd/) not do what somebody tells you to do; not obey: *She disobeyed her parents and went to the party.*
disobedient /ˌdɪsəˈbiːdiənt/ adjective A person who is disobedient does not do what somebody tells him/her to do: *a disobedient child*
disobedience /ˌdɪsəˈbiːdiəns/ noun (no plural) not doing what somebody tells you to do

dispensary /dɪsˈpensəri/ *noun* (**dispensaries**) a place where you can get medicine

display /dɪˈspleɪ/ *verb* (**displays, displaying, displayed** /dɪˈspleɪd/) show something so that people can see it: *Our pictures were displayed on the wall.*
display *noun* (*plural* **displays**) something that people look at: *a display of traditional dancing* **on display** in a place where people can look at it: *The paintings are on display in the museum.*

dispose /dɪˈspəʊz/ *verb* (**disposes, disposing, disposed** /dɪˈspəʊzd/) **dispose of something** throw something away or give something away because you do not want it: *Where can I dispose of this rubbish?*
disposal /dɪˈspəʊzl/ *noun* (no plural) *the disposal of nuclear waste*

dispute /dɪˈspjuːt/ *noun* an angry talk between people with different ideas: *There was a dispute about which driver caused the accident.*

dissatisfied /ˌdɪsˈsætɪsfaɪd/ *adjective* not pleased with something: *I am very dissatisfied with your work*

distance /ˈdɪstəns/ *noun* **1** how far it is from one place to another place: *It's a short distance from my house to the station.* ○ *We usually measure distance in miles or kilometres.* **2** a place that is far from somebody or something: *From a distance, he looks quite young.* **in the distance** far away: *I could see a light in the distance.*

distant /ˈdɪstənt/ *adjective* far away in space or time: *distant countries*

distinct /dɪˈstɪŋkt/ *adjective* **1** easy to hear, see or smell; clear: *There is a distinct smell of burning in this room.* **2** clearly different: *The African and the Indian elephant are two distinct species.*
distinctly *adverb* clearly: *I distinctly heard him say his name was Robert.*

distinguish /dɪˈstɪŋgwɪʃ/ *verb* (**distinguishes, distinguishing, distinguished** /dɪˈstɪŋgwɪʃt/) see, hear, etc the difference between two things or people: *Some people can't distinguish between me and my twin sister.* ○ *Can you distinguish a South African accent from an English one?*

distinguished /dɪˈstɪŋgwɪʃt/ *adjective* famous or important: *a distinguished actor*

distract /dɪˈstrækt/ *verb* (**distracts, distracting, distracted**) If a person or thing distracts you, he/she/it stops you thinking about what you are doing: *The noise distracted me from my homework.*

distress /dɪˈstres/ *noun* (no plural) **1** a strong feeling of pain or sadness **2** being in danger and needing help: *a ship in distress*

distribute /dɪˈstrɪbjuːt/ (**distributes, distributing, distributed**) give or send things to each person: *New books are distributed on the first day of school.*
distribution /ˌdɪstrɪˈbjuːʃn/ *noun* (no plural) *the distribution of newspapers*

district /ˈdɪstrɪkt/ *noun* a part of a country or town: *Bungoma district is in Western Kenya.*

disturb /dɪˈstɜːb/ *verb* (**disturbs, disturbing, disturbed** /dɪˈstɜːbd/) **1** stop somebody doing something, for example thinking, working or sleeping: *My brother always disturbs me when I'm trying to do my homework.* ○ *Do not disturb.* (a notice that you put on a door to tell people not to come in) **2** worry somebody: *We were disturbed by the news that our teacher was ill.*

disturbance /dɪˈstɜːbəns/ *noun* **1** a thing that stops you doing something, for example thinking, working or sleeping **2** when a group of people fight or make a lot of noise and trouble: *The football fans were causing a disturbance outside the stadium.*

ditch /dɪtʃ/ *noun* (*plural* **ditches**) a long narrow hole at the side of a road or field that carries away water

dive /daɪv/ *verb* (**dives, diving, dived** /daɪvd/) **1** jump into water with your arms and head first: *Sam dived into the pool.* **2** go under water: *The birds were diving for fish.*

dive

diving (no plural) the sport of jumping into water or swimming under water

diversion /daɪˈvɜːʃn/ *noun* a way that you must go when the usual way is closed: *There was a diversion around Nile Avenue because of a road accident.*

divert /daɪˈvɜːt/ *verb* (**diverts, diverting, diverted**) make something go a different way: *Our flight was diverted to another airport because of the bad weather.*

divide /dɪˈvaɪd/ *verb* (**divides, dividing, divided**) **1** share or cut something into smaller parts: *The teacher divided the class into groups of three.* ○ *The book is divided into ten chapters.* **2** go into parts: *When the road divides, go left.* **3** find out how many times one number goes into a bigger number: *36 divided by 4 is 9 (36 ÷ 4 = 9).*

divine /dɪˈvaɪn/ *adjective* of, like or from God or a god: *a divine message*

division /dɪˈvɪʒn/ *noun* **1** (no plural) finding out how many times one number goes into a bigger number **2** (no plural) sharing or cutting something into parts: *the division of Germany after the Second World War* **3** (*plural* **divisions**) one of the parts of a big company: *He works in the sales division.*

divorce /dɪˈvɔːs/ *noun* the end of a marriage by law: *She is getting a divorce.*

divorce *verb* (**divorces, divorcing, divorced** /dɪˈvɔːst/) *He divorced his wife.* ✪ We often say **get divorced**: *They got divorced last year.*

divorced *adjective*: *I'm not married – I'm divorced.*

dizzy /ˈdɪzi/ *adjective* (**dizzier, dizzi-est**) If you feel dizzy, you feel that everything is turning round and round and that you are going to fall: *The room was very hot and I started to feel dizzy.*

DJ /ˌdiː ˈdʒeɪ/ *short for* disc jockey

do[1] /duː/, /də/ *verb* **1** a word that you use with another verb to make a question: *Do you want a drink?* **2** a word that you use with another verb when you are saying 'not': *I like watching football but I don't* (= do not) *like playing it.* **3** a word that you use in place of saying something again: *She doesn't speak English, but I do* (= I speak English). **4** a word that you use before another verb to make its meaning stronger: *You do look nice!*

do[2] /duː/ *verb* (**does** /dʌz/, **doing, did** /dɪd/, **has done** /dʌn/) **1** carry out an action: *What are you doing?* ○ *He did the cooking.* ○ *What did you do with my key?* (= where did you put it?) **2** finish something; find the answer: *I have done my homework.* ○ *I can't do this sum – it's too difficult.* **3** have a job or study something: *'Tell me what he does.' 'He's a doctor.'* ○ *She's doing Economics at Makerere University.* **4** be good enough; be enough: *I couldn't find any rope, but will this string do?* **be** or **have to do with somebody** or **something** be connected with somebody or something: *I'm not sure what his job is – I think it's something to do with computers.* ○ *Don't read that letter. It has nothing to do with you!* **could do with something** want or need something: *I could do with a drink.* **do up 1** fasten something: *Do up the buttons on your shirt.* ✪ opposite: **undo 2** clean and repair something to make it look newer: *They bought an old house and now they are doing it up.*

do[1]			
present tense		*negative short forms*	*past tense* **did** /dɪd/
I	**do**	I	**don't**	
you	**do**	you	**don't**	*present participle* **doing**
he/she/it	**does** /dʌz/	he/she/it	**doesn't**	*past participle* **done** /dʌn/
we	**do**	we	**don't**	
you	**do**	you	**don't**	
they	**do**	they	**don't**	

dock /dɒk/ *noun* a place by the sea or a river where ships go so that people can move things on and off them or repair them

doctor /ˈdɒktə(r)/ *noun* **1** a person whose job is to make sick people well again: *Doctor Baucha sees patients every morning.* **2** a person who has the highest degree from a university ✪ When you write 'Doctor' as part of a person's name the short form is **Dr**.

document /ˈdɒkjumənt/ *noun* a paper with important information on it: *a legal document*

documentary /ˌdɒkjuˈmentri/ *noun* (*plural* **documentaries**) a film about true things: *I watched an interesting documentary about Japan on TV last night.*

dodge /dɒdʒ/ *verb* (**dodges**, **dodging**, **dodged** /dɒdʒd/) move quickly to avoid something or somebody: *He ran across the busy road, dodging the cars.*

does *form of* **do**

doesn't /ˈdʌznt/ = **does not**

dog /dɒg/ *noun* an animal that many people keep as a pet or to do work ✪ A young dog is called a **puppy**.

doll /dɒl/ *noun* a toy like a very small person

dollar /ˈdɒlə(r)/ *noun* money that people use in the USA, Zimbabwe and some other countries. There are 100 **cents** in a dollar. ✪ We write **$**: *This shirt costs $30.*

dolphin

dolphin /ˈdɒlfɪn/ *noun* an intelligent animal that lives in the sea

dome /dəʊm/ *noun* the round roof of a building

domestic /dəˈmestɪk/ *adjective* **1** of or about the home or family: *Cooking and cleaning are domestic jobs.* ○ *Many cats and dogs are domestic animals* (= animals that live in your home with you). **2** of or inside a country: *a domestic flight* (= to a place in the same country)

dominate /ˈdɒmɪneɪt/ *verb* (**dominates**, **dominating**, **dominated**) control somebody or something because you are stronger or more important: *He dominates his younger brother.*

donate /dəʊˈneɪt/ *verb* (**donates**, **donating**, **donated**) give something to people who need it: *They donated one million shillings to the hospital.*

donation /dəʊˈneɪʃn/ *noun* something that you give to people who need it: *a donation of money*

done *form of* **do**

donkey /ˈdɒŋki/ *noun* (*plural* **donkeys**) an animal like a small horse with long ears

don't /dəʊnt/ = **do not**

door /dɔː(r)/ *noun* the way into a building or room; a piece of wood, glass or metal that you use to open and close the way in to a building, room, cupboard, car, etc: *Can you close the door, please?* ○ *Maria knocked on the door. 'Come in,' Peter said.* ○ *There is somebody at the door.* ☛ picture at **house**. A house often has a **front door** and a **back door**. **answer the door** go to open the door when somebody knocks or rings the bell **next door** in the next house, room or building: *Mary lives next door to us.* **out of doors** outside; not in a building: *Farmers spend a lot of time out of doors.*

doorbell /ˈdɔːbel/ *noun* a bell outside a house that you ring to tell people inside that you want to go in

doorway /ˈdɔːweɪ/ *noun* an opening for going into a building or room: *Mike was waiting in the doorway when they arrived.*

dormitory /ˈdɔːmətri/ *noun* (*plural* **dormitories**) a big bedroom for a lot of people

dose /dəʊs/ *noun* an amount of medicine that you take at one time: *Take a large dose of medicine before you go to bed.*

dot /dɒt/ *noun* a small round mark: *The letter 'i' has a dot over it.* **on the dot** at exactly the right time: *Please be here at nine o'clock on the dot.*

dotted line /ˌdɒtɪd ˈlaɪn/ *noun* a line of

dots that sometimes shows where you have to write something: *Please sign* (= write your name) *on the dotted line.*

double /ˈdʌbl/ *adjective* **1** two times as much or as many; twice as much or as many: *You get paid double for working nights.* **2** with two parts that are the same: *double doors* **3** for two people: *a double bed* ○ *a double room* **4** You use 'double' before a letter or a number to show that it comes two times: *'How do you spell your name, Mr Ninsiima?' 'N, I, N, S, double I, M, A.'* ○ *The phone number is double four nine five one* (44951). ☛ Look at **single**.

double *verb* (**doubles**, **doubling**, **doubled** /ˈdʌbld/) make something twice as much or as many; become twice as much or as many: *The price has doubled: last year it was 500 shillings and this year it's 1 000.*

doubt[1] /daʊt/ *noun* a feeling that you are not sure about something: *She says the story is true but I have my doubts about it.* **in doubt** not sure: *If you are in doubt, ask your teacher.* **no doubt** I am sure: *Paul isn't here yet, but no doubt he will come later.*

doubt[2] /daʊt/ *verb* (**doubts**, **doubting**, **doubted**) not feel sure about something; think that something is probably not true or probably will not happen: *I doubt if he will come.*

doubtful /ˈdaʊtfl/ *adjective* not certain or not likely: *It is doubtful whether he will walk again.*

doubtless /ˈdaʊtləs/ *adverb* almost certainly: *Doubtless she'll be late!*

dough /dəʊ/ *noun* (no plural) flour, water and other things mixed together, for making bread

dove /dʌv/ *noun* a bird that is often used as a sign of peace

down /daʊn/ *preposition, adverb* **1** in or to a lower place; not up: *The sun goes down in the evening.* ○ *We ran down the hill.* ○ *Put that box down on the floor.* ☛ picture on page A2 **2** from standing to sitting or lying: *Sit down.* ○ *Lie down on the bed.* **3** in a way that is smaller, less strong, etc: *Prices are going down.* ○ *Turn that music down!* (= so that it is not so loud) **4** along:

'Can you tell me where the bank is, please?' 'Go down this road, then turn right at the end.' **5** on paper: *Write these words down.*

downhill /ˌdaʊnˈhɪl/ *adverb* down, towards the bottom of a hill: *My bicycle can go fast downhill.*

downstairs /ˌdaʊnˈsteəz/ *adverb* to or on a lower floor of a building: *I ran downstairs and out of the building.*

downstairs *adjective*: *She lives in the downstairs flat.* ☻ opposite: **upstairs**

downwards /ˈdaʊnwədz/, **downward** /ˈdaʊnwəd/ *adverb* down; towards a lower place or towards the ground: *She was lying face downward on the grass.* ☻ opposite: **upwards**

dowry /ˈdaʊri/ *noun* **1** a gift that a man gives to the parents of the woman he is going to marry **2** the money and things that belong to a woman who is getting married

doze /dəʊz/ *verb* (**dozes**, **dozing**, **dozed** /dəʊzd/) sleep lightly for a short time: *My grandfather was dozing in his armchair.* **doze off** start dozing: *I dozed off in front of the television.*

doze *noun*: *She had a doze after lunch.*

dozen /ˈdʌzn/ *noun* (*plural* **dozen**) twelve: *a dozen red roses* ○ *two dozen boxes* ○ *half a dozen eggs* **dozens of** a lot of: *They've invited dozens of people to the party.*

Dr *short way of writing* **Doctor**

draft /drɑːft/, **drafty** /ˈdrɑːfti/ *American English for* **draught**, **draughty**

drag /dræg/ *verb* (**drags**, **dragging**, **dragged** /drægd/) **1** pull something along the ground slowly, often because it is heavy: *He couldn't lift the sack, so he dragged it out of the shop.* **2** If something drags, it seems to go slowly because it is not interesting: *Time drags when you're waiting for a bus.*

drag

dragon /'drægən/ *noun* a big dangerous animal with fire in its mouth, that you find only in stories

drain¹ /dreɪn/ *noun* a pipe that carries away dirty water from a building: *The drain is blocked.*

drain² /dreɪn/ *verb* (**drains, draining, drained** /dreɪnd/) **1** let liquid flow away from something, so that it becomes dry: *Boil the rice in water and then drain it.* **2** become dry because liquid is flowing away: *Let the dishes drain.* **3** flow away: *The water drained away slowly.*

drama /'drɑːmə/ *noun* **1** (*plural dramas*) a story that you watch in the theatre or on television, or listen to on the radio: *a TV drama* **2** (no plural) the study of plays and acting: *She went to drama school.* **3** (*plural dramas*) an exciting thing that happens: *There was a big drama at school when one of the teachers fell in the river!*

dramatic /drə'mætɪk/ *adjective* **1** of plays or the theatre: *a dramatic society* **2** sudden, great or exciting: *The finish of the race was very dramatic.*

dramatically /drə'mætɪkli/ *adverb*: *Prices went up dramatically.*

dramatist /'dræmətɪst/ *noun* a person who writes plays

drank *form of* **drink¹**

draught /drɑːft/ *noun* cold air that comes into a room: *Can you shut the window? I can feel a draught.*

draughty /'drɑːfti/ *adjective* (**draughtier, draughtiest**) *a draughty house*

draughts /drɑːfts/ *noun* (plural) a game that two people play with round flat pieces on a board that has black and white squares on it: *Do you want a game of draughts?*

draw¹ /drɔː/ *verb* (**draws, drawing, drew** /druː/, **has drawn** /drɔːn/) **1** make a picture with a pencil, pen, chalk, etc: *She drew a picture of a horse.* ○ *He has drawn a car.* ○ *My sister draws well.* **2** pull or take something from a place: *He drew a knife from his pocket.* **3** move or come: *The train drew into the station.* **4** pull something to make it move: *The plough was drawn by two oxen.* **5** end a game with the same

number of points for both players or teams: *Ghana and Morocco drew in last Saturday's match.* **6** open or close curtains: *I switched on the light and drew the curtains.* **draw out** take money out of a bank: *She drew out all her money and bought a ticket to London.* **draw up** come to a place and stop: *A taxi drew up outside the house.* **draw something up** write something: *They drew up a list of people who they wanted to invite to the conference.*

draw² /drɔː/ *noun* the result of a game when both players or teams have the same number of points: *The football match ended in a 1-1 draw.*

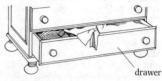

drawer

drawer /drɔː(r)/ *noun* a thing like a box that you can pull out from a cupboard or desk, for example

drawing /'drɔːɪŋ/ *noun* **1** (*plural drawings*) a picture made with a pencil, pen, chalk, etc **2** (no plural) making pictures with a pencil, pen, chalk, etc: *Karim is very good at drawing.*

drawing-pin /'drɔːɪŋ pɪn/ *noun* a short pin with a flat round top that you use for attaching paper to a wall or board: *I put the poster up with drawing-pins.*

drawn *form of* **draw¹**

dreadful /'dredfl/ *adjective* very bad: *I had a dreadful journey – my train was twelve hours late!*

dreadfully /'dredfəli/ *adverb* very: *I'm dreadfully sorry, but I must go now.*

dream /driːm/ *verb* (**dreams, dreaming, dreamt** /dremt/ or **dreamed** /driːmd/, **has dreamt** or **has dreamed**) **1** have a picture or idea in your mind when you are asleep: *I dreamt about you last night.* ○ *I dreamt that I met the president.* **2** hope for something nice in the future: *She dreams of becoming a famous actress.*

dream *noun* **1** pictures or ideas in your mind when you are asleep: *I had a dream about school last night.* ✪ A bad or frightening dream is called a **nightmare**. **2** something nice that you hope for

dress¹ /dres/ noun **1** (plural **dresses**) a piece of clothing with a top part and a skirt, that a woman or girl wears **2** (no plural) clothes: *The group of dancers wore national dress.*

dress² /dres/ verb (**dresses**, **dressing**, **dressed** /drest/) **1** put clothes on yourself or another person: *She dressed quickly and went out.* ○ *He washed and dressed the baby.* ✪ opposite: **undress** **2** wear clothes: *She dresses like a film star.* **dressed in something** wearing something: *He was dressed in black.*
dress up 1 put on your best clothes: *They dressed up to go to the wedding.* **2** put on special clothes for fun, so that you look like another person or a thing: *The children dressed up as ghosts.*
get dressed put on your clothes: *I got up, got dressed and ran to school.* ✪ opposite: **get undressed**

dressing /'dresɪŋ/ noun a thing for covering a part of your body that is hurt: *You should put a dressing on that cut.*

dressing-table /'dresɪŋ teɪbl/ noun a piece of bedroom furniture like a table with drawers and a mirror

drew form of **draw**¹

dried form of **dry**²

drier² /'draɪə(r)/ noun a machine for drying clothes: *Take the clothes out of the washing-machine and put them in the drier.* ☛ Look also at **hair-drier**.

dries form of **dry**²

driest form of **dry**¹

drift /drɪft/ verb (**drifts**, **drifting**, **drifted**) move slowly in the air or on water: *The empty boat drifted along on the sea.* ○ *The balloon drifted away.*

drill /drɪl/ noun a tool that you use for making holes: *They used a big drill to break up the road.*
drill verb (**drills**, **drilling**, **drilled** /drɪld/) make a hole using a drill: *He was drilling a hole in a piece of wood.*

drink¹ /drɪŋk/ verb (**drinks**, **drinking**, **drank** /dræŋk/, **has drunk** /drʌŋk/) **1** take in liquid, for example water, milk or coffee, through your mouth:

What do you want to drink? ○ *She was drinking a cup of tea.* **2** drink alcohol: *'Would you like some wine?' 'No, thank you. I don't drink.'*

drink² /drɪŋk/ noun **1** liquid, for example water, milk or coffee, that you take in through your mouth: *Would you like a drink?* ○ *Can I have a drink of water?* **2** drink with alcohol in it, for example beer or wine: *There was lots of food and drink at the party.*

drip /drɪp/ verb (**drips**, **dripping**, **dripped** /drɪpt/) **1** fall slowly in small drops: *Water was dripping through the roof.* **2** have liquid falling from it in small drops: *The tap is dripping.*

drive¹ /draɪv/ verb (**drives**, **driving**, **drove** /drəʊv/, **has driven** /'drɪvn/) **1** control a car, bus, etc and make it go where you want to go: *Can you drive?* ○ *Don't drive too fast!* **2** take somebody to a place in a car: *My uncle drove us to school in his pick-up.*

drive² /draɪv/ noun a journey in a car: *It's a long drive from Nakuru to Nairobi.*

drive-in /'draɪv ɪn/ noun a place where you can go to eat or to watch a film while you are sitting in your car

driver /'draɪvə(r)/ noun a person who controls a car, bus, train, etc: *John is a good driver.* ○ *a taxi-driver*

driving /'draɪvɪŋ/ noun (no plural) controlling a car, bus, etc: *Driving at night can be dangerous.*

driving-licence /'draɪvɪŋ laɪsns/ noun a piece of paper that shows that you are allowed to drive a car, etc

driving test /'draɪvɪŋ test/ noun a test that you have to pass before you get your **driving-licence**

droop /druːp/ verb (**droops**, **drooping**, **drooped** /druːpt/) bend or hang down: *Flowers droop if they don't get water.*

drop¹ /drɒp/ verb (**drops**, **dropping**, **dropped** /drɒpt/) **1** let something fall: *I dropped my watch and it broke.* **2** fall: *The glass dropped from her hands.* **3** become lower or less: *The temperature has dropped.* **4** stop your car and let somebody get out: *Could you drop me at the next corner?* **5** stop doing something: *I'm going to drop geography at school next year.* **drop in** visit somebody who does not know that you are coming: *I'll drop in to see you next week some time.* **drop off** fall asleep: *She dropped off in class.* **drop out** stop doing something with a group of people: *I dropped out of the football team when my father got ill.*

drop² /drɒp/ *noun* **1** a very small amount of liquid: *a drop of blood* ☛ picture on page A15 **2** a fall; going down: *a drop in temperature* ○ *a drop in prices*

drought /draʊt/ *noun* a long time when there is not enough rain: *Thousands of people died in the drought.*

drove *form of* **drive**¹

drown /draʊn/ *verb* (**drowns**, **drowning**, **drowned** /draʊnd/) **1** die under water because you cannot breathe: *The boy fell in the river and drowned.* **2** make a person or an animal die by putting them under water so that they cannot breathe: *They drowned the kittens.*

drug /drʌg/ *noun* **1** something that makes you better when you are ill: *They are looking for a drug that can cure AIDS.* **2** something that people eat, smoke or inject because it makes them feel happy or excited. In many countries it is against the law to use drugs: *She takes drugs.*

drug addict /ˈdrʌg ædɪkt/ *noun* a person who cannot stop using drugs

drums

drum /drʌm/ *noun* **1** a musical instrument that you hit with sticks or with your hands: *He sometimes plays the drum for hours.* **2** a big round container for oil: *an oil drum*

drummer /ˈdrʌmə(r)/ *noun* a person who plays a drum

drunk¹ *form of* **drink**¹

drunk² /drʌŋk/ *adjective* If a person is drunk, they have drunk too much alcohol.

dry¹ /draɪ/ *adjective* (**drier**, **driest**) **1** with no liquid in it or on it; not wet:

The washing isn't dry yet. ☛ picture on page A11 **2** with no rain: *dry weather* ○ *the dry season*

dry² /draɪ/ *verb* (**dries**, **drying**, **dried** /draɪd/, **has dried**) **1** become dry: *Our clothes were drying in the sun.* **2** make something dry: *Dry your hands on this towel.* **dry out** become completely dry: *Leave your shoes in the sun to dry out.* **dry up 1** become completely dry: *There was no rain for several months and all the rivers dried up.* **2** dry things like plates, knives and forks with a towel after you have washed them: *If I wash the dishes, could you dry up?* ✪ You can also say **do the drying-up**.

dry-clean /ˌdraɪ ˈkliːn/ *verb* (**dry-cleans**, **dry-cleaning**, **dry-cleaned** /ˌdraɪ ˈkliːnd/) make clothes clean by using chemicals, not water: *I had my suit dry-cleaned.*

dry-cleaner's *noun* a shop where clothes and other things are dry-cleaned

duck¹ /dʌk/ *noun* a bird that lives on and near water ✪ A young duck is called a **duckling**.

duck² /dʌk/ *verb* (**ducks**, **ducking**, **ducked** /dʌkt/) move your head down quickly, so

duck

that something does not hit you or so that somebody does not see you: *He saw the stone coming towards him and ducked.*

duckling /ˈdʌklɪŋ/ *noun* a young duck

due /djuː/ *adjective* **1** If something is due at a certain time, you expect it to happen or come then: *What time is the train due?* ○ *The new road is due to open in April.* **2** If an amount of money is due, you must pay it: *My rent is due at the beginning of the month.* **due for something** ready for something: *My car is due for a service.* **due to something** because of something: *The accident was due to bad driving.*

duet /djuˈet/ *noun* music for two people to sing or play on musical instruments: *James and Sarah sang a duet.*

dug *form of* **dig**

duke /djuːk/ *noun* a man who has a special title ☛ Look at **duchess**.

dull /dʌl/ *adjective* (**duller**, **dullest**)
1 not bright: *It was a dull, cloudy day.*
2 not strong or loud: *a dull pain* **3** not interesting or exciting: *Life is never dull in a big city.*

dumb /dʌm/ *adjective* not able to speak: *There are special schools for children who are deaf and dumb.*

dump /dʌmp/ *verb* (**dumps**, **dumping**, **dumped** /dʌmpt/) **1** take something to a place and leave it there because you do not want it: *They dumped their rubbish by the side of the road.* **2** put something down without being careful: *Don't dump your clothes on the floor!*

dump *noun* a place where you can take and leave things that you do not want

dune /djuːn/ *noun* a small hill of sand near the sea or in a desert

dung /dʌŋ/ *noun* (no plural) waste material from the bodies of large animals: *Cattle dung is a valuable fertilizer.*

dungarees /ˌdʌŋɡəˈriːz/ *noun* (plural) trousers with a part that covers the top of your body: *a new pair of dungarees*

during /ˈdjʊərɪŋ/ *preposition* **1** all the time that something is happening: *The sun gives us light during the day.* **2** at some time while something else is happening: *She died during the night.* ○ *I fell asleep during the film.*

dusk /dʌsk/ *noun* (no plural) the time in the evening when it is nearly dark

dust /dʌst/ *noun* (no plural) dry dirt that is like powder: *The old table was covered in dust.*

dust *verb* (**dusts**, **dusting**, **dusted**) take dust off something with a cloth: *I dusted the furniture.*

dustbin /ˈdʌstbɪn/ *noun* a thing that you put rubbish in outside your house

dustbin

duster /ˈdʌstə(r)/ *noun* a cloth that you use for taking the dust off furniture

dustman /ˈdʌstmən/ *noun* (*plural* **dustmen** /ˈdʌstmən/) a person whose job is to take away rubbish from outside people's houses

dusty /ˈdʌsti/ *adjective* (**dustier**, **dustiest**) covered with dust: *The furniture was very dusty.*

duty[1] /ˈdjuːti/ *noun* (*plural* **duties**) something that you must do because it is part of your job or because you think it is right: *It's your duty to look after your parents when they get older.* ○ *One of the duties of a secretary is to type letters.* **off duty** not working: *The police officer was off duty.* **on duty** working: *Some nurses at the hospital are on duty all night.*

duty[2] /ˈdjuːti/ *noun* (*plural* **duties**) money (a **tax**) that you pay to the government when you bring things into a country from another country

duty-free /ˌdjuːti ˈfriː/ *adjective*, *adverb* that you can bring into a country without paying money to the government. You can buy duty-free goods on planes or ships and at airports.

dwarf /dwɔːf/ *noun* a person who is much smaller than the usual size

dye /daɪ/ *noun* stuff that you use to change the colour of something, for example cloth or hair

dye *verb* (**dyes**, **dyeing**, **dyed** /daɪd/) change the colour of something: *We dyed the cloth red.*

dying *form of* **die**. **be dying for something** want to have something very much: *It's so hot! I'm dying for a drink.* **be dying to** want to do something very much: *My brother is dying to meet you.*

dysentery /ˈdɪsəntri/ *noun* (no plural) a serious illness that gives you very bad diarrhoea

Ee

each /iːtʃ/ *adjective, pronoun* every person or thing in a group: *Each student has to give a short talk to the class.* ○ *He gave a present to each of the children.*

each *adverb* for one: *These envelopes cost 5 shillings each.* **each other** words that show that somebody does the same thing as another person: *Connie and William looked at each other* (= Connie looked at William and William looked at Connie).

eager /ˈiːɡə(r)/ *adjective* If you are eager to do something, you want to do it very much: *We were all eager to hear the president's speech.*

eagerly *adverb*: *The crowd were waiting eagerly for the match to begin.*

eagle /ˈiːɡl/ *noun* a large bird that catches and eats small birds and animals

ear /ɪə(r)/ *noun* one of the two parts of a person or an animal that are used for hearing: *Elephants have big ears.* ☛ picture on page A4

early /ˈɜːli/ *adjective, adverb* (**earlier, earliest**) **1** before the usual or right time: *The train arrived ten minutes early.* ○ *I was early for the lesson.* **2** near the beginning of a time: *the early afternoon* ○ *She was in her early twenties* (= between the ages of 20 and about 23 or 24). ○ *I have to get up early tomorrow.* ✪ opposite: **late. an early night** an evening when you get to bed earlier than usual

earn /ɜːn/ *verb* (**earns, earning, earned** /ɜːnd/) **1** get money by working: *How much do teachers earn in your country?* ○ *I earn about 10 000 shillings a month.* **2** get something because you have worked well or done something good: *You've earned a rest!*

earnings /ˈɜːnɪŋz/ *noun* (plural) money that you get for working

earphones /ˈɪəfəʊnz/ *noun* (plural) things that you put over your head and ears for listening to a radio, cassette player, etc

earring /ˈɪərɪŋ/ *noun* a pretty thing that you wear on your ear

earth /ɜːθ/ *noun* (no plural) **1** this world; the planet that we live on: *The moon travels round the earth.* **2** what you grow plants in; soil: *Cover the seeds with earth.* **on earth** You use 'on earth' in questions with words like 'how' and 'what' when you are very surprised or do not know what the answer will be: *Where on earth is Paul? He's two hours late!* ○ *What on earth are you doing?*

earthquake /ˈɜːθkweɪk/ *noun* a sudden strong shaking of the ground

ease /iːz/ *noun* (no plural) **with ease** with no difficulty: *She answered the questions with ease.*

easily /ˈiːzəli/ *adverb* with no difficulty: *The cinema was almost empty so we easily found a seat.*

east /iːst/ *noun* (no plural) **1** where the sun comes up in the morning: *Which way is east?* ☛ picture at **north. 2 the far east** (no plural) the countries of Asia, for example China and Japan

east *adjective, adverb*: *Tanzania is on the east coast of Africa.* ○ *an east wind* (= that comes from the east) ○ *We travelled east from Kisumu to Nakuru.*

eastern /ˈiːstən/ *adjective* in or of the east part of a place: *eastern Kenya*

east coast fever /ˈiːst kəʊst fiːvə/ *noun* (no plural) a serious illness that cattle get from small insects (called **ticks**)

Easter /ˈiːstə(r)/ *noun* (no plural) a Sunday in March or April and the days around it, when Christians think about Christ coming back to life

easy /ˈiːzi/ *adjective* (**easier, easiest**) **1** If something is easy, you can do or understand it without any difficulty: *The homework was very easy.* ○ *Swahili is an easy language to learn.* **2** without problems or pain: *He has had an easy life.* ✪ opposite: **difficult** or **hard. take it easy, take things**

easy not worry or work too much: *After my exams I'm going to take it easy for a few days.*

eat /iːt/ *verb* (**eats**, **eating**, **ate** /et/, **has eaten** /ˈiːtn/) take in food through your mouth: *Have you eaten all the bread?* ○ *Do you want something to eat?*

ebola /eˈbəʊlə/ *noun* (no plural) a very dangerous illness that makes you feel very hot and makes you bleed inside your body

echo /ˈekəʊ/ *noun* (*plural* **echoes**) a sound that a wall sends back so that you hear it again

echo *verb* (**echoes**, **echoing**, **echoed** /ˈekəʊd/) *His footsteps echoed in the empty hall.*

eclipse /iˈklɪps/ *noun* **1** a time when the moon comes between the earth and the sun so that we cannot see the sun's light **2** a time when the earth comes between the sun and the moon so that we cannot see the moon's light

ecology /iˈkɒlədʒi/ *noun* (no plural) the study of the connection between living things and everything around them

ecological /ˌiːkəˈlɒdʒɪkl/ *adjective*: *The destruction of the rain forests is causing serious ecological problems.*

ecologist /iˈkɒlədʒɪst/ *noun* a person who studies or knows a lot about ecology

economic /ˌiːkəˈnɒmɪk/ *adjective* about the way that a country spends its money and makes, buys and sells things: *The country is in serious economic difficulties.*

economical /ˌiːkəˈnɒmɪkl/ *adjective* If something is economical, it does not cost a lot of money to use it: *This car is very economical to run* (= it does not use a lot of petrol).

economics /ˌiːkəˈnɒmɪks/ *noun* (no plural) the study of the way that countries spend money and make, buy and sell things

economist /iˈkɒnəmɪst/ *noun* a person who studies or knows a lot about economics

economy /iˈkɒnəmi/ *noun* (*plural* **economies**) **1** the way that a country spends its money and makes, buys and sells things: *the economy of Japan* **2** using money or things well and carefully

edge /edʒ/ *noun* the part along the end or side of something: *Don't sit on the edge of your chair – you might fall!*

edition /iˈdɪʃn/ *noun* one form of a book, magazine or newspaper: *The story was in the Sunday edition of the newspaper.*

editor /ˈedɪtə(r)/ *noun* a person whose job is to prepare or control a magazine, newspaper, book or film

educate /ˈedʒukeɪt/ *verb* (**educates**, **educating**, **educated**) teach somebody about things like reading, writing and mathematics at school or college: *Where was she educated?*

education /ˌedʒuˈkeɪʃn/ *noun* (no plural) teaching somebody about things like reading, writing and mathematics at school or college: *He had a good education.* ○ *The government spends a lot of money on education.*

educational /ˌedʒuˈkeɪʃənl/ *adjective*: *an educational visit to a factory*

eel /iːl/ *noun* a long fish that looks like a snake

effect /iˈfekt/ *noun* a change that happens because of something: *We are studying the effects of heat on different metals.* **have an effect on something** make something change: *His problems had a bad effect on his health.*

effective /iˈfektɪv/ *adjective* Something that is effective works well: *Running is an effective way of keeping fit.*

efficient /iˈfɪʃnt/ *adjective* A person or thing that is efficient works well and in the best way: *Our secretary is very efficient.* ✪ opposite: **inefficient**

efficiency /iˈfɪʃnsi/ *noun* (no plural) being efficient

efficiently *adverb*: *You must use your time more efficiently.*

effort /ˈefət/ *noun* trying hard to do something; hard work: *Thank you for all your efforts.* **make an effort** try hard to do something: *He made an effort to arrive on time.*

eg /ˌiː ˈdʒiː/ *short for* **for example**: *She travels to a lot of European countries, eg Spain, Greece and Italy.*

egg
eggcup

egg /eg/ *noun* **1** a round or oval thing that has a baby bird, fish, insect or snake inside it: *The hen has laid an egg.* **2** an egg from a hen that we eat

eight /eɪt/ *number* 8

eighth /eɪtθ/ *adjective, adverb, noun* **1** 8th **2** one of eight equal parts of something; ⅛

eighteen /ˌeɪˈtiːn/ *number* 18

eighteenth /ˌeɪˈtiːnθ/ *adjective, adverb, noun* 18th

eighty /ˈeɪti/ *number* **1** 80 **2** **the eighties** (plural) the numbers, years or temperature between 80 and 89 **in your eighties** between the ages of 80 and 89

eightieth /ˈeɪtiəθ/ *adjective, adverb, noun* 80th

either¹ /ˈaɪðə(r)/, /ˈiːðə(r)/ *adjective, pronoun* **1** one of two things or people: *There is fish and meat. You can have either.* ○ *Either of us will help you.* **2** each: *There are trees along either side of the street.*

either² /ˈaɪðə(r)/, /ˈiːðə(r)/ (used in sentences with 'not') also: *Henry can't swim and I can't (swim) either.* **either ... or** words that show two different things or people that you can choose: *You can have either tea or coffee.* ○ *I'll see you either tomorrow or Thursday.*

elaborate /ɪˈlæbərət/ *adjective* not simple; with a lot of different parts: *Her kanga has a very elaborate pattern on it.*

elastic /ɪˈlæstɪk/ *noun* (no plural) material that becomes longer when you pull it and then goes back to its usual size: *His trousers have elastic in the top to stop them falling down.*
elastic *adjective*: *elastic material*

elastic band /ɪˌlæstɪk ˈbænd/ *noun* a thin circle of rubber that you use for holding things together

elbow /ˈelbəʊ/ *noun* the part in the middle of your arm where it bends
☞ picture on page A4

elder¹ /ˈeldə(r)/ *adjective* older of two people: *My elder brother is at university and my younger brother is in Standard Four.*

elder² /ˈeldə(r)/ *noun* an older member of a clan or village, who makes decisions, gives advice, etc: *The council of village elders met to settle the dispute.*

elderly /ˈeldəli/ *adjective* quite old: *She is elderly and can't hear very well.*

eldest /ˈeldɪst/ *adjective* oldest of three or more people: *Their eldest son is at university but the other two are at school.*

elect /ɪˈlekt/ *verb* (**elects**, **electing**, **elected**) choose somebody to be a leader (by **voting**): *The new president was elected in 1990.*

election /ɪˈlekʃn/ *noun* a time when people choose somebody to be a leader by voting: *The election will be held on Wednesday.*

electric /ɪˈlektrɪk/ *adjective* using electricity to make it work: *an electric drill* ○ *an electric guitar*

electrical /ɪˈlektrɪkl/ *adjective* of or using electricity: *an electrical engineer*

electrician /ɪˌlekˈtrɪʃn/ *noun* a person whose job is to work with electricity: *This light isn't working – we need an electrician to mend it.*

electricity /ɪˌlekˈtrɪsəti/ *noun* (no plural) power that comes through wires. Electricity can make heat and light and makes things work.

electronic /ɪˌlekˈtrɒnɪk/ *adjective* Things like computers, calculators and radios are electronic. They use **microchips** or **transistors** to make them work: *an electronic typewriter*

electronics /ɪˌlekˈtrɒnɪks/ *noun* (no plural) using **microchips** or **transistors** to make things like computers, calculators and radios: *the electronics industry*

elegant /ˈelɪɡənt/ *adjective* with a beautiful style or shape: *She looked very elegant in her best clothes.*

element /ˈelɪmənt/ *noun* a simple chemical, for example oxygen or gold: *Water is made of the elements hydrogen and oxygen.*

elementary /ˌelɪ'mentri/ *adjective* for beginners; not difficult to do or understand: *an elementary dictionary*

elephant

tusk

trunk

elephant /'elɪfənt/ *noun* a very big wild animal from Africa or Asia, with a long nose (called a **trunk**) that hangs down

eleven /ɪ'levn/ *number* 11

eleventh /ɪ'levnθ/ *adjective, adverb, noun* 11th

else /els/ *adverb* **1** more; extra: *What else would you like?* ○ *Is anyone else coming with us?* **2** different; other: *If you don't like it here we can go somewhere else.* ○ *It's not mine – it must be somebody else's.* ○ *There was nothing else to eat so we had porridge again.* ✪ You use **else** after words like **anybody**, **nothing** and **somewhere**, and after question words like **where** and **who**. **or else** if not, then: *Go now, or else you'll be late.*

elsewhere /els'weə(r)/ *adverb* in or to another place: *He can't find a job in Kisumu so he's looking elsewhere for work.*

embarrass /ɪm'bærəs/ *verb* (**embarrasses**, **embarrassing**, **embarrassed** /ɪm'bærəst/) make somebody feel shy or worried about what other people think of them: *Daniel embarrassed his friends by singing very loudly on the bus.*

embarrassed *adjective* If you are embarrassed, you feel shy or worried about what other people think of you: *Everyone laughed when I fell off my chair – I was really embarrassed!*

embarrassing *adjective* Something that is embarrassing makes you feel embarrassed: *I couldn't remember her name – it was so embarrassing!*

embarrassment *noun* the feeling that you have when you are embarrassed; a

person or thing that embarrasses you: *He hid his face in embarrassment.*

embassy /'embəsi/ *noun* (*plural* **embassies**) a place where people work whose job is to speak and act for their government in another country: *To get a visa to travel in America, you should apply to the American embassy.*

embroider /ɪm'brɔɪdə(r)/ *verb* (**embroiders**, **embroidering**, **embroidered** /ɪm'brɔɪdəd/) make pictures with thread on cloth

embroidered *adjective*: *an embroidered blouse*

embroidery /ɪm'brɔɪdəri/ *noun* (no plural) something that has been embroidered

emerald /'emərəld/ *noun* a green jewel: *an emerald ring*

emerald, emerald green *adjective* bright green in colour

emerge /ɪ'mɜːdʒ/ *verb* (**emerges**, **emerging**, **emerged** /ɪ'mɜːdʒd/) come out from a place: *The moon emerged from behind the clouds.*

emergency /ɪ'mɜːdʒənsi/ *noun* (*plural* **emergencies**) a sudden dangerous situation, when people must help quickly: *Come quickly, doctor! It's an emergency!* ○ *I can lend you some money in an emergency.*

emigrate /'emɪɡreɪt/ *verb* (**emigrates**, **emigrating**, **emigrated**) leave your country to live in another country: *They emigrated to Britain in the 1960s to find work.*

emigration /ˌemɪ'ɡreɪʃn/ *noun* (no plural) *the emigration of Soviet Jews to Israel*

emotion /ɪ'məʊʃn/ *noun* a strong feeling, for example love or anger

emotional /ɪ'məʊʃənl/ *adjective* **1** about feelings: *She's got emotional problems – her boyfriend has left her.* **2** If you are emotional, you have strong feelings and you show them: *He got very emotional when we said goodbye.*

emperor /'empərə(r)/ *noun* a man who rules a group of countries (called an **empire**): *Emperor Haile Selassie of Ethiopia* ☞ Look at **empress**.

emphasize /'emfəsaɪz/ *verb* (**emphasizes**, **emphasizing**, **emphasized**

/'emfəsaɪzd/) say something strongly to show that it is important: *She emphasized the importance of hard work.*

empire /'empaɪə(r)/ *noun* a group of countries that is controlled by one country: *the Roman Empire*

employ /ɪm'plɔɪ/ *verb* (**employs, employing, employed** /ɪm'plɔɪd/) pay somebody to do work for you: *The factory employs 800 workers.* ☛ Look at **unemployed.**

employee /ɪm'plɔɪi:/ *noun* a person who is paid to work: *This company treats its employees very well.*

employer /ɪm'plɔɪə(r)/ *verb* a person or company that pays other people to do work

employment /ɪm'plɔɪmənt/ *noun* (no plural) having a job that you are paid to do: *He went to Nairobi and found employment as a taxi-driver.* ☛ Look at **unemployment.**

empress /'emprəs/ *noun* (*plural* **empresses**) a woman who rules a group of countries (called an **empire**), or the wife of an emperor

empty[1] /'empti/ *adjective* (**emptier, emptiest**) with nothing or nobody inside or on it: *My glass is empty.* ○ *The cinema was almost empty.* ☛ picture at **full**

empty[2] /'empti/ *verb* (**empties, emptying, emptied** /'emptid/, **has emptied**) **1** take everything out of something: *The waiter emptied the ashtrays.* ○ *We emptied our bags out onto the floor.* **2** become empty: *The film finished and the cinema started to empty.*

enable /ɪ'neɪbl/ *verb* (**enables, enabling, enabled** /ɪ'neɪbld/) make it possible for somebody to do something: *Your help enabled me to finish the job.*

enclose /ɪn'kləʊz/ *verb* (**encloses, enclosing, enclosed** /ɪn'kləʊzd/) **1** put something inside a letter or parcel: *I enclose a map and instructions how to get here.* **2** put something, for example a wall or fence, around a place on all sides: *The prison is enclosed by a high wall.*

encourage /ɪn'kʌrɪdʒ/ *verb* (**encourages, encouraging, encouraged** /ɪn'kʌrɪdʒd/) give somebody hope or help so that they do something or continue doing something: *We encouraged him to write a letter to the newspaper.*

encouragement /ɪn'kʌrɪdʒmənt/ *noun* (no plural) giving somebody hope or help so that they do something or continue doing something: *Brenda's parents gave her a lot of encouragement when she was taking her exams.*

encouraging *adjective* Something that is encouraging gives encouragement: *Kaburo's school report is very encouraging.*

encyclopedia /ɪn,saɪklə'pi:diə/ *noun* (*plural* **encyclopedias**) a book or set of books that gives information about a lot of different things from A to Z: *an encyclopedia of world history*

end[1] /end/ *noun* the furthest or last part of something: *Turn right at the end of the street.* ○ *They were sitting at the other end of the room.* ○ *I'm getting married at the end of June.* **come to an end** stop: *The holiday was coming to an end and we started to think about going back to school.* **end to end** in a line with the ends touching: *They put the tables end to end.* **for ... on end** for a very long time: *He practices heading the ball for hours on end.* **in the end** finally; at last: *I looked for the keys for hours and in the end I found them in the drawer.* **make ends meet** have enough money for your needs: *After her husband died it was difficult to make ends meet.* **put an end to something** stop something happening: *We must put an end to this terrible war.*

end[2] /end/ *verb* (**ends, ending, ended**) **1** stop: *What time does the film end?* ○ *The road ends here.* ○ *Most adverbs in English end in '-ly'.* **2** finish something: *We ended the meeting with a song.* **end up** finally be in a place or doing something when you did not plan it: *If she continues to steal, she'll end up in prison.* ○ *He ended up as a teacher.*

ending /'endɪŋ/ *noun* the last part of something, for example a word, story or film: *All these words have the same ending: criticize, organize and realize.* ○ *The film has a happy ending.*

endless /'endləs/ *adjective* never stopping

or finishing; very long: *The journey seemed endless.*

endlessly *adverb*: *He talks endlessly about nothing.*

enemy /ˈenəmi/ *noun* (*plural* **enemies**) **1** a person who hates you: *He was a kind man with no enemies.* **2** **the enemy** (no plural) the army or country that your country is fighting against in a war: *The enemy is attacking from the north.* **make enemies** do things that make people hate you: *In business, you often make enemies.*

energetic /ˌenəˈdʒetɪk/ *adjective* full of energy so that you can do a lot of things

energy /ˈenədʒi/ *noun* (no plural) **1** the power that your body has to do things: *He ran out of energy at the end of the race.* **2** the power from electricity, gas, coal, etc that is used to make machines work and to make heat and light: *It is important to try to save energy.* ○ *solar energy*

engaged /ɪnˈɡeɪdʒd/ *adjective* **1** If two people are engaged, they have agreed to get married: *Louise is engaged to Michael.* ○ *They got engaged last year.* **2** (used about a telephone) being used: *I tried to phone him but his number was engaged.*

engagement /ɪnˈɡeɪdʒmənt/ *noun* an agreement to marry somebody

engine /ˈendʒɪn/ *noun* **1** a machine that makes things move: *a car engine* **2** the front part of a train which pulls the rest.

engineer /ˌendʒɪˈnɪə(r)/ *noun* a person whose job is to plan, make or repair things like machines, roads or bridges: *My brother is an electrical engineer.*

engineering /ˌendʒɪˈnɪərɪŋ/ *noun* (no plural) planning and making things like machines, roads or bridges: *She's studying engineering at college.* ○ *He works in chemical engineering.*

enjoy /ɪnˈdʒɔɪ/ *verb* (**enjoys**, **enjoying**, **enjoyed** /ɪnˈdʒɔɪd/) like something very much: *I enjoy playing football.* ○ *Did you enjoy your dinner?* **enjoy yourself** have a happy time; have fun: *I really enjoyed myself at the party last night. Did you?*

enjoyable /ɪnˈdʒɔɪəbl/ *adjective* Something that is enjoyable makes you happy: *Thank you for a very enjoyable evening.*

enjoyment /ɪnˈdʒɔɪmənt/ *noun* (no plural) a feeling of enjoying something; pleasure: *I get a lot of enjoyment from travelling.*

enlarge /ɪnˈlɑːdʒ/ *verb* (**enlarges**, **enlarging**, **enlarged** /ɪnˈlɑːdʒd/) make something bigger: *We had the photograph enlarged.*

enlargement /ɪnˈlɑːdʒmənt/ *noun* a photograph that somebody has made bigger.

enormous /ɪˈnɔːməs/ *adjective* very big: *an enormous dog*

enormously /ɪˈnɔːməsli/ *adverb* very or very much: *This town has changed enormously since I was a child.*

enough /ɪˈnʌf/ *adjective*, *adverb*, *pronoun* as much or as many as you need: *There isn't enough food for ten people.* ○ *You're too thin – you don't eat enough.* ○ *Is she old enough to get married?*

enquire /ɪnˈkwaɪə(r)/, **enquiry** /ɪnˈkwaɪəri/ = **inquire**, **inquiry**

enrol /ɪnˈrəʊl/ *verb* (**enrols**, **enrolling**, **enrolled** /ɪnˈrəʊld/) join a group, for example a school, college, course or club. You usually pay money (a **fee**) when you enrol: *I've enrolled for French classes at the college.*

ensure /ɪnˈʃʊə(r)/ *verb* (**ensures**, **ensuring**, **ensured** /ɪnˈʃʊəd/) make certain: *Please ensure that all the lights are switched off before you leave.*

enter /ˈentə(r)/ *verb* (**enters**, **entering**, **entered** /ˈentəd/) **1** come or go into a place: *They stopped talking when she entered the room.* ○ *Do not enter without knocking.* ✪ In this sense, it is more usual to say **go in(to)** or **come in(to)**. **2** write a name or other information: *Please enter your name, address and date of birth at the bottom of the form.* **3** give your name to somebody because you want to do something like take an examination or run in a race: *I entered a competition last month and won 500 shillings.*

enterprise /ˈentəpraɪz/ *noun* a plan to

do something new and difficult, often to get money: *a business enterprise*

entertain /ˌentə'teɪn/ *verb* (**entertains**, **entertaining**, **entertained** /ˌentə'teɪnd/) **1** make somebody have a good time: *She entertained us all with her funny stories.* **2** give food and drink to visitors in your house: *We're entertaining friends this evening.*

entertaining /ˌentə'teɪnɪŋ/ *adjective* funny or interesting: *The play was really entertaining.*

entertainment /ˌentə'teɪnmənt/ *noun* anything that entertains people, for example films, plays or concerts: *There isn't much entertainment for young people in this town.*

enthusiasm /ɪn'θjuːziæzəm/ *noun* (no plural) a strong feeling of wanting to do something or liking something: *They didn't show much enthusiasm when I asked them to help me with the shopping.*

enthusiastic /ɪnˌθjuːzi'æstɪk/ *adjective* full of enthusiasm: *She's starting a new job next week and she's very enthusiastic about it.*

entire /ɪn'taɪə(r)/ *adjective* whole or complete; with no parts missing: *We spent the entire day trying to repair the engine.*

entirely /ɪn'taɪəli/ *adverb* completely: *She looks entirely different from her sister.* ○ *I entirely agree with you.*

entrance /'entrəns/ *noun* **1** (*plural* **entrances**) where you go into a place: *I'll meet you at the entrance to the museum.* **2** (*plural* **entrances**) coming or going into a place: *He made his entrance onto the stage.* **3** (no plural) the right to go into a place: *Entrance to the museum costs 50 shillings.*

entry /'entri/ *noun* (*plural* **entries**) **1** (no plural) the right to go into a place: *You can't go into that room – there's a sign on the door that says 'No Entry'.* **2** (*plural* **entries**) where you go into a place

envelope /'envələʊp/ *noun* a paper cover for a letter: *Have you written his address on the envelope?* ☞ picture on page A13

envied, **envies** *forms of* **envy**

envious /'enviəs/ *adjective* wanting what somebody else has: *She's envious of her sister's success.*

environment /ɪn'vaɪərənmənt/ *noun* **1** everything around you: *The children need a happy home environment.* **2** **the environment** (no plural) the air, water, land, animals and plants around us: *We must do more to protect the environment.*

environmental /ɪnˌvaɪərən'mentl/ *adjective*: *We talked about pollution and other environmental problems.*

envy /'envi/ *noun* (no plural) a sad or angry feeling of wanting what another person has: *I was filled with envy when I saw her new bike.*

envy *verb* (**envies**, **envying**, **envied** /'envid/, **has envied**) *I envy you! You always seem so happy!*

epidemic /ˌepɪ'demɪk/ *noun* a disease that many people in a place have at the same time: *The cholera epidemic has claimed thousands of victims.*

episode /'epɪsəʊd/ *noun* a programme on radio or television that is part of a longer story: *You can see the final episode of the series on Monday.*

equal[1] /'iːkwəl/ *adjective* the same; as big, as much or as good as another: *The women were demanding equal pay for equal work.* ○ *I tried to give everyone an equal amount of food.*

equal[2] /'iːkwəl/ *verb* (**equals**, **equalling**, **equalled** /'iːkwəld/) **1** be exactly the same amount as something: *Two plus two equals four (2 + 2 = 4).* **2** be as good as somebody or something: *He ran the race in 19.32 seconds, equalling the world record.*

equality /ɪ'kwɒləti/ *noun* (no plural) being the same or having the same rights: *In some countries black people are still fighting for equality.*

equally /'iːkwəli/ *adverb* **1** in equal parts: *Don't eat all the stew yourself – share it out equally!* **2** in the same way: *He's equally good at running and football.*

equator /ɪ'kweɪtə(r)/ *noun* (no plural) the line on maps around the middle of the world. Countries near the equator are very hot.

equip /ɪ'kwɪp/ *verb* (**equips**, **equipping**, **equipped** /ɪ'kwɪpt/) give somebody, or put in a place, all the things that are needed for doing something: *The bus is equipped with a rack for carrying luggage on the roof.* ○ *The kitchen is well equipped.*

equipment /ɪ'kwɪpmənt/ *noun* (no plural) special things that you need for doing something: *sports equipment*

erode /ɪ'rəʊd/ *verb* (**erodes**, **eroding**, **eroded**) **1** to destroy something very slowly: *If there is no vegetation, wind and rain will erode the soil.* ○ *Over the years, the weather has eroded the rock away.* **2** when something erodes, the wind and rain destroy it slowly: *Gabions were placed on the hillside to prevent the soil from eroding.*

erosion /ɪ'rəʊʒn/ *noun* (no plural) *soil erosion*

error /'erə(r)/ *noun* a thing that is done wrongly; a mistake: *The letter was sent to the wrong address because of a computer error.*

erupt /ɪ'rʌpt/ *verb* (**erupts**, **erupting**, **erupted**) When a **volcano** erupts, very hot liquid rock (called **lava**) suddenly comes out: *The volcano erupted and buried the village.*

eruption /ɪ'rʌpʃn/ *noun: a volcanic eruption*

escalator /'eskəleɪtə(r)/ *noun* stairs that move and carry people up and down

escape /ɪ'skeɪp/ *verb* (**escapes**, **escaping**, **escaped** /ɪ'skeɪpt/) **1** get free from somebody or something: *The bird escaped from the cage.* ○ *The prisoner escaped, but he was caught.* **2** If a liquid or gas escapes, it comes out of a place.

escape *noun* **make your escape** get free; get away from a place: *They jumped out of a window and made their escape.*

escort /ɪ'skɔːt/ *verb* (**escorts**, **escorting**, **escorted**) go with somebody, for example to make sure that they arrive somewhere: *The police escorted him out of the building.*

especially /ɪ'speʃəli/ *adverb* **1** very; more than usual or more than others: *I like bright colours, especially red.* ○ *I*

like a lot of sports, but I especially enjoy athletics. **2** for a particular person or thing: *I made this food especially for you.*

essay /'eseɪ/ *noun* a short piece of writing about a subject: *Our teacher asked us to write an essay on food production.*

essential /ɪ'senʃl/ *adjective* If something is essential, you must have or do it: *It is essential that you work hard for this exam.*

establish /ɪ'stæblɪʃ/ *verb* (**establishes**, **establishing**, **established** /ɪ'stæblɪʃt/) start something new: *This company was established in 1852.*

estate /ɪ'steɪt/ *noun* **1** land with a lot of houses or factories on it: *We live on a housing estate.* ○ *an industrial estate* **2** a large piece of land in the country that one person or family owns

estate agent /ɪ'steɪt eɪdʒənt/ *noun* a person whose job is to sell buildings and land for other people

estate car /ɪ'steɪt kɑː(r)/ *noun* a long car with a door at the back and space behind the back seat for carrying things

estimate /'estɪmeɪt/ *verb* (**estimates**, **estimating**, **estimated**) say how much you think something will cost, how big something is, how long it will take to do something, etc: *The council estimated that it would take a week to repair the road.*

estimate /'estɪmət/ *noun: The estimate for repairing the roof was 3 000 shillings.*

estuary /'estʃuəri/ *noun* (plural **estuaries**) the wide part of a river where it goes into the sea: *the estuary of the river Gambia*

etc /et'setərə/You use 'etc' at the end of a list to show that there are other things but you are not going to name them all: *I bought coffee, meat, oil, etc at the market.*

ethnic /'eθnɪk/ *adjective* of or from another country or race: *There are a lot of different ethnic groups in East Africa.*

eucalyptus /juːkə'lɪptəs/ *noun* (plural **eucalyptus** or **eucalyptuses**) a tree with leaves that are green all year. Eucalyptuses give oil that we can use as a medicine

evacuate /ɪ'vækjueɪt/ *verb* (**evacu-**

ates, **evacuating**, **evacuated**) take people away from a dangerous place to a safer place: *The area near the factory was evacuated after the explosion.*

evacuation /ɪˌvækjuˈeɪʃn/ *noun*: the evacuation of cities during the war

evaporate /ɪˈvæpəreɪt/ *verb* (**evaporates**, **evaporating**, **evaporated**) If a liquid evaporates, it changes into a gas: *Water evaporates if you heat it.*

eve /iːv/ *noun* the day before a special day: *24 December is Christmas Eve.* ○ *I went to a party on New Year's Eve* (= 31 December).

even[1] /ˈiːvn/ *adjective* **1** flat and smooth: *I fell over because the floor wasn't even.* ✪ opposite: **uneven**. **2** the same; equal: *Sara won the first game and I won the second, so we're even.* **3** Even numbers can be divided exactly by two: *4, 6 and 8 are even numbers.* ✪ opposite: **odd**. **get even with somebody** hurt somebody who has hurt you

even[2] /ˈiːvn/ *adverb* **1** a word that you use to say that something is surprising: *The game is so easy that even a child can play it.* ○ *He didn't laugh — he didn't even smile.* **2** a word that you use to make another word stronger: *That car is big, but this one is even bigger.* **even if** it does not change anything if: *Even if you run, you won't catch the bus.* **even so** although that is true: *I didn't have any lunch today, but even so I'm not hungry.* **even though** although: *I went to the party, even though I was tired.*

evening /ˈiːvnɪŋ/ *noun* the part of the day between the afternoon and when you go to bed: *What are you doing this evening?* ○ *We went for a long walk and in the evening we saw a film.* ○ *John came on Monday evening.*

event /ɪˈvent/ *noun* **1** something important that happens: *My sister's wedding was a big event for our family.* **2** a race or competition: *The next event will be the high-jump.*

eventually /ɪˈventʃuəli/ *adverb* after a long time: *I waited for him for three hours, and eventually he came.*

ever /ˈevə(r)/ *adverb* at any time: 'Have

you ever been to Marsabit?' 'No, I haven't.' ○ *Do you ever see Peter?* **ever since** in all the time since: *I have known Lucy ever since we were children.* **ever so**, **ever such** a very: *I'm ever so hot.* ○ *It's ever such a good film.* **for ever** for all time; always: *I will love you for ever.*

evergreen /ˈevəɡriːn/ *noun* a tree that has green leaves all the year

every /ˈevri/ *adjective* **1** all of the people or things in a group: *She knows every student in the school.* **2** once in each: *He phones every evening.* **every now and then**, **every now and again**, **every so often** sometimes, but not often: *I see Robert every now and then.* **every other**: *She comes every other day* (= for example on Monday, Wednesday and Friday but not on Tuesday or Thursday).

everybody /ˈevribɒdi/, **everyone** /ˈevriwʌn/ *pronoun* each person; all people: *Everybody at school likes my coat.* ○ *If everybody is here then we can start.*

everyday /ˈevrideɪ/ *adjective* normal; not special: *Computers are now part of everyday life.*

everything /ˈevriθɪŋ/ *pronoun* each thing; all things: *Everything in that shop is very expensive.*

everywhere /ˈevriweə(r)/ *adverb* in all places or to all places: *I've looked everywhere for my pen, but I can't find it.*

evidence /ˈevɪdəns/ *noun* (no plural) a thing that makes you believe that something has happened or that helps you know who did something: *The police searched the room, looking for evidence.* ○ *a piece of evidence* **give evidence** tell what you know about somebody or something in a court of law: *The man who saw the accident will give evidence in court.*

evident /ˈevɪdənt/ *adjective* easy to see or understand: *It was evident that he was lying, because he didn't look at me when he was speaking.*

evidently *adverb* clearly

evil /ˈiːvl/ *adjective* very bad: *an evil person*

exact /ɪɡˈzækt/ *adjective* completely

correct; without any mistakes: *Have you got the exact time?*

exactly /ɪɡˈzæktli/ *adverb* **1** You use 'exactly' when you are asking for or giving information that is completely correct: *Can you tell me exactly what happened?* ○ *It cost 500 shillings exactly.* **2** just: *This shirt is exactly what I wanted.* **3** You use 'exactly' to agree with somebody: *'So you've never met this man before?' 'Exactly.'*

exaggerate /ɪɡˈzædʒəreɪt/ *verb* (**exaggerates, exaggerating, exaggerated**) say that something is bigger, better, worse, etc than it really is: *Don't exaggerate! I was only two minutes late, not twenty.*

exaggeration /ɪɡˌzædʒəˈreɪʃn/ *noun*: *It's an exaggeration to say he never does any work — he sometimes does a little.*

examination /ɪɡˌzæmɪˈneɪʃn/ *noun* **1** (*also* **exam**) a test of what you know or can do: *We've got an exam in English next week.*

> ✪ You **sit** or **take** an examination. If you do well, you **pass** and if you do badly, you **fail**.: *I took an examination at the end of the year.* ○ *Did she pass all her exams?*

2 looking carefully at somebody or something: *She went into hospital for an examination.*

examine /ɪɡˈzæmɪn/ *verb* (**examines, examining, examined** /ɪɡˈzæmɪnd/) **1** ask questions to find out what somebody knows or what they can do: *You will be examined on everything you have learnt this year.* **2** look carefully at something or somebody: *I had my chest examined by the doctor.* ○ *I examined the car before I bought it.*

example /ɪɡˈzɑːmpl/ *noun* something that shows what other things of the same kind are like: *This dictionary gives many examples of how words are used in sentences.* **for example** let me give you an example: *Many different kinds of crop are grown in the region, for example maize, wheat and coffee.*

exceed /ɪkˈsiːd/ *verb* (**exceeds, exceeding, exceeded**) do or be more than something: *The price will not exceed 200 shillings.*

excellent /ˈeksələnt/ *adjective* very good: *She speaks excellent French.*

except /ɪkˈsept/ *preposition* but not: *The restaurant is open every day except Sunday.* ○ *Everyone went to the party except for me.* **except that** only that: *I don't know what he looks like, except that he's very tall.*

exception /ɪkˈsepʃn/ *noun* a person or thing that is not the same as the others: *Most of his family are tall but he is an exception.* **with the exception of somebody** or **something** if you do not count somebody or something: *I like all sports with the exception of swimming.*

exceptional /ɪkˈsepʃənl/ *adjective* **1** not usual: *It's exceptional to have so much rain at this time of year.* **2** very good: *She is an exceptional athlete.*

exceptionally /ɪkˈsepʃənəli/ *adverb*: *He was an exceptionally good student.*

exchange /ɪksˈtʃeɪndʒ/ *verb* (**exchanges, exchanging, exchanged** /ɪksˈtʃeɪndʒd/) give one thing and get another thing for it: *My new radio didn't work so I exchanged it for another one.* ○ *We exchanged addresses before saying goodbye.*

exchange *noun* **in exchange for something** If you get one thing in exchange for another thing, you give one thing and get another thing for it: *I worked for them in exchange for a room in their house.*

exchange rate /ɪksˈtʃeɪndʒ reɪt/ *noun* how much money from one country you can buy with money from another country: *The exchange rate is about 60 shillings to one US dollar.*

excite /ɪkˈsaɪt/ *verb* (**excites, exciting, excited**) make somebody have strong feelings of happiness or interest so that they are not calm: *Please don't excite the children too much or they won't sleep tonight.*

excited *adjective* not calm, for example because you are happy about something that is going to happen: *He's getting very excited about his holiday.*

excitement /ɪkˈsaɪtmənt/ *noun* (no plural) a feeling of being excited: *There was great excitement in the stadium before the match began.*

exciting *adjective* Something that is

exciting makes you have strong feelings of happiness or interest: *an exciting film* ○ *She's got a very exciting job – she travels all over the world and meets lots of famous people.*

exclaim /ɪk'skleɪm/ *verb* (**exclaims**, **exclaiming**, **exclaimed** /ɪk'skleɪmd/) say something suddenly and loudly because you are surprised, angry, etc: *'I don't believe it!' she exclaimed.*

exclamation /ˌeksklə'meɪʃn/ *noun*

exclamation mark /ˌeksklə'meɪʃn mɑːk/ *noun* a mark (!) that you use in writing to show loud or strong words, or surprise

exclude /ɪk'skluːd/ *verb* (**excludes**, **excluding**, **excluded**) shut or keep a person or thing out: *We cannot exclude the students from the meeting. Their ideas are important.* ☛ Look at **include**.

excluding *preposition* without; if you do not count: *It costs 2 500 shillings, excluding tax.*

excursion /ɪk'skɜːʃn/ *noun* a short journey to see something interesting or to enjoy yourself: *We're going on an excursion to the seaside on Sunday.*

excuse[1] /ɪk'skjuːs/ *noun* words you say or write to explain why you have done something wrong: *You're late! What's your excuse this time?*

excuse[2] /ɪk'skjuːz/ *verb* (**excuses**, **excusing**, **excused** /ɪk'skjuːzd/) say that it is not important that a person has done something wrong: *Please excuse us for being late.* **excuse me** You use 'excuse me' when you want to stop somebody who is speaking, or when you want to speak to somebody you don't know. You can also use 'excuse me' to say that you are sorry: *Excuse me, could you tell me the time, please?* ○ *Did I stand on your foot? Excuse me.*

execute /'eksɪkjuːt/ *verb* (**executes**, **executing**, **executed**) kill somebody to punish them

execution /ˌeksɪ'kjuːʃn/ *noun*: *the execution of prisoners*

executive /ɪg'zekjʊtɪv/ *noun* an important businessman or businesswoman

exercise[1] /'eksəsaɪz/ *noun* **1** (*plural exercises*) a piece of work that you do to learn something: *The teacher asked us to do exercises 1 and 2 for homework.* **2** (no plural) moving your body to keep it strong and well: *Swimming is very good exercise.* **3** (*plural exercises*) a special movement that you do to keep your body strong and well: *Touch your toes and stand up 20 times. This exercise is good for your legs, stomach and back.*

exercise book /'eksəsaɪz bʊk/ *noun* a book with clean pages that you use at school for writing in

exercise[2] /'eksəsaɪz/ *verb* (**exercises**, **exercising**, **exercised** /'eksəsaɪzd/) move your body to keep it strong and well: *They exercise in the park every morning.*

exhaust[1] /ɪg'zɔːst/ *verb* (**exhausts**, **exhausting**, **exhausted**) make somebody very tired: *The long journey exhausted us.*

exhausted *adjective* very tired: *I'm exhausted – I think I'll go to bed.*

exhaust[2] /ɪg'zɔːst/ *noun* a pipe that takes gas out from an engine, for example on a car

exhibition /ˌeksɪ'bɪʃn/ *noun* a group of things in a place so that people can look at them: *an exhibition of paintings by local schoolchildren*

exile /'eksaɪl/ *noun* **1** (no plural) having to live away from your own country, for example as a punishment: *the former president spent the last years of his life in exile.* **2** (*plural exiles*) a person who must live away from his/her own country

exist /ɪg'zɪst/ *verb* (**exists**, **existing**, **existed**) be real; live: *Does life exist on other planets?* ○ *That word does not exist.*

existence /ɪg'zɪstəns/ *noun* (no plural) being real; existing: *Do you believe in the existence of God?*

exit /'eksɪt/ *noun* a way out of a building: *Where is the exit?* **make an exit** go out of a place: *He made a quick exit.*

exotic /ɪg'zɒtɪk/ *adjective* strange or interesting because it comes from another country: *exotic fruits*

expand /ɪk'spænd/ *verb* (**expands**, **expanding**, **expanded**) become bigger or make something bigger: *Metals expand when they are heated.*

expansion /ɪkˈspænʃn/ *noun* (no plural) getting bigger: *The company needs bigger offices because of the expansion.*

expect /ɪkˈspekt/ *verb* (**expects**, **expecting**, **expected**) **1** think that somebody or something will come or that something will happen: *I expect she'll be late. She usually is.* ○ *Everyone expected Germany to win the game, but they lost 3-0.* ○ *She's expecting* (= she is going to have) *a baby in June.* **2** think that something is probably true: *They haven't had lunch yet, so I expect they're hungry.* **3** If you are expected to do something, you must do it: *I am expected to work until midnight every day.* **I expect so** You say 'I expect so' when you think that something will happen or that something is true: *'Is Wanja coming?' 'Oh yes, I expect so.'*

expedition /ˌekspəˈdɪʃn/ *noun* a journey to find or do something special: *They went on a hunting expedition in the bush.*

expel /ɪkˈspel/ *verb* (**expels**, **expelling**, **expelled** /ɪkˈspeld/) send somebody away from a school or club: *The boys were expelled from school for fighting.*

expense /ɪkˈspens/ *noun* **1** the cost of something: *Having a car is a big expense.* **2 expenses** (plural) money that you spend on a certain thing: *The company pays our travelling expenses.* **at somebody's expense** If you do something at somebody's expense, they pay for it: *We had dinner at the company's expense.*

expensive /ɪkˈspensɪv/ *adjective* Something that is expensive costs a lot of money: *expensive clothes* ✪ opposite: **cheap** or **inexpensive**

experience /ɪkˈspɪəriəns/ *noun* **1** (no plural) knowing about something because you have seen it or done it: *She has four years' teaching experience.* ○ *Do you have much experience of working with children?* **2** (plural **experiences**) something that has happened to you: *He wrote a book about his experiences in prison.* ○ *What's the*

most frightening experience you have ever had?*

experienced /ɪkˈspɪəriənst/ *adjective* If you are experienced, you know about something because you have done it many times before: *She's an experienced driver.* ✪ opposite: **inexperienced**

experiment /ɪkˈsperɪmənt/ *noun* You do an experiment to find out what will happen or to see if something is true: *They are doing experiments to find out if the drug is safe for humans.*

experiment *verb* (**experiments**, **experimenting**, **experimented**) *I don't think it's right to experiment on animals.*

expert /ˈekspɜːt/ *noun* a person who knows a lot about something: *He's an expert on metals.* ○ *a computer expert*

explain /ɪkˈspleɪn/ *verb* (**explains**, **explaining**, **explained** /ɪkˈspleɪnd/) **1** tell somebody about something so that they understand it: *The teacher usually explains the new words to us.* ○ *He explained how to use the machine.* **2** give a reason for something: *I explained why we needed the money.*

explanation /ˌekspləˈneɪʃn/ *noun* telling somebody about something so that they understand it, or giving a reason for something: *What explanation did they give for being late?*

explode /ɪkˈspləʊd/ *verb* (**explodes**, **exploding**, **exploded**) burst suddenly with a very loud noise: *A bomb exploded in the city centre, killing two people.* ✪ The noun is **explosion**.

exploit /ɪkˈsplɔɪt/ *verb* (**exploits**, **exploiting**, **exploited**) treat somebody badly to get what you want: *People who work for that company are exploited – they work long hours for very little money.*

explore /ɪkˈsplɔː(r)/ *verb* (**explores**, **exploring**, **explored** /ɪkˈsplɔːd/) travel around a new place to learn about it: *The boys found an old, empty building and went inside to explore.*

exploration /ˌekspləˈreɪʃn/ *noun: the exploration of space*

explorer *noun* a person who travels around a new place to learn about it:

The first European explorers arrived in America in the 15th century.

explosion /ɪkˈspləʊʒn/ *noun* bursting suddenly with a very loud noise: *There was an explosion and pieces of glass flew everywhere.* ✪ The verb is **explode**.

explosive /ɪkˈspləʊsɪv/ *adjective* Something that is explosive can cause an explosion: *an explosive gas*

explosive *noun* a substance that can make things explode: *Dynamite is an explosive.*

export /ɪkˈspɔːt/ *verb* (**exports, exporting, exported**) sell things to another country: *Kenya exports coffee to Britain.*

export /ˈekspɔːt/ *noun* **1** (no plural) selling things to another country: *These cars are made for export.* **2** (*plural* **exports**) something that you sell to another country: *The country's biggest exports are tea and cotton.* ✪ opposite: **import**

expose /ɪkˈspəʊz/ *verb* (**exposes, exposing, exposed** /ɪkˈspəʊzd/) show something that is usually covered or hidden: *A baby's skin should not be exposed to the sun for too long.* ○ *The newspaper exposed his terrible secret.*

express¹ /ɪkˈspres/ *verb* (**expresses, expressing, expressed** /ɪkˈsprest/) say or show how you think or feel: *She expressed her ideas well.*

express² /ɪkˈspres/ *adjective* that goes or is sent very quickly: *an express letter*
express *adverb*: *I sent the parcel express.*

express³ (*plural* **expresses**), **express train** *noun* a fast train that does not stop at all stations

expression /ɪkˈspreʃn/ *noun* **1** a word or group of words; a way of saying something: *The expression 'to drop off' means 'to fall asleep'.* **2** the look on your face that shows how you feel: *an expression of surprise*

extend /ɪkˈstend/ *verb* (**extends, extending, extended**) **1** make something longer or bigger: *The company have extended the contract for another 6 months.* **2** continue or stretch: *The park extends as far as the river.*

extension /ɪkˈstenʃn/ *noun* **1** a part

that you add to something to make it bigger: *They've built an extension on the back of the house.* **2** one of the telephones in a building that is connected to the main telephone: *Can I have extension 4110, please?*

extent /ɪkˈstent/ *noun* (no plural) how big something is: *I didn't know the full extent of the problem* (= how big it was) *until he explained it to me.* ✪ You use expressions like **to a certain extent** and **to some extent** to show that you do not think something is completely true.: *I agree with you to a certain extent.*

exterior /ɪkˈstɪəriə(r)/ *noun* the outside part: *We painted the exterior of the house white.*
exterior *adjective*: *an exterior door*
✪ opposite: **interior**

external /ɪkˈstɜːnl/ *adjective* on, of or from the outside: *external walls*
✪ opposite: **internal**

extinct /ɪkˈstɪŋkt/ *adjective* If a type of animal or plant is extinct, it does not exist now: *Dinosaurs became extinct millions of years ago.*

extra /ˈekstrə/ *adjective, adverb* more than what is usual: *I have put an extra blanket on your bed because it's cold tonight.* ○ *The room costs 150 shillings and you have to pay extra for breakfast.*

extraordinary /ɪkˈstrɔːdnri/ *adjective* very unusual or strange: *I had an extraordinary dream last night – I dreamt that I could fly.* ○ *Have you seen that extraordinary building with the pink roof?*

extraordinarily /ɪkˈstrɔːdnrəli/ *adverb* extremely: *She's extraordinarily clever.*

extravagant /ɪkˈstrævəgənt/ *adjective* **1** If you are extravagant, you spend too much money. **2** Something that is extravagant costs too much money: *He buys her a lot of extravagant presents.*

extreme /ɪkˈstriːm/ *adjective* **1** very great or strong: *the extreme cold of the Arctic* **2** as far away as possible: *They came from the extreme north of Uganda.* **3** If you say that a person is extreme, you mean that his/her ideas are too strong.

extremely *adverb* very: *He's extremely*

eye 106

good-looking and charming.

eye /aɪ/ *noun* one of the two parts in your head that you see with: *She's got beautiful eyes.* ○ *Open your eyes!* ☛ picture on page A4. **catch somebody's eye 1** If you catch somebody's eye, you make them look at you: *Try to catch the waiter's eye the next time he comes this way.* **2** If something catches your eye, you see it suddenly: *Her bright yellow clothes caught my eye.* **in somebody's eyes** as somebody thinks: *Nyiva is 42, but in his mother's eyes, he's still a little boy!* **keep an eye on somebody** or **something** look after or watch somebody or something:

Keep an eye on your money at the market – there are thieves around. **see eye to eye with somebody** agree with somebody: *Mr Masagazi doesn't always see eye to eye with his neighbours.*

eyebrow /'aɪbraʊ/ *noun* one of the two lines of hair above your eyes ☛ picture on page A4

eyelash /'aɪlæʃ/ *noun* (*plural* **eyelashes**) one of the hairs that grow in a line on your eyelid: *She's got beautiful long eyelashes.* ☛ picture on page A4

eyelid /'aɪlɪd/ *noun* the piece of skin that can move to close your eye

eyesight /'aɪsaɪt/ *noun* (no plural) the power to see: *Your eyesight is very good.*

Ff

F *short way of writing* **Fahrenheit**

fable /'feɪbl/ *noun* a short story, usually about animals, that teaches people something

fabulous /'fæbjʊləs/ *adjective* very good; wonderful: *The food smells fabulous!*

face[1] /feɪs/ *noun* **1** the front part of your head: *Have you washed your face?* ○ *She had a smile on her face.* **2** the front or one side of something: *a clock face* ○ *He put the cards face down on the table.* **face to face** If two people are face to face, they are looking straight at each other: *They stood face to face.* **keep a straight face** not smile or laugh when something is funny: *I couldn't keep a straight face when he dropped his watch in the soup!* **make** or **pull a face** move your mouth and eyes to show that you do not like something: *She made a face when she saw what I had made for dinner.*

face[2] /feɪs/ *verb* (**faces, facing, faced** /feɪst/) **1** have the face or the front towards something: *Can you all face the front of the class, please?* ○ *My bedroom faces the garden.* **2** be brave enough to meet somebody unfriendly or do something difficult: *I can't face going to work today – I feel too ill.* **let's**

face it we must agree that it is true: *Let's face it – you're not very good at maths.*

facilities /fə'sɪlətiz/ *noun* (plural) things in a place for you to use: *Our school has very good sports facilities.*

fact /fækt/ *noun* something that you know has happened or is true: *It's a fact that the earth travels around the sun.* **in fact, in actual fact** words that you use to show that something is true; really: *I thought she was Moroccan, but in actual fact she's from Algeria.* ○ *I think I saw him – I'm certain, in fact.*

factory /'fæktəri/ *noun* (*plural* **factories**) a place where people make things, usually with machines: *He works at the car factory.*

fade /feɪd/ *verb* (**fades, fading, faded**) become less bright and colourful: *Will this shirt fade when I wash it?* ○ *faded jeans*

faeces /'fiːsiːz/ *noun* (plural) solid waste material that you pass from your body

Fahrenheit /'færənhaɪt/ *noun* (no plural) a way of measuring temperature. Water freezes at 32° Fahrenheit and boils at 212° Fahrenheit. ✪ The short way of writing 'Fahrenheit' is **F**: *110° F*

fail /feɪl/ *verb* (**fails**, **failing**, **failed** /feɪld/) **1** not pass an exam or test: *She failed her driving test again.* ○ *How many students failed last term?* **2** try to do something but not be able to do it: *He played quite well but failed to win the match.* **3** not do something that you should do: *The driver failed to stop at a red light.*

fail *noun* **without fail** certainly: *Be there at twelve o'clock without fail!*

failure /'feɪljə(r)/ *noun* **1** (no plural) not being successful: *The search for the missing children ended in failure.* **2** (*plural* **failures**) a person or thing that does not do well: *I felt that I was a failure because I didn't have a job.*

faint[1] /feɪnt/ *adjective* (**fainter**, **faintest**) **1** not clear or strong: *We could hear the faint sound of music in the distance.* **2** If you feel faint, you feel that you are going to fall, for example because you are ill or tired.

faint[2] /feɪnt/ *verb* (**faints**, **fainting**, **fainted**) fall down suddenly, for example because you are weak, ill or shocked: *She almost fainted when she saw the blood on her leg.*

fair[1] /feə(r)/ *adjective* (**fairer**, **fairest**) **1** Somebody or something that is fair treats people equally or in the right way: *a fair judge* ○ *It's not fair! I have to go to bed but you can stay up and watch TV!* ✪ opposite: **unfair**. **2** with a light colour: *He's got fair hair.* ○ *He is fair-haired.* ✪ opposite: **dark**. **3** quite good or quite large: *They've invited a fair number of people to their party.*

fair[2] /feə(r)/ *noun* a place outside where you can ride on big machines and play games to win prizes. Fairs usually travel from town to town.

fairly /'feəli/ *adverb* **1** in a way that is right and honest: *This company treats its workers fairly.* ✪ opposite: **unfairly**. **2** quite; not very: *She speaks French fairly well.* ○ *I'm fairly certain it was him.*

fairy /'feəri/ *noun* (*plural* **fairies**) a very small person in stories. Fairies have wings and can do magic.

fairy tale /'feəri teɪl/, **fairy story** /'feəri stɔːri/ (*plural* **fairy stories**)

noun a story for children that is about magic

faith /feɪθ/ *noun* **1** (no plural) feeling sure that somebody or something is good, right, honest, etc: *I've got great faith in your ability to do the job* (= I'm sure that you can do it). **2** (*plural* **faiths**) a religion: *the Muslim faith*

faithful /'feɪθfl/ *adjective* always ready to help your friends and to do what you have promised to do: *a faithful friend*

faithfully /'feɪθfəli/ *adverb* **Yours faithfully** words that you write at the end of a letter, before your name

fake /feɪk/ *noun* a copy of something, made to trick people: *This painting is not really by Van Gogh – it's a fake.*

fake *adjective*: *a fake thousand-shilling note*

fall[1] /fɔːl/ *verb* (**falls**, **falling**, **fell** /fel/, **has fallen** /'fɔːlən/) **1** go down quickly; drop: *The book fell off the table.* ○ *She fell down the steps and broke her arm.* **2** (*also* **fall over**) suddenly stop standing: *He slipped on the ice and fell.* ○ *I fell over and hurt my leg.* **3** become lower or less: *In the desert the temperature falls at night.* ○ *Prices have fallen again.* ✪ opposite: **rise**. **4** come or happen: *Darkness was falling.* **fall apart** break into pieces: *The chair fell apart when I sat on it.* **fall asleep** start sleeping: *She was so tired that she fell asleep in the armchair.* **fall behind** become slower than others, or not do something when you should do it: *She's falling behind with her school work because she goes out every evening.* **fall for somebody** start to love somebody: *He has fallen for someone he met on holiday.* **fall out with somebody** argue with somebody so that you stop being friends: *John has fallen out with his girlfriend.* **fall through** If a plan falls through, it does not happen.

fall[2] /fɔːl/ *noun* **1** a sudden drop from a higher place to a lower place: *He had a fall from his bicycle.* **2** becoming lower or less: *a fall in the price of oil* **3** **falls** (plural) a place where water falls from a high place to a low place: *the Victoria Falls* **4** *American English for* **autumn**

false /fɔːls/ *adjective* **1** not true; wrong: *A spider has eight legs – true or false?*

○ *She gave a false name to the police.*
2 not real or not natural: *People who have lost their own teeth wear false teeth* (= teeth that are made of plastic).

false alarm /ˌfɔːls əˈlɑːm/ *noun* a warning about something bad that does not happen: *Everyone thought there was a fire, but it was just a false alarm.*

fame /feɪm/ *noun* (no plural) being known by many people ✪ The adjective is **famous**.

familiar /fəˈmɪliə(r)/ *adjective* that you know well: *I heard a familiar voice in the next room.* **be familiar with something** know something well: *I'm not familiar with this computer.* ✪ opposite: **unfamiliar**

family /ˈfæməli/ *noun* (*plural* **families**) **1** parents and children: *How many people are there in your family?* ○ *My family are all very tall.* ○ *His family lives on a farm.* ✪ Sometimes 'family' means not just parents and children but other people too, for example grandparents, aunts, uncles and cousins. **2** a group of plants or animals: *Lions belong to the cat family.*

family tree /ˌfæməli ˈtriː/ *noun* a plan that shows all the people in a family

famine /ˈfæmɪn/ *noun* A famine happens when there is not enough food in a country: *Thousands of people died in the famine.*

famous /ˈfeɪməs/ *adjective* known by many people: *Oxford is famous for its university.* ○ *Henry Rono was a famous athlete.* ✪ The noun is **fame**.

fan[1] /fæn/ *noun* a thing that moves the air to make you cooler: *an electric fan on the ceiling*

fan *verb* (**fans**, **fanning**, **fanned** /fænd/) make somebody or something cooler by moving the air: *I fanned my face with the newspaper.*

fan[2] /fæn/ *noun* a person who likes somebody or something, for example a singer or a sport, very much: *She was a fan of the Beatles.* ○ *football fans*

fancy[1] /ˈfænsi/ *verb* (**fancies**, **fancying**,

fancied /ˈfænsid/, **has fancied**) **1** feel that you would like something: *Do you fancy a drink?* **2** a word that shows you are surprised: *Fancy seeing you here!*

fancy[2] /ˈfænsi/ *adjective* (**fancier**, **fanciest**) not simple or ordinary: *She wore a very fancy hat to the wedding.*

fantastic /fænˈtæstɪk/ *adjective* **1** very good; wonderful: *We had a fantastic holiday.* **2** strange or difficult to believe: *He told us fantastic stories about his adventures.*

fantasy /ˈfæntəsi/ *noun* (*plural* **fantasies**) something nice that you think about and that you hope will happen

far[1] /fɑː(r)/ *adjective* (**farther** /ˈfɑːðə(r)/ or **further** /ˈfɜːðə(r)/, **farthest** /ˈfɑːðɪst/ or **furthest** /ˈfɜːðɪst/) **1** a long way away: *Let's walk – it's not far.* **2** other: *They live on the far side of town.*

far[2] /fɑː(r)/ *adverb* (**farther** /ˈfɑːðə(r)/ or **further** /ˈfɜːðə(r)/, **farthest** /ˈfɑːðɪst/ or **furthest** /ˈfɜːðɪst/) **1** a long way: *My house isn't far from the school.* ○ *It's too far to walk in one day.* ○ *I walked much farther than you.* **2** You use 'far' to ask about the distance from one place to another place: *How far is it to Dar es Salaam from here?* ✪ We usually use 'far' only in questions and negative sentences, and after 'too' and 'so'. In other sentences we use **a long way**: *It's a long way to walk – let's take the bus.* **3** very much: *He's far taller than his brother.* ○ *That's far too expensive.* **as far as** to a place: *We walked as far as the village and then came back.* **as far as I know** words that you use when you think something is true but you are not certain: *As far as I know, she's well, but I haven't seen her for a long time.* **by far** You use 'by far' to show that a person or thing is much better, bigger, etc than anybody or anything else: *She's by far the best player in the team.* **far apart** If two things or people are far apart, they are a long way from each other: *I don't see him very often because we live too far apart.* **far from** not at all: *I'm far from certain.* **so far** until now: *So far the work has been easy.*

fare /feə(r)/ *noun* the money that you

pay to travel by bus, train, plane, etc: *How much is the train fare to Kisumu?*

farewell /ˌfeəˈwel/ *noun* saying goodbye: *We are having a farewell party for Mike because he is going to live in Australia.*

farm /fɑːm/ *noun* land and buildings where people keep animals and grow crops: *They work on a farm.* ○ *farm animals*

farm *verb* (**farms**, **farming**, **farmed** /fɑːmd/) *He farms in the north of the country.*

farmer *noun* a person who owns or looks after a farm

farmhouse /ˈfɑːmhaʊs/ *noun* the house on a farm where the farmer lives

farmyard /ˈfɑːmjɑːd/ *noun* the outside space near a farmhouse. A farmyard has buildings or walls around it.

farther, **farthest** *forms of* **far**

fascinating /ˈfæsɪneɪtɪŋ/ *adjective* very interesting: *She told us fascinating stories about her journey through the mountains.*

fashion /ˈfæʃn/ *noun* **1** a way of dressing or doing something that people like and try to copy for a short time: *What style of clothes are in fashion at the moment?* **2** the way you do something: *He spoke in a very strange fashion.* **in fashion** If something is in fashion, people like it at the moment: *Long hair is coming into fashion again.* **out of fashion** If something is out of fashion, people do not like it at the moment: *Bright colours have gone out of fashion.*

fashionable /ˈfæʃnəbl/ *adjective* in the newest fashion: *She was wearing a fashionable black hat.* ✪ opposite: **unfashionable** or **old-fashioned**

fashionably /ˈfæʃnəbli/ *adverb*: *He was fashionably dressed.*

fashion designer /ˈfæʃn dɪzaɪnə(r)/ *noun* a person whose job is to design clothes

fast[1] /fɑːst/ *adjective* (**faster**, **fastest**) **1** A person or thing that is fast can move quickly: *a fast car* **2** If a clock or watch is fast, it shows a time that is later than the real time: *My watch is*

five minutes fast. ✪ opposite: **slow**

fast food /ˌfæsˈfɑːst ˈfuːd/ *noun* (no plural) food like hamburgers and chips that can be cooked and eaten quickly

fast[2] /fɑːst/ *adverb* (**faster**, **fastest**) quickly: *Don't talk so fast – I can't understand what you're saying.* ✪ opposite: **slowly**. **fast asleep** sleeping very well: *The baby was fast asleep.*

fast[3] /fɑːst/ *verb* (**fasts**, **fasting**, **fasted**) not eat food for a certain time: *Muslims fast during Ramadan.*

fasten /ˈfɑːsn/ *verb* (**fastens**, **fastening**, **fastened** /ˈfɑːsnd/) **1** close something so that it will not come open: *Please fasten your seat-belts.* ○ *Can you fasten this suitcase for me?* **2** join one thing to another thing: *Fasten this badge to your jacket.*

fat[1] /fæt/ *adjective* (**fatter**, **fattest**) with a large round body: *You'll get fat if you eat too much chocolate.* ✪ opposite: **thin**. ☛ picture on page A10

fat[2] /fæt/ *noun* **1** (no plural) the oily substance under the skins of animals and people: *Cut the fat off the meat.* **2** (*plural* **fats**) oil that you use for cooking: *Heat some fat in a frying-pan.*

fatal /ˈfeɪtl/ *adjective* **1** Something that is fatal causes death: *a fatal car accident* **2** Something that is fatal has very bad results: *I made the fatal mistake of signing a paper I had not read properly.*

fatally /ˈfeɪtəli/ *adverb*: *She was fatally injured in the crash.*

fate /feɪt/ *noun* **1** (no plural) the power that some people believe controls everything that happens **2** (*plural* **fates**) what will happen to somebody or something: *What will be the fate of the prisoners?*

father /ˈfɑːðə(r)/ *noun* a man who has a child: *Where do your mother and father live?* ☛ Look at **dad** and **daddy**.

father-in-law /ˈfɑːðər ɪn lɔː/ *noun* (*plural* **fathers-in-law**) the father of your husband or wife

fault /fɔːlt/ *noun* **1** (no plural) If something bad is your fault, you made it happen: *It's Mbogori's fault that we are*

There is a serious fault in the machine.

faulty *adjective* not working well: *This light doesn't work – the switch is faulty.*

favour /'feɪvə(r)/ *noun* something that you do to help somebody: *Would you do me a favour and open the door?* ○ *Could I ask you a favour – will you take me to the station this evening?* **be in favour of something** like or agree with something: *Are you in favour of higher taxes on cigarettes?*

favourite /'feɪvərɪt/ *adjective* Your favourite person or thing is the one that you like more than any other: *What's your favourite food?*

favourite *noun* a person or thing that you like more than any other: *I like all subjects at school but science is my favourite.*

fax /fæks/ *verb* (**faxes, faxing, faxed** /fækst/) send a copy of something like a letter or picture using telephone lines and a machine called a **fax machine**: *The drawings were faxed from New York.*

fax *noun* (*plural* **faxes**) a copy of something that is sent by a fax machine

fear /fɪə(r)/ *noun* the feeling that you have when you think that something bad might happen: *I have a terrible fear of dogs.*

fear *verb* (**fears, fearing, feared** /fɪəd/) **1** be afraid of somebody or something: *We all fear illness and death.* **2** feel that something bad might happen: *I fear we will be late.* ✪ It is more usual to say **be afraid (of)** or **be frightened (of)**.

feast /fiːst/ *noun* a large special meal for a lot of people: *a wedding feast*

feat /fiːt/ *noun* something you do that is clever, difficult or dangerous: *Breaking the world record was an amazing feat.*

feather /'feðə(r)/ *noun* Birds have feathers on their bodies to keep them warm and to help them fly.

feather

feature /'fiːtʃə(r)/ *noun* **1** an important part of something:

Pictures are a feature of this dictionary. **2 features** (plural) the parts of the face, for example the eyes, nose or mouth **3** an important piece of writing in a magazine or newspaper, or a programme on TV: *The magazine has a special feature on volcanoes on the centre pages.*

February /'februari/ *noun* the second month of the year

fed *form of* **feed**

federal /'fedərəl/ *adjective* A federal country has several smaller countries or states that are joined together: *the Federal Government of the United States*

federation /,fedə'reɪʃn/ *noun* a group of states or companies that work together

fed up /,fed 'ʌp/ *adjective* unhappy or bored because you have had or done too much of something: *I'm fed up with waiting for Eva – let's go without her.*

fee /fiː/ *noun* **1** money that you pay to somebody for special work: *The lawyer's fee was very high.* **2** money that you pay to do something, for example to join a club: *How much is the entrance fee?* **3 fees** (plural) the money that you pay for lessons at school, college or university: *Who pays your college fees?*

feeble /'fiːbl/ *adjective* (**feebler, feeblest**) not strong; weak: *a feeble old man*

feed /fiːd/ *verb* (**feeds, feeding, fed** /fed/, **has fed**) give food to a person or an animal: *The baby's crying – I'll go and feed her.*

feeder road /'fiːdə rəʊd/ *noun* a small road that joins villages to the main road system

feel /fiːl/ *verb* (**feels, feeling, felt** /felt/, **has felt**) **1** know something because your body tells you: *How do you feel?* ○ *I don't feel well.* ○ *I'm feeling tired.* ○ *He felt somebody touch his arm.* **2** be rough, smooth, wet, dry, etc when you touch it: *The water felt cold.* ○ *A snake's skin looks wet but feels dry if you touch it.* **3** think; believe: *I feel that we should talk about this.* **4** touch something to learn about it: *Feel this wool – it's really soft.* **feel for something** If you feel for something, you try to get something you cannot see with your hands: *She felt in her pocket for her money.* **feel like** want something: *Do you feel like a cup of tea? ○ I don't feel like studying tonight.*

feeling /ˈfiːlɪŋ/ *noun* **1** (*plural* **feelings**) something that you feel inside yourself, like happiness or anger: *a feeling of sadness* **2** (no plural) the ability to feel in your body: *I was so cold that I had no feeling in my feet.* **3** (*plural* **feelings**) an idea that you are not certain about: *I have a feeling that she isn't telling the truth.* **hurt somebody's feelings** do or say something that makes somebody sad: *Don't tell him you don't like his shirt – you'll hurt his feelings.*

feet *plural of* **foot**

fell *form of* **fall**[1]

fellow[1] /ˈfeləʊ/ *noun* a man: *What is that fellow doing?*

fellow[2] /ˈfeləʊ/ *adjective* a word that you use to talk about people who are the same as you: *She doesn't know many of her fellow students.*

felt *form of* **feel**

felt-pen /ˌfelt ˈpen/, **felt-tip pen** /ˌfelt tɪp ˈpen/ *noun* a pen with a soft point

female /ˈfiːmeɪl/ *adjective* A female animal or person belongs to the sex that can have babies.
female *noun*: *That elephant is a female.* ☞ Look at **male**.

feminine /ˈfemənɪn/ *adjective* of or like a woman; right for a woman: *feminine clothes* ☞ Look at **masculine**.

fence

fence /fens/ *noun* a thing like a wall that is made of pieces of wood or metal. Fences are put round gardens and fields.

ferocious /fəˈrəʊʃəs/ *adjective* very fierce and wild: *A rhinoceros is a ferocious animal.*

ferry /ˈferi/ *noun* (*plural* **ferries**) a boat that takes people or things on short journeys across a river or sea: *We travelled to Kisumu by ferry.*

fertile /ˈfɜːtaɪl/ *adjective* where plants grow well: *fertile soil* ✪ opposite: **infertile**

fertilizer /ˈfɜːtəlaɪzə(r)/ *noun* food for plants

festival /ˈfestɪvl/ *noun* **1** a time when people do special things because they are happy about something: *Christmas is an important Christian festival.* **2** a time when there are a lot of plays, concerts, etc in one place: *a festival of music and dance*

fetch /fetʃ/ *verb* (**fetches**, **fetching**, **fetched** /fetʃt/) **1** go and bring back somebody or something: *Can you fetch me the books from the cupboard? ○ I went to fetch my little brother from school.* ☞ picture at **bring**. **2** If something fetches a certain price, somebody pays this price for it: *That old cow won't fetch much.*

fever /ˈfiːvə(r)/ *noun* If you have a fever, your body is too hot because you are ill.

feverish /ˈfiːvərɪʃ/ *adjective* If you are feverish, your body is too hot because you are ill.

few /fjuː/ *adjective, pronoun* (**fewer**, **fewest**) not many: *Few people live to the age of 100. ○ There are fewer buses in the evenings.* **a few** some but not many: *Only a few people came to the meeting. ○ She has written a lot of books, but I have only read a few of them.*

fiancé /fiˈɒnseɪ/ *noun* A woman's fiancé is the man she is going to marry: *Can I introduce my fiancé, David? We've just got engaged.*

fiancée /fiˈɒnseɪ/ *noun* A man's fiancée is the woman he is going to marry.

fib /fɪb/ *noun* something you say that you know is not true; a small lie: *Don't tell fibs!*
fib *verb* (**fibs**, **fibbing**, **fibbed** /fɪbd/) *I was fibbing when I said I liked her hat.*
fibber *noun* a person who tells fibs

fiction /ˈfɪkʃn/ *noun* (no plural) stories that somebody writes and that are not true: *I enjoy reading fiction.*

fiddle /ˈfɪdl/ *verb* (**fiddles**, **fiddling**,

fiddled /'fɪdld/) touch something a lot with your fingers: *Stop fiddling with your pen and do some work!*

field /fiːld/ *noun* **1** a piece of land where people grow crops: *a field of corn* **2** one thing that you study: *Dr Mugabe is one of the most famous scientists in his field.* **3** a piece of land used for something special: *a sports field* ○ *an airfield* (= a place where aeroplanes land and take off) **4** a place where people work for oil, gold, etc: *the oil-fields of Saudi Arabia*

fierce /fɪəs/ *adjective* (**fiercer, fiercest**) **1** angry and wild: *a fierce dog* **2** very strong: *the fierce heat of the sun*

fifteen /ˌfɪf'tiːn/ *number* 15

fifteenth /ˌfɪf'tiːnθ/ *adjective, adverb, noun* 15th

fifth /fɪfθ/ *adjective, adverb, noun* **1** 5th **2** one of five equal parts of something; $\frac{1}{5}$

fifty /'fɪfti/ *number* **1** 50 **2** **the fifties** (plural) the numbers, years or temperature between 50 and 59: *He was born in the fifties* (= in the 1950s). **in your fifties** between the ages of 50 and 59

fiftieth /'fɪftiəθ/ *adjective, adverb, noun* 50th

fig /fɪg/ *noun* a soft sweet fruit that is full of small seeds

fight¹ /faɪt/ *verb* (**fights, fighting, fought** /fɔːt/, **has fought**) **1** When people fight, they try to hurt or kill each other using their hands, knives or guns: *What are the children fighting about?* **2** try very hard to stop something: *He fought against the illness for two years.* **3** talk in an angry way; argue **fight for something** try very hard to do or get something: *The workers are fighting for better pay.*

fighter *noun* **1** a person who fights as a sport **2** a small aeroplane that shoots other aeroplanes

fight² /faɪt/ *noun* an act of fighting: *There was a fight outside the restaurant last night.*

figure /'fɪgə(r)/ *noun* **1** one of the symbols (0–9) that we use to show numbers: *Shall I write the numbers in words or figures?* **2** an amount or price: *What*

are our sales figures for last month? **3** the shape of a person's body: *She's got a good figure.* **4** a shape of a person that you cannot see clearly: *I saw a tall figure outside the window.* **5** **figures** (plural) working with numbers to find an answer; arithmetic: *I'm not very good at figures.* **figure of speech** words that you use in an unusual way to make your meaning stronger: *I didn't really mean that she was mad – I was just a figure of speech.*

file¹ /faɪl/ *noun* **1** a box or cover for keeping papers in **2** a collection of information on a computer

file

file *verb* (**files, filing, filed** /faɪld/) put papers into a file: *Can you file these letters, please?*

file² /faɪl/ *noun* a tool with rough sides that you use for making things smooth: *a nail-file*

file *verb* (**files, filing, filed** /faɪld/) make something smooth with a file: *She filed her nails.*

file³ /faɪl/ *verb* (**files, filing, filed** /faɪld/) walk in a line, one behind the other: *The students filed into the classroom.* **in single file** in a line with each person following the one in front: *The children walked into the hall in single file.*

fill /fɪl/ *verb* (**fills, filling, filled** /fɪld/) **1** make something full: *Can you fill this glass with water, please?* **2** become full: *His eyes filled with tears.* **fill in** write facts or answers in the spaces that have been left for them: *She gave me a form and told me to fill it in.* **fill up** become or make something completely full: *He filled up the tank with petrol.*

film¹ /fɪlm/ *noun* **1** moving pictures that you see at a cinema or on television: *There's a good film on at the cinema this week.* **2** the special thin plastic that you use in a camera for taking photographs: *I bought a roll of black and white film.*

film² /fɪlm/ *verb* (**films, filming, filmed** /fɪlmd/) use a camera to make moving pictures of a story, news, etc: *A TV company are filming outside my house.*

filter /'fɪltə(r)/ *noun* a thing used for holding back the solid parts in a liquid or gas: *a coffee filter*

filter *verb* (**filters**, **filtering**, **filtered** /'fɪltəd/) *You should filter the water before you drink it.*

filthy /'fɪlθi/ *adjective* (**filthier**, **filthiest**) very dirty: *Go and wash your hands. They're filthy!*

fin /fɪn/ *noun* one of the thin flat parts on a fish that help it to swim ☛ picture at **fish**

final¹ /'faɪnl/ *adjective* last; at the end: *The final word in this dictionary is 'zoom'.*

final² /'faɪnl/ *noun* **1** the last game in a competition to decide who wins **2 finals** (plural) the last examinations that you take at university

finally /'faɪnəli/ *adverb* **1** after a long time; in the end: *After a long wait the bus finally arrived.* **2** You use 'finally' before saying the last thing in a list: *And finally, I would like to thank my parents for all their help.*

finance /'faɪnæns/ *noun* **1** (no plural) money; planning how to get, save and use money for a business, country, etc: *the Minister of Finance* **2 finances** (plural) the money you have that you can spend: *My finances aren't very good* (= I haven't got much money).

finance *verb* (**finances**, **financing**, **financed** /'faɪnænst/) give money to pay for something: *The building was financed by the government.*

financial /faɪ'nænʃl/ *adjective* of or about money: *financial problems*

find /faɪnd/ *verb* (**finds**, **finding**, **found** /faʊnd/, **has found**) **1** see or get something after looking or trying: *I can't find my glasses.* ○ *She hasn't found a job yet.* ○ *Has anybody found the answer to this question?* **2** see or get something that you did not expect: *I found some money in the street.* ○ *I woke up and found myself in hospital.* **3** think or have an idea about something because you have felt, tried, seen it, etc: *I didn't find that book very interesting.* ○ *He finds it difficult to sleep at night.* **find out** discover something, for example by asking or studying: *Can*

you find out what time the train leaves? ○ *Has she found out that you broke the window?*

fine¹ /faɪn/ *adjective* (**finer**, **finest**) **1** well or happy: *'How are you?' 'Fine thanks. And you?'* **2** good enough; okay: *'Let's meet on Monday.' 'Fine.'* ○ *'Do you want some more milk in your coffee?' 'No, that's fine.'* **3** beautiful or of good quality: *There's a fine view from the top floor of the building.* ○ *That was one of Rono's finest races.* **4** in very thin pieces: *fine thread* ✪ opposite: **thick**. **5** in very small pieces: *Salt is finer than sugar.* ✪ opposite: **coarse**

fine² /faɪn/ *noun* money that you must pay because you have done something wrong: *You'll get a fine if you park your car there.*

fine *verb* (**fines**, **fining**, **fined** /faɪnd/) make somebody pay a fine: *He was fined 1 000 shillings for stealing.*

finger /'fɪŋɡə(r)/ *noun* one of the five parts at the end of each hand: *She wears a ring on her little* (= smallest) *finger.* ☛ picture on page A4. **keep your fingers crossed** hope that somebody or something will be successful: *I'll keep my fingers crossed for you in your exams.*

fingernail /'fɪŋɡəneɪl/ *noun* the hard part at the end of your finger ☛ picture on page A4

fingerprint /'fɪŋɡəprɪnt/ *noun* the mark that a finger makes when it touches something: *The police found his fingerprints on the gun.*

finish¹ /'fɪnɪʃ/ *verb* (**finishes**, **finishing**, **finished** /'fɪnɪʃt/) **1** stop happening: *School finishes at four o'clock.* **2** stop doing something; come to the end of something: *I finish work at half past five.* ○ *Hurry up and finish your dinner!* ○ *Have you finished cleaning your room?* **finish off** do or eat the last part of something: *He finished off all the milk.* **finish with somebody or something** not want or need somebody or something any more: *Can I read this book when you've finished with it?*

finish² /'fɪnɪʃ/ *noun* (*plural* **finishes**) the last part of something; the end: *the finish of a race* ✪ opposite: **start**

fir /fɜː (r)/, **fir-tree**/ˈfɜː triː/ *noun* a tall tree with thin sharp leaves (called **needles**) that usually grows in cold countries

fire[1] /ˈfaɪə(r)/ *noun* **1** the heat and bright light that comes from burning things: *Many animals are afraid of fire.* ○ *There was a big fire at the factory last night.* **2** burning wood or coal that you use for keeping a place warm or for cooking: *They lit a fire to keep warm.* **3** a thing that uses electricity or gas to keep a room warm: *Switch on the fire.* **catch fire** start to burn: *She dropped her cigarette and the chair caught fire.* **on fire** burning: *My house is on fire!* **put out a fire** stop something from burning: *We put out the fire with buckets of water.* **set fire to something**, **set something on fire** make something start to burn: *Somebody set the house on fire.*

fire[2] /ˈfaɪə(r)/ *verb* (**fires**, **firing**, **fired** /ˈfaɪəd/) **1** shoot with a gun: *The soldiers fired at the enemy.* **2** tell somebody to leave their job: *He was fired because he was always late for work.*

fire-alarm /ˈfaɪər əlɑːm/ *noun* a bell that rings to tell people that there is a fire

fire brigade /ˈfaɪə brɪˌɡeɪd/ *noun* a group of people whose job is to stop fires: *Call the fire brigade!*

fire-engine /ˈfaɪər endʒɪn/ *noun* a vehicle that takes people and equipment to stop fires

fire-escape /ˈfaɪər ɪskeɪp/ *noun* stairs on the outside of a building where people can leave quickly when there is a fire inside

fire extinguisher /ˈfaɪər ɪkˌstɪŋɡwɪʃə(r)/ *noun* a metal container full of chemicals for stopping a fire

fireman /ˈfaɪəmən/ (*plural* **firemen** /ˈfaɪəmən/), **fire-fighter**/ˈfaɪə faɪtə(r)/ *noun* a person whose job is to stop fires

fireplace /ˈfaɪəpleɪs/ *noun* the place in a room where you can have a fire to make the room warm

fire station /ˈfaɪə steɪʃn/ *noun* a building where fire-engines are kept

firework /ˈfaɪəwɜːk/ *noun* a container with special powder in it that sends out coloured lights and smoke or makes a loud noise when you burn it: *We watched a firework display in the park.*

firm[1] /fɜːm/ *adjective* (**firmer**, **firmest**) **1** Something that is firm is quite hard or does not move easily: *Wait until the glue is firm.* ○ *The shelf isn't very firm, so don't put too many books on it.* **2** showing that you will not change your ideas: *She's very firm with her children* (= she makes them do what she wants). ○ *a firm promise*

firmly *adverb*: *Nail the pieces of wood together firmly.*

firm[2] /fɜːm/ *noun* a group of people working together in a business; a company: *My father works for a building firm.*

first[1] /fɜːst/ *adjective* before all the others: *January is the first month of the year.*

firstly *adverb* a word that you use when you are giving the first thing in a list: *We were angry firstly because he didn't come, and secondly because he didn't telephone.*

first[2] /fɜːst/ *adverb* **1** before all the others: *I arrived at the house first.* **2** for the first time: *I first met Paul in 1986.* **3** before doing anything else: *First fry the onions, then add the potatoes.* **at first** at the beginning: *At first she was afraid of the water, but she soon learned to swim.* **first of all** before anything else: *I'm going to cook dinner, but first of all I need to buy some food.*

first[3]/fɜːst/ *noun* (no plural) a person or thing that comes earliest or before all others: *I was the first to arrive at the party.* ○ *Today is the first of May (May 1st).*

first aid /ˌfɜːst ˈeɪd/ *noun* (no plural) quick simple help that you give to a person who is hurt, before a doctor comes

first class /ˌfɜːst ˈklɑːs/ *noun* (no plural) **1** the part of a train, plane, etc that it is more expensive to travel in: *I got a seat in first class.* **2** the fastest, most expensive way of sending letters

first-class /ˌfɜːst ˈklɑːs/ *adjective*, *adverb*: *a first-class stamp* ○ *It costs more to travel first-class.* ☞ Look at

second class and at the Note at **stamp**.

first name /ˈfɜːst neɪm/ *noun* the name that your parents choose for you when you are born: *'What is Mr Mwangi's first name?' 'Paul.'* ☛ Note at **name**.

fin   **fish**
tail

fish[1] /fɪʃ/ *noun* (*plural* **fish** or **fishes**) an animal that lives and breathes in water and uses its fins and tail for swimming: *I caught a big fish.* ○ *We had fish for dinner.*

fish[2] /fɪʃ/ *verb* (**fishes**, **fishing**, **fished** /fɪʃt/) try to catch fish ✪ When you talk about spending time fishing as a sport, you often say **go fishing**: *I go fishing at weekends..*

fishing *noun* (no plural) catching fish

fisherman /ˈfɪʃəmən/ *noun* (*plural* **fishermen** /ˈfɪʃəmən/) a person who catches fish as a job or sport

fist /fɪst/ *noun* a hand with the fingers closed tightly: *She banged on the door with her fist.*

fit[1] /fɪt/ *adjective* (**fitter**, **fittest**) **1** healthy and strong: *All her children are fit and well.* **2** good enough; right: *This food isn't fit to eat.* ○ *Do you think she's fit for the job?* ✪ opposite: **unfit**

fitness /ˈfɪtnəs/ *noun* (no plural) being healthy and strong

fit[2] /fɪt/ *verb* (**fits**, **fitting**, **fitted**) **1** be the right size and shape for somebody or something: *These shoes don't fit me – they're too tight.* ○ *This key doesn't fit the lock.* **2** putting something in the right place: *Can you fit these pieces of the bicycle together?* **fit in 1** have space for somebody or something: *I can only fit five people in the car.* **2** have time to do something or see somebody: *I have a job and a family and so it's hard to fit in studying.*

fit[3] /fɪt/ *noun* **1** a sudden illness **2** doing something suddenly that you cannot stop: *He was so funny – we were in fits of laughter.* ○ *I had a coughing fit.*

five /faɪv/ *number* 5

fix /fɪks/ *verb* (**fixes**, **fixing**, **fixed** /fɪkst/) **1** put something in a place so that it will not move: *We fixed the shelf to the wall.* **2** repair something: *The light isn't working – can you fix it?* **3** decide something; make a plan for something: *We fixed a date for the wedding.*

fixed *adjective* Something that is fixed does not change or move: *a fixed price*

fizz /fɪz/ *verb* (**fizzes**, **fizzing**, **fizzed** /fɪzd/) If a drink fizzes, it makes a lot of small bubbles.

fizzy *adjective* (**fizzier**, **fizziest**) *Do you like fizzy drinks?*

flag /flæg/ *noun* a piece of cloth with a special pattern on it joined to a stick (called a **flagpole**). Every country has its own flag.

flag

flake /fleɪk/ *noun* a small thin piece of something: *snowflakes* ○ *Flakes of paint were coming off the wall.*

flake *verb* (**flakes**, **flaking**, **flaked** /fleɪkt/) *Paint was flaking off the wall.*

flame /fleɪm/ *noun* a hot bright pointed piece of fire ☛ picture at **candle**. **in flames** burning: *The house was in flames.*

flamingo /fləˈmɪŋɡəʊ/ *noun* (*plural* **flamingos** or **flamingoes**) a large pink and red bird that has long legs and stands in water

flap[1] /flæp/ *noun* a flat piece of something that hangs down, for example to cover an opening. A flap is joined to something by one side: *the flap of an envelope*

flap[2] /flæp/ *verb* (**flaps**, **flapping**, **flapped** /flæpt/) move quickly up and down or from side to side: *Birds flap their wings when they fly.* ○ *The sails of the boat flapped in the wind.*

flare /fleə(r)/ *verb* (**flares**, **flaring**, **flared** /fleəd/) **flare up** If a fire flares up, it suddenly burns more brightly or strongly.

flash[1] /flæʃ/ *verb* (**flashes**, **flashing**, **flashed** /flæʃt/) **1** send out a bright light that comes and goes quickly: *The* *police car's lights flashed on and off.* **2** make something send out a sudden bright light: *She flashed a torch into the dark room.* **3** come and go very quickly: *I saw something flash past the window.*

flash[2] /flæʃ/ *noun* (*plural* **flashes**) **1** a bright light that comes and goes quickly: *a flash of lightning* **2** a bright light that you use with a camera for taking photographs **in a flash** very quickly: *Wait for me – I'll be back in a flash.*

flat[1] /flæt/ *noun* a group of rooms for living in. A flat is usually on one floor of a house or big building. ✪ A tall building with a lot of flats in it is called a **block of flats**.

flat[2] /flæt/ *adjective* (**flatter**, **flattest**) **1** smooth, with no parts that are higher or lower than the rest: *The land around here is very flat.* ○ *A table has a flat top.* **2** A tyre that is flat does not have enough air inside it.

flat *adverb* with no parts that are higher or lower than the rest: *He lay flat on his back on the floor.*

flatten /'flætn/ *verb* (**flattens**, **flattening**, **flattened** /'flætnd/) make something flat: *I sat on the box and flattened it.*

flatter /'flætə(r)/ *verb* (**flatters**, **flattering**, **flattered** /'flætəd/) **1** try to please somebody by saying too many nice things about them that are not completely true **2** If you are flattered by something, you like it because it makes you feel important: *I felt flattered when she asked for my advice.*

flattery /'flætəri/ *noun* (no plural) saying too many nice things about somebody to please them

flavour /'fleɪvə(r)/ *noun* the taste of food: *This stew doesn't have much flavour.*

flavour *verb* (**flavours**, **flavouring**, **flavoured** /'fleɪvəd/) *rice flavoured with spices*

flea /fliː/ *noun* a very small insect without wings that can jump and that lives on and bites animals and people: *Our cat has got fleas.*

flee /fliː/ *verb* (**flees**, **fleeing**, **fled** /fled/, **has fled**) run away from something bad or dangerous: *During the*

war, thousands of people fled the country.

fleet /fliːt/ *noun* a big group of ships

flesh /fleʃ/ *noun* (no plural) the soft part of your body under your skin ✪ The flesh of an animal that we eat is called **meat**.

flew *form of* **fly**[2]

flex /fleks/ *noun* (*plural* **flexes**) a long piece of wire covered with plastic that brings electricity to things like lamps, irons, etc

flexible /'fleksəbl/ *adjective* **1** that can bend easily without breaking **2** that can change easily: *It's not important to me when we go – my plans are quite flexible.*

flies 1 *plural of* **fly**[1] **2** *form of* **fly**[2]

flight /flaɪt/ *noun* **1** (*plural* **flights**) a journey in an aeroplane: *Our flight from Entebbe leaves at 10 a.m.* ○ *a direct flight from Nairobi to London* **2** (no plural) flying: *Have you ever seen an eagle in flight?*

flight of stairs /ˌflaɪt əv 'steəz/ *noun* a group of steps

fling /flɪŋ/ *verb* (**flings**, **flinging**, **flung** /flʌŋ/, **has flung**) throw something strongly or without care: *She flung a book and it hit me.*

flirt /flɜːt/ *verb* (**flirts**, **flirting**, **flirted**) show somebody that you like them in a sexual way: *Who was that boy she was flirting with at the party?*

flirt *noun* a person who flirts a lot

float /fləʊt/ *verb* (**floats**, **floating**, **floated**) **1** stay on top of a liquid: *Wood floats on water.* ☞ Look at **sink**. **2** move slowly in the air: *Clouds were floating across the sky.*

flock /flɒk/ *noun* a group of birds, sheep or goats: *a flock of seagulls*

flood /flʌd/ *noun* **1** When there is a flood, a lot of water covers the land: *Many homes were destroyed in the flood.* **2** a lot of something: *My dad had a flood of cards when he was in hospital.*

flood *verb* (**floods**, **flooding**, **flooded**) *A pipe burst and flooded the kitchen.*

floor /flɔː(r)/ *noun* **1** the part of a room that you walk on: *There weren't any chairs so we sat on the floor.* **2** all the rooms at the same height in a building:

I live on the top floor. ○ *Our hotel room was on the sixth floor.*

floppy disk /ˌflɒpi ˈdɪsk/ *noun* a small flat piece of plastic that stores information for a computer ☛ picture at **computer**

florist /ˈflɒrɪst/ *noun* a person who sells flowers ✪ A shop that sells flowers is called a **florist's**.

flour /ˈflaʊə(r)/ *noun* (no plural) soft white or brown powder that we use to make bread, cakes, etc

flourish /ˈflʌrɪʃ/ *verb* (**flourishes**, **flourishing**, **flourished** /ˈflʌrɪʃt/) **1** grow well: *The garden flourished after all the rain.* **2** become strong or successful: *Their business is flourishing.*

flow /fləʊ/ *verb* (**flows**, **flowing**, **flowed** /fləʊd/) move along like a river: *This river flows into Lake Victoria.*
flow *noun* (no plural) *I used a handkerchief to stop the flow of blood.*

flower /ˈflaʊə(r)/ *noun* the brightly coloured part of a plant that comes before the seeds or fruit ☛ picture at **plant**
flowery /ˈflaʊəri/, **flowered** /ˈflaʊəd/ *adjective* with a pattern of flowers on it: *a flowery dress*

flown *form of* **fly**²

flu /fluː/ *noun* (no plural) an illness like a bad cold that makes you ache and feel very hot: *I think I've got flu.*

fluent /ˈfluːənt/ *adjective* **1** able to speak easily and correctly: *Rose is fluent in English and French.* **2** spoken easily and correctly: *He speaks fluent German.*
fluently *adverb*: *She speaks five languages fluently.*

fluff /flʌf/ *noun* (no plural) soft light stuff that comes off wool, animals, etc

fluid /ˈfluːɪd/ *noun* anything that can flow; a liquid: *Water is a fluid.*

flung *form of* **fling**

flush /flʌʃ/ *verb* (**flushes**, **flushing**, **flushed** /flʌʃt/) clean something by sending water through it: *Please flush the toilet.*

flute /fluːt/ *noun* a musical instrument with holes, that you blow

fly¹ /flaɪ/ *noun* (*plural* **flies**) a small insect with two wings

fly

fly² /flaɪ/ *verb* (**flies**, **flying**, **flew** /fluː/, **has flown** /fləʊn/) **1** move through the air: *Ostriches cannot fly.* **2** make an aircraft move through the air: *A pilot is a person who flies an aircraft.* **3** travel in an aeroplane: *How much would it cost to fly to America?* **4** move quickly: *The door suddenly flew open and John came in.* ○ *A stone came flying through the window.*

flying /ˈflaɪɪŋ/ *adjective* able to fly: *flying insects*

flying saucer /ˌflaɪɪŋ ˈsɔːsə(r)/ *noun* a flying object that some people think they have seen, and that may come from another planet

flyover /ˈflaɪəʊvə(r)/ *noun* a bridge that carries a road over other roads

foal /fəʊl/ *noun* a young horse

foam /fəʊm/ *noun* (no plural) a lot of very small white bubbles that you see when you move liquid quickly

focus /ˈfəʊkəs/ *verb* (**focuses**, **focusing**, **focused** /ˈfəʊkəst/) move parts of a camera, microscope, etc so that you can see things through it clearly
focus *noun* (no plural) **in focus** If a photograph is in focus, it is clear. **out of focus** If a photograph is out of focus, it is not clear: *Your face is out of focus in this photo.*

foil /fɔɪl/ *noun* (no plural) metal that is very thin like paper. Foil is often used for covering food.

fold¹ /fəʊld/ *verb* (**folds**, **folding**, **folded**) **1** (*also* **fold up**) bend something so that one part is on top of another part: *I folded the letter and put it in the envelope.* ○ *Fold up your clothes.* ✪ opposite: **unfold**. **2** If you fold your arms, you cross them in front of your chest.
folding *adjective* that can be made flat: *a folding bed*

fold² /fəʊld/ *noun* a line that is made when you bend cloth or paper

folder /ˈfəʊldə(r)/ *noun* a cover made of cardboard or plastic for keeping papers in

folk /fəʊk/ *noun* (plural) people: *There*

are a lot of old folk living in this village.

folk-dance /ˈfəʊk dɑːns/ *noun* an old dance of the people of a particular place: *the folk-dances of Turkey*

folk-song /ˈfəʊk sɒŋ/ *noun* an old song of the people of a particular place

follow /ˈfɒləʊ/ *verb* (**follows**, **following**, **followed** /ˈfɒləʊd/) **1** come or go after somebody or something: *Follow me and I'll show you the way.* ○ *I think that car is following us!* **2** go along a road, path, etc: *Follow this road for about a mile and then turn right.* **3** do what somebody says you should do: *Did you follow my advice?* **4** understand something: *Has everyone followed the lesson so far?* **as follows** as you will now hear or read: *The dates of the meetings will be as follows: 21 March, 3 April, 19 April.*

following /ˈfɒləʊŋ/ *adjective* next: *I came back from my uncle's on Sunday and went to work on the following day.*

fond /fɒnd/ *adjective* (**fonder**, **fondest**) **be fond of somebody** or **something** like somebody or something a lot: *They are very fond of their uncle.*

food /fuːd/ *noun* (no plural) People and animals eat food so that they can live and grow: *Let's go and get some food – I'm hungry.* ○ *They gave the horses food and water.*

fool[1] /fuːl/ *noun* a person who is silly or who does something silly: *You fool! You forgot to lock the door!* **make a fool of somebody** do something that makes somebody look silly: *He always makes a fool of himself at parties.*

fool[2] /fuːl/ *verb* (**fools**, **fooling**, **fooled** /fuːld/) make somebody think something that is not true; trick somebody: *You can't fool me! I know you're lying!* **fool about**, **fool around** do silly things: *Stop fooling about with that knife.*

foolish /ˈfuːlɪʃ/ *adjective* stupid; silly: *a foolish mistake*

foolishly *adverb*: *I foolishly forgot to bring any money.*

foot /fʊt/ *noun* **1** (*plural* **feet** /fiːt/) the part of your leg that you stand on: *I've been walking all day and my feet hurt.* ☛ picture on page 216 **2** (*plural* **foot** or **feet**) a measure of length (= 30·48

centimetres). There are twelve **inches** in a foot, and three feet in a **yard**: *'How tall are you?' 'Five foot six* (= five feet and six inches).*'* ✪ The short way of writing 'foot' is **ft**. **3** the lowest part; the bottom: *She was standing at the foot of the stairs.* **on foot** walking: *Shall we go by car or on foot?* **put your feet up** rest: *If you're tired, put your feet up and listen to the radio.* **put your foot down** say strongly that something must or must not happen: *My father put his foot down and said I had to study every evening.*

football /ˈfʊtbɔːl/ *noun* **1** (no plural) a game for two teams of eleven players who try to kick a ball into a **goal** on a field called a **pitch**: *He plays football for Nigeria.* ○ *I'm going to a football match on Saturday.* **2** (*plural* **footballs**) a ball for playing this game

footballer *noun* a person who plays football

footpath /ˈfʊtpɑːθ/ *noun* a path in the country for people to walk on

footprint /ˈfʊtprɪnt/ *noun* a mark that your foot or shoe makes on the ground

footstep /ˈfʊtstep/ *noun* the sound of a person walking: *I heard footsteps, and then a knock on the door.*

for[1] /fə(r)/, /fɔː(r)/ *preposition* **1** a word that shows who will get or have something: *These flowers are for you.* **2** a word that shows how something is used or why something is done: *We had fish for dinner.* ○ *Take this medicine for your cold.* ○ *He was sent to prison for murder.* **3** a word that shows how long: *She has lived here for 20 years.* ☛ Note at **since 4** a word that shows how far: *We walked for miles.* **5** a word that shows where a person or thing is going: *Is this the train for Kampala?* **6** a word that shows the person or thing you are talking about: *It's time for us to go.* **7** a word that shows how much something is: *I bought this book for 200 shillings.* **8** a word that shows that you like an idea: *Some people were for the strike and others were against it.* **9** on the side of somebody or something: *He plays football for Italy.* **10** with the meaning of: *What is the word for 'table' in Swahili?*

for[2] /fə(r)/ *conjunction* because: *She was crying, for she knew they could never meet again.* ○ **Because** and **as** are the words that we usually use.

forbid /fə'bɪd/ *verb* (**forbids**, **forbidding**, **forbade** /fə'bæd/, **has forbidden** /fə'bɪdn/) say that somebody must not do something: *My parents have forbidden me to see him again.* ○ *Smoking is forbidden* (= not allowed) *inside the building.*

force[1] /fɔːs/ *noun* **1** (no plural) power or strength: *He was killed by the force of the explosion.* **2** (*plural* **forces**) a group of people, for example police or soldiers, who do a special job: *the police force* **by force** using a lot of strength, for example by pushing, pulling or hitting: *I lost the key so I had to open the door by force.*

force[2] /fɔːs/ *verb* (**forces**, **forcing**, **forced** /fɔːst/) **1** make somebody do something that they do not want to do: *They forced him to give them the money.* **2** do something by using a lot of strength: *The thief forced the window open.*

forecast /'fɔːkɑːst/ *noun* what somebody thinks will happen: *The weather forecast said that the rains would start today.*

foreground /'fɔːɡraʊnd/ *noun* the part of a picture that seems nearest to you: *The man in the foreground is my father.* ○ opposite: **background**

forehead /'fɒhed/ *noun* the part of your face above your eyes ☛ picture on page A4

foreign /'fɒrən/ *adjective* of or from another country: *We've got some foreign students staying at our house.* ○ *a foreign language*

foreigner *noun* a person from another country ☛ Note at **stranger**.

forest /'fɒrɪst/ *noun* a big piece of land with a lot of trees: *We went for a walk in the forest.* ○ A **forest** is larger than a **wood**. A **jungle** is a forest in a very hot country.

forever /fər'evə(r)/ *adverb* **1** for all time; always: *I will love you forever.* **2** very often: *I can't read because he is forever asking me questions!*

forgave *form of* **forgive**

forge /fɔːdʒ/ *verb* (**forges**, **forging**, **forged** /fɔːdʒd/) make a copy of something because you want to trick people and make them think it is real: *He was put in prison for forging money.*

forgery /'fɔːdʒəri/ *noun* **1** (no plural) making a copy of something to trick people: *Forgery is a crime.* **2** (*plural* **forgeries**) a copy of something made to trick people: *This painting is not really by Picasso – it's a forgery.*

forget /fə'get/ *verb* (**forgets**, **forgetting**, **forgot** /fə'gɒt/, **has forgotten** /fə'gɒtn/) **1** not remember something; not have something in your mind any more: *I've forgotten her name.* ○ *Don't forget to feed the cat.* **2** not bring something with you: *I couldn't see the film very well because I had forgotten my glasses.* **3** stop thinking about something: *Forget about your exams and enjoy yourself!*

forgive /fə'gɪv/ *verb* (**forgives**, **forgiving**, **forgave** /fə'geɪv/, **has forgiven** /fə'gɪvn/) stop being angry with somebody for a bad thing that they did: *He never forgave me for forgetting his birthday.*

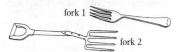

fork 1

fork 2

fork /fɔːk/ *noun* **1** a thing with long points at one end, that you use for putting food in your mouth **2** a large tool with points at one end, that you use for digging the ground **3** a place where a road or river divides into two parts: *When you get to the fork in the road, go left.*

form[1] /fɔːm/ *noun* **1** a type of something: *Cars, trains and buses are all forms of transport.* **2** a piece of paper with spaces for you to answer questions: *You need to fill in this form to get a new passport.* **3** the shape of a person or thing: *In the dark, we could just see her familiar form coming towards us.* **4** one of the ways you write or say a word: *'Forgot' is a form of 'forget'.* **5** a class in a school: *Which form are you in?*

form[2] /fɔːm/ *verb* (**forms**, **forming**, **formed** /fɔːmd/) **1** make something or give a shape to something: *We formed a line outside the cinema.* ○ *In English we usually form the past tense by adding 'ed'.* **2** grow; take shape: *Ice forms when water freezes.* **3** start a group, etc: *They formed a club for African people living in London.*

formal /'fɔːml/ *adjective* You use formal language or behave in a formal way at important or serious times and with people you do not know very well: *'Yours faithfully' is a formal way of ending a letter.* ○ *I wore a suit and tie because it was a formal dinner.* ✪ opposite: **informal**

formally /'fɔːməli/ *adverb*: *He was dressed formally for his interview.*

former /'fɔːmə(r)/ *adjective* of a time before now: *countries of the former Soviet Union*

former *noun* (no plural) the first of two things or people: *I have visited both Morocco and Tunisia, and I prefer the former.* ☞ Look at **latter**.

formerly /'fɔːməli/ *adverb* before this time: *Sri Lanka was formerly called Ceylon.*

formula /'fɔːmjulə/ *noun* (*plural* **formulae** /'fɔːmjuliː/ *or* **formulas**) **1** a group of letters, numbers or symbols that show a rule in mathematics or science: *The formula for finding the area of a circle is* πr^2. **2** a list of the substances that you need to make something: *a formula for a new drug*

fort /fɔːt/ *noun* a strong building that was made to protect a place against its enemies

fortieth /'fɔːtiəθ/ *adjective*, *adverb*, *noun* 40th

fortnight /'fɔːtnaɪt/ *noun* two weeks: *It took a fortnight for my letter to get there.*

fortnightly *adjective*, *adverb*: *We have fortnightly meetings.*

fortress /'fɔːtrəs/ *noun* (*plural* **fortresses**) a large strong building that was made to protect a place against its enemies

fortunate /'fɔːtʃənət/ *adjective* lucky: *I was very fortunate to get the job.*

✪ opposite: **unfortunate**

fortunately *adverb*: *There was an accident but fortunately nobody was hurt.*

fortune /'fɔːtʃuːn/ *noun* **1** (no plural) things that happen that you cannot control; luck: *I had the good fortune to get the job.* **2** (*plural* **fortunes**) a lot of money: *He made a fortune selling cars.*

tell somebody's fortune say what will happen to somebody in the future: *The old lady said she could tell my fortune by looking at my hand.*

forty /'fɔːti/ *number* **1** 40 **2** the **forties** (plural) the numbers, years or temperature between 40 and 49 **in your forties** between the ages of 40 and 49

forward[1] /'fɔːwəd/, **forwards** /'fɔːwədz/ *adverb* **1** in the direction that is in front of you: *Move forwards to the front of the train.* ✪ opposite: **backwards**. **2** to a later time: *When you travel from Senegal to Tanzania, you need to put your watch forward.* **look forward to something** wait for something with pleasure: *We're looking forward to seeing you again.*

forward[2] /'fɔːwəd/ *verb* (**forwards**, **forwarding**, **forwarded**) send a letter to somebody at their new address: *Could you forward all my post to me while I'm in London?*

fossil /'fɒsl/ *noun* a part of a dead plant or an animal that has been in the ground for a very long time and has become hard

fought *form of* **fight**

foul[1] /faʊl/ *adjective* dirty, or with a bad smell or taste: *What a foul smell!*

foul[2] /faʊl/ *noun* something you do that is against the rules of a game, for example football: *He was sent off the field for a foul against the goalkeeper.*

foul *verb* (**fouls**, **fouling**, **fouled** /faʊld/) *Fish was fouled twice.*

found[1] *form of* **find**

found[2] /faʊnd/ *verb* (**founds**, **founding**, **founded**) start something, for example a school or business: *This school was founded in 1968.*

founder *noun* a person who founds something

foundation /faʊn'deɪʃn/ *noun* **1** (no

plural) starting a group, building, etc: *the foundation of a new school* **2 foundations** (plural) the strong parts of a building which you build first under the ground

fountain

/ˈfaʊntən/ *noun* water that shoots up into the air and then falls down again.

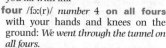

fountain

fountain-pen

/ˈfaʊntən pen / *noun* a pen that you fill with ink

four /fɔː(r)/ *number* 4 **on all fours** with your hands and knees on the ground: *We went through the tunnel on all fours.*

four-legged /ˌfɔː ˈlegɪd/ *adjective* with four legs. A horse is a four-legged animal.

fourteen /ˌfɔːˈtiːn/ *number* 14

fourteenth /ˌfɔːˈtiːnθ/ *adjective, adverb, noun* 14th

fourth /fɔːθ/ *adjective, adverb, noun* 4th

fowl /faʊl/ *noun* (plural **fowl** or **fowls**) a bird, especially a hen, that people keep on farms

fox /fɒks/ *noun* (plural **foxes**) a wild animal that looks like a dog and has a long thick tail and red fur

fraction /ˈfrækʃn/ *noun* **1** an exact part of a number ¼ (= a quarter) *and* ⅓ (= a third) *are fractions.* **2** a very small part of something: *For a fraction of a second I thought you were my sister.*

fracture /ˈfræktʃə(r)/ *verb* (**fractures, fracturing, fractured** /ˈfræktʃəd/) break a bone in your body: *She fell and fractured her leg.*

fracture *noun*: *a fracture of the arm*

fragile /ˈfrædʒaɪl/ *adjective* A thing that is fragile breaks easily: *Be careful with those glasses. They're very fragile.*

fragment /ˈfrægmənt/ *noun* a very small piece that has broken off something: *The window broke and fragments of glass went everywhere.*

frail /freɪl/ *adjective* (**frailer, frailest**) not strong or healthy: *a frail old woman*

frame[1] /freɪm/ *noun* **1** a thin piece of

wood or metal round the edge of a picture, window, mirror, etc **2** strong pieces of wood or metal that give something its shape: *They made a shelter of plastic sheets on a wooden frame.*

frame of mind /ˌfreɪm əv ˈmaɪnd/ *noun* how you feel: *I'm not in the right frame of mind for singing.*

frame[2] /freɪm/ *verb* (**frames, framing, framed** /freɪmd/) put a picture in a frame: *She had her daughter's photograph framed.*

framework /ˈfreɪmwɜːk/ *noun* the strong part of something that gives it shape: *The bridge has a steel framework.*

frank /fræŋk/ *adjective* (**franker, frankest**) If you are frank, you say exactly what you think: *To be frank, I don't really like that shirt you're wearing.*

frankly *adverb*: *Tell me frankly what you think of my work.*

fraud /frɔːd/ *noun* **1** (no plural) doing things that are not honest to get money: *Two of the company directors were sent to prison for fraud.* **2** (plural **frauds**) a person or thing that is not what he/she/it seems to be: *He said he was a police officer but I knew he was a fraud.*

freckles /ˈfreklz/ *noun* (plural) small light brown spots on a person's skin: *A lot of people with red hair have freckles.*

free[1] /friː/ *adjective, adverb* (**freer, freest**) **1** If you are free, you can go where you want and do what you want: *After five years in prison she was finally free.* **2** If something is free, you do not have to pay for it: *We've got some free tickets for the concert.* ○ *Children under five travel free on trains.* **3** not busy: *Are you free this afternoon?* ○ *I don't have much free time.* **4** not being used: *Excuse me, is this seat free?* **5** not fixed: *Take the free end of the rope in your left hand.* **free from something, free of something** without something bad: *It's nice to be on holiday, free from all your worries.* **set free** let a person or animal go out of a prison or cage: *We set the bird free and it flew away.*

free[2] /friː/ *verb* (**frees, freeing, freed** /friːd/) make somebody or something

free: *He was freed after ten years in prison.*

freedom /ˈfriːdəm/ *noun* (no plural) being free: *They gave their children too much freedom.*

freeze /friːz/ *verb* (**freezes**, **freezing**, **froze** /frəʊz/, **has frozen** /ˈfrəʊzn/) **1** become hard because it is so cold. When water freezes, it becomes ice. **2** make food very cold so that it stays fresh for a long time: *frozen food* **3** stop suddenly and stay very still: *The cat froze when it saw the bird.* **freeze to death** be so cold that you die

freezer /ˈfriːzə(r)/ *noun* a big metal box for making food very cold, like ice, so that you can keep it for a long time

freezing /ˈfriːzɪŋ/ *adjective* very cold: *It's freezing at night in the desert.*

freight /freɪt/ *noun* (no plural) things that lorries, ships, trains and aeroplanes carry from one place to another: *a freight train*

frequent /ˈfriːkwənt/ *adjective* Something that is frequent happens often: *How frequent is the Eldoret bus?*

frequently *adverb* often: *Tuva is frequently late for school.*

fresh /freʃ/ *adjective* (**fresher**, **freshest**) **1** made or picked not long ago; not old: *I love the smell of fresh bread.* ○ *These beans are fresh – I picked them this morning.* **2** new or different: *fresh ideas* **3** not frozen or from a tin: *fresh fruit* **4** clean and cool: *Open the window and let some fresh air in.*

fresh water /ˌfreʃ ˈwɔːtə/ *noun* not sea water

freshly *adverb*: *freshly baked bread*

Friday /ˈfraɪdeɪ/ *noun* the sixth day of the week, next after Thursday

fridge /frɪdʒ/ *noun* a big metal box for keeping food and drink cold and fresh

fried *form of* **fry**

friend /frend/ *noun* a person that you like and know very well: *David is my best friend.* ○ *We are very good friends.* **make friends with somebody** become a friend of somebody: *Have you made friends with any of the students in your class?*

friendly /ˈfrendli/ *adjective* (**friendlier**, **friendliest**) A person who is friendly is kind and helpful: *My neighbours are very friendly.* ✪ opposite: **unfriendly**. **be friendly with somebody** If you are friendly with somebody, he/she is your friend: *Jane is friendly with a girl who lives in the same street.*

friendship /ˈfrendʃɪp/ *noun* being friends with somebody

fries *form of* **fry**

fright /fraɪt/ *noun* a sudden feeling of fear: *Why didn't you knock on the door before you came in? You gave me a fright!*

frighten /ˈfraɪtn/ *verb* (**frightens**, **frightening**, **frightened** /ˈfraɪtnd/) make somebody feel afraid: *Sorry, did I frighten you?*

frightened *adjective* If you are frightened, you are afraid of something: *He's frightened of spiders.*

frightening /ˈfraɪtnɪŋ/ *adjective* Something that is frightening makes you feel afraid: *That was the most frightening film I have ever seen.*

fringe /frɪndʒ/ *noun* **1** the short hair that hangs down above your eyes ➡ picture at **hair** **2** threads that hang from the edge of a piece of material **3** the edge of a place: *We live on the fringes of town.*

fro /frəʊ/ *adverb* **to and fro** first one way and then the other way, many times: *She travels to and fro between Mombasa and Nairobi.*

frog /frɒg/ *noun* a small animal that lives in and near water. Frogs have long back legs and they can jump.

frog

from /frəm/, /frɒm/ *preposition* **1** a word that shows where something starts: *We travelled from Kisumu to Mombasa.* **2** a word that shows where somebody lives or was born: *I come from Uganda.* **3** a word that shows when somebody or something starts: *The shop is open from 9.30 until 5.30.* **4** a word that shows who gave or sent something: *I had a letter from Grace.* ○ *I borrowed a dress from my sister.* **5** a word that shows the place where you find something: *He took the money from my bag.* **6** a word that shows how far away something is: *The house is two miles from the village.* **7** a word that shows how something changes: *The sky changed from blue to grey.* **8** a word that shows the lowest number or price: *The tickets cost from 50 to 100 shillings.* **9** a word that shows what is used to make something: *Paper is made from wood.* **10** a word that shows difference: *My book is different from yours.* **11** a word that shows why: *Children are dying from this disease.*

front /frʌnt/ *noun* the side or part of something that faces forwards and that you usually see first: *The book has a picture of a lion on the front.* ○ *John and I sat in the front of the car and the children sat in the back.* ☛ picture at **back**. **in front of somebody** or **something 1** further forward than another person or thing: *Alice was sitting in front of the television.* ☛ picture on page A1. **2** when other people are there: *Please don't talk about it in front of my parents.*

front *adjective*: *the front door* ○ *the front seat of a car*

frontier /ˈfrʌntɪə(r)/ *noun* the line where one country joins another country

frost /frɒst/ *noun* in cold countries, ice like white powder that covers the ground when the weather is very cold: *There was a frost last night.*

frosty *adjective* (**frostier**, **frostiest**) *a frosty morning*

frown /fraʊn/ *verb* (**frowns**, **frowning**, **frowned** /fraʊnd/) move your eyebrows together to make lines on your forehead. You frown when you are worried, angry or thinking hard: *John frowned at me when I came in. 'You're late,' he said.*

frown *noun*: *She looked at me with a frown.*

froze, **frozen** *forms of* **freeze**

frozen food /ˌfrəʊzn ˈfuːd/ *noun* (no plural) food that is very cold, like ice, when you buy it. You keep frozen food in a **freezer**.

fruit /fruːt/ *noun* the part of a plant or tree that holds the seeds and that you can eat. Bananas, oranges and apples are kinds of fruit. ✪ Be careful! We do not usually say 'a fruit'. We say 'a piece of fruit' or 'some fruit': *Would you like a piece of fruit?* ○ *'Would you like some fruit?' 'Yes please – I'll have a banana.'*

frustrating /frʌˈstreɪtɪŋ/ *adjective* If something is frustrating, it makes you angry because you cannot do what you want to do: *It's very frustrating when you can't say what you mean in a foreign language.*

fry /fraɪ/ *verb* (**fries**, **frying**, **fried** /fraɪd/, **has fried**) cook something or be cooked in hot oil: *Fry the onions in butter.* ○ *fried eggs*

fry-pan /ˈfraɪ pæn/ *American English for* **frying-pan**

frying-pan /ˈfraɪŋ pæn/ *noun* a flat metal container with a long handle that you use for frying food

frying-pan

ft *short way of writing* **foot** 2

fuel /ˈfjuːəl/ *noun* (no plural) anything that you burn to make heat or power. Wood, coal and oil are kinds of fuel.

fulfil /fʊlˈfɪl/ *verb* (**fulfils**, **fulfilling**, **fulfilled** /fʊlˈfɪld/) do what you have planned or promised to do: *Jane fulfilled her dream of travelling around the world.*

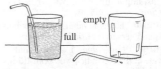
empty

full

full /fʊl/ *adjective* (**fuller**, **fullest**) **1** with a lot of people or things in it, so that there is no more space: *My glass is full.* ○ *The bus was full so we waited for the next one.* ○ *These socks are full of holes.* **2** complete; with nothing missing: *Please tell me the full story.* **3** as much, big, etc as possible: *The train was travelling at full speed.* **full up** with no space for anything or anybody else: *'Would you like anything else to eat?' 'No thank you, I'm full up.'* **in full** completely; with nothing missing: *Please write your name in full.*

full stop /ˌfʊl ˈstɒp/ *noun* a mark ( )

that you use in writing to show the end of a sentence, or after the short form of a word

full-time /ˌfʊl ˈtaɪm/ *adjective, adverb* for all the normal working hours of the day or week: *My mother has a full-time job.* ○ *Do you work full-time?* ☞ Look at **part-time**.

fully /ˈfʊli/ *adverb* completely; totally: *'Do you have a room for tonight, please?' 'No, I'm sorry, we're fully booked.'*

fun /fʌn/ *noun* (no plural) something that you enjoy; pleasure: *Cooking is fun if you don't have to do it every day.* ○ *We had great fun at the party.* ○ *Have fun!* (= enjoy yourself!) **for fun** to enjoy yourself: *I don't enter races – I run just for fun.* **make fun of somebody** laugh about somebody in an unkind way: *The other children make fun of him because he wears glasses.*

function /ˈfʌŋkʃn/ the special work that a person or thing does: *The function of the heart is to send blood round the body.*

function *verb* (**functions, functioning, functioned** /ˈfʌŋkʃnd/) work: *The engine will not function without oil.*

fund /fʌnd/ *noun* money that will be used for something special: *The money from the concert will go into a fund to build a new hospital.*

fundamental /ˌfʌndəˈmentl/ *adjective* most important; basic: *You are making a fundamental mistake.*

funeral /ˈfjuːnərəl/ *noun* the time when a dead person is buried or burned

funnel /ˈfʌnl/ *noun* **1** a tube that is wide at the top to help you pour things into bottles **2** a large pipe on a ship or railway engine that smoke comes out of

funny /ˈfʌni/ *adjective* (**funnier, funniest**) **1** A person or thing that is funny makes you laugh or smile: *a funny story* **2** strange or surprising: *There's a funny smell in this room.*

fur /fɜː(r)/ *noun* the soft thick hair on animals. Cats and rabbits have fur.

furry /ˈfɜːri/ *adjective* (**furrier, furriest**) *a furry animal*

furious /ˈfjʊəriəs/ *adjective* very angry: *My parents are furious with me when*

I came home late again.

furnace /ˈfɜːnɪs/ *noun* a very hot fire in a closed place, used for heating metals, making glass, etc

furnished /ˈfɜːnɪʃt/ *adjective* with furniture already in it: *I live in a furnished flat.* ☯ opposite: **unfurnished**

furniture /ˈfɜːnɪtʃə(r)/ *noun* (no plural) tables, chairs, beds, etc: *They've bought some furniture for their new house.* ○ *All the furniture is very old.* ○ *The only piece of furniture in the room was a large bed.*

furrow /ˈfʌrəʊ/ *noun* a long cut that a plough makes in the soil

further /ˈfɜːðə(r)/ *adjective, adverb* **1** more far: *Which is further from here – Cape Town or Cairo?* ○ *We couldn't go any further because the road was closed.* **2** more; extra: *Do you have any further questions?*

further education /ˌfɜːðər edʒuˈkeɪʃn/ *noun* studying that you do after you finish secondary school

furthest *form of* **far**

fuse /fjuːz/ *noun* a small piece of wire that stops too much electricity going through something. Plugs usually have fuses in them.

fuss¹ /fʌs/ *noun* (no plural) a lot of excitement or worry about small things that are not important: *He makes a fuss when I'm five minutes late.* **make a fuss of somebody** be kind to somebody; do a lot of small things for somebody: *I like visiting my grandfather because he always makes a fuss of me.*

fussy *adjective* (**fussier, fussiest**) A fussy person cares a lot about small things that are not important, and is difficult to please: *William is fussy about his food – he won't eat anything with onions in it.*

fuss² /fʌs/ *verb* (**fusses, fussing, fussed** /fʌst/) worry and get excited about a lot of small things that are not important: *Stop fussing!*

future¹ /ˈfjuːtʃə(r)/ *noun* **1** the time that will come: *Nobody knows what will happen in the future.* ○ *The company's future is uncertain.* **2 the future** (no plural) the form of a verb that shows what will happen after now in

future after now: *You must work harder in future.* ☛ Look at **past** and **present**.

future[2] /ˈfjuːtʃə(r)/ *adjective* of the time that will come: *Have you met John's future wife?*

Gg

g short way of writing **gram**

gabion /ˈɡæbɪən/ *noun* a container made of wire mesh that you fill with large stones. *We put gabions on the side of a hill to prevent rain washing away the soil.*

gadget /ˈɡædʒɪt/ *noun* a small machine or tool: *Their kitchen is full of electrical gadgets.*

gain /ɡeɪn/ *verb* (**gains**, **gaining**, **gained** /ɡeɪnd/) **1** get more of something: *She gained useful experience from her last job.* ○ *I have gained a lot of weight.* **2** get what you want or need: *The police are trying to gain more information about the robbery.*

galaxy /ˈɡæləksi/ *noun* (*plural* **galaxies**) a very large group of stars and planets

gale /ɡeɪl/ *noun* a very strong wind: *The trees were blown down in the gale.*

gallery /ˈɡæləri/ *noun* (*plural* **galleries**) a building or room where people can go to look at paintings

gallon /ˈɡælən/ *noun* a measure of liquid (= 4·5 litres). There are eight **pints** in a gallon: *a gallon of petrol* ☛ Note at **pint**

gallop /ˈɡæləp/ *verb* (**gallops**, **galloping**, **galloped** /ˈɡæləpt/) When a horse gallops, it runs very fast: *The horses galloped round the field.*

gallop *noun*: *I took the horse for a gallop.*

gamble /ˈɡæmbl/ *verb* (**gambles**, **gambling**, **gambled** /ˈɡæmbld/) **1** try to win money by playing games that need luck: *He gambled a lot of money on the last race.* **2** do something, although there is a chance that you might lose: *I gambled on running the first part of the race very fast.*

gamble *noun* something that you do without knowing if you will win or lose

gambler /ˈɡæmblə(r)/ *noun* a person who tries to win money by playing games that need luck

gambling /ˈɡæmblɪŋ/ *noun* (no plural) playing games that need luck, to try to win money

game /ɡeɪm/ *noun* **1** (*plural* **games**) something you play that has rules: *Shall we have a game of football?* ○ *We played a game of cards, and I won.* **2** (no plural) wild animals or birds: *a game reserve* ○ *He's a game ranger in a national park.* **3** **games** (plural) sports that you play at school or in a competition: *the Olympic Games*

gang /ɡæŋ/ *noun* **1** a group of people who do bad things together: *a street gang* **2** a group of friends who often meet: *The whole gang is coming to the party tonight.* **3** a group of workers: *a gang of road menders*

gang *verb* (**gangs**, **ganging**, **ganged** /ɡæŋd/) **gang up on** or **against somebody** join together against another person: *The other boys ganged up on Tim because he was much smaller than them.*

gangster /ˈɡæŋstə(r)/ *noun* one of a group of dangerous criminals: *Al Capone was a famous Chicago gangster.*

gangway /ˈɡæŋweɪ/ *noun* **1** a bridge from the side of a ship to the land so that people can go on and off **2** the long space between two rows of seats in a cinema, theatre, etc

gaol /dʒeɪl/ = **jail**

gap /ɡæp/ *noun* a space in something or between two things; a space where something should be: *The sheep got out through a gap in the fence.* ○ *Write the correct word in the gap.*

gape /geɪp/ *verb* (**gapes**, **gaping**, **gaped** /geɪpt/) look at somebody or something with your mouth open because you are surprised: *She gaped at me when I said I was getting married.*

gaping *adjective* wide open: *There was a gaping hole in the ground.*

garage /ˈgærɑːʒ/ *noun* **1** a building where you keep your car **2** a place where cars are repaired **3** a place where you can buy petrol

garden /ˈgɑːdn/ *noun* **1** a piece of land by your house where you can grow fruit and vegetables **2 gardens** (plural) a public park: *Jeevanjee Gardens*

garlic /ˈgɑːlɪk/ *noun* (no plural) a plant like a small onion with a strong taste and smell, that you use in cooking

gas /gæs/ *noun* **1** (*plural* **gases**) anything that is like air: *Hydrogen and oxygen are gases.* **2** (no plural) a gas with a strong smell, that you burn to make heat: *a gas fire*

gasp /gɑːsp/ *verb* (**gasps**, **gasping**, **gasped** /gɑːspt/) breathe in quickly and noisily through your mouth: *She gasped in surprise when she heard the news.* ○ *He was gasping for air when they pulled him out of the water.*

gasp *noun*: *a gasp of surprise*

gate

gate /geɪt/ *noun* **1** a kind of door in a fence or wall outside: *We closed the gate to stop the cows getting out of the field.* **2** a door in an airport that you go through to reach the aeroplane: *Please go to gate 15.*

gateway /ˈgeɪtweɪ/ *noun* a way in or out of a place that has a gate to close it

gather /ˈgæðə(r)/ *verb* (**gathers**, **gathering**, **gathered** /ˈgæðəd/) **1** come together in a group; meet: *A*

crowd gathered to watch the fight. **2** take things that are in different places and bring them together: *I gathered up all the books and papers and put them in my bag.* **3** understand something: *I gather that you know my sister.*

gathering /ˈgæðərɪŋ/ *noun* a time when people come together: *There was a large gathering outside the palace.*

gauge /geɪdʒ/ *noun* an instrument that measures how much of something there is: *Where is the petrol gauge in this car?*

gauge *verb* (**gauges**, **gauging**, **gauged** /geɪdʒd/) measure something

gave *form of* **give**

gay /geɪ/ *adjective* **1** attracted to people of the same sex; homosexual **2** happy and full of fun ✪ We do not often use 'gay' with this meaning now.

gaze /geɪz/ *verb* (**gazes**, **gazing**, **gazed** /geɪzd/) look at somebody or something for a long time: *She sat and gazed out of the window.* ○ *He was gazing at her.*

gazelle /gəˈzel/ *noun* (*plural* **gazelle** or **gazelles**) a kind of small antelope

gear /gɪə(r)/ *noun* **1** (*plural* **gears**) a set of wheels that work together in a machine to pass power from one part to another. The gears of a car or bicycle help to control it when it goes up and down hills and help it to go faster or slower: *You need to change gear to go round the corner.* **2** (no plural) special clothes or things that you need for a job or sport: *camping gear*

geese *plural of* **goose**

gem /dʒem/ *noun* a beautiful stone that is very valuable; a jewel

general[1] /ˈdʒenrəl/ *adjective* **1** of, by or for most people or things: *Is this car park for general use?* **2** not in detail: *The back cover gives you a general idea of what the book is about.* **in general** usually: *I don't eat much meat in general.*

general election /ˌdʒenrəl ɪˈlekʃn/ *noun* a time when people choose a new government: *Did you vote in the last general election?*

general knowledge /ˌdʒenrəl ˈnɒlɪdʒ/ *noun* (no plural) what you know about a lot of different things

general[2] /'dʒenrəl/ *noun* a very important officer in the army

generally /'dʒenrəli/ *adverb* usually; mostly: *I generally get up at about six o'clock.*

generate /'dʒenəreɪt/ *verb* (**generates**, **generating**, **generated**) make heat, electricity, etc: *Power stations generate electricity.*

generation /ˌdʒenə'reɪʃn/ *noun* **1** the children, or the parents, or the grandparents, in a family: *This photo shows three generations of my family.* **2** all the people who were born at about the same time: *The older and the younger generations listen to different music.*

generator /'dʒenəreɪtə(r)/ *noun* a machine that produces electricity

generosity /ˌdʒenə'rɒsəti/ *noun* (no plural) liking to give things to other people

generous /'dʒenərəs/ *adjective* **1** always ready to give things or to spend money: *She is very generous – she often buys me presents.* **2** large: *generous amounts of food*

generously *adverb*: *He always gives generously to charities.*

genius /'dʒiːniəs/ *noun* (*plural* **geniuses**) a very clever person: *Einstein was a genius.*

gentle /'dʒentl/ *adjective* (**gentler**, **gentlest**) quiet and kind; not rough: *Be gentle with the baby.* ○ *a gentle voice* ○ *It was a hot day, but there was a gentle breeze* (= a soft wind).

gently /'dʒentli/ *adverb*: *Close the door gently or you'll wake the children up.*

gentleman /'dʒentlmən/ *noun* (*plural* **gentlemen** /'dʒentlmən/) **1** a polite way of saying 'man': *There is a gentleman here to see you.* **2** a man who is polite and kind to other people ☞ Look at **lady**.

genuine /'dʒenjuɪn/ *adjective* real and true: *Those aren't genuine diamonds – they're pieces of glass!*

genuinely *adverb* really: *Do you think he's genuinely sorry?*

geography /dʒi'ɒgrəfi/ *noun* (no plural) the study of the earth and its countries, mountains, rivers, weather, etc

geographical /ˌdʒiːə'græfɪkl/ *adjective*: *geographical names* (= names of countries, seas, cities, etc)

geology /dʒi'ɒlədʒi/ *noun* (no plural) the study of rocks and soil and how they were made

geologist /dʒi'ɒlədʒɪst/ *noun* a person who studies or knows a lot about geology

geometry /dʒi'ɒmətri/ *noun* (no plural) the study of things like lines, angles and shapes

geranium /dʒə'reɪniəm/ *noun* a plant with red, white or pink flowers

germ /dʒɜːm/ *noun* a very small living thing that can make you ill: *flu germs*

gesture /'dʒestʃə(r)/ *noun* a movement of your head or hand to show how you feel or what you want

get /get/ *verb* (**gets**, **getting**, **got** /gɒt/, **has got**) **1** buy or take something: *Will you get some bread when you go shopping?* **2** receive something: *I got a lot of presents for my birthday.* **3** become: *He is getting fat.* ○ *Mum got angry.* ○ *It's getting cold.* **4** go and bring back somebody or something: *Jenny will get the children from school.* **5** arrive somewhere: *We got to Kasese at ten o'clock.* **6** start to have an illness: *I think I'm getting a cold.* **7** understand or hear something: *I don't get the joke.* **8** a word that you use with part of another verb to show that something happens to somebody or something: *She got caught by the police.* **9** travel on a train, bus, etc: *I didn't walk – I got the train.* **10** make somebody do something: *I got Peter to help me.* **get away with something** do something bad and not be punished for it: *He lied but he got away with it.* **get back** return: *When did you get back from your holiday?* **get in** come to a place: *My train got in at 7.15.* **get in, get into something** climb into a car: *Tom got into the car.* **get off** leave a train, bus, bicycle, etc: *Where did you get off the bus?* **get on 1** words that you use to say or ask how well somebody does something: *Patrick is getting on well at school.* ○ *How did you get on in the exam?* **2** become late: *I must go home –*

the time is getting on. **3** become old: *My grandfather is getting on — he's nearly 70.* **get on, get onto something** climb onto a bus, train or bicycle: *I got on the train.* **get on with somebody** live or work in a friendly way with somebody: *We get on well with our neighbours.* **get out** leave a car, etc: *I opened the door and got out.* **get out of something** not do something that you do not like: *I'll come swimming with you if I can get out of cleaning my room.* **get something out** take something from the place where it was: *She opened her bag and got out a pen.* **get over something** become well or happy again after you have been ill or sad: *He still hasn't got over his wife's death.* **get through** be able to speak to somebody on the telephone; be connected: *I tried to ring the police station but I couldn't get through.* **get through something 1** use or finish a certain amount of something: *I got through a lot of work today.* **2** pass an examination, etc **get together** meet; come together in a group: *The whole family got together for Christmas.* **get up** stand up; get out of bed: *What time do you usually get up?* **get up to something 1** do something, usually something bad: *I must go and see what the children are getting up to.* **2** come as far as a place in a book, etc: *I've got up to page 180.* **have got** have something: *She has got brown eyes.* ○ *Have you got any money?* **have got to** If you have got to do something, you must do it: *I have got to leave soon.*

ghee /giː/ *noun* (no plural) liquid butter that we use in cooking

ghost /ɡəʊst/ *noun* the form of a dead person that a living person thinks he/she sees: *Do you believe in ghosts?*

ghostly *adjective* of or like a ghost: *She could hear ghostly noises.*

giant /ˈdʒaɪənt/ *noun* a very big tall person in stories: *Goliath was a giant.*

giant *adjective* very big: *a giant insect*

gift /ɡɪft/ *noun* **1** something that you give to or get from somebody; a present: *wedding gifts* **2** something that you can do well or learn easily: *She has a gift for languages.*

gigantic /dʒaɪˈɡæntɪk/ *adjective* very big

giggle /ˈɡɪɡl/ *verb* (**giggles**, **giggling**, **giggled** /ˈɡɪɡld/) laugh in a silly way: *The children couldn't stop giggling.*

giggle *noun*: *There was a giggle from the back of the class.*

gill /ɡɪl/ *noun* the part on each side of a fish that it breathes through ☛ picture at **fish**

ginger /ˈdʒɪndʒə(r)/ *noun* (no plural) a plant with a very hot strong taste, that is used in cooking

gipsy /ˈdʒɪpsi/ = **gypsy**

giraffe /dʒəˈrɑːf/ *noun* a big animal with a very long neck and long legs

girl /ɡɜːl/ *noun* a female child; a young woman

girlfriend /ˈɡɜːlfrend/ *noun* a girl or woman who is somebody's special friend: *Have you got a girlfriend?*

Girl Guide /ˌɡɜːl ˈɡaɪd/ *noun* a member of a special club for girls

give /ɡɪv/ *verb* (**gives**, **giving**, **gave** /ɡeɪv/, **has given** /ˈɡɪvn/) **1** let somebody have something: *She gave me a watch for my birthday.* ○ *I gave my ticket to the man at the door.* ○ *I gave John 1 000 shillings for his old bike.* **2** make somebody have or feel something: *That noise is giving me a headache.* ○ *Jo gave me an angry look.* ○ *He gave a shout.* ○ *She gave him a kiss.* **give away** give something to somebody without getting money for it: *I've given all my old clothes away.* **give somebody back something, give something back to somebody** return something to somebody: *Can you give me back the book I lent you last week?* **give in** say that you will do something that you do not want to do, or agree that you will not win: *I had to give in and ask for the answer to the puzzle.* **give something in** give work, etc to somebody: *The teacher asked us to give in our essays today.* **give out** give something to many people: *Could you give out these books to the class, please?* **give up** stop trying to do something, because you know that you cannot do it: *I give up — what's the answer?* **give**

something up stop doing or having something: *I'm trying to give up smoking.*

glacier /ˈglæsiə(r)/ *noun* a large river of ice that moves slowly down a mountain

glad /glæd/ *adjective* happy; pleased: *He was glad to see us.*

gladly *adverb* If you do something gladly, you are happy to do it: *I'll gladly help you.*

glance /glɑːns/ *verb* (glances, glancing, glanced /glɑːnst/) look quickly at somebody or something: *Fatima glanced at her watch.*

glance *noun: a glance at the newspaper* **at a glance** with one look: *I could see at a glance that he was ill.*

glare /gleə(r)/ *verb* (glares, glaring, glared /gleəd/) **1** look angrily at somebody: *He glared at the children.* **2** shine with a strong light that hurts your eyes: *The sun glared down.*

glare *noun* **1** (no plural) strong light that hurts your eyes: *the glare of the car's headlights* **2** (plural glares) a long angry look: *I tried to say something, but he gave me a glare.*

glass /glɑːs/ *noun* **1** (no plural) hard stuff that you can see through. Bottles and windows are made of glass: *I cut myself on some broken glass.* ○ *a glass jar* **2** (plural glasses) a thing made of glass that you drink from: *a glass of orange juice* ○ *a wineglass*

glass

glasses /ˈglɑːsɪz/ *noun* (plural) two pieces of special glass (called lenses) in a frame that people wear over their eyes to help them see better: *Does she wear glasses?* ☛ Look also at **sunglasses**. ✪ Be careful! You cannot say 'a glasses'. You can say **a pair of glasses**: *I need a new pair of glasses.*(or: *I need (some) new glasses.*)

gleam /gliːm/ *verb* (gleams, gleaming, gleamed /gliːmd/) shine with a soft light: *The lake gleamed in the moonlight.*

gleam *noun: I could see a gleam of light through the trees.*

glide /glaɪd/ *verb* (glides, gliding, glided) move smoothly and silently: *The bird glided through the air.*

glider /ˈglaɪdə(r)/ *noun* an aeroplane without an engine

gliding *noun* (no plural) flying in a glider as a sport

glimmer /ˈglɪmə(r)/ *verb* (glimmers, glimmering, glimmered /ˈglɪməd/) shine with a small, weak light

glimmer *noun: the glimmer of a candle*

glimpse /glɪmps/ *verb* (glimpses, glimpsing, glimpsed /glɪmpst/) see somebody or something quickly, but not clearly: *I just glimpsed a plane between the clouds.*

glimpse *noun* **catch a glimpse of** somebody or something see somebody or something quickly, but not clearly: *I caught a glimpse of myself in the mirror as I walked past.*

glisten /ˈglɪsn/ *verb* (glistens, glistening, glistened /ˈglɪsnd/) shine because it is wet or smooth: *His eyes glistened with tears.*

glitter /ˈglɪtə(r)/ *verb* (glitters, glittering, glittered /ˈglɪtəd/) shine brightly with a lot of small flashes of light: *The broken glass glittered in the sun.* ○ *glittering diamonds*

glitter *noun* (no plural) *the glitter of jewels*

global /ˈgləʊbl/ *adjective* of or about the whole world: *Pollution is a global problem.*

globe /gləʊb/ *noun* **1** a ball with a map of the world on it **2 the globe** (no plural) the earth: *He's travelled all over the globe.*

gloomy /ˈgluːmi/ *adjective* (gloomier, gloomiest) **1** dark and sad: *What a gloomy day!* **2** sad and without hope: *He's feeling very gloomy because he can't get a job.*

gloomily /ˈgluːmɪli/ *adverb: She looked gloomily out of the window at the rain.*

glorious /ˈglɔːriəs/ *adjective* **1** wonderful or beautiful: *The weather was glorious.* **2** famous and full of glory: *a glorious history*

glory /ˈglɔːri/ *noun* (no plural) **1** fame and respect that you get when you do great things: *the glory of winning at the Olympics* **2** great beauty: *Early morning* *is the best time to see the forest in all its glory.*

glossy /ˈglɒsi/ *adjective* (**glossier**, **glossiest**) smooth and shiny: *glossy hair*

glove /glʌv/ *noun* a thing that you wear to keep your hand warm or safe: *a pair of goalkeeping gloves* ○ *rubber gloves*

gloves

glow /gləʊ/ *verb* (**glows**, **glowing**, **glowed** /gləʊd/) send out soft light or heat without flames or smoke: *His cigarette glowed in the dark.*

glow *noun*: *the glow of the sky at sunset*

glue /gluː/ *noun* (no plural) a thick liquid that you use for sticking things together

glue *verb* (**glues**, **gluing**, **glued** /gluːd/) stick one thing to another thing with glue: *Glue the two pieces of wood together.*

gnaw /nɔː/ *verb* (**gnaws**, **gnawing**, **gnawed** /nɔːd/) bite something for a long time: *The dog was gnawing a bone.*

go[1] /gəʊ/ *verb* (**goes**, **going**, **went** /went/, **has gone** /gɒn/) **1** move from one place to another: *I went to Nairobi by train.* ○ *Her new car goes very fast.* **2** travel to a place to do something: *Paul has gone to school.* ○ *Are you going to the meeting tomorrow?* ○ *I'll go and make some coffee.* **3** leave a place: *What time does the bus go?* ○ *I must go now – it's four o'clock.* **4** become: *Her hair has gone grey.* **5** have as its place: *'Where do these plates go?' 'In that cupboard.'* **6** lead to a place: *Does this road go to the lake?* **7** work: *Jane dropped the clock and now it doesn't go.* **8** happen in a certain way: *How is your new job going?* ○ *The week went very quickly.* **9** disappear: *My headache has gone.* **10** be or look good with something else: *Do these shoes go with my dress?* **11** make a certain sound: *Cows go 'moo'.* **go ahead** begin or continue to do something: *'Can I borrow your pen?' 'Yes, go ahead.'* **go away** leave: *Go away! I'm doing my homework.* ○ *They have gone away for a few days.* **go back** go again to a place where you were before; return: *We're going back to*

school tomorrow. **go by** pass: *The holidays went by very quickly.* **go down well** be something that people like: *The speech went down very well with the crowd.* **go off 1** explode: *A bomb went off in the station.* **2** when food or drink goes of, it becomes too old to eat or drink: *This meat has gone off – it smells horrible.* **go off somebody** or **something** stop liking somebody or something **go on 1** happen: *What's going on?* **2** continue; not stop: *I went on working.* **3** words that you use when you want somebody to do something: *Oh, go on! Come to the party with me!* **go out 1** leave the place where you live or work: *I went out for a walk.* ○ *We're going out tonight.* **2** stop shining or burning: *The fire has gone out.* **go out with somebody** have somebody as a boyfriend or girlfriend: *She's going out with a boy at school.* **go over something** look at or explain something carefully from the beginning to the end: *Go over your work before you give it to the teacher.* **go round 1** be enough for everybody: *Is there enough wine to go round?* **2** go to somebody's home: *We're going round to Maalim's this evening.* **go through something 1** look at or explain something carefully from the beginning to the end: *The teacher went through our homework.* **2** suffer something: *She went through a difficult time when her husband was ill.* **go up** become higher or more: *The price of petrol has gone up again.*

go[2] /gəʊ/ *noun* (*plural* **goes**) the time when you can or should do something: *Get off the bike – it's my go!* **have a go** try to do something: *I'll have a go at mending your bike.* **in one go** with one try: *There are too many books here to carry in one go.*

---

been or gone?

If somebody has **been** to a place, they have travelled there and come back again:

I've **been** to Italy three times.

If somebody has **gone** to a place, they have travelled there and they are there now:

Judy isn't here. She has **gone** to Italy.

goal /gəʊl/ *noun* **1** the place where the ball must go to win a point in a game like football: *He kicked the ball into the goal.* **2** a point that a team wins in a game like football when the ball goes into the goal: *Tunisia won by three goals to two.* ○ *Hassan has scored another goal.*

goalkeeper

goal

goalkeeper /ˈgəʊlkiːpə(r)/ *noun* a player in a game like football who must stop the ball from going into the goal

horn

goat

kid

goat /gəʊt/ *noun* an animal with horns. People keep goats for their milk. ✪ A young goat is called a **kid**.

god /gɒd/ *noun* **1** (*plural* **gods**) a being that people believe controls them and nature **2** **God** (no plural) the one great being that Christians, Jews and Muslims believe made the world and controls everything

goddess /ˈgɒdes/ *noun* (*plural* **goddesses**) a female god

goes *form of* go¹

goggles /ˈgɒglz/ *noun* (plural) big glasses that you wear so that water, dust, wind, etc cannot get in your eyes: *a pair of goggles*

going *form of* go¹ **be going to 1** words that show what you plan to do in the future: *Joe's going to cook the dinner tonight.* **2** words that you use when you are sure that something will happen: *It's going to rain.*

gold /gəʊld/ *noun* (no plural) a yellow metal that is very valuable: *Is your ring made of gold?* ○ *a gold watch*

gold *adjective* with the colour of gold: *gold paint*

golden /ˈgəʊldən/ *adjective* **1** made of gold: *a golden crown* **2** with the colour of gold: *golden hair*

golf /gɒlf/ *noun* (no plural) a game that you play by hitting a small ball into holes with a long stick (called a **golf club**)

golf-course /ˈgɒlf kɔːs/ *noun* a large piece of land, covered in grass, where people play golf

gone *form of* go¹

good¹ /gʊd/ *adjective* (**better**, **best**) **1** that does what you want; done or made very well: *It's a good knife — it cuts very well.* ○ *The film was really good.* **2** that you enjoy; nice: *Have a good evening!* ○ *The weather was very good.* **3** able to do something well: *He's a good driver.* **4** kind, or doing the right thing: *It's good of you to help.* ○ *The children were very good while you were out.* **5** right or suitable: *This is a good place for a picnic.* **6** big, long, complete, etc: *Take a good look at this photo.* **7** a word that you use when you are pleased: *Is everyone here? Good. Now let's begin.* ✪ The adverb is **well**. **good at something** able to do something well: *James is very good at boxing.* **good for you** If something is good for you, it makes you well, happy, etc.: *Fresh fruit and vegetables are good for you.*

good² /gʊd/ *noun* (no plural) something that is right or helpful **be no good**, **not be any good** not be useful: *These shoes aren't any good. They are too small.* ○ *It's no good asking mum for money — she hasn't got any.* **do somebody good** make somebody well or happy: *It will do you good to go to bed early tonight.* **for good** for all time; for ever: *She has given up her job for good.*

good afternoon /ˌgʊd ɑːftəˈnuːn/ words that you say when you see or speak to somebody in the afternoon ✪ Often we just say **Afternoon**: '*Good afternoon, Mr Buke.*' '*Afternoon, Mike.*'

goodbye /ˌgʊdˈbaɪ/ a word that you say when somebody goes away, or when you go away: *Goodbye! See you tomorrow.*

good evening /ˌgʊd ˈiːvnɪŋ/ words that you say when you see or speak to somebody in the evening ✪ Often we just say **Evening.**: *'Good evening, Mr Muben.' 'Evening, Miss Njoro.'*

Good Friday /ˌgʊd 'fraɪdeɪ/ *noun* the Friday before Easter when Christians remember the death of Christ

good-looking /ˌgʊd 'lʊkɪŋ/ *adjective* nice to look at; handsome: *He's a good-looking boy.* ☛ Note at **beautiful**.

good morning /ˌgʊd 'mɔːnɪŋ/ words that you say when you see or speak to somebody in the morning ✪ Often we just say **Morning**: *'Good morning, Eva.' 'Morning.'*

good-natured /ˌgʊd 'neɪtʃəd/ *adjective* friendly and kind

goodness /'gʊdnəs/ *noun* (no plural) **1** something in food that is good for your health: *Fresh vegetables have a lot of goodness in them.* **2** being good or kind **for goodness' sake** words that show anger: *For goodness' sake, hurry up!* **goodness, goodness me** words that show surprise: *Goodness! What a big crowd!* **thank goodness** words that show you are happy because a problem or danger has gone away: *Thank goodness it's stopped raining.*

good night /ˌgʊd 'naɪt/ words that you say when you leave somebody in the evening

goods /gʊdz/ *noun* (plural) **1** things that you buy or sell: *That shop sells electrical goods.* **2** things that a train or lorry carries: *a goods train*

good-tempered /ˌgʊd 'tempəd/ *adjective* not often angry: *My dad is very good-tempered.*

goose /guːs/ *noun* (*plural* **geese** /giːs/) a big bird with a long neck. People keep geese on farms for their eggs and meat.

gorgeous /'gɔːdʒəs/ *adjective* very good; wonderful: *The weather was gorgeous!* ○ *What a gorgeous dress!*

gorilla /gə'rɪlə/ *noun* an animal like a very big black monkey with no tail

gorilla

gosh /gɒʃ/ a word that shows surprise: *Gosh! What a big house!*

gossip /'gɒsɪp/ *noun* (no plural) talk about other people that is often unkind: *Don't believe all the gossip you hear.*

gossip *verb* (**gossips, gossiping, gossiped** /'gɒsɪpt/) *They were gossiping about Beatrice's new boyfriend.*

got *form of* **get**

gourd /gɔːd/, /gʊəd/ *noun* a large fruit that grows on the ground; we use the hard, dried skin of a gourd (a **calabash**) as a container for water, food, etc

govern /'gʌvn/ *verb* (**governs, governing, governed** /'gʌvnd/) control a country or part of a country: *Kenyatta governed Kenya until 1978.*

government /'gʌvənmənt/ *noun* a group of people who control a country: *The leaders of all the European governments will meet today in Brussels.* ○ *The Government have discussed the plan.*

governor /'gʌvənə(r)/ *noun* **1** a person who controls part of a country **2** a person who controls a place like a prison or hospital

gown /gaʊn/ *noun* **1** a long dress that a woman wears at a special time **2** a long loose piece of clothing that people wear to do a special job. Judges and university teachers sometimes wear gowns.

grab /græb/ *verb* (**grabs, grabbing, grabbed** /græbd/) take something quickly and roughly: *The thief grabbed her bag and ran away.*

grace /greɪs/ *noun* (no plural) **1** a beautiful way of moving: *She dances with grace.* **2** thanks to God that people say before or after they eat

graceful /'greɪsfl/ *adjective* A person or thing that is graceful moves in a beautiful way: *a graceful dancer*
gracefully /'greɪsfəli/ *adverb*: *He moves very gracefully.*

grade[1] /greɪd/ *noun* **1** how good something is; the level or quality of something: *Which grade of petrol does your car use?* **2** a number or letter that a teacher gives for your work to show how good it is: *She got very good grades in all her exams.*

grade[2] /greɪd/ *verb* (**grades**, **grading**, **graded**) sort things or people into sizes, kinds, etc: *The eggs are graded by size.*

gradual /ˈgrædʒʊəl/ *adjective* Something that is gradual happens slowly: *I am making gradual progress with my work.*

gradually /ˈgrædʒʊəli/ *adverb*: *We all become gradually older.*

graduate[1] /ˈgrædʒuət/ *noun* a person who has finished studying at a university or college and who has passed his/her last exams: *a graduate of Makerere University*

graduate[2] /ˈgrædʒueɪt/ *verb* (**graduates**, **graduating**, **graduated**) finish your studies at a university or college and pass your last exams: *I graduated from Kenyatta University in 1997.*

graffiti /grəˈfiːti/ *noun* (plural) funny, rude or angry words or pictures that people write or draw on walls: *The walls of the old building were covered with graffiti.*

graft /grɑːft/ *noun* **1** a piece of a living plant that is fixed onto another plant so that they will grow together **2** a piece of living skin, bone, etc that is fixed onto a damaged part of somebody's body in a medical operation: *a skin graft*

grain /greɪn/ *noun* **1** (no plural) the seeds of a plant like wheat or rice that we eat **2** (*plural* **grains**) a seed or a small hard piece of something: *grains of rice* ○ *a grain of sand*

gram, **gramme** /græm/ *noun* a measure of weight. There are 1 000 grams in a **kilogram**. ✪ The short way of writing 'gram' is **g**: *30g of butter*

grammar /ˈgræmə(r)/ *noun* (no plural) the rules that tell you how to put words together when you speak or write

grammatical /grəˈmætɪkl/ *adjective* **1** of or about grammar: *What is the grammatical rule for making plurals in English?* **2** correct because it follows the rules of grammar: *The sentence 'They is happy' is not grammatical.*

✪ opposite: **ungrammatical**

grammatically /grəˈmætɪkli/ *adverb*: *The sentence is not grammatically correct.*

gran /græn/ *noun* grandmother

grand /grænd/ *adjective* (**grander**, **grandest**) very big, important, rich, etc: *a grand house*

grandad /ˈgrændæd/ *noun* grandfather

grandchild /ˈgræntʃaɪld/ *noun* (*plural* **grandchildren** /ˈgræntʃɪldrən/) the child of your child

granddaughter /ˈgrændɔːtə(r)/ *noun* the daughter of your child

grandfather /ˈgrænfɑːðə(r)/ *noun* the father of your mother or father

grandma /ˈgrænmɑː/ *noun* grandmother

grandmother /ˈgrænmʌðə(r)/ *noun* the mother of your mother or father

grandpa /ˈgrænpɑː/ *noun* grandfather

grandparents /ˈgrænpeərənts/ *noun* (plural) the mother and father of your mother or father

grandson /ˈgrænsʌn/ *noun* the son of your child

grandstand /ˈgrændstænd/ *noun* lines of seats, with a roof over them, where you sit to watch a sport

granny, **grannie** /ˈgræni/ *noun* (*plural* **grannies**) grandmother

grant[1] /grɑːnt/ *noun* money that you give for a special reason: *The government gives grants to some young people so they can study at university.*

grant[2] /grɑːnt/ *verb* (**grants**, **granting**, **granted**) give somebody what they have asked for: *They granted him a visa to leave the country.*

a bunch of grapes

grape /greɪp/ *noun* a small green or purple fruit that we eat or make into wine: *a bunch of grapes*

grapefruit /ˈgreɪpfruːt/ *noun* (plural

grapefruit or **grapefruits**) a fruit that looks like a big orange, but is yellow

grapevine /ˈgreɪpvaɪn/ *noun* **the grapevine** the way that news is passed from one person to another: *I heard it on the grapevine that you are getting married.*

graph /grɑːf/ *noun* a picture that shows how numbers, amounts, etc are different from each other

graph

grasp /grɑːsp/ *verb* (**grasps**, **grasping**, **grasped** /grɑːspt/) **1** hold something tightly: *Harriet grasped my arm to stop herself from falling.* **2** understand something: *He could not grasp what I was saying.*

grasp *noun* (no plural) *The ball fell from my grasp.*

grass /grɑːs/ *noun* (no plural) a plant with thin green leaves that covers fields and gardens. Cows and sheep eat grass: *Don't walk on the grass.*

grassy *adjective* covered with grass

grate /greɪt/ *verb* (**grates**, **grating**, **grated**) If you grate food you rub it over a metal tool (called a **grater**) so that it is in very small pieces: *Can you grate some coconut?* ○ *grated carrot*

grateful /ˈgreɪtfl/ *adjective* If you are grateful, you feel or show thanks to somebody: *We are grateful to you for the help you have given us.* ✪ opposite: **ungrateful**

gratitude /ˈgrætɪtjuːd/ *noun* (no plural) the feeling of being grateful: *We gave David a present to show our gratitude for all his help.*

grave[1] /greɪv/ *adjective* (**graver**, **gravest**) very bad or serious ✪ **Serious** is the word that we usually use.

grave[2] /greɪv/ *noun* a hole in the ground where a dead person's body is put: *We put flowers on the grave.*

gravestone /ˈgreɪvstəʊn/ *noun* a piece of stone on a grave that shows the name of the dead person

graveyard /ˈgreɪvjɑːd/ *noun* a piece of land near a church where dead people are put in the ground

gravel /ˈgrævl/ *noun* (no plural) very small stones that are used for making roads

gravity /ˈgrævəti/ *noun* (no plural) the force that pulls everything towards the earth

gravy /ˈgreɪvi/ *noun* (no plural) a hot brown liquid that you eat with meat and vegetables

graze[1] /greɪz/ *verb* (**grazes**, **grazing**, **grazed** /greɪzd/) hurt your skin by rubbing it against something rough: *He fell and grazed his arm.*

graze *noun*: *Her legs were covered with grazes.*

graze[2] /greɪz/ *verb* (**grazes**, **grazing**, **grazed** /greɪzd/) eat grass: *The sheep were grazing in the fields.*

grease /griːs/ *noun* (no plural) fat from animals, or any thick stuff that is like oil: *You will need very hot water to get the grease off these plates.*

greasy /ˈgriːsi/ *adjective* (**greasier**, **greasiest**) with a lot of grease on or in it: *Greasy food is not good for you.* ○ *greasy hair*

great[1] /greɪt/ *adjective* (**greater**, **greatest**) **1** very large or very much: *It's a great pleasure to meet you.* **2** important or special: *Henry Rono was a great runner.* **3** very; very good: *They are great friends.* ○ *There's a great big dog in the garden!* **4** very good; wonderful: *I had a great weekend.* ○ *It's great to see you!* **a great many** very many: *He knows a great many people.*

great-[2] /greɪt/ *prefix* a word that you put before other words to show some parts of a family. For example, your **great-grandmother** is the mother of your grandmother or grandfather, and your **great-grandson** is the son of your grandson or granddaughter.

greatly /ˈgreɪtli/ *adverb* very much: *I wasn't greatly surprised to see her.*

greed /griːd/ *noun* (no plural) the feeling that you want more of something than you need

greedy *adjective* (**greedier**, **greediest**) A person who is greedy wants or takes more of something than he/she needs: *She's so greedy – she's eaten the whole melon!*

whole melon!

green /griːn/ *adjective* (**greener**, **greenest**) with the colour of leaves and grass: *dark green*

green *noun* **1** the colour of leaves and grass: *She was dressed in green.* **2** a place in the centre of a village that is covered with grass

greengrocer /'griːnɡrəʊsə(r)/ *noun* a person who sells fruit and vegetables in a small shop (called a **greengrocer's**)

greenhouse /'griːnhaʊs/ *noun* (*plural* **greenhouses** /'griːnhaʊzɪz/) a building made of glass, where plants grow

greet /griːt/ *verb* (**greets**, **greeting**, **greeted**) say or do something when you meet somebody: *He greeted me with a smile.*

greeting /'griːtɪŋ/ *noun* **1** words that you say when you meet somebody: *'Hello' and 'Good morning' are greetings.* **2 greetings** (plural) words that you write to somebody at a special time: *a greetings card* (= a card that you send at Christmas or on a birthday, for example)

grew *form of* **grow**

grey /ɡreɪ/ *adjective* (**greyer**, **greyest**) with a colour like black and white mixed together: *My grandmother has grey hair.* ○ *a grey-haired old man* ○ *The sky was grey.*

grey *noun*: *He was dressed in grey.*

grid /ɡrɪd/ *noun* lines that cross each other to make squares, for example on a map

grief /ɡriːf/ *noun* (no plural) great sadness

grieve /ɡriːv/ *verb* (**grieves**, **grieving**, **grieved** /ɡriːvd/) feel great sadness: *She is grieving for her dead son.*

grill /ɡrɪl/ *verb* (**grills**, **grilling**, **grilled** /ɡrɪld/) cook meat, fish, etc on metal bars under or over heat: *grilled steak*

grill *noun* the part of a cooker, or a special metal thing, where you grill food

grin /ɡrɪn/ *verb* (**grins**, **grinning**, **grinned** /ɡrɪnd/) have a big smile on your face: *She grinned at me.*

grin *noun*: *He had a big grin on his face.*

grind /ɡraɪnd/ *verb* (**grinds**, **grinding**,

ground /ɡraʊnd/, **has ground**) make something into very small pieces or powder by crushing it: *They ground the wheat into flour.* ○ *ground coffee*

grip /ɡrɪp/ *verb* (**grips**, **gripping**, **gripped** /ɡrɪpt/) hold something tightly: *Marie gripped my hand as we crossed the road.*

grip *noun* (no plural) *He kept a tight grip on the rope.*

grit /ɡrɪt/ *noun* (no plural) very small pieces of stone

groan /ɡrəʊn/ *verb* (**groans**, **groaning**, **groaned** /ɡrəʊnd/) make a deep sad sound, for example because you are unhappy or in pain: *'I've got a headache,' he groaned.*

groan *noun*: *'I've got to do my homework,' she said with a groan.*

groceries /'ɡrəʊsəriz/ *noun* (plural) food that you buy in packets, tins, jars, etc

groom /ɡruːm/ *noun* **1** a person whose job is to look after horses **2** a man on the day of his wedding; a bridegroom

groove /ɡruːv/ *noun* a long thin cut: *The needle moves along a groove in the record.*

grope /ɡrəʊp/ *verb* (**gropes**, **groping**, **groped** /ɡrəʊpt/) try to find something by using your hands, when you cannot see: *I groped in the dark for the door.*

ground¹ *form of* **grind**

ground² /ɡraʊnd/ *noun* **1** (no plural) the top part of the earth: *We sat on the ground and rested.* **2** (*plural* **grounds**) a piece of land that is used for something special: *a sports ground* ○ *a playground* (= a place where children play) **3 grounds** (plural) the land around a large building: *the grounds of the hospital*

ground floor /ˌɡraʊnd 'flɔː(r)/ *noun* the part of a building that is at the same height as the street: *My office is on the ground floor.*

groundnut /'ɡraʊndnʌt/ (*also* **peanut**) *noun* a kind of nut that grows under the ground. You can eat groundnuts or use their oil.

group /ɡruːp/ *noun* **1** a number of people or things together: *A group of people were standing outside the shop.*

grow /grəʊ/ *verb* (**grows**, **growing**, **grew** /gruː/, **has grown** /grəʊn/)
1 become bigger: *Children grow very quickly.* **2** When a plant grows somewhere, it lives there: *Oranges grow in warm countries.* **3** plant something in the ground and look after it: *We grow potatoes and maize in our shamba.* **4** let something grow: *Joshua has grown a beard.* **5** become: *It was growing dark.* ✪ In this sense, it is more usual to say **get** or **become**. **grow into something** get bigger and become something: *Kittens grow into cats.* **grow out of something** become too big to do or wear something: *She's grown out of her shoes.* **grow up** become an adult; change from a child to a man or woman: *I want to be a doctor when I grow up.*

growl /graʊl/ *verb* (**growls**, **growling**, **growled** /graʊld/) If an animal growls, it makes a low angry sound: *The dog growled at the stranger.*
growl *noun*: *The dog gave a fierce growl.*

grown-up /ˈgrəʊn ʌp/ *noun* a man or woman, not a child; an adult: *Ask a grown-up to help you.*
grown-up /ˌgrəʊn ˈʌp/ *adjective*: *She has a grown-up son.*

growth /grəʊθ/ *noun* (no plural) getting bigger; growing: *the growth of a baby*

grubby /ˈgrʌbi/ *adjective* (**grubbier**, **grubbiest**) dirty: *grubby hands*

grumble /ˈgrʌmbl/ *verb* (**grumbles**, **grumbling**, **grumbled** /ˈgrʌmbld/) say many times that you do not like something: *My parents are always grumbling about prices.*

grumpy /ˈgrʌmpi/ *adjective* (**grumpier**, **grumpiest**) a little angry; bad-tempered: *She gets grumpy when she's tired.*

grunt /grʌnt/ *verb* (**grunts**, **grunting**, **grunted**) make a short rough sound, like a pig makes
grunt *noun*: *She didn't say anything — she just gave a grunt.*

guarantee /ˌgærənˈtiː/ *noun* **1** a special promise on paper that a company will repair a thing you have bought, or give you a new one, if it goes wrong:

This watch has a two-year guarantee. **2** a promise that something will happen: *I want a guarantee that you will do the work today.*

guarantee *verb* (**guarantees**, **guaranteeing**, **guaranteed** /ˌgærənˈtiːd/)
1 say that you will repair a thing that somebody buys, or give them a new one, if it goes wrong: *The television is guaranteed for three years.* **2** promise something: *I can't guarantee that I will be able to help you, but I'll try.*

guard[1] /gɑːd/ *verb* (**guards**, **guarding**, **guarded**) keep somebody or something safe from other people, or stop somebody from escaping: *The house was guarded by two large dogs.*

guard[2] /gɑːd/ *noun* **1** a person who keeps somebody or something safe from other people, or who stops somebody from escaping: *There are guards outside the palace.* **2** a person whose job is to look after people and things on a train **on guard** guarding: *The soldiers were on guard outside the airport.*

guardian /ˈgɑːdiən/ *noun* a person who looks after a child with no parents

guava /ˈgwɑːvə/ *noun* (*plural* **guava** or **guavas**) a fruit that has yellow skin and is pink inside

guerrilla /gəˈrɪlə/ *noun* a person who is not in an army but who fights secretly against the government or an army

guess /ges/ *verb* (**guesses**, **guessing**, **guessed** /gest/) give an answer when you do not know if it is right: *Can you guess how old he is?*
guess *noun* (*plural* **guesses**) *If you don't know the answer, have a guess!*

guest /gest/ *noun* **1** a person that you invite to your home, to a party, etc: *There were 200 guests at the wedding.* **2** a person who is staying in a hotel
guest-house /ˈgest haʊs/ *noun* (*plural* **guest-houses** /ˈgest haʊzɪz/) a small hotel

guidance /ˈgaɪdns/ *noun* (no plural) help and advice: *I want some guidance on how to find a job.*

guide[1] /gaɪd/ *noun* **1** a person who shows other people where to go and tells them about a place: *The guide took us round the town.* **2** (*also* **guidebook**) a book that tells you about a town, country, etc **3** a book that tells you about something, or how to do something: *a guide to computing* **4 Guide = Girl Guide**

guide² /gaɪd/ *verb* (**guides**, **guiding**, **guided**) show somebody where to go or what to do: *He guided us through the busy streets to our hotel.*

guilt /gɪlt/ *noun* (no plural) **1** having done something wrong: *The police could not prove his guilt.* ✪ opposite: **innocence**. **2** the feeling that you have when you know that you have done something wrong: *She felt terrible guilt after stealing the money.*

guilty /ˈgɪlti/ *adjective* (**guiltier**, **guiltiest**) **1** If you are guilty, you have done something wrong: *He is guilty of murder.* ✪ opposite: **innocent**. **2** If you feel guilty, you feel that you have done something wrong: *I feel guilty about lying to her.*

guinea fowl /ˈgɪni faʊl/ *noun* (*plural* **guinea fowl** or **guinea fowls**) a large bird that you can eat with grey feathers and white spots

guinea-pig /ˈgɪni pɪg/ *noun* **1** a small animal that people keep as a pet **2** a person who is used in an experiment

Guinea worm /ˈgɪni wɛm/ *noun* a long worm that lives under a person's skin

guitar /gɪˈtɑː(r)/ *noun* a musical instrument with strings: *I play the guitar in a band.*

guitarist /gɪˈtɑːrɪst/ *noun* a person who plays the guitar

gulf /gʌlf/ *noun* a large area of sea that has land almost all the way around it: *the Gulf of Mexico*

gull /gʌl/ *noun* a large grey or white bird that lives by the sea; a seagull

gulp /gʌlp/ *verb* (**gulps**, **gulping**, **gulped** /gʌlpt/) eat or drink something quickly: *He gulped down a cup of tea and left.*

gulp *noun*: *She took a gulp of coffee.*

gum /gʌm/ *noun* **1** (*plural* **gums**) Your gums are the hard pink parts of your mouth that hold the teeth. **2** (no plural) thick liquid that you use for sticking pieces of paper together ☞ Look also at **chewing-gum**.

gun /gʌn/ *noun* a thing that shoots out pieces of metal (called **bullets**) to kill or hurt people or animals: *He pointed the gun at the bird and fired.*

gun

gunman /ˈgʌnmən/ *noun* (*plural* **gunmen** /ˈgʌnmən/) a man who shoots another person with a gun

gunpowder /ˈgʌnpaʊdə(r)/ *noun* (no plural) powder that explodes. It is used in guns and fireworks.

gush /gʌʃ/ *verb* (**gushes**, **gushing**, **gushed** /gʌʃt/) flow out suddenly and strongly: *Blood was gushing from the cut in her leg.*

gust /gʌst/ *noun* a sudden strong wind: *A gust of wind blew his hat off.*

gutter /ˈgʌtə(r)/ *noun* **1** a pipe under the edge of a roof to carry away rainwater **2** the part at the edge of a road where water is carried away

guy /gaɪ/ *noun* a man: *He's a nice guy!*

gymnasium /dʒɪmˈneɪziəm/ *noun* a room where you do exercises for your body ✪ The short form is **gym**.

gymnastics /dʒɪmˈnæstɪks/ *noun* (plural) exercises for your body ✪ The short form is **gym**.

habit /ˈhæbɪt/ *noun* something that you do very often: *Smoking is a bad habit.* ○ *She's got a habit of touching her hair when she talks.*

habitat /ˈhæbɪtæt/ *noun* the natural place where a plant or animal lives

had *form of* **have**

hadn't /ˈhædnt/ = **had not**

ha! ha! /ˌhɑː ˈhɑː/ *words that you write to show that somebody is laughing*

hair /heə(r)/ *noun* **1** (*plural* **hairs**) one of the long thin things that grow on the skin of people and animals: *There's a hair in my food.* **2** (no plural) all the hairs on a person's head: *She's got long hair.* ☛ picture on page A4

> ✪ You wash your hair with **shampoo** and make it tidy with a **hairbrush** or a **comb**. Some words that you can use to talk about the colour of a person's hair are **black**, **dark**, **brown**, **red**, **fair**, **blond** and **grey**.

hairbrush /ˈheəbrʌʃ/ *noun* (*plural* **hairbrushes**) a brush that you use to make your hair tidy

haircut /ˈheəkʌt/ *noun* **1** when somebody cuts your hair: *I need a haircut.* **2** the way that your hair is cut: *I like your new haircut.*

hairdresser /ˈheədresə(r)/ *noun* a person whose job is to wash, cut and arrange hair ✪ The place where a hairdresser works is called a **hairdresser's**: *I'm going to the hairdressers to get my hair cut.*

hairstyle /ˈheəstaɪl/ *noun* the way that your hair is cut and arranged

hairy /ˈheəri/ *adjective* (**hairier**, **hairiest**) covered with hair: *He has got hairy legs.*

half /hɑːf/ *noun* (*plural* **halves** /hɑːvz/) *adjective, pronoun* one of two equal parts of something; ½: *Half of six is three.* ○ *I lived in Britain for two and a half years.* ○ *The journey takes an hour and a half.* ○ *She gave me half of her food.* **in half** so that there are two equal parts: *Cut the melon in half.*

half *adverb* 50%; partly: *The bottle is half empty.* **half past** 30 minutes after an hour on the clock: *It's half past nine.* ☛ Look at page A8.

half-price /ˌhɑːf ˈpraɪs/ *adjective, adverb* for half the usual price: *Children travel half-price on this bus.*

half-time /ˌhɑːf ˈtaɪm/ *noun* (no plural) a short time in the middle of a game like football, when you are not playing

halfway /ˌhɑːfˈweɪ/ *adverb* in the middle: *They live halfway between Mombasa and Nairobi.* ○ *She went out halfway through the lesson.*

hall /hɔːl/ *noun* **1** a big room or building where a lot of people meet: *a concert hall* ○ *We did our exams in the school hall.* **2** the room in a house that is near the front door and has doors to other rooms: *You can leave your coat in the hall.*

hallo = **hello**

halt /hɔːlt/ *noun* (no plural) **come to a halt** stop: *The car came to a halt.*

halve /hɑːv/ *verb* (**halves**, **halving**, **halved** /hɑːvd/) divide something into two parts that are the same: *There were two of us, so I halved the orange.*

halves *plural of* **half**

ham /hæm/ *noun* (no plural) meat from a pig's leg that you can keep for a long time because salt or smoke was used to prepare it ☛ Note at **pig**.

hamburger /ˈhæmbɜːgə(r)/ *noun* meat cut into very small pieces and made into a flat round shape, that you eat between two pieces of bread: *A hamburger and chips, please.*

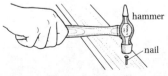

hammer

nail

hammer /ˈhæmə(r)/ *noun* a tool with a handle and a heavy metal part, that you use for hitting **nails** into things

hammer *verb* (**hammers**, **hammer-**

ing, **hammered** /ˈhæməd/) **1** hit something with a hammer: *I hammered the nail into the wood.* **2** hit something hard: *He hammered on the door until somebody opened it.*

hammock /ˈhæmək/ *noun* a bed made of cloth or rope that you hang up at the two ends

hand[1] /hænd/ *noun* **1** the part at the end of your arm: *She held the letter in her hand.* ☞ picture on page A4. **2** one of the parts of a clock or watch that move to show the time **a hand** some help: *Could you give me a hand with my homework?* **by hand** without using a machine: *These shoes are made by hand.* **get out of hand** become difficult to control: *The party got out of hand.* **hand in hand** with your hand in another person's hand **hands up 1** put one hand in the air if you can answer the question **2** put your hands in the air because somebody has a gun **hold hands** have another person's hand in your hand **in good hands** well looked after: *Don't worry — your son is in good hands.* **on hand** near and ready to help: *There is a doctor on hand 24 hours a day.* **on the one hand... on the other hand** words that show the good and bad things about an idea: *On the one hand it's a very interesting job, but on the other hand it's not well-paid.*

hold hands

hand[2] /hænd/ *verb* (**hands**, **handing**, **handed**) put something into somebody's hand: *Can you hand me the scissors, please?* ○ *I handed my homework to the teacher.* **hand down** pass a thing, story, etc from an older person to a younger one: *He never had new clothes — they were handed down from his older brothers.* **hand in** give something to somebody: *The teacher asked us to hand in our homework.* **hand out** give something to many people: *Please hand out these books.* **hand over** give something to somebody: *'Hand over that knife!' said the police officer.*

handbag /ˈhændbæg/ *noun* a small bag for carrying things like money and keys

handcuffs /ˈhændkʌfs/ *noun* (plural) two metal rings with a chain that are put on a prisoner's arms so that he/she cannot use his/her hands

handful /ˈhændfʊl/ *noun* **1** as much as you can hold in one hand: *a handful of stones* **2** a small number: *Only a handful of people came to the meeting.*

handicap /ˈhændikæp/ *noun* something that stops you doing well: *a school for children with physical handicaps*

handicapped /ˈhændikæpt/ *adjective* not able to use a part of your body well: *They have a handicapped son.*

handkerchief /ˈhæŋkətʃɪf/ *noun* a square piece of cloth or paper that you use for cleaning your nose

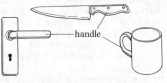

handle

handle[1] /ˈhændl/ *noun* the part of a thing that you hold in your hand: *I turned the handle and opened the door.* ○ *Hold that knife by the handle.*

handle[2] /ˈhændl/ *verb* (**handles**, **handling**, **handled** /ˈhændld/) **1** touch something with your hands: *Please wash your hands before you handle the food.* **2** control somebody or something: *That dog is too big for a small child to handle.* **3** look after something and do what is necessary: *My secretary handles all letters.*

handlebars /ˈhændlbɑːz/ *noun* (plural) the part at the front of a bicycle or motor cycle that you hold when you are riding it ☞ picture at **bicycle**

handmade /ˌhændˈmeɪd/ *adjective* made by a person, not by a machine: *handmade clothes*

handsome /ˈhænsəm/ *adjective* good-looking: *a handsome man* ☞ Note at **beautiful**.

handwriting /ˈhændraɪtɪŋ/ *noun* (no

plural) the way you write: *Her hand-writing is difficult to read.*

handy /'hændi/ *adjective* (**handier**, **handiest**) **1** useful: *This bag will be handy for carrying my books.* **2** near and easy to find or reach: *Have you got a pen handy?* **come in handy** be useful: *Don't throw that box away — it might come in handy for something.*

hang /hæŋ/ *verb* **1** (**hangs**, **hanging**, **hung** /hʌŋ/, **has hung**) fix something, or be fixed at the top so that the lower part is free: *Hang your coat (up) on the hook.* ○ *I hung the washing on the line to dry.* **2** (**hangs**, **hanging**, **hanged** /hæŋd/, **has hanged**) kill somebody by holding them above the ground by a rope around the neck: *He was hanged for murder.* **hang about**, **hang around** stay somewhere with nothing special to do: *My plane was late so I had to hang about in the airport all morning.* **hang on** wait: *Hang on — I'm not ready.* **hang on to somebody** or **something** hold something firmly: *Hang on to your purse.* **hang up** end a telephone call by putting the telephone down

hanger /'hæŋə(r)/ *noun* a coat-hanger; a piece of metal, wood or plastic with a hook. You use it for hanging clothes on. ☛ picture at **coat-hanger**

hanky, **hankie** /'hæŋki/ *noun* (*plural* **hankies**) a handkerchief

happen /'hæpən/ *verb* (**happens**, **happening**, **happened** /'hæpənd/) take place: *How did the accident happen?* ○ *Did you hear what happened to me yesterday?* **happen to** do something by chance: *I happened to meet Tim yesterday.*

happy /'hæpi/ *adjective* (**happier**, **happiest**) **1** If you are happy, you feel very pleased. People often laugh or smile when they are happy: *She looks very happy.* ○ *That was one of the happiest days of my life.* ✪ opposite: **unhappy** or **sad** ☛ picture on page A10. **2** a word that you use to say that you hope somebody will enjoy a special time: *Happy New Year!* ○ *Happy Christmas!* ○ *Happy Birthday!* ✪ **Many happy returns (of the day)** means the same as **Happy Birthday**.

happily /'hæpɪli/ *adverb* **1** in a happy way **2** it is lucky that: *Happily, the accident was not serious.*

happiness /'hæpɪnəs/ *noun* (no plural) being happy

harambee /'hɑːrɑːmbeɪ/ *noun* (no plural) a Swahili word that means 'pull together'. In Kenya, a harambee meeting is a meeting held to raise money for something: *The school committee held a harambee meeting to raise funds for two new classrooms.*

harbour /'hɑːbə(r)/ *noun* a place where ships can stay safely in the water

hard[1] /hɑːd/ *adjective* (**harder**, **hardest**) **1** not soft; firm: *These apples are very hard.* ○ *I couldn't sleep because the bed was too hard.* ✪ opposite: **soft**. ☛ picture on page A11. **2** difficult to do or understand: *The exam was very hard.* ○ *hard work* ☛ Look at **easy**. **3** full of problems: *He's had a hard life.* **4** not kind or gentle: *She is very hard on her children.*

hard[2] /hɑːd/ *adverb* **1** a lot: *She works very hard.* ○ *You must try harder!* **2** strongly: *It's raining hard.* ○ *She hit him hard.*

hardback /'hɑːdbæk/ *noun* a book with a hard cover ☛ Look at **paperback**.

hard disk /ˌhɑːd 'dɪsk/ *noun* a plastic part inside a computer that stores information

harden /'hɑːdn/ *verb* (**hardens**, **hardening**, **hardened** /'hɑːdnd/) become hard: *Wait for the cement to harden.*

hardly /'hɑːdli/ *adverb* almost not; only just: *She spoke so quietly that I could hardly hear her.* ○ *There's hardly any* (= almost no) *coffee left.*

hare /heə(r)/ *noun* an animal like a big rabbit. Hares have long ears and can run very fast.

harm[1] /hɑːm/ *noun* (no plural) hurt or damage **come to harm** be hurt or damaged: *Make sure the children don't come to any harm.* **there is no harm in** nothing bad will happen if you do something: *I don't know if she'll help you, but there's no harm in asking.*

harm[2] /hɑːm/ *verb* (**harms**, **harming**,

harmed /hɑːmd/) hurt or damage somebody or something: *The dog won't harm you.*

harmful /'hɑːmfl/ *adjective* Something that is harmful can hurt or damage people or things: *Strong sunlight can be harmful to young babies.*

harmless /'hɑːmləs/ *adjective* not dangerous: *Don't be frightened – these insects are harmless.*

harmony /'hɑːməni/ *noun* **1** (no plural) having the same ideas, etc, with no arguments: *The different races live together in harmony.* **2** (plural **harmonies**) musical notes that sound nice together: *They sang in harmony.*

harsh /hɑːʃ/ *adjective* (**harsher**, **harshest**) **1** rough and unpleasant to see or hear: *a harsh voice* **2** not kind; cruel: *a harsh punishment*

harvest /'hɑːvɪst/ *noun* **1** the time when fruit, corn or vegetables are ready to cut or pick: *Extra workers are needed at harvest time.* **2** all the fruit, corn or vegetables that are cut or picked: *We had a good harvest this year.*

harvest *verb* (**harvests**, **harvesting**, **harvested**) *When does the farmer harvest his wheat?*

has *form of* **have**

hasn't /'hæznt/ = **has not**

haste /heɪst/ *noun* (no plural) doing things too quickly: *In his haste to get up, he knocked over the chair.* **in haste** quickly; in a hurry: *The letter was written in haste.*

hasty /'heɪsti/ *adjective* (**hastier**, **hastiest**) **1** If you are hasty, you do something too quickly: *Don't be too hasty. This is a very important decision.* **2** said or done quickly: *We ate a hasty lunch, then left.*

hastily /'heɪstɪli/ *adverb*: *He put the money hastily into his pocket.*

hats

hat /hæt/ *noun* a thing that you wear on your head: *She's wearing a hat.*

hatch /hætʃ/ *verb* (**hatches**, **hatching**, **hatched** /hætʃt/) When baby birds, insects, fish, etc hatch, they come out of an egg.

hate /heɪt/ *verb* (**hates**, **hating**, **hated**) have a very strong feeling of not liking somebody or something: *Most cats hate water.* ○ *I hate waiting for buses.*

hate, **hatred** /'heɪtrɪd/ *noun* (no plural) a very strong feeling of not liking somebody or something

haul /hɔːl/ *verb* (**hauls**, **hauling**, **hauled** /hɔːld/) pull something heavy: *They hauled the boat out of the river.*

haunt /hɔːnt/ *verb* (**haunts**, **haunting**, **haunted**) **1** If a ghost haunts a place, it visits it often: *A ghost haunts the village.* **2** If something sad or unpleasant haunts you, you often think of it: *Her unhappy face still haunts me.*

haunted *adjective* often visited by ghosts: *a haunted house*

have[1] /həv/, /hæv/ *verb* a word that you use with parts of other verbs to

have[1]

present tense		short forms		negative short forms	
I	**have**	I**'ve**		I	**haven't**
you	**have**	you**'ve**		you	**haven't**
he/she/it	**has** /hæz/	he**'s**/she**'s**/it**'s**		he/she/it	**hasn't**
we	**have**	we**'ve**		we	**haven't**
you	**have**	you**'ve**		you	**haven't**
they	**have**	they**'ve**		they	**haven't**

past tense **had** /hæd/

present participle **having**

past participle **had**

show that something happened or started in the past: *I have seen that man before.* ○ *We have been here for two hours.* ○ *When we arrived, Nelima had already left.* ✪ verb table on previous page

have² /hæv/ *verb* (**has** /hæz/, **having**, **had** /hæd/, **has had**) **1** (*also* **have got**) own or keep something: *She has lovely eyes.* ○ *They have got a big farm.* ○ *Do you have any brothers and sisters?* **2** be ill with something; feel something: *She has got a headache.* **3** eat or drink something: *What time do you have breakfast?* **4** a word that shows that something happens to somebody or something: *I had a shower.* ○ *He has had an accident.* ○ *Did you have a good journey?* **5** (*also* **have got**) a word that you use with some nouns: *I have an idea.* ○ *Have you got time to help me?* **have to, have got to** must: *I have to/ have got to go to school tomorrow.* ○ *We don't have to/ haven't got to get up early tomorrow.* ○ *Do we have to/ have we got to pay for this now?* **have something done** let somebody do something for you: *I had my hair cut yesterday.* ○ *Have you had your car mended?*

haven't /ˈhævnt/ = **have not**

hawk /hɔːk/ *noun* a big bird that catches and eats other birds and small animals

hay /heɪ/ *noun* (no plural) dry grass that is used as food for farm animals

hay fever /ˈheɪ fiːvə(r)/ *noun* (no plural) an illness like a cold. Grass and other plants can cause hay fever.

hazard /ˈhæzəd/ *noun* a danger: *Animals are a hazard for drivers.*

hazardous /ˈhæzədəs/ *adjective* dangerous: *a hazardous journey*

he /hiː/ *pronoun* (*plural* **they**) the man or boy that the sentence is about: *I saw Mike when he arrived.* ○ *'Where is John?' 'He's* (= he is) *at home.'*

head¹ /hed/ *noun* **1** the part of your body above your neck, that has your eyes, ears, nose and mouth in it: *She turned her head to look at me.* ☞ picture on page A4. **2** what you use for thinking: *A strange thought came into his head.* **3** the top, front or most important part: *She sat at the head of the table.*

4 the most important person: *Mrs Ogonwe is head of the council.* **5** **heads** (plural) the side of a coin that has the head of a person on it ✪ You say **heads or tails** when you are throwing a coin in the air to decide something, for example who will start a game. **a head, per head** for one person: *The meal cost 150 shillings a head.* **go to your head** make you too pleased with yourself: *Winning a prize for his painting went to his head, and he began to think he was a great artist.* **head first** with your head before the rest of your body

> ✪ You **nod** your head (move it up and down) to say 'yes' or to show that you agree, and you **shake** your head (move it from side to side) to say 'no' or to show that you disagree.

head² /hed/ *verb* (**heads**, **heading**, **headed**) **1** be at the front or top of a group: *Michael's name heads the list.* **2** hit a ball with your head: *Okocha headed Nigeria's second goal.* **head for** go towards a place: *Let's head for home.*

headache /ˈhedeɪk/ *noun* a pain in your head: *I've got a headache.*

heading /ˈhedɪŋ/ *noun* the words at the top of a piece of writing to show what it is about; a title

headlight /ˈhedlaɪt/ (*also* **headlamp**) /ˈhedlæmp/ *noun* one of the two big strong lights on the front of a car ☞ picture at **car**

headline /ˈhedlaɪn/ *noun* **1** words in big letters at the top of a newspaper story **2** **the headlines** (plural) the most important news on radio or television: *Here are the news headlines.*

headmaster /ˌhedˈmɑːstə(r)/ *noun* a man who is in charge of a school

headmistress /ˌhedˈmɪstrəs/ *noun* (*plural* **headmistresses**) a woman who is in charge of a school

headphones /ˈhedfəʊnz/ *noun*

headphones

(plural) things that you put over your head and ears for listening to a radio, cassette player, etc

headquarters /ˌhedˈkwɔːtəz/ *noun* (plural) the main offices where the leaders work: *The company's headquarters are in London.* ✪ The short form is **HQ.**

headway /ˈhedweɪ/ *noun* (no plural) **make headway** go forward: *We haven't made much headway in our discussions.*

heal /hiːl/ *verb* (**heals**, **healing**, **healed** /hiːld/) become well again; make something well again: *The cut on his leg healed slowly.*

health /helθ/ *noun* (no plural) how well your body is; how you are: *Smoking is bad for your health.*

healthy /ˈhelθi/ *adjective* (**healthier**, **healthiest**) **1** well; not ill: *healthy children* **2** that helps to make or keep you well: *healthy food* ✪ opposite: **unhealthy**

heap /hiːp/ *noun* **1** a lot of things on top of one another in an untidy way; a large amount of something: *She left her clothes in a heap on the floor.* **2 heaps** (plural) a lot: *heaps of time*

heap *verb* (**heaps**, **heaping**, **heaped** /hiːpt/) put a lot of things on top of one another: *She heaped food onto my plate.*

hear or **listen**?

Hear and **listen** are used in different ways. When you **hear** something, sounds come to your ears:

*I **heard** the door close.*

When you **listen to** something, you are trying to hear it:

*I **listen to** the radio every morning.*

hear /hɪə(r)/ *verb* (**hears**, **hearing**, **heard** /hɜːd/, **has heard**) **1** get sounds with your ears: *Can you hear that noise?* ○ *I heard somebody laughing in the next room.* **2** learn about something with your ears: *Have you heard the news?* **hear from somebody** get a letter or a phone call from somebody: *Have you heard from your sister?* **hear of somebody** or **something** know about somebody or something: *Who is he? I've never heard of him.* **will not**

hear of something will not agree to something: *My father wouldn't hear of me paying for the meal.*

hearing /ˈhɪərɪŋ/ *noun* (no plural) the power to hear: *Speak louder – her hearing isn't very good.*

heart /hɑːt/ *noun* **1** the part of a person's or animal's body that makes the blood go round inside: *Your heart beats faster when you run.* ☛ picture on page A4. **2** your feelings: *She has a kind heart.* **3** the centre; the middle part: *They live in the heart of the countryside.* **4** the shape ♥ **5 hearts** (plural) the playing-cards that have red shapes like hearts on them: *the six of hearts* **break somebody's heart** make somebody very sad: *It broke his heart when his wife died.* **by heart** so that you know every word: *I have learned the poem by heart.* **lose heart** stop hoping: *Don't lose heart – you can still win if you try.* **your heart sinks** you suddenly feel unhappy: *My heart sank when I saw the first question on the exam paper.*

heart attack /ˈhɑːt ətæk/ *noun* a sudden dangerous illness, when your heart stops working properly: *She had a heart attack and died.*

heartbeat /ˈhɑːtbiːt/ *noun* the movement or sound of your heart as it pushes blood around your body: *The doctor listened to my heartbeat.*

heartless /ˈhɑːtləs/ *adjective* not kind; cruel

heat /hiːt/ *noun* **1** (no plural) the feeling of something hot: *the heat of the sun* **2** (*plural* **heats**) one of the first parts of a race or competition: *The winner of this heat will run in the final.*

heat, **heat up** *verb* (**heats**, **heating**, **heated**) make something hot; become hot: *I heated some water in a saucepan.* ○ *Wait for the oven to heat up before you put the food in.*

heath /hiːθ/ *noun* a big piece of wild land where there are no farms

heave /hiːv/ *verb* (**heaves**, **heaving**, **heaved** /hiːvd/) lift or pull something heavy: *We heaved the suitcase up the stairs.*

heaven /ˈhevn/ *noun* (no plural) Many

people believe that God lives in heaven and that good people go to heaven when they die. ☞ Look at **hell**. **Good Heavens!** words that you use to show surprise: *Good Heavens! I've won first prize!*

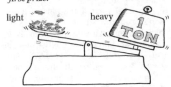

light   heavy

heavy /'hevi/ *adjective* (**heavier**, **heaviest**) **1** with a lot of weight, so it is difficult to lift or move: *I can't carry this bag — it's too heavy.* **2** larger, stronger or more than usual: *heavy rain* ○ *The traffic was very heavy this morning.* ✪ opposite: **light**

heavy metal /ˌhevi 'metl/ *noun* (no plural) a kind of very loud rock music

heavily /'hevəli/ *adverb*: *It was raining heavily.*

hectare /'hekteə(r)/ *noun* a measure of land. There are 10 000 **square metres** in a hectare.

hectic /'hektɪk/ *adjective* very busy: *I had a hectic day at work.*

he'd /hi:d/ **1** = **he had** **2** = **he would**

hedge /hedʒ/ *noun* a line of small trees that makes a kind of wall around a garden or field

heel /hi:l/ *noun* **1** the back part of your foot ☞ picture on page A4. **2** the back part of a shoe under the heel of your foot **3** the part of a sock that covers the heel of your foot

height /haɪt/ *noun* **1** (*plural* **heights**) how far it is from the bottom to the top of somebody or something: *What is the height of this mountain?* ○ *The wall is two metres in height.* ○ *She asked me my height, weight and age.* ☞ picture on page A5. **2** (*plural* **heights**) a high place: *I'm afraid of heights.* **3** (no plural) the strongest or most important part of something: *the height of summer*

heir /eə(r)/ *noun* a person who receives money, goods, etc when another person dies: *Prince Charles is Queen Elizabeth's heir.*

heiress /'eəres/ *noun* (*plural* **heiresses**) an heir who is a woman

held *form of* **hold**[1]

helicopter

helicopter /'helɪkɒptə(r)/ *noun* a kind of small aircraft that can go straight up in the air. It has long metal parts on top that turn to help it fly.

he'll /hi:l/ = **he will**

hell /hel/ *noun* (no plural) Some people believe that bad people go to hell when they die. ☞ Look at **heaven**.

hello /hə'ləʊ/ a word that you say when you meet somebody or when you answer the telephone

helmet /'helmɪt/ *noun* a hard hat that keeps your head safe: *The motor cyclist survived the crash because he was wearing a helmet.*

help /help/ *verb* (**helps**, **helping**, **helped** /helpt/) **1** do something useful for somebody; make somebody's work easier: *Will you help me with the washing-up?* ○ *She helped me to carry the box.* **2** a word that you shout when you are in danger: *Help! I can't swim!* **can't help** If you can't help doing something, you can't stop yourself doing it: *It was so funny that I couldn't help laughing.* **help yourself** take what you want: *Help yourself to a drink.* ○ *'Can I have a drink?' 'Of course. Help yourself!'*

help *noun* (no plural) **1** helping somebody: *Thank you for all your help.* ○ *Do you need any help?* **2** a person or thing that helps: *He was a great help to me when I was ill.*

helpful /'helpfl/ *adjective* A person or thing that is helpful gives help: *The woman in the shop was very helpful.* ○ *helpful advice* ✪ opposite: **unhelpful**

helpless /'helpləs/ *adjective* not able to do things without help: *Babies are totally helpless.*

hem /hem/ *noun* the bottom edge of something like a shirt or trousers, that is folded and sewn

hemisphere /'hemɪsfɪə(r)/ *noun* one half of the earth: *the northern/southern hemisphere*

hen /hen/ *noun* **1** a female bird that people keep on farms for its eggs ➥ Note at **chicken**. **2** any female bird ✪ A male bird is a **cock**.

hepatitis /ˌhepə'taɪtɪs/ *noun* (no plural) a serious illness of the liver

her[1] /hɜː(r)/ *pronoun* (*plural* **them**) a word that shows a woman or a girl: *Tell your mother that I'll see her tonight.* ○ *I wrote to her yesterday.*

her[2] /hɜː(r)/ *adjective* the woman or girl that you have just talked about: *That's her book.* ○ *Mrs Rono has hurt her leg.*

herb /hɜːb/ *noun* a plant that people use to make food taste good, or in medicine

herd /hɜːd/ *noun* a big group of animals of the same kind: *a herd of cows* ○ *a herd of elephants*

here /hɪə(r)/ *adverb* in, at or to this place: *Your glasses are here.* ○ *Come here, please.* ○ *Here's my car.* ○ *Where's Daniel? Oh, here he is.* **here and there** in different places: *There were groups of people here and there along the beach.* **here goes** words that you say before you do something exciting or dangerous: *'Here goes,' said Henry, and jumped into the river.* **here you are** words that you say when you give something to somebody: *'Can I borrow a pen, please?' 'Yes, here you are.'*

here's /hɪəz/ = **here is**

hero /'hɪərəʊ/ *noun* (*plural* **heroes**) **1** a person who has done something brave or good: *Everybody said that Kiprotich was a hero after he rescued his sister from the fire.* **2** the most important man or boy in a book, play or film

heroic /hə'rəʊɪk/ *adjective* very brave

heroin /'herəʊɪn/ *noun* (no plural) a very strong drug that can be dangerous

heroine /'herəʊɪn/ *noun* **1** a woman who has done something brave or good **2** the most important woman or girl in a book, play or film

hers /hɜːz/ *pronoun* something that belongs to her: *Mrs Naddangira says this book is hers.* ○ *Are these keys hers?*

herself /hɜː'self/ *pronoun* (*plural* **themselves** /ðəm'selvz/) **1** a word that shows the same woman or girl that you have just talked about: *She fell and hurt herself.* **2** a word that makes 'she' stronger: *'Who told you that Jane was married?' 'She told me herself.'* **by herself 1** alone; without other people: *She lives by herself.* **2** without help: *She can carry the box by herself.*

he's /hiːz/ **1** = **he is 2** = **he has**

hesitate /'hezɪteɪt/ *verb* (**hesitates**, **hesitating**, **hesitated**) stop for a moment before you do or say something because you are not sure about it: *He hesitated before answering the question.*

hesitation /ˌhezɪ'teɪʃn/ *noun* (no plural) *They agreed without hesitation.*

hexagon /'heksəgən/ *noun* a shape with six sides

hexagonal /hek'sægənl/ *adjective* with six sides: *a hexagonal box*

hey /heɪ/ a word that you shout to make somebody listen to you, or when you are surprised: *Hey! Where are you going?*

hi /haɪ/ a word that you say when you meet somebody; hello: *Hi Hassan! How are you?*

hiccup, **hiccough** /'hɪkʌp/ *noun* a sudden noise that you make in your throat. You sometimes get hiccups when you have eaten or drunk too quickly.

hide[1] /haɪd/ *verb* (**hides**, **hiding**, **hid** /hɪd/, **has hidden** /'hɪdn/) **1** put something where people cannot find it: *I hid the money under the bed.* **2** be or get in a place where people cannot see or find you: *Somebody was hiding behind the door.* **3** not tell or show something to somebody: *She tried to hide her feelings.*

hide-and-seek /ˌhaɪd n 'siːk/ *noun* (no plural) a game that children play. Some children hide and one child tries to find them.

hide[2] /haɪd/ *noun* the skin of a large animal

hideous /'hɪdiəs/ *adjective* very ugly: *That shirt is hideous!*

hiding /'haɪdɪŋ/ *noun* (no plural) **be in hiding**, **go into hiding** be in, or go into a place where people will not find you: *The prisoners escaped and went into hiding.*

high /haɪ/ *adjective* (**higher, highest**) **1** Something that is high goes up a long way: *a high wall* ○ *Mount Everest is the highest mountain in the world.* ✪ opposite: **low.** ☞ picture on page A10. **2** You use 'high' to say or ask how far something is from the bottom to the top: *The table is 80 cm high.* ☞ picture on page A5. ✪ We use **tall**, not **high**, to talk about people.: *How tall are you?* ○ *He's 1·72 metres tall.* **3** far from the ground: *a high shelf* **4** great: *The car was travelling at high speed.* ○ *high temperatures* **5** at the top of sound; not deep: *I heard the high voice of a child.* ☞ Look at **low.**

high *adverb* a long way above the ground: *The plane flew high above the clouds.* **high and low** everywhere: *I've looked high and low for my keys, but I can't find them anywhere.*

high-jump /ˈhaɪ dʒʌmp/ *noun* (no plural) a sport where people jump over a high bar

highlands /ˈhaɪləndz/ *noun* (plural) the part of a country with hills and mountains: *the Kenyan Highlands*

highlight /ˈhaɪlaɪt/ *noun* the best or most exciting part of something: *The highlight of the show was when everyone sang together.*

highly /ˈhaɪli/ *adverb* **1** very or very much: *Their children are highly intelligent.* ○ *She has a highly paid job.* **2** very well: *I think very highly of your work* (= I think it is very good).

Highness /ˈhaɪnəs/ *noun* (plural **Highnesses**) a word that you use when speaking to or about a royal person: *His Highness the Prince of Wales*

high school /ˈhaɪ skuːl/ *noun* a kind of secondary school in some countries that you go to until you are 18 or 19 years old

high street /ˈhaɪ striːt/ *noun* the biggest or most important street in a town

highway /ˈhaɪweɪ/ *noun* a big road between towns ✪ **Highway** is used mostly in American English.

hijack /ˈhaɪdʒæk/ *verb* (**hijacks, hijacking, hijacked** /ˈhaɪdʒækt/) take control of an aeroplane or a car and make the pilot or driver take you somewhere

hijacker *noun* a person who hijacks a plane or car

hill /hɪl/ *noun* a high piece of land that is not as high as a mountain: *I pushed my bike up the hill.* ○ *Their house is at the top of the hill.* ☞ Look also at **uphill** and **downhill.**

hilly *adjective* (**hillier, hilliest**) with a lot of hills: *The countryside is very hilly where I live.*

him /hɪm/ *pronoun* (plural **them**) a word that shows a man or boy: *Where's Mohammed? I can't see him.* ○ *I spoke to him yesterday.*

himself /hɪmˈself/ *pronoun* (plural **themselves** /ðəmˈselvz/) **1** a word that shows the same man or boy that you have just talked about: *Paul looked at himself in the mirror.* **2** a word that makes 'he' stronger: *Did he make this himself?* **by himself 1** alone; without other people: *Dad went shopping by himself.* **2** without help: *He did it by himself.*

Hindu /ˈhɪnduː/ *noun* a person who follows one of the religions of India, called **Hinduism**

hinge /hɪndʒ/ *noun* a piece of metal that joins two sides of a box, door, etc together so that it can open and close

hint /hɪnt/ *verb* (**hints, hinting, hinted**) say something, but not in a direct way: *Sarah looked at her watch, hinting that she wanted to go home.*

hint *noun* **1** something that you say, but not in a direct way: *When he said he had no money, it was a hint that he wanted to borrow some from you.* **2** a small amount of something: *There was a hint of anger in her voice.*

hip /hɪp/ *noun* the place where your leg joins the side of your body ☞ picture on page A4

hippopotamus /ˌhɪpəˈpɒtəməs/ *noun* (plural **hippopotamuses** or **hippopotami** /ˌhɪpəˈpɒtəmaɪ/) a large animal with thick skin that lives in and near water ✪ The short form is **hippo.**

hire /ˈhaɪə(r)/ *verb* (**hires**, **hiring**, **hired** /ˈhaɪəd/) **1** pay to use something for a short time: *We had to hire some machinery when we built the house.* **2** pay somebody to do a job for you: *We hired somebody to mend the roof.* **hire out** let somebody hire something from you: *They hire out forklifts.*

hire *noun* (no plural) *Have you got any boats for hire?*

his /hɪz/ *adjective* of him: *John came with his sister.* ○ *He has hurt his arm.*

his *pronoun* something that belongs to him: *Are these books yours or his?*

hiss /hɪs/ *verb* (**hisses**, **hissing**, **hissed** /hɪst/) make a noise like a very long **S**: *The cat hissed at me.*

hiss *noun* (*plural* **hisses**) *the hiss of steam*

historic /hɪˈstɒrɪk/ *adjective* important in history: *It was a historic moment when man first walked on the moon.*

historical /hɪˈstɒrɪkl/ *adjective* of or about past times: *Mandela's release from prison was an important historical event.*

history /ˈhɪstri/ *noun* (no plural) **1** the study of things that happened in the past: *History is my favourite subject at school.* **2** all the things that happened in the past: *It was an important moment in history.*

hit[1] /hɪt/ *verb* (**hits**, **hitting**, **hit**, **has hit**) touch somebody or something hard: *He hit me on the head with a book.* ○ *The car hit a wall.*

hit[2] /hɪt/ *noun* **1** touching somebody or something hard: *That was a good hit!* (in a game of cricket or baseball, for example) **2** a person or a thing that a lot of people like: *This song was a hit last year.*

hitchhike /ˈhɪtʃhaɪk/, (*also* **hitch**) *verb* (**hitchhikes**, **hitchhiking**, **hitchhiked** /ˈhɪtʃhaɪkt/, **hitches**, **hitching**, **hitched** /hɪtʃt/) travel by asking for free rides in cars and lorries: *We hitchhiked to the coast.*

hitchhiker *noun* a person who hitchhikes

HIV /ˌeɪtʃ aɪ ˈviː/ *noun* (no plural) a very small living thing (a **virus**) that can make a person get a very serious illness (called AIDS): *He is HIV positive* (= he has the virus in his body).

hive /haɪv/ *noun* a box where bees live

hoard /hɔːd/ *noun* a secret store of something, for example food or money

hoard *verb* (**hoards**, **hoarding**, **hoarded**) save and keep things secretly: *The old man hoarded the money in a box under his bed.*

hoarse /hɔːs/ *adjective* If your voice is hoarse, it is rough and quiet, for example because you have a cold.

hoax /həʊks/ *noun* (*plural* **hoaxes**) a trick that makes somebody believe something that is not true: *There wasn't really a bomb in the station – it was a hoax.*

hobby /ˈhɒbi/ *noun* (*plural* **hobbies**) something that you like doing when you are not working: *My hobbies are reading and football.*

hockey /ˈhɒki/ *noun* (no plural) a game for two teams of eleven players who hit a small ball with long curved sticks on a field (called a **pitch**)

hold[1] /həʊld/ *verb* (**holds**, **holding**, **held** /held/, **has held**) **1** have something in your hand or arms: *She was holding a gun.* ○ *He held the baby in his arms.* **2** keep something in a certain way: *Hold your hand up.* **3** have space for a certain number or amount: *The car holds five people.* **4** make something happen: *The meeting was held in the town hall.* **5** have something: *He holds a Ugandan passport.* **hold somebody** or **something back** stop somebody or something from moving forwards: *The police held back the crowd.* **Hold it!** Wait! Don't move! **hold on 1** wait: *Hold on, I'm coming.* **2** not stop holding something tightly: *The child held on to her mother's hand.* **hold up 1** make somebody or something late: *The bus was held up for two hours.* **2** try to steal from a place, using a gun: *Two men held up a bank in Nairobi today.*

hold[2] /həʊld/ *noun* (no plural) having something in your hand: *Can you get hold of* (= take and hold) *the other end of the table and help me move it?* **get hold of somebody** find somebody so that you can speak to them: *I'm trying* to get hold of Peter but he's not at home. **get hold of something** find something: I can't get hold of the book I need.

hold³ /həʊld/ noun the part of a ship or an aeroplane where you keep goods

hole /həʊl/ noun an empty space or opening in something: I'm going to dig a hole in the garden. ○ They are filling in the holes in the road. ○ My socks are full of holes.

holiday /ˈhɒlɪdeɪ/ noun a day or days when you do not go to work or school, and when you may go and stay away from home: The school holiday starts next week. ○ The teacher gave us our holiday homework **on holiday** not at work or school: Mrs Gombe isn't here this week. She's on holiday.

hollow /ˈhɒləʊ/ adjective with an empty space inside: A drum is hollow.

holy /ˈhəʊli/ adjective (**holier, holiest**) **1** very special because it is about God or a god: The Bible is the holy book of Christians. **2** A holy person lives a good and religious life.

home¹ /həʊm/ noun **1** the place where you live: Simon left home at the age of 18. **2** a place where they look after people, for example children who have no parents, or old people: My grandmother lives in a home. **at home** in your house or flat: I stayed at home yesterday. ○ Is Sara at home?

home² /həʊm/ adverb to the place where you live ✪ Be careful! We do not use **to** before home: Let's go home. ○ What time did you arrive home last night?

home³ /həʊm/ adjective of your home or your country: What is your home address?

homeless /ˈhəʊmləs/ adjective If you are homeless, you have nowhere to live: The floods made many people homeless.

home-made /ˌhəʊm ˈmeɪd/ adjective made in your house, not bought in a shop: home-made bread

homesick /ˈhəʊmsɪk/ adjective sad because you are away from home

homework /ˈhəʊmwɜːk/ noun (no plural) work that a teacher gives you

to do at home: Have you done your history homework? ☞ Note at **housework**.

homosexual /ˌhəʊməˈsekʃuəl/ adjective attracted to people of the same sex

honest /ˈɒnɪst/ adjective A person who is honest says what is true and does not steal or cheat: She's a very honest person. ○ Be honest – do you really like this dress? ✪ opposite: **dishonest**

honestly adverb: Try to answer the questions honestly. ○ Honestly, I don't know where your money is.

honesty /ˈɒnəsti/ noun (no plural) being honest

honey /ˈhʌni/ noun (no plural) the sweet food that bees make

honour /ˈɒnə(r)/ noun (no plural) **1** something that makes you proud and pleased: It was a great honour to be invited to meet the president. **2** the respect from other people that a person or country gets because of something very good that they have done: They are fighting for the honour of their country. **in honour of somebody** to show that you respect somebody: There is a party tonight in honour of our visitors.

hood /hʊd/ noun the part of a coat or jacket that covers your head and neck

hoof /huːf/ noun (plural **hoofs** or **hooves** /huːvz/) the hard part of the foot of horses and some other animals ☞ picture at **horse**

hook /hʊk/ noun a curved piece of metal or plastic for hanging things on, or for catching something: Hang your coat on that hook. ○ a fish-hook

hooks

off the hook If a telephone is off the hook, the part that you speak into (the **receiver**) is not in place so that the telephone will not ring.

hooligan /ˈhuːlɪɡən/ noun a young person who behaves in a noisy way and fights other people: football hooligans

hoot /huːt/ noun the sound that an owl or a car's horn makes

hoot verb (**hoots, hooting, hooted**)

make this sound: *The driver hooted at the dog.*

hooves *plural of* **hoof**

hop /hɒp/ *verb* (**hops**, **hopping**, **hopped** /hɒpt/) **1** jump on one foot **2** jump with two or all feet together: *The frog hopped onto the stone.*

hope[1] /həʊp/ *noun* **1** a feeling of wanting something to happen and thinking that it will: *He hasn't worked very hard so there is not much hope that he will pass the exam.* **2** a person or thing that gives you hope: *Can you help me? You're my only hope.* **give up hope** stop thinking that what you want will happen: *Don't give up hope. The letter may come tomorrow.*

hope[2] /həʊp/ *verb* (**hopes**, **hoping**, **hoped** /həʊpt/) want something that may happen: *I hope you have a nice holiday.* ○ *I hope to see you tomorrow.* ○ *We're hoping that you will come to the party.* ○ *She's hoping for a letter from her friend.* **I hope not** I do not want that to happen: *'Do you think we'll lose the match?' 'I hope not.'* **I hope so** I want that to happen: *'Will you be at the party?' 'I'm not sure — I hope so.'*

hopeful /ˈhəʊpfl/ *adjective* If you are hopeful, you think that something that you want will happen: *I'm hopeful about getting a job.*

hopefully /ˈhəʊpfəli/ *adverb* **1** in a hopeful way: *The cat looked hopefully at our plates.* **2** I hope: *Hopefully he won't be late.*

hopeless /ˈhəʊpləs/ *adjective* **1** very bad: *I'm hopeless at tennis.* **2** useless: *It's hopeless trying to work when my brother is here — he's so noisy!*

hopelessly *adverb*: *We got hopelessly lost in the desert.*

horizon /həˈraɪzn/ *noun* the line between the earth or sea and the sky: *We could see a ship on the horizon.*

horizontal /ˌhɒrɪˈzɒntl/ *adjective* Something that is horizontal goes from side to side, not up and down: *a horizontal line* ☛ picture on page A5

horn /hɔːn/ *noun* **1** one of the hard pointed things that some animals have on their heads ☛ picture at **goat**. **2** a thing in a car, ship, etc that makes a loud sound to warn people: *Don't sound your horn late at night.* **3** a musical instrument that you blow

horoscope /ˈhɒrəskəʊp/ *noun* something that tells you what will happen, using the planets and your date of birth: *Have you read your horoscope today?* (in a newspaper, for example)

horrible /ˈhɒrəbl/ *adjective* **1** Something that is horrible makes you feel afraid or shocked: *There was a horrible murder here last week.* **2** very bad: *What horrible weather!*

horrid /ˈhɒrɪd/ *adjective* very bad or unkind: *Don't be so horrid!*

horrify /ˈhɒrɪfaɪ/ *verb* (**horrifies**, **horrifying**, **horrified** /ˈhɒrɪfaɪd/, **has horrified**) shock and frighten somebody: *We were horrified by the photos of the car crash.*

horror /ˈhɒrə(r)/ *noun* (no plural) a feeling of fear or shock: *They watched in horror as the child ran in front of the bus.*

horror film /ˈhɒrə fɪlm/ *noun* a film that shows frightening things

horse

hoof

horse /hɔːs/ *noun* a big animal that can carry people and pull heavy things: *Can you ride a horse?* ✿ A young horse is called a **foal**. **on horseback** sitting on a horse

horseshoe /ˈhɔːs ʃuː/ *noun* a piece of metal like a U that a horse wears on its foot

horticulture /ˈhɔːtɪkʌltʃə(r)/ *noun* (no plural) growing fruit, vegetables and flowers

horticultural /ˌhɔːtɪˈkʌltʃərəl/ *adjective*

hose /həʊz/, **hose-pipe** /ˈhəʊz paɪp/ *noun* a long soft tube that you use to bring water, for example in the garden or when there is a fire

hospital /ˈhɒspɪtl/ *noun* a place where doctors and nurses look after people who are ill or hurt: *My brother is in hospital – he's broken his leg.* ○ *The ambulance took her to hospital.*

❂ A room in a hospital where people sleep is called a **ward**. A person who is staying in hospital is called a **patient**.

hospitality /ˌhɒspɪˈtæləti/ *noun* (no plural) being friendly to people who are visiting you, and looking after them well: *We thanked them for their hospitality.*

host /həʊst/ *noun* a person who invites guests, for example to a party: *The host offered me a drink.*

hostage /ˈhɒstɪdʒ/ *noun* a prisoner that you keep until people give you what you want: *The hijackers have freed all the hostages.* **hold somebody hostage** keep somebody as a hostage: *They held his daughter hostage until he paid them the money.* **take somebody hostage** catch somebody and keep them as a hostage

hostel /ˈhɒstl/ *noun* a place like a cheap hotel where people can stay: *a youth hostel*

hostess /ˈhəʊstəs/ *noun* (plural **hostesses**) a woman who invites guests, for example to a party ☛ Look also at **air-hostess**.

hostile /ˈhɒstaɪl/ *adjective* very unfriendly: *a hostile army*

hot /hɒt/ *adjective* (**hotter**, **hottest**) **1** not cold. A fire is hot: *I'm hot. Can you open the window?* ○ *It's hot today, isn't it?* ○ *hot water* ☛ picture on page A11. **2** Food that is hot has a strong, burning taste: *a hot curry*

hotel /həʊˈtel/ *noun* a place where you pay to sleep and eat: *The journalists stayed at a hotel near the airport.*

hour /ˈaʊə(r)/ *noun* **1** a measure of time. There are 60 **minutes** in an hour: *The journey took two hours.* ○ *I've been waiting for an hour.* ○ *half an hour* **2 hours** (plural) the time when somebody is working, or when a shop or office is open: *Our office hours are 9 a.m. to 5 p.m.*

hourly /ˈaʊəli/ *adjective, adverb* that happens or comes on an hour: *There is an hourly news bulletin on the radio.*

house /haʊs/ *noun* (plural **houses** /ˈhaʊzɪz/) **1** a building where a person or a family lives. A house has more than one floor: *How many rooms are there in your house?* ○ *We're going to my grandmother's house tomorrow.* ☛ Look at **bungalow** and **flat**. **2** a building for a special use: *a warehouse*

housewife /ˈhaʊswaɪf/ *noun* (plural **housewives** /ˈhaʊswaɪvz/) a woman who works for her family in the house

housework /ˈhaʊswɜːk/ *noun* (no plural) work that you do in your house, for example cleaning and washing

❂ Be careful! Work that a teacher gives you to do at home is called **homework**.

housing /ˈhaʊzɪŋ/ *noun* (no plural) flats and houses for people to live in: *The government is spending a lot of money on new housing.*

housing estate /ˈhaʊzɪŋ ɪsteɪt/ *noun* a big group of houses that were built at the same time: *We live on a housing estate.*

hover /ˈhɒvə(r)/ *verb* (**hovers**, **hovering**, **hovered** /ˈhɒvəd/) stay in the air in one place: *An eagle was hovering above us.*

hovercraft /ˈhɒvəkrɑːft/ *noun* (plural **hovercraft**) a kind of boat that moves over the top of water on air that it pushes out

how /haʊ/ *adverb* **1** in what way: *How does this machine work?* ○ *She told me how to get to the station.* ○ *Do you know how to spell 'elementary'?* **2** a word that you use to ask if somebody is well: *'How is your sister?' 'She's very well, thank you.'* ❂ You use 'how' only when you are asking about somebody's health. When you are asking somebody to describe another person or a thing you use **what… like?**: *'What is your sister like?' 'She's tall with brown hair.'* **3** a word that you use to ask if something is good: *How was the film?* **4** a word that you use to ask questions about amount, etc: *How old are you?* ○ *How many brothers and sisters have you got?* ○ *How much does this cost?* ○ *How long have you lived here?* **5** a word that shows surprise or strong feeling: *How kind of you to help!* **how about …?** words that you use when you suggest something: *How about a drink?* ○ *How about going for a walk?*

how are you? do you feel well?: *'How are you?' 'Fine, thanks.'* **how do you do?** polite words that you say when you meet somebody for the first time ✪ When somebody says 'How do you do?', you also answer 'How do you do?'

however[1] /haʊˈevə(r)/ *adverb* **1** it does not matter how: *I never win, however hard I try.* **2** a way of saying 'how' more strongly: *However did you find me?*

however[2] /haʊˈevə(r)/ *conjunction* but: *She's very intelligent. However, she's quite lazy.*

howl /haʊl/ *noun* a long loud sound, like a dog makes

howl *verb* (**howls, howling, howled** /haʊld/) make this sound: *The dogs howled all night.* ○ *The wind howled around the house.*

HQ /ˌeɪtʃ ˈkjuː/ *short for* **headquarters**

hug /hʌg/ *verb* (**hugs, hugging, hugged** /hʌgd/) put your arms around somebody to show that you love them: *She hugged her parents and said goodbye.*

hug *noun: He gave his brother a hug.*

huge /hjuːdʒ/ *adjective* very big: *He caught a huge fish.*

hullo = **hello**

hum /hʌm/ *verb* (**hums, humming, hummed** /hʌmd/) **1** make a sound like bees **2** sing with your lips closed: *If you don't know the words of the song, hum it.*

human /ˈhjuːmən/ *adjective* of or like people, not animals or machines: *the human body*

human (*also* **human being**) *noun* a person: *Human beings have lived on earth for thousands of years.*

the human race /ðə ˌhjuːmən ˈreɪs/ *noun* (no plural) all the people in the world

humble /ˈhʌmbl/ *adjective* A humble person does not think he/she is better or more important than other people: *Becoming rich and famous has not changed her – she is still very humble.*

humorous /ˈhjuːmərəs/ *adjective* A person or thing that is humorous makes you smile or laugh: *a humorous story*

humour /ˈhjuːmə(r)/ *noun* (no plural) being funny: *a story full of humour*

have a sense of humour be able to laugh and make other people laugh at funny things: *Dave has a good sense of humour.*

hump /hʌmp/ *noun* a round lump: *A camel has a hump on its back.*

hundred /ˈhʌndrəd/ *number* 100: *We invited a hundred people to the party.* ○ *two hundred pounds* ○ *four hundred and twenty* ○ *hundreds of people*

hundredth /ˈhʌndrədθ/ *adjective, adverb, noun* 100th

hung *form of* **hang**[1]

hunger /ˈhʌŋgə(r)/ *noun* (no plural) the feeling that you want or need to eat

hungry /ˈhʌŋgri/ *adjective* (**hungrier, hungriest**) If you are hungry, you want to eat: *Let's eat soon – I'm hungry!*

hunt /hʌnt/ *verb* (**hunts, hunting, hunted**) chase animals to kill them as a sport or for food: *Young lions have to learn to hunt.* ✪ When you talk about spending time hunting, you say **go hunting**: *They went hunting in the bush.* **hunt for something** try to find something: *I've hunted everywhere for my book but I can't find it.*

hunt *noun: a hunt for my keys*

hunter *noun* a person who chases and kills animals

hunting *noun* (no plural) chasing and killing animals

hurl /hɜːl/ *verb* (**hurls, hurling, hurled** /hɜːld/) throw something strongly: *She hurled the book across the room.*

hurray, hooray /həˈreɪ/, **hurrah** /həˈrɑː/ a word that you shout when you are very pleased about something: *Hurray! She's won!*

hurricane /ˈhʌrɪkən/ *noun* a storm with very strong winds

hurry[1] /ˈhʌri/ *noun* **in a hurry** If you are in a hurry, you need to do something quickly: *I can't talk to you now – I'm in a hurry.*

hurry[2] /ˈhʌri/ *verb* (**hurries, hurrying, hurried** /ˈhʌrid/) move or do something quickly: *We hurried home after school.* **hurry up** move or do something more quickly: *Hurry up or we'll be late!*

hurt /hɜːt/ *verb* (**hurts, hurting, hurt, has hurt**) **1** make somebody or something feel pain: *I fell and hurt my leg.* ○ *Did you hurt yourself?* ○ *You hurt her feelings* (= made her unhappy) *when you said she was stupid.* ○ *These shoes hurt – they are too small.* **2** feel pain: *My leg hurts.*

husband /ˈhʌzbənd/ *noun* the man that a woman is married to ☛ picture on page A3

husk /hʌsk/ *noun* the hard outside part of nuts and seeds: *coconut husks*

hut /hʌt/ *noun* a small building with one room. Huts are usually made of wood or metal.

hydroelectric /ˌhaɪdrəʊɪˈlektrɪk/ *adjective* **1** using the power of water to produce electricity: *a hydroelectric dam*

2 power produced by moving water

hydrogen /ˈhaɪdrədʒən/ *noun* (no plural) a light gas that you cannot see or smell: *Water is made of hydrogen and oxygen.*

hyena /haɪˈiːnə/ *noun* (plural **hyenas** or **hyena**) a wild dog that has short back legs and longer front legs

hygiene /ˈhaɪdʒiːn/ *noun* (no plural) keeping yourself and things around you clean: *Good hygiene is very important when you are preparing food.*

hygienic /haɪˈdʒiːnɪk/ *adjective* clean ✪ opposite: **unhygienic**

hymn /hɪm/ *noun* a song that Christians sing in church

hyphen /ˈhaɪfn/ *noun* a mark (-) that you use in writing. It joins words together (for example **ice-cream**) or shows that a word continues on the next line.

Ii

I /aɪ/ *pronoun* (plural **we**) the person who is speaking: *I am Tanzanian.* ○ *I'll* (= I will) *see you tomorrow.* ○ *I'm early, aren't I?*

ice /aɪs/ *noun* (no plural) water that has become hard because it is very cold: *Do you want ice in your drink?*

iceberg /ˈaɪsbɜːg/ *noun* a very big piece of ice in the sea

ice-cream /ˌaɪs ˈkriːm/ *noun* very cold sweet food made from milk: *Do you like ice-cream?* ○ *Two chocolate ice-creams, please.*

ice-cube /ˈaɪs kjuːb/ *noun* a small piece of ice that you put in a drink to make it cold

iced /aɪst/ *adjective* **1** very cold: *iced water* **2** covered with **icing**: *iced cakes*

ice lolly /ˌaɪs ˈlɒli/ *noun* (plural **ice lollies**) a piece of sweet ice on a stick

icing /ˈaɪsɪŋ/ *noun* (no plural) sweet stuff that you use for covering cakes: *a cake with pink icing*

icy /ˈaɪsi/ *adjective* (**icier, iciest**) **1** covered with ice: *icy roads* **2** very cold: *an icy wind*

I'd /aɪd/ **1** = I had **2** = I would

ID /ˌaɪ ˈdiː/ *short for* **identification**[2]

idea /aɪˈdɪə/ *noun* **1** a plan or new thought: *It was a good idea to bring some water with us.* ○ *I've got an idea. Let's go swimming!* **2** a picture in your mind: *The pictures give you a good idea of what Algeria is like.* ○ *I've got no idea* (= I do not know) *where she is.* **3** what you believe: *My parents have very strict ideas about who I go out with.*

ideal /aɪˈdiːəl/ *adjective* the best or exactly right: *This is an ideal place for a fire.*

identical /aɪˈdentɪkl/ *adjective* exactly the same: *These two cameras are identical.* ○ *identical twins*

identify /aɪˈdentɪfaɪ/ *verb* (**identifies, identifying, identified** /aɪˈdentɪfaɪd/, **has identified**) say or know who somebody is or what something is: *The police have not identified the dead man yet.*

identification /aɪˌdentɪfɪˈkeɪʃn/ *noun* (no plural) **1** identifying somebody or something: *The identification of bodies after the accident was difficult.* **2** something that shows who you are, for example a passport: *Do you have any identification?* ✪ The short form is **ID**.

identity /aɪ'dentəti/ *noun (plural identities)* who or what a person or thing is: *The identity of the killer is not known.*

identity card /aɪ'dentəti kɑːd/ *noun* a card that shows who you are

idiom /'ɪdiəm/ *noun* a group of words with a special meaning: *The idiom 'break somebody's heart' means 'make somebody very unhappy'.*

idiomatic /ˌɪdiə'mætɪk/ *adjective* using idioms: *idiomatic English*

idiot /'ɪdiət/ *noun* a person who is stupid or does something silly: *I was an idiot to forget my key.*

idol /'aɪdl/ *noun* **1** something that people worship as a god **2** a famous person that people love: *Ronaldo is the idol of millions of football fans.*

ie /ˌaɪ 'iː/ this is what I mean: *You can buy hot drinks, ie tea and coffee, on the train.* ✪ **ie** is usually used in writing.

if /ɪf/ *conjunction* **1** a word that you use to say what is possible or true when another thing happens or is true: *If you press this button, the machine starts.* ○ *If you see him, give him this letter.* ○ *If your feet were smaller, you could wear my shoes.* ○ *If I won the lottery, I would buy a big house.* ○ *I may see you tomorrow. If not, I'll see you next week.* **2** a word that shows a question; whether: *Do you know if Paul is at home?* ○ *She asked me if I wanted to go to a party.* **as if** in a way that makes you think something: *She looks as if she has been on holiday.* **if only** words that show that you want something very much: *If only I could drive!*

ignorance /'ɪɡnərəns/ *noun* (no plural) not knowing about something: *Her ignorance surprised me.*

ignorant /'ɪɡnərənt/ *adjective* If you are ignorant, you do not know about something: *I'm very ignorant about computers.*

ignore /ɪɡ'nɔː(r)/ *verb* (**ignores**, **ignoring**, **ignored** /ɪɡ'nɔːd/) know

about somebody or something, but do not do anything about it: *He ignored the warning and swam a long way from the shore.* ○ *I said hello to her, but she ignored me!*

---

il- *prefix*

You can add **il-** to the beginning of some words to give them the opposite meaning, for example:
illegal = not legal

I'll /aɪl/ = **I shall** = **I will**

ill /ɪl/ *adjective* **1** not well; not in good health: *Mark is in bed because he is ill.* ○ *I feel too ill to go to work.* ✪ The noun is **illness**. **2** bad: *ill health* **be taken ill** become ill: *Margaret was taken ill at work.*

illegal /ɪ'liːɡl/ *adjective* not allowed by the law; not legal: *It is illegal to carry a gun.*

illegally /ɪ'liːɡəli/ *adverb*: *She came into the country illegally.*

illness /'ɪlnəs/ *noun* (plural **illnesses**) being ill: *Cancer is a serious illness.* ○ *He could not come to the meeting because of illness.*

ill-treat /ˌɪl'triːt/ *verb* (**ill-treats**, **ill-treating**, **ill-treated**) do unkind things to a person or an animal: *This dog has been ill-treated.*

illustrate /'ɪləstreɪt/ *verb* (**illustrates**, **illustrating**, **illustrated**) add pictures to show something more clearly: *The book is illustrated with colour photographs.*

illustration /ˌɪlə'streɪʃn/ *noun* a picture: *This dictionary has a lot of illustrations.*

---

im- *prefix*

You can add **im-** to the beginning of some words to give them the opposite meaning, for example:
impatient = not patient

I'm /aɪm/ = **I am**

image /'ɪmɪdʒ/ *noun* **1** a picture in people's minds of somebody or something: *A lot of people have an image of London as cold and rainy.* **2** a picture on paper or in a mirror: *images of war*

imaginary /ɪ'mædʒɪnəri/ *adjective* not

real; only in your mind: *The film is about an imaginary country.*

imagination /ɪˌmædʒɪˈneɪʃn/ *noun* being able to think of new ideas or make pictures in your mind: *You need a lot of imagination to write stories for children.* ○ *You didn't really see a ghost – it was just your imagination.*

imagine /ɪˈmædʒɪn/ *verb* (**imagines**, **imagining**, **imagined** /ɪˈmædʒɪnd/) **1** make a picture of something in your mind: *Can you imagine what the world was like one million years ago?* ○ *I closed my eyes and imagined I was lying on a beach.* **2** think that something will happen or that something is true: *I imagine Mehmet will come by car.*

imitate /ˈɪmɪteɪt/ *verb* (**imitates**, **imitating**, **imitated**) try to do the same as somebody or something; copy somebody or something: *He imitated his teacher's voice.*

imitation /ˌɪmɪˈteɪʃn/ *noun* something that you make to look like another thing; a copy: *It's not a diamond, it's only a glass imitation.* ○ *imitation leather*

immediate /ɪˈmiːdiət/ *adjective* happening at once: *I can't wait – I need an immediate answer.*

immediately /ɪˈmiːdiətli/ *adverb* now; at once: *Come to my office immediately!*

immense /ɪˈmens/ *adjective* very big: *immense problems*

immensely /ɪˈmensli/ *adverb* very or very much: *We enjoyed the party immensely.*

immigrant /ˈɪmɪɡrənt/ *noun* a person who comes to another country to live there: *Many immigrants to East Africa have come from Asia.*

immigration /ˌɪmɪˈɡreɪʃn/ *noun* (no plural) coming to another country to live there

immune /ɪˈmjuːn/ *adjective* safe, so that you cannot get a disease: *You're immune to measles if you've had it before.*

impatience /ɪmˈpeɪʃns/ *noun* (no plural) not being calm when you are waiting: *He showed his impatience by looking at his watch five or six times.*

impatient /ɪmˈpeɪʃnt/ *adjective* If you

are impatient, you do not want to wait for something: *Don't be so impatient! The bus will be here soon.*

impatiently *adverb*: *'Hurry up!' she said impatiently.*

imperative /ɪmˈperətɪv/ *noun* the form of a verb that you use for telling somebody to do something: *'Listen!' and 'Go away!' are in the imperative.*

imply /ɪmˈplaɪ/ *verb* (**implies**, **implying**, **implied** /ɪmˈplaɪd/, **has implied**) mean something without saying it: *He asked if I had any work to do. He was implying that I was lazy.*

import /ɪmˈpɔːt/ *verb* (**imports**, **importing**, **imported**) buy things from another country and bring them into your country: *Britain imports coffee from Kenya.* ✪ opposite: **export**

import /ˈɪmpɔːt/ *noun* a thing that is imported ✪ opposite: **export**

importer /ɪmˈpɔːtə(r)/ *noun* a person, company or country that imports things

important /ɪmˈpɔːtnt/ *adjective* **1** If something is important, you must do, have or think about it: *It is important to sleep well the night before an exam.* ○ *I think that happiness is more important than money.* **2** powerful or special: *The prime minister is a very important person.* ✪ opposite: **unimportant**

importance /ɪmˈpɔːtns/ *noun* (no plural) being important; value: *Oil is of great importance to industry.*

impossible /ɪmˈpɒsəbl/ *adjective* If something is impossible, you cannot do it, or it cannot happen: *It is impossible to finish this work by five o'clock.* ○ *The house was impossible to find.*

impossibility /ɪmˌpɒsəˈbɪləti/ *noun* (plural **impossibilities**) *I can't lend you 100 000 shillings. It's an impossibility!*

impress /ɪmˈpres/ *verb* (**impresses**, **impressing**, **impressed** /ɪmˈprest/) make somebody have good feelings or thoughts about you or about something that is yours: *He was so impressed by our singing that he asked us to sing on the radio.*

impressive /ɪmˈpresɪv/ *adjective* If something is impressive, it impresses people, for example because it is very good or very big: *an impressive building* ○ *Your work is very impressive.*

impression /ɪmˈpreʃn/ *noun* feelings or thoughts you have about somebody or something: *My first impressions of the city were not very good.* ○ *What's your impression of the new teacher?* **make an impression** give somebody a certain idea of yourself: *He made a good impression on his first day at work.*

imprison /ɪmˈprɪzn/ *verb* (**imprisons**, **imprisoning**, **imprisoned** /ɪmˈprɪznd/) put somebody in prison: *He was imprisoned for killing his wife.*

imprisonment /ɪmˈprɪznmənt/ *noun* (no plural) being in prison: *two years' imprisonment*

improve /ɪmˈpruːv/ *verb* (**improves**, **improving**, **improved** /ɪmˈpruːvd/) become better or make something better: *Your writing has improved a lot this year.* ○ *You must improve your spelling.*

improvement /ɪmˈpruːvmənt/ *noun* a change that makes something better than it was before: *There has been a big improvement in Sam's work.*

impulse /ˈɪmpʌls/ *noun* a sudden strong wish to do something: *She felt an impulse to run away.*

in¹ /ɪn/ *adverb* **1** to a place, from outside: *I opened the door and went in.* **2** at home or at work: *'Can I speak to Rita, please?' 'I'm sorry – she's not in.'*

in² /ɪn/ *preposition* **1** a word that shows where: *Entebbe is in Uganda.* ○ *He put his hand in the water* ○ *Julie is in bed.* ☛ picture on page A1. **2** a word that shows when: *My birthday is in May.* ○ *He started school in 1994.* ☛ Look at page A9. **3** a word that shows how long; after: *I'll be ready in ten minutes.* **4** a word that shows how somebody or something is: *This room is in a mess.* ○ *Miriam was in tears* (= she was crying). **5** a word that shows what clothes somebody is wearing: *He was dressed in a suit.* **6** a word that shows which way, what language, etc: *Write your name in capital letters.* ○ *They were speaking in French.* **7** a word that shows somebody's job: *He's in the army.* **8** making something: *There are 100 centimetres in a metre.* ○ *Sit in a circle.*

in-³ *prefix*
You can add **in-** to the beginning of some words to give them the opposite meaning, for example:
incomplete = not complete

inability /ˌɪnəˈbɪləti/ *noun* (no plural) not being able to do something: *He has an inability to talk about his problems.*

inaccurate /ɪnˈækjərət/ *adjective* not correct; with mistakes in it: *The report in the newspaper was inaccurate.*

inadequate /ɪnˈædɪkwət/ *adjective* not as much as you need, or not good enough: *These tyres are inadequate for this road.* ○ *inadequate food*

inch /ɪntʃ/ *noun* (*plural* **inches**) a measure of length (= 2·54 centimetres). There are twelve inches in a **foot**: *I am five foot six inches tall.* ○ *a twelve-inch ruler* ☛ Note at **foot**.

incident /ˈɪnsɪdənt/ *noun* something that happens: *Esther told us about a funny incident at school, when her teacher fell off the chair!*

incidentally /ˌɪnsɪˈdentəli/ *adverb* a word that you say when you are going to talk about something different: *Jama helped us to move the table. Incidentally, he has a new car.*

inclined /ɪnˈklaɪnd/ *adjective* **be inclined to 1** be likely to do something: *I don't want to tell Rosa about this – she's inclined to get angry.* **2** want to do something: *I'm inclined to agree with you.*

include /ɪnˈkluːd/ *verb* (**includes**, **including**, **included**) **1** have somebody or something as one part of the whole: *The price of the room includes breakfast.* **2** make somebody or something part of a group: *Have you included tea on the list of things to buy?* ☛ Look at **exclude**.

including *preposition* with; if you count: *There were five people in the car, including the driver.*

income /ˈɪnkʌm/ *noun* all the money that you receive for your work, for example: *What was your income last year?*

income tax /ˈɪnkʌm tæks/ *noun* (no plural) the money that you pay to the government from the money that you earn

incomplete /ˌɪnkəmˈpliːt/ *adjective* not finished; with parts missing: *This list is incomplete.*

inconsiderate /ˌɪnkənˈsɪdərət/ *adjective* A person who is inconsiderate does not think or care about other people and their feelings: *It's inconsiderate of you to make so much noise when people are asleep.*

inconsistent /ˌɪnkənˈsɪstənt/ *adjective* not always the same: *She's very inconsistent – sometimes her work is good and sometimes it's bad.*

inconvenience /ˌɪnkənˈviːniəns/ *noun* (no plural) problems or difficulty: *The repairs to the road caused a lot of inconvenience to drivers.*

inconvenient /ˌɪnkənˈviːniənt/ *adjective* If something is inconvenient, it gives you problems or difficulty: *She came at an inconvenient time – I was just going out.*

incorrect /ˌɪnkəˈrekt/ *adjective* not correct; not right or true: *It is incorrect to say that two plus two equals five.*

incorrectly *adverb*: *The name was incorrectly spelt.*

increase /ɪnˈkriːs/ *verb* (**increases**, **increasing**, **increased** /ɪnˈkriːst/) become bigger or more; make something bigger or more: *The number of women who go to work has increased.*

increase /ˈɪnkriːs/ *noun*: *There has been an increase in road accidents.* ○ *a price increase* ✪ opposite: **decrease**

incredible /ɪnˈkredəbl/ *adjective* **1** surprising and very difficult to believe: *Mike told us an incredible story about his grandmother catching a thief.* **2** very great: *She earns an incredible amount of money.*

incredibly /ɪnˈkredəbli/ *adverb* extremely: *He's incredibly clever.*

indeed /ɪnˈdiːd/ *adverb* **1** a word that makes 'very' stronger: *Thank you very much indeed.* ○ *She's very happy indeed.* **2** really; certainly: *'Did you have a good holiday?' 'I did indeed.'*

indefinite /ɪnˈdefɪnət/ *adjective* not definite; not clear or certain: *They are staying for an indefinite length of time.*

indefinitely /ɪnˈdefɪnətli/ *adverb* for a long time, perhaps for ever: *I can't wait indefinitely.*

independence /ˌɪndɪˈpendəns/ *noun* (no plural) being free from another person, thing or country: *Kenya gained full independence in 1963.*

independent /ˌɪndɪˈpendənt/ *adjective* **1** not controlled by another person, thing or country: *Zimbabwe has been independent since 1980.* **2** A person who is independent does not need help: *She lives alone now and she is very independent.*

index /ˈɪndeks/ *noun* (*plural* **indexes**) a list of words from A to Z at the end of a book. It tells you what things are in the book and where you can find them.

indicate /ˈɪndɪkeɪt/ *verb* (**indicates**, **indicating**, **indicated**) **1** show something, usually by pointing with your finger: *Can you indicate your school on this map?* **2** give a sign about something: *Black clouds indicate that it's going to rain.* **3** show that your car is going to turn by using a light: *You should indicate left now.*

indication /ˌɪndɪˈkeɪʃn/ *noun* something that shows something: *He gave no indication that he was angry.*

indicator /ˈɪndɪkeɪtə(r)/ *noun* a light on a car that shows that it is going to turn left or right

indignant /ɪnˈdɪgnənt/ *adjective* angry because somebody has done or said something that you do not like or agree with: *She was indignant when I said she was lazy.*

indignantly *adverb*: *'I'm not late,' he said indignantly.*

indignation /ˌɪndɪgˈneɪʃn/ *noun* (no plural) a feeling of anger and surprise

indirect /ˌɪndəˈrekt/ *adjective* not straight or direct: *We came an indirect way to avoid the city centre.*

indirectly *adverb* in an indirect way

individual[1] /ˌɪndɪˈvɪdʒuəl/ *adjective* **1** for only one person or thing: *He had individual lessons to help him learn to read.* **2** single and different: *Each individual country has its own flag.*

individually /ˌɪndɪˈvɪdʒuəli/ *adverb* separately; alone; not together: *The* *teacher spoke to each student individually.*

individual² /ˌɪndɪˈvɪdʒuəl/ *noun* one person: *Teachers must treat each child as an individual.*

indoor /ˈɪndɔː(r)/ *adjective* done or used inside a building: *an indoor swimming-pool* ○ *indoor games* ✪ opposite: **outdoor**

indoors /ˌɪnˈdɔːz/ *adverb* in or into a building: *Let's go indoors.* ✪ opposite: **outdoors**

industrial /ɪnˈdʌstriəl/ *adjective* **1** of or about making things in factories: *industrial machines* **2** with a lot of factories: *This is an important industrial centre.*

industry /ˈɪndəstri/ *noun* **1** (no plural) the work of making things in factories: *Is there much industry in your country?* **2** (*plural* **industries**) all the companies that make the same thing: *the textile industry*

inefficient /ˌɪnɪˈfɪʃnt/ *adjective* A person or thing that is inefficient does not work well or in the best way: *This machine is very old and inefficient.*

inevitable /ɪnˈevɪtəbl/ *adjective* If something is inevitable, it will certainly happen: *The accident was inevitable – he was driving too fast.*

inevitably /ɪnˈevɪtəbli/ *adverb*: *Building the new hospital inevitably cost a lot of money.*

inexperienced /ˌɪnɪkˈspɪəriənst/ *adjective* If you are inexperienced, you do not know about something because you have not done it many times before: *a young inexperienced driver*

infect /ɪnˈfekt/ *verb* (**infects**, **infecting**, **infected**) give a disease to somebody: *He infected the other children in the class with his cold.*

infected *adjective* full of small living things (called **germs**) that can make you ill: *Clean that cut or it could become infected.*

infection /ɪnˈfekʃn/ *noun* a disease: *Mike has an ear infection.*

infectious /ɪnˈfekʃəs/ *adjective* that goes easily from one person to another: *This disease is infectious.*

inferior /ɪnˈfɪəriə(r)/ *adjective* not as good or important as another person

or thing: *Esther's work is so good that she makes the other students feel inferior.* ✪ opposite: **superior**

infinite /ˈɪnfɪnət/ *adjective* with no end; too much or too many to count or measure: *There is an infinite number of stars in the sky.*

infinitive /ɪnˈfɪnətɪv/ *noun* the simple form of a verb: *'Eat', 'go' and 'play' are all infinitives.*

inflate /ɪnˈfleɪt/ *verb* (**inflates**, **inflating**, **inflated**) fill something with air or gas to make it bigger: *He inflated the tyre.* ✪ It is more usual to say **blow up** or **pump up**.

inflation /ɪnˈfleɪʃn/ *noun* (no plural) a general rise in prices in a country: *The government is trying to control inflation.*

influence /ˈɪnfluəns/ *noun* **1** (no plural) the power to change what somebody believes or does: *Television has a strong influence on people.* **2** (*plural* **influences**) a person or thing that can change somebody or something: *Paul's new girlfriend is a good influence on him.*

influence *verb* (**influences**, **influencing**, **influenced** /ˈɪnfluənst/) change somebody or something; make somebody do what you want: *She is easily influenced by her friends.*

inform /ɪnˈfɔːm/ *verb* (**informs**, **informing**, **informed** /ɪnˈfɔːmd/) tell something to somebody: *You should inform the police of the accident.*

informal /ɪnˈfɔːml/ *adjective* You use informal language or behave in an informal way in situations that are friendly and easy, not serious or important, and with people that you know well. You do not usually use informal words when you write (except in letters to people that you know well): *I wear a suit when I'm at work, but more informal clothes at weekends.* ○ *an informal letter*

informally /ɪnˈfɔːməli/ *adverb*: *The students talked informally to each other.*

information /ˌɪnfəˈmeɪʃn/ *noun* (no plural) what you tell somebody; facts: *Can you give me some information about buses to Mombasa?* ✪ Be careful!

You cannot say 'an information'. You can say 'some information' or 'a piece of information': *She gave me an interesting piece of information.*

ingredient /ɪnˈgriːdiənt/ *noun* one of the things that you put in when you make something to eat: *The ingredients for this cake are flour, butter, sugar and eggs.*

inhabitant /ɪnˈhæbɪtənt/ *noun* a person or an animal that lives in a place: *The town has 30 000 inhabitants.*

inhabited /ɪnˈhæbɪtɪd/ *adjective* be inhabited have people or animals living there: *The South Pole is inhabited by penguins.*

inherit /ɪnˈherɪt/ *verb* (**inherits**, **inheriting**, **inherited**) receive something from somebody who has died: *Sabine inherited some money from her grandmother.*

inheritance /ɪnˈherɪtəns/ *noun* something that you inherit

initial /ɪˈnɪʃl/ *adjective* first: *Our initial idea was to go by bus, but then we decided to take the train.*

initially /ɪˈnɪʃəli/ *adverb* in the beginning; at first: *Initially I hated maths, but now I love it!*

initials /ɪˈnɪʃlz/ *noun* (plural) the first letters of your names: *Julie Mwangola's initials are J. M.*

inject /ɪnˈdʒekt/ *verb* (**injects**, **injecting**, **injected**) use a special needle to put a drug into a person's body

injection /ɪnˈdʒekʃn/ *noun*: *The doctor gave the baby an injection.*

injure /ˈɪndʒə(r)/ *verb* (**injures**, **injuring**, **injured** /ˈɪndʒəd/) hurt somebody or something: *She injured her arm when she was climbing a tree.* ○ *Daudi was injured in a car accident.*

injured *adjective*: *The injured woman was taken to hospital.*

injury /ˈɪndʒəri/ *noun* (plural **injuries**) damage to the body of a person or an animal: *He had serious head injuries.*

injustice /ɪnˈdʒʌstɪs/ *noun* (no plural) not being fair or right: *People are angry about the injustice of the new tax.*

ink /ɪŋk/ *noun* a coloured liquid for writing and printing: *The words on this page are printed in black ink.*

inland /ˈɪnlənd/ *adjective* in the middle of a country, not near the sea: *an inland lake*

inland /ˌɪnˈlænd/ *adverb* in or towards the middle of a country

inner /ˈɪnə(r)/ *adjective* of the inside; in the centre: *the inner city* ✪ opposite: **outer**

innocent /ˈɪnəsnt/ *adjective* If you are innocent, you have not done wrong: *The police say John stole the money, but I think he's innocent.* ✪ opposite: **guilty**

innocence /ˈɪnəsns/ *noun* (no plural) *The prisoner's family are sure of her innocence.* ✪ opposite: **guilt**

inquire /ɪnˈkwaɪə(r)/ *verb* (**inquires**, **inquiring**, **inquired** /ɪnˈkwaɪəd/) ask: *I inquired about buses to Kisumu.* ○ *'Are you hungry?' he inquired.* ✪ **Ask** is the word that we usually use. **inquire into something** try to find out more about something that happened: *The police are inquiring into the murder.*

inquiry /ɪnˈkwaɪəri/ *noun* (plural **inquiries**) a question that you ask about something: *The police are making inquiries about the robbery.*

insane /ɪnˈseɪn/ *adjective* mad

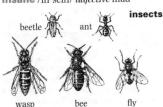

insects

beetle   ant

wasp   bee   fly

insect /ˈɪnsekt/ *noun* a very small animal that has six legs: *Ants, flies, butterflies and beetles are all insects.*

insecticide /ɪnˈsektɪsaɪd/ *noun* a substance that is used to kill insects on crops

insecure /ˌɪnsɪˈkjʊə(r)/ *adjective* **1** not safe or firm: *An actor's job is very insecure.* **2** worried and not sure about yourself: *Since their father left, the children have felt very insecure.*

insecurity /ˌɪnsɪˈkjʊərəti/ *noun* (no plural) *She had feelings of insecurity.*

insert /ɪnˈsɜːt/ *verb* (**inserts**, **inserting**, **inserted**) put something into something or between two things: *Insert the key into the lock.*

inside[1] /ɪnˈsaɪd/ *noun* the part near the middle of something: *The inside of a coconut is white and the outside is brown.* ○ *He did not see the inside of the house before he bought it.*

inside out with the wrong side on the outside: *You've got your shirt on inside out.*

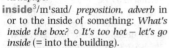
inside out

inside[2] /ˈɪnsaɪd/ *adjective* in or near the middle: *the inside pages of a newspaper*

inside[3] /ɪnˈsaɪd/ *preposition, adverb* in or to the inside of something: *What's inside the box?* ○ *It's too hot — let's go inside* (= into the building).

insist /ɪnˈsɪst/ *verb* (**insists, insisting, insisted**) **1** say very strongly that you must do or have something or that something must happen: *I said I could carry the box myself, but Lwanga insisted on helping me.* **2** say very strongly that something is true, when somebody does not believe you: *My sister insists that she saw a ghost.*

inspect /ɪnˈspekt/ *verb* (**inspects, inspecting, inspected**) **1** look at something carefully: *I inspected the car before I bought it.* **2** visit a place or a group of people to see that work is done well: *The kitchens are inspected every week.*

inspection /ɪnˈspekʃn/ *noun:* *The police made an inspection of the house.*

inspector /ɪnˈspektə(r)/ *noun* **1** a person whose job is to see that things are done correctly: *On the train, the inspector asked to see my ticket.* ○ *a factory inspector* **2** a police officer

inspiration /ˌɪnspəˈreɪʃn/ *noun* a person or thing that gives you ideas which help you do something good, for example write or paint: *The beauty of the mountains is a great inspiration to many artists.*

inspire /ɪnˈspaɪə(r)/ *verb* (**inspires, inspiring, inspired** /ɪnˈspaɪəd/) **1** give somebody ideas that help them do something good, for example write or paint: *His wife inspired him to write this poem.* **2** make somebody feel or think something: *Her words inspired us all with hope.*

install /ɪnˈstɔːl/ *verb* (**installs, installing, installed** /ɪnˈstɔːld/) put a new thing in its place so it is ready to use: *They installed a water tank in the school.*

instalment /ɪnˈstɔːlmənt/ *noun* **1** one part of a long story on radio or television, or in a magazine: *Did you read the last instalment?* **2** a part of the cost of something that you pay each week or month, for example: *She's paying for her new car in twelve monthly instalments.*

instance /ˈɪnstəns/ *noun* an example: *There have been many instances of forest fires this year.* **for instance** as an example: *There are many things to see in Kenya — for instance Mount Kenya and Amboseli National Park.*

instant[1] /ˈɪnstənt/ *adjective* **1** that happens very quickly; immediate: *The film was an instant success.* **2** quick and easy to prepare: *an instant meal*

instant coffee /ˌɪnstənt ˈkɒfi/ *noun* (no plural) coffee that you make quickly with coffee powder and hot water

instantly *adverb* immediately; at once: *I asked him a question and he replied instantly.*

instant[2] /ˈɪnstənt/ *noun* a very short time; a moment: *She thought for an instant before she answered.*

instead /ɪnˈsted/ *adverb* in the place of somebody or something: *We haven't got any coffee. Would you like tea instead?* ○ *Mukasa can't go to the meeting so I will go instead.*

instead of *preposition* in the place of: *He's been playing football all afternoon instead of studying.* ○ *Can you come at 7.30 instead of 8.00?*

instinct /ˈɪnstɪŋkt/ *noun* something that makes people and animals do certain things without thinking or learning about them: *Birds build their nests by instinct.*

instinctive /ɪnˈstɪŋktɪv/ *adjective*: *Animals have an instinctive fear of fire.*

institute /ˈɪnstɪtjuːt/ *noun* a group of people who meet to study or talk about a special thing; the building where they meet: *the Institute of Science*

institution /ˌɪnstɪˈtjuːʃn/ *noun* a big building like a bank, hospital, prison or school, and all the people in it: *Makerere University is one of the largest institutions in East Africa.*

instruct /ɪnˈstrʌkt/ *verb* (**instructs**, **instructing**, **instructed**) **1** tell somebody what they must do: *He instructed the driver to take him to the airport.* **2** teach somebody: *She instructed me in how to use the computer.*

instruction /ɪnˈstrʌkʃn/ *noun* **1** (*plural* **instructions**) words that tell you what you must do or how to do something: *Read the instructions on the box before you make the cake.* **2** (no plural) teaching or being taught something: *driving instruction*

instructor /ɪnˈstrʌktə(r)/ *noun* a person who teaches you how to do something: *a driving instructor*

instrument /ˈɪnstrəmənt/ *noun* **1** a thing that you use for doing a special job: *A telescope is an instrument used for looking at things that are a long way away.* ○ *medical instruments* (= used by doctors) **2** a thing that you use for playing music: *Violins and trumpets are musical instruments.* ○ *What instrument do you play?*

insult /ɪnˈsʌlt/ *verb* (**insults**, **insulting**, **insulted**) be rude to somebody: *She insulted my brother by saying he was ugly.*
insult /ˈɪnsʌlt/ *noun* something rude that you say or do to somebody: *The boys shouted insults at each other.*

insurance /ɪnˈʃʊərəns/ *noun* (no plural) an agreement where you pay money to a company so that it will give you a lot of money if something bad happens: *When I crashed my car, the insurance paid for the repairs.*

insure /ɪnˈʃʊə(r)/ *verb* (**insures**, **insuring**, **insured** /ɪnˈʃʊəd/) pay money to a company, so that it will give you money if something bad happens: *Have you insured your house against fire?* ○ *My car isn't insured.*

intelligence /ɪnˈtelɪdʒəns/ *noun* (no plural) being able to think, learn and understand quickly and well: *He is a man of great intelligence.* ○ *an intelligence test*

intelligent /ɪnˈtelɪdʒənt/ *adjective* able to think, learn and understand quickly and well: *Their daughter is very intelligent.*

intend /ɪnˈtend/ *verb* (**intends**, **intending**, **intended**) plan to do something: *When do you intend to go to Addis Ababa?* **be intended for somebody** or **something** be for somebody or something: *This dictionary is intended for elementary learners of English.*

intense /ɪnˈtens/ *adjective* very great or strong: *intense pain* ○ *The heat from the fire was intense.*

intention /ɪnˈtenʃn/ *noun* what you plan to do: *They have no intention of getting married.*

intentional /ɪnˈtenʃənl/ *adjective* that you want and plan to do, and do not do by mistake: *I'm sorry I upset you – it wasn't intentional!* ✪ opposite: **unintentional**

intentionally /ɪnˈtenʃənəli/ *adverb*: *They broke the window intentionally – it wasn't an accident.*

interest[1] /ˈɪntrəst/ *noun* **1** (no plural) wanting to know or learn about somebody or something: *He read the story with interest.* **2** (*plural* **interests**) something that you like doing or learning about: *His interests are computers and rock music.* **3** (no plural) the extra money that you pay back if you borrow money or that you receive if you put money in a bank **take an interest in somebody** or **something** want to know about somebody or something: *He takes no interest in politics.*

interest[2] /ˈɪntrəst/ *verb* (**interests**, **interesting**, **interested**) make somebody want to know more: *Religion doesn't interest her.*

interested *adjective* If you are interested in somebody or something, you want to know more about them: *Are you interested in cars?* ✪ opposite: **uninterested**

interesting *adjective* A person or thing that is interesting makes you want to know more about him/her/it: *This book is very interesting.* ○ *That's an interesting idea!* ✪ opposite: **uninteresting** or **boring**

interfere /ˌɪntəˈfɪə(r)/ *verb* (**interferes**, **interfering**, **interfered** /ˌɪntəˈfɪəd/) **1** try to do something with or for somebody, when they do not want your help: *Don't interfere! Let John decide what he wants to do.* **2** stop something from being done well: *His interest in football often interferes with his studies.* **3** change or touch something without asking if you can: *Who's been interfering with the clock? It's stopped.*

interference /ˌɪntəˈfɪərəns/ *noun*: *Go away! I don't want any interference when I'm working!*

interior /ɪnˈtɪəriə(r)/ *noun* the inside part: *We painted the interior of the house white.*

interior *adjective*: *interior walls* **✪** opposite: **exterior**

intermediate /ˌɪntəˈmiːdiət/ *adjective* that comes between two people or things; in the middle: *She's in an intermediate class.*

internal /ɪnˈtɜːnl/ *adjective* of or on the inside: *He has internal injuries* (= inside his body). **✪** opposite: **external**

internally /ɪnˈtɜːnəli/ *adverb* on the inside

international /ˌɪntəˈnæʃnəl/ *adjective* between different countries: *an international football match* ∘ *an international flight*

interpret /ɪnˈtɜːprɪt/ *verb* (**interprets**, **interpreting**, **interpreted**) say in one language what somebody has said in another language: *I can't speak Arabic – can you interpret for me?*

interpreter *noun* a person who interprets: *The President had an interpreter when he went to China.*

interrupt /ˌɪntəˈrʌpt/ *verb* (**interrupts**, **interrupting**, **interrupted**) **1** stop somebody speaking or doing something by saying or doing something yourself: *Please don't interrupt me when I'm speaking.* **2** stop something for a time: *The war interrupted travel between the two countries.*

interruption /ˌɪntəˈrʌpʃn/ *noun*: *I can't do my homework here. There are too many interruptions.*

interval /ˈɪntəvl/ *noun* a short time be-

tween two parts of a play or concert: *We bought drinks in the interval.*

interview /ˈɪntəvjuː/ *noun* **1** a meeting when somebody asks you questions to decide if you will have a job: *I've got an interview for a new job tomorrow.* **2** a meeting when somebody answers questions for a newspaper or for a television or radio programme: *There was an interview with the Prime Minister on TV last night.*

interview *verb* (**interviews**, **interviewing**, **interviewed** /ˈɪntəvjuːd/) ask somebody questions in an interview: *They interviewed six people for the job.*

interviewer *noun* a person who asks questions in an interview: *The interviewer asked me why I wanted the job.*

into /ˈɪntə/, /ˈɪntu/, /ˈɪntuː/ *preposition* **1** to the middle or the inside of something: *Come into the house.* ∘ *I went into town.* ∘ *He fell into the river.* ➥ picture on page A2. **2** a word that shows how somebody or something changes: *When it is very cold, water changes into ice.* ∘ *They made the room into a bedroom.* **3** against something: *The car crashed into a tree.* **4** a word that you use when you divide a number: *4 into 12 is 3.* **be into something** like something; be interested in something: *What sort of music are you into?*

introduce /ˌɪntrəˈdjuːs/ *verb* (**introduces**, **introducing**, **introduced** /ˌɪntrəˈdjuːst/) **1** bring people together for the first time and tell each of them the name of the other: *She introduced me to her brother.* **2** bring in something new: *This law was introduced in 1990.*

introduce yourself tell somebody your name: *He introduced himself to me.*

introduction /ˌɪntrəˈdʌkʃn/ *noun* **1** (*plural* **introductions**) bringing people together to meet each other **2** (*plural* **introductions**) a piece of writing at the beginning of a book that tells you about the book **3** (no plural) bringing in something new: *the introduction of computers into schools*

invade /ɪnˈveɪd/ *verb* (**invades**, **invading**, **invaded**) go into another country to attack it: *They invaded the country* *with tanks and guns.*

invader *noun* a person who invades

invalid /'ɪnvəlɪd/ *noun* a person who is very ill and needs another person to look after him/her: *She has been an invalid since the accident.*

invaluable /ɪn'væljuəbl/ *adjective* very useful: *Your help was invaluable.*

invariably /ɪn'veəriəbli/ *adverb* almost always: *He invariably arrives late.*

invasion /ɪn'veɪʒn/ *noun* a time when an army from one country goes into another country to attack it: *Germany's invasion of Poland in 1939*

invent /ɪn'vent/ *verb* (**invents, inventing, invented**) **1** make or think of something for the first time: *Who invented the bicycle?* **2** tell something that is not true: *She invented a story about where she was last night.*

inventor /ɪn'ventə(r)/ *noun* a person who makes or thinks of something new

invention /ɪn'venʃn/ *noun* **1** (*plural* inventions) a thing that somebody has made for the first time **2** (no plural) inventing something: *The invention of the telephone changed the world.*

inverted commas /ɪnˌvɜːtɪd 'kɒməz/ *noun* (plural) the signs " " or ' ' that you use in writing before and after words that somebody said

invest /ɪn'vest/ *verb* (**invests, investing, invested**) give money to a business or bank so that you will get more money back: *He invested all his money in the company.*

investment /ɪn'vestmənt/ *noun* investing money; money that you invest: *an investment of one million shillings*

investigate /ɪn'vestɪɡeɪt/ *verb* (**investigates, investigating, investigated**) try to find out about something: *The police are investigating the murder.*

investigation /ɪnˌvestɪ'ɡeɪʃn/ *noun*: *The police are holding an investigation into the fire.*

invisible /ɪn'vɪzəbl/ *adjective* If something is invisible, you cannot see it: *Wind is invisible.*

invitation /ˌɪnvɪ'teɪʃn/ *noun* If you have an invitation to go somewhere, somebody has spoken or written to you and asked you to go: *Muanga sent me an invitation to his wedding.*

invite /ɪn'vaɪt/ *verb* (**invites, inviting, invited**) ask somebody to come to a party or a meeting, for example: *Sarah invited me to her party.* ○ *Let's invite them for dinner.*

invoice /'ɪnvɔɪs/ *noun* a list that shows how much you must pay for things that somebody has sold you, or for work that somebody has done for you

involve /ɪn'vɒlv/ *verb* (**involves, involving, involved** /ɪn'vɒlvd/) **1** have something as a part: *The job involves using a computer.* **2** make somebody take part in something: *A lot of people were involved in planning the wedding.*

inward /'ɪnwəd/, **inwards**/'ɪnwədz/ *adverb* towards the inside or centre: *The doors open inwards.* ✪ opposite: **outward** or **outwards**

---

ir- *prefix*
You can add **ir-** to the beginning of some words to give them the opposite meaning, for example:
irregular = not regular

---

iron /'aɪən/ *noun* **1** (no plural) a strong hard metal: *The gates are made of iron.* ○ *an iron bar* **2** (*plural* irons) an electrical thing that gets hot and that you use for making clothes smooth

iron *verb* (**irons, ironing, ironed** /'aɪənd/) make clothes smooth with an iron: *Can you iron this shirt for me?* ✪ When we talk about ironing a lot of clothes, we often say **do the ironing.**: *I've done the ironing.*

ironing *noun* (no plural) clothes that you must iron: *There's a pile of ironing on the chair.*

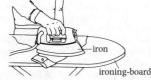

ironing-board /'aɪənɪŋ bɔːd/ *noun* a special long table where you iron clothes

irregular /ɪˈregjələ(r)/ *adjective* **1** that happens again and again, but with different amounts of time in between: *Their visits were irregular.* **2** A word that is irregular does not have the usual verb forms or plural: *'Catch' is an irregular verb.*

irrelevant /ɪˈreləvənt/ *adjective* not connected with something and not important: *We are good friends. She is older than me, but that is irrelevant.*

irrigate /ˈɪrɪgeɪt/ *verb* (**irrigates, irrigating, irrigated**) make water go to land where crops grow

irrigation /ˌɪrɪˈgeɪʃn/ *noun* (no plural)

irritate /ˈɪrɪteɪt/ *verb* (**irritates, irritating, irritated**) **1** make somebody quite angry: *He irritates me when he asks so many questions.* **2** make a part of your body hurt a little: *Cigarette smoke irritates my eyes.*

irritation /ˌɪrɪˈteɪʃn/ *noun*: *This plant causes irritation to your skin.*

is *form of* **be**

Islam /ˈɪzlɑːm/ *noun* (no plural) the religion of Muslim people. Islam teaches that there is only one God and that Muhammad is his messenger.

Islamic /ɪzˈlæmɪk/ *adjective*: *Islamic law*

island /ˈaɪlənd/ *noun* a piece of land with water all around it: *Zanzibar is an island.*

Isle /aɪl/ *noun* an island: *the British Isles* ✪ **Isle** is usually used in names of islands.

isn't /ˈɪznt/ = **is not**

isolated /ˈaɪsəleɪtɪd/ *adjective* far from other people or things: *an isolated house in the mountains*

isolation /ˌaɪsəˈleɪʃn/ *noun* (no plural) being away from other people or things: *A lot of old people live in isolation.*

issue[1] /ˈɪʃuː/ *noun* **1** an important problem that people talk about: *Pollution is a serious issue.* **2** a magazine or newspaper of a particular day, week, or month: *Have you read this week's issue of the magazine?*

issue[2] /ˈɪʃuː/ *verb* (**issues, issuing, issued** /ˈɪʃuːd/) give something to people: *The soldiers were issued with uniforms.*

it /ɪt/ *pronoun* (*plural* **they, them**) **1** a word that shows a thing or animal: *I've got a new shirt. It's* (= it is) *blue.* ○ *Where is the coffee? I can't find it.* **2** a word that points to an idea that follows: *It is difficult to learn Arabic.* **3** a word that shows who somebody is: *'Who's on the telephone?' 'It's Jo.'* **4** a word at the beginning of a sentence about time, the weather, distance, etc: *It's six o'clock.* ○ *It's hot today.* ○ *It's 100 kilometres to Mombasa.*

italics /ɪˈtælɪks/ *noun* (plural) letters that lean to the side: *This sentence is in italics.*

itch /ɪtʃ/ *verb* (**itches, itching, itched** /ɪtʃt/) have a feeling on your skin that makes you want to rub or scratch it: *My nose itches.* ○ *This shirt makes me itch.*

itch *noun* (*plural* **itches**) *I've got an itch.*

itchy *adjective* If something is itchy, it itches or it makes you itch: *itchy skin*

it'd /ˈɪtəd/ **1** = **it had 2** = **it would**

item /ˈaɪtəm/ *noun* **1** one thing in a list or group of things: *She had the most expensive item on the menu.* ○ *an item of clothing* **2** a piece of news: *There was an interesting item on TV about South Africa.*

it'll /ˈɪtl/ = **it will**

it's /ɪts/ **1** = **it is 2** = **it has**

its /ɪts/ *adjective* of the thing or animal that you have just talked about: *The dog has hurt its leg.* ○ *The company has its factory in Nakuru.*

itself /ɪtˈself/ *pronoun* (*plural* **themselves** /ðəmˈselvz/) **1** a word that shows the same thing or animal that you have just talked about: *The cat was washing itself.* **2** a word that makes 'it' stronger: *The hotel itself was nice but I didn't like the town.* **by itself 1** alone: *The house stands by itself in the forest.* **2** without being controlled by a person: *The machine will start by itself.*

I've /aɪv/ = **I have**

ivory /ˈaɪvəri/ *noun* (no plural) the hard white stuff that an elephant's **tusks** are made of

jack /dʒæk/ *noun* the playing-card that has a picture of a young man on it: *the jack of hearts*

jackal /'dʒækl/ *noun* a wild dog with long legs and pointed ears. Jackals hunt in groups or look for dead animals to eat.

jacket /'dʒækɪt/ *noun* a short coat with sleeves ☛ picture at **suit**

jagged /'dʒægɪd/ *adjective* rough, with a lot of sharp points: *jagged rocks*

jaguar /'dʒægjʊə(r)/ *noun* a wild animal like a big cat. It has yellow fur with black spots.

jail /dʒeɪl/ *noun* a prison: *He was sent to jail for two years.*

jail *verb* (**jails**, **jailing**, **jailed** /dʒeɪld/) put somebody in prison: *She was jailed for killing her husband.*

jam¹ /dʒæm/ *noun* (no plural) food made from fruit and sugar. You eat jam on bread: *a jar of strawberry jam*

jam² /dʒæm/ *verb* (**jams**, **jamming**, **jammed** /dʒæmd/) **1** push something into a place where there is not much space: *She jammed all her clothes into a suitcase.* **2** fix something or become fixed so that you cannot move it: *I can't open the window. It's jammed.*

jam³ /dʒæm/ *noun* a lot of people or things in a place, so that it is difficult to move: *a traffic jam*

January /'dʒænjuəri/ *noun* the first month of the year

jar /dʒɑː(r)/ *noun* a glass container for food: *a jar of coffee* ☛ picture at **container**

javelin /'dʒævəlɪn/ *noun* a long pointed stick that people throw as a sport

jaw /dʒɔː/ *noun* one of the two bones in the head of a person or an animal that hold the teeth ☛ picture on page A4

jazz /dʒæz/ *noun* (no plural) a kind of music with a strong beat

jealous /'dʒeləs/ *adjective* **1** angry or sad because you want what another person has: *Ben was jealous of his brother's new car.* **2** angry or sad because you are afraid of losing somebody's love: *Sarah's boyfriend gets jealous if she speaks to other boys.*

jealousy /'dʒeləsi/ *noun* (no plural) being jealous

jeans /dʒiːnz/ *noun* (plural) trousers made of strong cotton material, called **denim**. Jeans are usually blue: *a pair of jeans* ○ *She wore jeans and a T-shirt.*

Jeep /dʒiːp/ *noun* a strong car that can go well over rough land ✪ **Jeep** is a trade mark.

jelly /'dʒeli/ *noun* (plural **jellies**) a soft food made from fruit juice and sugar that shakes when you move it

jellyfish /'dʒelifɪʃ/ *noun* (plural **jellyfish** or **jellyfishes**) a soft, round sea animal that you can see through: *I saw a jellyfish on the beach.*

jembe /'dʒembe/ *noun* (an East African word) a farming tool used for turning and breaking up soil

jerk /dʒɜːk/ *noun* a sudden pull or other movement: *The bus started with a jerk.*

jerk *verb* (**jerks**, **jerking**, **jerked** /dʒɜːkt/) *The car jerked forward.* ○ *She jerked the door open.*

jet /dʒet/ *noun* **1** an aeroplane that flies when its engines push out hot gas **2** liquid or gas that is coming very fast out of a small hole: *a jet of gas* ○ *jets of water*

jet lag /'dʒet læg/ *noun* (no plural) a very tired feeling that you may have after a long journey by aeroplane

Jew /dʒuː/ *noun* a person who follows the old religion of Israel, called **Judaism**

Jewish /'dʒuːɪʃ/ *adjective*: *She is Jewish.*

jewel /'dʒuːəl/ *noun* a beautiful stone, for example a diamond, that is very valuable

jeweller *noun* a person who sells, makes or repairs jewellery and watches ✪ A shop that sells jewellery and watches is called a **jeweller's**.

jewellery /'dʒuːəlri/ *noun* (no plural)

things like rings, bracelets and necklaces: *She wears a lot of jewellery.*

jigsaw puzzle

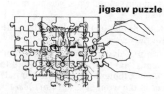

jigsaw, **jigsaw puzzle**/ˈdʒɪgsɔː pʌzl/ *noun* a picture in many pieces that you must put together

jiko /ˈdʒiːkɒ/ *noun* (an East African word) a metal stove that burns charcoal, kerosene or gas

job /dʒɒb/ *noun* **1** the work that you do for money: *He has left school but he hasn't got a job.* ○ *She's looking for a new job.* **2** a piece of work that you must do: *I have a lot of jobs to do in the house.* **a good job** a good or lucky thing: *It's a good job that I was at home when you phoned.* **make a good job of something** do something well: *You made a good job of the painting.* **out of a job** If you are out of a job, you do not have work that you are paid to do.

jockey /ˈdʒɒki/ *noun* (*plural* **jockeys**) a person who rides horses in races

jog /dʒɒg/ *verb* (**jogs**, **jogging**, **jogged** /dʒɒgd/) **1** run slowly for exercise: *I jogged round the park.* ✪ We often say **go jogging**: *I go jogging every morning.* **2** push or touch something a little, so that it moves: *She jogged my arm and I spilled my drink.*

jog *noun* (no plural) a slow run for exercise: *I went for a jog.*

jogger *noun* a person who jogs

jogging *noun* (no plural) running slowly for exercise

join /dʒɔɪn/ *verb* (**joins**, **joining**, **joined** /dʒɔɪnd/) **1** bring or fix one thing to another thing: *The new road joins the two villages.* ○ *Join the two pieces of wood together.* **2** come together with somebody or something: *This road joins the highway soon.* ○ *Will you join us for dinner?* **3** become a member of a group: *He joined the army.* **join in** do something with other people: *We're playing football.*

Do you want to join in?

joint[1] /dʒɔɪnt/ *noun* **1** a part of the body where two bones come together. Elbows and knees are joints. **2** a place where two parts of something join together: *the joints of a pipe* **3** a big piece of meat that you cook: *a joint of beef*

joint[2] /dʒɔɪnt/ *adjective* that people do or have together: *Nigeria won, and Spain and Denmark finished joint second.*

joke[1] /dʒəʊk/ *noun* something that you say or do to make people laugh: *She told us a joke.* **play a joke on somebody** do something to somebody to make other people laugh; trick somebody: *They played a joke on their teacher – they hid his books.*

joke[2] /dʒəʊk/ *verb* (**jokes**, **joking**, **joked** /dʒəʊkt/) say things that are not serious; say funny things: *I didn't really mean what I said – I was only joking.*

jolly /ˈdʒɒli/ *adjective* (**jollier**, **jolliest**) happy and full of fun

jolt /dʒəʊlt/ *noun* a sudden movement: *The train stopped with a jolt.*

jolt *verb* (**jolts**, **jolting**, **jolted**) make something or somebody move suddenly: *The car stopped suddenly and the passengers were jolted forwards.*

jot /dʒɒt/ *verb* (**jots**, **jotting**, **jotted**) **jot down** write something quickly: *I jotted down his phone number.*

journal /ˈdʒɜːnl/ *noun* a magazine about one special thing: *a medical journal*

journalism /ˈdʒɜːnəlɪzəm/ *noun* (no plural) the work of writing about the news for newspapers, magazines, television or radio

journalist /ˈdʒɜːnəlɪst/ *noun* a person whose job is to write about the news for newspapers, magazines, television or radio

journey /ˈdʒɜːni/ *noun* (*plural* **journeys**) going from one place to another: *Did you have a good journey?* ○ *The bus journey took about 12 hours.*

joy /dʒɔɪ/ *noun* (no plural) a very happy feeling: *Their children give them so much joy.*

joystick /ˈdʒɔɪstɪk/ a handle that you move to control something, for example a computer or an aeroplane

☞ picture at **computer**

jua kali /ˌdʒʊə ˈkæli/ *noun* (no plural) a Swahili phrase used for talking about informal jobs that people do to earn a living, especially making useful things to sell from old metal and wood: *the jua kali industry* ○ *a jua kali mechanic*

Judaism /ˈdʒuːdeɪɪzəm/ *noun* (no plural) the religion of the Jewish people

judge[1] /dʒʌdʒ/ *noun* **1** the person in a court of law who decides how to punish somebody: *The judge sent the man to prison for 20 years for killing his wife.* **2** a person who chooses the winner of a competition

judge[2] /dʒʌdʒ/ *verb* (judges, judging, judged /dʒʌdʒd/) **1** decide if something is good or bad, right or wrong, for example **2** decide who or what wins a competition: *The headmaster judged the painting competition.*

judgement /ˈdʒʌdʒmənt/ *noun* **1** what a judge in a court of law decides **2** what you think about somebody or something: *In my judgement, she will do the job very well.*

judo /ˈdʒuːdəʊ/ *noun* (no plural) a sport where two people fight and try to throw each other onto the floor

jug /dʒʌg/ *noun* a container with a handle that you use for holding or pouring water or milk, for example

jug

juggle /ˈdʒʌgl/ *verb* (juggles, juggling, juggled /ˈdʒʌgld/) keep two or more things in the air by throwing and catching them quickly: *The clown juggled three oranges.*

juggle

juggler /ˈdʒʌglə(r)/ *noun* a person who juggles

juice /dʒuːs/ *noun* (no plural) the liquid from fruit and vegetables: *a glass of orange juice* ○ *lemon juice*

juicy /ˈdʒuːsi/ *adjective* (juicier, juiciest) with a lot of juice: *big juicy tomatoes*

jukebox /ˈdʒuːkbɒks/ *noun* (plural jukeboxes) a machine in a café or bar that plays music when you put money in it

July /dʒuˈlaɪ/ *noun* the seventh month of the year

jumble /ˈdʒʌmbl/ *verb* (jumbles, jumbling, jumbled /ˈdʒʌmbld/) jumble up mix things so that they are untidy or in the wrong place: *I can't find the photo I was looking for – they are all jumbled up in this box.*

jumble *noun* (no plural) a lot of things that are mixed together in an untidy way: *a jumble of old clothes and books*

jumble sale /ˈdʒʌmbl seɪl/ *noun* a sale of things that people do not want any more. Clubs, churches and schools often have jumble sales to get money.

jump /dʒʌmp/ *verb* (jumps, jumping, jumped /dʒʌmpt/) **1** move quickly off the ground, using your legs to push you up: *The cat jumped onto the table.* ○ *The horse jumped over the wall.* **2** move quickly: *He jumped into the car and drove away.* **3** move suddenly because you are surprised or frightened: *A loud noise made me jump.*

jump

jump *noun*: *With one jump, the horse was over the fence.*

jumper /ˈdʒʌmpə(r)/ *noun* a warm piece of clothing with sleeves, that you wear on the top part of your body. Jumpers are often made of wool. ☞ picture at **coat**

junction /ˈdʒʌŋkʃn/ *noun* a place where roads or railway lines meet: *Turn right at the next junction.*

June /dʒuːn/ *noun* the sixth month of the year

jungle /ˈdʒʌŋgl/ *noun* a thick forest in a hot part of the world: *There are jungles in South America.*

junior /ˈdʒuːniə(r)/ *adjective* **1** less important: *He's a junior officer in the army.* **2** younger: *a junior pupil* ✪ opposite: **senior**

junior school /'dʒu:nɪə sku:l/ *noun* a school for children between the ages of seven and eleven

junk /dʒʌŋk/ *noun* (no plural) things that are old or useless: *The cupboard is full of junk.*

junk food /'dʒʌŋk fu:d/ *noun* food that is not very good for you, but that is easy to prepare or ready to eat

jury /'dʒʊəri/ *noun* (*plural* **juries**) a group of people in a court of law who decide if somebody has done something wrong or not: *The jury decided that the woman was guilty of killing her husband.*

just[1] /dʒʌst/ *adverb* **1** a very short time before: *Jim isn't here – he's just gone out.* **2** at this or that moment; now or very soon: *I'm just going to make some coffee.* ○ *She phoned just as I was going to bed.* **3** only: *It's just a small present.*

4 almost not: *I ran to the station and I just caught the train.* **5** a word that makes what you say stronger: *Just look at that funny little dog!* **just a minute**, **just a moment** wait for a short time: *Just a minute – there's someone at the door.* **just now 1** at this time; now: *I can't talk to you just now. I'm busy.* **2** a short time before: *Where's Liz? She was here just now.*

just[2] /dʒʌst/ *adjective* fair and right: *a just punishment* ✪ opposite: **unjust**

justice /'dʒʌstɪs/ *noun* (no plural) **1** being fair and right: *Justice for all!* ✪ opposite: **injustice 2** the law: *British justice*

justify /'dʒʌstɪfaɪ/ *verb* (**justifies**, **justifying**, **justified** /'dʒʌstɪfaɪd/, **has justified**) be or give a good reason for something: *Can you justify what you did?*

Kk

kanga /'kæŋgæ/, **leso** *noun* (an East African word) a piece of loose clothing for a woman or girl that she ties round her body.

kangaroo

kangaroo /ˌkæŋgə'ru:/ *noun* (*plural* **kangaroos**) an animal in Australia that jumps on its strong back legs

karate /kə'rɑ:ti/ *noun* (no plural) a Japanese sport where people fight with their hands and feet

keen /ki:n/ *adjective* (**keener**, **keenest**) **1** If you are keen, you want to do something and are interested in it: *Sintamei was keen to go out but I wanted to stay at home.* ○ *Rosa is a keen swimmer.* **2** very good or strong: *keen eyesight* **be keen on somebody** or

something like somebody or something very much: *My brother is keen on football.*

keep /ki:p/ *verb* (**keeps**, **keeping**, **kept** /kept/, **has kept**) **1** have something and not give it to another person: *You can keep that book – I don't need it.* **2** continue in the same way and not change: *Keep still – I want to take your photograph.* **3** make somebody or something stay the same and not change: *Keep this door closed.* ○ *You must keep the baby warm.* **4** have something in a special place: *Where do you keep the coffee?* **5** not stop doing something; do something many times: *Keep walking until you see the school, then turn left.* ○ *She keeps forgetting my name.* **6** look after and buy food and other things for a person or an animal: *It costs a lot to keep a family of four.* ○ *They keep sheep and goats on their farm.* **7** stay fresh: *Will this fish keep until tomorrow?* **keep away from somebody** or **something** not go near somebody or something: *Keep away from the river please, children.*

keep somebody from stop somebody from doing something: *You can't keep me from going out!* **keep going** continue; not stop: *I was very tired but I kept going to the end of the race.* **keep off something** not go on something: *Keep off the grass!* **keep on** not stop doing something; do something many times: *We kept on studying all night!* ○ *That man keeps on looking at me.* **keep out** stay outside: *The sign on the door said 'Danger. Keep out!'* **keep somebody or something out** stop somebody or something from going in: *We put a fence round the garden to keep the goats out.* **keep up with somebody or something** go as fast as another person or thing so that you are together: *Don't walk so quickly – I can't keep up with you.*

keeper /ˈkiːpə(r)/ *noun* a person who looks after something: *He's a keeper at the zoo – he looks after the lions.* ☞ Look also at **goalkeeper**.

kennel /ˈkenl/ *noun* a small house where a dog sleeps

kept *form of* **keep**

kerb /kɜːb/ *noun* the edge of a path next to a road: *They stood on the kerb waiting to cross the road.*

kerosene /ˈkerəsiːn/ *noun* (no plural) a type of oil that we use in stoves, lamps, etc

ketchup /ˈketʃəp/ *noun* (no plural) a cold sauce made from tomatoes: *Do you want ketchup on your chips?*

kettle /ˈketl/ *noun* a metal or plastic pot that you use for making water hot: *Put the kettle on* (= fill it with water and make it start to get hot).

key[1] /kiː/ *noun* **1** a piece of metal that opens or closes a lock: *He turned the key and opened the door.* **2** one of the parts of a typewriter, computer, piano, etc that you press with your fingers: *Pianos have black and white keys.* **3** answers to questions: *Check your answers with the key at the back of the book.*

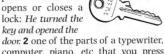
key

key[2] /kiː/ *verb* (**keys**, **keying**, **keyed** /kiːd/) **key in** put words or numbers into a computer by pressing the keys: *Key in your name.*

keyboard /ˈkiːbɔːd/ *noun* **1** all the keys on a piano, computer or typewriter, for example ☞ picture at **computer** **2** a musical instrument like a small electrical piano: *a keyboard player*

keyhole /ˈkiːhəʊl/ *noun* a hole in a lock where you put a key

kg *short way of writing* **kilogram**

kick[1] /kɪk/ *verb* (**kicks**, **kicking**, **kicked** /kɪkt/) **1** hit somebody or something with your foot: *I kicked the ball to Chris.* **2** move your foot or feet up quickly: *The child was kicking and screaming.* **kick off** start a game of football **kick somebody out** make somebody leave a place: *The boys were kicked out of the cinema because they were noisy*

kick[2] /kɪk/ *noun* **1** hitting something or somebody with your foot, or moving your foot or feet up quickly: *John gave the ball a kick.* **2** a feeling of excitement

kick-off /ˈkɪk ɒf/ *noun* the start of a game of football: *The kick-off is at 2.30.*

kid /kɪd/ *noun* **1** a child: *How old are your kids?* ✪ This is an informal word. **2** a young goat ☞ picture at **goat**

kidnap /ˈkɪdnæp/ *verb* (**kidnaps**, **kidnapping**, **kidnapped** /ˈkɪdnæpt/) take somebody away and hide them, so that their family or friends will pay you money to free them: *The son of a rich businessman was kidnapped today.*

kidnapper *noun* a person who kidnaps somebody

kidney /ˈkɪdni/ *noun* (*plural* **kidneys**) one of two parts inside your body ☞ picture on page A4

kill /kɪl/ *verb* (**kills**, **killing**, **killed** /kɪld/) make somebody or something die: *The police do not know who killed the old man.* ○ *Three people were killed in the accident.*

killer *noun* a person, animal or thing that kills

kilogram, **kilogramme** /ˈkɪləɡræm/, **kilo** /ˈkiːləʊ/ (*plural* **kilos**) *noun* a measure of weight. There are 1 000 grams in a kilogram: *I bought two kilos of potatoes.* ✪ The short way of writing 'kilogram' is **kg**: *1 kg of bananas*

kilometre /ˈkɪləmiːtə(r)/, /kɪˈlɒmɪtə(r)/ *noun* a measure of length. There are 1000 **metres** in a kilometre. ✪ The short way of writing 'kilometre' is **km**: *They live 100 km from Kampala.*

kilt /kɪlt/ *noun* a skirt that men in Scotland sometimes wear

kind[1] /kaɪnd/ *adjective* (**kinder**, **kindest**) friendly and good to other people: *'Can I carry your bag?' 'Thanks. That's very kind of you.'* ○ *Be kind to animals.* ✪ opposite: **unkind**

kind-hearted /ˌkaɪnd ˈhɑːtɪd/ *adjective* A person who is kind-hearted is kind and gentle to other people.

kindness /ˈkaɪndnəs/ *noun* (no plural) being kind: *Thank you for your kindness.*

kind[2] /kaɪnd/ *noun* a group of things or people that are the same in some way; a sort or type: *What kind of car do you have?* ○ *There are three different kinds of mosquito.* **kind of** words that you use when you are not sure about something: *He looks kind of tired.*

kindly[1] /ˈkaɪndli/ *adverb* in a kind way: *She kindly helped me cook the dinner.*

kindly[2] /ˈkaɪndli/ *adjective* (**kindlier**, **kindliest**) kind and friendly: *a kindly old man*

king /kɪŋ/ *noun* a man who rules a country and who is from a royal family: *King Hussein of Jordan* ☛ Look at **queen**.

kingdom /ˈkɪŋdəm/ *noun* a country where a king or queen rules: *the United Kingdom*

kiosk /ˈkiːɒsk/ *noun* a small shop in a street where you can buy things like sweets and newspapers through an open window ☛ Look also at **telephone kiosk**.

kiss /kɪs/ *verb* (**kisses**, **kissing**, **kissed** /kɪst/) touch somebody with your lips to show love or to say hello or goodbye: *She kissed me on the cheek.*

kiss (*plural* **kisses**) *noun*: *Give me a kiss!*

kit /kɪt/ *noun* **1** all the clothes or other things that you need to do something or to play a sport: *Where is my football kit?* ○ *a tool kit* **2** a set of small pieces

that you put together to make something: *a kit for making a model aeroplane*

kitchen /ˈkɪtʃɪn/ *noun* a room where you cook food

kite /kaɪt/ *noun* a light toy made of paper or cloth on a long string. You can make a kite fly in the wind: *The children were flying kites on the hill.*

kitten /ˈkɪtn/ *noun* a young cat ☛ picture at **cat**

km *short way of writing* **kilometre**

knee /niː/ *noun* the part in the middle of your leg where it bends: *I fell and cut my knee.* ☛ picture on page A4

kneel /niːl/ *verb* (**kneels**, **kneeling**, **knelt** /nelt/ or **kneeled** /niːld/, **has knelt** or **has kneeled**) go down or stay with your knees on the ground: *He knelt down to pray.* ○ *Jane was kneeling on the floor.*

kneel

knew *form of* **know**

knickers /ˈnɪkəz/ *noun* (plural) a small piece of clothing that a woman or girl wears under her other clothes, between the middle of her body and the top of her legs: *a pair of knickers*

knife

knife /naɪf/ *noun* (*plural* **knives** /naɪvz/) a sharp metal thing with a handle that you use to cut things or to fight

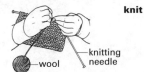
knit

wool — knitting needle

knit /nɪt/ *verb* (**knits**, **knitting**, **knitted**) use long sticks (called **knitting-needles**) to make clothes from wool: *My grandmother knitted this hat for me.*

knitting *noun* (no plural) **1** making clothes from wool: *Her hobbies are knit-*

ting and football. **2** something that you are knitting

knitting-needle /'nɪtɪŋ niːdl/ *noun* a long metal or plastic stick that you use for knitting

knives *plural of* **knife**

knob /nɒb/ *noun* **1** a round handle on a door or drawer: *a wooden doorknob* **2** a round thing that you turn to control part of a machine

knock[1] /nɒk/ *verb* (**knocks, knocking, knocked** /nɒkt/) **1** hit something to make a noise: *I knocked on the door, but nobody answered.* **2** hit something hard: *I knocked my head on the door.* ○ *She knocked a glass off the table.* **knock somebody down, knock somebody over** hit somebody so that they fall onto the ground: *The little boy was knocked down by a car.* **knock something down** break a building so that it falls down: *They knocked down the old houses and built a school in their place.* **knock somebody out** hit somebody hard so that they cannot get up again for a while **knock something over** hit something so that it falls: *I knocked over a jug and broke it.*

knock[2] /nɒk/ *noun* hitting something hard or the sound that this makes: *I heard a knock at the door.*

knot /nɒt/ *noun* a place where you have tied two ends of rope, string, etc tightly together: *I tied a knot in the rope.* ○ *Can you undo this knot (= make it loose)?*

knot

knot *verb* (**knots, knotting, knotted**) tie a knot in something: *He knotted the ends of the rope together.*

know /nəʊ/ *verb* (**knows, knowing, knew** /njuː/, **has known** /nəʊn/) **1** have something in your head, because you have learned it: *I don't know her name.* ○ *He knows a lot about cars.* ○ *Do you know how to use this machine?* ○ *'You're late!' 'Yes, I know.'* **2** have met or seen somebody or something before, perhaps many times: *I have known Mario for six years.* ○ *I know that part of the country quite well.* **get to know somebody** start to know somebody well: *I liked him when I got to know him.* **let somebody know** tell somebody: *Let me know if you need any help.* **you know** words that you use when you are thinking about what to say next ✪ You use expressions like **God knows** and **Heaven knows** to show very strongly that you do not know something: *'Where is Lisa?' 'God knows!'*

knowledge /'nɒlɪdʒ/ *noun* (no plural) what you know and understand about something: *He has a good knowledge of African history.*

knuckle /'nʌkl/ *noun* the bones where your fingers join your hand and where your hands bend

kph a way of measuring how fast something is moving. 'Kph' is short for **kilometres per hour**.

kwashiorkor /ˌkwæʃɪˈɔːkə(r)/ *noun* (no plural) (an African word) a serious illness that babies can get if they do not eat enough protein

l *short way of writing* **litre**

lab /læb/ *short for* **laboratory**

label /'leɪbl/ *noun* a piece of paper or plastic on something that tells you about it: *The label on the bottle says 'Made in Mexico'.*

label *verb* (**labels**, **labelling**, **labelled** /'leɪbld/) put a label on something: *I labelled all the boxes with my name and address.*

laboratory /lə'bɒrətri/ *noun* (*plural* **laboratories**) a special room where scientists work ✪ The short form of 'laboratory' is **lab**.

labour /'leɪbə(r)/ *noun* (no plural) hard work that you do with your hands and body

labourer /'leɪbərə(r)/ *noun* a person who does hard work with his/her hands and body: *a farm labourer*

lace /leɪs/ *noun* (*plural* **laces**) a string that you tie to close a shoe

lack /læk/ *verb* (**lacks**, **lacking**, **lacked** /lækt/) not have something, or not have enough of something: *The children lacked the food they needed.* **be lacking** be needed: *Money is lacking for a new school.*

lack *noun* (no plural) *There is a lack of good teachers.*

lad /læd/ *noun* a boy or young man

ladder /'lædə(r)/ *noun* two tall pieces of metal or wood with shorter pieces (called **rungs**) between them. You use a ladder for climbing up something.

lady /'leɪdi/ *noun* (*plural* **ladies**) a polite way of saying 'woman': *an old lady* ☞ Look at **gentleman**.

laid *form of* **lay**²

lain *form of* **lie**²

lake /leɪk/ *noun* a big area of water with land all around it: *Lake Victoria* ○ *We went swimming in the lake.*

lamb /læm/ *noun* **1** (*plural* **lambs**) a young sheep ☞ picture at **sheep**. **2** (no plural) meat from a lamb

lame /leɪm/ *adjective* If an animal is lame, it cannot walk well because it has hurt its leg or foot: *The ox went lame and couldn't work.*

lamp /læmp/ *noun* a thing that gives light: *It was dark, so I switched on the lamp.*

lamppost /'læmppəʊst/ *noun* a tall thing in the street with a light on the top

lampshade /'læmpʃeɪd/ *noun* a cover for a lamp

land¹ /lænd/ *noun* **1** (no plural) the part of the earth that is not the sea: *After two weeks in a boat, we were happy to see land.* **2** (no plural) a piece of ground: *They have bought some land and they are going to build a house on it.* ○ *farming land* **3** (*plural* **lands**) a country: *She returned to the land where she was born.* ✪ In this sense, **country** is the word that we usually use.

land² /lænd/ *verb* (**lands**, **landing**, **landed**) **1** come onto the ground from the air or from the sea: *The plane landed at Entebbe airport.* ○ *The boat has landed.* **2** bring an aircraft down onto the ground: *The pilot landed the plane safely.*

landing /'lændɪŋ/ *noun* **1** coming down onto the ground: *The plane made a safe landing in a field.* **2** a flat place at the top of stairs in a building: *There's a telephone on the landing.*

landlady /'lændleɪdi/ *noun* (*plural* **landladies**) **1** a woman who has a house and lets you live there if you pay her money **2** a woman who has a small hotel

landlord /ˈlændlɔːd/ *noun* **1** a man who has a house and lets you live there if you pay him money **2** a man who has a small hotel

landmark /ˈlændmaːk/ *noun* a big building or another thing that you can see easily from far away: *Mount Kilimanjaro is Tanzania's most famous landmark.*

landscape /ˈlændskeɪp/ *noun* everything you can see in an area of land: *The landscape around Lake Victoria is very beautiful.*

landslide /ˈlændslaɪd/ *noun* a large amount of earth and rock that falls down the side of a mountain: *Was anyone killed in the landslide?*

lane /leɪn/ *noun* one part of a wide road: *We were driving in the middle lane of the highway.*

language /ˈlæŋgwɪdʒ/ *noun* **1** (no plural) words that people say or write **2** (*plural* **languages**) words that a certain group of people say and write: *'Do you speak any foreign languages?' 'Yes, I speak French and Italian.'*

lap[1] /læp/ *noun* the flat part at the top of your legs when you are sitting: *The child sat on his mother's lap.*

lap[2] /læp/ *noun* going once round the track in a race: *The runner fell on the last lap.*

large /lɑːdʒ/ *adjective* (**larger**, **largest**) big: *They live in a large house.* ○ *She has a large family.* ○ *Have you got this shirt in a large size?* ✪ opposite: **small**
☛ picture on page A10

largely /ˈlɑːdʒli/ *adverb* mostly; mainly: *The room is largely used for meetings.*

larva /ˈlɑːvə/ *noun* (*plural* **larvae** /ˈlɑːviː/) an insect that has come out of an egg and looks like a short fat worm

laser /ˈleɪzə(r)/ *noun* an instrument that makes a very strong line of light (called a **laser beam**). Some lasers are used to cut metal and others are used by doctors in operations.

last[1] /lɑːst/ *adjective* **1** after all the others: *December is the last month of the year.* **2** just before now: *It's June now, so last month was May.* ○ *I was at school*

last week, but this week I'm on holiday. **3** only one left: *Can the last person in the room switch off the light, please?*
last night yesterday in the evening or in the night: *Did you go out last night?*

lastly *adverb* finally, as the last thing: *Lastly, I want to thank my parents for all their help.*

last[2] /lɑːst/ *adverb* **1** after all the others: *He finished last in the race.* **2** at a time that is nearest to now: *I last saw Karim in 1997.*

last[3] /lɑːst/ *noun* (no plural) a person or thing that comes after all the others; what comes at the end: *I was the last to arrive at the party.* **at last** in the end; after some time: *She waited all week, and at last the letter arrived.*

last[4] /lɑːst/ *verb* (**lasts**, **lasting**, **lasted**) **1** continue for a time: *The film lasted for three hours.* ○ *I hope the good weather will last until the weekend.* **2** be enough for a certain time: *We have enough food to last us till next week.*

late /leɪt/ *adjective, adverb* (**later**, **latest**) **1** after the usual or right time: *I went to bed late last night.* ○ *I was late for school today* (= I arrived late). ○ *My train was late.* ✪ opposite: **early** **2** near the end of a time: *They arrived in the late afternoon.* ○ *She's in her late twenties* (= between the ages of 25 and 29). ✪ opposite: **early** **3** no longer alive; dead: *Her late husband was a doctor.* **a late night** an evening when you go to bed later than usual **at the latest** not later than: *Please be here by twelve o'clock at the latest.* **later on** at a later time: *Bye – I'll see you later on.*

lately /ˈleɪtli/ *adverb* not long ago; recently: *Have you seen Mark lately?* ○ *The weather has been very bad lately.*

latest /ˈleɪtɪst/ *adjective* newest: *the latest fashions*

latrine /ləˈtriːn/ *noun* a hole in the ground that is used as a toilet

latter /ˈlætə(r)/ *adjective* last: *She couldn't walk very well in the latter part of her life.*

latter *noun* (no plural) the second of two things or people: *If I had to choose between an interesting job and a well-paid job, I would choose the latter.*

☞ Look at **former**.

laugh /lɑːf/ verb (**laughs, laughing, laughed** /lɑːft/) make sounds that show you are happy or that you think something is funny: *His jokes always make me laugh.* **laugh at somebody** or **something** laugh to show that you think somebody or something is funny or silly: *The children laughed at the clown.* ○ *They all laughed at me when I said I was frightened of dogs.*

laugh noun: *My brother has a loud laugh.* ○ *She told us a joke and we all had a good laugh.* **for a laugh** as a joke; for fun: *The boys put a spider in her bed for a laugh.*

laughter /ˈlɑːftə(r)/ noun (no plural) the sound of laughing: *I could hear laughter in the next room.*

launch /lɔːntʃ/ verb (**launches, launching, launched** /lɔːntʃt/) **1** put a ship into the water or a spacecraft into the sky: *This ship was launched in 1967.* **2** start something new: *The magazine was launched last year.*

laundry /ˈlɔːndri/ noun **1** (no plural) clothes that you must wash or that you have washed: *a laundry basket* **2** (plural **laundries**) a place where you send things like sheets and clothes so that somebody can wash them for you

lava /ˈlɑːvə/ noun (no plural) hot liquid rock that comes out of a **volcano**

lavatory /ˈlævətri/ noun (plural **lavatories**) a large bowl with a seat that you use when you need to empty waste from your body. The room that it is in is also called a **lavatory**: *Where's the lavatory, please?* ✪ **Toilet** is the word that we usually use.

law /lɔː/ noun **1** a rule of a country that says what people may and may not do: *There is a law against stealing.* ☞ Look at **legal**. **2 the law** (no plural) all the laws of a country **against the law** not allowed by the rules of a country: *Murder is against the law.* **break the law** do something that the laws of a country say you must not do: *I have never broken the law.*

lawcourt /ˈlɔːkɔːt/ noun a place where people (a **judge** or **jury**) decide if somebody has done something wrong, and what the punishment will be

lawn /lɔːn/ noun a piece of short grass in a garden or park: *They were sitting on the lawn.*

lawnmower /ˈlɔːnməʊə(r)/ noun a machine that cuts grass

lawyer /ˈlɔːjə(r)/ noun a person who has studied the law and who helps people or talks for them in a court of law

lay[1] form of **lie**[2]

lay[2] /leɪ/ verb (**lays, laying, laid** /leɪd/, **has laid**) **1** put something carefully on another thing: *I laid the papers on the desk.* **2** make an egg: *Birds and insects lay eggs.*

layer /ˈleɪə(r)/ noun something flat that lies on another thing or that is between other things: *The table was covered with a thin layer of dust.* ○ *It was so cold at night we had to wear four layers of clothing.*

lazy /ˈleɪzi/ adjective (**lazier, laziest**) A person who is lazy does not want to work: *Don't be so lazy – come and help me!* ○ *My teacher said I was lazy.*

lazily /ˈleɪzɪli/ adverb in a slow, lazy way: *She walked lazily across the room.*

laziness /ˈleɪzɪnəs/ noun (no plural) being lazy

lb short way of writing **pound**[2]

lead[1] /led/ noun **1** (no plural) a soft grey metal that is very heavy. Lead is used to make things like water-pipes. **2** (plural **leads**) the grey part inside a pencil

lead[2] /liːd/ verb (**leads, leading, led** /led/, **has led**) **1** take a person or an animal somewhere by going in front: *He led me to my room.* **2** be the first or the best, for example in a race or game: *Who's leading in the race?* **3** go to a place: *This path leads to the river.* **4** control a group of people: *The team was led by Joseph Muben.* **lead to something** make something happen: *Smoking can lead to heart disease.*

lead[3] /liːd/ noun (no plural) going in front or doing something first **be in the lead** be in front: *Gebreselassie was in the lead right from the start of the race.*

lead[4] /liːd/ noun **1** a long piece of leather or a chain that you tie to a dog's neck so that it walks with you **2** a long piece of wire that brings electricity to things like lamps and machines

leader /'li:də(r)/ *noun* **1** a person who controls a group of people: *They chose a new leader.* **2** a person or group that is the first or the best: *The leader is ten metres in front of the other runners.*

leadership /'li:dəʃɪp/ *noun* (no plural) controlling a group of people: *The country is under new leadership* (= has new leaders).

leading /'li:dɪŋ/ *adjective* best or very important: *a leading writer*

leaf /li:f/ *noun* (plural **leaves** /li:vz/) one of the flat green parts that grow on a plant or tree ✪ pictures at **plant** and **tree**

leaflet /'li:flət/ *noun* a piece of paper with writing on it that tells you about something: *A young boy was handing out leaflets in the street.*

league /li:g/ *noun* **1** a group of teams that play against each other in a sport: *the football league* **2** a group of people or countries that work together to do something: *the Arab League*

leak /li:k/ *verb* (**leaks**, **leaking**, **leaked** /li:kt/) **1** have a hole that liquid or gas can go through: *The roof of our house leaks when it rains.* ○ *The boat is leaking.* **2** go out through a hole: *Water is leaking from the pipe.*

leak *noun*: *There's a leak in the roof.*

lean[1] /li:n/ *adjective* (**leaner**, **leanest**) **1** thin but strong: *He is tall and lean.* **2** Lean meat does not have very much fat.

lean[2] /li:n/ *verb* (**leans**, **leaning**, **leant** /lent/ or **leaned** /li:nd/, **has leant** or **has leaned**) **1** not be straight; bend forwards, backwards or to the side **2** put your body or a thing against another thing: *Lean your bike against the wall.*

leap /li:p/ *verb* (**leaps**, **leaping**, **leapt** /lept/ or **leaped** /li:pt/, **has leapt** or **has leaped**) make a big jump: *The cat leapt onto the table.*

leap *noun* a big jump: *With one leap, he was over the wall.*

leap year /'li:p jɪə(r)/ *noun* a year when February has 29 days. Leap years happen every four years.

learn /lɜ:n/ *verb* (**learns**, **learning**, **learnt** /lɜ:nt/ or **learned** /lɜ:nd/, **has learnt** or **has learned**) **1** find out

something, or how to do something, by studying or by doing it often: *Ali is learning to swim.* ○ *I learnt English at school.* ○ *Learn this list of words for homework* (= so you can remember them). ☛ Look at **teach**. **2** hear about something: *I was sorry to learn of your father's death.*

learner /'lɜ:nə(r)/ *noun* a person who is learning: *This dictionary is for learners of English.*

least[1] /li:st/ *adjective*, *pronoun* the smallest amount of something: *Rose earns a lot of money, Jane earns less, and Kate earns the least.* ☛ Look at **less**.

least[2] /li:st/ *adverb* less than all others: *This is the least expensive camera in the shop.* **at least 1** not less than: *It will cost at least 1 500 shillings.* **2** although other things are bad: *We're not rich, but at least we're happy.* **not in the least** not at all: *'Are you angry?' 'Not in the least!'*

leather /'leðə(r)/ *noun* (no plural) the skin of an animal that is used to make things like shoes, jackets or bags: *a leather jacket*

leave[1] /li:v/ *verb* (**leaves**, **leaving**, **left** /left/, **has left**) **1** go away from somebody or something: *The train leaves at 8.40.* ○ *I left my job in May.* **2** let somebody or something stay in the same place or in the same way: *John left the door open.* **3** not bring something with you: *I left my books at home.* **4** make something stay; not use something: *Leave some food for me!* **leave somebody alone** not speak to or touch somebody: *Leave me alone – I'm busy!* **leave something alone** not touch or take something: *Leave that bag alone – it's mine!* **leave somebody or something behind** not take somebody or something with you: *She went shopping and left the children behind.* **leave for** start a journey to a place: *Mrs Omenya is leaving for Cairo tomorrow.* **leave out** not put in or do something; not include somebody or something: *The other children left him out of the game.* ○ *I left out question 3 in the exam because it was too difficult.* **leave something to somebody 1** let somebody do a job for you: *I left the cooking* to my sister. **2** give something to somebody when you die: *She left all her money to her sons.*

leave² /liːv/ *noun* (no plural) a time when you do not go to work: *I have 25 days' leave each year.* **on leave** having a holiday from your job: *He's on leave from the army.*

leaves *plural of* **leaf**

lecture /ˈlektʃə(r)/ *noun* a talk to a group of people to teach them about something: *She gave an interesting lecture on Spanish history.*

lecture *verb* (**lectures**, **lecturing**, **lectured** /ˈlektʃəd/) *Professor Sims lectures on Modern Art.*

lecturer *noun* a person whose job is to lecture: *He is a university lecturer.*

led *form of* **lead²**

ledge /ledʒ/ *noun* a long narrow flat place, for example under a window or on the side of a mountain: *a window-ledge*

left¹ *form of* **leave¹** **be left** be there after the rest has gone: *There is not much food left.*

left² /left/ *adjective, adverb* opposite of right: *Turn left at the church.* ○ *My left leg hurts.*

left *noun* (no plural) *The house is on your left.* ○ *In Kenya we drive on the left.*

left-hand /ˈleft hænd/ *adjective* of or on the left: *Your heart is on the left-hand side of your body.*

left-handed /ˌleft ˈhændɪd/ *adjective* If you are left-handed, you use your left hand more easily than your right-hand, for example when you write.

leg /leg/ *noun* **1** one of the long parts of the body of a person or an animal that is used for walking and standing: *A dog has four legs.* ☛ picture on page A4 **2** one of the parts of a pair of trousers that covers your leg **3** one of the long parts that a table or chair stands on **pull somebody's leg** try to make somebody believe something that is not true, for fun: *I didn't really see a ghost – I was only pulling your leg!*

legal /ˈliːɡl/ *adjective* **1** allowed by the law: *In many parts of America, it is legal to carry a gun.* ✪ opposite: **illegal**

or **against the law 2** of or about the law: *legal advice*

legally /ˈliːɡəli/ *adverb*: *They are not legally married.*

legend /ˈledʒənd/ *noun* an old story that is perhaps not true: *the legend of Bimwili and the Zimwi*

leisure /ˈleʒə(r)/ *noun* (no plural) the time when you are not working and can do what you want

lemon /ˈlemən/ *noun* a yellow fruit with a sour taste

lemon

lemonade /ˌleməˈneɪd/ *noun* **1** (no plural) a sweet clear drink with bubbles in it **2** (*plural* **lemonades**) a glass of this drink

lend /lend/ *verb* (**lends**, **lending**, **lent** /lent/, **has lent**) give something to somebody for a short time: *Rick lent me his car for an hour.* ☛ picture at **borrow**

length /leŋθ/ *noun* (no plural) how long something is: *The table is two metres in length.* ○ *We measured the length of the room.* ☛ picture on page A5

lengthen /ˈleŋθn/ *verb* (**lengthens**, **lengthening**, **lengthened** /ˈleŋθnd/) become longer or make something longer

lengthy /ˈleŋθi/ *adjective* (**lengthier**, **lengthiest**) long: *a lengthy meeting*

lens /lenz/ *noun* (*plural* **lenses**) a special piece of glass in things like cameras, microscopes or glasses ☛ Look also at **contact lens**.

lent *form of* **lend**

lentil /ˈlentl/ *noun* a small round dried seed. You cook lentils in water before you eat them: *lentil soup*

leopard /ˈlepəd/ *noun* a wild animal like a big cat with yellow fur and dark spots

leopard

leso /'lesɒ/ *noun* = **kanga**

less[1] /les/ *adjective, pronoun* a smaller amount of something; not so much: *A poor person has less money than a rich person.* ○ *I'm too fat – I should eat less.* ☞ Look at **least**.

less[2] /les/ *adverb* not so much: *It rains less in summer.* ○ *He's less intelligent than his sister.* ☞ Look at **least**.

lesson /'lesn/ *noun* a time when you learn something with a teacher: *I was late for school and missed the first lesson.*

let[1] /let/ *verb* (**lets**, **letting**, **let**, **has let**) allow somebody or something to do something: *Her parents won't let her go out with her boyfriend.* ○ *Let me carry your bag.* ○ *Let the dog in* (= let it come in). **let somebody down** not do something that you promised to do for somebody: *Margaret has let me down. We agreed to meet at eight o'clock but she didn't come.* **let go of somebody** or **something**, **let somebody** or **something go** stop holding somebody or something: *Let go of my hand!* ○ *Hold the rope and don't let go.* **let somebody off** not punish somebody: *He wasn't sent to prison – the judge let him off.* **let's** You use 'let's' to ask somebody to do something with you: *Let's go to the cinema this evening.*

let[2] /let/ *verb* (**lets**, **letting**, **let**, **has let**) allow somebody to use your house or land if they pay you: *Have you got any rooms to let?*

letter /'letə(r)/ *noun* **1** a sign in writing: *Z is the last letter in the English alphabet.*

> ✪ A, B and C are **capital** letters, and a, b, and c are **small** letters. **2** a piece of writing that one person sends to another person: *Did you post my letter?* ○ *She wrote a·letter to her mother.*

letter-box /'letə bɒks/ *noun* (*plural* **letter-boxes**) **1** a hole for letters in the door of a building **2** a box for letters outside a house **3** a box in the street where you put letters that you want to send

lettuce /'letɪs/ *noun* a plant with big leaves that you eat without cooking, in salads

level[1] /'levl/ *adjective* **1** with no part higher than another part; flat: *We need level ground to play football on.* ○ *This shelf isn't level.* **2** with the same heights, points or positions, for example: *The two teams are level with 40 points each.* ○ *His head is level with his mother's shoulder.*

level[2] /'levl/ *noun* how high something is: *The town is 500 metres above sea level.* ○ *an elementary-level French class*

level crossing /ˌlevl 'krɒsɪŋ/ *noun* a place where a railway line goes over a road

lever /'liːvə(r)/ *noun* **1** a bar for lifting something heavy or opening something. You put one end under the thing you want to lift or open, and push the other end. **2** a thing that you pull or push to make a machine work: *Pull this lever.*

liable /'laɪəbl/ *adjective* If you are liable to do something, you usually do it or you will probably do it: *He's liable to get angry if you don't do what he says.*

liar /'laɪə(r)/ *noun* a person who says or writes things that are not true: *I don't believe her – she's a liar.*

liberal /'lɪbərəl/ *adjective* A person who is liberal lets other people do and think what they want: *Marion's parents are very liberal, but mine are quite strict.*

liberate /'lɪbəreɪt/ *verb* (**liberates**, **liberating**, **liberated**) make somebody or something free: *France was liberated in 1945.*

liberty /'lɪbəti/ *noun* (no plural) being free to go where you want and do what you want

library /'laɪbrəri/ *noun* (*plural* **libraries**) a room or building where you go to borrow or read books ✪ Be careful! You cannot buy books from a **library**. The place where you buy books is called a **bookshop**.

librarian /laɪ'breəriən/ *noun* a person who works in a library

licence /'laɪsns/ *noun* a piece of paper that shows you are allowed to do or have something: *Do you have a driving-licence?*

license /'laɪsns/ *verb* (**licenses**, **licensing**, **licensed** /'laɪsnst/) give somebody a licence: *This shop is licensed to sell guns.*

lick /lɪk/ *verb* (**licks**, **licking**, **licked** /lɪkt/) move your tongue over something: *The cat was licking its paws.*

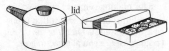
lid

lid /lɪd/ *noun* the top part of a box, pot or other container that covers it and that you can take off ☛ Look also at **eyelid**.

lie¹ /laɪ/ *verb* (**lies**, **lying**, **lied** /laɪd/, **has lied**) say something that you know is not true: *He lied about his age. He said he was 16 but really he's 14.*
lie *noun* something you say that you know is not true: *She told me a lie.* ✪ A person who lies is a **liar**.

lie² /laɪ/ *verb* (**lies**, **lying**, **lay** /leɪ/, **has lain** /leɪn/) **1** put your body flat on something so that you are not sitting or standing: *He lay on the bed.* **2** have your body flat on something: *The baby was lying on its back.* **3** be or stay on something: *His clothes lay on the floor where he left them.* **lie down** put or have your body flat on something: *She lay down on the bed.*

lieutenant /lef'tenənt/ *noun* an officer in the army or navy

life /laɪf/ *noun* **1** (no plural) People, animals and plants have life, but things like stone, metal and water do not: *Do you believe there is life after death?* ○ *Is there life on the moon?* **2** (*plural* **lives** /laɪvz/) being alive: *Many people lost their lives* (= died) *in the fire.* ○ *The doctor saved her life* (= stopped her dying). **3** (*plural* **lives**) the time that you have been alive: *He has lived here all his life.* **4** (no plural) the way that you live: *an unhappy life* **5** (no plural) energy; being busy and interested: *Young children are full of life.* **lead a life** live in a certain way: *She leads a busy life.*

lifebelt /'laɪfbelt/ *noun* a big ring that you hold or wear if you fall into water to stop you from drowning

lifeboat /'laɪfbəʊt/ *noun* a boat that goes to help people who are in danger at sea

life-jacket /'laɪf dʒækɪt/ *noun* a special jacket that you wear in a boat to stop you from drowning if you fall in the water

lifestyle /'laɪfstaɪl/ *noun* the way that you live: *They have a healthy lifestyle.*

lifetime /'laɪftaɪm/ *noun* all the time that you are alive: *There have been a lot of changes in my grandmother's lifetime.*

lift¹ /lɪft/ *verb* (**lifts**, **lifting**, **lifted**) move somebody or something up: *I can't lift this box. It's too heavy.* ○ *Lift your arm.*

lift² /lɪft/ *noun* **1** a machine that takes people and things up and down in a high building: *Shall we use the stairs or take the lift?* **2** a free journey in another person's car: *Can you give me a lift to Nairobi?*

light¹ /laɪt/ *noun* **1** (no plural) Light comes from the sun, fire and lamps. It makes us able to see things: *sunlight* ○ *The light was not very good so it was difficult to read.* **2** (*plural* **lights**) a thing that gives light, for example an electric lamp ☛ Look also at **traffic-lights**.

> ✪ A light can be **on** or **off**. You can **put**, **turn** or **switch** a light **on**, **off** or **out**: *Turn the lights off before you go to bed.* ○ *It's getting dark. Shall I switch the light on?*

3 (no plural) something, for example a match, that you use to start a cigarette burning: *Have you got a light?* **set light to something** make something start to burn

light² /laɪt/ *adjective* (**lighter**, **lightest**) **1** with a lot of light; not dark: *In summer it's light until about ten o'clock.* ○ *The room has a lot of windows so it's very light.* **2** with a pale colour; not dark: *a light-blue shirt*

light³ /laɪt/ *verb* (**lights**, **lighting**, **lit** /lɪt/ or **lighted**, **has lit** or **has lighted**) **1** make something start to burn: *Will you light the fire?* **2** give light to something: *The room is lit by two big lamps.* **3** easy to lift or move; not heavy: *Will you carry this bag for me? It's very light.* ☛ picture at **heavy** **4** not very much or not very strong: *light rain* ○ *I had a light breakfast.*

lightly *adverb*: *She touched me lightly on the arm.*

light-bulb /ˈlaɪt bʌlb/ *noun* the glass part of an electric lamp that gives light

lighter /ˈlaɪtə(r)/ *noun* a thing for lighting cigarettes

lighthouse /ˈlaɪthaʊs/ *noun* (*plural* **lighthouses** /ˈlaɪthaʊzɪz/) a tall building by or in the sea, with a strong light to show ships that there are rocks

lighting /ˈlaɪtɪŋ/ *noun* (no plural) the kind of lights that a place has: *street lighting*

lightning /ˈlaɪtnɪŋ/ *noun* (no plural) a sudden bright light in the sky when there is a storm: *He was struck* (= hit) *by lightning.* ☛ Look at **thunder**.

like[1] /laɪk/ *verb* (**likes**, **liking**, **liked** /laɪkt/) feel that somebody or something is good or nice; enjoy something: *Do you like Jane's new boyfriend?* ○ *I don't like carrots.* ○ *I like playing tennis.* ✪ opposite: **dislike**. **if you like** if you want: *'Shall we go out?' 'Yes, if you like.'* ✪ **Would like** is a more polite way of saying **want**: *Would you like some coffee?* ○ *I'd like to speak to the manager.*

like[2] /laɪk/ *preposition*, *conjunction* **1** the same as somebody or something: *She is wearing a dress like mine.* ○ *John looks like his father.* ☛ Look at **unlike**. **2** in the same way as somebody or something: *She acted like a child.* **3** for example: *I bought a lot of things, like books and clothes.* **what is ... like?** words that you say when you want to know more about somebody or something: *'What's that book like?' 'It's very interesting.'*

likely /ˈlaɪkli/ *adjective* (**likelier**, **likeliest**) If something is likely, it will probably happen: *It's likely that she will agree.* ○ *They are likely to be late.* ✪ opposite: **unlikely**

likeness /ˈlaɪknəs/ *noun* (no plural) being or looking the same: *There's a strong likeness between John and his brother.*

likewise /ˈlaɪkwaɪz/ *adverb* the same: *I sat down and Mohammed did likewise.*

lily /ˈlɪli/ *noun* (*plural* **lilies**) a plant with big flowers

limb /lɪm/ *noun* an arm or a leg

lime /laɪm/ *noun* a small green fruit like a lemon

limestone /ˈlaɪmstəʊn/ *noun* (no plural) a kind of rock, used for building and for making cement

limit /ˈlɪmɪt/ *noun* the most that is possible or allowed: *What is the speed limit* (= how fast are you allowed to go)?

limit *verb* (**limits**, **limiting**, **limited**) do or have no more than a certain amount or number: *There's only room for 100 people, so we must limit the number of tickets we sell.*

limp /lɪmp/ *verb* (**limps**, **limping**, **limped** /lɪmpt/) walk with difficulty because you have hurt your foot or leg

limp *noun* (no plural) *She walks with a limp.*

line[1] /laɪn/ *noun* **1** a long thin mark like this ——: *Draw a straight line.* ○ *The ball crossed the line, so it was a goal.* **2** people or things beside each other or one after the other: *Stand in a line.* **3** all the words that are beside each other on a page: *How many lines are there on this page?* ○ *I don't know the next line of the poem.* **4** a long piece of string or rope: *Hang the washing on the line to dry.* **5** what a train moves along **6** a very long wire for telephones or electricity: *I tried to phone him but the line was busy.*

line[2] /laɪn/ *verb* (**lines**, **lining**, **lined** /laɪnd/) **1** stand or be in lines along something: *People lined the street to watch the race.* **2** cover the inside of something with a different material: *The stove is made of metal lined with clay.* **line up** stand in a line or make a line: *We lined up to buy tickets.*

linen /ˈlɪnɪn/ *noun* (no plural) **1** a kind of strong cloth: *a white linen jacket* **2** things like tablecloths and sheets that are made of cotton or linen

liner /ˈlaɪnə(r)/ *noun* **1** a big ship that carries people a long way **2** a bag that you put inside something to keep it clean: *a dustbin liner*

linger /ˈlɪŋɡə(r)/ *verb* (**lingers**, **lingering**, **lingered** /ˈlɪŋɡəd/) stay somewhere for a long time: *They lingered in* *the park after the end of the concert.*

lining /ˈlaɪnɪŋ/ *noun* material that covers the inside of something: *My coat has a thick lining so it's very warm.*

link /lɪŋk/ *noun* **1** something that joins things or people together: *There's a link between smoking and heart disease.* **2** one of the round parts in a chain

link *verb* (**links, linking, linked** /lɪŋkt/) join two people or things: *A new railway line links the two cities.*

lioness

lion

lion /ˈlaɪən/ *noun* a wild animal like a big cat with yellow fur. Lions live in Africa and parts of Asia.

✪ A female lion is called a **lioness** and a young lion is called a **cub**.

lip /lɪp/ *noun* one of the two soft red parts above and below your mouth ☞ picture on page A4

lipstick /ˈlɪpstɪk/ *noun* colour that you put on your lips: *I put on some lipstick.*

liquid /ˈlɪkwɪd/ *noun* anything that is not a solid or a gas. Water, oil and milk are liquids.

liquid *adjective*: *liquid gold*

list /lɪst/ *noun* a lot of names or other things that you write, one after another: *a shopping list* (= of things that you must buy)

list *verb* (**lists, listing, listed**) write or say a list: *The teacher listed all our names.*

listen /ˈlɪsn/ *verb* (**listens, listening, listened** /ˈlɪsnd/) hear something when you are trying to hear it: *I was listening to the radio.* ○ *Listen! I want to tell you something.* ☞ Note at **hear**.

lit *form of* **light³**

literature /ˈlɪtrətʃə(r)/ *noun* (no plural) books, plays and poetry: *He is studying African literature.*

litre /ˈliːtə(r)/ *noun* a measure of liquid. There are 100 **centilitres** in a litre: *ten litres of petrol* ✪ The short way of

writing 'litre' is **l**: *20 l*

litter¹ /ˈlɪtə(r)/ *noun* **1** (no plural) pieces of paper and other things that people leave on the ground: *The park was full of litter after the concert.* **2** (plural **litters**) all the baby animals that are born to the same mother at the same time: *The dog had a litter of six puppies.*

litter² /ˈlɪtə(r)/ *verb* (**litters, littering, littered** /ˈlɪtəd/) be or make something untidy with litter: *My desk was littered with papers.*

little¹ /ˈlɪtl/ *adjective* **1** not big; small: *a little village* ☞ picture on page A10 **2** young: *a little girl* **3** not much: *We have very little money.* **a little** some but not much: *I speak a little French.*

little² /ˈlɪtl/ *adverb* I'm tired – I slept very little last night. **a little** quite; rather: *This skirt is a little too short for me.* **little by little** slowly: *Little by little she started to feel better.*

little³ /ˈlɪtl/ *pronoun* a small amount; not much: *There wasn't much food so we all just had a little.* ○ *I did very little today.*

live¹ /lɪv/ *verb* (**lives, living, lived** /lɪvd/) **1** be or stay alive: *You can't live without water.* ○ *He lived to the age of 93.* **2** have your home somewhere: *Where do you live?* **3** spend your life in a certain way: *They live a quiet life in the country.* **live on something 1** eat or drink only one thing: *Cows live on grass.* **2** have a certain amount of money: *They live on £70 a week.*

live² /laɪv/ *adjective* **1** not dead: *The snake ate a live mouse.* **2** If a radio or television programme is live, you see or hear it at the same time as it happens: *a live football match* **3** with electricity passing through it: *Don't touch that wire – it's live!*

lively /ˈlaɪvli/ *adjective* (**livelier, liveliest**) full of life; always moving or doing things: *The children are very lively.*

liver /ˈlɪvə(r)/ *noun* the part inside the body of a person or an animal that cleans the blood ☞ picture on 126

lives *plural of* **life**

livestock /ˈlaɪvstɒk/ *noun* (no plural)

animals that people keep on farms

living[1] /ˈlɪvɪŋ/ *adjective* alive; not dead: *Some people say he is the greatest living writer.*

living[2] /ˈlɪvɪŋ/ *noun* **1** the way that you get money: *What do you do for a living?* **2** the way that you live

living-room /ˈlɪvɪŋ ruːm/ *noun* a room in a house where people sit and watch television or talk, for example

lizard

lizard /ˈlɪzəd/ *noun* a small animal that has four legs, a long tail and rough skin

load[1] /ləʊd/ *noun* **1** something that is carried: *The lorry brought another load of wood.* **2 loads** (plural) a lot: *We've got loads of time.*

load[2] /ləʊd/ *verb* (**loads**, **loading**, **loaded**) **1** put things in or on something, for example a car or ship, that will carry them: *Two men loaded the furniture into the van.* ○ *They're loading the plane now.* ✪ opposite: **unload** **2** put bullets in a gun or film in a camera

loaf /ləʊf/ *noun* (*plural* **loaves** /ləʊvz/) a big piece of bread: *a loaf of bread*

loan /ləʊn/ *noun* money that somebody lends you: *The bank gave me a loan of 200 000 shillings to buy a car.*

loan *verb* (**loans**, **loaning**, **loaned** /ləʊnd/) lend something: *This book is loaned from the library.*

lobster /ˈlɒbstə(r)/ *noun* a sea animal with a hard shell, two big claws, eight legs and a long tail

local /ˈləʊkl/ *adjective* of a place near you: *Her children go to the local school.* ○ *a local newspaper* ○ *local government*

locally /ˈləʊkəli/ *adverb*: *Do you work locally?*

located /ləʊˈkeɪtɪd/ *adjective* in a place: *The factory is located just outside Mombasa.*

location /ləʊˈkeɪʃn/ *noun* a place: *The house is in a quiet location on top of a hill.*

lock[1] /lɒk/ *noun* a metal thing that keeps a door, gate, box, etc closed so that you cannot open it without a key

lock

lock[2] /lɒk/ *verb* (**locks**, **locking**, **locked** /lɒkt/) close with a key: *Don't forget to lock the door when you leave.* ✪ opposite: **unlock** **lock away** put something in a place that you close with a key: *The paintings are locked away at night.* **lock in** lock a door so that somebody cannot go out: *The prisoners are locked in.* **lock out** lock a door so that somebody cannot go in **lock up** lock all the doors and windows of a building

locker /ˈlɒkə(r)/ *noun* a small cupboard, with a lock, for keeping things in, for example in a school or at a station

locust /ˈləʊkəst/ *noun* an insect that flies in very large groups and destroys crops

lodge /lɒdʒ/ *verb* (**lodges**, **lodging**, **lodged** /lɒdʒd/) pay to live in another person's house: *I lodged with a family when I was studying in Nairobi.*

lodger *noun* a person who pays to live in another person's house

loft /lɒft/ *noun* the room or space under the roof of a house: *My old books are in a box in the loft.*

log /lɒg/ *noun* a thick round piece of wood from a tree: *Put another log on the fire.*

log

lollipop /ˈlɒlipɒp/, **lolly** /ˈlɒli/ (*plural* **lollies**) *noun* a big sweet on a stick ☛ Look also at **ice lolly**.

lonely /ˈləʊnli/ *adjective* (**lonelier**, **loneliest**) **1** unhappy because you are not with other people: *I was very lonely when I first came to this town.* **2** far from other places: *a lonely house in the hills*

loneliness /ˈləʊnlinəs/ *noun* (no plural) being lonely

long[1] /lɒŋ/ *adjective* (**longer** /ˈlɒŋgə(r)/, **longest** /ˈlɒŋgɪst/) **1** far from one end to the other: *This is the longest road in Uganda.* ○ *She has long black hair.* ✪ opposite: **short** ☛ picture on page A10 **2** You use 'long' to say or ask how far something is from one end to the other: *How long is the table?* ○ *The wall is 5 m long.* ☛ picture on page A5 **3** that continues for a lot of time: *a long film* ✪ opposite: **short 4** You use 'long' to say or ask about the time from the beginning to the end of something: *How long is the lesson?*

long² /lɒŋ/ *adverb* for a lot of time: *I can't stay long.* **as long as**, **so long as** if: *You can borrow the book as long as you promise not to lose it.* **long after** at a time much after **long ago** many years in the past: *Long ago there were no cars.* **long before** at a time much before: *My grandfather died long before I was born.* **no longer**, **not any longer** not now; not as before: *She doesn't live here any longer.*

long³ /lɒŋ/ *noun* (no plural) a lot of time: *She went shopping but she was not out for long.*

long⁴ /lɒŋ/ *verb* (**longs**, **longing**, **longed** /lɒŋd/) want something very much: *I long to see my family again.* ○ *She's longing for a letter from her boyfriend.*

longing *noun* a strong feeling of wanting something

long-jump /ˈlɒŋ dʒʌmp/ *noun* (no plural) a sport where you try to jump as far as you can

look¹ /lʊk/ *verb* (**looks**, **looking**, **looked** /lʊkt/) **1** turn your eyes towards somebody or something and try to see them: *Look at this picture.* ○ *You should look both ways before you cross the road.* **2** seem to be; appear: *You look tired!* **3** You say 'look' to make somebody listen to you: *Look, I need some money.* **look after somebody** or **something** take care of somebody or something: *Can you look after my children for a few hours?* **look as if**, **look as though** seem or appear: *It looks as if it's going to rain.* **look for somebody** or **something** try to find somebody or something: *I'm looking for my keys.* **look forward to something** wait for something with pleasure: *I'm looking forward to seeing you again.* **look into something** study something carefully: *We will look into the problem.* **look like somebody** or

something 1 seem to be something: *That looks like a good book.* **2** words that you use to ask about somebody's appearance: *'What does he look like?'* *'He's tall and very good-looking.'* **3** have the same appearance as somebody or something: *She looks like her mother.* **look out!** be careful!: *Look out! There's a car coming!* **look out for somebody** or **something** pay attention and try to see somebody or something: *Look out for thieves!* **look round** visit a place: *We looked round the museum.*

look² /lʊk/ *noun* **1** turning your eyes towards somebody or something; looking: *Paul gave me an angry look!* **2** the way something seems: *I don't like the look of that dog. I think it wants to attack us.* **3 looks** (plural) how a person's face and body is: *good looks* **have a look 1** see something: *Can I have a look at your photos?* **2** try to find something: *I've had a look for your pen, but I can't find it.* **have a look round** see many parts of a place: *We had a look round the museum.*

loop /luːp/ *noun* a round shape made by something like string or rope

loop

loose /luːs/ *adjective* (**looser**, **loosest**) **1** not tied or fixed: *The dog broke its chain and got loose.* ○ *One of his teeth is loose.* **2** not tight: *a loose white dress* ☛ picture on page A11

loosely *adverb* not tightly or firmly: *The rope was tied loosely round a tree.*

loosen /ˈluːsn/ *verb* (**loosens**, **loosening**, **loosened** /ˈluːsnd/) become looser or make something looser: *Can you loosen this knot? It's too tight.* ✪ opposite: **tighten**

loquat /ˈləʊkwɒt/ *noun* a small yellow fruit like an egg

Lord /lɔːd/ *noun* **the Lord** (no plural) God or Jesus Christ

lorry /ˈlɒri/ *noun* (plural **lorries**) a big vehicle for carrying heavy things

lorry

lose /luːz/ *verb* (**loses, losing, lost** /lɒst/, **has lost**) **1** not be able to find something: *I can't open the door because I've lost my key.* **2** not have somebody or something that you had before: *I lost my job when the factory closed.* **3** not win: *Our team lost the match.*

loser /ˈluːzə(r)/ *noun* a person who does not win a game, race or competition ✪ opposite: **winner**

loss /lɒs/ *noun* (*plural* **losses**) **1** losing something: *She hasn't recovered from the loss* (= death) *of her husband.* ○ *job losses* **2** how much money a business loses: *The company made a huge loss last year.* **at a loss** If you are at a loss, you do not know what to do or say.

lost[1] *form of* **lose**

lost[2] /lɒst/ *adjective* **1** If you are lost, you do not know where you are: *I took the wrong road and now I'm lost.* ○ *Take this map so that you don't get lost!* **2** If something is lost, you cannot find it.

lost property /ˌlɒst ˈprɒpəti/ *noun* (no plural) things that people have lost: *I left my bag on the train, so I went to the lost property office at the station.*

lot[1] /lɒt/ *noun* **a lot** very much; a big amount or number: *We ate a lot.* **a lot of, lots of** a big number or amount of something: *She's got a lot of friends.* ○ *Lots of love from Jane* (= words at the end of a letter).

lot[2] /lɒt/ *adverb* **a lot** very much or often: *Your flat is a lot bigger than mine.* ○ *I go to the cinema a lot.*

lotion /ˈləʊʃn/ *noun* liquid that you put on your skin: *suntan lotion*

loud /laʊd/ *adjective, adverb* (**louder, loudest**) that makes a lot of noise; not quiet: *I couldn't hear what he said because the music was too loud.* ○ *loud voices* ○ *Please speak a bit louder – I can't hear you.* ☛ picture on page A11. **out loud** so that other people can hear it: *I read the story out loud.*

loudly *adverb*: *She laughed loudly.*

loudspeaker /ˌlaʊdˈspiːkə(r)/ *noun* an instrument for making sounds louder: *Music was coming from the loud speakers.*

lounge /laʊndʒ/ *noun* a room in a house or hotel where you can sit in comfortable chairs

love[1] /lʌv/ *verb* (**loves, loving, loved** /lʌvd/) **1** have a strong warm feeling for somebody: *I love him very much.* ○ *She loves her parents.* **2** like something very much: *I love swimming.* ○ *I would love to go to America.*

love[2] /lʌv/ *noun* **1** (no plural) a strong warm feeling of liking somebody or something: *Their love for each other was very strong.* ○ *a love of football* **2** (*plural* **loves**) a person that you love: *Yes, my love.* **3** (no plural) (*also* **love from**) a way of ending a letter to somebody that you know well: *Lots of love from Peter.* **4** (no plural) a word in tennis that means zero: *The score is 15-love.* **be in love with somebody** love somebody: *He says he is in love with her and they are going to get married.* **fall in love with somebody** begin to love somebody: *He fell in love with Anne the first time they met.*

lovely /ˈlʌvli/ *adjective* (**lovelier, loveliest**) beautiful or very nice: *That's a lovely dress.* ○ *The evening sky looks lovely.* ○ *It's lovely to see you again.*

loving /ˈlʌvɪŋ/ *adjective* feeling or showing love: *loving parents*

low /ləʊ/ *adjective* (**lower, lowest**) **1** near the ground; not high: *There was a low wall round the garden.* ○ *a low bridge* ☛ picture on page A10 **2** less than usual: *low temperatures* ○ *low pay* **3** soft and quiet: *I heard low voices in the next room.* **4** deep; not high: *a low sound*

low *adverb* near the ground: *The plane flew low over the fields.*

lower[1] /ˈləʊə(r)/ *verb* (**lowers, lowering, lowered** /ˈləʊəd/) **1** move somebody or something down: *They lowered the flag.* **2** make something less: *Please lower your voice* (= speak more quietly). ✪ opposite: **raise**

lower[2] /ˈləʊə(r)/ *adjective* that is under another; bottom: *the lower lip* ✪ opposite: **upper**

loyal /ˈlɔɪəl/ *adjective* A person who is loyal does not change his/her friends or beliefs: *a loyal friend* ○ *He is loyal to the company he works for.*

loyalty /'lɔɪəlti/ *noun* (no plural) being loyal: *Loyalty to your friends is very important.*

luck /lʌk/ *noun* (no plural) **1** things that happen to you that you cannot control; chance **2** good things that happen to you that you cannot control: *Wish me luck for my exams!* **bad luck, hard luck** words that you say to somebody when you are sorry that they did not have good luck **be in luck** have good things happen to you: *I was in luck – the shop had the book I wanted.* **good luck** words that you say to somebody when you hope that they will do well: *Good luck! I'm sure you'll get the job.*

lucky /'lʌki/ *adjective* (**luckier, luckiest**) **1** If you are lucky, you have good luck: *She had a bad accident and she is lucky to be alive.* **2** Something that is lucky brings good luck: *My lucky number is 3.* ✪ opposite: **unlucky**

luckily /'lʌkɪli/ *adverb* it is lucky that: *I was late, but luckily they waited for me.*

luggage /'lʌgɪdʒ/ *noun* (no plural) bags and suitcases that you take with you when you travel: *'How much luggage have you got?' 'Only one suitcase.'*

lump /lʌmp/ *noun* **1** a hard piece of something: *two lumps of sugar* ○ *a lump of coal* ➡ picture on page A15 **2** a part in or on your body which has become hard and bigger: *I've got a lump on my head where I hit it.*

lunch /lʌntʃ/ *noun* (*plural* **lunches**) a meal that you eat in the middle of the day: *What would you like for lunch?* ○ *What time do you usually have lunch?*

lunch-time /'lʌntʃ taɪm/ *noun* the time when you eat lunch: *I'll meet you at lunch-time.*

lung /lʌŋ/ *noun* one of the two parts inside your body that you use for breathing ➡ picture on page A4

luxurious /lʌg'ʒʊəriəs/ *adjective* very comfortable and expensive: *a luxurious hotel*

luxury /'lʌkʃəri/ *noun* **1** (no plural) a way of living when you have all the expensive and beautiful things that you want: *They live in luxury in a beautiful house in Kololo.* ○ *a luxury hotel* **2** (*plural* **luxuries**) something that is very nice and expensive that you do not really need: *Eating in a restaurant is a luxury for most people.*

lying *form of* **lie**

Mm

m *short way of writing* **metre**

machine /məˈʃiːn/ *noun* a thing with parts that move to do work or to make something. Machines often use electricity: *a washing-machine* ○ *This machine does not work.*

machine-gun /məˈʃiːn gʌn/ *noun* a gun that can send out a lot of bullets very quickly

machinery /məˈʃiːnəri/ *noun* (no plural) **1** the parts of a machine: *the machinery inside a clock* **2** a group of machines: *The factory has bought some new machinery.*

mad /mæd/ *adjective* (**madder, maddest**) **1** ill in your mind **2** very stupid; crazy: *I think you're mad to go out in this storm!* **3** very angry: *He was mad at me for losing his watch.* **be mad about somebody** or **something** like somebody or something very much: *Ali is mad about football.* ○ *He's mad about her.* **drive somebody mad** make somebody very angry: *This noise is driving me mad!* **go mad 1** become ill in your mind: *He went mad and killed himself.* **2** become very angry: *Your mother will go mad when she finds out what you did at school.*

madam /ˈmædəm/ *noun* (no plural) **1** a polite way of speaking to a woman, instead of using her name: *'Can I help you, madam?' asked the shop assistant.* **2** **Madam** a word that you use at the beginning of a business letter to a woman: *Dear Madam ...* ☛ Look at **sir**.

made *form of* **make¹** **made of something** from this material: *This shirt is made of cotton.*

madness /ˈmædnəs/ *noun* (no plural) being ill in your mind

magazine /ˌmæɡəˈziːn/ *noun* a kind of thin book with a paper cover that you can buy every week or every month. It has a lot of different stories and pictures inside.

magic /ˈmædʒɪk/ *noun* (no plural) **1** a special power that can make strange or impossible things happen: *The witch changed the prince into a frog by magic.* **2** clever tricks that somebody can do to surprise people

magic (*also* **magical**) /ˈmædʒɪkl/ *adjective*: *magic tricks* ○ *The witch had magical powers.*

magician /məˈdʒɪʃn/ *noun* **1** a man in stories who has strange, unusual powers: *The magician turned the boy into a dog.* **2** a person who does clever tricks to surprise people

magistrate /ˈmædʒɪstreɪt/ *noun* a judge in a court of law who decides how to punish people for small crimes

magnet /ˈmæɡnət/ *noun* a piece of metal that can make other metal things move towards it

magnetic /mæɡˈnetɪk/ *adjective* with the power of a magnet: *Is this metal magnetic?*

magnificent /mæɡˈnɪfɪsnt/ *adjective* very good or beautiful: *What a magnificent view!*

magnify /ˈmæɡnɪfaɪ/ *verb* (**magnifies, magnifying, magnified** /ˈmæɡnɪfaɪd/, **has magnified**) make something look bigger than it really is: *We magnified the insect under a microscope.*

magnifying glass /ˈmæɡnɪfaɪɪŋ ɡlɑːs/ *noun* (*plural* **magnifying glasses**) a special piece of glass that you hold in your hand. It makes things look bigger than they really are.

magnifying glass

maid /meɪd/ *noun* a woman who does work like cleaning in a hotel or large house

mail /meɪl/ *noun* (no plural) **2** the way of sending and receiving letters, parcels, etc; post: *airmail* **2** letters and parcels that you send or receive; post: *Is there any mail for me?*

mail *verb* (**mails, mailing, mailed** /meɪld/) send something in the mail: *I'll mail the money to you.*

Prepositions 1

Prepositions of place

The lamp is **above** the table.

The meat is **on** the table.

The cat is **under** the table.

The lorry is **in front of** the car.

The car is **behind** the lorry.

The bird is **in/inside** the cage.

Sam is **between** Tom and Kim.
Kim is **next to/beside** Sam.

The temperature is **below** zero.

The girl is leaning **against** the wall.

Kim is **opposite** Tom.

The house is **among** the trees.

Prepositions 2

Prepositions of movement

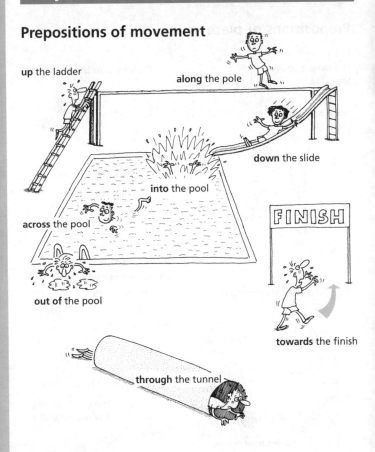

up the ladder

along the pole

down the slide

into the pool

across the pool

out of the pool

towards the finish

FINISH

through the tunnel

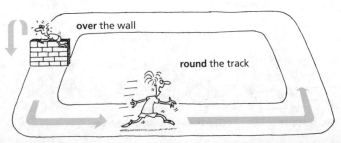

over the wall

round the track

East Africa

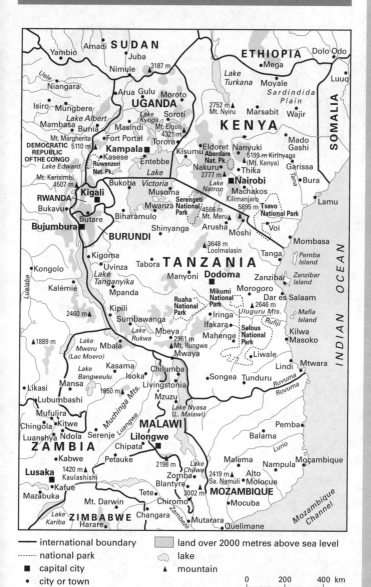

— international boundary

········· national park

■ capital city

• city or town

☐ land over 2000 metres above sea level

◇ lake

▲ mountain

0   200   400 km

The Human Body

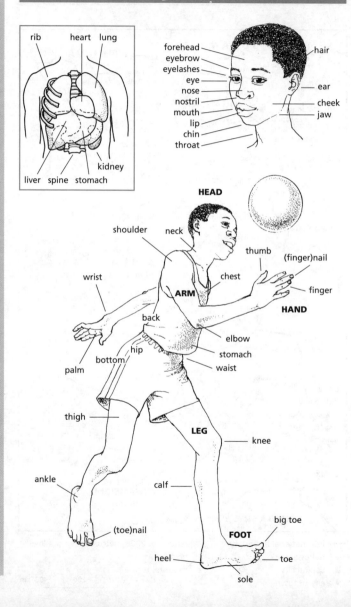

Shapes and sizes

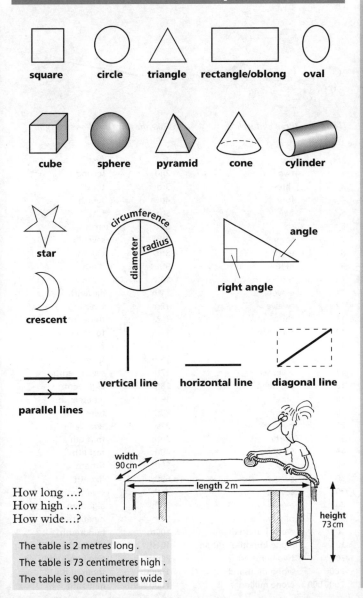

square   **circle**   **triangle**   **rectangle/oblong**   **oval**

cube   **sphere**   **pyramid**   **cone**   **cylinder**

star

crescent

circumference
diameter
radius

angle

right angle

parallel lines   **vertical line**   **horizontal line**   **diagonal line**

width 90 cm

length 2 m

height 73 cm

How long ...?
How high ...?
How wide...?

The table is 2 metres long .

The table is 73 centimetres high .

The table is 90 centimetres wide .

Numbers

*He has got **three** children.*

*Take the **third** road on the right.*

1	one	1st	first
2	two	2nd	second
3	three	3rd	third
4	four	4th	fourth
5	five	5th	fifth
6	six	6th	sixth
7	seven	7th	seventh
8	eight	8th	eighth
9	nine	9th	ninth
10	ten	10th	tenth
11	eleven	11th	eleventh
12	twelve	12th	twelfth
13	thirteen	13th	thirteenth
14	fourteen	14th	fourteenth
15	fifteen	15th	fifteenth
16	sixteen	16th	sixteenth
17	seventeen	17th	seventeenth
18	eighteen	18th	eighteenth
19	nineteen	19th	nineteenth
20	twenty	20th	twentieth
21	twenty-one	21st	twenty-first
30	thirty	30th	thirtieth
40	forty	40th	fortieth
50	fifty	50th	fiftieth
60	sixty	60th	sixtieth
70	seventy	70th	seventieth
80	eighty	80th	eightieth
90	ninety	90th	ninetieth
100	a/one hundred	100th	hundredth
101	a/one hundred and one	101st	hundred and first
200	two hundred	200th	two hundredth
1 000	a/one thousand	1 000th	thousandth
1 000 000	a/one million	1 000 000th	millionth

Saying numbers

267 — two hundred and sixty-seven

4 302 — four thousand, three hundred and two

Writing numbers ✎

We put a small space or a comma (,) between *thousands* and *hundreds* in numbers, for example:

15 000 or 15,000

Saying '0'

We usually say **nought** or **zero**:

nought point five (0.5)

In telephone numbers, we usually say **o** (you say it like **oh**):

My telephone number is 29035 (two nine **o** three five).

When we talk about temperature, we use **zero**:

It was very cold ~ the temperature was below **zero**.

In scores of games like football, we say **nil**:

The score was two-**nil**.

Fractions

◖	1/2	a half
◕	1/3	a/one third
◔	1/4	a/one quarter
◔	1/8	an/one eighth
◔	1/16	a/one sixteenth
◕	3/4	three quarters
●◔	1 2/5	one and two fifths

> To find out more about how to say **telephone numbers**, look at page A14.
> To find out more about how to say and write **numbers in dates**, look at page A9.

We use **.** (NOT **,**) in **decimals**.

Symbols		We write:	We say:
.	point	3.2	three point two
+	plus	5 + 6	five plus six
-	minus	10 - 4	ten minus four
x	multiplied by/ times	4 x 6	four multiplied by six four times six
÷	divided by	4 ÷ 2	four divided by two
%	per cent	78%	seventy-eight per cent
=	equals	1 + 3 = 4	one plus three equals four

Time

10:00 ten o'clock

5:15 (a) quarter past five
five fifteen

6:30 half past six
six thirty

3:45 (a) quarter to four
three forty-five

11:10 ten past eleven
eleven ten

11:40 twenty to twelve
eleven forty

14:07 seven minutes past two
two o seven *

What time is it?

What's the time?

It's ten o'clock.

To show what part of the day we mean, we can use:

a.m. *or* **in the morning**

The meeting is at 10 a.m.
The telephone rang at four o'clock in the morning.

p.m. *or* **in the afternoon**
         in the evening
         at night

The shop closes at 6 p.m.
She came home at eight o'clock in the evening.

---

* We do not often use the 'twenty-four hour clock' when we say times (so we do not say 'fourteen o seven'). We occasionally use it when we are reading a time from a bus or train timetable.

60 seconds	= 1 minute
60 minutes	= 1 hour
24 hours	= 1 day

Dates

Saying dates

How do you say… ?:

the twenty-fourth of January,
two thousand and one

or January the twenty-fourth,
two thousand and one

1999 — nineteen ninety-nine

1800 — eighteen hundred

Writing dates

Here are some ways of writing the date:

24 January
January 24
24th January
January 24th

Sometimes we just write numbers:

24 January 2001

24/1/01
(in Britain)

1/24/01
(in the USA)

on, in or at?

on	5 August Monday Wednesday morning my birthday
in	August 2003 (the) summer the morning/afternoon/evening
at	the beginning of June the weekend Christmas night six o'clock

Months

January
February
March
April
May
June
July
August
September
October
November
December

Days

Sunday
Monday
Tuesday
Wednesday
Thursday
Friday
Saturday

Opposites

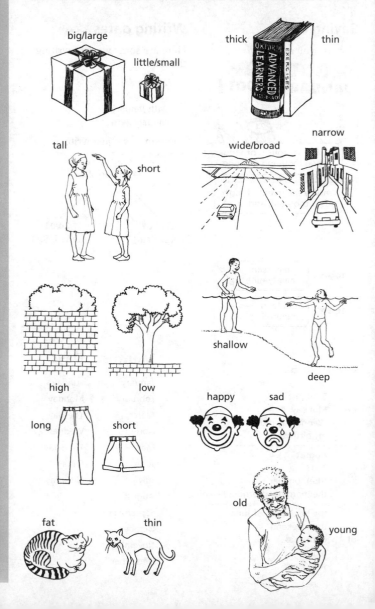

Opposites

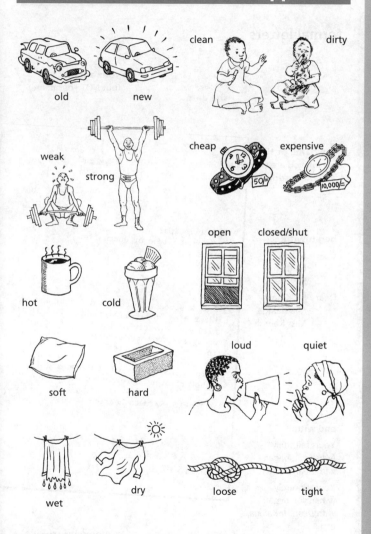

old · new

clean · dirty

weak · strong

cheap · expensive

open · closed/shut

hot · cold

soft · hard

loud · quiet

wet · dry

loose · tight

We give opposites for many of the words in this dictionary.
If you want to know the opposite of **tidy**, for example, look up
this word and you will find ☉ opposite: **untidy** after it.

Letter-writing

formal letters

your address
(but NOT your name)

the date

the name or title of the person you are writing to, and **their address**

P.O.Box 711
Meru
Kenya

5th December 2001

begin with:

Dear   Sir
          Madam
          Sirs

Dear   Mr Kainga
          Mrs Kainga
          Miss Kainga

The Principal
Nairobi College of Journalism
P.O.Box 2828
Nairobi

Dear Sir or Madam

I am a student in Standard Eight, and am interested in becoming a journalist in the future. I am trying to find out what qualifications and experience I would need in order to train when I finish school. I would be grateful if you could send me information about your college and any other relevant information or advice.

I look forward to hearing from you.

Yours faithfully

Rukia Mulaki

Rukia Mulaki

end with:

Yours faithfully
(when you began
with *Dear Sir*, etc)

Yours sincerely
(when you began
with *Dear Mr Kainga*,
etc)

Yours truly (US)
Sincerely yours (US)

your signature

Letter-writing

informal letters

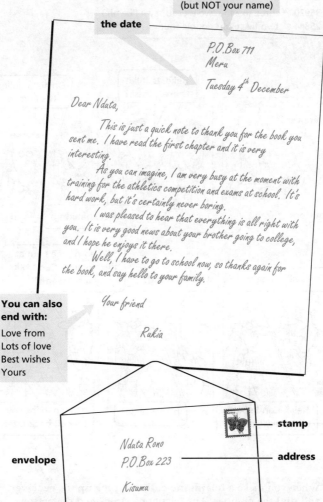

the date

your address
(but NOT your name)

P.O.Box 711
Meru

Tuesday 4ᵗʰ December

Dear Nduta,

This is just a quick note to thank you for the book you sent me. I have read the first chapter and it is very interesting.

As you can imagine, I am very busy at the moment with training for the athletics competition and exams at school. It's hard work, but it's certainly never boring.

I was pleased to hear that everything is all right with you. It is very good news about your brother going to college, and I hope he enjoys it there.

Well, I have to go to school now, so thanks again for the book, and say hello to your family.

Your friend

Rakia

You can also end with:

Love from
Lots of love
Best wishes
Yours

stamp

Kenya

Nduta Rono
P.O.Box 223

Kisumu

envelope

address

Telephoning

Saying telephone numbers

36920 three six nine two o (You say it like **oh**.)
25844 two five eight double four

When you make a **telephone call**, you **pick up** the **receiver** and **dial** the number. The telephone **rings**, and the person you are telephoning **answers** it. If he/she is already using the telephone, it is **engaged**.

Words that go together 1

a **pair** of shoes

a **string** of beads

a **bar** of chocolate

a **row** of houses

a **bundle** of newspapers

a **drop** of water

a **ball** of string

a **bunch** of flowers

a **crowd** of people

a **slice/piece** of pizza

a **pile** of books

a **queue** (of people)

a **lump** of coal

This dictionary tells you about words that often go together.
Do you know what word is missing in each of these
expressions? You can use the dictionary (look up **soap**, **grape**
and **shorts** and read the example sentences) to find out.

a **?** of soap

a **?** of grapes

a **?** of shorts

Words that go together 2

She has ____?____ a lot of mistakes.

When you learn a new word it is important to remember what other words you often see with it. This dictionary can help you to decide what word goes with another word. For example, if you look up **mistake** in the dictionary, you will see:

mistake¹ /mɪˈsteɪk/ *noun*
something that you think or do that is wrong: *You have made a lot of spelling mistakes in this letter.* ◊ *It was a mistake to go by bus – the journey took two hours!*
by mistake when you did not plan to do it: *I took your book by mistake – I thought*

The example sentence shows you that you use **make** with **mistake**.

You can use your dictionary to check which words below go together. Find the words in **B** and use the example sentences.

A	B
make	a story
take	fun
tell	a mistake
do	a question
have	homework
ask	a photograph

main /meɪn/ *adjective* most important: *My main reason for learning English is to get a better job.*

main road /ˌmeɪn ˈrəʊd/ *noun* a big important road between towns

mainly *adverb* mostly: *The students here are mainly between 19 and 23 years old.* ○ *She eats mainly vegetables.*

maintain /meɪnˈteɪn/ *verb* (**maintains**, **maintaining**, **maintained** /meɪnˈteɪnd/) **1** continue with something: *If he can maintain this speed, he'll win the race.* **2** keep something working well: *The roads are well maintained.*

maintenance /ˈmeɪntənəns/ *noun* (no plural) things that you do to keep something working well: *maintenance of a machine*

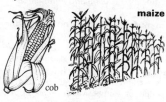

maize

cob

maize /meɪz/ *noun* (no plural) a tall plant with big yellow or white seeds that you can eat or use to make flour

Majesty /ˈmædʒəsti/ *noun* (*plural* **Majesties**) a word that you use to talk to or about a king or queen: *Her Majesty Queen Elizabeth II*

major¹ /ˈmeɪdʒə(r)/ *adjective* very large, important or serious: *There are airports in all the major cities.* ○ *major problems* ✪ opposite: **minor**

major² /ˈmeɪdʒə(r)/ *noun* an officer in the army

majority /məˈdʒɒrəti/ *noun* (no plural) most things or people in a group: *The majority of Africans can speak more than one language.* ☛ Look at **minority**.

make¹ /meɪk/ *verb* (**makes**, **making**, **made** /meɪd/, **has made**) **1** put things together so that you have a new thing: *They make cars in that factory.* ○ *He made a box out of some pieces of wood.* **2** cause something to be or to happen;

produce something: *The plane made a loud noise when it landed.* ○ *Running makes you tired.* ○ *That film made me cry.* ○ *I made a mistake.* **3** force somebody to do something: *My father made me stay at home.* **4** a word that you use with money, numbers and time: *She makes* (= earns) *a lot of money.* ○ *Five and seven make twelve.* ○ *'What's the time?' 'I make it six o'clock.'* **5** give somebody a job: *They made him President.* **6** be able to go somewhere: *I'm sorry, but I can't make the meeting on Friday.* **make do with something** use something that is not very good, because there is nothing better: *We didn't have a table, but we made do with some boxes.* **make something into something** change something so that it becomes a different thing: *They made the office into a classroom.* **make out** be able to see or understand something that is not clear: *It was dark and I couldn't make out the words on the sign.* **make up 1** tell something that is not true: *Nobody believes that story – he made it up!* **2** end a quarrel with somebody: *Chakava and Baluma had an argument last week, but they've made up now.*

make² /meɪk/ *noun* the name of the company that made something: *'What make is that car?' 'It's a Ford.'*

maker /ˈmeɪkə(r)/ *noun* a person or company that makes something: *a film maker*

make-up /ˈmeɪk ʌp/ *noun* (no plural) special powders and creams that you put on your face to make yourself more beautiful. Actors also wear make-up to make themselves look different: *She put on her make-up.*

makuti /mæˈkuːti/ *noun* (no plural) (an East African word) the leaves of a palm tree. Makuti can be used to make fences, baskets, etc or as a roof covering

malaria /məˈleəriə/ *noun* (no plural) a dangerous illness that you get from mosquitoes

male /meɪl/ *adjective* A male animal or person belongs to the sex that cannot have babies: *A cock is a male chicken.*

male *noun*: *If you look at these fish you*

can see that the males are bigger than the females. ☞ Look at **female**.

malnutrition /ˌmælnjuːˈtrɪʃn/ *noun* (no plural) illness that you get when you don't eat enough food

mammal /ˈmæml/ *noun* any animal that drinks milk from its mother's body when it is young: *Dogs, horses, whales and people are all mammals.*

man /mæn/ *noun* **1** (*plural* **men** /men/) a grown-up male person: *I saw a tall man with a beard.* **2** (*plural* **men**) any person: *All men must have water to live.* **3** (no plural) all human beings; people: *How long has man lived on the earth?*

manage /ˈmænɪdʒ/ *verb* (**manages**, **managing**, **managed** /ˈmænɪdʒd/) **1** be able to do something that is difficult: *The box was heavy but she managed to carry it.* **2** control somebody or something: *She manages a department of 30 people.*

management /ˈmænɪdʒmənt/ *noun* **1** (no plural) control of something, for example a business, and the people who work in it: *good management* **2** (*plural* **management**) all the people who control a business: *The management have decided to close the factory.*

manager /ˈmænɪdʒə(r)/ *noun* a person who controls a business, bank or hotel, for example: *Kilasi is the manager of a shop.* ○ *a bank manager*

manageress /ˌmænɪdʒəˈres/ *noun* a woman who controls a shop or restaurant

managing director /ˌmænɪdʒɪŋ dəˈrektə(r)/ *noun* the person who controls a big business

mane /meɪn/ *noun* the long hair on the neck of a horse or lion

mango /ˈmæŋgəʊ/ *noun* (*plural* **mangoes** or **mangos**) a fruit that is yellow or red on the outside and yellow on the inside.

mankind /mænˈkaɪnd/ *noun* (no plural) all the people in the world

man-made /ˌmæn ˈmeɪd/ *adjective* made by people; not natural: *man-made materials*

manner /ˈmænə(r)/ *noun* **1** the way that you do something or the way that something happens: *Don't get angry.*

Let's try to talk about this in a calm manner. **2 manners** (plural) the way you behave when you are with other people: *It's bad manners to talk with your mouth full.*

manual[1] /ˈmænjuəl/ *adjective* that you do with your hands: *Do you prefer manual work or office work?*

manually /ˈmænjuəli/ *adverb* using your hands: *This machine is operated manually.*

manual[2] /ˈmænjuəl/ *noun* a book that tells you how to do something: *It'll be difficult to fix the engine without a manual.*

manufacture /ˌmænjuˈfæktʃə(r)/ *verb* (**manufactures**, **manufacturing**, **manufactured** /ˌmænjuˈfæktʃəd/) make things in a factory using machines: *The company manufactures radios.*

manufacture *noun* (no plural) *the manufacture of plastic from oil*

manufacturer *noun: If it doesn't work, send it back to the manufacturer.*

many /ˈmeni/ *adjective* (**many**, **more**, **most**) *pronoun* a large number of people or things: *Many people in this country are very poor.* ○ *There aren't many students in my class.* ○ *Many of these books are very old.* ○ *There are too many mistakes in your homework.* **as many as** the same number that: *Take as many cakes as you want.* **how many ...?** words that you use to ask about the number of people or things: *How many brothers and sisters have you got?* ☞ Look at **much**.

map /mæp/ *noun* a drawing of a town, a country or the world. It shows things like mountains, rivers and roads: *Can you find Japan on the map?* ○ *a street map of Dar es Salaam* ✪ A book of maps is called an **atlas**.

marathon /ˈmærəθən/ *noun* a very long race when people run about 42 kilometres

marble /ˈmɑːbl/ *noun* **1** (no plural) very hard stone that is used to make buildings and statues: *Marble is always cold when you touch it.* **2** (*plural* **marbles**) a small glass ball that you use in a children's game: *they are playing marbles*

March /mɑːtʃ/ *noun* the third month of the year

march /mɑːtʃ/ *verb* (**marches, marching, marched** /mɑːtʃt/) **1** walk like a soldier: *The soldiers marched along the road.* **2** walk with a large group of people to show that you have strong feelings about something: *They marched through the town shouting 'Stop the war!'*

march *noun* (*plural* **marches**) **1** marching: *The soldiers were tired after the long march.* **2** a long walk by a large group of people to show that they have strong feelings about something: *a peace march*

margarine /ˌmɑːdʒəˈriːn/ *noun* (no plural) soft yellow food that looks like butter, but is not made of milk. You put it on bread or use it in cooking.

margin /ˈmɑːdʒɪn/ *noun* the space at the side of a page that has no writing or pictures in it

mark[1] /mɑːk/ *noun* **1** a spot or line that makes something less good than it was before: *There's a dirty mark on the front of your shirt.* **2** a shape or special sign on something: *The marks on her face show that she's married.* **3** a number or letter that a teacher gives for your work to show how good it is: *She got very good marks in the exam.*

mark[2] /mɑːk/ *verb* (**marks, marking, marked** /mɑːkt/) **1** put a sign on something by writing or drawing on it: *The price is marked on the bottom of the box.* **2** put a tick ✔ or cross (X) on school work to show if it is right or wrong, or write a number or letter to show how good it is: *The teacher marked all my answers wrong.* **3** show where something is: *This cross marks the place where he died.*

market /ˈmɑːkɪt/ *noun* **1** a place where people go to buy and sell things, usually outside: *There is a fruit and vegetable market in the town* **2** the people who want to buy something: *Britain is an important market for Kenyan coffee.*

marriage /ˈmærɪdʒ/ *noun* **1** the time when two people are together as husband and wife: *They had a long and happy marriage.* **2** the time when a man and woman become husband and

wife; a wedding: *The marriage will take place in church.*

marry /ˈmæri/ *verb* (**marries, marrying, married** /ˈmærid/, **has married**) take somebody as your husband or wife: *Will you marry me?* ○ *They married when they were very young.* ✪ It is more usual to say **get married**.

married *adjective*: *How long have you been married?* ○ *Joshua is married to Ruth.* ✪ opposite: **single** or **unmarried**. **get married** take somebody as your husband or wife: *Saeed and Shahida got married last year.*

marsh /mɑːʃ/ *noun* (*plural* **marshes**) soft wet ground

marvellous /ˈmɑːvələs/ *adjective* very good; wonderful: *I had a marvellous holiday.*

masculine /ˈmæskjʊlɪn/ *adjective* of or like a man; right for a man: *a masculine voice* ➨ Look at **feminine**.

mash /mæʃ/ *verb* (**mashes, mashing, mashed** /mæʃt/) press and mix food to make it soft: *mashed potatoes*

mask /mɑːsk/ *noun* a thing that you wear over your face to hide or protect it: *The thieves were wearing masks.* ○ *The doctors and nurses all wore masks.*

Mass /mæs/ *noun* (*plural* **Masses**) a service in the Roman Catholic church

mass /mæs/ *noun* (*plural* **masses**) a large amount or number of something: *a mass of rock* ○ *masses of people*

massacre /ˈmæsəkə(r)/ *noun* the cruel killing of a lot of people

massacre *verb* (**massacres, massacring, massacred** /ˈmæsəkəd/) *The army massacred hundreds of women and children.*

massive /ˈmæsɪv/ *adjective* very big: *The house is massive – it has 16 bedrooms!*

mast /mɑːst/ *noun* **1** a tall piece of wood or metal that holds the sails on a boat **2** a very tall metal thing that sends out sounds or pictures for radio or television

master[1] /ˈmɑːstə(r)/ *noun* a man who has people or animals in his control: *The dog ran to its master.*

master[2] /ˈmɑːstə(r)/ *verb* (**masters,**

mastering, mastered /ˈmɑːstəd/ learn how to do something well: *It takes a long time to master a foreign language.*

masterpiece /ˈmɑːstəpiːs/ *noun* a very good painting, book, film, etc: *His new book is a masterpiece.*

mat /mæt/ *noun* **1** a small thing that covers a part of the floor: *Wipe your feet on the mat before you go in.* **2** a small thing that you put on a table under a hot dish or cup or a glass: *a table-mat*

matatu /mæˈtætuː/ *noun* (in Kenya) a small bus

match[1] /mætʃ/ *noun* (*plural* **matches**) a special short thin piece of wood that makes fire when you rub it on something rough: *He struck a match and lit his cigarette.* ○ *a box of matches*

matches

matchbox /ˈmætʃbɒks/ *noun* a small box for matches

match[2] /mætʃ/ *noun* (*plural* **matches**) a game between two people or teams: *a football match* ○ *a boxing match*

match[3] /mætʃ/ *verb* (**matches, matching, matched** /mætʃt/) **1** have the same colour, shape or pattern as something else, or look good with something else: *Her socks match her dress.* **2** find something that is like another thing or that you can put with it: *Match the word with the right picture.*

match *noun* (no plural) something that looks good with something else, for example because it has the same colour, shape or pattern: *Your shoes and dress are a good match.*

matching *adjective*: *She was wearing a blue skirt and matching jacket.*

mate /meɪt/ *noun* **1** a friend: *He went out with his mates last night.* ✪ This is an informal word. **2** a person who lives, works or studies with you: *Ahmed is one of my classmates.* ○ *a flatmate* **3** one of two animals that come together to make young animals: *The bird is looking for a mate.*

mate *verb* (**mates, mating, mated**) When animals mate, they come together to make young animals.

material /məˈtɪəriəl/ *noun* **1** what you use for making or doing something: *Wood and stone are building materials.* ○ *writing materials* (= pens, pencils and paper, for example) **2** stuff that is made of wool, cotton, etc and that you use for making clothes and other things; cloth: *I don't have enough material to make a dress.*

mathematics /ˌmæθəˈmætɪks/, **maths** /mæθs/ *noun* (no plural) the study of numbers, measurements and shapes: *Maths is my favourite subject.*

mathematical /ˌmæθəˈmætɪkl/ *adjective*: *a mathematical problem*

matoke /mæˈtɒkə/ *noun* (no plural) (an East African word) a kind of food that we make from boiled bananas

matter[1] /ˈmætə(r)/ *noun* something that you must talk about or do: *There is a matter I would like to discuss with you.* **as a matter of fact** words that you use when you say something true, important or interesting: *I'm going home early today. As a matter of fact, it's my birthday.* **be the matter with somebody** or **something** be the reason for problems or unhappiness, for example: *Julie is crying. What's the matter with her?* ○ *There is something the matter with my eye.* **no matter how, what, when, who, etc** however, whatever, whenever, whoever, etc: *No matter how hard I try, I can't open the door.*

matter[2] /ˈmætə(r)/ *verb* (**matters, mattering, mattered** /ˈmætəd/) be important: *It doesn't matter if you're late – we'll wait for you.*

mattress

mattress /ˈmætrəs/ *noun* (*plural* **mattresses**) the thick soft part of a bed

mature /məˈtjʊə(r)/ *adjective* like an adult; fully grown

mauve /məʊv/ *adjective* purple

maximum /ˈmæksɪməm/ *noun* (no

plural) the most; the biggest possible size, amount or number: *This plane can carry a maximum of 150 people.*

maximum *adjective*: *We drove at a maximum speed of 110 kilometres per hour.* ✪ opposite: **minimum**

May /meɪ/ *noun* the fifth month of the year

may /meɪ/ *modal verb* **1** a word that shows what will perhaps happen or what is possible: *I may go to Mombasa on Saturday.* ○ *He may not be here.* **2** be allowed to do something: *May I open the window?* ○ *You may stay here tonight.* **3** hope something will happen: *May you be happy in your new house.* ☛ Look at the Note on page 195 to find out more about **modal verbs**.

maybe /ˈmeɪbi/ *adverb* perhaps; possibly: *'Are you going out tonight?' 'Maybe.'* ○ *Maybe you should phone him.*

mayor /meə(r)/ *noun* the leader of a **council** (a group of people who control a town or city)

mayoress /meəˈres/ *noun* (*plural* **mayoresses**) a mayor who is a woman, or the wife of a mayor

me /miː/ *pronoun* (*plural* **us**) the person who is speaking: *When he saw me he told me about the accident.* ○ *'Who broke the window?' 'It was me.'*

meadow /ˈmedəʊ/ *noun* a field of grass

meal /miːl/ *noun* food that you eat at a certain time of the day: *Breakfast is the first meal of the day.*

> ✪ **Breakfast**, **lunch** and **dinner** (and sometimes **tea** and **supper**) are the usual meals of the day.

mean[1] /miːn/ *verb* (**means**, **meaning**, **meant** /ment/, **has meant**) **1** say or show something in a different way; have as a meaning: *What does 'medicine' mean?* ○ *The red light means that you have to stop here.* **2** plan or want to say something: *She said 'yes' but she really meant 'no'.* ○ *I don't understand what you mean.* **3** plan or want to do something: *I didn't mean to hurt you.* ○ *I meant to phone you, but I forgot.* **4** make something happen: *This storm means there will be no sport*

today. **be meant to 1** If you are meant to do something, you should do it: *You're not meant to smoke on the train.* **2** If something is meant to be true, people say it is true: *This is meant to be a good film.* **mean something to somebody** be important to somebody: *My family means a lot to me.*

mean[2] /miːn/ *adjective* (**meaner**, **meanest**) **1** A person who is mean does not like to give things or to spend money: *Mungai is very mean – he hates spending his money on other people.* ✪ opposite: **generous**. **2** unkind: *It was mean of you to say that Peter was ugly.*

meaning /ˈmiːnɪŋ/ *noun* what something means or shows: *This word has two different meanings.*

means /miːnz/ *noun* (*plural* **means**) a way of doing something; a way of going somewhere: *I don't have a car and there are no trains, so I haven't got any means of getting to Arusha* **by means of something** by using something: *They chose the best student by means of a written test and interview.* **by no means** not at all: *I am by no means certain that I can come.*

meant *form of* **mean**[1]

meantime /ˈmiːntaɪm/ *noun* (no plural) **in the meantime** in the time between two things happening: *The police will be here soon, in the meantime you should stay calm.*

meanwhile /ˈmiːnwaɪl/ *adverb* **1** at the same time as another thing is happening: *My mother cooked the dinner and meanwhile I cleaned the house.* **2** in the time between two things happening: *I'm going to buy a bed next week, but meanwhile I'm sleeping on the floor.*

measles /ˈmiːzlz/ *noun* (no plural) an illness that makes small red spots come on your skin: *My little brother has got measles.*

measure[1] /ˈmeʒə(r)/ *verb* (**measures**, **measuring**, **measured** /ˈmeʒəd/) **1** find the size, weight or amount of somebody or something: *I measured the box with a ruler.* **2** be a certain size or amount: *This room measures six metres across.*

measure[2] /ˈmeʒə(r)/ *noun* a way of showing the size or amount of something: *A metre is a measure of length.*

measurement /ˈmeʒəmənt/ *noun* how long, wide, high, etc something is: *What are the measurements of the kitchen?*

meat /miːt/ *noun* (no plural) the parts of an animal's body that you can eat: *You can buy meat at a butcher's.*

mechanic /məˈkænɪk/ *noun* a person whose job is to repair or work with machines: *a car mechanic*

mechanical /məˈkænɪkl/ *adjective* moved, done or made by a machine: *They used a mechanical drill to break up the road.*

mechanics /məˈkænɪks/ *noun* (no plural) the study of how machines work

medal /ˈmedl/ *noun* a piece of metal with words and pictures on it that is given to somebody who has done something very good: *She won a gold medal in the Olympic Games.*

media /ˈmiːdiə/ *noun* (plural) **the media** television, radio and newspapers: *The media are always interested in the lives of film stars.*

medical /ˈmedɪkl/ *adjective* of or about medicine, hospitals or doctors: *a medical student* ○ *medical treatment*

medicine /ˈmedsn/ *noun* **1** (no plural) the science of understanding illnesses and making sick people well again: *He studied medicine for five years before becoming a doctor.* **2** (*plural* **medicines**) pills or special drinks that help you to get better when you are ill: *Take this medicine every morning.*

medium /ˈmiːdiəm/ *adjective* not big and not small; middle: *What size shirt do you need – small, medium or large?* ○ *He is of medium height.*

meet /miːt/ *verb* (**meets**, **meeting**, **met** /met/, **has met**) **1** come together at a certain time and place when you have planned it: *Let's meet outside the Town Hall at eight o'clock.* **2** see and say hello to somebody: *I met Kate in the library today.* **3** see and speak to somebody for the first time: *Have you met*

Anne? **4** go to a place and wait for somebody to arrive: *Can you meet me outside school at five?* **5** join together with something: *The two paths meet on the other side of the hill.*

meeting /ˈmiːtɪŋ/ *noun* **1** a time when a group of people come together for a special reason: *We had a meeting to talk about the plans for the new clinic.* **2** two or more people coming together: *Do you remember your first meeting with your husband?*

melody /ˈmelədi/ *noun* (*plural* **melodies**) a group of musical notes that make a nice sound when you play or sing them together; a tune: *This song has a lovely melody.*

melon /ˈmelən/ *noun* a big round yellow or green fruit with a lot of seeds inside

melt /melt/ *verb* (**melts**, **melting**, **melted**) warm something so that it becomes liquid; get warmer so that it becomes liquid: *Melt the butter in a saucepan.* ○ *The ice melted in his drink.*

member /ˈmembə(r)/ *noun* a person who is in a group: *I'm a member of the school football team.*

Member of Parliament /ˌmembər əv ˈpɑːləmənt/ *noun* a person that the people of a town or city choose to speak for them in politics ✪ The short form is **MP**.

membership /ˈmembəʃɪp/ *noun* (no plural) being in a group: *Membership of the club costs 200 shillings a year.*

memo /ˈmeməʊ/ *noun* (*plural* **memos**), (*also* **memorandum**) /ˌmeməˈrændəm/ (*plural* **memoranda**) a note that you write to a person who works with you: *I sent you a memo about the meeting on Friday.*

memorable /ˈmemərəbl/ *adjective* easy to remember because it is special in some way: *Their wedding was a very memorable day.*

memorial /məˈmɔːriəl/ *noun* something that people build or do to help us remember somebody, or something that happened: *The statue is a memorial to all the soldiers who died in the war.*

memorize /ˈmeməraɪz/ *verb* (**memorizes**, **memorizing**, **memorized**

/ˈmeməraɪzd/) learn something so that you can remember it exactly: *We have to memorize a poem for homework.*

memory /ˈmeməri/ *noun (plural memories)* **1** the power to remember things: *She's got a very good memory – she never forgets people's names.* **2** something that you remember: *I have very happy memories of my childhood.* **3** the part of a computer that holds information

men *plural of* **man**

mend /mend/ *verb* (**mends, mending, mended**) make something good again when it was broken; repair something: *Can you mend this chair?*

mental /ˈmentl/ *adjective* of or in your mind: *mental illness*
   mentally /ˈmentəli/ *adverb*: *He is mentally ill.*

mention /ˈmenʃn/ *verb* (**mentions, mentioning, mentioned** /ˈmenʃnd/) speak or write a little about something: *When I spoke to Rita, she mentioned that her son had started school.* ○ *He didn't mention Anna in his letter.* **don't mention it** polite words that you say when somebody says 'thank you': *'Thanks very much.' 'Don't mention it.'*
   mention *noun*: *There was no mention of the accident in the newspaper.*

menu /ˈmenjuː/ *noun (plural menus)* **1** a list of the food that you can choose in a restaurant: *What's on the menu?* ○ *Can I have the menu, please?* **2** a list on the screen of a computer that shows what you can do

merchant /ˈmɜːtʃənt/ *noun* a person who buys and sells things, especially from and to other countries: *She's a wine merchant.*

mercy /ˈmɜːsi/ *noun* (no plural) being kind and not hurting somebody who has done wrong: *The prisoners asked the president for mercy.* **be at the mercy of somebody** or **something** have no power against somebody or something: *Farmers are at the mercy of the weather.*

mere /mɪə(r)/ *adjective* only; not more than: *She was a mere child when her parents died.*

merely *adverb* only: *I don't want to buy the book – I am merely asking how much it costs.*

merge /mɜːdʒ/ *verb* (**merges, merging, merged** /mɜːdʒd/) join together with something else: *The two small companies merged into one large one.*

merit /ˈmerɪt/ *noun* what is good about somebody or something: *What are the merits of this plan?*

mermaid /ˈmɜːmeɪd/ *noun* a woman in stories who has a fish's tail and lives in the sea

merry /ˈmeri/ *adjective* (**merrier, merriest**) happy and full of fun: *Merry Christmas!*

mesh /meʃ/ *noun* (no plural) a material like a strong net that is made of wire, plastic or thread: *We made a fence from wire mesh.*

mess[1] /mes/ *noun* (no plural) **1** a lot of untidy or dirty things all in the wrong place: *There was a terrible mess after the party.* **2** a person or thing that is untidy or dirty: *My hair is a mess!* **be in a mess 1** be untidy: *this classroom is in a mess.* **2** have problems: *She's in a mess – she's got no money and nowhere to live.*

mess[2] /mes/ *verb* (**messes, messing, messed** /mest/) **mess about, mess around** do something in a silly way; play when you should be working: *Stop messing around and finish your work!* **mess up 1** do something badly or make something go wrong: *The bad weather messed up our plans for the weekend.* **2** make something untidy or dirty

message /ˈmesɪdʒ/ *noun* words that one person sends to another: *Could you give a message to Mwari, please? Please tell her I will be late.* ○ *Mr Baucha is not here at the moment. Can I take a message?*

messenger /ˈmesɪndʒə(r)/ *noun* a person who brings a message

messy /ˈmesi/ *adjective* (**messier, messiest**) **1** untidy or dirty: *a messy kitchen* **2** that makes you untidy or dirty: *Painting is a messy job.*

met *form of* **meet**

metal /ˈmetl/ *noun* Iron, lead, tin and

gold are all metals: *This chair is made of metal.* ○ *a metal box*

meter /ˈmiːtə(r)/ *noun* a machine that measures or counts something: *An electricity meter shows how much electricity you have used.*

method /ˈmeθəd/ *noun* a way of doing something: *What is the best method of cooking lamb?*

metre /ˈmiːtə(r)/ *noun* a measure of length. There are 100 **centimetres** in a metre: *The wall is eight metres long.* ✪ The short way of writing 'metre' is **m.**: *2 m*

metric /ˈmetrɪk/ *adjective* using metres, grams, litres, etc to measure things

miaow /miˈaʊ/ *noun* a sound that a cat makes

miaow *verb* (**miaows**, **miaowing**, **miaowed** /miˈaʊd/) make this sound

mice *plural of* **mouse**

microchip /ˈmaɪkrəʊtʃɪp/ *noun* a very small thing inside a computer, for example, that makes it work

microcomputer /ˈmaɪkrəʊkəmpjuːtə(r)/ *noun* a small computer

microphone

microphone /ˈmaɪkrəfəʊn/ *noun* an electrical thing that makes sounds louder or records them so you can listen to them later

microscope /ˈmaɪkrəskəʊp/ *noun* an instrument with special glass in it, that makes very small things look much bigger: *The scientist looked at the hair under the microscope.*

microscope

microwave /ˈmaɪkrəweɪv/, **microwave oven** /ˌmaɪkrəweɪv ˈʌvn/ *noun* a special oven that cooks food very quickly

mid, **mid-** /mɪd/ *adjective* (in) the middle of: *I'm going on holiday in mid July.* ○ *mid-morning coffee*

midday /ˌmɪdˈdeɪ/ *noun* (no plural) twelve o'clock in the day: *We met at midday.*

middle /ˈmɪdl/ *noun* **1** the part that is the same distance from the sides, edges or ends of something: *A mango has a seed in the middle.* **2** the time after the beginning and before the end: *The storm started in the middle of the night.*
be in the middle of be busy doing something: *I can't speak to you now – I'm in the middle of cooking dinner.*

middle *adjective*: *There are three houses and ours is the middle one.*

middle-aged /ˌmɪdl ˈeɪdʒd/ *adjective* not old and not young; between the ages of about 40 and 60: *a middle-aged man*

midnight /ˈmɪdnaɪt/ *noun* (no plural) twelve o'clock at night: *We left the party at midnight.*

midway /ˌmɪdˈweɪ/ *adverb* in the middle: *The village is midway between Tabora and Dodoma.*

might /maɪt/ *modal verb* **1** a word for 'may' in the past: *He said he might be late, but he was early.* **2** a word that shows what will perhaps happen or what is possible: *Don't run because you might fall.* ○ *'Where's Anne?' 'I don't know – she might be in the kitchen.'*
☛ Look at the Note on page 195 to find out more about **modal verbs**.

mighty /ˈmaɪti/ *adjective* (**mightier**, **mightiest**) very great, strong or powerful: *a mighty ocean*

mild /maɪld/ *adjective* (**milder**, **mildest**) gentle; not strong or extreme: *This curry has a mild taste.* ○ *The temperature in this region ranges from very hot to mild.*

mile /maɪl/ *noun* a measure of length that is used in some countries (= 1·6 kilometres): *We live three miles from the sea.* ☛ Note at **foot**.

military /ˈmɪlətri/ *adjective* of or for soldiers or the army: *a military camp* ○ *military action*

milk /mɪlk/ *noun* (no plural) the white liquid that a mother makes in her body to give to her baby. People drink the milk that cows and some other animals make: *Do you want milk in your coffee?*

milk *verb* (**milks**, **milking**, **milked** /mɪlkt/) take milk from a cow or another animal

milkman /'mɪlkmən/ *noun* (*plural* **milkmen** /'mɪlkmən/) a person who brings milk to your house

milky /'mɪlki/ *adjective* with a lot of milk in it: *milky coffee*

mill /mɪl/ *noun* **1** a building where a machine makes corn into flour ☛ Look also at **windmill**. **2** a factory for making things like steel or paper: *a paper-mill*

millet /'mɪlɪt/ *noun* (no plural) a kind of grass with very small seeds that you can eat or use to make flour

millimetre /'mɪlɪmiːtə(r)/ *noun* a measure of length. There are ten millimetres in a **centimetre**. ✪ The short way of writing 'millimetre' is **mm.**: *60 mm*

million /'mɪljən/ *number* 1 000 000; one thousand thousand: *About 29 million people live in this country.* ○ *millions of dollars* ○ *six million shillings*

millionth /'mɪljənθ/ *adjective, adverb, noun* 1 000 000th

millionaire /ˌmɪljə'neə(r)/ *noun* a very rich person who has more than a million pounds, dollars, etc

mime /maɪm/ *verb* (**mimes**, **miming**, **mimed** /maɪmd/) tell something by your actions, not by speaking

mince /mɪns/ *verb* (**minces**, **mincing**, **minced** /mɪnst/) cut meat into very small pieces, using a special machine: *minced beef*

mince *noun* (no plural) meat in very small pieces

mind[1] /maɪnd/ *noun* the part of you that thinks and remembers: *He has a very quick mind.* **change your mind** have an idea, then decide to do something different: *I planned to study last night but then changed my mind and went for a walk.* **have something on your mind** be worried about something: *I've got a lot on my mind at the moment.* **make up your mind** decide something: *Shall I buy the blue shirt or the red one? I can't make up my mind.*

mind[2] /maɪnd/ *verb* (**minds**, **minding**, **minded**) **1** feel unhappy or angry about something: *'Do you mind if I smoke?' 'No, I don't mind.'* (= you may smoke) **2** be careful of somebody or something: *Mind the step!* ○ *Mind! There's a dog in the road.* **do you mind ...?, would you mind ...?** please could you...?: *It's cold – would you mind closing the window?* **I don't mind** it is not important to me which thing: *'Do you want tea or coffee?' 'I don't mind.'* **never mind** don't worry; there is no problem; it doesn't matter: *'I forgot your book.' 'Never mind, I don't need it today.'*

mine[1] /maɪn/ *noun* a very big hole in the ground where people work to get things like coal, gold or diamonds: *a coalmine*

mine *verb* (**mines**, **mining**, **mined** /maɪnd/) dig in the ground for things like coal or gold

miner *noun* a person who works in a mine

mine[2] /maɪn/ *pronoun* something that belongs to me: *That bike is mine.* ○ *Are those books mine or yours?*

mineral /'mɪnərəl/ *noun* Minerals are things like coal, gold, salt or oil that come from the ground and that people use.

mini- /'mɪni/ *prefix* very small: *The school has a minibus that can carry twelve people.*

miniature /'mɪnətʃə(r)/ *noun* a very small copy of something larger: *The children made a miniature village.*

minimum /'mɪnɪməm/ *noun* (no plural) the smallest size, amount or number that is possible: *We need a minimum of six people to play this game.*

minimum *adjective*: *What is the minimum age for leaving school in your country?* ✪ opposite: **maximum**

minister /'mɪnɪstə(r)/ *noun* **1** one of the most important people in a government: *the Minister of Education* **2** a

priest in some Christian churches

ministry /ˈmɪnɪstri/ *noun* (*plural* **ministries**) a part of the government that controls one special thing: *the Ministry of Defence*

minor /ˈmaɪnə(r)/ *adjective* not very big or important: *Don't worry – it's only a minor problem.* ○ *a minor road* ✪ opposite: **major**

minority /maɪˈnɒrəti/ *noun* (no plural) the smaller part of a group: *Only a minority of the people in Burundi speak English.* ☞ Look at **majority**.

mint /mɪnt/ *noun* **1** (no plural) a small plant with a strong fresh taste and smell, that you put in food and drinks: *mint tea* **2** (*plural* **mints**) a sweet made from this

minus /ˈmaɪnəs/ *preposition* **1** less; when you take away: *Six minus two is four* (6 - 2 = 4). ☞ Look at **plus**. **2** below zero: *The temperature will fall to minus ten degrees.*

minute¹ /ˈmɪnɪt/ *noun* a measure of time. There are 60 **seconds** in a minute and 60 minutes in an **hour**: *It's nine minutes past six.* ○ *The train leaves in ten minutes.* **in a minute** very soon: *I'll be ready in a minute.* **the minute** as soon as: *Phone me the minute you arrive.*

minute² /maɪˈnjuːt/ *adjective* very small: *I can't read his writing – it's minute.*

miracle /ˈmɪrəkl/ *noun* a wonderful and surprising thing that happens and that you cannot explain: *It's a miracle that he wasn't killed when he fell from the window.*

miraculous /mɪˈrækjʊləs/ *adjective* wonderful and surprising: *a miraculous escape*

mirror

mirror /ˈmɪrə(r)/ *noun* a piece of special glass where you can see yourself: *Look in the mirror.*

mis- *prefix*
You can add **mis-** to the beginning of some words to show that something is done wrong or badly, for example:
misbehave = behave badly
misunderstand = not understand correctly

miserable /ˈmɪzrəbl/ *adjective* **1** If you are miserable, you are very sad: *I waited in the rain for an hour, feeling wet and miserable.* **2** If something is miserable, it makes you very sad: *That's miserable news.*

misery /ˈmɪzəri/ *noun* (no plural) great unhappiness

misfortune /ˌmɪsˈfɔːtʃuːn/ *noun* something bad that happens; bad luck: *She had the misfortune to crash her car and lose her job on the same day.*

mislead /ˌmɪsˈliːd/ *verb* (**misleads**, **misleading**, **misled** /ˌmɪsˈled/, **has misled**) make somebody believe something that is not true: *You misled me when you said you could give me a job.*

Miss /mɪs/ a word that you use before the name of a girl or woman who is not married: *Dear Miss Buke, …* ☞ Look at **Mrs** and **Ms**.

miss /mɪs/ *verb* (**misses**, **missing**, **missed** /mɪst/) **1** not hit or catch something: *I tried to hit the ball but I missed.* **2** feel sad about somebody or something that has gone: *I'll miss you when you go away.* **3** be too late for a train, bus, plane or boat: *I just missed my bus.* **4** not see, hear, etc something: *You missed a good football match on TV last night.* **miss out** not put in or do something; not include something: *I didn't finish the exam – I missed out two questions.*

missile /ˈmɪsaɪl/ *noun* a thing that you throw or send through the air to hurt somebody: *The boys were throwing stones, bottles and other missiles.* ○ *nuclear missiles*

missing /ˈmɪsɪŋ/ *adjective* lost, or not in the usual place: *The police are looking for the missing child.* ○ *My purse is missing. Have you seen it?*

mission /ˈmɪʃn/ *noun* a journey to do a special job: *They were sent on a mission to the moon.*

missionary /ˈmɪʃənri/ *noun* (*plural* **missionaries**) a person who goes to another country to teach people about a religion

mist /mɪst/ *noun* thin cloud near the ground, that is difficult to see through: *Early in the morning, the lake was covered in mist.*

misty *adjective* (**mistier**, **mistiest**) *a misty morning*

mistake¹ /mɪˈsteɪk/ *noun* something that you think or do that is wrong: *You have made a lot of spelling mistakes in this letter.* ○ *It was a mistake to go by bus – the journey took two hours!* **by mistake** when you did not plan to do it: *I took your book by mistake – I thought it was mine.*

mistake² /mɪˈsteɪk/ *verb* (**mistakes**, **mistaking**, **mistook** /mɪˈstʊk/, **has mistaken** /mɪˈsteɪkən/) think that somebody or something is a different person or thing: *I'm sorry – I mistook you for someone else.*

mistaken *adjective* wrong: *I said she was Algerian but I was mistaken – she's from Morocco.*

misunderstand /ˌmɪsˌʌndəˈstænd/ *verb* (**misunderstands**, **misunderstanding**, **misunderstood** /ˌmɪsˌʌndəˈstʊd/, **has misunderstood**) not understand something correctly: *I'm sorry, I misunderstood what you said.*

misunderstanding *noun* not understanding something correctly: *I think there's been a misunderstanding. I ordered two tickets, not four.*

mix /mɪks/ *verb* (**mixes**, **mixing**, **mixed** /mɪkst/) **1** put different things together to make something new: *Mix yellow and blue paint together to make green.* **2** join together to make something new: *Oil and water don't mix.* **3** be with and talk to other people: *In my job, I mix with a lot of different people.* **mix up 1** think that one person or thing is a different person or thing: *People often mix Mark up with his brother.* **2** make things untidy: *Don't mix up my papers!*

mixed /mɪkst/ *adjective* of different kinds: *He is African and his wife is Chinese, so their children are of mixed race.* ○ *a mixed class* (of boys and girls together)

mixer /ˈmɪksə(r)/ *noun* a machine that mixes things: *a cement-mixer*

mixture /ˈmɪkstʃə(r)/ *noun* something that you make by mixing different things together: *Air is a mixture of gases.*

mm *short way of writing* **millimetre**

moan /məʊn/ *verb* (**moans**, **moaning**, **moaned** /məʊnd/) **1** make a long sad sound when you are hurt or very unhappy: *He was moaning with pain.* **2** talk a lot about something that you do not like: *He's always moaning about his job.*

moan *noun*: *I heard a loud moan.*

mob /mɒb/ *noun* a big noisy group of people who are shouting or fighting

mobile /ˈməʊbaɪl/ *adjective* able to move easily from place to place: *A mobile dentist visits the village every few months.*

modal verb /ˌməʊdl ˈvɜːb/ *noun* a verb, for example 'might', 'can' or 'must', that you use with another verb

---

Modal verbs

Can, could, may, might, should, must, will, shall, would and **ought to** are modal verbs.

Modal verbs do not have an 's' in the 'he/she' form:

She can drive. (NOT: *She cans drive.*)

After modal verbs (except **ought to**), you use the infinitive without 'to':

I must go now. (NOT: *I must to go.*)

You make questions and negative sentences without 'do' or 'did':

Will you come with me? (NOT: *Do you will come?*)

They might not know. (NOT: *They don't might know.*)

---

model¹ /ˈmɒdl/ *noun* **1** a small copy of something: *a model aeroplane* **2** a person who wears clothes at a special show or for photographs, so that people will see them and buy them **3** one of the cars, machines, etc that a certain company makes: *This pick-up is the very latest model.* **4** a person who sits or stands so that an artist can draw, paint or photograph him/her

model² /ˈmɒdl/ *verb* (**models, modelling, modelled** /ˈmɒdld/) wear and show clothes as a model: *The company asked Kate to model their clothes.*

moderate /ˈmɒdərət/ *adjective* in the middle; not too much and not too little; not too big and not too small: *Kenya's chances of qualifying for the World Cup are only moderate.*

modern /ˈmɒdn/ *adjective* of the present time; of the kind that is usual now: *modern methods of farming* ○ *The airport is very modern.*

modest /ˈmɒdɪst/ *adjective* A person who is modest does not talk much about good things that he/she has done or about things that he/she can do well: *You didn't tell me you could sing so well – you're very modest!*

modestly *adverb*: *He spoke quietly and modestly about his success.*

modesty /ˈmɒdəsti/ *noun* (no plural) being modest

moist /mɔɪst/ *adjective* a little wet: *Keep the earth moist or the plant will die.*

moisture /ˈmɔɪstʃə(r)/ *noun* (no plural) small drops of water on something or in the air

mole /məʊl/ *noun* a small dark spot on a person's skin

moment /ˈməʊmənt/ *noun* a very short time: *He thought for a moment before he answered.* ○ *Can you wait a moment?* **at the moment** now: *She's away at the moment, but she'll be back next week.* **in a moment** very soon: *He'll be here in a moment.* **the moment** as soon as: *Tell Joseph to phone me the moment he arrives.*

monarch /ˈmɒnək/ *noun* a king or queen

monarchy /ˈmɒnəki/ *noun* (plural **monarchies**) a country that has a king or queen

monastery /ˈmɒnəstri/ *noun* (plural **monasteries**) a place where religious men, called **monks**, live, work and pray

Monday /ˈmʌndeɪ/ *noun* the second day of the week, next after Sunday

money /ˈmʌni/ *noun* (no plural) small round metal things (called **coins**) and pieces of paper (called **notes**) that you use when you buy or sell something: *How much money did you spend?* ○ *This jacket cost a lot of money.* **make money** get or earn money

mongoose

mongoose /ˈmɒŋguːs/ *noun* a small animal with fur that eats snakes, rats, etc

monk /mʌŋk/ *noun* a religious man who lives with other religious men in a **monastery**

monkey

monkey /ˈmʌŋki/ *noun* (plural **monkeys**) an animal with a long tail, that can climb trees

monster /ˈmɒnstə(r)/ *noun* an animal in stories that is big, ugly and frightening: *A dragon is a kind of monster.*

month /mʌnθ/ *noun* **1** one of the twelve parts of a year: *December is the last month of the year.* ○ *We went on holiday last month.* ○ *My exams start at the end of the month.* **2** about four weeks: *She was in hospital for a month.*

monthly /ˈmʌnθli/ *adjective, adverb* that happens or comes every month or once a month: *a monthly magazine* ○ *I am paid monthly.*

monument /ˈmɒnjumənt/ *noun* a thing that is built to help people remember a person or something that happened: *This is a monument to Nelson Mandela.*

moo /muː/ *noun* the sound that a cow makes

moo *verb* (**moos, mooing, mooed** /muːd/) make this sound

mood /muːd/ *noun* how you feel: *The teacher is in a bad mood because he's lost his glasses.* ○ *Our teacher was in a very good mood today.* **be in the mood for something** feel that you want something: *I'm not in the mood for a party.*

moon /muːn/ *noun* **the moon** (no plural) the big thing that shines in the sky at night

full moon /ˌfʊl ˈmuːn/ *noun* the time when you can see all of the moon

new moon /ˌnjuː ˈmuːn/ *noun* the time when you can see only the first thin part of the moon

moonlight /ˈmuːnlaɪt/ *noun* (no plural) the light from the moon

moor /mʊə(r)/ *verb* (**moors, mooring, moored** /mʊəd/) tie a boat or ship to something so that it will stay in one place

mop /mɒp/ *noun* a thing with a long handle that you use for washing floors

mop *verb* (**mops, mopping, mopped** /mɒpt/) clean something with a cloth or mop: *I mopped the floor.*

moral[1] /ˈmɒrəl/ *adjective* about what you think is right or wrong: *Some people do not eat meat for moral reasons.* ○ *a moral problem*

morally /ˈmɒrəli/ *adverb*: *It's morally wrong to tell lies.*

moral[2] /ˈmɒrəl/ *noun* a lesson about what is right and wrong, that you can learn from a story or from something that happens: *The moral of the story is that we should be kind to animals.*

more[1] /mɔː(r)/ *adjective, pronoun* a bigger amount or number of something: *You've got more money than I have.* ○ *Can I have some more bread?* ○ *We need two more chairs.* ○ *There aren't any more pens.* ☛ Look at **most**.

more[2] /mɔː(r)/ *adverb* **1** a word that makes an adjective or adverb stronger: *Your book was more expensive than mine.* ○ *Please speak more slowly.* **2** a bigger amount or number: *I like Anna more than her brother.* ☛ Look at **most**. **more or less** almost, but not exactly: *We are more or less the same age.* **not any more** not as before; not any longer:

They don't live here any more. **once more** again: *Let's practise the song once more and we'll be ready for the concert.*

morning /ˈmɔːnɪŋ/ *noun* the first part of the day, between the time when the sun comes up and midday: *I went swimming this morning.* ○ *I'm going to Zanzibar tomorrow morning.* ○ *The letter arrived on Tuesday morning.* ○ *I felt ill all morning.* **in the morning 1** not in the afternoon or evening: *I start work at nine o'clock in the morning.* **2** tomorrow during the morning: *I'll see you in the morning.*

mortar /ˈmɔːtə(r)/ *noun* **1** (no plural) a mixture of cement, sand and water that you put between bricks when you are building something **2** a strong bowl in which we pound things with a **pestle**

mortgage /ˈmɔːgɪdʒ/ *noun* money that you borrow to buy a house

Moslem /ˈmɒzləm/ = **Muslim**

mosque /mɒsk/ *noun* a building where Muslims go to pray

mosquito /məˈskiːtəʊ/ *noun* (plural **mosquitoes**) a small flying insect that bites people and animals and drinks their blood

moss /mɒs/ *noun* (no plural) a soft green plant that grows like a carpet on things like trees and stones

most[1] /məʊst/ *adjective, pronoun* the biggest amount or number of something: *Ali did a lot of work, but I did the most.* ○ *He was ill for most of last week.* ☛ Look at **more**. **at most, at the most** not more than; but not more: *We can stay two days at the most.* **make the most of something** use something in the best way: *We only have one free day, so let's make the most of it.*

most[2] /məʊst/ *adverb* more than all others: *She's the most beautiful girl I have ever seen.* ○ *Which match of the World Cup did you most enjoy?*

mostly /ˈməʊstli/ *adverb* almost all: *The students in my class are mostly 14 years old.*

motel /məʊˈtel/ *noun* a hotel for people who are travelling by car

moth /mɒθ/ *noun* an insect with big wings that flies at night

moth

mother /'mʌðə(r)/ *noun* a woman who has a child: *My mother was 18 when I was born.*

mother-in-law /'mʌðər ɪn lɔː/ *noun* (*plural* **mothers-in-law**) the mother of your husband or wife

motion /'məʊʃn/ *noun* (no plural) **in motion** moving: *Don't put your head out of the window while the train is in motion.*

motive /'məʊtɪv/ *noun* a reason for doing something: *Was there a motive for the murder?*

motor /'məʊtə(r)/ *noun* the part inside a machine that makes it move or work: *an electric motor*

motor bike

motor bike /'məʊtə baɪk/, **motor cycle** /'məʊtə saɪkl/ *noun* a large bicycle with an engine

motor cyclist /'məʊtə saɪklɪst/ *noun* a person who rides a motor cycle

motor boat /'məʊtə bəʊt/ *noun* a small fast boat that has an engine

motorist /'məʊtərɪst/ *noun* a person who drives a car

mould[1] /məʊld/ *noun* (no plural) soft green, grey or blue stuff that grows on food that is too old

mouldy *adjective* covered with mould: *mouldy bread*

mould[2] /məʊld/ *verb* (**moulds**, **moulding**, **moulded**) make something soft into a certain shape: *The children moulded the animals out of clay.*

mould *noun* an empty container for making things into a certain shape: *They poured the hot metal into the mould.*

mound /maʊnd/ *noun* **1** a small hill **2** a pile of things: *a mound of old books and newspapers*

Mount /maʊnt/ *noun* You use 'Mount' before the name of a mountain: *Mount Kenya* ✪ The short way of writing 'Mount' is **Mt**: *Mt Kilimanjaro*

mountain /'maʊntən/ *noun* a very high hill: *Everest is the highest mountain in the world.* ○ *We climbed the mountain.*

mountaineer /ˌmaʊntə'nɪə(r)/ *noun* a person who climbs mountains

mountaineering /ˌmaʊntə'nɪərɪŋ/ *noun* (no plural) the sport of climbing mountains

mourn /mɔːn/ *verb* (**mourns**, **mourning**, **mourned** /mɔːnd/) feel very sad, usually because somebody has died: *She is still mourning for her husband.*

mourning /'mɔːnɪŋ/ *noun* (no plural) a time when people are very sad because somebody has died: *They are in mourning for their son.*

mouse /maʊs/ *noun* (*plural* **mice** /maɪs/) **1** a small animal with a long tail: *Our cat caught a mouse.* **2** a thing that you move with your hand to tell a computer what to do ☛ picture at **computer**

mouse

moustache /mə'stɑːʃ/ *noun* the hair above a man's mouth, below his nose: *He has got a moustache.*

mouth /maʊθ/ *noun* (*plural* **mouths** /maʊðz/) **1** the part of your face below your nose that you use for eating and speaking: *Open your mouth, please!* ☛ picture on page A4. **2** the place where a river goes into the sea

mouthful /'maʊθfʊl/ *noun* the amount of food or drink that you can put in your mouth at one time: *a mouthful of food*

move[1] /muːv/ *verb* (**moves**, **moving**, **moved** /muːvd/) **1** go from one place to another; change the way you are standing or sitting: *Don't get off the bus while it's moving.* ○ *She moved closer to the fire because she was cold.* **2** put something in another place or another way: *Can you move your chair, please?* **3** go to live in another place: *When his company moved from Kisumu to Nai-*

robi he had to move too. ○ *We are moving house soon.* **move in** go to live in a house or flat: *I've got a new flat – I'm moving in next week.* **move out** leave a house or flat where you were living

move[2] /muːv/ *noun* **1** going from one place to another; changing the way you are standing or sitting: *The police are watching every move she makes.* **2** going to live in a new place: *We need a big van for the move.* **get a move on** hurry: *Get a move on or you'll be late for work!*

movement /'muːvmənt/ *noun* **1** moving or being moved: *The old man's movements were slow and painful.* **2** a group of people who have the same ideas or beliefs: *a political movement*

movie /'muːvi/ *noun* **1** a film that you see at the cinema: *Would you like to see a movie?* **2 the movies** (plural) the cinema: *We went to the movies last night.*

mow /məʊ/ *verb* (**mows**, **mowing**, **mowed** /məʊd/, **has mown** /məʊn/) cut grass: *They are mowing the grass before the big football match.*

mower *noun* a machine that cuts grass; a lawnmower

MP /ˌem 'piː/ *short for* **Member of Parliament**

mph a way of measuring how fast something is moving. 'Mph' is short for **miles per hour**: *The train was travelling at 125 mph.*

Mr /'mɪstə(r)/ a word that you use before the name of a man: *Mr Seth Otieno* ○ *Mr Chepkwony*

Mrs /'mɪsɪz/ a word that you use before the name of a woman who is married: *Mrs Meg Njehu* ○ *Mrs Karomo* ☛ Look at **Miss** and **Ms**.

Ms /məz/, /mɪz/ a word that you use before the name of a woman, instead of **Mrs** or **Miss**: *Ms Catherine Wambui*

Mt *short way of writing* **Mount**

much[1] /mʌtʃ/ *adjective* (**much**, **more**, **most**) *pronoun* a big amount of something; a lot of something: *I haven't got much money.* ○ *There was so much food that we couldn't eat it all.* ○ *'Do you like it?' 'No, not much.'* ✪ We usually use 'much' only in negative

sentences, in questions, and after 'too', 'so', 'as' and 'how'. In other sentences we use **a lot (of)**.: *She's got a lot of money.* ☛ Look at **many**. **as much as** the same amount that: *Take as much paper as you need.* **how much ...? 1** what amount?: *How much meat do you want?* **2** what price?: *How much is this shirt?*

much[2] /mʌtʃ/ *adverb* a lot: *I don't like him very much.* ○ *I am much older than him.*

mud /mʌd/ *noun* (no plural) soft wet earth: *Phil came home from the football match covered in mud.*

muddle /'mʌdl/ *verb* (**muddles**, **muddling**, **muddled** /'mʌdld/) **muddle somebody up** mix somebody's ideas so that they cannot understand or think clearly: *Don't ask so many questions – you're muddling me up.* **muddle somebody** or **something up** think that one person or thing is a different person or thing: *I always muddle Mwende up with her sister.* **muddle something up** make something untidy: *You've muddled all my papers up!*

muddle *noun* **in a muddle** untidy or not thinking clearly: *Your room is in a terrible muddle.* ○ *I was in such a muddle that I couldn't find anything.*

muddy /'mʌdi/ *adjective* (**muddier**, **muddiest**) covered with mud: *When it rains, the roads get very muddy.*

mug[1] /mʌg/ *noun* a big cup with straight sides: *a mug of tea*

mug

mug[2] /mʌg/ *verb* (**mugs**, **mugging**, **mugged** /mʌgd/) attack somebody in the street and take their money

mugger *noun* a person who mugs somebody

mule /mjuːl/ *noun* an animal whose parents were a horse and a donkey

multicoloured /ˌmʌlti'kʌləd/ *adjective* with many colours: *multicoloured birds*

multiply /'mʌltɪplaɪ/ *verb* (**multiplies**, **multiplying**, **multiplied** /'mʌltɪplaɪd/, **has multiplied**) make a number bigger by a certain number of times: *Two multiplied by three is six* (2 x 3 = 6).

○ *Multiply three and seven together.*

multiplication /ˌmʌltɪplɪˈkeɪʃn/ *noun* (no plural) multiplying a number

multi-storey /ˌmʌlti ˈstɔːri/ *adjective* with many floors: *a multi-storey car park*

mumble /ˈmʌmbl/ *verb* (**mumbles**, **mumbling**, **mumbled** /ˈmʌmbld/) speak quietly in a way that is not clear, so that people cannot hear you well: *She mumbled something about a party, but I didn't hear what she said.*

murder /ˈmɜːdə(r)/ *verb* (**murders**, **murdering**, **murdered** /ˈmɜːdəd/) kill somebody when you have decided to do it: *Police believe the dead man was murdered.*

murder *noun* murdering somebody: *He was sent to prison for the murder of a police officer.*

murderer *noun* a person who has murdered somebody: *The police have caught the murderer.*

murmur /ˈmɜːmə(r)/ *verb* (**murmurs**, **murmuring**, **murmured** /ˈmɜːməd/) speak in a low quiet voice or make a low sound that is not very clear: *'I love you,' she murmured in his ear.*

murmur *noun: I heard the murmur of voices from the next room.* ○ *the murmur of the wind in the trees*

murram /ˈmʌrəm/ *noun* (no plural) (an East African word) a type of hard soil that is full of small stones. We use murram to make small roads.

muscle /ˈmʌsl/ *noun* one of the parts inside your body that become tight or loose to help you move

museum /mjuˈziːəm/ *noun* a building where people can look at old or interesting things: *Have you ever been to the National Museum?*

mushroom
/ˈmʌʃrum/ *noun* a plant that you can eat, with a flat top and no leaves

music /ˈmjuːzɪk/ *noun* (no plural)
1 the sounds that you make by singing, or by playing instruments: *What sort of music do you like?* **2** signs on paper to show people what to sing or play: *Can*

you read music?

✪ Some types of music are **pop**, **rock**, **jazz**, **soul**, **reggae**, **rap** and **classical**.

musical /ˈmjuːzɪkl/ *adjective* **1** of music: *musical instruments* (= the guitar or the trumpet, for example) **2** good at making music: *She's a very musical child— she's always singing and dancing.*

musician /mjuˈzɪʃn/ *noun* a person who writes music or plays a musical instrument

Muslim /ˈmʊzlɪm/ *noun* a person who follows the religion of **Islam**

Muslim *adjective: the Muslim way of life*

must /məst/, /mʌst/ *modal verb* **1** a word that you use to tell somebody what to do or what is necessary: *You must look before you cross the road.* **2** a word that shows that you are sure something is true: *You must be tired after your long journey.* ○ *I can't find my keys. I must have left them at home.*
☞ Look at the Note on page 195 to find out more about **modal verbs**.

✪ You use **must not** or the short form **mustn't** to tell people <u>not</u> to do something:

You **mustn't** be late.

When you want to say that somebody can do something if they want, but that it is not necessary, you use **don't have to**:

You **don't have to** do your homework today (= you can do it if you want, but it is not necessary).

mustard /ˈmʌstəd/ *noun* (no plural) a thick yellow sauce with a very strong taste, that you eat with meat

mustn't /ˈmʌsnt/ = must not

mutter /ˈmʌtə(r)/ *verb* (**mutters**, **muttering**, **muttered** /ˈmʌtəd/) speak in a low quiet voice that is difficult to hear: *He muttered something about going home, and left the room.*

mutton /ˈmʌtən/ *noun* (no plural) meat from a sheep

my /maɪ/ *adjective* of me: *Where is my watch?* ○ *These are my books, not yours.* ○ *I've hurt my arm.*

myself /maɪˈself/ *pronoun* (*plural* **our-selves**) **1** a word that shows the same person as the one who is speaking: *I hurt myself.* ○ *I bought myself a new shirt.* **2** a word that makes 'I' stronger: *'Did you buy this bread?' 'No, I made it myself.'* **by myself 1** alone; without other people: *I live by myself.* **2** without help: *When I was eight years old my mother let me cook by myself.*

mysterious /mɪˈstɪəriəs/ *adjective* Something that is mysterious is strange and you do not know about it or understand it: *We saw some mysterious lights in the sky.*

mysteriously *adverb*: *The plane disappeared mysteriously.*

mystery /ˈmɪstri/ *noun* (*plural* **mysteries**) something strange that you cannot understand or explain: *The police say that the man's death is still a mystery.*

myth /mɪθ/ *noun* **1** a very old story **2** a story or belief that is not true

Nn

nagana /nəˈɡɑːnə/ *noun* (no plural) (an East African word) a serious illness that cattle get from tsetse flies

nail /neɪl/ *noun* **1** the hard part at the end of a finger or toe: *toenails* ○ *fingernails* ☛ picture on page A4. **2** a small thin piece of metal with one sharp end which you hit into wood (with a **hammer**) to fix things together ☛ picture at **hammer**

nail *verb* (**nails**, **nailing**, **nailed** /neɪld/) fix something to another thing with a nail: *I nailed the pieces of wood together.*

naked /ˈneɪkɪd/ *adjective* If you are naked, you are not wearing any clothes.

name¹ /neɪm/ *noun* a word or words that you use to call or talk about a person or thing: *My name is Gloria Mutungi.* ○ *What's your name?* ○ *Do you know the name of this flower?*

❖ Your **first name** is the name that your parents give you when you are born. In Christian countries this is also called your **Christian name**. Your **surname** is the name that everybody in your family has. A **nickname** is a name that your friends or family sometimes call you instead of your real name. **call somebody names** say bad, unkind words about somebody: *Joseph cried because the other children were calling him names.*

name² /neɪm/ *verb* (**names**, **naming**, **named** /neɪmd/) **1** give a name to somebody or something: *They named their baby Margaret.* ○ *They named him Shariff after his grandfather* (= gave him the same name as his grandfather). **2** know and say the name of somebody or something: *The headmaster could name every one of his 600 pupils.*

namely /ˈneɪmli/ *adverb* You use 'namely' when you are going to name a person or thing that you have just said something about: *Only two students were late, namely Fred and Bogere.*

nap /næp/ *noun* a short sleep that you have during the day: *I had a nap after lunch.*

napkin /ˈnæpkɪn/ *noun* a piece of cloth or paper that you use when you are eating to clean your mouth and hands and to keep your clothes clean

nappy /ˈnæpi/ *noun* (*plural* **nappies**) a piece of cloth or strong paper that a baby wears around its bottom and between its legs

narrow /ˈnærəʊ/ *adjective* (**narrower**, **narrowest**) not far from one side to the other: *The road was too narrow for two cars to pass.* ❖ opposite: **wide** or **broad**. ☛ picture on page A10. **have a narrow escape** If you have a narrow escape, something bad almost happens to you: *You had a very narrow escape – your car nearly hit a tree.*

narrowly *adverb* only just: *The car narrowly missed hitting me.*

nasty /ˈnɑːsti/ *adjective* (**nastier**, **nastiest**) bad; not nice: *There's a nasty smell in this room.* ○ *Don't be so nasty!*

nation /ˈneɪʃn/ *noun* a country and all the people who live in it

national /ˈnæʃnəl/ *adjective* of or for all of a country: *the national athletics championship* ○ *national newspapers*

national anthem /ˌnæʃnəl ˈænθəm/ *noun* the song of a country

national park /ˌnæʃnəl ˈpɑːk/ *noun* a large area of beautiful land that the government looks after

nationality /ˌnæʃəˈnæləti/ *noun* (*plural* **nationalities**) belonging to a certain country: *'What nationality are you?' 'I'm Ugandan.'*

native /ˈneɪtɪv/ *adjective* (of) the place where you were born: *I returned to my native country.*

native *noun* a person who was born in a place: *He lives in Nairobi but he's a native of Mombasa.*

natural /ˈnætʃrəl/ *adjective* **1** made by nature, not by people: *This part of the country is an area of great natural beauty.* ○ *Earthquakes and floods are natural disasters.* **2** normal or usual: *It's natural for parents to feel sad when their children leave home.* ♦ opposite: **unnatural**

naturally /ˈnætʃrəli/ *adverb* **1** in a way that is not made or caused by people: *Is your hair naturally straight?* **2** of course: *You didn't answer the telephone, so I naturally thought you were out.* **3** in a normal way: *Try to stand naturally while I take a photo.*

nature /ˈneɪtʃə(r)/ *noun* **1** (no plural) everything in the world that was not made by people: *the beauty of nature* **2** (*plural* **natures**) the way a person or thing is: *Our cat has a very friendly nature.*

naughty /ˈnɔːti/ *adjective* (**naughtier**, **naughtiest**) You say that a child is naughty when he/she does bad things or does not do what you ask him/her to do: *She's the naughtiest child in the class.*

naval /ˈneɪvl/ *adjective* of a navy: *a naval officer*

navigate /ˈnævɪgeɪt/ *verb* (**navigates**, **navigating**, **navigated**) use a map, etc to find which way a ship, an aeroplane or a car should go: *Long ago, sailors used the stars to navigate.*

navigator /ˈnævɪgeɪtə(r)/ *noun* a person who navigates

navy /ˈneɪvi/ *noun* (*plural* **navies**) the ships that a country uses when there is a war, and the people who work on them: *Samuel is in the navy.*

navy blue /ˌneɪvi ˈbluː/ *adjective* dark blue

near /nɪə(r)/ *adjective, adverb* (**nearer**, **nearest**) not far; close: *Let's walk to my house. It's quite near.* ○ *Where's the nearest hospital?* ○ *My parents live quite near.*

near *preposition* close to somebody or something: *I live very near my school – just five minutes' walk.*

nearby /ˈnɪəbaɪ/ *adjective* not far away; close: *We took her to a nearby hospital.*

nearby /nɪəˈbaɪ/ *adverb*: *After school I went to see my grandmother, who lives nearby.*

nearly /ˈnɪəli/ *adverb* almost; not quite: *I'm nearly 16 – it's my birthday next week.* ○ *She was so ill that she nearly died.* **not nearly** not at all: *The test wasn't nearly as difficult as I thought it would be.*

neat /niːt/ *adjective* (**neater**, **neatest**) with everything in the right place; tidy: *Keep your room neat and tidy.*

neatly *adverb*: *Write your name neatly.*

necessarily /ˌnesəˈserəli/ *adverb* **not necessarily** not always: *Big names aren't necessarily strong.*

necessary /ˈnesəsəri/ *adjective* If something is necessary, you must have or do it: *Warm clothes are necessary for camping.*

necessity /nəˈsesəti/ *noun* (*plural* **necessities**) something that you must have: *Food and clothes are necessities of life.*

neck /nek/ *noun* **1** the part of your body between your shoulders and your head: *Beatrice usually wears a chain*

round her neck. ☛ picture on page A4.
2 the part of a jumper, T-shirt, etc that goes round your neck **3** the thin part at the top of a bottle

necklace /ˈneklǝs/ *noun* a pretty thing that you wear round your neck: *a gold necklace*

need[1] /niːd/ *verb* (**needs**, **needing**, **needed**) **1** must have something; want something important and necessary that is not there: *All plants and animals need water.* ○ *You don't need to bring money – I'll pay.* **2** If you need to do something, you must do it, or it is very important to do it: *James is very ill. He needs to go to hospital.* ○ *'Do we need to pay now, or can we pay next week?' 'You needn't pay now.'/'You don't need to pay now.'*

need[2] /niːd/ *noun* **be in need of something** want something important and necessary that is not there: *She's in need of a rest.*

needle /ˈniːdl/ *noun* **1** a small thin piece of metal with a hole at one end and a sharp point at the other. You use a needle for sewing: *If you give me a needle and cotton, I'll sew the button on your shirt.* ☛ picture at **sew**. **2** something that is like a needle: *the needle of a compass* **3** a very thin pointed leaf. **Pine trees** and **fir-trees** have needles. ☛ Look also at **knitting-needle**.

needn't /ˈniːdnt/ = **need not**

negative /ˈnegǝtɪv/ *adjective* using words like 'no', 'not' and 'never': *'I don't like beer' is a negative sentence.*

negative *noun* a piece of film that you use to make a photograph. On a negative, dark things are light and light things are dark.

neglect /nɪˈglekt/ *verb* (**neglects**, **neglecting**, **neglected**) not take care of somebody or something: *The dog was dirty and thin because its owner had neglected it.*

neglect *noun* (no plural) *The house was in a state of neglect.*

neigh /neɪ/ *noun* the sound that a horse makes

neigh *verb* (**neighs**, **neighing**, **neighed** /neɪd/) make this sound

neighbour /ˈneɪbǝ(r)/ *noun* a person who lives near you: *Don't make so much noise or you'll wake the neighbours.* ✪ Your **next-door neighbour** is the person who lives in the house next door to your house.

neighbouring *adjective* that is near: *We played football against a team from the neighbouring village.*

neighbourhood /ˈneɪbǝhʊd/ *noun* a part of a town: *They live in a friendly neighbourhood.*

neither[1] /ˈnaɪðǝ(r)/, /ˈniːðǝ(r)/ *adjective, pronoun* not one and not the other of two things or people: *Neither book was very interesting.* ○ *Neither of the children can swim.*

neither[2] /ˈnaɪðǝ(r)/, /ˈniːðǝ(r)/ *adverb* (used in sentences with 'not') also not: *Lydia can't run very fast and neither can I.* ○ *'I don't like football.' 'Neither do I.'* **neither ... nor** not ... and not: *Neither Paul nor I went to the party.*

nephew /ˈnefjuː/ *noun* the son of your brother or sister

nerve /nɜːv/ *noun* **1** (*plural* **nerves**) one of the long thin things inside your body that carry feelings and messages to and from your brain **2 nerves** (plural) being worried or afraid: *John breathed deeply to calm his nerves.* **3** (no plural) being brave or calm when there is danger: *You need a lot of nerve to catch a snake.* **get on somebody's nerves** annoy somebody: *Stop making that noise – you're getting on my nerves!*

nervous /ˈnɜːvǝs/ *adjective* **1** worried or afraid: *I'm quite nervous about starting my new job.* **2** of the nerves in your body: *the nervous system*

nervously *adverb*: *He laughed nervously because he didn't know what to say.*

nervousness /ˈnɜːvǝsnǝs/ *noun* (no plural) being nervous

nest /nest/ *noun* a place where a bird, a snake, an insect, etc lives and lays its eggs or keeps its babies: *a bird's nest*

nest *verb* (**nests**, **nesting**, **nested**) make and live in a nest: *The ducks are nesting by the river.*

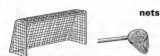

nets

net /net/ *noun* material that is made of long pieces of string, etc with holes between them: *a fishing net* ○ *a tennis net*

netball /'netbɔːl/ *noun* (no plural) a game where two teams of seven players try to throw a ball through a high round net

network /'netwɜːk/ *noun* a large group of things that are connected to one another across a country, etc: *the railway network*

never /'nevə(r)/ *adverb* not at any time; not ever: *She never works on Saturdays.* ○ *I've never been to Kampala.* ○ *I will never forget you.*

nevertheless /ˌnevəðə'les/ *conjunction, adverb* but; however; although that is true: *They played very well. Nevertheless, they didn't win.*

new /njuː/ *adjective* (**newer**, **newest**)
1 Something that is new has just been made or bought: *I bought a new pair of shoes yesterday.* ○ *Do you like my new hairstyle?* ☛ picture on page A11.
2 that you have not seen, had, learnt, etc before: *Our new flat is much bigger than our old one.* ○ *The teacher usually explains the new words to us.* **new to something** If you are new to something, you are at a place or doing something for the first time: *They are new to the town and they don't have any friends there.* **new year** the beginning of the year; the time around 1 January: *Happy New Year!* ✪ 1 January is called **New Year's Day** and 31 December is called **New Year's Eve**.

newcomer /'njuːkʌmə(r)/ *noun* a person who has just come to a place

newly /'njuːli/ *adverb* not long ago; recently: *Our school is newly built.*

news /njuːz/ *noun* (no plural) **1** words that tell people about things that have just happened: *Have you heard the news? Chakava is getting married.* ○ *I've got some good news for you.* ✪ Be careful! You cannot say 'a news'. You can say 'some news' or 'a piece of news': *Msakuzi told us an interesting piece of news.* **2** **the news** (no plural) a programme on television or radio that tells people about important things that have just happened: *We heard about the plane crash on the news.* **break the news** tell somebody about something important that has happened: *Have you broken the news to your wife?*

newspaper /'njuːspeɪpə(r)/ *noun* large pieces of paper with news, advertisements and other things printed on them, that you can buy every day or every week

next[1] /nekst/ *adjective* **1** that comes after this one: *I'm starting my new job next week.* ○ *Go straight on, then take the next road on the right.* **2** nearest to this one: *I live in the next village.* **next to** at the side of somebody or something; beside: *The bank is next to the post office.* ☛ picture on page A1

next[2] /nekst/ *adverb* after this; then: *I've finished this work. What shall I do next?*

next[3] /nekst/ *noun* (no plural) the person or thing that comes after this one: *Agnes came first and Paul was the next to arrive.*

next door /ˌnekst 'dɔː(r)/ *adjective, adverb* in or to the nearest house: *Who lives next door?* ○ *next-door neighbours*

nibble /'nɪbl/ *verb* (**nibbles**, **nibbling**, **nibbled** /'nɪbld/) eat something in very small bites: *The rabbit was nibbling some leaves.*

nice /naɪs/ *adjective* (**nicer**, **nicest**) pleasant, good or kind: *Did you have a nice trip?* ○ *I met a nice boy at the party.* ○ *It's nice to see you.* **nice and ...** words that show that you like something: *It's nice and warm by the fire.*

nicely *adverb*: *The party was going nicely until the fight started.*

nickname /'nɪkneɪm/ *noun* a name that your friends or family sometimes call you instead of your real name

niece /niːs/ *noun* the daughter of your brother or sister

night /naɪt/ *noun* **1** the time when it is dark because there is no light from the sun: *She stayed at my house last night.*

○ *The baby cried all night.* **2** the part of the day between the afternoon and when you go to bed: *We went to a party on Saturday night.* ✪ **Tonight** means the night or evening of today.

nightclub /'naɪtklʌb/ *noun* a place where you can go late in the evening to drink and dance, for example

nightdress /'naɪtdres/ (*plural* **nightdresses**), **nightie** /'naɪti/ *noun* a loose dress that a woman or girl wears in bed

nightly /'naɪtli/ *adjective, adverb* that happens or comes every night: *a nightly TV show*

nightmare /'naɪtmeə(r)/ *noun* **1** a dream that frightens you: *I had a nightmare last night.* **2** something that is very bad or frightening: *Crossing the river in the dark was a nightmare.*

night-time /'naɪt taɪm/ *noun* (no plural) the time when it is dark: *She is afraid to go out at night-time.*

nil /nɪl/ *noun* (no plural) nothing: *Our team won the match by two goals to nil.*

nine /naɪn/ *number* 9

ninth /naɪnθ/ *adjective, adverb, noun* **1** 9th **2** one of nine equal parts of something; $\frac{1}{9}$

nineteen /ˌnaɪn'ti:n/ *number* 19

nineteenth /ˌnaɪn'ti:nθ/ *adjective, adverb, noun* 19th

ninety /'naɪnti/ *number* **1** 90 **2** **the nineties** (plural) the numbers, years or temperatures between 90 and 99 **in your nineties** between the ages of 90 and 99: *My grandmother is in her nineties.*

ninetieth /'naɪntiəθ/ *adjective, adverb, noun* 90th

nitrogen /'naɪtrədʒən/ *noun* (no plural) a gas in the air

no¹, No *short way of writing* **number** 1

no² /nəʊ/ *adjective* **1** not one; not any: *I have no money – my purse is empty.* **2** a word that shows you are not allowed to do something: *The sign said 'No Smoking'.*

no *adverb* not any: *I'm a good swimmer but I'm no better than you.*

no³ /nəʊ/ a word that you use to show that something is not right or true, or that you do not want something; not

yes: *'Do you want a drink?' 'No, thank you.'* ○ *'He's from Zimbabwe.' 'No he isn't. He's South African.'* **oh no!** words that you say when something bad happens: *Oh no! I've broken my watch!*

nobody /'nəʊbədi/ *pronoun* no person; not anybody: *Nobody in our class speaks French.* ○ *There was nobody at home.*

nod /nɒd/ *verb* (**nods, nodding, nodded**) move your head down and up again quickly as a way of saying 'yes' or 'hello' to somebody: *'Do you understand?' asked the teacher, and everybody nodded.*

nod *noun*: *I'll give you a nod when it's time to start the show.*

noise /nɔɪz/ *noun* **1** something that you hear; a sound: *I heard a noise upstairs.* **2** a loud sound that you do not like: *Don't make so much noise!* ○ *What a terrible noise!*

noisy /'nɔɪzi/ *adjective* (**noisier, noisiest**) **1** full of loud noise: *The restaurant was too noisy.* **2** If a person or thing is noisy, he/she/it makes a lot of noise: *The children are very noisy.* ✪ *opposite:* **quiet**

noisily /'nɔɪzɪli/ *adverb*: *He ate his dinner noisily.*

nomad /'nəʊmæd/ *noun* a member of a group of people who move from place to place with their animals to find water and grass

nomadic /nəʊ'mædɪk/ *adjective*: *Many pastoralists have changed from a nomadic to a settled life.*

---

non- /nɒn/ *prefix*
You can add **non-** to the beginning of some words to give them the opposite meaning, for example:

a **non-smoker** = a person who does not smoke

a **non-stop** train = a train that goes from one place to another without stopping at the other stations in between

---

none /nʌn/ *pronoun* not any; not one: *She has eaten all the bananas – there are none in the box.* ○ *I went to every bookshop, but none of them had the book I wanted.*

nonsense /'nɒnsns/ *noun* (no plural) words or ideas that have no meaning or that are not true: *It's nonsense to say that Saidi is lazy.*

noon /nuːn/ *noun* (no plural) twelve o'clock in the middle of the day: *I met Athumani at noon.*

no one /'nəʊ wʌn/ *pronoun* no person; not anybody: *There was no one in the classroom.* ○ *No one saw me go into the house.*

nor /nɔː(r)/ *conjunction* (used after 'neither' and 'not') also not: *If Mwalimu doesn't go, nor will Miraji.* ○ *'I don't like eggs.' 'Nor do I.'* ○ *Neither Nazir nor I eat meat.*

normal /'nɔːml/ *adjective* usual and ordinary; not different or special: *I will be home at the normal time.*

normally /'nɔːməli/ *adverb* **1** usually: *I normally go to bed at about eleven o'clock.* **2** in a normal way: *He isn't behaving normally.*

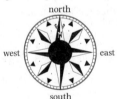

north

west   east

south

north /nɔːθ/ *noun* (no plural) the direction that is on your left when you watch the sun come up in the morning: *the north of Tanzania*

north *adjective, adverb*: *North Africa* ○ *a north wind* (= that comes from the north) ○ *We travelled north from Nairobi to Nanyuki.*

northern /'nɔːðən/ *adjective* in or of the north part of a place: *Mwanza is in northern Tanzania.*

nose /nəʊz/ *noun* **1** the part of your face, above your mouth, that you use for breathing and smelling ☞ picture on page A4. **2** the front part of a plane **blow your nose** blow air through your nose to empty it, into a piece of cloth or paper (a **handkerchief** or a **tissue**)

nostril /'nɒstrəl/ *noun* one of the two holes in your nose ☞ picture on page A4

nosy /'nəʊzi/ *adjective* (**nosier**, **nosiest**) too interested in other people's lives and in things that you should not be interested in: *'Where are you going?' 'Don't be so nosy!'*

not /nɒt/ *adverb* a word that gives the opposite meaning to another word or a sentence: *I'm not hungry.* ○ *They did not arrive.* ○ *I can come tomorrow, but not on Tuesday.* ○ *'Are you angry with me?' 'No, I'm not.'* ✪ We often say and write **n't**: *John isn't* (= is not) *here.* ○ *I haven't* (= have not) *got any sisters.*
not at all 1 no; not a little bit: *'Are you tired?' 'Not at all.'* **2** polite words that you say when somebody has said 'thank you': *'Thanks for your help.' 'Oh, not at all.'*

note[1] /nəʊt/ *noun* **1** some words that you write quickly to help you remember something: *I made a note of her address.* **2** a short letter: *Maria sent me a note to thank me for the present.* **3** a piece of paper money: *He gave me a 50 shilling note.* **4** a short piece of extra information about something in a book: *Look at the note on page 39.* **5** one sound in music, or a mark on paper that shows a sound in music: *I can play a few notes of this song.* **take notes** write when somebody is speaking so that you can remember their words later: *The teacher asked us to take notes in the lesson.*

note[2] /nəʊt/ *verb* (**notes**, **noting**, **noted**) notice and remember something: *Please note that all the shops are closed on Sundays.* **note down** write something so that you can remember it: *The police officer noted down my name and address.*

notebook /'nəʊtbʊk/ *noun* a small book where you write things that you want to remember

notepad /'nəʊtpæd/ *noun* some pieces of paper that are joined together at one edge, where you write things that you want to remember

notepaper /'nəʊtpeɪpə(r)/ *noun* (no plural) paper that you write letters on

nothing /'nʌθɪŋ/ *pronoun* not anything; no thing: *There's nothing in this bottle – it's empty.* ○ *I've finished all my work and I've got nothing to do.*

for nothing 1 for no money; free: *You can have these books for nothing. I don't want them.* **2** without a good result: *I went to the station for nothing – she wasn't on the train.* **have nothing on** If you have nothing on, you are not wearing any clothes. **nothing but** only: *He talks about nothing but his job.* **nothing like** not the same as somebody or something in any way: *He's nothing like his brother.*

notice[1] /ˈnəʊtɪs/ *noun* **1** (*plural* **notices**) a piece of writing that tells people something: *The notice on the wall says 'NO SMOKING'.* **2** (no plural) a warning that something is going to happen: *Our teacher gave us two weeks' notice of the history exam.* **at short notice** with not much time to get ready: *I was asked to play at short notice and I didn't have time to get my football boots.* **give in** or **hand in your notice** tell the person you work for that you are going to leave your job **take no notice of somebody** or **something** not listen to or look at somebody or something; not pay attention to somebody or something: *Take no notice of what she said – she's not feeling well.*

notice[2] /ˈnəʊtɪs/ *verb* (**notices**, **noticing**, **noticed** /ˈnəʊtɪst/) see somebody or something: *Did you notice what she was wearing?* ○ *I noticed that he was driving a new car.*

noticeable /ˈnəʊtɪsəbl/ *adjective* easy to see: *I've got a mark on my shirt. Is it noticeable?*

notice-board /ˈnəʊtɪs bɔːd/ *noun* a flat piece of wood on a wall. You put papers on a notice-board so everybody can read them: *The teacher put the exam results on the notice-board.*

nought /nɔːt/ *noun* the number 0: *We say 0·5 as 'nought point five'.*

noun /naʊn/ *noun* a word that is the name of a person, place, thing or idea: *'Anne', 'Africa', 'cat' and 'happiness' are all nouns.*

novel /ˈnɒvl/ *noun* a book that tells a story about people and things that are not real: *'A Grain of Wheat' is a novel by Ngugi wa Thiong'o.*

novelist /ˈnɒvəlɪst/ *noun* a person who writes novels

November /nəʊˈvembə(r)/ *noun* the eleventh month of the year

now[1] /naʊ/ *adverb* **1** at this time: *I can't see you now – can you come back later?* ○ *She was in Dar es Salaam but she's living in Arusha now.* ○ *Don't wait – do it now!* **2** a word that you use when you start to talk about something new, or to make people listen to you: *I've finished writing this letter. Now, what shall we have for dinner?* ○ *Be quiet, now!* **from now on** after this time; in the future: *From now on your teacher will be Mr Rashidi.* **now and again**, **now and then** sometimes, but not often: *We go to the cinema now and again.*

now[2] /naʊ/ *conjunction* because something has happened: *Now that Michael has arrived we can start dinner.*

nowadays /ˈnaʊədeɪz/ *adverb* at this time: *A lot of people work with computers nowadays.*

nowhere /ˈnəʊweə(r)/ *adverb* not anywhere; at, in or to no place: *There's nowhere to stay in this village.* **nowhere near** not at all: *I'm nowhere near as tall as my brother.*

nuclear /ˈnjuːklɪə(r)/ *adjective* **1** of or about the inside part of **atoms**: *nuclear physics* **2** using the great power that is made by breaking or joining parts of atoms: *nuclear energy* ○ *nuclear weapons*

nudge /nʌdʒ/ *verb* (**nudges**, **nudging**, **nudged** /nʌdʒd/) touch or push somebody or something with your elbow: *Nudge me if I fall asleep in class.*

nudge *noun*: *Agatha gave me a nudge.*

nuisance /ˈnjuːsns/ *noun* a person or thing that causes you trouble: *I've lost my keys. What a nuisance!*

numb /nʌm/ *adjective* not able to feel anything: *My fingers were numb with cold.*

number /ˈnʌmbə(r)/ *noun* **1** a word like 'two' or 'fifteen', or a symbol or group of symbols like 7 or 130: *Choose a number between ten and one hundred.* ○ *Our telephone number is Nairobi 453653.* ✪ We sometimes write **No** or **no**: *I live at no 47.* **2** a group of more than one person or thing: *A large* number of people were waiting for the bus. ○ There are a number of ways you can cook an egg.

number verb (**numbers, numbering, numbered** /'nʌmbəd/) give a number to something: Number the pages from one to ten.

number-plate /'nʌmbə pleɪt/ noun the flat piece of metal on the front and back of a car that has numbers and letters on it (its **registration number**) ☛ picture at **car**

numerous /'nju:mərəs/ adjective very many: He writes a lot of letters because he has numerous friends.

nun /nʌn/ noun a religious woman who lives with other religious women in a **convent**

nurse¹ /nɜ:s/ noun a person whose job is to look after people who are sick or hurt: My sister works as a nurse in a hospital.

nurse² /nɜ:s/ verb (**nurses, nursing, nursed** /nɜ:st/) look after somebody who is sick or hurt: I nursed my father when he was ill.

nursery /'nɜ:səri/ noun (plural **nurseries**) **1** a place where young children can stay when their parents are at work **2** a place where people grow and sell plants

nursery school /'nɜ:səri sku:l/ noun a school for children between the ages of three and five

nursing /'nɜ:sɪŋ/ noun (no plural) the job of being a nurse: He has decided to go into nursing when he leaves school.

nut /nʌt/ noun **1** the hard fruit of a tree, plant or bush: coconuts, groundnuts and cashew nuts **2** a small piece of metal with a hole in the middle that you put on the end of a long piece of metal (called a **bolt**). You use nuts and bolts for fixing things together.

nuts

nylon /'naɪlɒn/ noun (no plural) very strong material made by machines. Nylon is used for making clothes and other things: nylon thread

Oo

O /əʊ/ **1** = **Oh 2** a way of saying the number '0'

oak /əʊk/ noun **1** (plural **oaks**) a kind of large tree **2** (no plural) the wood of an oak tree: an oak table

oar /ɔ:(r)/ noun a long piece of wood with one flat end. You use oars to move a small boat through water (to **row**). ☛ picture at **row**

oasis /əʊ'eɪsɪs/ noun (plural **oases** /əʊ'eɪsi:z/) a place in a desert that has trees and water

oath /əʊθ/ noun a serious promise: I took an oath in front of a lawyer.

oats /əʊts/ noun (plural) a plant with seeds that we use as food for people and animals: We make porridge from oats.

obedient /ə'bi:diənt/ adjective An obedient person does what somebody tells him/her to do: He was an obedient child. ✪ opposite: **disobedient**

obedience /ə'bi:diəns/ noun (no plural) being obedient

obediently adverb: I called the dog and it followed me obediently.

obey /ə'beɪ/ verb (**obeys, obeying, obeyed** /ə'beɪd/) do what somebody or something tells you to do: You must obey the law.

object¹ /'ɒbdʒɪkt/ noun **1** a thing that you can see and touch: There was a small round object on the table. **2** what you plan to do: His object in life is to become as rich as possible. **3** In the sentence 'Jane painted the door', the object of the sentence is 'the door'.

object² /əb'dʒekt/ verb (**objects, objecting, objected**) not like something or not agree with something: I object to the plan.

objection /əb'dʒekʃn/ noun saying or feeling that you do not like something or that you do not agree with something: *I have no objections to the plan.*

obligation /ˌɒblɪ'geɪʃn/ noun something that you must do: *We have an obligation to help.*

oblige /ə'blaɪdʒ/ noun (**obliges**, **obliging**, **obliged** /ə'blaɪdʒd/) **be obliged to** If you are obliged to do something, you must do it: *You are not obliged to come if you do not want to.*

oblong /'ɒblɒŋ/ noun a shape with two long sides, two short sides and four angles of 90 degrees ☛ picture on page A5

oblong adjective: *This page is oblong.*

observation /ˌɒbzə'veɪʃn/ noun (no plural) watching or being watched carefully **be under observation** be watched carefully: *The police kept the house under observation.*

observe /əb'zɜːv/ verb (**observes**, **observing**, **observed** /əb'zɜːvd/) watch somebody or something carefully; see somebody or something: *The police observed a man leaving the house.*

obsess /əb'ses/ verb (**obsesses**, **obsessing**, **obsessed** /əb'sest/) **be obsessed with somebody** or **something** think about somebody or something all the time: *Paul is obsessed with football.*

obsession /əb'seʃn/ noun a person or thing that you think about all the time: *Cars are his obsession.*

obstacle /'ɒbstəkl/ noun **1** something that is in front of you, that you must go over or round before you can go on: *The horse jumped over the obstacle.* **2** a problem that stops you doing something

obstinate /'ɒbstɪnət/ adjective An obstinate person does not change his/her ideas or do what other people want him/her to do: *He's too obstinate to say he's sorry.*

obstruct /əb'strʌkt/ verb (**obstructs**, **obstructing**, **obstructed**) be in the way so that somebody or something cannot get past: *Please move your car — you're obstructing the traffic.*

obstruction /əb'strʌkʃn/ noun a thing that stops somebody or something from going past: *The train had to stop because there was an obstruction on the line.*

obtain /əb'teɪn/ verb (**obtains**, **obtaining**, **obtained** /əb'teɪnd/) get something: *Where can I obtain a visa for Egypt?* ✪ **Get** is the word that we usually use.

obvious /'ɒbvɪəs/ adjective very clear and easy to see or understand: *It's obvious that she's not happy.*

obviously adverb it is easy to see or understand that; clearly: *He obviously trains very hard — he's so much better than the other runners.*

occasion /ə'keɪʒn/ noun **1** a time when something happens: *I've been to Kampala on three or four occasions.* **2** a special time: *A wedding is a big family occasion.*

occasional /ə'keɪʒənl/ adjective that happens sometimes, but not very often: *We get the occasional storm at this time of year.*

occasionally /ə'keɪʒənəli/ adverb sometimes, but not often: *I go to Nakuru occasionally.*

occupation /ˌɒkju'peɪʃn/ noun **1** (plural **occupations**) a job: *What is your father's occupation?* ✪ **Job** is the word that we usually use. **2** (plural **occupations**) something that you do in your free time: *Fishing is his favourite occupation.* **3** (no plural) living in a house, room, etc: *The new house is now ready for occupation.* **4** (no plural) taking and keeping a town or country in war

occupy /'ɒkjupaɪ/ verb (**occupies**, **occupying**, **occupied** /'ɒkjupaɪd/, **has occupied**) **1** live or be in a place: *That building is occupied by students.* **2** make somebody busy; take somebody's time: *The children occupy most of her free time.* **3** take and keep control of a country, town, etc in a war: *The Americans occupied Japan from 1945 to '52.*

occupied adjective **1** busy: *This work will keep me occupied all week.* **2** being used: *Excuse me — is this seat occupied?*

occur /ə'kɜː(r)/ verb (**occurs**, **occurring**, **occurred** /ə'kɜːd/) happen: *The accident occurred this morning.* **occur to**

somebody come into somebody's mind: *It occurred to me that she didn't know our new address.*

ocean /ˈəʊʃn/ *noun* a very big sea: *the Indian Ocean*

o'clock /əˈklɒk/ *adverb* a word that you use after the numbers one to twelve for saying what time it is ✪ Be careful! 'O'clock' is only used with full hours.: *I left home at four o'clock and arrived in Mombasa at half past five (NOT at half past five o'clock).* ☛ picture on page A8

October /ɒkˈtəʊbə(r)/ *noun* the tenth month of the year

octopus /ˈɒktəpəs/ *noun* (*plural* **octopuses**) a sea animal with eight arms

odd /ɒd/ *adjective* (**odder**, **oddest**) **1** strange or unusual: *It's odd that he left without telling anybody.* **2** Odd numbers cannot be divided exactly by two: *1, 3, 5 and 7 are all odd numbers.* ✪ opposite: **even**. **3** part of a pair when the other one is not there: *You're wearing odd socks! One is black and the other is green!* **the odd one out** one that is different from all the others: *'Apple', 'orange', 'cabbage' – which is the odd one out?*

oddly *adverb* strangely: *She behaved very oddly.*

odds and ends /ˌɒdz ənd ˈendz/ *noun* (plural) different small things that are not important: *Sarah went out to buy a few odds and ends that she needed.*

of /əv/, /ɒv/ *preposition* **1** a word that shows who or what has or owns something: *the back of the chair* ○ *What's the name of this mountain?* ○ *the plays of Shakespeare* **2** a word that you use after an amount, etc: *a litre of water* ○ *the fourth of July* **3** a word that shows what something is or what is in something: *a piece of wood* ○ *a cup of tea* ○ *Is this shirt made of cotton?* **4** a word that shows who: *That's very kind of you.* **5** a word that shows that somebody or something is part of a group: *One of her friends is a doctor.* **6** a word that you use with some adjectives and verbs: *I'm proud of you.* ○ *This perfume smells of roses.*

off /ɒf/ *preposition, adverb* **1** down or away from something: *He fell off the roof.* ○ *We got off the bus.* ○ *The thief ran off.* **2** away from the place where it was: *If you're hot, take your coat off.* ○ *Clean that mud off your face.* **3** not working; not being used: *All the lights are off.* **4** away: *My birthday is not far off.* **5** not at work or school: *I had the day off yesterday.* **6** joined to something: *The village is just off the highway.* **7** not fresh: *This milk is off.*

offence /əˈfens/ *noun* something you do that is against the law: *It is an offence to drive at night without lights.* **take offence** become angry or unhappy: *He took offence because I said his spelling was bad.*

offend /əˈfend/ *verb* (**offends**, **offending**, **offended**) make somebody feel angry or unhappy; hurt somebody's feelings: *She was offended when you said she was silly.*

offer /ˈɒfə(r)/ *verb* (**offers**, **offering**, **offered** /ˈɒfəd/) say or show that you will do or give something if another person wants it: *She offered me a cake.* ○ *I offered to help her.*

offer *noun: Thanks for the offer, but I don't need any help.*

office /ˈɒfɪs/ *noun* **1** a room or building with desks and telephones, where people work: *I work in an office.* **2** a room or building where you can buy something or get information: *The ticket office is at the front of the station.* ○ *the post office* **3** one part of the government: *the Foreign Office*

officer /ˈɒfɪsə(r)/ *noun* **1** a person in the army, navy or air force who gives orders to other people: *a naval officer* **2** a person who does important work, especially for the government: *a prison officer* ○ *police officers*

official¹ /əˈfɪʃl/ *adjective* of or from the government or somebody who is important: *an official report* ○ *The news is now official – they are getting married!* ✪ opposite: **unofficial**

officially *adverb: I think I've got the job, but they will tell me officially on Friday.*

official² /əˈfɪʃl/ *noun* a person who does important work, especially for the government: *government officials*

often /ˈɒfn/ *adverb* many times: *We often play football on Sundays.* ○ *I've often seen her at the market.* ○ *I don't write to him very often.* ○ *How often do you visit her?* **every so often** sometimes, but not often: *Every so often she phones me.*

oh /əʊ/ **1** a word that shows a strong feeling, like surprise or fear: *Oh no! I've lost my keys!* **2** a word that you say before other words: *'What time is it?' 'Oh, about two o'clock.'* **Oh dear** words that show that you are surprised or unhappy: *Oh dear – have you hurt yourself?* **Oh well** words that you use when you are not happy about something, but you cannot change it: *'I'm too busy to go out tonight.' 'Oh well, I'll see you tomorrow then.'*

oil /ɔɪl/ *noun* (no plural) **1** a thick liquid that comes from plants or animals and that you use in cooking: *Fry the onions in oil.* **2** a thick liquid that comes from under the ground or the sea. We burn oil or use it in machines.

oil-painting /ˈɔɪl peɪntɪŋ/ *noun* a picture that has been done with paint made from oil

oily /ˈɔɪli/ *adjective* (**oilier, oiliest**) like oil or covered with oil: *This fish is very oily.* ○ *an oily liquid*

OK, okay /ˌəʊ ˈkeɪ/ yes; all right: *'Do you want to go to a party?' 'OK.'*

OK, okay *adjective, adverb* all right; good or well enough: *Is it okay to sit here?*

okra /ˈɒkrə/ *noun* (no plural) a small, thin, green vegetable with seeds inside

old /əʊld/ *adjective* (**older, oldest**) **1** If you are old, you have lived for a long time: *My grandfather is very old.* ○ *My sister is older than me.* ○ opposite: **young.** ☞ picture on page A10. **2** made or bought a long time ago: *an old house* ○ opposite: **new.** ☞ picture on page A11. **3** You use 'old' to show the age of somebody or something: *He's nine years old.* ○ *How old are you?* ○ *a six-year-old boy* **4** that you did or had before now: *My old job was more interesting than this one.* ○ opposite: **new. 5** that you have known for a long time: *Jane is an old friend – we were at school together.*

the old *noun* (plural) old people

old age /ˌəʊld ˈeɪdʒ/ *noun* (no plural) the part of your life when you are old

old-fashioned /ˌəʊld ˈfæʃnd/ *adjective* not modern; that people do not often use or wear now: *Clothes from the 1970s look old-fashioned now.*

olive /ˈɒlɪv/ *noun* a small green or black fruit, that people eat or make into oil

omelette /ˈɒmlət/ *noun* eggs that you mix together and cook in oil

omit /əˈmɪt/ *verb* (**omits, omitting, omitted**) not include something; leave something out: *Omit question 2 and do question 3.* ✪ It is more usual to say **leave out.**

on /ɒn/ *preposition, adverb* **1** a word that shows where: *Your book is on the table.* ○ *The number is on the door.* ○ *We watched the race on television.* ○ *I've got a cut on my hand.* ☞ picture on page A1. **2** a word that shows when: *My birthday is on 6 May.* ○ *I'll see you on Monday.* ☞ Look at page A9. **3** a word that shows that somebody or something continues: *You can't stop here – drive on.* **4** about: *a book on cars* **5** working; being used: *Is the light on or off?* **6** using something: *I spoke to Shariff on the telephone.* ○ *I came here on foot* (= walking). **7** covering your body: *Put your coat on.* **8** happening: *What's on at the cinema?* **9** when something happens: *On her return from holiday she found a pile of work on her desk.* **on and on** without stopping: *He went* (= talked) *on and on about his girlfriend.*

once /wʌns/ *adverb* **1** one time: *I've only been to Kampala once.* ○ *He phones us once a week* (= once every week). **2** at some time in the past: *This house was once a school.* **at once 1** immediately; now: *Come here at once!* **2** at the same time: *I can't do two things at once!* **for once** this time only: *For once I agree with you.* **once again, once more** again, as before: *Can you explain it to me once more?* **once or twice** a few times; not often: *I've only met them once or twice.*

once *conjunction* as soon as: *Once you've finished your homework you can go out.*

one¹ /wʌn/ *noun, adjective* **1** the number 1: *One and one make two* (1 + 1 = 2). ○ *Only one person spoke.* ○ *One of my friends is an actress.* **2** a: *I saw her one day last week.* **3** only: *You are the one person I can trust.* **4** the same: *All the birds flew in one direction.* **one by one** first one, then the next, etc; one at a time: *Please come in one by one.*

one² /wʌn/ *pronoun* a word that you say instead of the name of a person or thing: *I've got some bananas. Do you want one?* ○ *'Which shirt do you prefer?' 'This one.'* ○ *Here are some books – take the ones you want.* **one another** words that show that somebody does the same thing as another person: *John and Peter looked at one another* (= John looked at Peter and Peter looked at John.)

one³ /wʌn/ *pronoun* any person; a person: *One can get to Nairobi in three hours.* ✪ It is formal to use 'one' in this way. We usually use **you**.

oneself /wʌn'self/ *pronoun* **1** a word that shows the same person as 'one' in a sentence: *One should be careful not to hurt oneself.* **2** a word that makes 'one' stronger: *One can do it oneself.* **by oneself 1** alone; without other people **2** without help

one-way /ˌwʌn 'weɪ/ *adjective* **1** A one-way street is a street where you can drive in one direction only. **2** A one-way ticket is a ticket to travel to a place, but not back again. ✪ opposite: **return**

onion /'ʌnɪən/ *noun* a round vegetable with a strong taste and smell: *Cutting onions can make you cry.*

onion

only¹ /'əʊnli/ *adjective* with no others: *She's the only girl in her class – all the other students are boys.* **an only child** a child who has no brothers or sisters

only² /'əʊnli/ *adverb* and nobody or nothing else; no more than: *She has six sons and only one daughter.* ○ *We can't have dinner now. It's only four o'clock!* ○ *We only waited five minutes.* **only just 1** a short time before: *We've only just arrived.* **2** almost not: *We only just*

had enough money to pay for the bus.

only³ /'əʊnli/ *conjunction* but: *I'd like to come with you, only I don't have time.*

onto, on to /'ɒntə/, /'ɒntu/, /'ɒntuː/ *preposition* to a place on somebody or something: *The cat jumped on to the table.* ○ *The bottle fell onto the floor.*

onwards /'ɒnwədz/, **onward** /'ɒnwəd/ *adverb* **1** and after: *I shall be at home from eight o'clock onwards.* **2** forward; further: *The soldiers marched onwards until they came to a bridge.*

open¹ /'əʊpən/ *adjective* **1** not closed, so that people or things can go in or out: *Leave the windows open.* ☞ picture on page A11. **2** not closed or covered, so that you can see inside: *The book lay open on the table.* ○ *an open box* **3** ready for people to go in: *The bank is open from 9 a.m.to 4.30 p.m.* **4** that anybody can do or visit, for example: *The competition is open to all children under the age of 14.* **5** with not many buildings, trees, etc: *open fields* **in the open air** outside: *We had our lunch in the open air.*

open² /'əʊpən/ *verb* (**opens, opening, opened** /'əʊpənd/) **1** move so that people or things can go in, out or through: *It was hot, so I opened a window.* ○ *The door opened and a man came in.* **2** move so that something is not closed or covered: *Open your eyes!* **3** fold something out or back, to show what is inside: *Open your books.* **4** be ready for people to use; start: *Banks don't open on Sundays.* **5** say that something can start or is ready: *The President opened the new hospital.* ✪ opposite: **close** or **shut**

open³ /'əʊpən/ *noun* (no plural) **in the open** outside: *I like sleeping out in the open.*

open-air /ˌəʊpən 'eə(r)/ *adjective* outside: *an open-air concert*

opener /'əʊpnə(r)/ *noun* a thing that you use for opening tins or bottles: *a bottle-opener*

opening /'əʊpnɪŋ/ *noun* **1** a hole or space in something where people or things can go in and out; a hole: *The sheep got out of the field through an opening in the fence.* **2** when something is opened: *the opening of the new theatre*

openly /ˈəʊpənli/ *adverb* not secretly; without trying to hide anything: *She told me openly that she didn't agree.*

opera /ˈɒprə/ *noun* a play where the actors sing most of the words

operate /ˈɒpəreɪt/ *verb* (**operates, operating, operated**) **1** work or make something work: *How do you operate this machine?* ○ *I don't know how this machine operates.* **2** cut a person's body to take out or mend a part inside: *The doctor will operate on her leg tomorrow.*

✪ A doctor who operates is called a **surgeon**. A surgeon's work is called **surgery**.

operation /ˌɒpəˈreɪʃn/ *noun* **1** cutting a person's body to take out or mend a part inside: *He had an operation on his eye.* **2** something that happens, that needs a lot of people or careful planning: *a military operation*

operator /ˈɒpəreɪtə(r)/ *noun* **1** a person who makes a machine work: *She's a computer operator.* **2** a person who works for a telephone company and helps people to make calls: *The operator put me through to the number I wanted.*

opinion /əˈpɪnɪən/ *noun* what you think about something: *What's your opinion of his work?* ○ *In my opinion,* (= I think that) *she's wrong.*

opponent /əˈpəʊnənt/ *noun* a person that you fight or argue with, or play a game against: *The team beat their opponents easily.*

opportunity /ˌɒpəˈtjuːnəti/ *noun* (*plural* **opportunities**) a time when you can do something that you want to do; a chance: *I've seen her many times but I've never had the opportunity to talk to her.*

oppose /əˈpəʊz/ *verb* (**opposes, opposing, opposed** /əˈpəʊzd/) try to stop or change something because you do not like it: *A lot of people opposed the new law.* **as opposed to something** words that you use to show that you are talking about one thing, not something different: *She teaches at the college, as opposed to the university.* **be opposed to something** disagree strongly with something: *I am opposed to the plan.*

opposite[1] /ˈɒpəzɪt/ *adjective, adverb, preposition* **1** across from where somebody or something is; on the other side: *The church is on the opposite side of the road from the school.* ○ *You sit here, and I'll sit opposite.* ○ *The bank is opposite the supermarket.* ☛ picture on page A1. **2** as different as possible: *North is the opposite direction to south.*

opposite[2] /ˈɒpəzɪt/ *noun* a word or thing that is as different as possible from another word or thing: *'Hot' is the opposite of 'cold'.*

opposition /ˌɒpəˈzɪʃn/ *noun* (no plural) disagreeing with something and trying to stop it: *There was a lot of opposition to the plan.*

optician /ɒpˈtɪʃn/ *noun* a person who finds out how well you can see and sells you glasses ✪ The place where an optician works is called an **optician's**.

optimism /ˈɒptɪmɪzəm/ *noun* (no plural) thinking that good things will happen ✪ opposite: **pessimism**

optimist /ˈɒptɪmɪst/ *noun* a person who always thinks that good things will happen

optimistic /ˌɒptɪˈmɪstɪk/ *adjective* If you are optimistic, you think that good things will happen: *I'm optimistic about winning.*

option /ˈɒpʃn/ *noun* a thing that you can choose: *If you're going to Kisumu, there are two options – you can go by bus or by train.*

optional /ˈɒpʃənl/ *adjective* that you can choose or not choose: *All students must learn English, but French is optional.* ✪ opposite: **compulsory**

or /ɔː(r)/ *conjunction* **1** a word that joins the words for different things that you can choose: *Is it blue or green?* ○ *Are you coming or not?* ○ *We can buy meat, chicken or fish.* **2** if not, then: *Go now, or you'll be late.*

oral /ˈɔːrəl/ *adjective* spoken, not written: *an oral test in English*

orange[1] /ˈɒrɪndʒ/ *noun* a round fruit with a colour between red and yellow, and a thick skin: *orange juice*

orange

orange[2] /ˈɒrɪndʒ/ *adjective* with a colour that is between red and yellow: *orange paint*

orange *noun*: *Orange is my favourite colour.*

orbit /ˈɔːbɪt/ *noun* the path of one thing that is moving round another thing in space

orbit *verb* (**orbits**, **orbiting**, **orbited**) move round something in space: *The spacecraft is orbiting the moon.*

orchard /ˈɔːtʃəd/ *noun* a place where a lot of fruit trees grow

orchestra /ˈɔːkɪstrə/ *noun* a big group of people who play different musical instruments together

ordeal /ɔːˈdiːl/ *noun* a very bad or painful thing that happens to somebody: *He was lost in the mountains for a week without food or water – it was a terrible ordeal.*

order[1] /ˈɔːdə(r)/ *noun* **1** (no plural) the way that you place people or things together: *The names are in alphabetical order* (= with the names that begin with A first, then B, then C, etc). **2** (no plural) when everything is in the right place or everybody is doing the right thing: *Our teacher likes order in the classroom.* **3** (plural **orders**) words that tell somebody to do something: *Soldiers must always obey orders.* **4** (plural **orders**) asking somebody to make, send or bring you something: *The waiter came and took our order* (= we told him what we wanted to eat). **in order** with everything in the right place: *Are these papers in order?* **in order to** so that you can do something: *We arrived early in order to buy our tickets.* **out of order** not working: *I couldn't ring you – the phone was out of order.*

order[2] /ˈɔːdə(r)/ *verb* (**orders**, **ordering**, **ordered** /ˈɔːdəd/) **1** tell somebody that they must do something: *The doctor ordered me to stay in bed.* **2** say that you want something to be made, sent, brought, etc: *The shop didn't have the book I wanted, so I ordered it.* ○ *When the waiter came I ordered an omelette.*

ordinary /ˈɔːdnri/ *adjective* normal; not special or unusual: *Simon was wearing a suit, but I was in my ordinary clothes.* **out of the ordinary** unusual; strange: *Did you see anything out of the ordinary?*

ore /ɔː(r)/ *noun* rock or earth from which you get metal: *iron ore*

organ /ˈɔːgən/ *noun* **1** a part of the body that has a special purpose, for example the heart or the liver **2** a big musical instrument like a piano, with pipes that air goes through to make sounds

organic /ɔːˈgænɪk/ *adjective* **1** of living things: *organic chemistry* **2** grown in a natural way, without using chemicals: *organic vegetables*

organization /ˌɔːgənaɪˈzeɪʃn/ *noun* **1** (plural **organizations**) a group of people who work together for a special purpose: *He works for an organization that helps old people.* **2** (no plural) planning or arranging something: *She's busy with the organization of her daughter's wedding.*

organize /ˈɔːgənaɪz/ *verb* (**organizes**, **organizing**, **organized** /ˈɔːgənaɪzd/) plan or arrange something: *Our teacher has organized a visit to the museum.*

oriental /ˌɔːriˈentl/ *adjective* of or from eastern countries, for example China or Japan: *oriental art*

origin /ˈɒrɪdʒɪn/ *noun* the beginning; the start of something: *Many English words have Latin origins.*

original /əˈrɪdʒənl/ *adjective* **1** first; earliest: *They say the new model of this car is better, but I prefer the original.* **2** new and different: *His poems are very original.* **3** real, not copied: *original paintings*

original *noun*: *This is a copy of the letter – the original is in the National Museum.*

originally /əˈrɪdʒənəli/ *adverb* in the beginning; at first: *This building was originally the home of a rich family, but now it's a hotel.*

ornament /ˈɔːnəmənt/ *noun* a thing that we have because it is beautiful, not because it is useful

ornamental /ˌɔːnəˈmentl/ *adjective*

orphan /ˈɔːfn/ *noun* a child whose mother and father are dead

ostrich /ˈɒstrɪtʃ/ *noun* (plural **ostriches**) a very big African bird.

Ostriches have very long legs and can run fast, but they cannot fly.

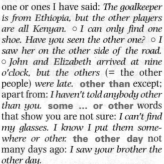

ostrich

other /ˈʌðə(r)/ *adjective, pronoun* as well as or different from the one or ones I have said: *The goalkeeper is from Ethiopia, but the other players are all Kenyan.* ○ *I can only find one shoe. Have you seen the other one?* ○ *I saw her on the other side of the road.* ○ *John and Elizabeth arrived at nine o'clock, but the others (= the other people) were late.* **other than** except; apart from: *I haven't told anybody other than you.* **some ... or other** words that show you are not sure: *I can't find my glasses. I know I put them somewhere or other.* **the other day** not many days ago: *I saw your brother the other day.*

otherwise /ˈʌðəwaɪz/ *adverb* **1** in all other ways: *The house is a bit small, but otherwise it's perfect.* **2** in a different way: *Most people agreed, but Joyce thought otherwise.*

otherwise *conjunction* if not: *Hurry up, otherwise you'll be late.*

ouch /aʊtʃ/ You say 'ouch' when you suddenly feel pain: *Ouch! That hurts!*

ought to /ˈɔːt tə/, /ˈɔːt tu/, /ˈɔːt tuː/ *modal verb* **1** words that you use to tell or ask somebody what is the right thing to do: *It's late – you ought to go home.* ○ *Ought I to ring her?* **2** words that you use to say what you think will happen or what you think is true: *Mbarouk has worked very hard, so he ought to pass the exam.* ○ *These shoes ought to be good, because they were very expensive.* ☛ Look at the note on page 195 to find out more about **modal verbs.**

ounce /aʊns/ *noun* a measure of weight (= 28·35 grams). There are 16 ounces in a **pound**: *four ounces of flour* ☉ The short way of writing 'ounce' is **oz**: *6 oz butter* ☛ Note at **pound**

our /ɑː(r)/, /ˈaʊə(r)/ *adjective* of us: *This is our house.*

ours /ɑːz/, /ˈaʊəz/ *pronoun* something that belongs to us: *Your house is bigger than ours.*

ourselves /ɑːˈselvz/, /aʊəˈselvz/ *pronoun* (plural) **1** a word that shows the same people that you have just talked about: *We made ourselves some coffee.* **2** a word that makes 'we' stronger: *We built the house ourselves.* **by ourselves 1** alone; without other people: *We sat by ourselves while everyone else was dancing.* **2** without help

out /aʊt/ *adjective, adverb* **1** away from a place; from inside: *When you go out, please close the door.* ○ *She opened the box and took out a gun.* **2** not at home or not in the place where you work: *I phoned Wilson but he was out.* ○ *I can't go out tonight because I have to study.* **3** not burning or shining: *The fire went out.* **4** not hidden; that you can see: *Look! The sun is out!* ○ *All the flowers are out (= open).* **5** in a loud voice: *She cried out in pain.*

outbreak /ˈaʊtbreɪk/ *noun* the sudden start of something: *There have been outbreaks of fighting in the city.*

outdoor /ˈaʊtdɔː(r)/ *adjective* done or used outside a building: *Football and cricket are outdoor games.* ☉ opposite: **indoor**

outdoors /ˌaʊtˈdɔːz/ *adverb* outside a building: *In summer we sometimes eat outdoors.* ☉ opposite: **indoors**

outer /ˈaʊtə(r)/ *adjective* on the outside; far from the centre: *My outer clothes were wet but my underwear was dry.* ☉ opposite: **inner**

outfit /ˈaʊtfɪt/ *noun* a set of clothes that you wear together: *I like your outfit.*

outing /ˈaʊtɪŋ/ *noun* a short journey to enjoy yourself or to learn about a place: *We went on a school outing to a factory last week.*

outline /ˈaʊtlaɪn/ *noun* a line that shows the shape or edge of something: *It was dark, but we could see the outline of the trees on the hill.*

outlook /ˈaʊtlʊk/ *noun* what will probably happen: *With all these talented young runners, the outlook is good for Kenyan athletics.*

out of /ˈaʊt əv/ *preposition* **1** words that show where from: *She took a key* out of his pocket. ○ She got out of bed. ☛ picture on page A2. **2** not in: *Fish can't live out of water.* **3** by using something; from: *He made a table out of some old pieces of wood.* **4** from that number: *Nine out of ten people are scared of snakes.* **5** because of: *Ann helped us out of kindness.* **6** without: *She's been out of work for six months.*

output /ˈaʊtpʊt/ *noun* (no plural) the amount of things that somebody or something has made or done: *What was the factory's output last year?*

outside[1] /ˌaʊtˈsaɪd/ *noun* the part of something that is away from the middle: *The outside of a coconut is brown and the inside is white.*

outside[2] /ˌaʊtˈsaɪd/ *adjective* away from the middle of something: *the outside walls of the house were painted white.*

outside[3] /ˌaʊtˈsaɪd/ *preposition, adverb* not in; in or to a place that is not inside a building: *I left my bicycle outside the shop.* ○ *Come outside and see our animals!*

outskirts /ˈaʊtskɜːts/ *noun* (plural) the parts of a town or city that are far from the centre: *The airport is on the outskirts of the city.*

outstanding /ˌaʊtˈstændɪŋ/ *adjective* very good; much better than others: *Her work is outstanding.*

outward /ˈaʊtwəd/, **outwards** /ˈaʊt-wədz/ *adverb* towards the outside: *The windows open outwards.* ✪ opposite: **inward** or **inwards**

oval /ˈəʊvl/ *noun* a shape like an egg ☛ picture on page A5

oval *adjective* with a shape like an egg: *an oval mirror*

oven /ˈʌvn/ *noun* the part of a cooker that has a door. You put food inside an oven to cook it.

over[1] /ˈəʊvə(r)/ *adverb, preposition* **1** above something; higher than something: *A plane flew over our heads.* ○ *There is a sign over the door.* **2** on somebody or something so that it covers them: *She put a blanket over the sleeping child.* **3** down: *I fell over in the street.* **4** across; to the other side of something: *The dog jumped over the*

wall. ○ *a bridge over a river* ☛ picture on page A2. **5** so that the other side is on top: *Turn the cassette over.* **6** more than a number, price, etc: *She lived in Egypt for over 20 years.* ○ *This game is for children of ten and over.* **7** not used: *After shopping at the market, I still had a few shillings left over.* **8** from one place to another: *Come over and see us on Saturday.* **9** a word that shows that you repeat something: *He said the same thing over and over again* (= many times). ○ *The audience liked the song so much that she sang it all over again* (= again, from the beginning). **10** finished: *My exams are over.* **all over** in every part: *She travels all over the world.* **over here** here: *Come over here!* **over there** there: *Go over there and see if you can help.*

over-[2] /ˈəʊvə(r)/ *prefix*
You can add **over-** to the beginning of a lot of words to give them the meaning 'too much', for example:
overeat = eat too much
oversleep = sleep too long

overall[1] /ˌəʊvərˈɔːl/ *adjective* of everything; total: *The overall cost of the repairs will be about 5 000 shillings.*

overall *adverb*: *How much will it cost overall?*

overall[2] /ˈəʊvərɔːl/ *noun* a kind of coat that you wear over your clothes to keep them clean when you are working

overalls /ˈəʊvərɔːlz/ *noun* (plural) a piece of clothing that covers your legs, body and arms. You wear it over your other clothes to keep them clean when you are working.

overboard /ˈəʊvəbɔːd/ *adverb* over the side of a boat and into the water: *She fell overboard.*

overcome /ˌəʊvəˈkʌm/ *verb* (**overcomes**, **overcoming**, **overcame** /ˌəʊvəˈkeɪm/, **has overcome**) find an answer to a difficult thing in your life; control something: *He overcame his fear of water.*

overcrowded /ˌəʊvəˈkraʊdɪd/ *adjective* too full of people: *The buses are overcrowded at this time of day.*

overdue /ˌəʊvəˈdjuː/ *adjective* late: *Our landlady is angry because the rent is overdue.*

overflow /ˌəʊvəˈfləʊ/ *verb* (**overflows**, **overflowing**, **overflowed** /ˌəʊvəˈfləʊd/) come over the edge of something because there is too much in it: *After the rain, the river overflowed its banks.*

overgrown /ˌəʊvəˈɡrəʊn/ *adjective* covered with plants that have grown too big: *The house was empty and the garden was overgrown.*

overhead /ˈəʊvəhed/ *adjective* above your head: *an overhead light*
overhead /ˌəʊvəˈhed/ *adverb*: *A plane flew overhead.*

overhear /ˌəʊvəˈhɪə(r)/ *verb* (**overhears**, **overhearing**, **overheard** /ˌəʊvəˈhɜːd/, **has overheard**) hear what somebody is saying when they are speaking to another person, not to you: *I overheard Winnie saying that she was unhappy.*

overlap /ˌəʊvəˈlæp/ *verb* (**overlaps**, **overlapping**, **overlapped** /ˌəʊvəˈlæpt/) When two things overlap, part of one thing covers part of the other thing: *The tiles on the roof overlap.*

overlook /ˌəʊvəˈlʊk/ *verb* (**overlooks**, **overlooking**, **overlooked** /ˌəʊvəˈlʊkt/) **1** look down on something from above: *My room overlooks the river.* **2** not see or notice something: *He overlooked a spelling mistake.*

overnight /ˌəʊvəˈnaɪt/ *adjective, adverb* for or during the night: *They stayed at our house overnight.* ○ *an overnight journey*

oversleep /ˌəʊvəˈsliːp/ *verb* (**oversleeps**, **oversleeping**, **overslept** /ˌəʊvəˈslept/, **has overslept**) sleep too long and not wake up at the right time: *I overslept and was late for work.*

overtake /ˌəʊvəˈteɪk/ *verb* (**overtakes**, **overtaking**, **overtook** /ˌəʊvəˈtʊk/, **has overtaken** /ˌəʊvəˈteɪkən/) go past somebody or something that is going more slowly: *The car overtook a bus.*

overtime /ˈəʊvətaɪm/ *noun* (no plural) extra time that you spend at work: *I have done a lot of overtime this week.*

overweight /ˌəʊvəˈweɪt/ *adjective* too heavy or fat: *The doctor said I was overweight and that I should eat less.*

overwhelming /ˌəʊvəˈwelmɪŋ/ *adjective* very great or strong: *an overwhelming feeling of loneliness*

ow /aʊ/ You say 'ow' when you suddenly feel pain: *Ow! You're standing on my foot.*

owe /əʊ/ *verb* (**owes**, **owing**, **owed** /əʊd/) **1** have to pay money to somebody because they have given you something: *I lent you 50 shillings last week and 50 shillings the week before, so you owe me 100 shillings.* **2** feel that you have something because of what another person has done: *She owes her life to the man who pulled her out of the river.*

owing to /ˈəʊɪŋ tu/ *preposition* because of: *The train was late owing to an accident earlier in the day.*

owl /aʊl/ *noun* a bird that flies at night and eats small animals

owl

own[1] /əʊn/ *adjective, pronoun* You use 'own' to say that something belongs to a person or thing: *Is that your own camera or did you borrow it?* ○ *I would like to have my own room* (= for me and nobody else). ✪ Be careful! You cannot use 'own' after 'a' or 'the'. You cannot say: *I would like an own room.* You say: *I would like my own room.* (or: *I would like a room of my own.*) **get your own back on somebody** do something bad to somebody who has done something bad to you: *He said he would get his own back on me for breaking his watch.* **of your own** that belongs to you and not to anybody else: *I want a home of my own.* **on your own 1** alone: *She lives on her own.* **2** without help: *I can't move this box on my own – can you help me?*

own[2] /əʊn/ *verb* (**owns**, **owning**, **owned** /əʊnd/) have something that is yours: *We don't own our flat – we rent it.* **own up** say that you have done something wrong: *Nobody owned up to breaking the window.*

owner /ˈəʊnə(r)/ *noun* a person who has something: *Who is the owner of this pen?*

ox /ɒks/ *noun* (*plural* **oxen** /ˈɒksn/) a male cow. Oxen are sometimes used to pull or carry heavy things on farms.

oxygen /ˈɒksɪdʒən/ *noun* (no plural) a gas in the air. Plants and animals need oxygen to live.

oz *short way of writing* **ounce**

ozone /ˈəʊzəʊn/ *noun* (no plural) a gas in the air

Pp

p *short way of writing* **page** 1

pace /peɪs/ *noun* **1** a step: *Take two paces forward!* **2** how fast you do something or how fast something happens: *The race began at a fast pace.* **keep pace with somebody** or **something** go as fast as somebody or something: *She couldn't keep pace with the other runners.*

pack¹ /pæk/ *noun* **1** a group of things that you buy together: *I bought a pack of five exercise books.* **2** a group of animals that hunt together: *a pack of hyenas*

pack of cards /ˌpæk əv ˈkɑːdz/ *noun* a set of 52 playing-cards ☛ Look at **card**.

pack² /pæk/ *verb* (**packs**, **packing**, **packed** /pækt/) **1** put things into a bag or suitcase before you go somewhere: *Have you packed your suitcase?* ○ *Don't forget to pack your toothbrush.* **2** put things into a box, bag, etc: *Pack all these books into boxes.* ✪ opposite: **unpack**. **pack up 1** stop doing something: *At two o'clock we packed up and went home.* **2** If a machine packs up, it stops working.

package /ˈpækɪdʒ/ *noun* something that is wrapped in paper; a small parcel

packaging /ˈpækɪdʒɪŋ/ *noun* (no plural) material like paper, cardboard or plastic that is used to wrap things that you buy or that you send

packed /pækt/ *adjective* full: *The train was packed.*

packet /ˈpækɪt/ *noun* a small box or bag that you buy things in: *a packet of*

cigarettes ○ *an empty cigarette packet* ○ *a packet of biscuits* ☛ picture at **container**

pact /pækt/ *noun* an important agreement to do something: *The two countries signed a peace pact.*

pad /pæd/ *noun* **1** some pieces of paper that are joined together at one end: *a writing pad* **2** a thick flat piece of soft material: *Footballers wear pads on their legs to protect them.* ○ *I used a pad of cotton wool to clean the cut.*

paddle¹ /ˈpædl/ *noun* a piece of wood with a flat end, that you use for moving a small boat through water

paddle *verb* (**paddles**, **paddling**, **paddled** /ˈpædld/) move a small boat through water with a paddle: *We paddled up the river.*

paddle² /ˈpædl/ *verb* (**paddles**, **paddling**, **paddled** /ˈpædld/) walk in water that is not deep, with no shoes on your feet: *The children were paddling in the sea.*

padlock /ˈpædlɒk/ *noun* a lock that you use on things like gates and bicycles

page /peɪdʒ/ *noun* **1** one side of a piece of paper in a book, magazine or newspaper: *Please turn to page 120.* ○ *What page is the story on?* ✪ The short way of writing 'page' is **p**. **2** one piece of paper in a book, magazine or newspaper

paid *form of* **pay¹**

pain /peɪn/ *noun* **1** (*plural* **pains**) the feeling that you have in your body when you are hurt or ill: *I've got a pain in my leg.* ○ *He's in pain.* **2** (no plural) unhappiness

painful /'peɪnfl/ *adjective* Something that is painful gives pain: *I've cut my leg – it's very painful.*

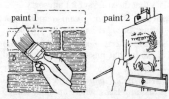

paint 1   paint 2

paint /peɪnt/ *noun* a coloured liquid that you put on things with a brush, to change the colour or to make a picture: *red paint ○ Is the paint dry yet?*

paint *verb* (**paints**, **painting**, **painted**) **1** put paint on something to change the colour: *We painted the walls grey.* **2** make a picture of somebody or something with paints: *I'm painting some flowers. ○ My sister paints very well.*

paintbrush /'peɪntbrʌʃ/ *noun* (*plural* **paintbrushes**) a brush that you use for painting

painter /'peɪntə(r)/ *noun* **1** a person whose job is to paint things like walls or houses **2** a person who paints pictures: *Edith is a talented painter.*

painting /'peɪntɪŋ/ *noun* a picture that somebody makes with paint: *The teacher put the children's paintings up on the wall.*

pair /peə(r)/ *noun* **1** two things of the same kind that you use together: *a pair of shoes ○ a pair of earrings* ☛ picture on page A15. **2** a thing with two parts that are joined together: *a pair of glasses ○ a pair of scissors ○ I bought two pairs of trousers.* **3** two people or animals together: *a pair of ducks* **in pairs** with two things or people together: *Shoes are only sold in pairs.*

palace /'pæləs/ *noun* a very large house where a king, queen or another important person lives: *The Queen lives at Buckingham Palace.*

pale /peɪl/ *adjective* (**paler**, **palest**) with a light colour; not strong or dark: *a pale-blue dress* ✿ *opposite* **dark** or **deep**

palm /pɑːm/ *noun* **1** the flat part of the front of your hand ☛ picture on page A4. **2** (*also* **palm-tree**) a tree that has no branches and a lot of big leaves at the top: *a coconut palm*

pan /pæn/ *noun* a metal pot that you use for cooking: *a frying-pan ○ a saucepan*

pancake /'pænkeɪk/ *noun* a very thin round thing that you eat. You make pancakes with flour, eggs and milk and cook them in a frying-pan.

panda /'pændə/ *noun* a large black and white bear, that lives in China

pane /peɪn/ *noun* a piece of glass in a window

panel /'pænl/ *noun* **1** a flat piece of wood, metal or glass that is part of a door, wall or ceiling **2** a flat part on a machine, where there are things to help you control it: *the control panel of an aircraft*

panga /'pæŋgæ/ *noun* (an East African word) a large, heavy knife

panic /'pænɪk/ *noun* a sudden feeling of fear that you cannot control and that makes you do things without thinking carefully: *There was panic in the shop when the fire started.*

panic *verb* (**panics**, **panicking**, **panicked** /'pænɪkt/) *Don't panic!*

pant /pænt/ *verb* (**pants**, **panting**, **panted**) take in and let out air quickly through your mouth, for example after running or because you are very hot: *The dog was panting.*

panther /'pænθə(r)/ *noun* a wild animal like a big cat. Panthers are usually black.

pants /pænts/ *noun* (plural) a small piece of clothing that you wear under your other clothes, between the middle of your body and the top of your legs: *a pair of pants*

papaya /pə'paɪæ/, **pawpaw** /'pɔːpɔː/ *noun* a large fruit that has a green skin and is orange on the inside with small black seeds

paper /'peɪpə(r)/ *noun* **1** (no plural) thin material for writing or drawing on or for wrapping things in: *The pages of this book are made of paper. ○ a sheet of paper ○ a paper bag* **2** (*plural* **papers**) a newspaper: *Have you seen today's* *paper?* **3 papers** (plural) important pieces of paper with writing on them: *The police officer asked to see my papers* (= for example, a passport or an identity card). **4** (*plural* **papers**) a group of questions in an examination: *The English paper was easy.*

paperback /ˈpeɪpəbæk/ *noun* a book with a paper cover ☞ Look at **hardback**.

paper-clip /ˈpeɪpə klɪp/ *noun* a small metal thing that you

paper-clip

use for holding pieces of paper together

parachute /ˈpærəʃuːt/ *noun* a thing like a big umbrella that you have on your back when you jump out of an aeroplane and that opens, so that you will fall to the ground slowly

parachute

parade /pəˈreɪd/ *noun* a line of people who are walking together for a special reason, while other people watch them: *a military parade*

paradise /ˈpærədaɪs/ *noun* (no plural) the place where some people think good people go after they die; heaven

paragraph /ˈpærəɡrɑːf/ *noun* a group of lines of writing. A paragraph always begins on a new line.

parallel /ˈpærəlel/ *adjective* Parallel lines are straight lines that are always the same distance from each other. ☞ picture on page A5

paralysed /ˈpærəlaɪzd/ *adjective* If you are paralysed, you cannot move your body or a part of it: *After the accident she was paralysed in both legs.*

parcel /ˈpɑːsl/ *noun* something with paper around it, that you send or carry: *She sent a parcel of books to her aunt.*

parcel

pardon /ˈpɑːdn/ *verb* (**pardons**, **pardoning**, **pardoned** /ˈpɑːdnd/) forgive somebody for something bad that

they have done ✪ **Forgive** is the word that we usually use. **pardon?** What did you say? **pardon me 1** What did you say? **2** I am sorry.

parent /ˈpeərənt/ *noun* a mother or father: *Both her parents are very nice.*

parish /ˈpærɪʃ/ *noun* (*plural* **parishes**) an area that has its own church and priest

park¹ /pɑːk/ *noun* a large place with grass and trees, where anybody can go to walk, play games, etc: *We went for a walk in Uhuru Park.*

park² /pɑːk/ *verb* (**parks, parking, parked** /pɑːkt/) stop and leave a car, lorry, etc somewhere for a time: *You can't park in this street.* ○ *My car is parked opposite the bank.*

parking *noun* (no plural) *The sign says 'No Parking'.* ○ *I can't find a parking space.*

parking-meter /ˈpɑːkɪŋ miːtə(r)/ *noun* a machine that you put money into to pay for parking a car next to it

parliament /ˈpɑːləmənt/ *noun* the people who make the laws in a country: *the Kenyan parliament*

parrot /ˈpærət/ *noun* a bird with very bright feathers that can copy what people say

parrot

parsley /ˈpɑːsli/ *noun* (no plural) a small plant that you use in cooking

part¹ /pɑːt/ *noun* **1** some, but not all of something; one of the pieces of something: *We spent part of the day on the beach.* ○ *Which part of Tanzania do you come from?* **2** a piece of a machine: *Is there a shop near here that sells bicycle parts?* **3** the person you are in a play or film: *She played the part of the old woman.* **take part in something** do something together with other people: *All the students took part in the concert.*

part² /pɑːt/ *verb* (**parts, parting, parted**) go away from each other: *We parted at the station. John got on the train and I went home.*

participate /pɑːˈtɪsɪpeɪt/ *verb* (**participates, participating, participated**) do something together with other people: *Ten countries participated in the discussions.*

participant /pɑːˈtɪsɪpənt/ *noun* a person who does something together with other people

participation /pɑːˌtɪsɪˈpeɪʃn/ *noun* (no plural) doing something together with other people

participle /ˈpɑːtɪsɪpl/ *noun* a form of a verb: *The present participle of 'eat' is 'eating' and the past participle is 'eaten'.*

particular /pəˈtɪkjələ(r)/ *adjective* **1** one only, and not any other: *You need a particular kind of flour to make bread.* **2** special or more than usual: *The road is very muddy, so take particular care when you are driving.* **3** If you are particular, you want something to be exactly right: *He's very particular about the food he eats.* **in particular** more than others: *Is there anything in particular you want to do this weekend?*

particularly /pəˈtɪkjələli/ *adverb* more than others; especially: *I'm particularly tired today.* ○ *I don't particularly like fish.*

parties plural of **party**

parting /ˈpɑːtɪŋ/ *noun* **1** a line that you make on your head by combing your hair in different directions **2** when people leave each other: *It was a sad parting for Sarah and Tom.*

partly /ˈpɑːtli/ *adverb* not completely but in some way: *The window was partly open.* ○ *The accident was partly my fault and partly the other driver's.*

partner /ˈpɑːtnə(r)/ *noun* **1** your husband, wife, boyfriend or girlfriend **2** a person you are dancing with, or playing a game with **3** one of the people who owns a business

partnership /ˈpɑːtnəʃɪp/ *noun* being partners: *The two sisters went into partnership and opened a shop.*

part of speech /ˌpɑːt əv ˈspiːtʃ/ *noun* 'Noun', 'verb', 'adjective' and 'adverb' are parts of speech.

part-time /ˌpɑːt ˈtaɪm/ *adjective, adverb* for only a part of the day or week: *I've got a part-time job as a secretary.*

○ *Jane works part-time.* ☞ Look at **full-time**.

party /ˈpɑːti/ *noun* (*plural* **parties**) **1** a meeting of friends, often in somebody's house, to eat, drink and perhaps dance: *We're having a party this Saturday. Can you come?* ○ *a birthday party* **2** a group of people who have the same ideas about politics **3** a group of people who are travelling or working together: *a party of tourists*

pass[1] /pɑːs/ *noun* (*plural* **passes**) **1** a special piece of paper or card that says you can go somewhere or do something: *You need a pass to get into the factory.* **2** doing well enough in an examination: *How many passes did you get in your exams?* **3** a road or way through mountains **4** kicking, throwing or hitting a ball to somebody in a game

pass[2] /pɑːs/ *verb* (**passes, passing, passed** /pɑːst/) **1** go by somebody or something: *She passed me in the street.* ○ *Do you pass any shops on your way to the station?* **2** give something to somebody: *Could you pass me the salt, please?* **3** go by: *A week passed before his letter arrived.* **4** do well enough in an examination or test: *Did you pass your driving test?* ♦ opposite: **fail. 5** spend time: *How did you pass the time in hospital?* **pass on** give or tell something to another person: *Will you pass on a message to Mike for me?* **pass through** go through a place: *The train passes through Nakuru on its way to Nairobi.*

passage /ˈpæsɪdʒ/ *noun* **1** a short part of a book or speech: *We studied a passage from the story for homework.* **2** a narrow way, for example between two buildings

passenger /ˈpæsɪndʒə(r)/ *noun* a person who is travelling in a car, bus, train, plane, etc, but not the person who is driving it: *The plane was carrying 200 passengers.*

passer-by /ˈpɑːsə baɪ/ *noun* (*plural* **passers-by**) a person who is walking past you in the street: *I asked a passer-by where the museum was.*

passion /ˈpæʃn/ *noun* a very strong

feeling, usually of love, but sometimes of anger or hate

passionate /'pæʃənət/ *adjective* with very strong feelings: *He's passionate about athletics.*

passion fruit /'pæʃn fruːt/ *noun* a sweet, round fruit that has a purple skin and is green on the inside

passive /'pæsɪv/ *noun* (no plural) the form of a verb that shows that the action is done by a person or thing to another person or thing: *In the sentence 'The car was stolen', the verb is in the passive.* ✪ opposite: **active**

passport /'pɑːspɔːt/ *noun* a small book with your name and photograph in it. You must take it with you when you travel to other countries.

password /'pɑːswɜːd/ *noun* a secret word that you must say to enter a place

past[1] /pɑːst/ *noun* (no plural) **1** the time before now, and the things that happened then: *We learn about the past in history lessons.* ○ *In the past, smoke signals were used as a form of communication.* **2** (*also* **past tense**) the form of a verb that you use to talk about the time before now: *The past tense of the verb 'go' is 'went'.* ☞ Look at **present** and **future**.

past *adjective* **1** of the time that has gone: *We will forget your past mistakes.* **2** last; just before now: *He has been ill for the past week.*

past[2] /pɑːst/ *preposition, adverb* **1** a word that shows how many minutes after the hour: *It's two minutes past four.* ○ *It's half past seven.* ☞ Look at page A8. **2** from one side of somebody or something to the other; by; on the other side of somebody or something: *Go past the park, then turn left.* ○ *The bus went past without stopping.*

paste /peɪst/ *noun* soft wet stuff, sometimes used for sticking paper to things: *Mix the powder with water to make a paste.*

pastime /'pɑːstaɪm/ *noun* something that you like doing when you are not working: *Painting is her favourite pastime.*

pastoral /'pɑːstərəl/ *adjective* of or about farming or keeping animals: *pas-*

-toral regions ○ *pastoral communities*

pastoralism /'pɑːstərəlɪzm/ *noun* (no plural) moving animals from place to place to find water and grass

pastoralist /'pɑːstərəlɪst/ *noun* a member of a group of people who move with their animals to find water and grass

pastry /'peɪstri/ *noun* (no plural) a mixture of flour, fat and water that is used for making pies

pasture /'pɑːstʃə(r)/ *noun* land that is covered with grass that cattle can eat: *During the hot dry season these nomads move their cattle to better pastures.*

pat /pæt/ *verb* (**pats**, **patting**, **patted**) touch somebody or something lightly with your hand flat: *She patted the dog on the head.*

pat *noun*: *He gave me a pat on the shoulder.*

patch /pætʃ/ *noun* (*plural* **patches**) **1** a piece of cloth that you use to cover a hole in things like clothes: *I sewed a patch on my jeans.* **2** a small piece of something that is not the same as the other parts: *a black cat with a white patch on its back*

path /pɑːθ/ *noun* (*plural* **paths** /pɑːðz/) a way across a piece of land, where people can walk: *a path through the woods*

patience /'peɪʃns/ *noun* (no plural) staying calm and not getting angry when you are waiting for something, or when you have problems: *Growing tea takes hard work and patience.* ✪ opposite: **impatience**. **lose patience with somebody** become angry with somebody: *She was walking so slowly that her sister finally lost patience with her.*

patient[1] /'peɪʃnt/ *adjective* able to stay calm and not get angry when you are waiting for something or when you have problems: *Just sit there and be patient. Your mum will be here soon.* ✪ opposite: **impatient**

patiently *adverb*: *She waited patiently for the bus.*

patient[2] /'peɪʃnt/ *noun* a sick person that a doctor is looking after

patrol /pəˈtrəʊl/ *noun* a group of people, ships, aircraft, etc that go round a place to see that everything is all right: *an army patrol* **on patrol** going round a place to see that everything is all right: *There are usually police on patrol in the park at night.*

patrol *verb* (**patrols**, **patrolling**, **patrolled** /pəˈtrəʊld/) *A guard patrols the gate at night.*

patter /ˈpætə(r)/ (**patters**, **pattering**, **pattered** /ˈpætəd/) make quick light sounds: *Rain pattered against the window.*

patter *noun*: *the patter of children's feet on the stairs*

pattern /ˈpætn/ *noun* **1** shapes and colours on something: *My favourite dress has a yellow flower pattern on a blue background.* **2** a thing that you copy when you make something: *I bought some material and a pattern to make a new skirt.*

patterned /ˈpætnd/ *adjective* with shapes and colours on it: *a patterned shirt*

pause /pɔːz/ *noun* a short stop: *She played for 30 minutes without a pause.*

pause *verb* (**pauses**, **pausing**, **paused** /pɔːzd/) stop for a short time: *He paused before answering my question.*

pavement /ˈpeɪvmənt/ *noun* the part at the side of a road where people can walk

paw /pɔː/ *noun* the foot of an animal, for example a dog, cat or lion ☞ *picture at* **cat**

pay¹ /peɪ/ *verb* (**pays**, **paying**, **paid** /peɪd/, **has paid**) **1** give money to get something: *She paid 1 000 shillings for the dress.* ○ *Are you paying in cash or by cheque?* **2** give money for work that somebody does: *I paid the builder for mending the roof.* **pay back** give back the money that somebody has lent to you: *Can you lend me 500 shillings? I'll pay you back* (= pay it back to you) *next week.* **pay somebody back** hurt somebody who has hurt you: *One day I'll pay her back for lying to me!* **pay for something** give money for what you buy: *He paid for the car in cash.*

pay² /peɪ/ *noun* (no plural) the money that you get for work

payment /ˈpeɪmənt/ *noun* **1** (no plural) paying or being paid: *This cheque is in payment for the work you have done.* **2** (*plural* **payments**) an amount of money that you pay: *I make monthly payments of 1 000 shillings.*

pay phone /ˈpeɪ fəʊn/ *noun* a telephone that you put money in to make a call

PC /ˌpiː ˈsiː/ *noun* a small computer. 'PC' is short for **personal computer**.

PE /ˌpiː ˈiː/ *short for* **physical education**

pea /piː/ *noun* a very small round green vegetable. Peas grow in **pods**.

peace /piːs/ *noun* (no plural) **1** a time when there is no war, fighting or trouble between people or countries **2** being quiet and calm: *the peace of the countryside at night* ○ *Go away and leave me in peace!* **make peace** agree to end a war or fight: *The two countries made peace.*

peaceful /ˈpiːsfl/ *adjective* **1** with no fighting: *a peaceful demonstration* **2** quiet and calm: *a peaceful evening*

peacefully /ˈpiːsfəli/ *adverb*: *She's sleeping peacefully.*

peach /piːtʃ/ *noun* (*plural* **peaches**) a soft round fruit with a yellow and red skin and a large seed in the centre

peach

peacock /ˈpiːkɒk/ *noun* a large bird with beautiful long blue and green feathers in its tail

peak /piːk/ *noun* **1** the pointed top of a mountain **2** the time when something is highest, biggest, etc: *The traffic is at its peak between five and six in the evening.* **3** the pointed front part of a hat that is above your eyes

peanut /ˈpiːnʌt/ *noun* a nut that you can eat

pear /peə(r)/ *noun* a fruit that is green or yellow on the outside and white on the inside

pear

pearl /pɜːl/ *noun* a small round white thing that comes from an **oyster** (a kind of shellfish). Pearls are used to make things like necklaces and earrings: *a pearl necklace*

pebble /ˈpebl/ *noun* a small round stone

peck /pek/ *verb* (**pecks**, **pecking**, **pecked** /pekt/) When a bird pecks something, it eats or bites it with its beak: *The hens were pecking at the corn.*

peculiar /prˈkjuːliə(r)/ *adjective* strange; not usual: *What's that peculiar smell?*

pedal /ˈpedl/ *noun* a part of a bicycle or other machine that you move with your feet ☞ picture at **bicycle**

pedestrian /pəˈdestriən/ *noun* a person who is walking in the street

pedestrian crossing /pəˌdestriən ˈkrɒsɪŋ/ *noun* a place where cars must stop so that people can cross the road

peel /piːl/ *noun* (no plural) the outside part of some fruit and vegetables: *orange peel*

peel *verb* (**peels**, **peeling**, **peeled** /piːld/) **1** take the outside part off a fruit or vegetable: *Can you peel the potatoes?* **2** come off in thin pieces: *The paint is peeling off the walls.*

peep /piːp/ *verb* (**peeps**, **peeping**, **peeped** /piːpt/) **1** look at something quickly or secretly: *I peeped through the window and saw her.* **2** come out for a short time: *The moon peeped out from behind the clouds.*

peer /pɪə(r)/ *verb* (**peers**, **peering**, **peered** /pɪəd/) look closely at something because you cannot see well: *I peered outside but I couldn't see anything because it was dark.*

peg /peg/ *noun* **1** a small thing on a wall or door where you can hang clothes: *Your coat is on the peg.* **2** a small wooden or plastic thing that holds wet clothes on a line when they are drying: *a clothes-peg*

pen¹ /pen/ *noun* a thing that you use for writing with a coloured liquid (called **ink**)

pen² /pen/ *noun* a small place with a fence around it for keeping animals in

penalty /ˈpenlti/ *noun* (*plural* **penalties**) a punishment: *The penalty for travelling without a ticket is 50*

shillings. (= you must pay 50 shillings).

pencil /ˈpensl/ *noun* a thin piece of wood with grey or coloured stuff inside it. Pencils are used for writing or drawing.

pen-friend /ˈpen frend/, **pen-pal** /ˈpen pæl/ *noun* a person that you write to but have probably never met

penguin

/ˈpeŋgwɪn/ *noun* a black and white bird that lives in very cold places. Penguins can swim but they cannot fly.

penguin

penknife

/ˈpennaɪf/ *noun* (*plural* **penknives** /ˈpennaɪvz/) a small knife that you can carry in your pocket

penknife

pension /ˈpenʃn/ *noun* money that you get from a government or a company when you are old and do not work any more (when you are **retired**)

pensioner /ˈpenʃənə(r)/ *noun* a person who has a pension

people /ˈpiːpl/ *noun* (plural) more than one person: *How many people came to the meeting?* ○ *People in this region are famous for being friendly.*

pepper /ˈpepə(r)/ *noun* **1** (no plural) powder with a hot taste that you put on food: *salt and pepper* **2** (*plural* **peppers**) a red, green or yellow vegetable with a lot of white seeds inside

peppermint /ˈpepəmɪnt/ *noun* **1** (no plural) a plant with a strong fresh taste and smell. It is used to make things like sweets and medicines. **2** (*plural* **peppermints**) a sweet made from this

per /pə(r)/ *preposition* for each; in each: *They pay me 500 shillings per day.* ○ *I was driving at 60 kilometres per hour.*

per cent /pə ˈsent/ *noun* (no plural) %; in each hundred: *90 per cent of the people who work here are men* (= in 100 people there are 90 men).

percentage /pəˈsentɪdʒ/ *noun*: '*What percentage of students passed the exam?' 'Oh, about eighty per cent.'*

perch /pɜːtʃ/ *noun* (*plural* **perches**) a place where a bird sits

perch *verb* (**perches**, **perching**, **perched** /pɜːtʃt/) sit on something narrow: *The bird perched on a branch.*

perfect /ˈpɜːfɪkt/ *adjective* **1** so good that it cannot be better; with nothing wrong: *Her English is perfect.* ○ *This soil is perfect for growing corn.* **2** made from 'has', 'have' or 'had' and the **past participle** of a verb: *perfect tenses*

perfectly /ˈpɜːfɪktli/ *adverb* **1** completely; very: *I'm perfectly all right.* **2** in a perfect way: *She played the piece of music perfectly.*

perform /pəˈfɔːm/ *verb* (**performs**, **performing**, **performed** /pəˈfɔːmd/) **1** do a piece of work: *The doctor performed an operation to save her life.* **2** be in a play, concert, etc: *The band is performing in the park tonight.*

performer *noun* a person who is in a play, concert, etc

performance /pəˈfɔːməns/ *noun* **1** (*plural* **performances**) a time when a play, etc. is shown, or music is played in front of a lot of people: *We went to the evening performance of the play.* **2** (no plural) how well you do something: *My parents were pleased with my performance in the exam.*

perfume /ˈpɜːfjuːm/ *noun* **1** a nice smell **2** a liquid with a nice smell that you put on your body: *a bottle of perfume*

perhaps /pəˈhæps/ *adverb* a word that you use when you are not sure about something: *I don't know where she is — perhaps she's still at work.* ○ *There were three men, or perhaps four.*

period /ˈpɪəriəd/ *noun* **1** an amount of time: *He was ill four times in a period of six months.* **2** a certain time in the life of a person or the history of a country: *What period of history are you studying?* **3** a lesson: *We have five periods of English a week.* **4** the time when a woman loses blood from her body each month:

permanent /ˈpɜːmənənt/ *adjective* Something that is permanent continues for ever or for a very long time and does not change: *I'm looking for a permanent job.* ☛ Look at **temporary**.

permanently *adverb*: *Has he left permanently or is he coming back?*

permission /pəˈmɪʃn/ *noun* (no plural) allowing somebody to do something: *She gave me permission to leave early.*

permit[1] /pəˈmɪt/ *verb* (**permits**, **permitting**, **permitted**) allow somebody to do something: *You are not permitted to smoke in the hospital.* ✪ **Allow** is the word that we usually use.

permit[2] /ˈpɜːmɪt/ *noun* a piece of paper that says you can do something or go somewhere: *Have you got a work permit?*

person /ˈpɜːsn/ *noun* (*plural* **people** /ˈpiːpl/) a man or woman: *I think she's the best person for the job.* **in person** seeing somebody, not just speaking on the telephone or writing a letter: *I want to speak to her in person.*

personal /ˈpɜːsənl/ *adjective* of or for one person; private: *This letter is personal, so I don't want anyone else to read it.*

personal stereo /ˌpɜːsənl ˈsteriəʊ/ *noun* (*plural* **personal stereos**) a small cassette player or radio with **headphones**, that is easy to carry

personality /ˌpɜːsəˈnæləti/ *noun* (*plural* **personalities**) **1** what sort of person you are; your character: *Fred has a great personality.* **2** a famous person: *a television personality*

personally /ˈpɜːsənəli/ *adverb* You say 'personally' when you are saying what you think about something: *Personally, I like her, but a lot of people don't.*

persuade /pəˈsweɪd/ *verb* (**persuades**, **persuading**, **persuaded**) make somebody think or do something by talking to them: *The man in the shop persuaded me to buy the most expensive pen.*

persuasion /pəˈsweɪʒn/ *noun* (no plural) persuading somebody or being persuaded: *After a lot of persuasion she agreed to come.*

pessimism /ˈpesɪmɪzəm/ *noun* (no plural) thinking that bad things will happen ✪ opposite: **optimism**

pessimist /ˈpesɪmɪst/ *noun* a person who always thinks that bad things will happen

pessimistic /ˌpesɪˈmɪstɪk/ *adjective* If you are pessimistic, you think that bad things will happen: *Don't be so pessimistic!*

pest /pest/ *noun* **1** an insect or animal that damages plants or food **2** a person or thing that makes you a little angry: *My sister won't leave me alone when I'm working – she's a real pest!*

pestle /pesl/ *noun* a wooden tool that we use to pound things in a strong bowl (a **mortar**)

pet /pet/ *noun* **1** an animal that you keep in your home: *I've got two pets – a cat and a dog.* **2** a child that a teacher or a parent likes best: *She's the teacher's pet.*

petal /ˈpetl/ *noun* one of the coloured parts of a flower

petition /pəˈtɪʃn/ *noun* a special letter, from a group of people, that asks for something: *Thousands of people signed the petition for a new clinic.*

petrol /ˈpetrəl/ *noun* (no plural) a liquid that you put in a car to make the engine work

petrol station /ˈpetrəl steɪʃn/ *noun* a place where you can buy petrol

phantom /ˈfæntəm/ *noun* a ghost

pharmacist /ˈfɑːməsɪst/ *another word for* **chemist** 1

phase /feɪz/ *noun* a time when something is changing or growing: *Many farmers watch the phases of the moon carefully.*

philosophy /fəˈlɒsəfi/ *noun* **1** (no plural) the study of ideas about the meaning of life **2** (*plural* **philosophies**) what one person thinks about life: *Enjoy yourself today and don't worry about tomorrow – that's my philosophy!*

philosopher /fəˈlɒsəfə(r)/ *noun* a person who studies philosophy

phone /fəʊn/ *noun* a telephone; an instrument that you use for talking to somebody who is in another place: *The phone's ringing – can you answer it?*

○ *What's your phone number?* ○ *I need to make a phone call.* **on the phone** using a telephone to speak to somebody: *Ann was on the phone for an hour.*

phone *verb* (**phones**, **phoning**, **phoned** /fəʊnd/) use a telephone: *I phoned my grandmother last night.*

phonetics /fəˈnetɪks/ *noun* (no plural) the study of the sounds that people make when they speak

phonetic *adjective* using special signs to show how to say words: *The phonetic alphabet is used to show pronunciation.*

photocopy /ˈfəʊtəʊkɒpi/ *noun* (*plural* **photocopies**) a copy of something on paper that you make with a special machine (called a **photocopier**)

photocopy *verb* (**photocopies**, **photocopying**, **photocopied** /ˈfəʊ təʊkɒpid/, **has photocopied**) *Can you photocopy this letter for me?*

photograph /ˈfəʊtəgrɑːf/, **photo** /ˈfəʊtəʊ/ (*plural* **photos**) *noun* a picture that you take with a camera: *I took a photo of Mount Kilimanjaro.*

photograph *verb* (**photographs**, **photographing**, **photographed** /ˈfəʊtəgrɑːft/) take a photograph of somebody or something: *The winner was photographed holding his prize.*

photographer /fəˈtɒgrəfə(r)/ *noun* a person who takes photographs

photographic /ˌfəʊtəˈgræfɪk/ *adjective* about photographs or photography: *photographic equipment*

photography /fəˈtɒgrəfi/ *noun* (no plural) taking photographs

phrase /freɪz/ *noun* a group of words that you use together as part of a sentence: *'First of all' and 'a piece of paper' are phrases.*

physical /ˈfɪzɪkl/ *adjective* You use 'physical' about things that you feel or do with your body: *physical exercise*

physically /ˈfɪzɪkli/ *adverb*: *I'm not physically fit.*

physical education /ˌfɪzɪkl edʒuˈkeɪʃn/ *noun* (no plural) sports that you do at school ✪ The short form is **PE**.

physics /ˈfɪzɪks/ *noun* (no plural) the study of things like heat, light and

sound

physicist /ˈfɪzɪsɪst/ *noun* a person who studies or knows a lot about physics

piano /pɪˈænəʊ/ *noun* (*plural* **pianos**) a big musical instrument that you play by pressing black and white bars (called **keys**):

pianist /ˈpiːənɪst/ *noun* a person who plays the piano

pick[1] /pɪk/ *verb* (**picks**, **picking**, **picked** /pɪkt/) **1** take the person or thing you like best; choose: *They picked Simon as their captain.* **2** take a flower, fruit or vegetable from the place where it grows: *Picking tea is very hard work.* **pick out** be able to see somebody or something in a lot of others: *Can you pick out my father in this photo?* **pick up 1** take and lift somebody or something: *She picked up the bags and put them on the table.* ○ *The phone stopped ringing just as I picked it up.* **2** come to take somebody or something away: *I picked up my post from the post office.* **3** learn something without really studying it: *Did you pick up any French while you were in West Africa?*

pick[2] /pɪk/ *noun* (no plural) what you choose; your choice **take your pick** choose what you like: *We've got red, green and blue shirts. Take your pick.*

picket /ˈpɪkɪt/ *verb* (**pickets**, **picketing**, **picketed**) stand outside the place where you work when there is a **strike**, and try to stop people going to work

picket *noun* a person or group of people who picket: *There was a picket outside the hospital.*

pickpocket /ˈpɪkpɒkɪt/ *noun* a person who steals things from people's pockets

pick-up /ˈpɪk ʌp/ *noun* a small lorry with no roof on the back

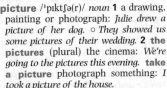
pick-up

picture /ˈpɪktʃə(r)/ *noun* **1** a drawing, painting or photograph: *Julie drew a picture of her dog.* ○ *They showed us some pictures of their wedding.* **2** **the pictures** (plural) the cinema: *We're going to the pictures this evening.* **take a picture** photograph something: *I took a picture of the house.*

pie /paɪ/ *noun* meat, fruit, vegetables, etc with pastry: *an apple pie*

pie

piece /piːs/ *noun* **1** a part of something: *We covered the hole with a piece of wood.* ○ *a piece of broken glass* ☛ picture on page A15. **2** one single thing: *Have you got a piece of paper?* ○ *That's an interesting piece of news.* **fall to pieces** break into pieces: *The chair fell to pieces when I sat on it.* **in pieces** broken: *The teapot lay in pieces on the floor.* **take something to pieces** divide something into its parts: *I took the bed to pieces because it was too big to go through the door.*

pier /pɪə(r)/ *noun* a long thing that is built from the land into the sea, where people can get on and off boats

pierce /pɪəs/ *verb* (**pierces**, **piercing**, **pierced** /pɪəst/) make a hole in something with a sharp point: *The nail pierced her skin.*

piercing /ˈpɪəsɪŋ/ *adjective* A piercing sound is very loud and sharp: *a piercing cry*

pig /pɪg/ *noun* a fat animal that people keep on farms for its meat

> ✪ A young pig is called a **piglet**. Meat from a pig is called **pork**, **bacon** or **ham**.

pigeon /ˈpɪdʒɪn/ *noun* a grey bird that you often see in towns

piglet /ˈpɪglət/ *noun* a young pig

pigsty /ˈpɪgstaɪ/ *noun* (*plural* **pigsties**) a small building where pigs live

pilau /pɪˈlaʊ/ *noun* (no plural) rice that is cooked with spices and meat or vegetables

pile /paɪl/ *noun* a lot of things on top of one another; a large amount of something: *There's a pile of clothes on the floor.* ○ *a pile of earth* ☛ picture on page A15

pile *verb* (**piles**, **piling**, **piled** /paɪld/) put a lot of things on top of one another: *She piled the boxes on the table.*

pilgrim /ˈpɪlgrɪm/ *noun* a person who travels a long way to a place because it has a special religious meaning

pilgrimage /'pɪlgrɪmɪdʒ/ *noun* a journey that a pilgrim makes

pill /pɪl/ *noun* a small round hard piece of medicine that you swallow: *Take one of these pills before every meal.*

pillar /'pɪlə(r)/ *noun* a tall strong piece of stone, wood or metal that holds up a building

pillow

pillow /'pɪləʊ/ *noun* a soft thing that you put under your head when you are in bed

pillowcase /'pɪləʊkeɪs/ *noun* a cover for a pillow

pilot /'paɪlət/ *noun* **1** a person who flies an aircraft **2** a person who guides a ship along a river, into a harbour, etc

pin¹ /pɪn/ *noun* a small thin piece of metal with a flat part at one end and a sharp point at the other. You use a pin for holding pieces of cloth or paper together. ☛ Look also at **drawing-pin** and **safety pin**.

pins and needles /ˌpɪnz ən 'niːdlz/ *noun* (plural) the strange feeling that you sometimes get in a part of your body when you have not moved it for a long time

pin² /pɪn/ *verb* (**pins**, **pinning**, **pinned** /pɪnd/) **1** fix things together with a pin or pins: *Pin the pieces of material together before you sew them.* ○ *Could you pin this notice to the board?* **2** hold somebody or something so that they cannot move: *He tried to get away, but they pinned him against the wall.*

pinch /pɪntʃ/ *verb* (**pinches**, **pinching**, **pinched** /pɪntʃt/) **1** press somebody's skin tightly between your thumb and finger: *Don't pinch me – it hurts!* **2** steal something: *Who's pinched my pen?* ☻ This is an informal use.

pinch *noun* (*plural* **pinches**) **1** pinching something: *He gave my leg a pinch.* **2** how much of something you can hold between your thumb and finger:

Add a pinch of salt to the stew.

pine /paɪn/, **pine tree** /'paɪn triː/ *noun* a tall tree with thin sharp leaves (called **needles**) that do not fall off in winter

pineapple
/'paɪnæpl/ *noun* a big fruit that has a rough brown skin and is yellow inside

pineapple

pink /pɪŋk/ *adjective* with a light red colour: *a pink jumper*
pink *noun*: *She was dressed in pink.*

pint /paɪnt/ *noun* a measure of liquid (= 0·57 litres). There are eight pints in a **gallon**: *a pint of beer* ○ *two pints of milk* ☻ The short way of writing 'pint' is **pt**.

pioneer /ˌpaɪə'nɪə(r)/ *noun* a person who goes somewhere or does something before other people: *Marie Curie was a pioneer in the field of medicine.*

pip /pɪp/ *noun* the seed of some fruits. Lemons, oranges and apples have pips.

pipe /paɪp/ *noun* **1** a long tube that takes water, oil, gas, etc from one place to another **2** a thing that you put tobacco in to smoke it **3** a musical instrument that you blow

pipeline /'paɪplaɪn/ *noun* a big pipe that carries oil or gas a long way

pirate /'paɪrət/ *noun* a person on a ship who robs other ships

pistol /'pɪstl/ *noun* a small gun

pit /pɪt/ *noun* **1** a deep hole in the ground **2** a deep hole that people make in the ground to take out coal

pitch¹ /pɪtʃ/ *noun* (*plural* **pitches**) **1** a piece of ground where you play games like football or cricket **2** how high or low a sound is

pitch² /pɪtʃ/ *verb* (**pitches**, **pitching**, **pitched** /pɪtʃt/) put up a tent: *We pitched our tent under a big tree.*

pity¹ /'pɪti/ *noun* (no plural) sadness for a person or an animal who is in pain or who has problems: *I felt pity for the old dog so I gave him some food.* **it's a pity**, **what a pity** it is sad: *It's a pity you can't come to the party.* **take pity on somebody** help somebody because you feel sad for them: *I took pity on her and gave her some money.*

pity² /ˈpɪti/ *verb* (**pities**, **pitying**, **pitied**, **has pitied** /ˈpɪtid/) feel sad for somebody who is in pain or who has problems: *I really pity people who haven't got anywhere to live.*

pizza /ˈpiːtsə/ *noun* (*plural* **pizzas**) a flat round piece of bread with tomatoes, cheese and other things on top, that is cooked in an oven

place¹ /pleɪs/ *noun* **1** where somebody or something is: *Put the book back in the right place.* **2** a building, town, country, etc: *Zanzibar is a very interesting place.* ○ *Do you know a good place to fish?* **3** a seat or space for one person: *An old man was sitting in my place.* **4** where you are in a race, test, etc: *Alice finished in second place.* **in place** where it should be; in the right place: *The glue held the paper in place.* **in place of somebody** or **something** instead of somebody or something: *Joseph became goalkeeper in place of Michael, who had broken his leg.* **take place** happen: *The wedding of John and Sara will take place on 22 May.*

place² /pleɪs/ *verb* (**places**, **placing**, **placed** /pleɪst/) put something somewhere: *I placed the eggs carefully on the table.*

plain¹ /pleɪn/ *adjective* (**plainer**, **plainest**) **1** with no pattern; all one colour: *She wore a plain blue dress.* **2** simple and ordinary: *plain food* **3** easy to see, hear or understand; clear: *It's plain that he's unhappy.* **4** not pretty: *She was a plain child.*

plainly *adverb* clearly: *They were plainly very angry.*

plain² /pleɪn/ *noun* a large piece of flat land

plait /plæt/ *verb* (**plaits**, **plaiting**, **plaited**) put long pieces of hair, rope, etc over and under each other to make one thick piece: *Her hair is plaited.*

plait *noun* a long piece of hair that somebody has plaited: *She wears her hair in plaits.*

plan¹ /plæn/ *noun* **1** something that you have decided to do, and how to do it: *What are your plans for next year?* ○ *They have plans to build a new school.* **2** a map: *a street plan of London* **3** a drawing for a new building, machine,

etc: *Have you seen the plans for the new shopping centre?*

plan² /plæn/ *verb* (**plans**, **planning**, **planned** /plænd/) decide what you are going to do and how you are going to do it: *They're planning a harambee meeting in the school next week.* ○ *I'm planning to go to university.*

plane /pleɪn/ *noun* an aeroplane: *From this hill you can watch planes taking off and landing at the airport.* ☞ picture at **aeroplane**

planet /ˈplænɪt/ *noun* a large round thing in space that moves around the sun: *Earth, Mars and Venus are planets.*

plank /plæŋk/ *noun* a long flat piece of wood

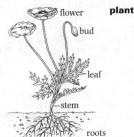

plant

flower

bud

leaf

stem

roots

plant¹ /plɑːnt/ *noun* anything that grows from the ground: *Don't forget to water the plants.*

plant² /plɑːnt/ *verb* (**plants**, **planting**, **planted**) put plants or seeds in the ground to grow: *We planted some potatoes.*

plantation /plɑːnˈteɪʃn/ *noun* a piece of land where things like tea, cotton or tobacco grow: *a sugar plantation*

plaster /ˈplɑːstə(r)/ *noun* **1** (no plural) soft stuff that becomes hard and smooth when it is dry. Plaster is used for covering walls. **2** (*plural* **plasters**) a small piece of sticky material that you put over a cut on your body to keep it clean **3** (no plural) white stuff that you put round a broken arm or leg. It becomes hard and keeps the arm or leg safe until it is better: *When I broke my leg it was in plaster for two months.*

plastic /ˈplæstɪk/ *noun* (no plural) a strong light material that is made in factories. Plastic is used for making a

plate 230

lot of different things: *This ball is made of plastic.*

plate /pleɪt/ *noun* a round flat thing that you put food on ☞ Look also at **number-plate**.

plate

platform /ˈplætfɔːm/ *noun* **1** the part of a railway station where you stand to wait for a train: *Which platform does the Mombasa train stop at?* **2** a place that is higher than the floor, where people stand so that other people can see and hear them: *The headmaster went up to the platform to make his speech.*

play[1] /pleɪ/ *verb* (**plays**, **playing**, **played** /pleɪd/) **1** have fun; do something to enjoy yourself: *The children were playing with the kitten.* **2** take part in a game: *I like playing hockey.* ○ *Do you know how to play chess?* **3** make music with a musical instrument: *My sister plays the guitar very well.* ✪ We always use **the** before the names of musical instruments.: *I'm learning to play the violin.* **4** put a record, tape or compact disc in a machine and listen to it: *Shall I play the tape again?* **5** be somebody in a play in the theatre or on television or radio: *The young woman was played by Meg Njehu.*

play[2] /pleɪ/ *noun* **1** (*plural* **plays**) a story that you watch in the theatre or on television, or listen to on the radio: *We went to see a play at the National Theatre.* **2** (no plural) games; what children do for fun: *work and play* ✪ Be careful! We **play** football, cards, etc or we **have a game of** football, cards, etc (NOT **a play**).

player /ˈpleɪə(r)/ *noun* **1** a person who plays a game: *hockey players* **2** a person who plays a musical instrument: *a trumpet player*

playground /ˈpleɪɡraʊnd/ *noun* a piece of land where children can play

playing-cards /ˈpleɪŋ kɑːdz/ *noun* a set of 52 cards that you use for playing games ☞ Look at **card**.

playing-field /ˈpleɪŋ fiːld/ *noun* a field for sports like football and cricket

plea /pliː/ *noun* asking for something

with strong feeling: *He made a plea for help.*

plead /pliːd/ *verb* (**pleads**, **pleading**, **pleaded**) ask for something in a very strong way: *He pleaded with his parents to buy him a guitar.* **plead guilty** say in a court of law that you did something wrong: *She pleaded guilty to murder.* **plead not guilty** say in a court of law that you did not do something wrong

pleasant /ˈpleznt/ *adjective* nice, enjoyable or friendly: *It's very pleasant to sit and relax with a cold drink.* ○ *He's a very pleasant person.* ✪ opposite: **unpleasant**

pleasantly *adverb*: *She smiled pleasantly.*

please /pliːz/ a word that you use when you ask politely: *What's the time, please?* ○ *Two cups of coffee, please.* ✪ You use **yes, please** to say that you will have something.: *'Would you like a drink?' 'Yes, please.'*

please *verb* (**pleases**, **pleasing**, **pleased** /pliːzd/) make somebody happy: *I wore my best clothes to please my mother.*

pleased /pliːzd/ *adjective* happy: *He wasn't very pleased to see me.* ○ *Are you pleased with your new shoes?*

pleasure /ˈpleʒə(r)/ *noun* **1** (no plural) the feeling of being happy or enjoying something: *I go fishing for pleasure, not for money.* **2** (*plural* **pleasures**) something that makes you happy: *It was a pleasure to meet you.* **it's a pleasure** You say 'it's a pleasure' as a polite way of answering somebody who thanks you: *'Thank you for your help.' 'It's a pleasure.'* **with pleasure** You say 'with pleasure' to show in a polite way that you are happy to do something: *'Can you help me move these boxes?' 'Yes, with pleasure.'*

pleat /pliːt/ *noun* a fold in a piece of cloth

plenty /ˈplenti/ *pronoun* as much or as many as you need; a lot: *Do you want to stay for dinner? There's plenty of food.*

pliers /ˈplaɪəz/ *noun* (plural) a tool for holding things tightly or for cutting wire: *Have you got a pair of pliers?*

plod /plɒd/ *verb* (**plods**, **plodding**, **plodded**) walk slowly in a heavy tired way: *We plodded up the hill in the rain.*

plot /plɒt/ *noun* **1** a secret plan to do something that is wrong: *a plot to kill the president* **2** what happens in a story, play or film: *This book has a very exciting plot.*

plot *verb* (**plots**, **plotting**, **plotted**) make a secret plan to do something that is wrong: *They plotted to rob the bank.*

plough /plaʊ/ *noun* a machine used on farms for digging and turning over the soil. Ploughs are pulled by animals or tractors.

plough *verb* (**ploughs**, **ploughing**, **ploughed** /plaʊd/) use a plough to dig and turn over the soil: *The farmer ploughed his fields.*

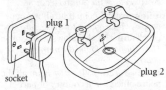

socket ... plug 1 ... plug 2

plug /plʌg/ *noun* **1** a thing that joins a lamp, machine, etc to a place in the wall (called a **socket**) where there is electricity **2** a round thing that you put in the hole in a wash-basin or bath, to stop the water going out

plug *verb* (**plugs**, **plugging**, **plugged** /plʌgd/) fill a hole with something: *I plugged the hole in the pipe with plastic.*

plug in put an electric plug into a place in the wall where there is electricity: *Can you plug the radio in, please?* ○ *The lamp isn't plugged in.* ❍ opposite: **unplug**

plumber /ˈplʌmə(r)/ *noun* a person whose job is to put in and repair things like water-pipes

plump /plʌmp/ *adjective* (**plumper**, **plumpest**) quite fat, in a nice way: *a plump baby*

plunge /plʌndʒ/ *verb* (**plunges**, **plunging**, **plunged** /plʌndʒd/) **1** jump or fall suddenly into something: *She plunged into the pool.* **2** push something suddenly and strongly into something

else: *I plunged my hand into the water.*

plural /ˈplʊərəl/ *noun* the form of a word that shows there is more than one: *The plural of 'child' is 'children'.*

plural *adjective*: *Most plural nouns in English end in 's'.* ☞ Look at **singular**.

plus /plʌs/ *preposition* added to; and: *Two plus three is five (2 + 3 = 5).* ○ *The bus can carry 52 passengers plus the driver.* ☞ Look at **minus**.

pm /ˌpiː ˈem/ You use p.m. after a time to show that it is between midday and midnight: *The train leaves at 3 p.m.* ❍ We use **a.m.** for times between midnight and midday.

pneumonia /njuːˈməʊniə/ *noun* (no plural) a serious illness of the lungs

poach[1] /pəʊtʃ/ *verb* (**poaches**, **poaching**, **poached** /pəʊtʃt/) cook food gently in or over water or milk: *a poached egg*

poach[2] /pəʊtʃ/ *verb* (**poaches**, **poaching**, **poached** /pəʊtʃt/) kill and steal animals, birds or fish from another person's land

poacher *noun* a person who poaches

PO Box /ˌpiː ˈəʊ bɒks/ *noun* (*plural* **PO Boxes**) a box in a post office for keeping the letters of a person or office: *The address is PO Box 40911, Nairobi.*

pocket

pocket /ˈpɒkɪt/ *noun* a small bag in your clothes for carrying things: *I put the key in my pocket.* **pick somebody's pocket** steal money from somebody's pocket or bag

pod /pɒd/ *noun* the long green part of some plants, that has seeds inside it. Peas grow in pods.

poem /ˈpəʊɪm/ *noun* a piece of writing, usually with short lines that may rhyme. Poems try to show feelings or ideas: *I have written a poem.*

poet /ˈpəʊɪt/ *noun* a person who writes poems: *Ken Saro-Wiwa was a famous Nigerian poet.*

poetic /pəʊˈetɪk/ *adjective* of or like poets or poetry: *poetic language*

poetry /ˈpəʊətri/ *noun* (no plural) poems: *Wordsworth wrote beautiful poetry.*

point¹ /pɔɪnt/ *noun* **1** a small round mark ( ) that shows part of a number: *2·5 (two point five)* **2** a certain time or place: *The other team scored a second goal and at that point I knew we couldn't win the match.* **3** the most important idea; the purpose or reason: *The point of going to school is to learn.* ○ *What's the point of phoning her? She's not at home.* **4** the sharp end of something: *the point of a needle* **5** a mark that you win in a game or sport: *Our team scored six points.* **be on the point of** If you are on the point of doing something, you are going to do it very soon: *I was on the point of going out when there was a knock at the door.* **point of view** your way of thinking about something: *I understand your point of view.* **there's no point in** there is no good reason to do something: *There's no point in waiting for Julie – she isn't coming.*

point² /pɔɪnt/ *verb* (**points**, **pointing**, **pointed**) show where something is using your finger, a stick, etc: *I asked him where the bank was and he pointed across the road.* ○ *There was a sign pointing towards the beach.* **point something at somebody or something** hold something towards somebody or something: *She was pointing a gun at his head.* **point out** tell or show something: *Eva pointed out that my bag was open.*

pointed /ˈpɔɪntɪd/ *adjective* with a sharp end: *He was making holes in the ground with a pointed stick.*

pointless /ˈpɔɪntləs/ *adjective* with no use or purpose: *It's pointless telling Paul anything – he never listens.*

poison /ˈpɔɪzn/ *noun* (no plural) something that will kill you or make you very ill if you eat or drink it: *rat poison*

poison *verb* (**poisons**, **poisoning**, **poisoned** /ˈpɔɪznd/) use poison to kill or hurt somebody or something

poisonous /ˈpɔɪzənəs/ *adjective* Something that is poisonous will kill you or make you very ill if you eat or drink it: *Some berries are poisonous.*

poke /pəʊk/ *verb* (**pokes**, **poking**, **poked** /pəʊkt/) **1** push somebody or something hard with your finger or another long thin thing: *She poked me in the eye with a pencil.* **2** push something quickly somewhere: *Daniel poked his head out of the window.*

poke *noun*: *I gave her a poke to wake her up.*

polar /ˈpəʊlə(r)/ *adjective* of the North or South Pole

pole¹ /pəʊl/ *noun* a long thin piece of wood or metal. Poles are often used to hold something up: *a flag-pole* ○ *tent poles*

pole² /pəʊl/ *noun* one of two places at the top and bottom of the earth: *the North Pole* ○ *the South Pole*

police /pəˈliːs/ *noun* (plural) a group of people whose job is to make sure that people do not break the laws of a country: *Have the police found the murderer?* ○ *a police car*

police force /pəˈliːs fɔːs/ *noun* all the police officers in a country or part of a country

policeman /pəˈliːsmən/ *noun* (plural **policemen** /pəˈliːsmən/) a man who works in the police

police officer /pəˈliːs ɒfɪsə(r)/ *noun* a policeman or policewoman

police station /pəˈliːs steɪʃn/ *noun* an office where police officers work

policy /ˈpɒləsi/ *noun* (plural **policies**) the plans of a group of people: *What is the government's policy on education?*

polish /ˈpɒlɪʃ/ *verb* (**polishes**, **polishing**, **polished** /ˈpɒlɪʃt/) rub something so that it shines: *Have you polished your shoes?*

polish *noun* (no plural) stuff that you put on something to make it shine: *furniture polish*

polite /pəˈlaɪt/ *adjective* If you are polite, you are helpful and kind to other people and you do not do or say things that make people sad or angry: *It is polite to say 'please' when you ask for something.* ✪ opposite: **impolite** or **rude**

politely adverb: He asked politely for a glass of water.

politeness /pə'laɪtnəs/ noun (no plural) being polite

political /pə'lɪtɪkl/ adjective of or about the work of government: A political party is a group of people who have the same ideas about how to control their country. ○ political beliefs

politically /pə'lɪtɪkli/ adverb: a politically powerful country

politician /ˌpɒlə'tɪʃn/ noun a person who works in the government or who wants to work in the government: Members of Parliament are politicians.

politics /'pɒlətɪks/ noun (no plural) **1** the work of government: Are you interested in politics? **2** the study of government: She studied Politics at university.

pollen /'pɒlən/ noun (no plural) the yellow powder in flowers

pollinate /'pɒlɪneɪt/ verb to carry the yellow powder (**pollen**) of a flower to another flower of the same type so that it can produce seeds. Insects, birds and the wind pollinate flowers.

pollute /pə'luːt/ verb (**pollutes**, **polluting**, **polluted**) make air, rivers, etc dirty and dangerous: Many rivers are polluted with chemicals from factories.

pollution /pə'luːʃn/ noun (no plural) **1** polluting air, rivers, etc: As the amount of traffic in the city grows, the pollution gets worse. **2** dirty and dangerous stuff from cars, factories, etc

pond /pɒnd/ noun a small area of water: There is a fish pond in the park.

pool /puːl/ noun **1** a little liquid or light on the ground: After the rain there were pools of water on the road. ○ She was lying in a pool of blood. **2** a place for swimming: Mului dived into the pool.

poor /pɔː(r)/ adjective (**poorer**, **poorest**) **1** with very little money ✪ opposite: **rich**. The noun is **poverty**. **2** a word that you use when you feel sad because somebody has problems: Poor Msakuzi! She's feeling ill. **3** not good: My grandfather is in very poor health.

poorly /'pɔːli/ adverb not well; badly: The street is poorly lit.

pop /pɒp/ noun (no plural) modern music that a lot of young people like: What's your favourite pop group? ○ pop music ○ a pop singer

pop³ /pɒp/ verb (**pops**, **popping**, **popped** /pɒpt/) make a short sharp sound; make something make a short sharp sound: The balloon will pop if you put a pin in it.

pope /pəʊp/ noun the most important person in the Roman Catholic Church: Pope John Paul

popular /'pɒpjələ(r)/ adjective liked by a lot of people: Football is a popular sport all over the world. ✪ opposite: **unpopular**

popularity /ˌpɒpju'lærəti/ noun (no plural) being liked by a lot of people

population /ˌpɒpju'leɪʃn/ noun the number of people who live in a place: What is the population of your country?

pork /pɔːk/ noun (no plural) meat from a pig ☞ Note at **pig**.

porridge /'pɒrɪdʒ/ noun (no plural) soft food that we make from pounded grain and hot water

port /pɔːt/ noun a town or city by the sea, where ships arrive and leave: Mombasa is the largest port on the coast of East Africa.

portable /'pɔːtəbl/ adjective that you can move or carry easily: a portable television

porter /'pɔːtə(r)/ noun **1** a person whose job is to carry people's bags in places like railway stations and hotels **2** a person whose job is to look after the entrance of a hotel or other large building

portion /'pɔːʃn/ noun a part of something that one person gets: He gave a portion of the money to each of his children. ○ a large portion of chips

portrait /'pɔːtreɪt/ noun a painting or picture of a person

position /pə'zɪʃn/ noun **1** the place where somebody or something is: Can you show me the position of your village on the map? **2** the way a person is sitting or lying, or the way a thing is standing: She was still sitting in the same position when I came back. **3** how things are at a certain time: He's in a *difficult position – he hasn't got enough money to finish his studies.* **in position** in the right place: *The dancers were in position, waiting for the music to start.*

positive /ˈpɒzətɪv/ *adjective* **1** completely certain: *Are you positive that you closed the door?* **2** that helps you or gives you hope: *The teacher was very positive about my work.*

positively *adverb* really; certainly: *The idea is positively stupid.*

possess /pəˈzes/ *verb* (**possesses**, **possessing**, **possessed** /pəˈzest/) have or own something: *He lost everything that he possessed in the fire.* ✪ **Have** and **own** are the words that we usually use.

possession /pəˈzeʃn/ *noun* **1** (no plural) having or owning something: *The possession of drugs is a crime.* **2** **possessions** (plural) the things that you have or own

possibility /ˌpɒsəˈbɪləti/ *noun* (*plural* **possibilities**) something that might happen: *There's a possibility that we'll have to wait a long time, so take a book.*

possible /ˈpɒsəbl/ *adjective* If something is possible, it can happen or you can do it: *Is it possible to get to Egypt by train?* ○ *I'll phone you as soon as possible.* ✪ opposite: **impossible**

possibly /ˈpɒsəbli/ *adverb* **1** perhaps: *'Will you be free tomorrow?' 'Possibly.'* **2** in a way that can be done: *I'll come as soon as I possibly can.*

post¹ /pəʊst/ *noun* a tall piece of wood or metal that stands in the ground to hold something or to show where something is: *Can you see a signpost anywhere?*

post² /pəʊst/ *noun* (no plural) **1** the way of sending and receiving letters, parcels, etc: *I sent your present by post.* **2** letters and parcels that you send or receive: *Did you get any post this morning?*

postage /ˈpəʊstɪdʒ/ *noun* (no plural) money that you must pay when you send a letter or parcel

postal /ˈpəʊstl/ *adjective* of the post: *postal collections*

postbox /ˈpəʊstbɒks/ *noun* (*plural*

postboxes) a box in the street where you put letters that you want to send

postcard

postcard /ˈpəʊstkɑːd/ *noun* a card with a picture on one side, that you write on and send by post

postman /ˈpəʊstmən/ *noun* (*plural* **postmen** /ˈpəʊstmən/) a man who takes (**delivers**) letters and parcels to people

post office /ˈpəʊst ɒfɪs/ *noun* a building where you go to send letters and parcels and to buy stamps

post³ /pəʊst/ *verb* (**posts**, **posting**, **posted**) **1** send a letter or parcel: *Could you post this letter for me?* **2** send somebody to a place to do a job: *Sara's company have posted her to Japan for two years.*

poster /ˈpəʊstə(r)/ *noun* a big piece of paper on a wall, with a picture or words on it

postpone /pəˈspəʊn/ *verb* (**postpones**, **postponing**, **postponed** /pəˈspəʊnd/) say that something will happen at a later time, not now: *John is not here, so we will postpone the meeting until tomorrow.*

pot /pɒt/ *noun* **1** a deep round container for cooking: *a big pot of soup* **2** a container that you use for a special thing: *a pot of paint* ○ *a plant pot*

potato /pəˈteɪtəʊ/ *noun* (*plural* **potatoes**) a round vegetable that grows under the ground, that is white on the inside and brown or yellow on the outside. You cook it before you eat it: *a baked potato*

pottery /ˈpɒtəri/ *noun* (no plural) **1** cups, plates and other things made from **clay** (heavy earth that becomes hard when it dries): *They make bowls in this factory.* **2** making cups, plates and other things from clay: *He makes his living from pottery.*

poultry /ˈpəʊltri/ *noun* (plural) birds

that people keep on farms for their eggs or their meat. Hens, ducks and geese are poultry.

pounce /paʊns/ *verb* (**pounces, pouncing, pounced** /paʊnst/) jump on somebody or something suddenly: *The cat pounced on the bird.*

pound[1] /paʊnd/ *noun* a measure of weight (= 0·454 kilograms). There are 16 **ounces** in a pound: *a hundred-pound sack of potatoes* ○ *two pounds of sugar* ✪ The short way of writing 'pound' is **lb**.

pound[2] /paʊnd/ *verb* make something into very small pieces or powder by hitting it many times. You pound things in a strong bowl (called a **mortar**) using a special tool (a **pestle**).

pour /pɔː(r)/ *verb* (**pours, pouring, poured** /pɔːd/) **1** make liquid flow out of or into something: *She poured water from the jug into a cup.*

pour

2 flow quickly: *Oil poured out of the damaged ship.* **it's pouring** it is raining very hard

poverty /ˈpɒvəti/ *noun* (no plural) being poor: *There are many people living in poverty in this city.*

powder /ˈpaʊdə(r)/ *noun* dry stuff that is made of a lot of very small pieces: *washing-powder* (= for washing clothes)

power /ˈpaʊə(r)/ *noun* **1** (no plural) being strong; being able to do something: *the power of the storm* ○ *I did everything in my power* (= everything I could do) *to help her.* **2** (no plural) being able to make people do what you want: *The president has a lot of power.* **3** (no plural) what makes things work; energy: *nuclear power* **4** (*plural* **powers**) the right to do something: *Police officers have the power to arrest people.* **5** (*plural* **powers**) a strong person or country: *There is a meeting of world powers in Rome next week.*

power point /ˈpaʊə pɔɪnt/ *noun* a place in a wall where you can push an electric plug

power station /ˈpaʊə steɪʃn/ *noun* a place where electricity is made

powerful /ˈpaʊəfl/ *adjective* **1** very strong; with a lot of power: *The car has a very powerful engine.* ○ *The president is very powerful.* **2** that you can smell or hear clearly, or feel strongly: *a powerful drug*

practical /ˈpræktɪkl/ *adjective* **1** that is about doing or making things, not just about ideas: *Have you got any practical experience of teaching?* **2** able to do useful things: *I'm not a very practical person.* **3** possible to do easily: *Your plan isn't practical.*

practically /ˈpræktɪkli/ *adverb* almost; nearly: *Don't go out – lunch is practically ready!* ○ *You've been late for school practically every day this month!*

practice /ˈpræktɪs/ *noun* (no plural) doing something many times so that you will do it well: *You need lots of practice when you're learning to play a musical instrument.* **out of practice** not good at something, because you have not done it for a long time

practise /ˈpræktɪs/ *verb* (**practises, practising, practised** /ˈpræktɪst/) do something many times so that you will do it well: *If you want to become a professional footballer, you must practise every day.*

praise /preɪz/ *verb* (**praises, praising, praised** /preɪzd/) say that somebody or something is good: *She was praised for her hard work.*

praise *noun* (no plural) *The book has received a lot of praise.*

pram

pram /præm/ *noun* a thing that a baby lies in to go out. It has wheels so that you can push it.

prawn /prɔːn/ *noun* a small pink sea animal that you can eat

pray /preɪ/ *verb* (**prays, praying, prayed** /preɪd/) speak to God or a god: *They prayed for help.*

prayer /preə(r)/ *noun* words that you say when you speak to God or a god: *They said a prayer for peace.*

preach /priːtʃ/ *verb* (**preaches**, **preaching**, **preached** /priːtʃt/) talk about God or a god to a group of people

precaution /prɪˈkɔːʃn/ *noun* something that you do so that bad things will not happen: *I took the precaution of closing all the windows when I went out.*

precious /ˈpreʃəs/ *adjective* **1** very valuable: *Diamonds are precious stones.* **2** that you love very much: *My family is very precious to me.*

precise /prɪˈsaɪs/ *adjective* exactly right: *I gave him precise instructions on how to get to my house.*

precisely *adverb* exactly: *They arrived at two o'clock precisely.*

predict /prɪˈdɪkt/ *verb* (**predicts**, **predicting**, **predicted**) say what you think will happen: *She predicted that it would rain, and she was right.*

prediction /prɪˈdɪkʃn/ *noun*: *His predictions were not correct.*

prefer /prɪˈfɜː(r)/ *verb* (**prefers**, **preferring**, **preferred** /prɪˈfɜːd/) like one thing or person better than another: *Would you prefer tea or coffee?* ○ *Jane wants to go for a walk but I would prefer to stay at home.* ○ *He prefers going out to studying.*

preference /ˈprefrəns/ *noun* liking one thing or person better than another: *We have mangoes and bananas – do you have a preference?*

preferable /ˈprefrəbl/ *adjective* better; that you like more: *I think living in the country is preferable to living in the city.*

preferably /ˈprefrəbli/ *adverb*: *Come and see us any day, but preferably not next Wednesday.*

prefix /ˈpriːfɪks/ *noun* (*plural* **prefixes**) a group of letters that you add to the beginning of a word to make another word: *The prefix 'im-' means 'not', so 'impossible' means 'not possible'.* ☛ Look at **suffix**.

pregnant /ˈpregnənt/ *adjective* If a woman is pregnant, she has a baby growing in her body.

prejudice /ˈpredʒədɪs/ *noun* a feeling of not liking somebody or something, before you know much about them: *she has a prejudice against foreigners*

prejudiced /ˈpredʒədɪst/ *adjective* with strong and unfair ideas about somebody or something, before you know much about them: *He is prejudiced against me because I'm a woman.*

preparation /ˌprepəˈreɪʃn/ *noun* **1** (no plural) making something ready: *the preparation of food* **2 preparations** (plural) what you do to get ready for something: *wedding preparations* **in preparation for something** to get ready for something: *I packed my bags in preparation for the journey.*

prepare /prɪˈpeə(r)/ *verb* (**prepares**, **preparing**, **prepared** /prɪˈpeəd/) make somebody or something ready; make yourself ready: *Martha is in the kitchen preparing the dinner.* ○ *I prepared well for the exam.* **prepared for something** ready for something difficult or bad: *I wasn't prepared for all these problems.* **prepared to** happy to do something: *I'm not prepared to give you any money.*

preposition /ˌprepəˈzɪʃn/ *noun* a word that you use before a noun or pronoun to show when, how, etc: *'In,' 'for,' 'after' and 'above' are all prepositions.* ○ *In the sentence 'He travelled from Kisumu to Mombasa', 'from' and 'to' are prepositions.*

prescribe /prɪˈskraɪb/ *verb* (**prescribes**, **prescribing**, **prescribed** /prɪˈskraɪbd/) say that somebody must take a medicine: *The doctor prescribed some tablets for her illness.*

prescription /prɪˈskrɪpʃn/ *noun* a piece of paper where a doctor writes what medicine you need. You take it to a **chemist's** and get the medicine there.

presence /ˈprezns/ *noun* (no plural) being in a place: *She was so quiet that I didn't notice her presence.* **in the presence of somebody** with another person or other people there: *She signed the papers in the presence of a lawyer.*

present[1] /ˈpreznt/ *adjective* **1** in a place: *There were 200 people present at the meeting.* **2** being or happening now: *What is your present job?*

present[2] /ˈpreznt/ *noun* (no plural) **1** the time now: *I can't help you at present — I'm too busy.* **2** (*also* **present tense**) the form of a verb that you use to talk about now ☞ Look at **past** and **future**.

present[3] /ˈpreznt/ *noun* something that you give to or get from somebody: *a birthday present*

present[4]/prɪˈzent/ *verb* (**presents**, **presenting**, **presented**) give something to somebody: *Who presented the prizes to the winners?*

presentation /ˌprezn̩ˈteɪʃn/ *noun* presenting something: *The presentation of the prizes will take place at 7.30.*

presently /ˈprezntli/ *adverb* **1** soon: *He will be here presently.* **2** now: *She's presently working in a hotel.*

preservation /ˌprezəˈveɪʃn/ *noun* (no plural) keeping something safe; making something stay the same: *the preservation of rare birds*

preserve /prɪˈzɜːv/ *verb* (**preserves**, **preserving**, **preserved** /prɪˈzɜːvd/) keep something safe; make something stay the same: *Parts of the town are new, but they have preserved many of the old buildings.*

president /ˈprezɪdənt/ *noun* **1** the leader in many countries that do not have a king or queen: *the President of Tanzania* **2** the most important person in a big company, club, etc

presidential /ˌprezɪˈdenʃl/ *adjective* of a president or his/her work: *the presidential elections*

press[1] /pres/ *verb* (**presses**, **pressing**, **pressed** /prest/) **1** push something: *If you press this button, the door will open.* ○ *She pressed her face against the window.* **2** make clothes flat and smooth using an iron: *This suit needs pressing.*

press[2] /pres/ *noun* **1** **the press** (no plural) newspapers and magazines and the people who write them: *She told her story to the press.* **2** (*plural* **presses**) pushing something: *Give the doorbell a press.* **3** (*plural* **presses**) a machine for printing things like books and newspapers

pressure /ˈpreʃə(r)/ *noun* **1** the force that presses on something: *the air pressure in a car tyre* **2** a feeling of worry or unhappiness, for example because you have too many things to do: *the pressures of city life*

presume /prɪˈzjuːm/ *verb* (**presumes**, **presuming**, **presumed** /prɪˈzjuːmd/) think that something is true but not be certain: *She's not home yet so I presume she's still at work.*

pretend /prɪˈtend/ *verb* (**pretends**, **pretending**, **pretended**) try to make somebody believe something that is not true: *He didn't want to talk, so he pretended to be asleep.*

pretty[1] /ˈprɪti/ *adjective* (**prettier**, **prettiest**) nice to look at: *a pretty little girl* ○ *These flowers are very pretty.* ☞ Note at **beautiful**.

pretty[2] /ˈprɪti/ *adverb* quite; fairly: *I feel pretty tired today.*

prevent /prɪˈvent/ *verb* (**prevents**, **preventing**, **prevented**) stop somebody from doing something or stop something happening: *Her parents want to prevent her from getting married.* ○ *It is easier to prevent disease than to cure it.*

prevention /prɪˈvenʃn/ *noun* (no plural) preventing something: *the prevention of crime*

previous /ˈpriːviəs/ *adjective* that happened or came before or earlier: *Who was the previous owner of the car?*

previously *adverb*: *I work in a factory now, but previously I was a secretary.*

prey /preɪ/ *noun* (no plural) an animal or bird that another animal or bird kills for food: *Zebra are prey for lions.*

price /praɪs/ *noun* how much money you pay to buy something: *The price is 150 shillings.* ○ *Prices in this country are very high.*

prick /prɪk/ *verb* (**pricks**, **pricking**, **pricked** /prɪkt/) make a very small hole in something, or hurt somebody, with a sharp point: *I pricked my finger on a needle.* ○ *Prick the potatoes with a fork before you cook them.*

prick *noun* a small sharp pain: *She felt the prick of a needle.*

prickle /ˈprɪkl/ *noun* a sharp point on a plant or an animal: *A porcupine has prickles.*

prickly /ˈprɪkli/ *adjective* covered with prickles: *a prickly bush*

pride /praɪd/ *noun* (no plural) **1** being pleased about something that you or others have done or about something that you have; being proud: *She showed us her painting with great pride.* **2** the feeling that you are better than other people

priest /priːst/ *noun* a person who leads people in their religion: *a Buddhist priest*

primary /ˈpraɪməri/ *adjective* first; most important: *What is the primary cause of the illness?*

primary school /ˈpraɪməri skuːl/ *noun* a school for children between the ages of five and twelve

prime minister /ˌpraɪm ˈmɪnɪstə(r)/ *noun* the leader of the government in some countries, for example in Britain

prince /prɪns/ *noun* **1** a man in a royal family, especially the son of a king or queen: *the Prince of Wales* **2** a man who is the ruler of a small country

princess /ˌprɪnˈses/ *noun* (*plural* **princesses**) a woman in a royal family, especially the daughter of a king or queen or the wife of a prince

principal[1] /ˈprɪnsəpl/ *adjective* most important: *My principal reason for going to Nairobi was to find a job.*

principal[2] /ˈprɪnsəpl/ *noun* a person who is in charge of a school or college

principally /ˈprɪnsəpli/ *adverb* mainly; mostly: *She sometimes travels to Europe, but she works principally in Africa.*

principle /ˈprɪnsəpl/ *noun* **1** a rule about how you should live: *He has very strong principles.* **2** a rule or fact about how something happens or works: *scientific principles*

print /prɪnt/ *verb* (**prints**, **printing**, **printed**) **1** put words or pictures onto paper using a machine. Books, newspapers and magazines are printed. **2** write with letters that are not joined together: *Please print your name and address clearly.*

print *noun* **1** (no plural) letters that a machine makes on paper: *The print is too small to read.* **2** (*plural* **prints**) a mark where something has pressed: *footprints in the sand* **3** (*plural* **prints**) a copy on paper of a painting or photograph

printer /ˈprɪntə(r)/ *noun* **1** a person or company that prints things like books or newspapers **2** a machine that prints words from a computer ☞ picture at **computer**

prison /ˈprɪzn/ *noun* a place where people must stay when they have done something that is wrong: *He was sent to prison for robbing a bank.* ○ *She was in prison for 15 years.*

prisoner /ˈprɪznə(r)/ *noun* a person who is in prison or any person who is not free

private /ˈpraɪvət/ *adjective* **1** for one person or a small group of people only, and not for anybody else: *The house has a private swimming-pool* (= that only the people who live in the house can use). ○ *You shouldn't read his letters – they're private.* **2** alone; without other people there: *I would like a private meeting with the manager.* **3** not of your job: *She never talks about her private life with the people at work.* **4** not controlled by the government: *private schools* (= you must pay to go there)
in private alone; without other people there: *Can I speak to you in private?*

privately *adverb*: *Let's go into my office – we can talk more privately there.*

privilege /ˈprɪvəlɪdʒ/ *noun* something special that only one person or a few people may do or have: *Pupils who behave well have special privileges.*

privileged /ˈprɪvəlɪdʒd/ *adjective*: *I felt very privileged when I was invited to meet the President.*

prize /praɪz/ *noun* something that you give to the person who wins a game, race, etc: *I won first prize in the painting competition.*

probable /ˈprɒbəbl/ *adjective* If something is probable, it will almost certainly happen or it is almost certainly true: *It is probable that he will be late.* ✪ opposite: **improbable**

probably /ˈprɒbəbli/ *adverb* almost certainly: *I will probably see you on Thursday.*

problem /ˈprɒbləm/ *noun* **1** something

that is difficult; something that makes you worry: *She has a lot of problems. Her husband is ill and her son is in prison.* ○ *I've got a problem with my knee – it hurts a lot.* **2** a question that you must answer by thinking about it: *I can't solve this problem.*

proceed /prə'si:d/ *verb* (**proceeds**, **proceeding**, **proceeded**) continue; go on: *If everyone is here, then we can proceed with the meeting.* ✪ **Continue** and **go on** are the words that we usually use.

process /'prəʊses/ *noun* (*plural* **processes**) a number of actions, one after the other for doing or making something: *He explained the process of building a boat.* ○ *Learning a language is usually a slow process.*

process *verb* make something ready to use, sell, etc: *The tea is taken to the factory to be processed.*

procession /prə'seʃn/ *noun* a line of people or cars that are moving slowly along: *There was a long procession of people at the funeral.*

produce[1] /prə'dju:s/ *verb* (**produces**, **producing**, **produced** /prə'dju:st/) **1** make or grow something: *This factory produces cars.* ○ *What does the farm produce?* **2** make something happen: *His hard work produced good results.* **3** bring something out to show it: *She produced a ticket from her pocket.* **4** organize something like a play or film: *The play was produced by Telly Otieno.*

produce[2] /'prɒdju:s/ *noun* (no plural) food that you grow on a farm or in a garden to sell: *fresh farm produce*

producer /prə'dju:sə(r)/ *noun* **1** a person who organizes something like a play or film: *a television producer* **2** a company or country that makes or grows something: *Brazil is an important producer of coffee.*

product /'prɒdʌkt/ *noun* something that people make or grow to sell: *Coffee is one of Kenya's most important products.*

production /prə'dʌkʃn/ *noun* **1** (no plural) making or growing something: *the production of oil* **2** (*plural* **productions**) a play, film, etc

profession /prə'feʃn/ *noun* a job that needs a lot of studying and special training: *She's a doctor by profession.*

professional /prə'feʃənl/ *adjective* **1** of or about somebody who has a profession: *I got professional advice from a lawyer.* **2** who does something for money as a job: *a professional athlete* ☛ Look at **amateur**.

professionally /prə'feʃənəli/ *adverb*: *He plays football professionally.*

professor /prə'fesə(r)/ *noun* an important teacher at a university: *Professor Banjo*

profile /'prəʊfaɪl/ *noun* the shape of a person's face when you see it from the side

profit /'prɒfɪt/ *noun* money that you get when you sell something for more than it cost to buy or make: *If you buy a bike for 800 shillings and sell it for 1000 shillings, you make a profit of 200 shillings.*

profitable /'prɒfɪtəbl/ *adjective* If something is profitable, it brings you money: *a profitable business*

program /'prəʊgræm/ *noun* a list of instructions that you give to a computer

program *verb* (**programs**, **programming**, **programmed** /'prəʊgræmd/) give instructions to a computer

programmer *noun* a person whose job is to write programs for a computer

programme /'prəʊgræm/ *noun* **1** something on television or radio: *Did you watch that programme about Japan on TV last night?* **2** a list of things that have been planned to happen: *The President will have a very full programme during his visit to our province.* ○ *What's your programme for tomorrow?*

progress[1] /'prəʊgres/ *noun* (no plural) moving forward or becoming better: *Thomas has made good progress in maths this year.* **in progress** happening: *Silence! Examination in progress.*

progress[2] /prə'gres/ *verb* (**progresses**, **progressing**, **progressed** /prə'grest/) move forward or become better: *I felt more tired as the day progressed.*

prohibit /prə'hɪbɪt/ *verb* (**prohibits**,

prohibiting, prohibited) say that people must not do something: *Smoking is prohibited in the theatre.*

project /ˈprɒdʒekt/ *noun* **1** a big plan to do something: *a project to build a new airport* **2** a piece of work that you do at school. You find out a lot about something and write about it: *We did a project on solar energy.*

projector /prəˈdʒektə(r)/ *noun* a machine that shows films or pictures on a wall or screen

prominent /ˈprɒmɪnənt/ *adjective* **1** easy to see, for example because it is bigger than usual: *prominent teeth* **2** important and famous: *a prominent writer*

promise[1] /ˈprɒmɪs/ *verb* (**promises, promising, promised** /ˈprɒmɪst/) say that you will certainly do or not do something: *She promised to give me the money today.* ○ *I promise I'll come.* ○ *Promise me that you won't be late!*

promise[2] /ˈprɒmɪs/ *noun* saying that you will certainly do or not do something **break a promise** not do what you promised **keep a promise** do what you promised **make a promise** say that you will certainly do or not do something

promote /prəˈməʊt/ *verb* (**promotes, promoting, promoted**) give somebody a more important job: *She worked hard, and after a year she was promoted to manager.*

promotion /prəˈməʊʃn/ *noun*: *The new job is a promotion for me.*

prompt /prɒmpt/ *adjective* quick: *She gave me a prompt answer.*

promptly *adverb* quickly; not late: *We arrived promptly at two o'clock.*

pronoun /ˈprəʊnaʊn/ *noun* a word that you use in place of a noun: *'He', 'it', 'me' and 'them' are all pronouns.*

pronounce /prəˈnaʊns/ *verb* (**pronounces, pronouncing, pronounced** /prəˈnaʊnst/) make the sound of a letter or word: *How do you pronounce your name?* ○ *You don't pronounce the 'b' at the end of 'comb'.*

pronunciation /prəˌnʌnsiˈeɪʃn/ *noun* how you say a word or words: *There are two different pronunciations for this* word. ○ *His pronunciation is very good.*

proof /pruːf/ *noun* (no plural) something that shows that an idea is true: *Do you have any proof that you are the owner of this car?* ❂ The verb is **prove**.

propeller /prəˈpelə(r)/ *noun* a thing that is joined to the engine on a ship or an aeroplane. It turns round fast to make the ship or aeroplane move.

proper /ˈprɒpə(r)/ *adjective* **1** right or correct: *I haven't got the proper tools to mend the car.* **2** real: *He hasn't got any proper friends.*

properly *adverb* well or correctly: *Close the door properly.*

property /ˈprɒpəti/ *noun* **1** (no plural) something that you have or own: *This book is the property of the school, so please be careful with it.* **2** (*plural* **properties**) a building and the land around it

prophet /ˈprɒfɪt/ *noun* a person that God chooses to give his message to people

proportion /prəˈpɔːʃn/ *noun* **1** a part of something: *A large proportion of people in Africa can speak two or more languages.* **2** the amount or size of one thing compared to another thing: *What is the proportion of men to women in the factory?*

proposal /prəˈpəʊzl/ *noun* **1** a plan or idea about how to do something: *a proposal to build a new station* **2** asking somebody to marry you

propose /prəˈpəʊz/ *verb* (**proposes, proposing, proposed** /prəˈpəʊzd/) **1** say what you think should happen or be done: *I propose that we should meet again on Monday.* **2** ask somebody to marry you: *Mike proposed to Vicky.*

protect /prəˈtekt/ *verb* (**protects, protecting, protected**) keep somebody or something safe: *Wear a hat to protect your head against the sun.* ○ *Parents try to protect their children from danger.*

protection /prəˈtekʃn/ *noun* (no plural) keeping somebody or something safe: *protection against disease*

protein /ˈprəʊtiːn/ *noun* a substance that is in food such as meat, fish and beans. It helps us to grow and be healthy.

protest /prəˈtest/ *verb* (**protests, protesting, protested**) say or show strongly that you do not like something: *They protested against the government's plans.*

protest/ˈprəʊtest/ *noun*: *They made a protest against the new tax.*

Protestant /ˈprɒtɪstənt/ *noun* a person who believes in the Christian God and who is not a Roman Catholic

proud /praʊd/ *adjective* (**prouder**, **proudest**) **1** If you feel proud, you are pleased about something that you or others have done or about something that you have: *They are very proud of their new house.* **2** A person who is proud thinks that he/she is better than other people: *She was too proud to say she was sorry.* ☻ The noun is **pride**.

proudly *adverb*: *'I made this myself,' he said proudly.*

prove /pruːv/ *verb* (**proves**, **proving**, **proved** /pruːvd/, **has proved** or **has proven** /ˈpruːvn/) show that something is true: *The blood on his shirt proves that he is the murderer.* ☻ The noun is **proof**.

proverb /ˈprɒvɜːb/ *noun* a short sentence that people often say, that gives help or advice: *'An eye is sharper than a razor'* is an East African proverb.

provide /prəˈvaɪd/ *verb* (**provides**, **providing**, **provided**) give something to somebody who needs it: *I'll provide the food for the party.* ○ *School provides you with many of the skills you need in life.*

provided /prəˈvaɪdɪd/, **providing** /prəˈvaɪdɪŋ/ *conjunction* only if: *Phone me when you get home, providing it's not too late.* ○ *I'll go provided that the children can come with me.*

province /ˈprɒvɪns/ *noun* a part of a country: *Kenya has eight provinces.*

provincial /prəˈvɪnʃl/ *adjective* of a province: *the provincial government*

PS /ˌpiː ˈes/ You write 'PS' at the end of a letter, after your name, when you want to add something: *... Love from Paul. PS I'll see you next week.*

psychiatrist /saɪˈkaɪətrɪst/ *noun* a doctor who helps people who are ill in the mind

psychology /saɪˈkɒlədʒi/ *noun* (no plural) the study of the mind and how

it works

psychologist /saɪˈkɒlədʒɪst/ *noun* a person who studies or knows a lot about psychology

pt *short way of writing* **pint**

PTO /ˌpiː tiː ˈəʊ/ please turn over; words at the bottom of a page that tell you to turn to the next page

public[1] /ˈpʌblɪk/ *adjective* of or for everybody: *a public telephone* ○ *The President always has bodyguards when he walks in a public place.*

public convenience /ˌpʌblɪk kənˈviːniəns/ *noun* a building or room with a toilet for anybody to use, for example in the street

public transport /ˌpʌblɪk ˈtrænspɔːt/ *noun* buses and trains that everybody can use: *I usually travel by public transport.*

publicly *adverb* to everybody; not secretly: *She spoke publicly about her friendship with the Prince.*

public[2] /ˈpʌblɪk/ *noun* **the public** (no plural) all people: *The palace is open to the public between 10 a.m. and 4 p.m.*
in public when other people are there: *I don't want to talk about it in public.*

publication /ˌpʌblɪˈkeɪʃn/ *noun* **1** (no plural) making and selling a book, magazine, etc: *He became very rich after the publication of his first book.* **2** (*plural* **publications**) a book, magazine, etc

publicity /pʌbˈlɪsəti/ *noun* (no plural) giving information about something so that people know about it: *There was a lot of publicity for the new film.*

publish /ˈpʌblɪʃ/ *verb* (**publishes**, **publishing**, **published** /ˈpʌblɪʃt/) prepare and print a book, magazine or newspaper for selling: *This dictionary was published by Oxford University Press.*

publisher *noun* a person or company that publishes books, magazines or newspapers

puddle /ˈpʌdl/ *noun* a little water on the ground

puff /pʌf/ *noun* a small amount of air, wind, smoke, etc that blows: *a puff of smoke*

puff *verb* (**puffs**, **puffing**, **puffed**

/pʌft/) **1** come out in puffs: *Smoke was puffing out of the chimney.* **2** breathe quickly: *She was puffing as she ran up the hill.*

pull

pull[1] /pʊl/ *verb* (**pulls, pulling, pulled** /pʊld/) **1** move somebody or something strongly towards you: *She pulled the drawer open.* **2** go forward, moving something behind you: *The cart was pulled by two oxen.* **3** move something somewhere: *He pulled up his trousers.* **pull down** destroy a building: *The old school has been pulled down.* **pull in** drive a car to the side of the road and stop: *I pulled in to look at the map.* **pull yourself together** control your feelings after being upset: *Pull yourself together and stop crying.* **pull up** stop a car: *The driver pulled up at the traffic lights.*

pull[2] /pʊl/ pulling something: *Give the rope a pull.*

pullover /ˈpʊləʊvə(r)/ *noun* a warm piece of clothing with sleeves, that you wear on the top part of your body. Pullovers are often made of wool.

pulse /pʌls/ *noun* the beating of your heart that you feel in different parts of your body, especially in your wrist: *The nurse felt his pulse.*

pump /pʌmp/ *noun* a machine that moves a liquid or gas into or out of something: *a bicycle-pump* ∘ *a petrol pump*

pump *verb* (**pumps, pumping, pumped** /pʌmpt/) move a liquid or gas with a pump: *Your heart pumps blood around your body.* **pump up** fill something with air, using a pump: *I pumped up my bicycle tyres.*

pumpkin /ˈpʌmpkɪn/ *noun* a very large round vegetable with a thick orange skin

pun /pʌn/ *noun* a funny use of a word that has two meanings, or that sounds

the same as another word

punch /pʌntʃ/ *verb* (**punches, punching, punched** /pʌntʃt/) **1** hit somebody or something hard with your closed hand (your **fist**): *She punched me in the stomach.* **2** make a hole in something with a special tool: *You have to punch your card in a machine when you arrive at work in the factory.*

punch *noun* (*plural* **punches**) a punch on the chin

punctual /ˈpʌŋktʃuəl/ *adjective* If you are punctual, you come or do something at the right time: *Please try to be punctual for your classes.*

punctually /ˈpʌŋktʃuəli/ *adverb*: *They arrived punctually at seven o'clock.*

punctuate /ˈpʌŋktʃueɪt/ *verb* (**punctuates, punctuating, punctuated**) put marks like commas, full stops and question marks in writing

punctuation /ˌpʌŋktʃu'eɪʃn/ *noun* (no plural) using punctuation marks when you are writing

punctuation mark /pʌŋktʃu'eɪʃn mɑːk/ *noun* one of the signs that you use when you are writing. Commas (,), full stops (.) and colons (:) are all punctuation marks.

puncture /ˈpʌŋktʃə(r)/ *noun* a hole in a tyre, that lets the air go out: *My bike has got a puncture.*

puncture *verb* (**punctures, puncturing, punctured** /ˈpʌŋktʃəd/) make a puncture in something: *A piece of glass punctured the tyre.*

punish /ˈpʌnɪʃ/ *verb* (**punishes, punishing, punished** /ˈpʌnɪʃt/) make somebody suffer because they have done something wrong: *The children were punished for telling lies.*

punishment /ˈpʌnɪʃmənt/ *noun*: *What is the punishment for murder in your country?* ∘ *The child was sent to bed as a punishment for being naughty.*

pupa /ˈpjuːpə/ *noun* (*plural* **pupae** /ˈpjuːpiː/) an insect at the time in its life when it is inside a hard case

pupil /ˈpjuːpl/ *noun* a person who is learning at school: *There are 30 pupils in the class.*

puppet /ˈpʌpɪt/ *noun* a doll that you move by pulling strings or by putting your hand inside it and moving your fingers

puppy /'pʌpi/ noun (plural **puppies**) a young dog

purchase /'pɜːtʃəs/ verb (**purchases**, **purchasing**, **purchased** /'pɜːtʃəst/) buy something: *The company has purchased three new shops.* ✪ **Buy** is the word that we usually use.

purchase noun buying something; something that you have bought: *She made several purchases and then left.*

pure /pjʊə(r)/ adjective (**purer**, **purest**) **1** not mixed with anything else; clean: *This shirt is pure cotton.* ○ *pure mountain air* **2** complete or total: *What she said was pure nonsense.*

purely adverb completely or only: *He doesn't like his job – he does it purely for the money.*

purple /'pɜːpl/ adjective with a colour between red and blue

purple noun: *She often wears purple.*

purpose /'pɜːpəs/ noun the reason for doing something: *What is the purpose of your visit?* **on purpose** because you want to; not by accident: *'You've broken my pen!' 'I'm sorry, I didn't do it on purpose.'*

purr /pɜː(r)/ verb (**purrs**, **purring**, **purred** /pɜːd/) When a cat purrs, it makes a low sound that shows that it is happy.

purse /pɜːs/ noun a small bag that you keep money in

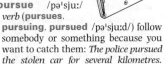
purse

pursue /pə'sjuː/ verb (**pursues**, **pursuing**, **pursued** /pə'sjuːd/) follow somebody or something because you want to catch them: *The police pursued the stolen car for several kilometres.* ✪ **Chase** is the word that we usually use.

push /pʊʃ/ verb (**pushes**, **pushing**, **pushed** /pʊʃt/) **1** move somebody or something strongly away from you:

push

The car broke down so we had to push it to a garage. **2** press something with your finger: *Push the button to ring the bell.*

push noun (plural **pushes**) *She gave him a push and he fell.*

put /pʊt/ verb (**puts**, **putting**, **put**, **has put**) move something to a place: *She put the book on the table.* ○ *He put his hand in his pocket.* ○ *Put* (= write) *your name at the top of the page.* **put away** put something in its usual place: *She put the box away in the cupboard.* **put down** put something on another thing, for example on the floor or a table **put somebody off** make you feel that you do not like somebody or something, or that you do not want to do something: *The accident put me off driving.* **put something off** not do something until a later time: *He put off his holiday because the children were ill.* **put on 1** take clothes and wear them: *Put on your coat.* ✪ opposite: **take off**. **2** press or turn something to make an electrical thing start working: *I put on the TV.* ○ *Put the lights on.* **3** make a record, cassette or compact disc start to play: *Let's put my new cassette on.* **put out** stop a fire or stop a light shining: *She put out the fire with a bucket of water.* **put somebody through** connect somebody on the telephone to the person that they want to speak to: *Can you put me through to the manager, please?* **put somebody up** let somebody sleep in your home: *Can you put me up for the night?* **put up with somebody** or **something** suffer pain or problems without complaining: *We can't change the bad weather, so we have to put up with it.*

puzzle¹ /'pʌzl/ noun **1** something that is difficult to understand or explain: *Joan's reason for leaving her job is a puzzle to me.* **2** a game that is difficult and makes you think a lot: *a crossword puzzle* ☞ Look also at **jigsaw puzzle**.

puzzle² /'pʌzl/ verb (**puzzles**, **puzzling**, **puzzled** /'pʌzld/) make you think a lot because you cannot understand or explain it: *Ayubu's illness puzzled the doctors.*

puzzled adjective If you are puzzled,

you cannot understand or explain something: *She was puzzled when he didn't answer her letter.*

puzzling /'pʌzlɪŋ/ *adjective* If something is puzzling, you cannot understand or explain it.

pyjamas /pə'dʒɑːməz/ *noun* (plural) a loose jacket and trousers that you wear in bed

pyramid /'pɪrəmɪd/ *noun* a shape with a flat bottom and three or four sides that come to a point at the top: *the pyramids of Egypt* ☛ picture on page A5.

pyrethrum /paɪ'riːθrəm/ *noun* a kind of flower used for making a substance that kills insects

Qq

quack /kwæk/ *noun* the sound that a duck makes

quack *verb* (**quacks, quacking, quacked** /kwækt/) make this sound

qualification /ˌkwɒlɪfɪ'keɪʃn/ *noun* an examination that you have passed, or training or knowledge that you need to do a special job: *He left school with no qualifications.*

qualify /'kwɒlɪfaɪ/ *verb* (**qualifies, qualifying, qualified** /'kwɒlɪfaɪd/, **has qualified**) get the right knowledge and training and pass exams so that you can do a certain job: *Nazir has qualified as a doctor.*

qualified *adjective*: *a qualified nurse*

quality /'kwɒləti/ *noun* (no plural) how good or bad something is: *This furniture isn't very good quality.*

quantity /'kwɒntəti/ *noun* (plural **quantities**) how much of something there is; amount: *I only bought a small quantity of cheese.*

quarrel /'kwɒrəl/ *verb* (**quarrels, quarrelling, quarrelled** /'kwɒrəld/) talk angrily with somebody because you do not agree: *They were quarrelling about money.*

quarrel *noun* a fight with words; an argument: *I had a quarrel with my brother.*

quarry /'kwɒri/ *noun* (plural **quarries**) a place where people cut stone out of the ground to make things like buildings or roads

quarter /'kwɔːtə(r)/ *noun* **1** one of four equal parts of something; $\frac{1}{4}$ *a mile and a quarter* ○ *You can walk there in three-quarters of an hour.* **2** three

months: *You get a telephone bill every quarter.* **3** a part of a town: *the student quarter* **(a) quarter past** 15 minutes after the hour: *It's quarter past two.* ○ *I'll meet you at a quarter past.* ☛ Look at page A8. **(a) quarter to** 15 minutes before the hour: *quarter to nine*

quarter-final /ˌkwɔːtə 'faɪnl/ *noun* In a competition, a quarter-final is one of the four games that are played to choose who will play in the **semi-finals.**

quay /kiː/ *noun* (plural **quays**) a place in a harbour where ships go so that people can move things on and off them

queen /kwiːn/ *noun* **1** a woman who rules a country and who is from a royal family: *Queen Elizabeth II* (= the second), *the Queen of England* **2** the wife of a king

query /'kwɪəri/ *noun* (plural **queries**) a question: *Phone me if you have any queries.*

query *verb* (**queries, querying, queried** /'kwɪərid/) ask a question about something that you think is wrong: *We queried the bill but the waitress said it was correct.*

question[1] /'kwestʃən/ *noun* **1** something that you ask: *They asked me a lot of questions.* ○ *She didn't answer my question.* ○ *What is the answer to question 3?* **2** a problem that needs an answer: *We need more money. The question is, where are we going to get it from?* **in question** that we are talking about: *On the day in question I was* *at my uncle's house.* **out of the question** not possible: *No, I won't give you any more money. It's out of the question!*

question mark /ˈkwestʃən mɑːk/ *noun* the sign (?) that you write at the end of a question

question tag /ˈkwestʃən tæg/ *noun* words that you put on the end of a sentence to make a question: *In the sentence 'You are from Uganda, aren't you?', 'aren't you' is a question tag.*

question[2] /ˈkwestʃən/ *verb* (**questions**, **questioning**, **questioned** /ˈkwestʃənd/) ask somebody questions about something: *The police questioned him about the stolen car.*

questionnaire /ˌkwestʃəˈneə(r)/ *noun* a list of questions for people to answer: *Please fill in* (= write the answers on) *the questionnaire.*

queue /kjuː/ *noun* a line of people who are waiting to do something: *There was a long queue in the bank.* ☛ picture on page A15

queue, **queue up** *verb* (**queues**, **queuing**, **queued** /kjuːd/) stand in a queue: *We queued for a bus.*

quick /kwɪk/ *adjective, adverb* (**quicker**, **quickest**) fast; that takes little time: *It's quicker to travel by plane than by train.* ○ *Can I make a quick telephone call?* ☛ Look at **slow**.

quickly *adverb*: *Come as quickly as you can!*

quiet /ˈkwaɪət/ *adjective* (**quieter**, **quietest**) **1** with little sound or no sound: *Be quiet – the baby's asleep.* ○ *a quiet voice* ✪ opposite: **loud** or **noisy**. ☛ picture on page A11. **2** without many people or without many things happening: *The streets are very quiet at night.*

quiet *noun* (no plural) being quiet: *I need quiet when I'm working.*

quietly *adverb*: *Please close the door quietly.*

quilt /kwɪlt/ *noun* a soft thick cover for a bed. Quilts often have feathers inside.

quite /kwaɪt/ *adverb* **1** not very; rather; fairly: *It's quite warm today, but it's not hot.* ○ *He plays the guitar quite well.* ○ *We waited quite a long time.* **2** completely: *Dinner is not quite ready.*

quite a few or **quite a lot of** a lot of something: *There were quite a few people at the meeting.* ○ *I study quite a lot in the evenings.*

quiz /kwɪz/ *noun* (*plural* **quizzes**) a game where you try to answer questions: *a quiz on television*

quotation /kwəʊˈteɪʃn/, **quote** /kwəʊt/ *noun* words that you say or write, that another person said or wrote before: *That's a quotation from a famous poem.*

quotation marks /kwəʊˈteɪʃn mɑːks/, **quotes** *noun* (plural) the signs " " or '' that you use in writing before and after words that someone has said

quote /kwəʊt/ *verb* (**quotes**, **quoting**, **quoted**) say or write something that another person said or wrote before: *She quoted from the Bible.*

rabbi /'ræbaɪ/ *noun* (*plural* **rabbis**) a teacher or leader of the Jewish religion

rabbit /'ræbɪt/ *noun* a small animal with long ears. Rabbits live in holes under the ground.

rabbit

race[1] /reɪs/ *noun* **1** a competition to see who can run, drive, ride, etc fastest: *Who won the race?* ○ *a horse-race* **2 the races** (plural) a time when there are a lot of horse-races in one place

racecourse /'reɪskɔːs/, **racetrack** /'reɪstræk/ *noun* a place where you go to see horse-races

race[2] /reɪs/ *verb* (**races**, **racing**, **raced** /reɪst/) run, drive, ride, etc in a competition to see who is the fastest: *The cars raced round the track.*

race[3] /reɪs/ *noun* a group of people of the same kind, for example with the same colour of skin: *People of many different races live together in this country.*

racial /'reɪʃl/ *adjective* of race: *racial differences*

racing /'reɪsɪŋ/ *noun* (no plural) a sport where horses, cars, etc race against each other: *a racing car*

racism /'reɪsɪzəm/ *noun* (no plural) the belief that some groups (**races**) of people are better than others

racist /'reɪsɪst/ *noun* a person who believes that some races of people are better than others

racist *adjective*: *a racist comment*

rack /ræk/ *noun* a kind of shelf, made of bars, that you put things in or on: *Put your bag in the luggage rack* (= on a bus or train).

racket, racquet /'rækɪt/ *noun* a thing that you use for hitting the ball in tennis, badminton and squash

racket

radar /'reɪdɑː(r)/ *noun* (no plural) a way of finding where a ship or an aircraft is and how fast it is travelling by using radio waves

radiation /ˌreɪdi'eɪʃn/ *noun* (no plural) dangerous energy that some substances send out

radiator /'reɪdieɪtə(r)/ *noun* **1** a metal thing with hot water inside that you use to make a room warm **2** a part of a car that has water in it to keep the engine cold

radio /'reɪdiəʊ/ *noun* **1** (no plural) sending or receiving sounds that travel a long way through the air by special waves: *The captain of the ship sent a message by radio.* **2** (plural **radios**) an instrument that brings voices or music from far away so that you can hear them: *We listened to an interesting programme on the radio.*

radius /'reɪdiəs/ *noun* (*plural* **radii** /'reɪdiaɪ/) the length of a straight line from the centre of a circle to the outside ☞ picture on page A5

raft /rɑːft/ *noun* a flat boat with no sides and no engine

rag /ræg/ *noun* **1** a small piece of old cloth that you use for cleaning **2 rags** (plural) clothes that are very old and torn: *She was dressed in rags.*

rage /reɪdʒ/ *noun* strong anger

raid /reɪd/ *noun* a sudden attack on a place: *a bank raid*

raid *verb* (**raids**, **raiding**, **raided**) *Police raided the house looking for drugs.*

rail /reɪl/ *noun* **1** (*plural* **rails**) a long piece of wood or metal that is fixed to a wall or to something else: *She held on to the rail as she came down the steps.* **2 rails** (plural) the long pieces of metal that trains go on **3** (no plural) trains as a way of travelling: *I travelled from Kisumu to Nairobi by rail* (= in a train).

railings /'reɪlɪŋz/ *noun* (plural) a fence made of long pieces of metal

railway /'reɪlweɪ/ *noun* **1** (also **railway line**) the metal lines that trains go on from one place to another **2** a train service that carries people and things: *a railway timetable*

railway station /ˈreɪlweɪ steɪʃn/ *noun* a place where trains stop so that people can get on and off

rain /reɪn/ *noun* **1** (no plural) the water that falls from the sky **2 the rains** (plural) in some countries, the only time of year when there is a lot of rain: *If the rains come late, the crops might fail.*

rain *verb* (**rains, raining, rained** /reɪnd/) When it rains, water falls from the sky: *It's raining.* ○ *It rained all day.*

rainbow /ˈreɪnbəʊ/ *noun* a half circle of bright colours that you sometimes see in the sky when rain and sun come together

rain forest /ˈreɪn fɒrɪst/ *noun* a forest in a hot part of the world where there is a lot of rain

rainy /ˈreɪni/ *adjective* (**rainier, rainiest**) with a lot of rain: *a rainy day* ○ *the rainy season*

raise /reɪz/ *verb* (**raises, raising, raised** /reɪzd/) **1** move something or somebody up: *Raise your hand if you want to ask a question.* **۞** opposite: **lower 2** make something bigger, higher, stronger, etc: *They've raised the price of petrol.* ○ *She raised her voice* (= spoke louder). **3** get money from other people: *We raised 50 000 shillings for the hospital.* **4** start to talk about something: *He raised an interesting question.*

raisin /ˈreɪzn/ *noun* a dried grape

rake /reɪk/ *noun* a tool with a long handle that you use in a garden for collecting leaves or for making the soil flat

rake *verb* (**rakes, raking, raked** /reɪkt/) *Rake up the dead leaves.*

rally /ˈræli/ *noun* (plural **rallies**) **1** a group of people walking or standing together to show that they feel strongly about something: *a peace rally* **2** a race for cars or motor cycles

ramp /ræmp/ *noun* a path that goes to a higher or lower place: *I pushed the wheelchair up the ramp.*

ran *form of* **run**[1]

random /ˈrændəm/ *adjective* at

random without any special plan: *She chose a few books at random.*

rang *form of* **ring**[2]

range[1] /reɪndʒ/ *noun* **1** different things of the same kind: *we study a range of subjects at school.* **2** how far you can see, hear, shoot, travel, etc: *The gun has a range of five miles.* **3** the amount between the highest and the lowest: *The age range of the children is between eight and twelve.* **4** a line of mountains or hills

range[2] /reɪndʒ/ *verb* (**ranges, ranging, ranged** /reɪndʒd/) be at different points between two things: *The ages of the students in the class range from 11 to 13.*

rank /ræŋk/ *noun* how important somebody is in a group of people, for example in an army: *General is one of the highest ranks in the army.*

ransom /ˈrænsəm/ *noun* money that you must pay so that a criminal will free a person that he/she has taken: *The kidnappers have demanded a ransom of a million shillings.*

rap /ræp/ *noun* **1** a quick knock: *I heard a rap at the door.* **2** a kind of music in which singers speak the words of a song very quickly

rap *verb* (**raps, rapping, rapped** /ræpt/) **1** hit something quickly and lightly: *She rapped on the door.* **2** speak the words of a song very quickly

rape /reɪp/ *verb* (**rapes, raping, raped** /reɪpt/) make somebody have sex when they do not want to

rape *noun: He was sent to prison for rape.*

rapid /ˈræpɪd/ *adjective* quick; fast: *rapid changes*

rapidly *adverb: Once she took the medicine she recovered rapidly.*

rare /reə(r)/ *adjective* (**rarer, rarest**) **1** If something is rare, you do not find or see it often: *Gorillas are rare animals.* ○ *It's rare to have rain in the dry season.* **2** Meat that is rare is only cooked a little.

rarely *adverb* not often: *I rarely go to bed very late.*

rash[1] /ræʃ/ *noun* (plural **rashes**) a lot of small red spots on your skin

rash[2] /ræʃ/ *adjective* (**rasher, rashest**)

If you are rash, you do things too quickly, without thinking: *You were very rash to leave your job before you had found a new one.*

raspberry /ˈrɑːzbəri/ *noun* (*plural* **raspberries**) a small soft red fruit: *raspberry jam*

rat /ræt/ *noun* an animal like a big mouse

rate /reɪt/ *noun* **1** the speed of something or how often something happens: *The crime rate was lower in 1997 than in 1996.* **2** the amount that something costs or that somebody is paid: *His rate of pay is 50 shillings an hour.* **at any rate** anyway; whatever happens: *I hope to be back before ten o'clock – I won't be late at any rate.*

rather /ˈrɑːðə(r)/ *adverb* more than a little but not very; quite: *We were rather tired after our long journey.* ○ *It's rather a small room.* **rather than** in the place of; instead of: *Can I have a banana rather than a mango?* **would rather** would prefer to do something: *I would rather go by train than by bus.*

ration /ˈræʃn/ *noun* a small amount of something that you are allowed to have when there is not enough for everybody to have what they want: *food rations*

rattle /ˈrætl/ *verb* (**rattles**, **rattling**, **rattled** /ˈrætld/) **1** make a lot of short sounds because it is shaking: *The windows were rattling all night in the wind.* **2** shake something so that it makes a lot of small sounds: *She rattled the money in the tin.*

rattle *noun* **1** the noise of things hitting each other: *the rattle of empty bottles* **2** a toy that a baby can shake to make a noise

raw /rɔː/ *adjective* **1** not cooked: *raw meat* **2** natural; as it comes from the soil, from plants, etc: *raw sugar*

ray /reɪ/ *noun* (*plural* **rays**) a line of light or heat: *the rays of the sun*

razor /ˈreɪzə(r)/ *noun* a sharp thing that people use to cut hair off their bodies (to **shave**): *It took me a long time to shave because the razor wasn't very sharp.*

razor-blade /ˈreɪzə bleɪd/ *noun* the thin metal part of a razor that cuts

re- *prefix*
You can add **re-** to the beginning of some words to give them the meaning 'again', for example:
rebuild = build again: *We rebuilt the fence after the storm.*
redo = do again: *Your homework is all wrong. Please redo it.*

reach /riːtʃ/ *verb* (**reaches**, **reaching**, **reached** /riːtʃt/) **1** arrive somewhere: *It was dark when we reached the town.* ○ *Have you reached the end of the book yet?* **2** put out your hand to do or get something; be able to touch something: *I reached for the telephone.* ○ *Can you get that book from the top shelf for me? I can't reach.*

reach *noun* (no plural) **beyond reach**, **out of reach** too far away to touch: *Keep this medicine out of the reach of children.* **within reach** near enough to touch or go to: *Do you live within reach of Kampala?*

react /riˈækt/ *verb* (**reacts**, **reacting**, **reacted**) say or do something when another thing happens: *How did your mother react to the news?*

reaction /riˈækʃn/ *noun* what you say or do because of something that has happened: *What was her reaction when you told her about the accident?*

read /riːd/ *verb* (**reads**, **reading**, **read** /red/, **has read**) **1** look at words and understand them: *Have you read this book? It's very interesting.* **2** say words that you can see: *I read a story to the children.* **read out** read something to other people: *The teacher read out the list of names.*

reading *noun* (no plural) *My interests are reading and football.*

reader /ˈriːdə(r)/ *noun* **1** a person who reads something **2** a book for reading at school

ready /ˈredi/ *adjective* **1** prepared so that you can do something: *I'll be ready to leave in five minutes.* **2** prepared so that you can use it: *Dinner will be ready soon.* **3** happy to do something: *He's always ready to help.* **get ready** make yourself ready for something: *I'm getting ready to go out.*

ready-made /ˌredi 'meɪd/ *adjective* prepared and ready to use: *ready-made soup*

real /rɪəl/ *adverb* **1** not just in the mind; that really exists: *The film is about something that happened in real life.* **2** true: *The name he gave to the police wasn't his real name.* **3** natural; not a copy: *This ring is real gold.* **4** big or complete: *I've got a real problem.*

reality /rɪˈæləti/ *noun* (*plural* **realities**), the way that something really is: *People think I have an interesting job, but in reality it's quite boring.*

realize /ˈrɪəlaɪz/ *verb* (**realizes**, **realizing**, **realized** /ˈrɪəlaɪzd/) understand or know something: *When I got home, I realized that I had lost my key.* ○ *I didn't realize you were American.*

realization /ˌrɪəlaɪˈzeɪʃn/ *noun* (no plural) understanding or knowing something

really /ˈrɪəli/ *adverb* **1** in fact; truly: *Do you really love him?* **2** very or very much: *I'm really hungry.* ○ *'Do you like this music?' 'Not really.'* **3** a word that shows you are interested or surprised: *'I'm going to have a baby.' 'Really?'*

rear /rɪə(r)/ *noun* (no plural) the back part: *The kitchen is at the rear of the house.*

rear *adjective* at the back: *the rear window of a car*

reason /ˈriːzn/ *noun* why you do something or why something happens: *The reason I didn't come to school was that I was ill.* ○ *Is there any reason why you were late?*

reasonable /ˈriːznəbl/ *adjective* **1** fair and willing to listen to what other people say: *Be reasonable! You can't ask one person to do all the work!* **2** fair or right: *I think 10 000 shillings is a reasonable price.* ✪ opposite: **unreasonable**

reasonably /ˈriːznəbli/ *adverb* **1** quite, but not very: *The food was reasonably good.* **2** in a reasonable way: *Don't get angry – let's talk about this reasonably.*

reassure /ˌriːəˈʃʊə(r)/ *verb* (**reassures**, **reassuring**, **reassured** /ˌriːəˈʃʊəd/) say or do something to make somebody feel safer or happier: *The doctor re-*

assured her that she was not seriously ill.

reassurance /ˌriːəˈʃʊərəns/ *noun* what you say to make somebody feel safer or happier: *He needs reassurance that he is right.*

rebel[1] /ˈrebl/ *noun* a person who fights against the people in control

rebel[2] /rɪˈbel/ *verb* (**rebels**, **rebelling**, **rebelled** /rɪˈbeld/) fight against the people in control: *She rebelled against her parents and went to live in Nairobi.*

rebellion /rɪˈbeliən/ *noun* a time when a lot of people fight against the people in control: *Hundreds of people died in the rebellion.*

recall /rɪˈkɔːl/ *verb* (**recalls**, **recalling**, **recalled** /rɪˈkɔːld/) remember something: *I can't recall the name of Maria's brother.* ✪ **Remember** is the word that we usually use.

receipt /rɪˈsiːt/ *noun* a piece of paper that shows you have paid for something: *Can I have a receipt?*

receive /rɪˈsiːv/ *verb* (**receives**, **receiving**, **received** /rɪˈsiːvd/) get something that somebody has given or sent to you: *Did you receive my letter?* ✪ **Get** is the word that we usually use.

receiver /rɪˈsiːvə(r)/ *noun* the part of a telephone that you use for listening and speaking ☞ picture on page A14

recent /ˈriːsnt/ *adjective* that happened a short time ago: *Is this a recent photo of your son?*

recently *adverb* not long ago: *I've been studying a lot recently – that's why I'm so tired.*

reception /rɪˈsepʃn/ *noun* **1** (no plural) the place where you go first when you arrive at a hotel, company, etc: *Leave your key at reception if you go out.* **2** (*plural* **receptions**) a big important party: *a wedding reception*

receptionist /rɪˈsepʃənɪst/ *noun* a person in a hotel, company, etc who helps you when you arrive and who may also answer the telephone

recipe /ˈresəpi/ *noun* a piece of writing that tells you how to cook something

reckless /ˈrekləs/ *adjective* A person who is reckless does dangerous things without thinking about what could happen: *reckless driving*

reckon /'rekən/ *verb* (**reckons**, **reckoning**, **reckoned** /'rekənd/) believe something because you have thought about it: *I reckon it will take us about 3 hours to get there.*

recognize /'rekəgnaɪz/ *verb* (**recognizes**, **recognizing**, **recognized** /'rekəgnaɪzd/) **1** know again somebody or something that you have seen or heard before: *I didn't recognize you without your glasses.* **2** know that something is true: *They recognize that there is a problem.*

recognition /,rekəg'nɪʃn/ *noun* (no plural) recognizing somebody or something

recommend /,rekə'mend/ *verb* (**recommends**, **recommending**, **recommended**) **1** tell somebody that a person or thing is good or useful: *Can you recommend a good book?* **2** tell somebody in a helpful way what you think they should do: *I recommend that you see a doctor.*

recommendation /,rekəmen'deɪʃn/ *noun*: *I read this book on my brother's recommendation* (= because he said it was good).

record[1] /'rekɔːd/ *noun* **1** notes about things that have happened: *Keep a record of all the money you spend.* **2** a round plastic thing that makes music when you play it on a **record player**: *Put another record on.* **3** the best, fastest, highest, lowest, etc that has been done in a sport: *She holds the world record for long jump.* ○ *He ran the race in record time.* **break a record** do better in a sport than anybody has done before

record[2] /rɪ'kɔːd/ *verb* (**records**, **recording**, **recorded**) **1** write notes about or make pictures of things that happen so you can remember them later: *In his diary he recorded everything that he did.* **2** put music or a film on a tape or record so that you can listen to or watch it later: *I recorded a concert from the radio.*

recorder /rɪ'kɔːdə(r)/ *noun* a musical instrument that you blow. Children often play recorders. ☛ Look also at **tape recorder** and **video recorder**.

recording /rɪ'kɔːdɪŋ/ *noun* sounds or pictures on a tape, record or film: *We listened to the recording of the concert.*

record-player /'rekɔːd pleɪə(r)/ *noun* a machine that makes music come out of records

recover /rɪ'kʌvə(r)/ *verb* (**recovers**, **recovering**, **recovered** /rɪ'kʌvəd/) **1** become well or happy again after you have been ill or sad: *She is slowly recovering from her illness.* **2** get back something that you have lost: *Police recovered the stolen car.*

recovery /rɪ'kʌvəri/ *noun* (no plural) *He made a quick recovery after his illness.*

rectangle /'rektæŋgl/ *noun* a shape with two long sides, two short sides and four angles of 90 degrees ☛ picture on page A5

rectangular /rek'tæŋjələ(r)/ *adjective* with the shape of a rectangle: *This page is rectangular.*

recycle /,riː'saɪkl/ *verb* (**recycles**, **recycling**, **recycled** /,riː'saɪkld/) do something to materials like paper and glass so that they can be used again: *Old newspapers can be recycled.*

red /red/ *adjective* (**redder**, **reddest**) **1** with the colour of blood: *She's wearing a bright red dress.* ○ *red wine* **2** Red hair has a colour between red, orange and brown.

red *noun*: *Lucy was dressed in red.*

reduce /rɪ'djuːs/ *verb* (**reduces**, **reducing**, **reduced** /rɪ'djuːst/) make something smaller or less: *I bought this shirt because the price was reduced from 200 shillings to 100.* ○ *Reduce speed now* (= words on a road sign).

reduction /rɪ'dʌkʃn/ *noun*: *price reductions* ✪ opposite: **increase**

redundant /rɪ'dʌndənt/ *adjective* without a job because you are not needed any more: *When the factory closed 300 people were made redundant.*

reed /riːd/ *noun* a tall plant, like grass, that grows in or near water

reel /riːl/ *noun* a thing with round sides that holds cotton for sewing, film for cameras, etc: *a reel of cotton*

reel

refer /rɪˈfɜ:(r)/ *verb* (**refers**, **referring**, **referred** /rɪˈfɜ:d/) **refer to somebody** or **something 1** talk about somebody or something: *When I said that some people are stupid, I wasn't referring to you!* **2** be used to mean something: *The word 'child' refers here to anybody under the age of 16.* **3** look in a book or ask somebody for information: *If you don't understand a word, you may refer to your dictionaries.*

referee /ˌrefəˈri:/ *noun* a person in a sport like football or boxing who controls the match

reference /ˈrefrəns/ *noun* **1** what somebody says or writes about something: *There are many references to my town in this book about Kenya.* **2** If somebody gives you a reference, they write about you to somebody who may give you a new job: *Did your boss give you a good reference?*

reference book /ˈrefrəns bʊk/ *noun* a book where you look for information: *A dictionary is a reference book.*

reflect /rɪˈflekt/ *verb* (**reflects**, **reflecting**, **reflected**) send back light, heat or sound: *A mirror reflects a picture of you when you look in it.*

reflection /rɪˈflekʃn/ *noun* **1** (*plural* **reflections**) a picture that you see in a mirror or in water: *He looked into the pool and saw a reflection of himself.* **2** (no plural) sending back light, heat or sound

reform /rɪˈfɔ:m/ *verb* (**reforms**, **reforming**, **reformed** /rɪˈfɔ:md/) change something to make it better: *The government wants to reform the education system in this country.*

reform *noun* a change to make something better: *political reform*

refresh /rɪˈfreʃ/ *verb* (**refreshes**, **refreshing**, **refreshed** /rɪˈfreʃt/) make somebody feel cooler, stronger or less tired: *A sleep will refresh you after your long journey.*

refreshing *adjective*: *a cool, refreshing drink*

refreshments /rɪˈfreʃmənts/ *noun* (plural) food and drinks that you can buy in a place like a cinema or theatre: *Refreshments will be sold in the interval.*

refrigerator /rɪˈfrɪdʒəreɪtə(r)/ *noun* a big metal box for keeping food and drink cold and fresh ✪ **Fridge** is the word that we usually use.

refuge /ˈrefju:dʒ/ *noun* a place where you are safe from somebody or something **take refuge from something** go to a safe place to get away from something bad or dangerous: *We took refuge from the hot sun under a tree.*

refugee /ˌrefjuˈdʒi:/ *noun* a person who must leave his/her country because of danger

refund /riˈfʌnd/ *verb* (**refunds**, **refunding**, **refunded**) pay back money: *When the match was cancelled they refunded our money.*

refund /ˈri:fʌnd/ *noun* money that is paid back to you: *The watch I bought was broken so I asked for a refund.*

refuse /rɪˈfju:z/ *verb* (**refuses**, **refusing**, **refused** /rɪˈfju:zd/) say 'no' when somebody asks you to do or have something: *I asked James to help, but he refused.* ○ *The shop assistant refused to give me my money back.*

refusal /rɪˈfju:zl/ *noun* saying 'no' when somebody asks you to do or have something: *a refusal to pay*

regard[1] /rɪˈgɑ:d/ *verb* (**regards**, **regarding**, **regarded**) think of somebody or something in a certain way: *I regard her as my best friend.*

regard[2] /rɪˈgɑ:d/ *noun* **1** (no plural) what you think about somebody or something: *I have a high regard for his work* (= I think it is very good). **2** (no plural) care: *She shows no regard for other people's feelings.* **3 regards** (plural) kind wishes: *Please give my regards to your parents.*

reggae /ˈregeɪ/ *noun* (no plural) a type of West Indian music: *Bob Marley was a famous reggae singer.*

regiment /ˈredʒɪmənt/ *noun* a group of soldiers in an army

region /ˈri:dʒən/ *noun* a part of a country or of the world: *There will be rain in northern regions today.*

regional /ˈri:dʒənl/ *adjective* of a certain region

register[1] /ˈredʒɪstə(r)/ *noun* a list of names: *The teacher keeps a register of* *all the students in the class.*

register² /ˈredʒɪstə(r)/ *verb* (**registers**, **registering**, **registered** /ˈredʒɪstəd/)
1 put a name on a list: *I would like to register for the English course.* **2** show a number or amount: *The thermometer registered 30°C.*

registration /ˌredʒɪˈstreɪʃn/ *noun* (no plural) putting a name on a list: *registration of births, marriages and deaths*

registration number /redʒɪˈstreɪʃn nʌmbə(r)/ *noun* the numbers and letters on the front and back of a car, etc

regret /rɪˈgret/ *verb* (**regrets**, **regretting**, **regretted**) feel sorry about something that you did: *He regrets selling his car.* ○ *I don't regret what I said to her.*

regret *noun*: *I don't have any regrets about leaving my job.*

regular /ˈregjələ(r)/ *adjective* **1** that happens again and again with the same amount of space or time in between: *We have regular meetings every Monday morning.* ○ *regular breathing* **2** who goes somewhere or does something often: *I've never seen him before – he's not one of my regular customers.* **3** usual: *Who is your regular doctor?* **4** A word that is regular has the usual verb forms or plural: *'Work' is a regular verb.* ☞ Look at **irregular**.

regularly *adverb*: *We meet regularly every Friday.*

regulation /ˌregjuˈleɪʃn/ *noun* something that controls what people do; a rule or law: *You can't smoke here – it's against fire regulations.*

rehearse /rɪˈhɜːs/ *verb* (**rehearses**, **rehearsing**, **rehearsed** /rɪˈhɜːst/) do or say something again and again before you do it in front of other people: *We are rehearsing for the concert.*

rehearsal /rɪˈhɜːsl/ *noun* a time when you rehearse: *There's a rehearsal for the play tonight.*

reign /reɪn/ *noun* a time when a king or queen rules a country: *The reign of Haile Selassie began in 1930.*

reign *verb* (**reigns**, **reigning**, **reigned** /reɪnd/) be king or queen of a country: *Emperor Haile Selassie reigned until 1974.*

rein /reɪn/ *noun* a long thin piece of leather that a horse wears on its head so that a rider can control it

reject /rɪˈdʒekt/ *verb* (**rejects**, **rejecting**, **rejected**) say that you do not want somebody or something: *He rejected my offer of help.*

related /rɪˈleɪtɪd/ *adjective* in the same family; connected: *'Are those two boys related?' 'Yes, they're brothers.'*

relation /rɪˈleɪʃn/ *noun* **1** a person in your family **2** a connection between two things: *There is no relation between the size of the countries and the number of people who live there.*

relationship /rɪˈleɪʃnʃɪp/ *noun* how people, things or ideas are connected to each other; feelings between people: *I have a good relationship with my parents.* ○ *The book is about the relationship between an Indian boy and an English girl.*

relative /ˈrelətɪv/ *noun* a person in your family

relatively /ˈrelətɪvli/ *adverb* quite: *This room is relatively small.*

relax /rɪˈlæks/ *verb* (**relaxes**, **relaxing**, **relaxed** /rɪˈlækst/) **1** rest and be calm; become less worried or angry: *After a hard day at work I spent the evening relaxing in front of the television.* **2** become less tight or make something become less tight: *Let your body relax.*

relaxation /ˌriːlækˈseɪʃn/ *noun* (no plural) *You need more rest and relaxation.*

relaxed *adjective*: *She felt relaxed after her holiday.*

release /rɪˈliːs/ *verb* (**release**, **releasing**, **released** /rɪˈliːst/) let a person or an animal go free: *We opened the cage and released the bird.*

release *noun*: *the release of the prisoners*

relevant /ˈreləvənt/ *adjective* connected with what you are talking or writing about; important: *We need somebody who can do the job well – your age is not relevant.* ✪ opposite: **irrelevant**

reliable /rɪˈlaɪəbl/ *adjective* that you can trust: *My car is very reliable.* ○ *He is a reliable person.* ✪ opposite: **unreliable**

relied *form of* **rely**

relief /rɪˈliːf/ *noun* (no plural) **1** what you feel when pain or worry stops: *It was a great relief to know she was safe.* **2** food or money for people who need it: *Many countries sent relief to the people who had lost their homes in the floods.*

relies *form of* **rely**

relieved /rɪˈliːvd/ *adjective* pleased because a problem or danger has gone away: *I was relieved to hear that you weren't hurt in the accident.*

religion /rɪˈlɪdʒən/ *noun* **1** (no plural) believing in a god **2** (*plural* **religions**) one of the ways of believing in a god, for example Christianity, Islam or Buddhism

religious /rɪˈlɪdʒəs/ *adjective* **1** of religion: *a religious leader* **2** with a strong belief in a religion: *I'm not very religious.*

reluctant /rɪˈlʌktənt/ *adjective* If you are reluctant to do something, you do not want to do it: *Ian was reluctant to give me the money.*

reluctance /rɪˈlʌktəns/ *noun* (no plural) being reluctant: *He agreed, but with great reluctance.*

reluctantly *adverb*: *Ann reluctantly agreed to help with the housework.*

rely /rɪˈlaɪ/ *verb* (**relies**, **relying**, **relied** /rɪˈlaɪd/, **has relied**) **rely on somebody** or **something 1** feel sure that somebody or something will do what they should do: *You can rely on him to help you.* **2** need somebody or something: *My parents rely on me for money.* ✪ The adjective is **reliable**.

remain /rɪˈmeɪn/ *verb* (**remains**, **remaining**, **remained** /rɪˈmeɪnd/) **1** stay after other people or things have gone: *After the fire, very little remained of the house.* **2** stay in the same way; not change: *I asked her a question but she remained silent.*

remains /rɪˈmeɪnz/ *noun* (plural) what is left when most of something has gone: *the remains of an old church*

remark /rɪˈmɑːk/ *verb* (**remarks**, **remarking**, **remarked** /rɪˈmɑːkt/) say something: *'It's cold today,' he remarked.*

remark *noun* something that you say: *He made a remark about the food.*

remarkable /rɪˈmɑːkəbl/ *adjective* unusual and surprising in a good way: *a remarkable discovery*

remarkably /rɪˈmɑːkəbli/ *adverb*: *She speaks French remarkably well.*

remedy /ˈremədi/ *noun* (*plural* **remedies**) a way of making something better: *a remedy for toothache*

remember /rɪˈmembə(r)/ *verb* (**remembers**, **remembering**, **remembered** /rɪˈmembəd/) keep something in your mind or bring something back into your mind; not forget something: *Can you remember his name?* ○ *I remember posting the letter.* ○ *Did you remember to go to the bank?*

remind /rɪˈmaɪnd/ *verb* (**reminds**, **reminding**, **reminded**) make somebody remember somebody or something: *This song reminds me of when I was little.* ○ *I reminded her to buy some bread.*

reminder *noun* something that makes you remember

remote /rɪˈməʊt/ *adjective* (**remoter**, **remotest**) far from other places: *They live in a remote village in the mountains.*

remove /rɪˈmuːv/ *verb* (**removes**, **removing**, **removed** /rɪˈmuːvd/) take somebody or something away or off: *The statue was removed from the museum.* ○ *Please remove your shoes before entering the temple.* ✪ It is more usual to use other words, for example **take out** or **take off**.

removal /rɪˈmuːvl/ *noun* removing something: *Vegetation prevents the removal of topsoil by rain.*

renew /rɪˈnjuː/ *verb* (**renews**, **renewing**, **renewed** /rɪˈnjuːd/) get or give something new in the place of something old: *My passport expires soon so I'll have to go and renew it.*

rent /rent/ *verb* (**rents**, **renting**, **rented**) **1** pay to live in a place or to use something that belongs to another person: *I rent a flat in the centre of town.* **2** let somebody live in a place or use something that belongs to you, if they pay you: *Mrs Kamau rents out rooms to students.*

rent *noun* the money that you pay to live in a place or to use something that belongs to another person: *My rent* *has gone up by 1000 shillings a month.*

repair /rɪˈpeə(r)/ *verb* (**repairs**, **repairing**, **repaired** /rɪˈpeəd/) make something that is broken good again; mend something: *Can you repair my bike?*

repair *noun: The shop is closed for repairs to the roof.*

repay /riˈpeɪ/ *verb* (**repays**, **repaying**, **repaid** /riˈpeɪd/, **has repaid**) **1** pay back money to somebody **2** do something for somebody to show your thanks: *How can I repay you for all your help?*

repayment /riˈpeɪmənt/ *noun* paying somebody back: *monthly repayments*

repeat /rɪˈpiːt/ *verb* (**repeats**, **repeating**, **repeated**) **1** say or do something again: *He didn't hear my question, so I repeated it.* **2** say what another person has said: *Repeat this sentence after me.*

repeat *noun* something that is done again: *There are a lot of repeats of old programmes on TV.*

repetition /ˌrepəˈtɪʃn/ *noun* saying or doing something again: *This book is boring – it's full of repetition.*

replace /rɪˈpleɪs/ *verb* (**replaces**, **replacing**, **replaced** /rɪˈpleɪst/) **1** put something back in the right place: *Please replace the books on the shelf when you have finished with them.* **2** take the place of somebody or something: *When Maldini was injured, Baggio replaced him as captain of the team.* **3** put a new or different person or thing in the place of another: *The watch was broken so the shop replaced it with a new one.*

replacement /rɪˈpleɪsmənt/ *noun* **1** (*plural* **replacements**) a new or different person or thing that takes the place of another: *Sue is leaving the company next month so we need to find a replacement.* **2** (no plural) putting a new or different person or thing in the place of another

reply /rɪˈplaɪ/ *verb* (**replies**, **replying**, **replied** /rɪˈplaɪd/, **has replied**) answer: *I have written to Jane but she hasn't replied.*

reply *noun* (*plural* **replies**) an answer: *Have you had a reply to your letter?* **in reply** as an answer: *What did you say in reply to his question?*

report[1] /rɪˈpɔːt/ *verb* (**reports**, **reporting**, **reported**) tell or write about something that has happened: *We reported the accident to the police.*

report[2] /rɪˈpɔːt/ *noun* **1** something that somebody says or writes about something that has happened: *Did you read the newspaper reports about the earthquake?* **2** something that teachers write about a student's work

reporter /rɪˈpɔːtə(r)/ *noun* a person who writes in a newspaper or speaks on the radio or television about things that have happened

represent /ˌreprɪˈzent/ *verb* (**represents**, **representing**, **represented**) **1** be a sign for something: *The yellow lines on the map represent roads.* **2** speak or do something for another person or other people: *Gebreselassie will represent Ethiopia at the Olympic Games.*

representative /ˌreprɪˈzentətɪv/ *noun* a person who speaks or does something for a group of people: *There were representatives from every country in Europe at the meeting.*

reproduce /ˌriːprəˈdjuːs/ *verb* (**reproduces**, **reproducing**, **reproduced** /ˌriːprəˈdjuːst/) When animals or plants reproduce, they have young ones.

reproduction /ˌriːprəˈdʌkʃn/ *noun* (no plural) *We are studying plant reproduction at school.*

reptile /ˈreptaɪl/ *noun* an animal with cold blood, that lays eggs. Snakes, lizards, crocodiles and tortoises are reptiles.

republic /rɪˈpʌblɪk/ *noun* a country where people choose the government and the leader (the **president**): *the Republic of South Africa*

reputation /ˌrepjuˈteɪʃn/ *noun* what people think or say about somebody or something: *This school has a good reputation.*

request /rɪˈkwest/ *verb* (**requests**, **requesting**, **requested**) ask for something: *Passengers are requested not to smoke* (= a notice in a bus). ✪ It is more usual to say **ask (for)**.

request *noun* asking for something: *They made a request for money.*

require /rɪˈkwaɪə(r)/ *verb* (**requires, requiring, required** /rɪˈkwaɪəd/) need something: *Do you require anything else?* **❸ Need** is the word that we usually use.

requirement /rɪˈkwaɪəmənt/ *noun* something that you need

rescue /ˈreskjuː/ *verb* (**rescues, rescuing, rescued**) save somebody or something from danger: *She rescued the child when he fell in the river.*

rescue *noun* **come** or **go to somebody's rescue** try to help somebody: *The police came to his rescue.*

research /rɪˈsɜːtʃ/ *noun* (no plural) studying something carefully to find out more about it: *scientific research*

research *verb* (**researches, researching, researched** /rɪˈsɜːtʃt/) study something carefully to find out more about it: *Scientists are researching the causes of the disease.*

resemble /rɪˈzembl/ *verb* (**resembles, resembling, resembled** /rɪˈzembld/) look like somebody or something: *Mary resembles her mother.* **❸** It is more usual to say **look like**.

resemblance /rɪˈzembləns/ *noun*: *There's no resemblance between my two brothers.*

resent /rɪˈzent/ *verb* (**resents, resenting, resented**) feel angry about something because it is not fair: *I resent Alan getting the job. He got it because he's the manager's son!*

resentment /rɪˈzentmənt/ *noun* (no plural) a feeling of anger about something that is not fair

reserve[1] /rɪˈzɜːv/ *verb* (**reserves, reserving, reserved** /rɪˈzɜːvd/) keep something for a special reason or to use later; ask somebody to keep something for you: *I would like to reserve a single room for tomorrow night, please.* ○ *Those seats are reserved.*

reservation /ˌrezəˈveɪʃn/ *noun* a room, seat or another thing that you have reserved: *You can't eat at that restaurant without a reservation.*

reserve[2] /rɪˈzɜːv/ *noun* **1** something that you keep to use later: *reserves of food* **2** a person who will play in a game if another person cannot play **in reserve** for using later: *Don't spend all the money – keep some in reserve.*

reservoir /ˈrezəvwɑː(r)/ *noun* a big lake where a town or city keeps water to use later

residence /ˈrezɪdəns/ *noun* **1** (no plural) living in a place: *Some birds have taken up residence in* (= started to live in) *our roof.* **2** (*plural* **residences**) the place where an important or famous person lives: *the Prime Minister's residence*

resident /ˈrezɪdənt/ *noun* a person who lives in a place

resign /rɪˈzaɪn/ *verb* (**resigns, resigning, resigned** /rɪˈzaɪnd/) leave your job: *The director has resigned.* **resign yourself to something** accept something that you do not like: *There were a lot of people at the doctor's so John resigned himself to a long wait.*

resignation /ˌrezɪɡˈneɪʃn/ *noun* saying that you want to leave your job **hand in your resignation** tell the person you work for that you are going to leave your job

resist /rɪˈzɪst/ *verb* (**resists, resisting, resisted**) **1** fight against somebody or something; try to stop somebody or something: *If he has a gun, don't try to resist.* **2** refuse to do or have something that you want to do or have: *I can't resist sweets.*

resistance /rɪˈzɪstəns/ *noun* (no plural) resisting somebody or something: *There was a lot of resistance to the plan to build a new dam.*

resolution /ˌrezəˈluːʃn/ *noun* something that you decide to do: *Julie made a resolution to stop smoking.*

resort /rɪˈzɔːt/ *noun* a place where a lot of people go on holiday: *Malindi is a popular tourist resort.* **a last resort** the only person or thing left that can help: *Nobody else will lend me the money, so I am asking you as a last resort.*

resources /rɪˈsɔːsɪz/ *noun* (plural) things that a person or a country has and can use: *Oil is one of our most important natural resources.*

respect[1] /rɪ'spekt/ *noun* (no plural)
1 thinking that somebody is very good or clever: *I have a lot of respect for your father.* **2** being polite to somebody: *You should treat old people with respect.*

respect[2] /rɪ'spekt/ *verb* (**respects**, **respecting**, **respected**) think that somebody is good or clever: *The students respect their teacher.*

respectable /rɪ'spektəbl/ *adjective* If a person or thing is respectable, people think he/she/it is good or correct: *She comes from a respectable family.*

respond /rɪ'spɒnd/ *verb* (**responds**, **responding**, **responded**) do or say something to answer somebody or something: *I said 'hello' and he responded by smiling.*

response /rɪ'spɒns/ *noun* an answer to somebody or something: *I wrote to them but I've had no response.*

responsible /rɪ'spɒnsəbl/ *adjective* **1** If you are responsible for somebody or something, you must look after them: *The driver is responsible for the lives of the people on the bus.* **2** A responsible person is somebody that you can trust: *We need a responsible person to look after our son.* ✪ opposite: **irresponsible**.
be responsible for something be the person who made something bad happen: *Who was responsible for the accident?*

responsibility /rɪ,spɒnsə'bɪləti/ *noun* **1** (no plural) being responsible for somebody or something; having to look after somebody or something: *She has responsibility for the whole department.* **2** (*plural* **responsibilities**) something that you must do; somebody or something that you must look after: *Fixing the engine is my brother's responsibility.*

rest[1] /rest/ *verb* (**rests**, **resting**, **rested**) **1** sleep or be still and quiet: *We worked all morning and then rested for an hour before starting work again.* **2** be on something; put something on or against another thing: *His arms were resting on the table.*

rest[2] /rest/ *noun* sleeping or being still and quiet: *After walking for an hour, we stopped for a rest.*

rest[3] /rest/ *noun* (no plural) **the rest**
1 what is there when a part has gone: *If you don't want the rest, I'll eat it.* ○ *I liked the beginning, but the rest of the film wasn't very good.* **2** the other people or things: *My sisters prepared the food and the rest of us went for a walk.*

restaurant /'restrɒnt/ *noun* a place where you buy a meal and eat it

restless /'restləs/ *adjective* not able to be still: *The children always get restless on long journeys.*

restore /rɪ'stɔː(r)/ *verb* (**restores**, **restoring**, **restored** /rɪ'stɔːd/) make something as good as it was before: *The old palace was restored.*

restrain /rɪ'streɪn/ *verb* (**restrains**, **restraining**, **restrained** /rɪ'streɪnd/) stop somebody or something from doing something; control somebody or something: *I couldn't restrain my anger.*

restrict /rɪ'strɪkt/ *verb* (**restricts**, **restricting**, **restricted**) allow only a certain amount, size, sort, etc: *The government has decided to restrict the number of immigrants entering the country.*

restriction /rɪ'strɪkʃn/ *noun* a rule to control somebody or something: *There are a lot of parking restrictions in the city centre.*

result /rɪ'zʌlt/ *noun* **1** what happens because something else has happened: *The accident was a result of bad driving.* **2** the score or mark at the end of a game, competition or exam: *football results* ○ *When will you know your exam results?* **as a result** because of something: *I got up late, and as a result I missed the train.*

result *verb* (**results**, **resulting**, **resulted**) **result in something** make something happen: *The accident resulted in the death of two drivers.*

retire /rɪ'taɪə(r)/ *verb* (**retires**, **retiring**, **retired** /rɪ'taɪəd/) stop working because you are a certain age: *My grandfather retired when he was 65.*

retired *adjective*: *a retired teacher*

retirement /rɪ'taɪəmənt/ *noun* (no plural) the time when a person stops working because he/she is a certain age: *What is the age of retirement in your country?*

retreat /rɪˈtriːt/ *verb* (**retreats**, **retreating**, **retreated**) move back or away from somebody or something, for example because you have lost a fight: *The enemy is retreating.*

retreat *noun* retreating: *The army is now in retreat.*

return[1] /rɪˈtɜːn/ *verb* (**returns**, **returning**, **returned** /rɪˈtɜːnd/) **1** come or go back to a place: *They returned from Kabale last week.* **2** give, put, send or take something back: *Will you return this book to the library?*

return[2] /rɪˈtɜːn/ *noun* **1** (no plural) coming or going back to a place: *A big crowd welcomed the team at the airport on their return home.* **2** (no plural) giving, putting, sending or taking something back: *the return of the stolen money* **3** (plural **returns**), **return ticket** a ticket to travel to a place and back again: *A return to London, please.* ➡ Look at **single**. **in return** If you do something in return for something else, you do it because somebody has helped you or given you something: *We have bought you a present in return for all your help.*

returns /rɪˈtɜːnz/ *noun* (plural) **many happy returns** words that you say on somebody's birthday

reunion /ˌriːˈjuːniən/ *noun* a meeting of people who have not seen each other for a long time: *We had a family reunion on my grandfather's birthday.*

reveal /rɪˈviːl/ *verb* (**reveals**, **revealing**, **revealed** /rɪˈviːld/) tell something that was a secret or show something that was hidden: *She refused to reveal any names to the police.*

revenge /rɪˈvendʒ/ *noun* (no plural) **get, have** or **take your revenge on somebody** do something bad to somebody who has done something bad to you: *He says he will take his revenge on the judge who sent him to prison.*

reverse[1] /rɪˈvɜːs/ *verb* (**reverses**, **reversing**, **reversed** /rɪˈvɜːst/) **1** make a car, etc go backwards: *I reversed the car into the garage.* **2** turn something the other way round: *Writing is reversed in a mirror.* **reverse the charges** make a telephone call that the person you are telephoning will pay for

reverse[2] /rɪˈvɜːs/ *noun* (no plural) the opposite thing or way **in reverse** in the opposite way; starting at the end and finishing at the beginning: *I wrote the story in reverse – I thought of the ending first and worked backwards.*

review /rɪˈvjuː/ *noun* **1** a piece of writing in a newspaper or magazine that says what somebody thinks about a book, film, play, etc: *The film got very good reviews.* **2** thinking again about something that happened before: *a review of all the important events of the year*

review *verb* (**reviews**, **reviewing**, **reviewed** /rɪˈvjuːd/) **1** write a review about a book, film, play, etc **2** think again about something that happened before: *Let's review what we have learned in this lesson.*

revise /rɪˈvaɪz/ *verb* (**revises**, **revising**, **revised** /rɪˈvaɪzd/) **1** study again something that you have learnt, before an exam: *I'm revising for the Geography test.* **2** change something to make it better or more correct: *The book was revised.*

revision /rɪˈvɪʒn/ *noun* (no plural) studying again something that you have learnt, before an exam: *I haven't done any revision for the maths exam.*

revive /rɪˈvaɪv/ *verb* (**revives**, **reviving**, **revived** /rɪˈvaɪvd/) become or make somebody or something well or strong again: *They pulled the boy out of the river and tried to revive him, but he was already dead.*

revolt /rɪˈvəʊlt/ *verb* (**revolts**, **revolting**, **revolted**) fight against the people in control: *The army is revolting against the government.*

revolt *noun* when people fight against the people in control

revolting /rɪˈvəʊltɪŋ/ *adjective* horrible; so bad that it makes you feel sick: *a revolting smell*

revolution /ˌrevəˈluːʃn/ *noun* **1** a fight by people against their government, to put a new government in its place: *The French Revolution was in 1789.* **2** a big change in the way of doing things: *the Industrial Revolution*

reward /rɪˈwɔːd/ *noun* a present or money that you give to thank somebody for something that they have done: *The police are offering a 50 000 shilling reward to anyone who finds the killer.*

reward *verb* (**rewards**, **rewarding**, **rewarded**) give a reward to somebody: *James's parents bought him a bike to reward him for passing his exam.*

rewind /riːˈwaɪnd/ *verb* (**rewinds**, **rewinding**, **rewound** /riːˈwaʊnd/, **has rewound**) make a tape (in a **tape recorder** or **video recorder**) go backwards: *Rewind the tape and play it again.*

rhinoceros

rhinoceros /raɪˈnɒsərəs/ *noun* (*plural* **rhinoceros** or **rhinoceroses**) a big wild animal with thick skin and a horn on its nose. Rhinoceroses live in Africa and Asia. ✪ The short form is **rhino**.

rhyme[1] /raɪm/ *noun* **1** when two words have the same sound, for example 'bell' and 'well': *Her poetry is written in rhyme.* **2** a short piece of writing where the lines end with the same sounds

rhyme[2] /raɪm/ *verb* (**rhymes**, **rhyming**, **rhymed** /raɪmd/) **1** have the same sound as another word: *'Moon' rhymes with 'spoon' and 'chair' rhymes with 'bear'.* **2** have lines that end with the same sounds: *This poem doesn't rhyme.*

rhythm /ˈrɪðəm/ *noun* a regular pattern of sounds that come again and again: *This music has a good rhythm.*

rib /rɪb/ *noun* one of the bones around your chest ☞ picture on page A4

ribbon /ˈrɪbən/ *noun* a long thin piece of pretty material for tying things: *She wore a ribbon in her hair.*

ribbon

rice /raɪs/ *noun* (no plural) white or brown seeds from a plant that grows in hot countries, that we use as food: *Would you like rice or potatoes with your chicken?*

rich /rɪtʃ/ *adjective* (**richer**, **richest**) **1** with a lot of money: *a rich family* ✪ opposite: **poor**. **2** with a lot of something: *Saudi Arabia is rich in oil.* **3** Food that is rich has a lot of fat or sugar in it: *a rich chocolate cake*

the rich *noun* (plural) people who have a lot of money

rid /rɪd/ *verb* **get rid of somebody** or **something** throw something away or become free of somebody or something: *I got rid of my old coat and bought a new one.* ○ *This dog is following me – I can't get rid of it.*

riddle /ˈrɪdl/ *noun* a question that has a clever or funny answer: *Here's a riddle: What has four legs but can't walk? The answer is a chair!*

ride /raɪd/ *verb* (**rides**, **riding**, **rode** /rəʊd/, **has ridden** /ˈrɪdn/) **1** sit on a horse or bicycle and control it as it moves: *My brother taught me to ride a bike.* ○ *I ride my bike to school.* **2** travel in a car, bus or train: *We rode in the back of the car.* ✪ When you control a car, bus or train, you **drive** it.

ride *noun* a journey on a horse or bicycle, or in a car, bus or train: *We went for a ride on our bikes.* ○ *a train ride*

rider *noun* a person who rides a horse or bicycle

riding *noun* (no plural) the sport of riding a horse

ridge /rɪdʒ/ *noun* a long thin part of something that is higher than the rest, for example along the top of hills or mountains: *We walked along the ridge looking down at the valley below.*

ridiculous /rɪˈdɪkjələs/ *adjective* so silly that it makes people laugh: *You can't play football with a coconut – that's ridiculous!*

rifle /ˈraɪfl/ *noun* a long gun that you hold against your shoulder when you fire it

right[1] /raɪt/ *adjective, adverb* opposite of left. Most people write with their right hand: *Turn right at the end of the street.*

right *noun* (no plural) *We live in the first house on the right.*

right² /raɪt/ *adjective* **1** correct or true: *That's not the right answer.* ○ *Are you Mr Kamotho?' 'Yes, that's right.'* **2** good; fair or what the law allows: *It's not right to leave young children alone in the house.* **3** best: *Is she the right person for the job?* ✪ opposite: **wrong**

right³ /raɪt/ *adverb* **1** correctly: *Have I spelt your name right?* ✪ opposite: **wrong. 2** exactly: *He was sitting right next to me.* **3** all the way: *Go right to the end of the road.* **4** immediately: *We left right after dinner.* **5** yes, I agree; yes, I will: *'I'll see you tomorrow.' 'Right.'* **6** You say 'right' to make somebody listen to you: *Are you ready? Right, let's go.* **right away** immediately; now: *Fetch the doctor right away!*

right⁴ /raɪt/ *noun* **1** (no plural) what is good or fair: *Young children have to learn the difference between right and wrong.* **2** (*plural* **rights**) what you are allowed to do, especially by law: *In Britain, everyone has the right to vote at 18.*

right angle /'raɪt æŋgl/ *noun* an angle of 90 degrees. A square has four right angles. ☞ picture on page A5

right-hand /'raɪt hænd/ *adjective* of or on the right: *The shop is on the right-hand side of the road.*

right-handed /ˌraɪt 'hændɪd/ *adjective* If you are right-handed, you use your right hand more easily than your left hand.

rightly /'raɪtli/ *adverb* correctly: *If I remember rightly, I arrived there on 15 June.*

rigid /'rɪdʒɪd/ *adjective* **1** hard and not easy to bend or move **2** not able to be changed; strict: *My school has very rigid rules.*

rim /rɪm/ *noun* the edge of something round: *the rim of a cup*

rind /raɪnd/ *noun* the thick hard skin of some fruits, or of bacon or cheese: *lemon rind*

ring¹ /rɪŋ/ *noun* **1** a circle of metal that you wear on your finger **2** a circle:

ring

Please stand in a ring. **3** a space with seats around it, for a circus or boxing match

ring² /rɪŋ/ *verb* (**rings**, **ringing**, **rang** /ræŋ/, **has rung** /rʌŋ/) **1** make a sound like a bell: *The telephone is ringing.* **2** press or move a bell so that it makes a sound: *We rang the bell again but nobody answered.* **3** telephone somebody: *I'll ring you on Sunday.* **ring somebody back** telephone somebody again: *I wasn't at my desk when Angela called, so I rang her back later.* **ring up** telephone somebody: *Your brother rang up while you were out.*

ring³ /rɪŋ/ *noun* the sound that a bell makes: *There was a ring at the door.* **give somebody a ring** telephone somebody: *I'll give you a ring later.*

rinse /rɪns/ *verb* (**rinses**, **rinsing**, **rinsed** /rɪnst/) wash something with water to take away dirt or soap: *Wash your hair and rinse it well.*

riot /'raɪət/ *noun* when a group of people fight and make a lot of noise and trouble: *There were riots in the streets after the football match.* **riot** *verb* (**riots**, **rioting**, **rioted**): *The prisoners are rioting.*

rip /rɪp/ *verb* (**rips**, **ripping**, **ripped** /rɪpt/) pull or tear quickly and roughly: *I ripped my shirt on a nail.* ○ *Joe ripped the letter open.* **rip up** tear something into small pieces: *She ripped the photo up.*

ripe /raɪp/ *adjective* (**riper**, **ripest**) Fruit that is ripe is ready to eat: *These melons aren't ripe – they're still hard.*

rise /raɪz/ *verb* (**rises**, **rising**, **rose** /rəʊz/, **has risen** /'rɪzn/) go up; become higher or more: *The sun rises in the east and sets* (= goes down) *in the west.* ○ *Prices are rising.* **rise** *noun* becoming higher or more: *a rise in the price of oil* ○ *a pay rise*

risk /rɪsk/ *noun* the possibility that something bad may happen; danger: *Do you think there's any risk of a landslide?* **at risk** in danger: *Children are at risk from this disease.* **take a risk** or **risks** do something when it is possible that something bad may happen because of it: *Don't take risks when you're driving.*

risk *verb* (**risks**, **risking**, **risked** /rɪskt/) **1** put somebody or something in danger: *He risked his life to save the child from the burning house.* **2** do something when there is a possibility that something bad may happen because of it: *If you don't work harder, you risk failing the exam.*

risky /ˈrɪski/ *adjective* (**riskier**, **riskiest**) dangerous

rival /ˈraɪvl/ *noun* a person who wants to do better than you or who is trying to take what you want: *John and Lucy are rivals for the manager's job.*

river /ˈrɪvə(r)/ *noun* a long wide line of water that flows into the sea: *the River Nile*

road /rəʊd/ *noun* the way from one place to another, where cars can go: *Is this the road to Nakuru?* ○ *The hotel is on Kamati Road.* **by road** in a car, bus, etc: *It's a long journey by road – the train is faster.*

roam /rəʊm/ *verb* (**roams**, **roaming**, **roamed** /rəʊmd/) walk or travel with no special plan: *Dogs were roaming the streets looking for food.*

roar /rɔː(r)/ *verb* (**roars**, **roaring**, **roared** /rɔːd/) make a loud deep sound: *The lion roared.* ○ *Everybody roared with laughter.*

roar *noun*: *the roar of an aeroplane's engines*

roast /rəʊst/ *verb* (**roasts**, **roasting**, **roasted**) cook or be cooked in an oven or over a fire: *Roast the chicken in a hot oven.*

roast *adjective*: *roast chicken*

rob /rɒb/ *verb* (**robs**, **robbing**, **robbed** /rɒbd/) take something that is not yours from a person or place: *They robbed a bank.* ☛ Note at **steal**.

robber *noun* a person who robs

robbery /ˈrɒbəri/ *noun* (*plural* **robberies**) taking something that is not yours from a bank, etc: *What time did the robbery take place?*

robot /ˈrəʊbɒt/ *noun* a machine that can work like a person: *This car was built by robots.*

rock[1] /rɒk/ *noun* **1** (no plural) the very hard stuff that is in the ground and in mountains **2** (*plural* **rocks**) a big piece of this: *The ship hit the rocks.*

rock[2] /rɒk/, **rock music** /ˈrɒk mjuːzɪk/ *noun* (no plural) a sort of modern music: *a rock concert*

rock[3] /rɒk/ *verb* (**rocks**, **rocking**, **rocked** /rɒkt/) move slowly backwards and forwards or from side to side; make somebody or something do this: *The boat was rocking gently on the lake.* ○ *I rocked the baby until she went to sleep.*

rocket /ˈrɒkɪt/ *noun* **1** an engine with long round sides that pushes a spacecraft up into space **2** a thing with long round sides that carries a bomb through the air **3** a **firework** that goes up into the air and then explodes

rocky /ˈrɒki/ *adjective* (**rockier**, **rockiest**) with a lot of rocks: *a rocky path*

rod /rɒd/ *noun* a thin straight piece of wood or metal: *a fishing-rod*

rode *form of* **ride**

role /rəʊl/ *noun* **1** the person you are in a play or film: *The role of the King was played by Bob Lewis.* **2** what a person does: *Your role is to tell other people what to do.*

roll

roll[1] /rəʊl/ *verb* (**rolls**, **rolling**, **rolled** /rəʊld/) **1** move along, turning over and over; make something go over and over: *The pencil rolled off the table on to the floor.* ○ *We rolled the rock down the path.* **2** move on wheels: *The car rolled down the hill.* **3** make something flat by moving something heavy on top of it: *Roll the dough into a large circle.* **roll over** turn your body a different way when you are lying down: *She rolled over.* **roll up** make something into a long round shape or the shape of a ball: *Can you help me to roll up this carpet?*

roll[2] /rəʊl/ *noun* something made into a long round shape by rolling it around itself many times:
a roll of material ○
a roll of film

roller-skate
/ˈrəʊlə skeɪt/ *noun*
a shoe with wheels
on the bottom, for

roller-skate

moving quickly on smooth ground

roller-skating *noun* (no plural) moving on roller-skates

Roman Catholic /ˌrəʊmən ˈkæθəlɪk/ *noun* a member of the Christian church that follows the Pope

romance /rəʊˈmæns/ *noun* **1** a time when two people are in love: *a romance between a doctor and a nurse* **2** a story about love: *She writes romances.*

romantic /rəʊˈmæntɪk/ *adjective* about love; full of feelings of love: *a romantic film*

roof /ruːf/ *noun* (*plural* **roofs**) the top of a building or car, that covers it

room /ruːm/ *noun* **1** (*plural* **rooms**) one of the spaces with walls round it in a building: *How many rooms are there in the hotel?* ○ *a classroom*

> ✪ A house or flat can have a **living-room** (or **sitting-room** or **lounge**), **bedrooms**, a **bathroom**, a **toilet**, a **kitchen**, a **hall** and perhaps a **dining-room**. **2** (no plural) space: *There's no room for you in the car.*

root /ruːt/ *noun* the part of a plant that is under the ground ☞ *picture at* **plant**

rope /rəʊp/ *noun* very thick strong string

rope

rose[1] *form of* **rise**

rose[2] /rəʊz/ *noun* a flower with a sweet smell. It grows on a bush that has sharp points (called **thorns**) on it.

rosy /ˈrəʊzi/ *adjective* (**rosier**, **rosiest**) pink: *rosy cheeks*

rot /rɒt/ *verb* (**rots**, **rotting**, **rotted**) become bad and soft, as things do when they die: *Nobody picked the mangoes so they rotted.*

rotate /rəʊˈteɪt/ *verb* (**rotates**, **rotating**, **rotated**) move in circles: *The earth rotates around the sun.*

rotten /ˈrɒtn/ *adjective* old and not fresh; bad: *These eggs are rotten – they smell horrible!*

rough /rʌf/ *adjective* (**rougher**, **roughest**) **1** not smooth or flat: *It was difficult to walk on the rough ground.* **2** not gentle or calm: *rough seas* **3** not

exactly correct; made or done quickly: *Can you give me a rough idea how much it will cost?* ○ *a rough drawing*

roughly /ˈrʌfli/ *adverb* **1** not gently: *He pushed me roughly away.* **2** about; not exactly: *The school will take roughly six months to build.*

round[1] /raʊnd/ *adjective* with the shape of a circle or a ball: *a round plate*

round[2] /raʊnd/ *adverb, preposition* **1** on or to all sides of something, often in a circle: *The earth moves round the sun.* ○ *We sat round the table.* ○ *He tied a rope round the goat's neck.* ☞ *picture on page A2.* **2** in the opposite direction or in another direction: *I turned round and went home again.* ○ *Turn your chair round.* **3** in or to different parts of a place: *I'd like to travel round the whole of Africa one day.* **4** from one person to another: *Pass these papers round the class.* **5** to somebody's house: *Come round* (= to my house) *at eight o'clock.* **6** to or on the other side of something: *There's a bank just round the corner.* **go round** be enough for everybody: *Are there enough plates to go round?* **round about** nearly; not exactly: *It will cost round about 10 000 shillings.* **round and round** round many times: *The bird flew round and round the room.*

round[3] /raʊnd/ *noun* **1** a lot of visits, one after another, for example as part of your job: *The doctor started his round early, visiting every patient in the hospital.* **2** one part of a game or competition: *the third round of the boxing match*

roundabout

roundabout /ˈraʊndəbaʊt/ *noun* **1** a place where roads meet, where cars must drive round in a circle **2** a big round machine at a fair. It has model animals or cars on it that children can ride on as it turns.

round trip /ˌraʊnd ˈtrɪp/ *noun* a journey to a place and back again

roundworm /ˈraʊndwɜːm/ *noun* a kind of worm that lives inside the bodies of people and pigs

route /ruːt/ *noun* a way from one place to another: *What is the quickest route from Kisumu to Kitale?*

routine /ruːˈtiːn/ *noun* your usual way of doing things: *My morning routine is to get up at seven, have breakfast, then go to work.*

row[1] /rəʊ/ *noun* a line of people or things: *We sat in the front row of the class* (= the front line of seats). ○ *a row of houses* ➡ picture on page A15

row[2] /rəʊ/ *verb* (**rows**, **rowing**, **rowed** /rəʊd/) move a boat through water using long pieces of wood with flat ends (called **oars**): *We rowed across the lake.*

rowing-boat /ˈrəʊɪŋ bəʊt/ *noun* a small boat that you move through water using oars

rowing

oar
rowing-boat

row[3] /raʊ/ *noun* **1** (*plural* **rows**) a noisy talk between people who do not agree about something: *She had a row with her boyfriend.* **2** (no plural) loud noise: *The children are making a terrible row.*

royal /ˈrɔɪəl/ *adjective* of or about a king or queen: *the royal family*

royalty /ˈrɔɪəlti/ *noun* (no plural) kings, queens and their families

rub /rʌb/ *verb* (**rubs**, **rubbing**, **rubbed** /rʌbd/) move something backwards and forwards on another thing: *I rubbed my hands together to keep them warm.* ○ *The cat rubbed its head against my leg.* **rub out** take writing or marks off something by using a rubber or a cloth: *I rubbed the word out and wrote it again.*

rub *noun* (no plural) *Give your shoes a rub.*

rubber /ˈrʌbə(r)/ *noun* **1** (no plural) material that we use to make things like car tyres **2** (*plural* **rubbers**) a small piece of rubber that you use for taking away marks that you have made with a pencil

rubber band /ˌrʌbə(r) ˈbænd/ *noun* a thin circle of rubber that you use for holding things together

rubbish /ˈrʌbɪʃ/ *noun* (no plural) **1** things that you do not want any more: *old boxes, bottles and other rubbish* ○ *Throw this rubbish in the bin.* **2** something that is bad, stupid or wrong: *You're talking rubbish!*

rucksack /ˈrʌksæk/ *noun* a bag that you carry on your back, for example when you are walking or climbing

rudder /ˈrʌdə(r)/ *noun* a flat piece of wood or metal at the back of a boat or an aeroplane. It moves to make the boat or aeroplane go left or right.

rude /ruːd/ *adjective* (**ruder**, **rudest**) **1** not polite: *It's rude to walk away when someone is talking to you.* **2** about things like sex or using the toilet: *rude words*

rudely *adverb:* *'Shut up!' she said rudely.*

rug

rug /rʌg/ *noun* **1** a small piece of thick material that you put on the floor **2** a thick piece of material that you put round your body to keep you warm

rugby /ˈrʌgbi/ *noun* (no plural) a game like football for two teams of 13 or 15 players. In rugby, you can kick and carry the ball.

ruin /ˈruːɪn/ *verb* (**ruins**, **ruining**, **ruined** /ˈruːɪnd/) damage something badly so that it is no longer good; destroy something completely: *I spilled coffee on my jacket and ruined it.* ○ *The bad news ruined my day.*

ruin *noun* a building that has been badly damaged: *The old building is now a ruin.* **in ruins** badly damaged or destroyed: *The city was in ruins after the war.*

rule[1] /ruːl/ *noun* **1** (*plural* **rules**) something that tells you what you must or must not do: *It's against the school rules to smoke.* ○ *break the rules* (= do something that you should not do) **2** (no plural) government: *India was once under British rule.*

rule[2] /ru:l/ *verb* (**rules**, **ruling**, **ruled** /ru:ld/) control a country: *Queen Victoria ruled Britain for many years.*

ruler

ruler /'ru:lə(r)/ *noun* **1** a long piece of plastic, metal or wood that you use for drawing straight lines or for measuring things **2** a person who rules a country

rumble /'rʌmbl/ *verb* (**rumbles**, **rumbling**, **rumbled** /'rʌmbld/) make a long deep sound: *I'm so hungry that my stomach is rumbling.*

rumble *noun* (no plural) *the rumble of thunder*

rumour /'ru:mə(r)/ *noun* something that a lot of people are talking about that is perhaps not true: *There's a rumour that our teacher is leaving.*

run[1] /rʌn/ *verb* (**runs**, **running**, **ran** /ræn/, **has run**) **1** move very quickly on your legs: *I was late, so I ran to the bus-stop.* **2** go; make a journey: *The buses don't run on Sundays.* **3** control something and make it work: *Who runs the company?* **4** pass or go somewhere: *The road runs across the fields.* **5** flow: *The river runs into Lake Victoria.* **6** work: *The car had stopped but the engine was still running.* **7** move something somewhere: *He ran his fingers through his hair.* **run after somebody** or **something** try to catch somebody or something: *The children ran after the ball.* **run away** go quickly away from a place: *She ran away from home when she was 14.* **run out of something** have no more of something: *We've run out of coffee. Will you go and buy some?* **run over somebody** or **something** drive over somebody or something: *The dog was run over by a bus.*

run[2] /rʌn/ *noun* moving very quickly on your legs: *I go for a run every morning.*

rung[1] *form of* **ring**[2]

rung[2] /rʌŋ/ *noun* one of the steps of a ladder ☞ picture at **ladder**

runner /'rʌnə(r)/ *noun* a person who runs

runner-up /ˌrʌnər'ʌp/ *noun* (plural **runners-up** /ˌrʌnəz'ʌp/) a person or team that comes second in a race or competition

running[1] /'rʌnɪŋ/ *noun* (no plural) the sport of running: *running shoes*

running[2] /'rʌnɪŋ/ *adjective* one after another: *We won the competition for three years running.*

runway /'rʌnweɪ/ *noun* (plural **runways**) a long piece of ground where aeroplanes take off and land

rural /'rʊərəl/ *adjective* of the country, not the town: *The book is about life in rural Kenya.*

rush /rʌʃ/ *verb* (**rushes**, **rushing**, **rushed** /rʌʃt/) **1** go or come very quickly: *The children rushed out of school.* **2** do something quickly or make somebody do something quickly: *We rushed to finish the work on time.* **3** take somebody or something quickly to a place: *She was rushed to hospital.*

rush *noun* (no plural) **1** a sudden quick movement: *At the end of the film there was a rush for the exits.* **2** a need to move or do something very quickly: *I can't stop now – I'm in a rush.*

the rush hour /ðə 'rʌʃ aʊə(r)/ *noun* the time when a lot of people are going to or coming from work

rust /rʌst/ *noun* (no plural) red-brown stuff that you sometimes see on metal that has been wet

rust *verb* (**rusts**, **rusting**, **rusted**) become covered with rust: *My bike rusted because I left it out in the rain.*

rusty *adjective* (**rustier**, **rustiest**) covered with rust: *a rusty nail*

rustle /'rʌsl/ *verb* (**rustles**, **rustling**, **rustled** /'rʌsld/) make a sound like dry leaves moving together; make something make this sound: *Stop rustling your newspaper – I can't hear the radio!*

rustle *noun* (no plural) *the rustle of leaves*

Ss

sack[1] /sæk/ *noun* a big strong bag for carrying heavy things: *a sack of rice*

sack[2] /sæk/ *verb* (**sacks**, **sacking**, **sacked** /sækt/) say that somebody must leave their job: *The manager sacked her because she was always late.*

sack *noun* (no plural) **get the sack** lose your job **give somebody the sack** say that somebody must leave their job

sacred /ˈseɪkrɪd/ *adjective* with a special religious meaning

sacrifice /ˈsækrɪfaɪs/ *verb* (**sacrifices**, **sacrificing**, **sacrificed** /ˈsækrɪfaɪst/) **1** kill an animal as a present to a god: *They sacrificed a lamb.* **2** stop doing or having something important so that you can help somebody or to get something else

sacrifice *noun*: *They made a lot of sacrifices to pay for their son to go to university.*

sad /sæd/ *adjective* (**sadder**, **saddest**) **1** unhappy: *The children were very sad when their dog died.* ☛ picture on page A10 **2** that makes you feel unhappy: *a sad story*

sadly *adverb*: *She looked sadly at the empty house.*

sadness /ˈsædnəs/ *noun* (no plural) the feeling of being sad

saddle /ˈsædl/ *noun* a seat on a horse or bicycle ☛ picture at **bicycle**

safari /səˈfɑːri/ *noun* (*plural* **safaris**) **1** a journey to look at or hunt wild animals, usually in Africa **2** a journey, especially a long one **3** (in Kenya) (*also* **Safari Rally**) a race for cars that takes place every year

safe[1] /seɪf/ *adjective* (**safer**, **safest**) **1** not in danger; not hurt: *Don't go out alone at night – you won't be safe.* **2** not dangerous: *Is it safe to swim in this river?* ○ *Always keep medicines in a safe place.* **safe and sound** not hurt or broken: *The child was found safe and sound.*

safely *adverb*: *Write to your parents to*

tell them you have arrived safely.

safe[2] /seɪf/ *noun* a strong metal box with a lock where you keep money or things like jewellery

safety /ˈseɪfti/ *noun* (no plural) being safe: *He is worried about the safety of his children.*

safety belt /ˈseɪfti belt/ *noun* a long thin piece of material that you put round your body in a car or an aeroplane to keep you safe in an accident

safety pin /ˈseɪfti pɪn/ *noun* a pin that you use for joining things together. It has a cover over the point so that it is not dangerous.

safety pin

sag /sæg/ *verb* (**sags**, **sagging**, **sagged** /sægd/) bend or hang down: *The bed is very old and it sags in the middle.*

said *form of* **say**[1]

sail[1] /seɪl/ *noun* a big piece of cloth on a boat. The wind blows against the sail and moves the boat along.

sail

sail[2] /seɪl/ *verb* (**sails**, **sailing**, **sailed** /seɪld/) **1** travel on water: *The ship sailed along the coast.* **2** control a boat with sails: *The crew sailed the dhow from Zanzibar to India.*

sailing *noun* (no plural) the sport of controlling a boat with sails

sailor /ˈseɪlə(r)/ *noun* a person who works on a ship

saint /seɪnt/ *noun* a very good and holy person: *Saint Nicholas* ✪ You usually say /sənt/ before names. The short way of writing 'Saint' before names is **St**: *St George's church*

sake /seɪk/ *noun* **for the sake of somebody** or **something**, **for somebody's** or **something's sake** to help somebody or something; because of somebody or something: *Chris and Jackie stayed together for the sake of their children.* ✪ You use expressions like **for goodness' sake**, **for God's sake** and **for Heaven's sake** to show that you are angry.: *For goodness' sake, be quiet!*

salad /ˈsæləd/ *noun* a dish of cold, usually raw vegetables

salary /ˈsæləri/ *noun* (*plural* **salaries**) money that you receive every month for the work that you do

sale /seɪl/ *noun* **1** (no plural) selling something **2** (*plural* **sales**) a time when a shop sells things for less money than usual: *In the sale, everything is half-price.* **for sale** If something is for sale, its owner wants to sell it: *Is this house for sale?* **on sale** If something is on sale, you can buy it in shops: *His new book is on sale in most bookshops from today.*

salesman /ˈseɪlzmən/ *noun* (*plural* **salesmen** /ˈseɪlzmən/), **saleswoman** /ˈseɪlzwʊmən/ (*plural* **saleswomen**), **salesperson**/ˈseɪlzpɜːsn/ (*plural* **salespeople**) a person whose job is selling things

salt /sɔːlt/ *noun* (no plural) white stuff that comes from sea water and from the earth. We put it on food to make it taste better: *Add a little salt and pepper.*

salty *adjective* (**saltier**, **saltiest**) with salt in it: *Sea water is salty.*

salute /səˈluːt/ *verb* (**salutes**, **saluting**, **saluted**) make the special sign that soldiers make, by lifting your hand to your head: *The soldiers saluted as the President walked past.*

salute *noun*: *The soldier gave a salute.*

same /seɪm/ *adjective* **the same** not different; not another: *My sister and I like the same kind of music.* ○ *I've lived in the same town all my life.* ○ *He went to the same school as me.*

same *pronoun* **all** or **just the same** anyway: *I understand why you're angry. All the same, I think you should say sorry.* **same to you** words that

you use for saying to somebody what they have said to you: *'Good luck in the exam.' 'Same to you.'* **the same** not a different person or thing: *Do these two words mean the same?* ○ *Your shoes are the same as mine.*

sample /ˈsɑːmpl/ *noun* a small amount of something that shows what the rest is like: *The shop was giving away free samples of shampoo.* ○ *The doctor took a blood sample for analysis.*

sand /sænd/ *noun* (no plural) powder made of very small pieces of rock, that you find next to the sea and in deserts

sandy *adjective* (**sandier**, **sandiest**) with sand: *a sandy beach*

sandal /ˈsændl/ *noun* a light open shoe

sandals

sane /seɪn/ *adjective* (**saner**, **sanest**) with a normal healthy mind; not mad ✪ opposite: **insane**

sang *form of* **sing**

sank *form of* **sink**²

sarcastic /sɑːˈkæstɪk/ *adjective* If you are sarcastic, you say the opposite of what you mean, in an unkind way.

sardine /sɑːˈdiːn/ *noun* a very small fish that you can eat

sari /ˈsɑːri/ *noun* (*plural* **saris**) a long piece of material that Indian women wear around their bodies as a dress

sat *form of* **sit**

satchel /ˈsætʃəl/ *noun* a bag that children use for carrying books to and from school

satellite /ˈsætəlaɪt/ *noun* **1** a thing in space that moves round a planet: *The moon is a satellite of the earth.* **2** a thing that people have sent into space. Satellites travel round the earth and send back pictures or television and radio signals: *satellite television*

satin /ˈsætɪn/ *noun* (no plural) very shiny smooth cloth

satisfaction /ˌsætɪsˈfækʃn/ *noun* (no plural) being pleased with what you or other people have done: *She finished painting the picture and looked at it with satisfaction.*

satisfactory /ˌsætɪsˈfæktəri/ *adjective*

good enough, but not very good: *Her work is not satisfactory.* ✪ opposite: **unsatisfactory**

satisfy /ˈsætɪsfaɪ/ *verb* (**satisfies**, **satisfying**, **satisfied** /ˈsætɪsfaɪd/, **has satisfied**) give somebody what they want or need; be good enough to make somebody pleased: *Nothing he does satisfies his father.*

satisfied *adjective* pleased because you have had or done what you wanted: *The teacher was not satisfied with my work.*

satisfying *adjective* Something that is satisfying makes you pleased because it is what you want: *a satisfying result*

Saturday /ˈsætədeɪ/ *noun* the seventh day of the week, next after Friday

sauce /sɔːs/ *noun* a thick liquid that you eat on or with other food: *tomato sauce*

saucepan
/ˈsɔːspən/ *noun* a round metal container for cooking

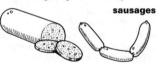
saucepan

saucer /ˈsɔːsə(r)/
noun a small round plate that you put under a cup ➙ picture at **cup**

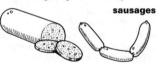
sausages

sausage /ˈsɒsɪdʒ/ *noun* meat that is cut into very small pieces and put inside a long, thin skin

savage /ˈsævɪdʒ/ *adjective* wild or fierce: *a savage attack by a large dog*

savanna, **savannah** /səˈvænə/ *noun* (no plural) dry land with a little grass and a few or no trees

save /seɪv/ *verb* (**saves**, **saving**, **saved** /seɪvd/) **1** take somebody or something away from danger: *He saved me from the fire.* ○ *The doctor saved her life.* **2** keep something, especially money, to use later: *I've saved enough money to buy a car.* ○ *Save some of the meat for tomorrow.* **3** use less of something: *She saves money by making her own clothes.* **4** stop somebody from scoring a goal, for example in football **save up for**

something keep money to buy something later: *I'm saving up for a new bike.*

savings /ˈseɪvɪŋz/ *noun* (plural) money that you are keeping to use later: *I keep my savings in the bank.*

saw

saw[1] *form of* **see**

saw[2] /sɔː/ *noun* a metal tool for cutting wood

saw *verb* (**saws**, **sawing**, **sawed** /sɔːd/, **has sawn** /sɔːn/) *She sawed a branch off the tree.*

sawdust /ˈsɔːdʌst/ *noun* (no plural) powder that falls when you saw wood

saxophone
/ˈsæksəfəʊn/ *noun* a musical instrument made of metal that you play by blowing into it

saxophone

---

say or **tell**?

Say and **tell** are not used in the same way. Look at these sentences:

*Jo **said** 'I'm ready.'*
*Jo **said** (that) she was ready.*
*Jo **said** to me that she was ready.*
*Jo **told** me (that) she was ready.*
*Jo **told** me to close the door.*

---

say[1] /seɪ/ *verb* (**says** /sez/, **saying**, **said** /sed/, **has said**) **1** make words with your mouth: *You say 'please' when you ask for something.* ○ *'This is my room,' he said.* ○ *She said that she was cold.* **2** give information: *The notice on the door said 'Private'.* ○ *The clock says half past three.* **that is to say** what I mean is... :*I'll see you in a week, that's to say next Monday.*

say[2] /seɪ/ *noun* **have a say** have the right to help decide something: *I would like to have a say in what we do with the money.*

saying /ˈseɪɪŋ/ *noun* a sentence that people often say, that gives advice about something: *'Look before you leap'* is an old saying.

scab /skæb/ noun a hard covering that grows over your skin where it is cut or broken

scaffolding /'skæfəldɪŋ/ noun (no plural) metal bars and pieces of wood joined together, where people like painters and builders can stand when they are working on high parts of a building

scald /skɔːld/ verb (scalds, scalding, scalded) burn somebody or something with very hot liquid

scale /skeɪl/ noun 1 a set of marks on something for measuring: *This ruler has one scale in centimetres and one scale in inches.* 2 how distances are shown on a map: *This map has a scale of one centimetre to ten kilometres.* 3 one of the flat hard things that cover the body of animals like fish and snakes

scales

scales /skeɪlz/ noun (plural) a machine for showing how heavy people or things are

scalp /skælp/ noun the skin on the top of your head, under your hair

scan /skæn/ verb (scans, scanning, scanned /skænd/) 1 look carefully because you are trying to find something: *They scanned the sea, looking for a boat.* 2 read something quickly: *Jane scanned the list until she found her name.*

scanner noun a machine that gives a picture of the inside of something. Doctors use one kind of scanner to look inside people's bodies.

scandal /'skændl/ noun 1 (plural scandals) something that makes a lot of people talk about it, perhaps in an angry way: *There was a big scandal when the referee admitted accepting money from the team.* 2 (no plural) unkind talk about somebody that gives

you a bad idea of them

scar /skɑː(r)/ noun a mark on your skin, that an old cut has left

scar verb (scars, scarring, scarred /skɑːd/) make a scar on skin: *His face was badly scarred by the accident.*

scarce /skeəs/ adjective (scarcer, scarcest) difficult to find; not enough: *Water is scarce in desert regions.*

scarcely /'skeəsli/ adverb almost not; only just: *He was so frightened that he could scarcely speak.*

scare /skeə(r)/ verb (scares, scaring, scared /skeəd/) make somebody frightened: *That noise scared me!*

scare noun a feeling of being frightened: *You gave me a scare!*

scared adjective frightened: *Martha is scared of the dark.*

scarf /skɑːf/ noun (plural scarves /skɑːvz/) a piece of material that you wear around your neck or head

scarlet /'skɑːlət/ adjective with a bright red colour

scatter /'skætə(r)/ verb (scatters, scattering, scattered /'skætəd/) 1 move quickly in different directions: *The crowd scattered when the lorry came towards them.* 2 throw things so that they fall in a lot of different places: *She scattered the seeds on the soil and covered them.*

scene /siːn/ noun 1 a place where something happened: *The police arrived at the scene of the crime.* 2 what you see in a place; a view: *He painted scenes of life in the countryside.* 3 part of a play or film: *Act 1, Scene 2 of 'Hamlet'*

scenery /'siːnəri/ noun (no plural) 1 the things like mountains, rivers and forests that you see around you in the countryside: *What beautiful scenery!* 2 things on the stage of a theatre that make it look like a real place

scent /sent/ noun 1 (plural scents) a smell: *This flower has no scent.* 2 (no plural) a liquid with a nice smell, that you put on your body: *a bottle of scent*

scented adjective with a nice smell: *scented soap*

schedule /'ʃedjuːl/ noun a plan or list of times when things will happen or be done: *I've got a busy schedule next week.*

behind schedule late: *We're behind schedule with the work.* **on schedule** with everything happening at the right time: *We are on schedule to finish the work in May.*

scheme /skiːm/ *noun* a plan: *a scheme to build more houses*

scholar /ˈskɒlə(r)/ *noun* a person who has learned a lot about something: *a famous history scholar*

scholarship /ˈskɒləʃɪp/ *noun* money that is given to a good student to help him/her to continue studying: *Adrian won a scholarship to Nairobi University.*

school /skuːl/ *noun* **1** (*plural* **schools**) a place where children go to learn: *Grace is at school.* ○ *Which school do you go to?* **2** (no plural) being at school: *I hate school!* ○ *He left school when he was 16.* ○ *School starts at nine o'clock.* **3** (*plural* **schools**) a place where you go to learn a special thing: *law school*

schoolboy /ˈskuːlbɔɪ/, **schoolgirl** /ˈskuːlɡɜːl/, **schoolchild** /ˈskuːl-tʃaɪld/ (*plural* **schoolchildren**) *noun* a boy or girl who goes to school

school days /ˈskuːldeɪz/ *noun* (plural) the time in your life when you are at school

science /ˈsaɪəns/ *noun* the study of natural things: *I'm interested in science.* ○ *Biology, chemistry and physics are all sciences.*

science fiction /ˌsaɪəns ˈfɪkʃn/ *noun* (no plural) stories about things like travel in space, life on other planets or life in the future

scientific /ˌsaɪənˈtɪfɪk/ *adjective* of or about science: *a scientific experiment*

scientist /ˈsaɪəntɪst/ *noun* a person who studies science or works with science

scissors

scissors /ˈsɪzəz/ *noun* (plural) a tool for cutting that has two sharp parts that are joined together: *These scissors aren't very sharp.* ✪ Be careful! You cannot say 'a scissors'. You can say a

pair of scissors: *I need a pair of scissors.* (or: *I need some scissors.*)

scoop /skuːp/ *verb* (**scoops**, **scooping**, **scooped** /skuːpt/) use a spoon or your hands to take something up or out: *I scooped some water out of the river with a bucket.*

scooter /ˈskuːtə(r)/ *noun* a light motor cycle with a small engine

score /skɔː(r)/ *noun* the number of points, goals, etc that you win in a game or competition: *The winner got a score of 320.*

score *verb* (**scores**, **scoring**, **scored** /skɔːd/) win a point in a game or competition: *McCarthy scored four goals against Namibia.*

scorn /skɔːn/ *noun* (no plural) the strong feeling you have when you think that somebody or something is not good enough: *He was full of scorn for my idea.*

scorpion /ˈskɔːpɪən/ *noun* an animal that has eight legs and lives in hot, dry places. A scorpion has a long tail with a poisonous sting

scorpion
tail
sting

Scout /skaʊt/ = Boy Scout

scramble /ˈskræmbl/ *verb* (**scrambles**, **scrambling**, **scrambled** /ˈskræmbld/) move quickly up or over something, using your hands to help you: *They scrambled over the wall.*

scrambled eggs /ˌskræmbld ˈeɡz/ *noun* (plural) eggs that you mix together with milk and cook in a pan with butter

scrap /skræp/ *noun* **1** (*plural* **scraps**) a small piece of something: *a scrap of paper* **2** (no plural) something you do not want any more but that is made of material that can be used again: *scrap paper* ○ *scrap metal*

scrape /skreɪp/ *verb* (**scrapes**, **scraping**, **scraped** /skreɪpt/) **1** move a rough or sharp thing across something: *I scraped the mud off my shoes with a knife.* **2** hurt or damage something by moving it against a rough or sharp thing: *I fell and scraped my knee on the wall.*

scratch¹ /skrætʃ/ *verb* (**scratches**, **scratching**, **scratched** /skrætʃt/) **1** cut or make a mark on something with a sharp thing: *The cat scratched me!* **2** move your fingernails across your skin: *She scratched her head.*

scratch² /skrætʃ/ *noun* (*plural* **scratches**) a cut or mark that a sharp thing makes: *Her hands were covered in scratches from the bush.* **from scratch** from the beginning: *I threw away the letter I was writing and started again from scratch.*

scream /skri:m/ *verb* (**screams**, **screaming**, **screamed** /skri:md/) make a loud high cry that shows you are afraid or hurt: *She saw the snake and screamed.* ○ *He screamed for help.*
scream *noun* a loud high cry: *a scream of pain*

screech /skri:tʃ/ *verb* (**screeches**, **screeching**, **screeched** /skri:tʃt/) make a loud high sound: *The car's brakes screeched as it stopped suddenly.*

screen /skri:n/ *noun* **1** the flat square part of a television or computer where you see pictures or words ☛ picture at **computer 2** the flat thing on the wall of a cinema, where you see films **3** a kind of thin wall that you can move around. Screens are used to keep away cold, light, etc or to stop people from seeing something: *The nurse put a screen around the bed.*

screwdriver　　screw

screw /skru:/ *noun* a small metal thing with a sharp end, that you use for fixing things together. You push it into something by turning it with a **screwdriver**.
screw *verb* (**screws**, **screwing**, **screwed** /skru:d/) **1** fix something to another thing using a screw **2** turn something to fix it to another thing: *Screw the lid on the jar.* ✪ opposite: **unscrew**. **screw up** make paper or material into a ball with your hand: *He screwed up the letter and threw it in the bin.*

screwdriver /ˈskru:draɪvə(r)/ *noun* a tool for turning screws

scribble /ˈskrɪbl/ *verb* (**scribbles**, **scribbling**, **scribbled** /ˈskrɪbld/) write something or make marks on paper quickly and without care: *The children scribbled in my book.*

script /skrɪpt/ *noun* the written words that actors speak in a play or film

scrub¹ /skrʌb/ *verb* (**scrubs**, **scrubbing**, **scrubbed** /skrʌbd/) rub something hard to clean it, usually with a brush and soap and water: *He scrubbed the floor.*

scrub² /skrʌb/ *noun* (no plural) small trees and plants that grow in hot dry places

scruffy /ˈskrʌfi/ *adjective* (**scruffier**, **scruffiest**) untidy and perhaps dirty: *She was wearing scruffy clothes.*

sculptor /ˈskʌlptə(r)/ *noun* a person who makes shapes from things like stone or wood

sculpture /ˈskʌlptʃə(r)/ *noun* **1** (no plural) making shapes from things like stone or wood **2** (*plural* **sculptures**) a shape made from things like stone or wood

sea /si:/ *noun* **1** (no plural) the salty water that covers large parts of the earth: *We went for a swim in the sea.* ○ *The sea is very rough today.* **2** (*plural* **seas**) a big area of salty water: *the Black Sea* **at sea** travelling on the sea: *We spent three weeks at sea.*

seafood /ˈsi:fu:d/ *noun* (no plural) fish and small animals from the sea that you can eat

seagull /ˈsi:gʌl/ *noun* a big grey or white bird with a loud cry, that lives near the sea

seal¹ /si:l/ *noun* an animal with short fur that lives in and near the sea, and that eats fish

seal² /si:l/ *verb* (**seals**, **sealing**, **sealed** /si:ld/) close something tightly by sticking two parts together: *She sealed the envelope.*

seam /si:m/ *noun* a line where two pieces of cloth are joined together

search /sɜ:tʃ/ *verb* (**searches**, **searching**, **searched** /sɜ:tʃt/) look carefully because you are trying to find somebody or something: *I searched everywhere for my pen.*

search *noun* (*plural* **searches**) *I found my key after a long search.* **in search of somebody** or **something** looking for somebody or something: *We drove round the town in search of a cheap hotel.*

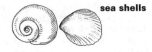

sea shells

sea shell /'si: ʃel/ *noun* the hard outside part of a small animal that lives in the sea

seashore /'si:ʃɔ:(r)/ *noun* (no plural) the land next to the sea; the beach

seasick /'si:sɪk/ *adjective* If you are seasick, you feel ill in your stomach because the boat you are on is moving a lot.

season /'si:zn/ *noun* **1** one of the four parts of the year in cool countries. The four seasons are **spring**, **summer**, **autumn** and **winter**. **2** a special time of the year for something: *The football season starts soon.*

seat /si:t/ *noun* something that you sit on: *the back seat of a car* ○ *We had seats at the front of the theatre.* **take a seat** sit down: *Please take a seat.*

seat belt /'si:t belt/ *noun* a long thin piece of material that you put round your body in a car or an aeroplane to keep you safe in an accident

seaweed /'si:wi:d/ *noun* (no plural) plants that grow in the sea

second[1] /'sekənd/ *adjective, adverb* next after first: *February is the second month of the year.*

secondly *adverb* a word that you use when you are giving the second thing in a list: *Firstly, it's too expensive and secondly, we don't really need it.*

second[2] /'sekənd/ *noun* (no plural) a person or thing that comes next after the first: *Today is the second of April (April 2nd).* ○ *I was the first to arrive, and John was the second.*

second[3] /'sekənd/ *noun* **1** a measure of time. There are 60 seconds in a **minute**. **2** a very short time: *Wait a second!*

○ *I'll be ready in a second.*

secondary school /'sekəndri sku:l/ *noun* a school for pupils between the ages of 13 and 19

second class /ˌsekənd 'klɑ:s/ *noun* (no plural) **1** the part of a train, plane, etc that it is cheaper to travel in: *We sat in second class.* **2** the cheapest but the slowest way of sending letters

second-class *adjective, adverb*: *a second-class ticket* ○ *I sent the letter second class.* ☛ Look at **first-class** and at the Note at **stamp**.

second-hand /ˌsekənd 'hænd/ *adjective, adverb* not new; used by another person before: *second-hand books* ○ *I bought this car second-hand.*

secrecy /'si:krəsi/ *noun* (no plural) not telling other people: *They worked in secrecy.*

secret[1] /'si:krət/ *adjective* If something is secret, other people do not or must not know about it: *They kept their plans secret* (= they did not tell anybody about them). ○ *a secret meeting*

secretly *adverb* without other people knowing: *We are secretly planning a big party for her.*

secret[2] /'si:krət/ *noun* something that you do not or must not tell other people: *I can't tell you where I'm going — it's a secret.* **in secret** without other people knowing: *They met in secret.* **keep a secret** not tell other people a secret: *Can you keep a secret?*

secretary /'sekrətri/ *noun* (*plural* **secretaries**) **1** a person who types letters, answers the telephone and does other things in an office **2** an important person in the government: *the Secretary of State for Education*

secretarial /ˌsekrə'teəriəl/ *adjective* of or about the work of a secretary: *a secretarial college*

secretary bird /'sekrətri bɜ:d/ *noun* a large bird with long legs that eats snakes

secretive /'si:krətɪv/ *adjective* If you are secretive, you do not like to tell other people about yourself or your plans: *Maalim is very secretive about his job.*

section /'sekʃn/ *noun* one of the parts

of something: *This section of the road is closed.*

secure /sɪˈkjʊə(r)/ *adjective* **1** safe: *Don't climb that ladder – it's not very secure* (= it may fall). ○ *Her job is secure* (= she will not lose it). **2** If you are secure, you feel safe and you are not worried: *Do you feel secure about the future?* ✪ opposite: **insecure 3** well locked or protected so that nobody can go in or out: *This gate isn't very secure.*

securely *adverb*: *Are all the windows securely closed?*

security /sɪˈkjʊərəti/ *noun* (no plural) **1** the feeling of being safe: *Children need love and security.* **2** things that you do to keep a place safe: *We need better security at airports.*

***

see or **look**?

See and **look** are used in different ways. When you **see** something, you know about it with your eyes, without trying:

*Suddenly I **saw** a bird fly past the window.*

When you **look** at something, you turn your eyes towards it because you want to see it:

***Look** at this picture carefully. Can you **see** the bird?*

***

see /siː/ *verb* (**sees**, **seeing**, **saw** /sɔː/, **has seen** /siːn/) **1** know something using your eyes: *It was so dark that I couldn't see anything.* ○ *Can you see that plane?* **2** visit or meet somebody: *I'll see you outside the station at ten o'clock.* **3** understand something: *'You have to turn the key this way.' 'I see.'* **4** find out about something: *Look in the newspaper to see what time the film starts.* **5** make certain about something: *Please see that everybody is here.* **I'll see** I will think about what you have said and tell you what I have decided later: *'Will you lend me the money?' 'I'll see.'* **seeing that**, **seeing as** because: *Seeing that you've got nothing to do, you can help me!* **see somebody off** go to an airport or a station to say goodbye to somebody who is leaving **see to somebody** or **something** do what you need to do for

somebody or something: *Sit down – I'll see to the dinner.* **see you**, **see you later** goodbye

seed /siːd/ *noun* the small hard part of a plant from which a new plant grows

seek /siːk/ *verb* (**seeks**, **seeking**, **sought** /sɔːt/, **has sought**) try to find or get something: *You should seek help.*

seem /siːm/ *verb* (**seems**, **seeming**, **seemed** /siːmd/) make you think that something is true: *She seems tired.* ○ *My mother seems to like you.* ○ *Margaret seems like* (= seems to be) *a nice girl.*

seen *form of* **see**

see-saw /ˈsiː sɔː/ *noun* a special piece of wood that can move up and down when a child sits on each end

seize /siːz/ *verb* (**seizes**, **seizing**, **seized** /siːzd/) take something quickly and strongly: *The thief seized my bag and ran away.*

seldom /ˈseldəm/ *adverb* not often: *It seldom rains in the desert.*

select /sɪˈlekt/ *verb* (**selects**, **selecting**, **selected**) take the person or thing that you like best; choose: *The manager has selected two new players for the team.* ✪ **Choose** is the word that we usually use.

selection /sɪˈlekʃn/ *noun* **1** (no plural) taking the person or thing you like best: *the selection of a new president* **2** (*plural* **selections**) a group of people or things that somebody has chosen, or a group of things that you can choose from: *This shop has a good selection of books.*

self- /self/ *prefix* by yourself; for yourself: *He is self-taught – he never went to university.*

self-confident /ˌself ˈkɒnfɪdənt/ *adjective* sure about yourself and what you can do

self-conscious /ˌself ˈkɒnʃəs/ *adjective* worried about what other people think of you: *She walked into the classroom feeling very self-conscious.*

self-employed /ˌself ɪmˈplɔɪd/ *adjective* If you are self-employed, you work for yourself, not for somebody else's company: *He's a self-employed electrician.*

selfish /'selfɪʃ/ *adjective* If you are self-ish, you think too much about what you want and not about what other people want: *It was selfish of you to go out when your mother was ill.* ✪ opposite: **unselfish**

selfishly *adverb*: *He behaved very selfishly.*

selfishness /'selfɪʃnəs/ *noun* (no plural) *Her selfishness made me very angry.*

self-service /ˌself 'sɜːvɪs/ *adjective* In a self-service shop or restaurant you take what you want and then pay for it.

sell /sel/ *verb* (**sells**, **selling**, **sold** /səʊld/, **has sold**) give something to somebody who pays you money for it: *I sold my guitar for 4 000 shillings.* ○ *He sold me a ticket.* ○ *Does that shop sell pencils?* ➡ Look at **buy**. **sell out** be sold completely so that there are no more left: *I went to the shop to buy a newspaper, but they had all sold out.* **sell out of something** sell all that you have of something: *We have oranges, but we have sold out of bananas.*

semi- /semi/ *prefix* half: *A semicircle is a half circle.*

semicolon /ˌsemiˈkəʊlən/ *noun* a mark (;) that you use in writing to separate parts of a sentence

semifinal /ˌsemiˈfaɪnl/ *noun* In a competition, a semifinal is one of the two games that are played to find out who will play in the **final**.

senate /'senət/ *noun* one of the parts of the government in some countries

senator /'senətə(r)/ *noun* a member of a senate

send /send/ *verb* (**sends**, **sending**, **sent** /sent/, **has sent**) **1** make something go somewhere: *I sent a letter to John.* ○ *Have you sent your parents a letter?* **2** make somebody go somewhere: *My company is sending me to Nairobi.* ○ *He was sent to prison for ten years.* **send for somebody** or **something** ask for somebody or something to come to you: *Send for a doctor!* **send off** post something: *I'll send the letter off today.*

senior /'siːniə(r)/ *adjective* **1** more important: *a senior officer in the army*

2 older: *a senior pupil* ✪ opposite: **junior**

sensation /sen'seɪʃn/ *noun* **1** a feeling: *I felt a burning sensation on my skin.* **2** great excitement or interest; something that makes people very excited: *The new film caused a sensation.*

sensational /sen'seɪʃənl/ *adjective* very exciting or interesting: *sensational news*

sense[1] /sens/ *noun* **1** (*plural* **senses**) the power to see, smell, taste or touch: *Dogs have a good sense of smell.* **2** (no plural) the ability to feel or understand something: *The boy had no sense of right and wrong.* **3** (no plural) the ability to think carefully about something and to do the right thing: *Did anybody have the sense to call the police?* **4** (*plural* **senses**) a meaning: *This word has four senses.* **make sense** be possible to understand: *What does this sentence mean? It doesn't make sense to me.*

sense[2] /sens/ *verb* (**senses**, **sensing**, **sensed** /senst/) understand or feel something: *I sensed that he was worried.*

sensible /'sensəbl/ *adjective* able to think carefully about something and to do the right thing: *It was very sensible of you to call the police when you saw the accident.*

sensibly /'sensəbli/ *adverb*: *This section of road is dangerous, so please drive sensibly.*

sensitive /'sensətɪv/ *adjective* **1** If you are sensitive about something, you easily become worried or unhappy about it: *Don't say anything bad about her work – she's very sensitive about it.* ✪ opposite: **insensitive 2** A person who is sensitive understands and is careful about other people's feelings: *He's a very sensitive man.* ✪ opposite: **insensitive 3** If something is sensitive, it is easy to hurt or damage: *sensitive skin*

sent *form of* **send**

sentence[1] /'sentəns/ *noun* a group of words that tells you something or asks a question. When a sentence is written, it always begins with a capital letter and usually ends with a full stop.

sentence[2] /'sentəns/ *noun* the punishment that a judge gives to somebody in a court of law

sentence *verb* (**sentences**, **sentencing**, **sentenced** /'sentənst/) tell somebody in a court of law what their punishment will be: *The judge sentenced the man to two years in prison.*

separate[1] /'seprət/ *adjective* **1** away from something; not together or not joined: *Cut the dough into eight separate pieces.* ○ *In my school, the older children are separate from the younger ones.* **2** different; not the same: *We stayed in separate rooms in the same hotel.*

separately *adverb*: *Shall we pay separately or together?*

separate[2] /'sepəreɪt/ *verb* (**separates**, **separating**, **separated**) **1** stop being together: *My parents separated when I was a baby.* **2** divide people or things; keep people or things away from each other: *The teacher separated the class into two groups.* **3** be between two things: *The Mediterranean separates Europe and Africa.*

separation /ˌsepə'reɪʃn/ *noun*: *The separation from my family and friends made me very unhappy.*

September /sep'tembə(r)/ *noun* the ninth month of the year

sergeant /'sɑːdʒənt/ *noun* an officer in the army or the police

serial /'sɪəriəl/ *noun* a story that is told in parts on television or radio, or in a magazine

series /'sɪəriːz/ *noun* (*plural* **series**) **1** a number of things of the same kind that come one after another: *I heard a series of shots and then silence.* **2** a number of television or radio programmes, often on the same subject, that come one after another: *a TV series on dinosaurs*

serious /'sɪəriəs/ *adjective* **1** very bad: *That was a serious mistake.* ○ *They had a serious accident.* **2** important: *a serious decision* **3** not funny: *a serious film* **4** If you are serious, you are not joking or playing: *Are you serious about going to live with your grandmother?* ○ *You look very serious. Is something wrong?*

seriously *adverb*: *She's seriously ill.*

take somebody or **something seriously** show that you know somebody or something is important: *Don't take what he says too seriously – he is always joking.*

seriousness /'sɪəriəsnəs/ *noun* (no plural) *The boy didn't understand the seriousness of his crime.*

sermon /'sɜːmən/ *noun* a talk that a priest gives in church

servant /'sɜːvənt/ *noun* a person who works in another person's house, doing work like cooking and cleaning

serve /sɜːv/ *verb* (**serves**, **serving**, **served** /sɜːvd/) **1** do work for other people: *During the war he served in the army.* **2** give food or drink to somebody: *Breakfast is served from 7.30 to 9.00 a.m.* **3** help somebody in a shop to buy things: *Which assistant served you when you bought the shoes?* **it serves you right** it is right that this bad thing has happened to you: *'I feel ill.' 'It serves you right for eating so much!'*

service /'sɜːvɪs/ *noun* **1** (*plural* **services**) a business that does useful work for all the people in a country or an area: *This town has a good bus service.* ○ *the postal service* **2** (no plural) help or work that you do for somebody: *She left the company after ten years of service.* **3** (no plural) the work that somebody does for customers in a shop, restaurant or hotel: *The food was good but the service was very slow.* **4** (*plural* **services**) a meeting in a church with prayers and singing: *We went to the evening service.* **5** (*plural* **services**) the time when somebody looks at a car or machine to see that it is working well: *He takes his car to the garage for a service every six months.*

serviette /ˌsɜːvi'et/ *noun* a piece of cloth or paper that you use when you are eating to clean your mouth and hands and to keep your clothes clean

session /'seʃn/ *noun* a time when people meet to do something: *The first training session is at nine o'clock.*

set[1] /set/ *noun* a group of things of the same kind, or a group of things that you use together: *a set of six glasses* ○ *My grandfather still has a full set of teeth.*

set[2] /set/ *verb* (**sets, setting, set, has set**) **1** put something somewhere: *Dad set the plate in front of me.* **2** make something ready to use or to start working: *I set my alarm clock for seven o'clock.* ○ *I set the table* (= put knives, forks, etc on it). **3** make something happen: *They set the school on fire* (= made it start to burn). **4** When the sun sets, it goes down from the sky. ✪ opposite: **rise 5** decide what something will be; fix something: *Let's set a date for the meeting.* **6** give somebody work to do: *Our teacher set us a lot of homework.* **7** become hard or solid: *Wait for the cement to set.* **set off, set out** start a journey: *We set off for Kisumu at two o'clock.* **set up** start something: *The company was set up in 1981.*

settee /se'ti:/ *noun* a long soft seat for more than one person

setting /'setɪŋ/ *noun* the place where something is or where something happens: *The house is in a beautiful setting on top of a hill.*

settle /'setl/ *verb* (**settles, settling, settled** /'setld/) **1** go to live in a new place and stay there: *Ruth left Nairobi and went to settle in the north of Kenya.* **2** decide something after talking with somebody; end a discussion or argument: *Have you settled your argument with Simon?* **3** come down and rest somewhere: *The bird settled on a branch.* **4** pay something: *Have you settled your bill?* **settle down 1** sit down or lie down so that you are comfortable: *I settled down in front of the television.* **2** become calm and quiet: *The children settled down and went to sleep.* **3** begin to have a calm life in one place: *When are you going to get married and settle down?* **settle in** start to feel happy in a new place: *We only moved to this flat last week and we haven't settled in yet.*

settlement /'setlmənt/ *noun* **1** an agreement about something after talking or arguing: *After long talks about pay, the workers and their boss reached a settlement.* **2** a group of homes in a place where no people have lived before: *a settlement in the mountains*

seven /'sevn/ *number* 7

seventh /'sevnθ/ *adjective, adverb, noun* **1** 7th **2** one of seven equal parts of something; $\frac{1}{7}$

seventeen /ˌsevn'ti:n/ *number* 17

seventeenth /ˌsevn'ti:nθ/ *adjective, adverb, noun* 17th

seventy /'sevnti/ *number* **1** 70 **2** **the seventies** (plural) the numbers, years or temperature between 70 and 79 **in your seventies** between the ages of 70 and 79

seventieth /'sevntiəθ/ *adjective, adverb, noun* 70th

several /'sevrəl/ *adjective, pronoun* more than two but not many: *I've read this book several times.* ○ *Several letters arrived this morning.* ○ *If you need a pen, there are several on the table.*

severe /sɪ'vɪə(r)/ *adjective* (**severer, severest**) **1** not kind or gentle: *severe punishment* **2** very bad: *a severe headache* ○ *a severe injury*

severely *adverb*: *They punished him severely.* ○ *She was severely injured in the accident.*

sew /səʊ/ *verb* (**sews, sewing, sewed** /səʊd/, **has sewed** or **has sewn** /səʊn/) use a needle and cotton to join pieces of material together or to join something to material: *He sewed a button on his shirt.* ○ *Can you sew?*

needle
cotton

sewing *noun* (no plural) something that you sew

sewing machine /'səʊɪŋ məʃi:n/ *noun* a machine that you use for sewing

sex /seks/ *noun* **1** (plural **sexes**) being a male or a female: *What sex is your dog?* ○ *the male sex* **2** (no plural) when two people put their bodies together, sometimes to make a baby: *She had sex with him.*

sh! /ʃ/ be quiet!: *Sh! You'll wake the baby up!*

shabby /'ʃæbi/ *adjective* (**shabbier, shabbiest**) old and untidy or dirty because you have used it a lot: *a shabby coat*

shabbily /'ʃæbɪli/ *adverb*: *She was shabbily dressed.*

shade[1] /ʃeɪd/ *noun* **1** (no plural) a place

where it is dark and cool because the sun doesn't shine there: *We sat in the shade of a big tree.* **2** (*plural* **shades**) a thing that keeps strong light from your eyes: *I bought a new shade for the lamp.* **3** (*plural* **shades**) how light or dark a colour is: *I'm looking for a shirt in a darker shade of green.*

shade² /ʃeɪd/ *verb* (**shades**, **shading**, **shaded**) stop light from shining on something: *He shaded his eyes with his hand.*

shadow /ˈʃædəʊ/ *noun* a dark shape that you see near somebody or something that is in front of the light

shady /ˈʃeɪdi/ *adjective* (**shadier**, **shadiest**) not in bright sunshine: *We sat in a shady area under the trees.*

shake /ʃeɪk/ *verb* (**shakes**, **shaking**, **shook** /ʃʊk/, **has shaken** /ˈʃeɪkən/) **1** move quickly from side to side or up and down: *The house shakes when trains go past.* ○ *He was shaking with fear.* **2** make something move quickly from side to side or up and down: *Shake the bottle before opening it.* ○ *An explosion shook the windows.* **shake hands** hold somebody's hand and move it up and down as a greeting **shake your head** move your head from side to side to say 'no'

shaky /ˈʃeɪki/ *adjective* (**shakier**, **shakiest**) **1** shaking because you are ill or frightened: *You've got shaky hands.* **2** not firm; not strong: *Don't sit in that chair — it's a bit shaky.*

shall /ʃəl/, /ʃæl/ *modal verb* **1** a word that you use instead of 'will' with 'I' and 'we' to show the future: *I shall see you tomorrow.* **2** a word that you use when you ask what is the right thing to do: *Shall I close the window?* ○ *What shall we do tomorrow?*

❂ The negative form of 'shall' is **shall not** or the short form **shan't** /ʃɑːnt/:
I shan't be there.
The short form of 'shall' is **'ll**. We often use this:
I'll (=I shall) *see you tomorrow.*
☞ Look at the Note on page 195 to find out more about **modal verbs**.

---

shallow /ˈʃæləʊ/ *adjective* (**shallower**, **shallowest**) not deep; with not much water: *This part of the river is shallow — we can walk across.* ☞ picture on page A10

shamba /ˈʃæmbə/ *noun* (an East African word) a small farm or a field that is used for growing crops

shame /ʃeɪm/ *noun* (no plural) the unhappy feeling that you have when you have done something wrong or stupid: *I was filled with* (= felt a lot of) *shame after I lied to my parents.* ❂ The adjective is **ashamed**. **it's a shame**, **what a shame** it is sad; I am sorry: *It's a shame that you have to leave now.*

shampoo /ʃæmˈpuː/ *noun* (*plural* **shampoos**) a special liquid for washing your hair: *a bottle of shampoo*

shan't /ʃɑːnt/ = shall not

shape¹ /ʃeɪp/ *noun* **1** (*plural* **shapes**) what you see if you draw a line round something; the form of something: *What shape is the table — round or square?* ○ *I made a bowl in the shape of a fish.* ○ *Circles, squares and triangles are all different shapes.* **2** (no plural) how good or bad something is; how healthy somebody is: *He was in bad shape after the accident.* **out of shape** not in the right shape: *My jumper went out of shape when I washed it.*

shape² /ʃeɪp/ *verb* (**shapes**, **shaping**, **shaped** /ʃeɪpt/) give a certain shape to something: *She shaped the clay into a pot.*

shaped *adjective* with a certain shape: *That rock is shaped like a cat.* ○ *an L-shaped room*

share¹ /ʃeə(r)/ *verb* (**shares**, **sharing**, **shared** /ʃeəd/) **1** give parts of something to different people: *Share these sweets with your friends.* ○ *We shared the stew between three of us.* **2** have or use something with another person: *I share a bedroom with my sister.*

share² /ʃeə(r)/ *noun* a part of something bigger that each person has: *Here is your share of the money.* ○ *I did my share of the work.*

shark

shark /ʃɑːk/ *noun* a big fish that lives in the sea. Some sharks have sharp teeth and are dangerous.

sharp[1] /ʃɑːp/ *adjective* (**sharper**, **sharpest**) **1** with an edge or point that cuts or makes holes easily: *a sharp knife* ○ *a sharp needle* ✪ opposite: **blunt** **2** strong and sudden: *a sharp bend in the road* ○ *I felt a sharp pain in my leg.* **3** clear and easy to see: *We could see the sharp outline of the mountains against the sky.* **4** with a taste like lemons or vinegar: *If your drink tastes too sharp, add some sugar.* **5** able to see, hear or learn well: *She's got a very sharp mind.* ○ *sharp eyes* **6** sudden and angry: *sharp words*

sharply *adverb*: *The road bends sharply to the left.* ○ *'Go away!' he said sharply.*

sharp[2] /ʃɑːp/ *adverb* **1** exactly: *Be here at six o'clock sharp.* **2** with a big change of direction: *Turn sharp right at the next corner.*

sharpen /ˈʃɑːpən/ *verb* (**sharpens**, **sharpening**, **sharpened** /ˈʃɑːpənd/) make something sharp or sharper: *sharpen a knife*

sharpener /ˈʃɑːpnə(r)/ *noun* a thing that you use for making something sharp: *a pencil-sharpener*

shatter /ˈʃætə(r)/ *verb* (**shatters**, **shattering**, **shattered** /ˈʃætəd/) break into very small pieces; break something into very small pieces: *The glass hit the floor and shattered.* ○ *The explosion shattered the windows.*

shave /ʃeɪv/ *verb* (**shaves**, **shaving**, **shaved** /ʃeɪvd/) cut hair off your face or body by cutting it very close with a **razor**: *He shaves every morning.*

shave *noun*: *I haven't had a shave today.*

shaver *noun* an electric tool that you use for shaving

shawl /ʃɔːl/ *noun* a big piece of cloth that a woman wears round her shoulders, or that you put round a baby

she /ʃiː/ *pronoun* (*plural* **they**) a woman or girl who the sentence is about: *'Where's your sister?' 'She's* (= she is) *at work.'*

she'd /ʃiːd/ **1** = she had **2** = she would

shed[1] /ʃed/ *noun* a small building where you keep things or animals: *We keep our tools in a small shed.*

shed[2] /ʃed/ *verb* (**sheds**, **shedding**, **shed**, **has shed**) let something fall off: *The snake shed its skin.*

sheep

lamb

sheep /ʃiːp/ (*plural* **sheep**) an animal that people keep on farms for its meat and its wool

✪ A young sheep is called a **lamb**. Meat from a young sheep is also called **lamb**.

sheer /ʃɪə(r)/ *adjective* **1** complete: *sheer nonsense* **2** very steep: *a sheer drop to the sea*

sheet /ʃiːt/ *noun* **1** a big piece of thin material for a bed: *I put some clean sheets on the bed.* **2** a thin flat piece of something like paper, glass or metal: *a sheet of writing paper*

shelf

shelf /ʃelf/ *noun* (*plural* **shelves** /ʃelvz/) a long flat piece of wood on a wall or in a cupboard, where things can stand: *Put the plates on the shelf.* ○ *bookshelves*

she'll /ʃiːl/ = she will

shell /ʃel/ *noun* the hard outside part of birds' eggs and nuts and of some animals, for example snails and crabs ☞ Look also at **sea shell**.

shellfish /ˈʃelfɪʃ/ *noun* (*plural* **shellfish**) a kind of animal that lives in water and that has a shell

shelter[1] /ˈʃeltə(r)/ *noun* **1** (no plural)

being safe from bad weather or danger: *We took shelter from the rain under a tree.* ○ *People ran for shelter when the bombs started to fall.* **2** (*plural* **shelters**) a place where you are safe from bad weather or danger: *a bus shelter* (= for people who are waiting at a bus-stop)

shelter² /ˈʃeltə(r)/ *verb* (**shelters**, **sheltering**, **sheltered** /ˈʃeltəd/) **1** make somebody or something safe from bad weather or danger: *The trees shelter the house from the wind.* **2** go to a place where you will be safe from bad weather or danger: *Let's shelter from the rain under that tree.*

shelves *plural of* **shelf**

shepherd /ˈʃepəd/ *noun* a person who looks after sheep

she's /ʃiːz/ **1** = she is **2** = she has

shield¹ /ʃiːld/ *noun* a big piece of metal, wood or leather that soldiers carried in front of their bodies when they were fighting in wars long ago. Some police officers carry shields now.

shield² /ʃiːld/ *verb* (**shields**, **shielding**, **shielded**) keep somebody or something safe from danger or from being hurt: *She shielded her eyes from the sun with her hand.*

shift¹ /ʃɪft/ *verb* (**shifts**, **shifting**, **shifted**) move something to another place: *Can you help me to shift the bed? I want to sweep the floor.*

shift² /ʃɪft/ *noun* a group of workers who begin work when another group finishes: *Each shift in the factory works for eight hours.* ○ *the night shift*

shifting cultivation /ˈʃɪftɪŋ kʌltɪˈveɪʃn/ *noun* (no plural) a way of farming in which a farmer grows crops on a piece of land for a long time until they do not grow well there any more, then the farmer uses a new piece of land

shilling /ˈʃɪlɪŋ/ *noun* money that people use in several East African countries: *A hundred cents make one shilling.* ○ *The car cost 200 shillings*

shine /ʃaɪn/ *verb* (**shines**, **shining**, **shone** /ʃɒn/, **has shone**) **1** give out light: *The sun is shining.* **2** be bright: *I polished my shoes until they shine.*

shine *noun* (no plural) brightness: *This shampoo will give your hair a lovely shine.*

shiny *adjective* (**shinier**, **shiniest**) *a shiny new car*

ship /ʃɪp/ *noun* a big boat for long journeys on the sea: *The coffee is carried to Europe by ship.*

ship *verb* (**ships**, **shipping**, **shipped** /ʃɪpt/) send something in a ship: *The company ships coffee to Europe.*

shipping /ˈʃɪpɪŋ/ *noun* (no plural) ships: *The port is now open to shipping.*

shipwreck /ˈʃɪprek/ *noun* an accident at sea when a ship breaks in bad weather or on rocks **be shipwrecked** be on a ship when it is in a shipwreck: *They were shipwrecked off the coast of Tanzania.*

shirt /ʃɜːt/ *noun* a thin piece of clothing that you wear on the top part of your body ☞ picture at **suit**

shiver /ˈʃɪvə(r)/ *verb* (**shivers**, **shivering**, **shivered** /ˈʃɪvəd/) shake because you are cold, frightened or ill: *We were shivering with cold.*

shock¹ /ʃɒk/ *noun* **1** a very bad surprise: *The news of his death was a shock to all of us.* **2** a sudden pain when electricity goes through your body: *Don't touch that wire – you'll get an electric shock.*

shock² /ʃɒk/ *verb* (**shocks**, **shocking**, **shocked** /ʃɒkt/) give somebody a very bad surprise; upset somebody: *She was shocked by his death.*

shocking /ˈʃɒkɪŋ/ *adjective* If something is shocking, it makes you feel upset, angry, or surprised in a very bad way: *a shocking crime*

shoes

shoe /ʃuː/ *noun* a covering made of leather or plastic that you wear on your foot: *a pair of shoes* ○ *What size are these shoes?* ○ *What size shoes do you take?* ○ *a shoe shop*

shoelace /ˈʃuːleɪs/ *noun* a string that you tie to close a shoe: *Tie your shoelaces.*

shone *form of* **shine**

shook *form of* **shake**

shoot[1] /ʃuːt/ *verb* (**shoots, shooting, shot** /ʃɒt/, **has shot**) **1** send a bullet from a gun or an arrow from a bow; hurt or kill a person or an animal with a gun: *She shot a bird.* ○ *The police officer was shot in the arm.* **2** move quickly or suddenly: *The car shot past us.* **3** make a film: *They are shooting a film about the war.*

shoot[2] /ʃuːt/ *noun* a new part of a plant: *The first shoots appear in spring.*

shop[1] *noun* a building where you buy things: *a bookshop* ○ *a clothes shop*

shop assistant /ˈʃɒp əsɪstənt/ *noun* a person who works in a shop

shopkeeper /ˈʃɒpkiːpə(r)/ *noun* a person who owns a small shop

shoplifter /ˈʃɒplɪftə(r)/ *noun* a person who steals things from shops

shoplifting /ˈʃɒplɪftɪŋ/ *noun* (no plural) stealing things from shops

shop[2] /ʃɒp/ *verb* (**shops, shopping, shopped** /ʃɒpt/) go to buy things from shops: *I'm shopping for some new clothes.* ❂ It is more usual to say **go shopping**.

shopper *noun* a person who is buying things: *The streets were full of shoppers.*

shopping /ˈʃɒpɪŋ/ *noun* (no plural) **1** buying things from shops: *She does her shopping after work.* **2** the things that you have bought in a shop: *Will you carry my shopping for me?* **go shopping** go to buy things from shops

shopping centre /ˈʃɒpɪŋ sentə(r)/ *noun* a place where there are a lot of shops together

shopping mall /ˈʃɒpɪŋ mɔːl/ *noun* a big building where there are a lot of shops together

shore /ʃɔː(r)/ *noun* the land next to the sea or a lake

short /ʃɔːt/ *adjective* (**shorter, shortest**) **1** very little from one end to the other: *Her hair is very short.* ○ *We live a short distance from the beach.* ❂ opposite: **long** ☛ picture on page A10 **2** very little from the bottom to the top: *I'm too short to reach the top shelf.* ○ *a short fat man* ❂ opposite: **tall** ☛ picture on page A10 **3** that only lasts for a

little time: *The film was very short.* ○ *a short rest* ❂ opposite: **long.** **be short of something** not have enough of something: *I'm short of money this month.* **for short** as a short way of saying or writing something: *My brother's name is Robert, but we call him 'Bob' for short.* **short for something** a short way of saying or writing something: *'Tom' is short for 'Thomas'.*

shortage /ˈʃɔːtɪdʒ/ *noun* when there is not enough of something: *a water shortage* ○ *There is a shortage of good teachers.*

short cut /ˌʃɔːt ˈkʌt/ *noun* a shorter way to get somewhere: *We took a short cut to school across the field.*

shorten /ˈʃɔːtn/ *verb* (**shortens, shortening, shortened** /ˈʃɔːtnd/) become shorter or make something shorter: *The trousers were too long, so I shortened them.*

shortly /ˈʃɔːtli/ *adverb* soon: *The doctor will see you shortly, Mr Githinji.* ○ *We left shortly after six o'clock.*

shorts

shorts /ʃɔːts/ *noun* (plural) short trousers that end above your knees: *a pair of shorts*

shot[1] *form of* **shoot**[1]

shot[2] /ʃɒt/ *noun* **1** firing a gun, or the noise that this makes: *He fired a shot.* **2** a photograph: *This is a good shot of you.* **3** kicking or hitting a ball in a sport like football

should /ʃʊd/ *modal verb* **1** a word that you use to tell or ask somebody what is the right thing to do: *If you feel ill, you should stay in bed.* ○ *Should I apologize to her for being so rude?* **2** a word that you use to say what you think will happen or what you think is true: *They should arrive soon.* **3** the word for 'shall' in the past: *We asked if we should help her.*

❂ The negative form of 'should' is **should not** or the short form **shouldn't** /ˈʃʊdnt/: *You shouldn't drive so fast.* ☛ Look at the Note on page 195 to find out more about **modal verbs**.

shoulder /ˈʃəʊldə(r)/ *noun* the part of

your body between your neck and your arm ☛ picture on page A4

shouldn't /'ʃʊdnt/ = should not

shout /ʃaʊt/ *verb* (**shouts, shouting, shouted**) speak very loudly: *Don't shout at me!* ○ *'Go back!' she shouted.*
shout *noun*: *We heard a shout for help.*

shove /ʃʌv/ *verb* (**shoves, shoving, shoved** /ʃʌvd/) push somebody or something in a rough way: *They shoved him through the door.*

shovel /'ʃʌvl/ *noun* a tool like a **spade** with a short handle, that you use for moving earth or sand, for example
shovel *verb* (**shovels, shovelling, shovelled** /'ʃʌvld/) move something with a shovel: *We shovelled the sand onto the lorry.*

show¹ /ʃəʊ/ *verb* (**shows, showing, showed** /ʃəʊd/, **has shown** /ʃəʊn/ or **has showed**) **1** let somebody see something: *She showed me her stamp collection.* ○ *You have to show your ticket on the train.* **2** make something clear; explain something to somebody: *Can you show me how to use the computer?* **3** appear or be seen: *The anger showed in his face.* **show off** talk loudly or do something silly to make people notice you: *Joyce is always talking about how much money she has, just to show off.* **show something off** let people see something that is new or beautiful: *James wanted to show off his new jacket.* **show somebody round** go with somebody and show them everything in a building: *David showed me round the school.* **show up** arrive: *What time did they show up?*

show² /ʃəʊ/ *noun* **1** something that you watch at the theatre or on television: *a comedy show* ○ *Did you enjoy the show?* **2** a group of things in one place that people go to see: *a flower show* **on show** in a place where people can see it: *The paintings are on show at the National Gallery until 15 May.*

shower /'ʃaʊə(r)/ *noun* **1** a place where you can wash by standing under water that falls from above you: *There's a shower in the bathroom.* **2** washing yourself in a shower: *I had a shower after work.* **3** rain that falls for a short time

shown *form of* **show¹**

shrank *form of* **shrink**

shred /ʃred/ *noun* a small thin piece torn or cut off something: *shreds of paper*

shriek /ʃriːk/ *verb* (**shrieks, shrieking, shrieked** /ʃriːkt/) make a loud high cry: *She shrieked in fear* (= because she was afraid).
shriek *noun*: *He gave a shriek of pain.*

shrill /ʃrɪl/ *adjective* (**shriller, shrillest**) A shrill sound is high and loud: *a shrill whistle*

shrimp /ʃrɪmp/ *noun* a small sea animal that you can eat

shrine /ʃraɪn/ *noun* a special holy place

shrink /ʃrɪŋk/ *verb* (**shrinks, shrinking, shrank** /ʃræŋk/ or **shrunk** /ʃrʌŋk/, **has shrunk**) become smaller or make something smaller: *My trousers shrank when I washed them.*

shrub /ʃrʌb/ *noun* a plant like a small low tree

shrug /ʃrʌg/ *verb* (**shrugs, shrugging, shrugged** /ʃrʌgd/) move your shoulders to show that you do not know or do not care about something: *I asked her where Sam was but she just shrugged.*
shrug *noun* (no plural) *He answered my question with a shrug.*

shrunk *form of* **shrink**

shudder /'ʃʌdə(r)/ *verb* (**shudders, shuddering, shuddered** /'ʃʌdəd/) shake, for example because you are afraid: *He shuddered when he saw the snake.*
shudder *noun*: *She felt a shudder of fear.*

shuffle /'ʃʌfl/ *verb* (**shuffles, shuffling, shuffled** /'ʃʌfld/) **1** walk slowly, without taking your feet off the ground: *The old man shuffled along the road.* **2** mix playing cards before a game

shut¹ /ʃʌt/ *verb* (**shuts, shutting, shut, has shut**) **1** move something so that it is not open: *Could you shut the door, please?* **2** move so that it is not open: *The door shut behind me.* **3** stop being open, so that people cannot go there: *The shops shut at 5.30.* **shut**

down close and stop working; make something close and stop working: *The factory shut down last year.* **shut up** stop talking: *Shut up and listen!* ✪ This expression is quite rude.

shut² /ʃʌt/ *adjective* closed; not open: *The school is shut today.* ○ *Is the door shut?* ☛ picture on page A11

shutter /ˈʃʌtə(r)/ *noun* a wooden or metal thing that covers the outside of a window: *Close the shutters.*

shuttle /ˈʃʌtl/ *noun* an aeroplane or a bus that goes to a place and then back again and again

shy /ʃaɪ/ *adjective* (**shyer**, **shyest**) not able to talk easily to people you do not know: *He was too shy to speak to her.*
shyness /ˈʃaɪnəs/ *noun* (no plural) being shy

sick /sɪk/ *adjective* (**sicker**, **sickest**) not well; ill: *She's looking after her sick mother.* **be sick** When you are sick, food comes up from your stomach and out of your mouth. **be sick of something** have had or done too much of something, so that you do not want it any longer: *I'm sick of being inside – let's go for a walk.* **feel sick** feel that food is going to come up from your stomach

sickle /ˈsɪkl/ *noun* a tool for cutting grass, corn, etc that has a handle and a long curved blade

sickle

sickness /ˈsɪknəs/ *noun* (no plural) being ill: *He could not work for a long time because of sickness.*

side /saɪd/ *noun* **1** one of the flat outside parts of something: *A box has six sides.* ○ *A piece of paper has two sides.* **2** the part of something that is not the front, back, top or bottom: *There is a door at the side of the house.* ☛ picture at **back 3** the edge of something; the part that is away from the middle: *I stood at the side of the road.* **4** the right or left part of something: *He lay on his side.* ○ *We drive on the left side of the road in Britain.* **5** one of two groups of people who fight or play a game against each other: *Which side won?* **be on somebody's side** agree with or help somebody in a fight or argu-

ment: *Rose said I was wrong, but Andy was on my side.* **side by side** next to each other: *They walked side by side.* **take sides** show that you agree with one person, and not the other, in a fight or an argument

sideways /ˈsaɪdweɪz/ *adjective, adverb* **1** to or from the side: *She looked sideways at the girl next to her.* **2** with one of the sides first: *We carried the table sideways through the door.*

siege /siːdʒ/ *noun* **1** when an army stays outside a town for a long time so that people and things cannot get in or out **2** when police stay outside a building for a long time to try to make a criminal come out

sigh /saɪ/ *verb* (**sighs**, **sighing**, **sighed** /saɪd/) breathe once very deeply when you are sad, tired or pleased, for example
sigh *noun*: '*I wish I had more money,*' *he said with a sigh.*

sight /saɪt/ *noun* **1** (no plural) the power to see: *She has poor sight* (= she cannot see well). **2** (no plural) seeing somebody or something: *When we reached the top of the hill we had our first sight of the city.* **2** (*plural* **sights**) something that you see: *The mountains were a beautiful sight.* **3** (*plural* **sights**) the interesting places to visit: *What are the main sights of Kenya?* **at first sight** when you see somebody or something for the first time: *He fell in love with her at first sight.* **catch sight of somebody** or **something** see somebody or something suddenly: *I caught sight of Fiona in the crowd.* **come into sight** come where you can see it: *The train came into sight.* **in sight** where you can see it: *Is the land in sight yet?* **lose sight of somebody** or **something** no longer be able to see somebody or something: *After an hour at sea we lost sight of land.* **out of sight** where you cannot see it: *We watched until the car was out of sight.*

sightseer /ˈsaɪtsiːə(r)/ *noun* a person who is visiting interesting places: *The town was full of sightseers.*

sightseeing /ˈsaɪtsiːɪŋ/ *noun* (no plural) visiting interesting places: *We did some sightseeing in Nairobi.*

signs

sign¹ /saɪn/ *noun* **1** a mark, shape or movement that has a special meaning: *+ and - are signs that mean 'plus' and 'minus'.* ○ *I put up my hand as a sign for him to stop.* **2** a thing with writing or a picture on it that tells you something: *The sign said 'No Smoking'.* ○ *a road sign* **3** something that tells you about another thing: *Dark clouds are a sign of rain.*

sign² /saɪn/ *verb* (**signs**, **signing**, **signed** /saɪnd/) write your name in your own way on something: *Sign here, please.* ○ *I signed the letter.* ✪ The noun is **signature**

signal /'sɪgnəl/ *noun* a light, sound or movement that tells you something without words: *A red light is a signal for cars to stop.* ○ *radio signals*

signal *verb* (**signals**, **signalling**, **signalled** /'sɪgnəld/) make a signal: *The policeman signalled to the children to cross the road.*

signature /'sɪgnətʃə(r)/ *noun* your name that you have written in your own way ☛ picture at **cheque**

significance /sɪg'nɪfɪkəns/ *noun* (no plural) the importance or meaning of something: *What is the significance of this discovery?*

significant /sɪg'nɪfɪkənt/ *adjective* important; with a special meaning: *The police say that the time of the robbery was very significant.*

signpost /'saɪnpəʊst/ *noun* a sign beside a road, that shows the way to a place and how far it is

Sikh /siːk/ *noun* a person who follows one of the religions of India, called **Sikhism**

silence /'saɪləns/ *noun* **1** (no plural) When there is silence, there is no sound: *I can only work in complete silence.* **2** (*plural* **silences**) a time when nobody speaks or makes a noise: *There was a long silence before she answered the question.* **in silence** without

speaking or making a noise: *We ate our dinner in silence.*

silent /'saɪlənt/ *adjective* **1** with no sound; completely quiet: *Everyone was asleep, and the house was silent.* **2** If you are silent, you are not speaking: *I asked him a question and he was silent for a moment before he answered.*

silently *adverb*: *The cat moved silently towards the bird.*

silk /sɪlk/ *noun* (no plural) thin smooth cloth that is made from the threads that an insect (called a **silkworm**) makes: *a silk shirt*

silly /'sɪli/ *adjective* (**sillier**, **silliest**) stupid; not clever: *Don't be so silly!* ○ *It was silly of you to leave the door open when you went out.*

silver /'sɪlvə(r)/ *noun* (no plural) **1** a shiny grey metal that is very valuable: *a silver necklace* **2** things that are made of silver, for example knives, forks and plates

silver *adjective* with the colour of silver: *silver paper*

similar /'sɪmələ(r)/ *adjective* the same in some ways but not completely the same: *Rats are similar to mice, but they are bigger.* ○ *Jane and her sister look very similar.*

similarity /ˌsɪmə'lærəti/ *noun* (*plural* **similarities**) a way that people or things are the same: *There are a lot of similarities between the two countries.* ✪ opposite: **difference**

simple /'sɪmpl/ *adjective* (**simpler**, **simplest**) **1** easy to do or understand: *This dictionary is written in simple English.* ○ *'How do you open that?' 'I'll show you – it's simple.'* **2** without a lot of different parts or extra things; plain: *She wore a simple black dress.* ○ *a simple meal*

simplicity /sɪm'plɪsəti/ *noun* (no plural) being simple: *I like the simplicity of these paintings.*

simplify /'sɪmplɪfaɪ/ *verb* (**simplifies**, **simplifying**, **simplified** /'sɪmplɪfaɪd/, **has simplified**) make something easier to do or understand: *The story has been simplified so that the children can understand it.*

simply /'sɪmpli/ *adverb* **1** in a simple

simsim /ˈsɪmsɪm/ (an East African word) (*also* **sesame**) /ˈsesəmi/ *noun* (no plural) a plant with small seeds. You can use simsim oil and seeds in cooking.

sin /sɪn/ *noun* something that your religion says you should not do, because it is very bad: *Stealing is a sin.*

sin *verb* (**sins**, **sinning**, **sinned** /sɪnd/) do something that your religion says is very bad

since /sɪns/ *preposition* in all the time after: *She has been ill since Sunday.* ○ *I haven't seen him since 1987.*

since *conjunction* **1** from the time when: *She has lived here since she was a child.* ○ *Jane hasn't written since she went to university.* **2** because: *Since it's your birthday, I'll buy you a drink.*

since *adverb* from then until now: *Andy left three years ago and we haven't seen him since.* **ever since** in all the time from then until now: *George went to Mombasa in 1974 and he has lived there ever since.*

sincere /sɪnˈsɪə(r)/ *adjective* If you are sincere, you are honest and you mean what you say: *Were you being sincere when you said that you loved me?*

sincerely *adverb* **Yours sincerely** words that you write at the end of a letter, before your name

sing /sɪŋ/ *verb* (**sings**, **singing**, **sang** /sæŋ/, **has sung** /sʌŋ/) make music with your voice: *She sang a song.* ○ *The birds were singing.*

singer *noun* a person who sings

single[1] /ˈsɪŋgl/ *adjective* **1** only one: *There wasn't a single cloud in the sky.* **2** not married: *Are you married or single?* **3** for one person: *I would like to book a single room, please.* ○ *a single bed* ☞ Look at **double**. **4** for a journey to a place, but not back again: *How much is a single ticket to Nairobi, please?* ☞ Look at **return**. **every single** each: *You answered every single question correctly.*

single[2] /ˈsɪŋgl/ *noun* a ticket for a journey to a place, but not back again: *A single to Kisumu, please.* ☞ Look at **return**.

singular /ˈsɪŋgjələ(r)/ *noun* (no plural) the form of a word that you use for one person or thing: *The singular of 'men' is 'man'.*

singular *adjective*: *'Table' is a singular noun.* ☞ Look at **plural**.

sink[1] /sɪŋk/ *noun* the place in a kitchen where you wash dishes

sink[2] /sɪŋk/ *verb* (**sinks**, **sinking**, **sank** /sæŋk/, **has sunk** /sʌŋk/) **1** go down under water: *If you throw a stone into water, it sinks.* ○ *The fishing boat sank to the bottom of the sea.* ☞ Look at **float**. **2** make a ship go down under water: *The ship was sunk by a bomb.* **3** go down: *The sun sank slowly behind the hills.*

sip /sɪp/ *verb* (**sips**, **sipping**, **sipped** /sɪpt/) drink something slowly, taking only a little each time: *She sipped her coffee.*

sip *noun*: *Can I have a sip of your drink?*

sir /sɜː(r)/ *noun* **1** (no plural) a polite way of speaking to a man, instead of using his name: *'Can I help you, sir?' asked the shop assistant.* ☞ Look at **madam**. **2** **Sir** (no plural) a word that you use at the beginning of a business letter to a man: *Dear Sir...* ☞ Look at **madam**.

siren /ˈsaɪərən/ *noun* a machine that makes a long loud sound to warn people about something. Police cars and fire-engines have sirens.

sisal /ˈsaɪsl/ *noun* (no plural) a plant with long leaves that we use to make rope, floor covering, etc

sister /ˈsɪstə(r)/ *noun* **1** Your sister is a girl or woman who has the same parents as you: *I've got two sisters and one brother.* ○ *Jane and Anne are sisters.* **2** a nurse in a hospital

sister-in-law /ˈsɪstər ɪn lɔː/ *noun* (*plural* **sisters-in-law**) **1** the sister of your wife or husband **2** the wife of your brother

sit /sɪt/ *verb* (**sits**, **sitting**, **sat** /sæt/, **has sat**) **1** rest on your bottom: *We sat in the garden all afternoon.* ○ *She was sitting on a bench.* **2** (*also* **sit down**) put yourself down on your bottom: *Come and sit next to me.* ○ *She came into the room and sat down.* **3** do an examination: *The students will sit their exams in June.* **sit up** sit when you have been lying: *He sat up in bed and looked at the clock.*

sitting room /ˈsɪtɪŋ ruːm/ *noun* a room in a house where people sit and watch television or talk, for example

site /saɪt/ *noun* a place where something is, was, or will be: *The station was built on the site of an old farm.* ○ *a campsite*

situated /ˈsɪtʃueɪtɪd/ *adjective* in a place: *The hotel is situated close to the beach.*

situation /ˌsɪtʃuˈeɪʃn/ *noun* the things that are happening in a certain place or at a certain time: *Sue is in a difficult situation – she can't decide what to do.*

six /sɪks/ *number* (*plural* **sixes**) 6

sixth /sɪksθ/ *adjective, adverb, noun* **1** 6th **2** one of six equal parts of something; $\frac{1}{6}$

sixteen /ˌsɪksˈtiːn/ *number* 16

sixteenth /ˌsɪksˈtiːnθ/ *adjective, adverb, noun* 16th

sixty /ˈsɪksti/ *number* **1** 60 **2 the sixties** (plural) the numbers, years or temperature between 60 and 69 **in your sixties** between the ages of 60 and 69

sixtieth /ˈsɪkstiəθ/ *adjective, adverb, noun* 60th

size /saɪz/ *noun* **1** (no plural) how big or small something is: *My bedroom is the same size as yours.* **2** (*plural* **sizes**) an exact measurement: *Have you got these shoes in a bigger size?*

skate /skeɪt/ *noun* a boot with wheels or a long sharp piece of metal under it, that you wear for moving on smooth ground or on ice: *a pair of roller skates* ○ *ice-skates*

skate *verb* (**skates, skating, skated**) move on skates

skateboard /ˈskeɪtbɔːd/ *noun* a long piece of wood or plastic on wheels. You stand on it as it moves over the ground.

skeleton /ˈskelɪtn/ *noun* the bones of a whole animal or person

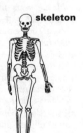
skeleton

sketch /sketʃ/ *verb* (**sketches, sketching, sketched** /sketʃt/) draw something quickly: *I sketched the house.*

sketch *noun* (*plural* **sketches**) a picture that you draw quickly

skid /skɪd/ *verb* (**skids, skidding, skidded**) If a car, lorry, etc skids, it moves suddenly and dangerously to the side, for example because the road is wet: *The lorry skidded on the icy road.*

skies plural of **sky**

skilful /ˈskɪlfl/ *adjective* very good at doing something: *a skilful tennis player*

skilfully /ˈskɪlfəli/ *adverb*: *The food was skilfully prepared.*

skill /skɪl/ *noun* **1** (no plural) being able to do something well: *You need great skill to fly a plane.* **2** (*plural* **skills**) a thing that you can do well: *What skills do you need for this job?*

skilled /skɪld/ *adjective* good at something because you have learned about or done it for a long time: *skilled workers* ✪ opposite: **unskilled**

skin /skɪn/ *noun* **1** (no plural) what covers the outside of a person or an animal's body: *She has dark skin.* **2** (*plural* **skins**) the outside part of some fruits and vegetables: *a banana skin*

skinny /ˈskɪni/ *adjective* (**skinnier, skinniest**) too thin: *He's very skinny – he doesn't eat enough.*

skip /skɪp/ *verb* (**skips, skipping, skipped** /skɪpt/) **1** move along quickly with little jumps from one foot to the other foot: *The child skipped along the road.* **2** jump many times over a rope that is turning **3** not do or have something that you should do or have: *I skipped my class today and went swimming.*

skip *noun* a little jump

skipping rope /ˈskɪpɪŋ rəʊp/ *noun* a rope that you use for skipping

skirt /skɜːt/ *noun* a piece of clothing for a woman or girl that hangs from the middle of the body

skull /skʌl/ *noun* the bones in the head of a person or an animal

sky /skaɪ/ *noun* (*plural* **skies**) the space

above the earth where you can see the sun, moon and stars: *a beautiful blue sky* ○ *There are no clouds in the sky.*

skyscraper /ˈskaɪskreɪpə(r)/ *noun* a very tall building: *He works on the 49th floor of a skyscraper.*

slab /slæb/ *noun* a thick flat piece of something: *slabs of stone* ○ *a big slab of meat*

slam /slæm/ *verb* (**slams**, **slamming**, **slammed** /slæmd/) close something or put something down with a loud noise: *She slammed the door angrily.* ○ *He slammed the book on the table and went out.*

slang /slæŋ/ *noun* (no plural) words that a certain group of people use when they are talking. You do not use slang when you need to be polite, and you do not usually use it in writing: *'Hop it!' is slang for 'Go away!'.*

slant /slɑːnt/ *verb* (**slants**, **slanting**, **slanted**) Something that slants has one side higher than the other or does not stand straight up: *My handwriting slants to the left.*

slap /slæp/ *verb* (**slaps**, **slapping**, **slapped** /slæpt/) hit somebody with the flat inside part of your hand: *He slapped me in the face.*

slap *noun*: *She gave me a slap across the face.*

slaughter /ˈslɔːtə(r)/ *verb* (**slaughters**, **slaughtering**, **slaughtered** /ˈslɔːtəd/) **1** kill an animal for food **2** kill a lot of people in a cruel way

slaughter *noun* (no plural) killing animals or people

slave /sleɪv/ *noun* a person who belongs to another person and must work for that person for no money

slavery /ˈsleɪvəri/ *noun* (no plural) **1** being a slave: *They lived in slavery.* **2** having slaves: *When did slavery end in America?*

sleep /sliːp/ *verb* (**sleeps**, **sleeping**, **slept** /slept/, **has slept**) rest with your eyes closed, as you do at night: *I sleep for eight hours every night.* ○ *Did you sleep well?*

sleep *noun* (no plural) *I didn't get any sleep last night.* **go to sleep** start to sleep: *I got into bed and soon went to sleep.*

> ✪ Be careful! We usually say **be asleep**, not **be sleeping**:
> *I was asleep when you phoned.*
> We use **go to sleep** or **fall asleep** to talk about starting to sleep.

sleeping sickness /ˈsliːpɪŋ sɪknəs/ *noun* (no plural) a serious illness that makes you want to sleep. You get sleeping sickness from tsetse flies.

sleepless /ˈsliːpləs/ *adjective* without sleep: *I had a sleepless night worrying about money.*

sleepy /ˈsliːpi/ *adjective* (**sleepier**, **sleepiest**) **1** tired and ready to sleep: *I felt sleepy after that big meal.* **2** quiet, with not many things happening: *a sleepy little village*

sleet /sliːt/ *noun* (no plural) snow and rain together

sleeve

sleeve /sliːv/ *noun* the part of a coat, dress or shirt, for example, that covers your arm: *a shirt with short sleeves*

slender /ˈslendə(r)/ *adjective* thin, in a nice way: *She has long, slender legs.*

slept *form of* **sleep**

slice /slaɪs/ *noun* a thin piece that you cut off bread, meat or other food: *a slice of lemon* ☞ picture on page A15

slice *verb* (**slices**, **slicing**, **sliced** /slaɪst/) cut something into slices: *Slice the onions.*

slide¹ /slaɪd/ *verb* (**slides**, **sliding**, **slid** /slɪd/, **has slid**) move smoothly or make something move smoothly across something: *The children were sliding in the mud.*

slide² /slaɪd/ *noun* **1** a long metal thing that children play on. They climb up steps, sit down, and then slide down the other side. **2** a small photograph that you show on a **screen**, using a **projector**

slight /slaɪt/ *adjective* (**slighter**, **slightest**) small; not important or serious: *I've got a slight problem.* ○ *a slight headache*

slightly /'slaɪtli/ *adverb* a little: *I'm feeling slightly better today.*

slim[1] /slɪm/ *adjective* (**slimmer**, **slimmest**) thin, but not too thin: *a tall slim man*

slim[2] /slɪm/ *noun* (no plural) a word used in Africa for **AIDS**

sling[1] /slɪŋ/ *noun* a piece of cloth that you wear to hold up an arm that is hurt: *She's got her arm in a sling.*

sling[2] /slɪŋ/ *verb* (**slings**, **slinging**, **slung** /slʌŋ/, **has slung**) throw something without care: *He got angry and slung the book at me.*

slip[1] /slɪp/ *verb* (**slips**, **slipping**, **slipped** /slɪpt/) **1** move smoothly over something by mistake and fall or almost fall: *He slipped in the mud and broke his leg.* **2** go quickly and quietly so that nobody sees you: *Ann slipped out of the room when the children were asleep.* **3** put something in a place quickly and quietly: *He slipped the money into his pocket.*

slip[2] /slɪp/ *noun* **1** a small piece of paper: *Write your address on this slip of paper.* **2** a small mistake: *I made a slip.*

slippery /'slɪpəri/ *adjective* so smooth or wet that you cannot move on it or hold it easily: *The road was wet and slippery.* ○ *The skin of a fish is slippery.*

slit /slɪt/ *noun* a long thin hole or cut

slit *verb* (**slits**, **slitting**, **slit**, **has slit**) make a long thin cut in something: *I slit the envelope open with a knife.*

slither /'slɪðə(r)/ *verb* (**slithers**, **slithering**, **slithered** /'slɪðəd/) move along like a snake: *The snake slithered across the floor.*

slogan /'sləʊgən/ *noun* a short sentence or group of words that is easy to remember. Slogans are used to make people believe something or buy something: *'Faster than light' is the slogan for the new car.*

slope /sləʊp/ *noun* a piece of ground that has one end higher than the other,

like the side of a hill: *We walked down the mountain slope.*

slope *verb* (**slopes**, **sloping**, **sloped** /sləʊpt/) have one end higher than the other: *The field slopes down to the river.* ○ *a sloping roof*

slot /slɒt/ *noun* a long thin hole that you push something through: *Put a coin in the slot and take your ticket.*

slot machine /'slɒt məʃiːn/ *noun* a machine that gives you things like drinks or sweets when you put money in a small hole

slow[1] /sləʊ/ *adjective* (**slower**, **slowest**) **1** A person or thing that is slow does not move or do something quickly: *a slow train* ○ *She hasn't finished her work yet – she's very slow.* **2** If a clock or watch is slow, it shows a time that is earlier than the real time: *My watch is five minutes slow.* ☛ Look at **quick** and **fast**.

slow *adverb* slowly: *Please drive slower.*

slowly *adverb*: *The old lady walked slowly up the hill.*

slow[2] /sləʊ/ *verb* (**slows**, **slowing**, **slowed** /sləʊd/) **slow down** start to go more slowly; make somebody or something start to go more slowly: *The train slowed down as it came into the station.* ○ *Don't talk to me when I'm working – it slows me down.*

slug /slʌg/ *noun* a small soft animal that moves slowly and eats plants

slum /slʌm/ *noun* a poor part of a city where people live in old dirty buildings

slung *form of* **sling**[2]

sly /slaɪ/ *adjective* A person who is sly tricks people or does things secretly.

smack /smæk/ *verb* (**smacks**, **smacking**, **smacked** /smækt/) hit somebody with the inside part of your hand: *They never smack their children.*

smack *noun*: *She gave her son a smack.*

small /smɔːl/ *adjective* (**smaller**, **smallest**) **1** not big; little: *This dress is too small for me.* ○ *My house is smaller than yours.* **2** young: *They have two small children.* ☛ picture on page A10

smart /smɑːt/ *adjective* (**smarter**, **smartest**) **1** right for a special or important time; clean and tidy: *She wore smart clothes for her job interview.* ○

He looks very smart in his new jacket.
2 clever: *a smart businesswoman*

smartly *adverb*: *She was very smartly dressed.*

smash /smæʃ/ *verb* (**smashes, smashing, smashed** /smæʃt/) **1** break something into many pieces: *The boys smashed the window.* **2** break into many pieces: *I dropped the plate but it didn't smash.*

smash *noun* the loud noise when something breaks into pieces: *The glass hit the floor with a smash.*

smear /smɪə(r)/ *verb* (**smears, smearing, smeared** /smɪəd/) spread soft stuff on something, making it dirty: *The child smeared porridge over his clothes.*

smear *noun* a dirty mark: *She had smears of paint on her dress.*

smell /smel/ *verb* (**smells, smelling, smelt** /smelt/ or **smelled** /smeld/, **has smelt** or **has smelled**) **1** notice something with your nose: *Can you smell smoke?* **2** If something smells, you notice it with your nose: *This fish smells bad.* ○ *The perfume smells of roses.* **3** have a bad smell: *Your feet smell!*

smell *noun* something that you notice with your nose: *There's a smell of gas in this room.*

smelly /'smeli/ *adjective* (**smellier, smelliest**) with a bad smell: *smelly socks*

smelt /smelt/ *verb* to get metal from rock or earth (**ore**) by making it very hot

smile /smaɪl/ *verb* (**smiles, smiling, smiled** /smaɪld/) move your mouth to show that you are happy or that you think something is funny: *He smiled at me.*

smile *noun*: *She had a big smile on her face.*

smoke¹ /sməʊk/ *noun* (no plural) the grey or black gas that you see in the air when something is burning: *The room was full of smoke.* ○ *cigarette smoke*

smoke² /sməʊk/ *verb* (**smokes, smoking, smoked** /sməʊkt/) have a cigarette, cigar or pipe in your mouth, and breathe the smoke in and out: *He was smoking a cigarette.* ○ *Do you smoke?*

smoking *noun* (no plural) *No smoking in the theatre.*

smoked /sməʊkt/ *adjective* prepared by putting it over a wood fire so that you can keep it for a long time: *smoked ham*

smoker /'sməʊkə(r)/ *noun* a person who smokes ✪ opposite: **non-smoker**

smoky /'sməʊki/ (**smokier, smokiest**) *adjective* full of smoke: *a smoky room*

smooth /smuːð/ *adjective* (**smoother, smoothest**) **1** flat; not rough: *Babies have smooth skin.* **2** moving gently: *The weather was good so we had a very smooth flight.*

smoothly *adverb*: *The plane landed smoothly.*

smother /'smʌðə(r)/ *verb* (**smothers, smothering, smothered** /'smʌðəd/) **1** kill somebody by covering their face so that they cannot breathe **2** cover a thing with too much of something: *He smothered his food with salt.*

smuggle /'smʌɡl/ *verb* (**smuggles, smuggling, smuggled** /'smʌɡld/) take things secretly into or out of a country: *They were trying to smuggle drugs into the country.*

smuggler /'smʌɡlə(r)/ *noun* a person who smuggles: *drug smugglers*

snack /snæk/ *noun* a small quick meal: *We had a snack on the train.*

snack bar /'snæk bɑː(r)/ *noun* a place where you can buy and eat snacks

snag /snæɡ/ *noun* a small problem: *The work will be finished tomorrow if there are no snags.*

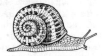

snail

snail /sneɪl/ *noun* a small soft animal with a hard shell on its back. Snails move very slowly.

snake

snake /sneɪk/ *noun* an animal with a long thin body and no legs: *Do these snakes bite?*

snap[1] /snæp/ *verb* (**snaps, snapping, snapped** /snæpt/) **1** break suddenly with a sharp noise: *He snapped the pencil in two.* **2** say something in a quick angry way: *'Go away – I'm busy!' she snapped.* **3** try to bite somebody or something: *The dog snapped at my leg.*

snap[2] /snæp/, **snapshot** /'snæpʃɒt/ *noun* a photograph: *She showed us her family snaps.*

snarl /snɑːl/ *verb* (**snarls, snarling, snarled** /snɑːld/) When an animal snarls, it shows its teeth and makes a low angry sound: *The dog snarled at the stranger.*

snatch /snætʃ/ *verb* (**snatches, snatching, snatched** /snætʃt/) take something quickly and roughly: *He snatched her money and ran away.*

sneak /sniːk/ *verb* (**sneaks, sneaking, sneaked** /sniːkt/) go somewhere very quietly so that nobody sees or hears you: *She sneaked out of the classroom while the teacher wasn't looking.*

sneer /snɪə(r)/ *verb* (**sneers, sneering, sneered** /snɪəd/) speak or smile in an unkind way to show that you do not like somebody or something or that you think they are not good enough: *I told her about my idea, but she just sneered at it.*

sneer *noun* an unkind smile

sneeze /sniːz/ *verb* (**sneezes, sneezing, sneezed** /sniːzd/) send air out of your nose and mouth with a sudden loud noise, for example because you have a cold: *Pepper makes you sneeze.*

sneeze *noun*: *She gave a loud sneeze.*

sniff /snɪf/ *verb* (**sniffs, sniffing, sniffed** /snɪft/) **1** make a noise by suddenly taking in air through your nose. People sometimes sniff when they have a cold or when they are crying. **2** smell something: *The dog was sniffing the meat.*

sniff *noun*: *I heard a loud sniff.*

snooze /snuːz/ *verb* (**snoozes, snoozing, snoozed** /snuːzd/) sleep for a short time

snooze *noun*: *I had a snooze after lunch.*

snore /snɔː(r)/ *verb* (**snores, snoring, snored** /snɔːd/) make a noise in your nose and throat when you are asleep: *He was snoring loudly.*

snort /snɔːt/ *verb* (**snorts, snorting, snorted**) make a noise by blowing air through the nose: *The horse snorted.*

snow /snəʊ/ *noun* (no plural) soft white stuff that falls from the sky in cool countries when it is very cold

snow *verb* (**snows, snowing, snowed** /snəʊd/) When it snows, snow falls from the sky: *It often snows in the mountains.*

snowy *adjective* (**snowier, snowiest**) with a lot of snow: *snowy weather*

so[1] /səʊ/ *adverb* **1** a word that you use when you say how much, how big, etc something is: *This bag is so heavy that I can't carry it.* ☞ Look at **such**. **2** a word that makes another word stronger: *Why are you so late?* **3** also: *Julie is a teacher and so is her husband.* ○ *'I like this music.' 'So do I.'* ✪ In negative sentences, we use **neither** or **nor**. **4** You use 'so' instead of saying words again: *'Is John coming?' 'I think so.'* (= I think that he is coming) **and so on** and other things like that: *The shop sells pens, paper and so on.* **not so ... as** words that show how two people or things are different: *He's not so tall as his brother.* **or so** words that you use to show that a number is not exactly right: *Forty or so people came to the party.*

so[2] /səʊ/ *conjunction* **1** because of this or that: *The shop is closed so I can't buy any bread.* **2** (also **so that**) in order that: *Speak louder so that everybody can hear you.* ○ *I'll draw you a map so you can find my house.* **so what?** why is that important or interesting?: *'It's late.' 'So what? There's no school tomorrow.'*

soak /səʊk/ *verb* (**soaks, soaking, soaked** /səʊkt/) **1** make somebody or something very wet: *It was raining when I went out. I got soaked!* **2** be in a liquid; let something stay in a liquid: *He left his dirty shirts to soak in soapy water.* **soak up** take in a liquid: *Soak the water up with a cloth.*

soaking *adjective* very wet: *This towel is soaking.*

soap /səʊp/ *noun* (no plural) stuff that you use with water for washing and cleaning: *a bar of soap*

soap opera /ˈsəʊp ɒprə/ *noun* a story about the lives of a group of people, that is on the TV or radio every day or several times each week

soap powder /ˈsəʊp paʊdə(r)/ *noun* (no plural) powder that you use for washing clothes

soapy *adjective* with soap in it: *soapy water*

soar /sɔː(r)/ *verb* (**soars**, **soaring**, **soared** /sɔːd/) **1** fly high in the sky **2** go up very fast: *Prices are soaring.*

sob /sɒb/ *verb* (**sobs**, **sobbing**, **sobbed** /sɒbd/) cry loudly, making short sounds

sob *noun*: *'She's left me!' he said with a sob.*

sober /ˈsəʊbə(r)/ *adjective* not drunk

so-called /ˌsəʊ ˈkɔːld/ *adjective* a word that you use to show that you do not think another word is correct: *Her so-called friends did not help her* (= they are not really her friends).

soccer /ˈsɒkə(r)/ *noun* (no plural) football

social /ˈsəʊʃl/ *adjective* of people together; of being with other people: *the social problems of big cities* ○ *Anne has a busy social life* (= she goes out with friends a lot).

social security /ˌsəʊʃl sɪˈkjʊərəti/ *noun* (no plural) money that a government pays to somebody who is poor, for example because they have no job

social worker /ˈsəʊʃl wɜːkə(r)/ *noun* a person whose job is to help people who have problems, for example because they are poor or ill

society /səˈsaɪəti/ *noun* **1** (no plural) a group of people living together, with the same ideas about how to live **2** (*plural* **societies**) a group of people who are interested in the same thing: *a music society*

sock /sɒk/ *noun* a thing that you wear on your foot, inside your shoe: *a pair of socks*

socks

socket /ˈsɒkɪt/ *noun* a place in a wall where you can push an electric plug ☞ picture at **plug**

sofa

sofa /ˈsəʊfə/ *noun* a long soft seat for more than one person: *Jane was sitting on the sofa.*

soft /sɒft/ *adjective* (**softer**, **softest**) **1** not hard or firm; that moves when you press it: *The ground is soft here.* ○ *a soft bed* ☞ picture on page A11 **2** smooth and nice to touch; not rough: *soft skin* ○ *My cat's fur is very soft.* **3** quiet or gentle; not loud: *soft music* ○ *He has a very soft voice.* **4** not bright or strong: *the soft light of a candle* **5** kind and gentle; not strict: *She's too soft with her class and they don't do any work.*

soft drink /ˌsɒft ˈdrɪŋk/ *noun* a cold drink with no alcohol in it, for example orange juice or lemonade

softly *adverb* gently or quietly: *She spoke very softly.*

software /ˈsɒftweə(r)/ *noun* (no plural) programs for a computer

soggy /ˈsɒgi/ *adjective* (**soggier**, **soggiest**) very wet

soil /sɔɪl/ *noun* (no plural) what plants and trees grow in; earth

solar /ˈsəʊlə(r)/ *adjective* of or using the sun: *solar energy*

the solar system /ðə ˈsəʊlə sɪstəm/ *noun* (no plural) the sun and the planets that move around it

sold *form of* **sell** **be sold out** When things are sold out, there are no more to sell: *I'm sorry – the bananas are sold out.*

soldier /ˈsəʊldʒə(r)/ *noun* a person in an army

sole[1] /səʊl/ *noun* the bottom part of your foot or of a shoe: *These boots have leather soles.* ☞ picture on page A4

sole

sole[2] /səʊl/ *adjective* only: *His sole interest is football.*

solemn /'sɒləm/ *adjective* serious: *slow, solemn music*

solemnly *adverb*: *'I've got some bad news for you,' he said solemnly.*

solid /'sɒlɪd/ *adjective* **1** hard, not like a liquid or a gas: *Water becomes solid when it freezes.* **2** with no empty space inside; made of the same material inside and outside: *a solid rubber ball* ○ *This ring is solid gold.*

solid *noun* not a liquid or gas: *Milk is a liquid and bread is a solid.*

solitary /'sɒlətri/ *adjective* without others; alone: *She went for a long solitary walk.*

solo /'səʊləʊ/ *noun* (*plural* **solos**) a piece of music for one person to sing or play: *a piano solo*

solo *adjective, adverb* alone; without other people: *She flew solo across the Atlantic.*

solution /sə'luːʃn/ *noun* the answer to a question, problem or puzzle: *I can't find a solution to this problem.*

solve /sɒlv/ *verb* (**solves, solving, solved** /sɒlvd/) find the answer to a question, problem or puzzle: *The police are still trying to solve the crime.*

some /sʌm/ *adjective, pronoun* **1** a number or amount of something: *I bought some tomatoes and some butter.* ○ *I've made some coffee. Do you want some?* ✪ In questions and after 'not' and 'if', we usually use **any**: *Did you buy any apples?* ○ *I didn't buy any meat.* **2** part of a number or amount of something: *Some of the children can swim, but the others can't.* **3** I do not know which: *There's some man at the door who wants to see you.* **some more** a little more or a few more: *Have some more coffee.* ○ *Some more people arrived.* **some time** quite a long time: *We waited for some time but she did not come.*

somebody /'sʌmbədi/ (*also* **someone**) /'sʌmwʌn/ *pronoun* a person; a person that you do not know: *There's somebody at the door.* ○ *Someone has broken the window.* ○ *Ask somebody else* (= another person) *to help you.*

somehow /'sʌmhaʊ/ *adverb* in some way that you do not know: *We must find her somehow.*

somersault /'sʌməsɔːlt/ *noun* a movement when you turn your body with your feet going over your head: *The children were doing somersaults.*

something /'sʌmθɪŋ/ *pronoun* a thing; a thing you cannot name: *There's something under the table. What is it?* ○ *I want to tell you something.* ○ *Would you like something else* (= another thing) *to eat?* **something like** the same as somebody or something, but not in every way: *A rat is something like a mouse, but bigger.*

sometime /'sʌmtaɪm/ *adverb* at a time that you do not know exactly: *I'll arrive sometime tomorrow.*

sometimes /'sʌmtaɪmz/ *adverb* not very often: *He sometimes writes to me.* ○ *Sometimes I walk to work and sometimes I go by bus.*

somewhere /'sʌmweə(r)/ *adverb* at, in or to a place that you do not know exactly: *They live somewhere near here.* ○ *'Did she go to Mombasa?' 'No, I think she went somewhere else* (= to another place) *on the coast.'*

son /sʌn/ *noun* a boy or man who is somebody's child: *They have a son and two daughters.*

song /sɒŋ/ *noun* **1** (*plural* **songs**) a piece of music with words that you sing: *a pop song* **2** (no plural) singing; music that a person or bird makes

son-in-law /'sʌn ɪn lɔː/ *noun* (*plural* **sons-in-law**) the husband of your daughter

soon /suːn/ *adverb* not long after now, or not long after a certain time: *John will be home soon.* ○ *She arrived soon after two o'clock.* ○ *Goodbye! See you soon!* **as soon as** at the same time that; when: *Phone me as soon as you get home.* **sooner or later** at some time in the future: *Don't worry – I'm sure he will write to you sooner or later.*

soot /sʊt/ *noun* (no plural) black powder that comes from smoke

soothe /suːð/ *verb* (**soothes, soothing, soothed** /suːðd/) make somebody feel calmer and less unhappy: *The baby was crying, so I tried to soothe her by singing to her.*

soothing *adjective*: *soothing music*

sore /sɔː(r)/ *adjective* If a part of your body is sore, it gives you pain: *My feet were sore after the long walk.* ○ *I've got a sore throat.*

sore *noun* a place on your skin that is painful because of infection: *His legs were covered in sores.*

sorghum /'sɔːgəm/ *noun* (no plural) a kind of grass with a lot of very small seeds that we can make into flour

sorrow /'sɒrəʊ/ *noun* sadness

sorry /'sɒri/ *adjective* **1** a word that you use when you feel bad about something you have done: *I'm sorry I didn't phone you.* ○ *Sorry I'm late!* ○ *I'm sorry for losing your pen.* **2** sad: *I'm sorry you can't come to the party.* **3** a word that you use to say 'no' politely: *I'm sorry – I can't help you.* **4** a word that you use when you did not hear what somebody said and you want them to say it again: *'My name is Philip Kiptoon.' 'Sorry? Philip who?'* **feel sorry for somebody** feel sad because somebody has problems: *I felt sorry for her when her father died.*

sort¹ /sɔːt/ *noun* a group of things or people that are the same in some way; a type or kind: *What sort of food do you like best?* ○ *We found all sorts of shells on the beach.* **sort of** words that you use when you are not sure about something: *It's sort of long and thin, a bit like a sausage.*

sort² /sɔːt/ *verb* (**sorts, sorting, sorted**) put things into groups: *The machine sorts the rocks into large ones and small ones.* **sort out 1** make something tidy: *I sorted out the kitchen.* **2** find an answer to a problem

SOS /ˌes əʊ 'es/ *noun* a call for help from a ship or an aeroplane that is in danger

sought *form of* **seek**

soul /səʊl/ *noun* **1** (*plural* **souls**) the part of a person that some people believe does not die when the body dies **2** (*also* **soul music**) (no plural) a kind of Black American music: *a soul singer* **not a soul** not one person: *I looked everywhere, but there wasn't a soul in the building.*

sound¹ /saʊnd/ *noun* something that you hear: *I heard the sound of a baby crying.* ○ *Light travels faster than sound.*

sound² /saʊnd/ *verb* (**sounds, sounding, sounded**) seem a certain way when you hear it: *He sounded angry when I spoke to him on the phone.* ○ *That sounds like a good idea.* ○ *She told me about the book – it sounds interesting.*

sound³ /saʊnd/ *adjective* **1** healthy or strong: *sound teeth* **2** right and good: *sound advice*

sound *adverb* **sound asleep** sleeping very well: *The children are sound asleep.*

soup /suːp/ *noun* (no plural) liquid food that you make by cooking things like vegetables or meat in water: *chicken soup*

sour /'saʊə(r)/ *adjective* **1** with a taste like lemons or vinegar: *If it's too sour, put some sugar in it.* **2** Sour milk tastes bad because it is not fresh: *This milk has gone sour.*

source /sɔːs/ *noun* a place where something comes from: *Our information comes from many sources.*

south /saʊθ/ *noun* (no plural) the direction that is on your right when you watch the sun come up in the morning ☛ picture at **north**

south *adjective, adverb*: *Brazil is in South America.* ○ *We drove south to the border.*

southern /'sʌðən/ *adjective* in or of the south part of a place: *Nairobi is in southern Kenya.*

souvenir /ˌsuːvə'nɪə(r)/ *noun* something that you keep to remember a place or something that happened: *I brought back this cowboy hat as a souvenir of America.*

sow /səʊ/ *verb* (**sows, sowing, sowed** /səʊd/, **has sown** /səʊn/ or **has sowed**) put seeds in the ground: *The farmer sowed the field with corn.*

space /speɪs/ *noun* **1** (no plural) a place that is big enough for somebody or something to go into or onto: *Is there space for me in your car?* **2** (*plural* **spaces**) an empty place between other things: *There is a space here for you to write your name.* **3** (no plural) the place far away outside the earth, where all the planets and stars are: *space travel*

spacecraft /'speɪskrɑːft/ *noun* (*plural* **spacecraft**) a vehicle that travels in space

spaceman /'speɪsmæn/ (*plural* **spacemen**), **spacewoman** /'speɪswʊmən/ (*plural* **spacewomen**) *noun* a person who travels in space

spaceship /'speɪsʃɪp/ *noun* a vehicle that travels in space

spacious /'speɪʃəs/ *adjective* with a lot of space inside: *a spacious house*

spade /speɪd/ *noun* **1** a tool that you use for digging ☞ picture at **dig** **2** **spades** (plural) the playing-cards that have the shape ♠ on them: *the queen of spades*

spaghetti /spə'geti/ *noun* (no plural) a kind of food made from flour and water, that looks like long pieces of string

spanner

spanner /'spænə(r)/ *noun* a tool that you use for turning **nuts** and **bolts**

spare[1] /speə(r)/ *adjective* **1** extra; that you do not need now: *Have you got a spare tyre in your car?* **2** spare time is time when you are not working: *What do you do in your spare time?*

spare[2] /speə(r)/ *verb* (**spares**, **sparing**, **spared** /speəd/) be able to give something to somebody: *I can't spare the time to help you today.* ○ *Can you spare any money?*

spark /spɑːk/ *noun* a very small piece of fire

sparkle /'spɑːkl/ *verb* (**sparkles**, **sparkling**, **sparkled** /'spɑːkld/) shine with a lot of very small points of light: *The sea sparkled in the sunlight.* ○ *Her eyes sparkled with excitement.*

sparkle *noun* (no plural) *the sparkle of diamonds*

sparrow /'spærəʊ/ *noun* a small brown bird

spat *form of* **spit**

speak /spiːk/ *verb* (**speaks**, **speaking**, **spoke** /spəʊk/, **has spoken**

/'spəʊkən/) **1** say words; talk to somebody: *Please speak more slowly.* ○ *Can I speak to John Kamotho, please?* (= words that you say on the telephone) **2** know and use a language: *Can you speak French?* **3** talk to a group of people: *The chairwoman spoke for an hour at the meeting.* **speak up** talk louder: *Can you speak up? I can't hear you!*

speaker /'spiːkə(r)/ *noun* **1** a person who is talking to a group of people **2** the part of a radio, cassette player, etc where the sound comes out

spear /spɪə(r)/ *noun* a long stick with a sharp point at one end, used for hunting or fighting

special /'speʃl/ *adjective* **1** not usual or ordinary; important for a reason: *It's my birthday today so we are having a special dinner.* **2** for a particular person or thing: *He goes to a special school for deaf children.*

specially /'speʃəli/ *adverb* **1** for a particular person or thing: *I made this cake specially for you.* **2** very; more than usual or more than others: *The food was not specially good.*

specialist /'speʃəlɪst/ *noun* a person who knows a lot about something: *She's a specialist in East African art.*

specialize /'speʃəlaɪz/ *verb* (**specializes**, **specializing**, **specialized** /'speʃəlaɪzd/) **specialize in something** study or know a lot about one special thing: *This doctor specializes in natural medicine.*

species /'spiːʃiːz/ *noun* (*plural* **species**) a group of animals or plants that are the same in some way: *a rare species of plant*

specific /spə'sɪfɪk/ *adjective* **1** particular: *Is there anything specific that you want to talk about?* **2** exact and clear: *He gave us specific instructions on how to get there.*

specifically /spə'sɪfɪkli/ *adverb*: *I specifically asked you to write in pencil, not pen.*

specimen /'spesɪmən/ *noun* a small amount or part of something that shows what the rest is like; one example of a group of things: *a specimen of rock* ○ *The doctor took a specimen of* *blood for testing.*

speck /spek/ *noun* a very small bit of something: *specks of dust*

spectacles /'spektəklz/ *noun* (plural) pieces of special glass that you wear over your eyes to help you see better: *a pair of spectacles* ✪ It is more usual to say **glasses**.

spectacular /spek'tækjulə(r)/ *adjective* wonderful to see: *There was a spectacular view from the top of the mountain.*

spectator /spek'teɪtə(r)/ *noun* a person who watches something that is happening: *There were 2 000 spectators at the football match.*

sped *form of* **speed**²

speech /spiːtʃ/ *noun* **1** (no plural) the power to speak, or the way that you speak **2** (*plural* **speeches**) a talk that you give to a group of people: *The President made a speech.*

speed¹ /spiːd/ *noun* how fast something goes: *The car was travelling at a speed of 50 miles an hour.* ○ *a high-speed train* (= that goes very fast)

speed limit /'spiːd lɪmɪt/ *noun* the fastest that you are allowed to travel on a road: *What's the speed limit in towns?*

speed² /spiːd/ *verb* (**speeds**, **speeding**, **sped** /sped/ or **speeded**, **has sped** or **has speeded**) **1** go or move very quickly: *He sped past me on his bike.* **2** drive too fast: *The police stopped me because I was speeding.* **speed up** go faster; make something go faster

spell¹ /spel/ *verb* (**spells**, **spelling**, **spelt** /spelt/ or **spelled** /speld/, **has spelt** or **has spelled**) use the right letters to make a word: *'How do you spell your name?' 'A-Z-I-Z.'* ○ *You have spelt this word wrong.*

spelling *noun* the right way of writing a word: *Look in your dictionary to find the right spelling.*

spell² /spel/ *noun* magic words **put a spell on somebody** say magic words to somebody to change them or to make them do what you want: *The witch put a spell on the prince.*

spend /spend/ *verb* (**spends**, **spending**, **spent** /spent/, **has spent**) **1** pay money for something: *Louise spends a lot of money on clothes.* **2** use time for

something: *I spent two weeks in hospital.* ○ *He spent a lot of time sleeping.*

sphere /sfɪə(r)/ *noun* any round thing that is like a ball: *The earth is a sphere.* ☞ picture on page A5

spice /spaɪs/ *noun* a powder or the seeds from a plant that you can put in food to give it a stronger taste. Pepper and ginger are spices.

spicy /'spaɪsi/ *adjective* (**spicier**, **spiciest**) with spices in it: *Indian food is usually spicy.*

spider — web

spider /'spaɪdə(r)/ *noun* a small animal with eight legs, that catches and eats insects: *Spiders spin webs to catch flies.*

spied *form of* **spy**

spies *form of* **spy**

spike /spaɪk/ *noun* a piece of metal with a sharp point: *The fence has spikes along the top.*

spill /spɪl/ *verb* (**spills**, **spilling**, **spilt** /spɪlt/ or **spilled** /spɪld/, **has spilt** or **has spilled**) If you spill a liquid, it flows out of something by accident: *I've spilt my tea!*

spill

spin /spɪn/ *verb* (**spins**, **spinning**, **spun** /spʌn/, **has spun**) **1** turn round quickly; turn something round quickly: *She spun a coin on the table.* **2** make thread from wool or cotton **3** make a web: *The spider spun a web.*

spinach /'spɪnɪtʃ/ *noun* (no plural) a vegetable with big green leaves

spine /spaɪn/ *noun* the line of bones in your back ☞ picture on page A4

spiral /'spaɪrəl/ *noun* a long shape that goes round and round as it goes up: *A spring is a spiral.*

spiral *adjective: a spiral staircase*

spirit /'spɪrɪt/ *noun* **1** the part of a person that is not the body. Some people think that your spirit does not die when your body dies. **2 spirits** (plural) alcoholic drinks. Whisky and brandy are spirits. **3 spirits** (plural) how you feel: *She's in high spirits* (= happy) *today*.

spit /spɪt/ *verb* (**spits**, **spitting**, **spat** /spæt/, **has spat**) send liquid or food out from your mouth: *He spat on the ground.* ○ *The baby spat her food out.*

spite /spaɪt/ *noun* (no plural) wanting to hurt somebody: *She broke my watch out of spite* (= because she wanted to hurt me). **in spite of something** although something is true; not noticing or not caring about something: *I slept well in spite of the noise.* ○ *In spite of the bad weather, we went out.*

splash /splæʃ/ *verb* (**splashes**, **splashing**, **splashed** /splæʃt/) **1** throw drops of liquid over somebody or something and make them wet: *The car splashed us as it drove past.* **2** move through water so that drops of it fly in the air: *The children were splashing around in the pool.*

splash *noun* (*plural* **splashes**) **1** the sound that a person or thing makes when they fall into water: *Tom jumped into the river with a big splash.* **2** a place where liquid has fallen: *There were splashes of paint on the floor.*

splendid /'splendɪd/ *adjective* very beautiful or very good: *a splendid view* ○ *What a splendid idea!*

splinter /'splɪntə(r)/ *noun* a thin sharp piece of wood or glass that has broken off a bigger piece: *I've got a splinter in my finger.*

split /splɪt/ *verb* (**splits**, **splitting**, **split**, **has split**) **1** break something into two parts: *I split the wood with an axe.* **2** break open: *His jeans split when he sat down.* **3** share something; give a part to each person: *We split the money between us.* **split up** stop being together: *He has split up with his wife.*

split *noun* a long cut or hole in something

spoil /spɔɪl/ *verb* (**spoils**, **spoiling**,

spoilt /spɔɪlt/ or **spoiled** /spɔɪld/, **has spoilt** or **has spoiled**) **1** make something less good than before: *The mud spoiled my shoes.* ○ *The bad news spoilt my day.* **2** give a child too much so that they think they can always have what they want: *She spoils her grandchildren.* ○ *a spoilt child*

spoke[1] *form of* **speak**

spoke[2] /spəʊk/ *noun* one of the thin pieces of wire that join the middle of a wheel to the outside, for example on a bicycle

spoken *form of* **speak**

spokesman /'spəʊksmən/ *noun* (*plural* **spokesmen** /'spəʊksmən/), **spokeswoman** /'spəʊkswʊmən/ (*plural* **spokeswomen**) *noun* a person who tells somebody what a group of people has decided

sponge /spʌndʒ/ *noun* **1** a soft thing with a lot of small holes in it, that you use for washing yourself or cleaning things **2** a soft light cake

sponsor /'spɒnsə(r)/ *verb* (**sponsors**, **sponsoring**, **sponsored** /'spɒnsəd/) give money so that something, for example a sports event, will happen: *The football match was sponsored by a large firm.*

sponsor *noun* a person or company that sponsors

spoon /spu:n/ *noun* a thing with a round end that you use for putting food in your mouth or for mixing: *a wooden spoon* ○ *a teaspoon*

spoon

spoonful /'spu:nfʊl/ *noun* the amount that you can put in one spoon: *Two spoonfuls of sugar in my tea, please.*

sport /spɔ:t/ *noun* a game that you do to keep your body strong and well and because you enjoy it: *Jane does a lot of sport.* ○ *Football, swimming, and athletics are all sports.*

sportsman /'spɔ:tsmən/ *noun* (*plural* **sportsmen** /'spɔ:tsmən/), **sportswoman** /'spɔ:tswʊmən/ (*plural* **sportswomen**) a person who plays sport

sports car /ˈspɔːts kɑː(r)/ *noun* a fast car, usually with a roof that you can open

spot[1] /spɒt/ *noun* **1** a small round mark: *a red dress with white spots* **2** a small red mark on your skin: *A lot of teenagers get spots on their face.* **3** a place: *This is a good spot for camping.*

spotted *adjective* with small round marks on it: *a spotted shirt*

spotted

spot

spotty *adjective* (**spottier**, **spottiest**) with small red marks on your skin: *a spotty face*

spot[2] /spɒt/ *verb* (**spots**, **spotting**, **spotted**) see somebody or something suddenly: *She spotted her friend in the crowd.*

spout /spaʊt/ *noun* the part of a container that is like a short tube, where liquid comes out. Teapots have spouts.

sprain /spreɪn/ *verb* (**sprains**, **spraining**, **sprained** /spreɪnd/) hurt part of your body by turning it suddenly: *William fell and sprained his ankle.*

sprang *form of* **spring**[3]

spray /spreɪ/ *noun* **1** (no plural) liquid in very small drops that flies through the air: *spray from the sea* **2** (plural **sprays**) liquid in a can that comes out in very small drops when you press a button: *hairspray*

spray

spray *verb* (**sprays**, **spraying**, **sprayed** /spreɪd/) make very small drops of liquid fall on something: *Somebody has sprayed paint on my car.*

spread /spred/ *verb* (**spreads**, **spreading**, **spread**, **has spread**) **1** open something so that you can see all of it: *The bird spread its wings and flew away.* ○ *Spread out the map on the table.* **2** put soft stuff all over something: *I spread butter on the bread.* **3** move to other places or to other people; make something do this: *Fire quickly spread to other parts of the building.* ○ *Rats spread disease.*

spread *noun* (no plural) *Doctors are trying to stop the spread of the disease.*

spring

spring[1] /sprɪŋ/ *noun* **1** a thin piece of metal that is bent round and round. A spring will go back to the same size and shape after you push or pull it. **2** a place where water comes out of the ground

spring[2] /sprɪŋ/ *noun* in cool countries, the part of the year after winter, when plants start to grow

spring[3] /sprɪŋ/ *verb* (**springs**, **springing**, **sprang** /spræŋ/, **has sprung** /sprʌŋ/) jump or move suddenly: *The cat sprang on the mouse.*

sprinkle /ˈsprɪŋkl/ *verb* (**sprinkles**, **sprinkling**, **sprinkled** /ˈsprɪŋkld/) throw drops or small pieces of something on another thing: *Sprinkle some sugar on the fruit.*

sprint /sprɪnt/ *verb* (**sprints**, **sprinting**, **sprinted**) run a short distance very fast

sprout[1] /spraʊt/ *noun* a Brussels sprout; a round green vegetable like a very small cabbage

sprout[2] /spraʊt/ *verb* (**sprouts**, **sprouting**, **sprouted**) start to grow: *New leaves are sprouting on the trees.*

sprung *form of* **spring**[3]

spun *form of* **spin**

spy /spaɪ/ *noun* (plural **spies**) a person who tries to learn secret things about another country, person or company

spy *verb* (**spies**, **spying**, **spied** /spaɪd/, **has spied**) try to learn secret things about somebody or something

spy on somebody watch somebody or something secretly

squad /skwɒd/ *noun* a small group of people who work together: *Morocco's football squad* ○ *a squad of police officers*

square /skweə(r)/ *noun* **1** a shape with four straight sides that are the same length ☞ picture on page A5 **2** an open space in a town with buildings around it: *the market square* ○ *Parliament Square*

square *adjective* with four straight sides that are the same length, and four right angles: *a square table* ✪ A **square metre** is an area that is one metre long on each side.

squash¹ /skwɒʃ/ *verb* (**squashes**, **squashing**, **squashed** /skwɒʃt/) **1** press something hard and make it flat: *She sat on my hat and squashed it.* **2** push a lot of people or things into a small space: *We squashed five people into the back of the car.*

squash³ /skwɒʃ/ *noun* (no plural) a game where two players hit a small ball against a wall in a special room (called a **court**): *Have you ever played squash?*

squat /skwɒt/ *verb* (**squats**, **squatting**, **squatted**) **1** sit with your feet on the ground, your legs bent and your bottom just above the ground: *I squatted down to light the fire.* **2** live in an empty building that is not yours and that you do not pay for

squatter *noun* a person who squats in an empty building

squeak /skwiːk/ *verb* (**squeaks**, **squeaking**, **squeaked** /skwiːkt/) make a short high sound like a mouse: *The door was squeaking, so I put some oil on it.*

squeak *noun*: *the squeak of a mouse*

squeaky *adjective*: *He's got a squeaky voice.*

squeal /skwiːl/ *verb* (**squeals**, **squealing**, **squealed** /skwiːld/) make a loud high sound like a pig: *The children squealed with excitement.*

squeal *noun*: *the squeal of a pig*

squeeze /skwiːz/ *verb* (**squeezes**, **squeezing**, **squeezed** /skwiːzd/) **1** press something hard between other things: *I squeezed an orange* (to make the juice come out). **2** go into a small space; push too much into a small space: *Can you squeeze another person into the back of your car?* ○ *Fifty people squeezed into the small room.*

squeeze

tube

squeeze *noun*: *She gave my arm a squeeze.*

squirrel /ˈskwɪrəl/ *noun* a small grey or brown animal with a big thick tail. Squirrels live in trees and eat nuts.

squirt /skwɜːt/ *verb* (**squirts**, **squirting**, **squirted**) **1** suddenly shoot out of something: *I opened the bottle and beer squirted everywhere.* **2** make liquid suddenly shoot out of something: *The elephant squirted the people with water.*

St 1 *short way of writing* **saint 2** *short way of writing* **street**

stab /stæb/ *verb* (**stabs**, **stabbing**, **stabbed** /stæbd/) push a knife or another sharp thing into somebody or something: *He was stabbed in the back.*

stable¹ /ˈsteɪbl/ *noun* a building where you keep horses

stable² /ˈsteɪbl/ *adjective* Something that is stable will not move, fall or change: *Don't stand on that table – it's not very stable.* ✪ *opposite:* **unstable**

stack /stæk/ *noun* a lot of things on top of one another: *a stack of books*

stack *verb* (**stacks**, **stacking**, **stacked** /stækt/) put things on top of one another: *I stacked the chairs after the concert.*

stadium /ˈsteɪdiəm/ *noun* a place with seats around it where you can watch sports matches: *a football stadium*

staff /stɑːf/ *noun* (plural) the group of people who work in a place: *The hotel staff were very friendly.*

staff room /ˈstɑːf ruːm/ *noun* a room in a school where teachers can work and rest

stage¹ /steɪdʒ/ *noun* the part of a theatre where actors, dancers, etc stand and move

stage² /steɪdʒ/ *noun* a certain time in a longer set of things that happen: *The first stage of the course lasts for two weeks.* **at this stage** now: *At this stage I don't know what I'll do when I leave school.*

stagger /ˈstægə(r)/ *verb* (**staggers**, **staggering**, **staggered** /ˈstægəd/) walk as if you are going to fall: *He staggered across the room with the heavy box.*

stain /steɪn/ *verb* (**stains**, **staining**, **stained** /steɪnd/) make coloured or dirty marks on something: *The coffee* *stained his shirt brown.*

stain *noun*: *She had blood stains on her shirt.*

stairs /steəz/ *noun* (plural) steps that lead up and down inside a building: *I ran up the stairs.* ☞ Look also at **downstairs** and **upstairs**.

staircase /'steəkeɪs/, **stairway** /'steəweɪ/ *noun* a big group of stairs

stale /steɪl/ *adjective* (**staler**, **stalest**) not fresh: *stale bread* ○ *stale air*

stalk /stɔːk/ *noun* one of the long thin parts of a plant that the flowers, leaves or fruit grow on

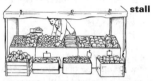

stall

stall /stɔːl/ *noun* a big table with things on it that somebody wants to sell, for example in a street or market: *a fruit stall*

stammer /'stæmə(r)/ *verb* (**stammers**, **stammering**, **stammered** /'stæməd/) say the same sound many times when you are trying to say a word: *'B-b-b-but wait for me,' she stammered.*

stamp[1] /stæmp/ *noun* **1** a small piece of paper that you put on a letter to show that you have paid to send it ☞ picture on page A13 **2** a small piece of wood or metal that you press on paper to make marks or words: *a date stamp*

stamp[2] /stæmp/ *verb* (**stamps**, **stamping**, **stamped** /stæmpt/) **1** put your foot down quickly and hard: *She stamped on the spider and killed it.* **2** walk by putting your feet down hard and loudly: *Mike stamped angrily out of the room.* **3** press a small piece of wood or metal on paper to make marks or words: *They stamped my passport at the airport.*

stand[1] /stænd/ *verb* (**stands**, **standing**, **stood** /stʊd/, **has stood**) **1** be on your feet: *She was standing by the door.* **2** (*also* **stand up**) get up on your feet: *The teacher asked us all to stand up.* **3** be

in a place: *The village stands on a hill.* **4** put something somewhere: *I stood the ladder against the wall.* **can't stand somebody** or **something** hate somebody or something: *I can't stand this music.* **stand by 1** watch but not do anything: *How can you stand by while those boys kick the cat?* **2** be ready to do something: *Stand by until I call you!* **stand by somebody** help somebody when they need it: *Julie's parents stood by her when she was in trouble.* **stand for something** be a short way of saying or writing something: *USA stands for 'the United States of America'.* **stand out** be easy to see: *Joseph stands out in a crowd because he is so tall.* **stand still** not move: *Stand still while I take your photograph.* **stand up for somebody** or **something** say that somebody or something is right; support somebody or something: *Everyone else said I was wrong, but my sister stood up for me.* **stand up to somebody** show that you are not afraid of somebody

stand[2] /stænd/ *noun* **1** a table or small shop where you can buy things or get information: *a news-stand* (= where you can buy newspapers and magazines) **2** a piece of furniture that you can put things on: *an umbrella stand*

standard[1] /'stændəd/ *noun* how good somebody or something is: *Her work is of a very high standard* (= very good).

standard of living /ˌstændəd əv 'lɪvɪŋ/ *noun* (*plural* **standards of living**) how rich or poor you are: *They have a low standard of living* (= they are poor).

standard[2] /'stændəd/ *adjective* normal; not special: *Clothes are sold in standard sizes.*

stank *form of* **stink**

staple /'steɪpl/ *noun* a small, very thin piece of metal that you push through pieces of paper to join them together, using a special tool (called a **stapler**)

staple *verb* (**staples**, **stapling**, **stapled** /'steɪpld/) *Staple the pieces of paper together.*

star[1] /stɑː(r)/ *noun* **1** one of the small bright lights that you see in the sky at night **2** a shape with points ☞ picture on page A5

star[2] /stɑː(r)/ *noun* a famous person, for example an actor or a singer: *a film star*

star *verb* (**stars**, **starring**, **starred** /stɑːd/) **1** be an important actor in a play or film: *He has starred in many films.* **2** have somebody as a star: *The film stars Leonardo di Caprio.*

stare /steə(r)/ *verb* (**stares**, **staring**, **stared** /steəd/) look at somebody or something for a long time: *Everybody stared at her hat.* ○ *He was staring out of the window.*

start[1] /stɑːt/ *verb* (**starts**, **starting**, **started**) **1** begin to do something: *I start work at nine o'clock.* ○ *It started raining.* ○ *She started to cry.* **2** begin to happen; make something begin to happen: *The film starts at 7.30.* ○ *The police do not know who started the fire.* **3** begin to work or move; make something begin to work or move: *The engine won't start.* ○ *I can't start the car.* **start off** begin: *The teacher started off by asking us our names.*

start[2] /stɑːt/ *noun* **1** the beginning or first part of something: *She arrived after the start of the meeting.* **2** starting something: *We have got a lot of work to do, so let's make a start.* **for a start** words that you use when you give your first reason for something: *'Why can't I go to school?' 'Well, for a start, you're not old enough yet.'*

starter /'stɑːtə(r)/ *noun* a small amount of food that you eat as the first part of a meal

startle /'stɑːtl/ *verb* (**startles**, **startling**, **startled** /'stɑːtld/) make somebody suddenly surprised or frightened: *You startled me when you knocked on the window.*

starve /stɑːv/ *verb* (**starves**, **starving**, **starved** /stɑːvd/) die because you do not have enough to eat: *Millions of people are starving in some parts of the world.* **be starving** be very hungry: *When will dinner be ready? I'm starving!*

starvation /stɑː'veɪʃn/ *noun* (no plural) *The child died of starvation.*

state[1] /steɪt/ *noun* **1** (no plural) how somebody or something is: *The room is in a terrible state!* (= untidy or dirty)

2 (*plural* **states**) a country and its government: *Many schools are owned by the state.* **3** (*plural* **states**) a part of a country: *Texas is a state in the USA.* **state of mind** how you feel: *What state of mind is he in?*

state[2] /steɪt/ *verb* (**states**, **stating**, **stated**) say or write something: *I stated in my letter that I was looking for a job.*

statement /'steɪtmənt/ *noun* something that you say or write: *The driver made a statement to the police about the accident.*

station /'steɪʃn/ *noun* **1** a railway station; a place where trains stop so that people can get on and off **2** a place where buses start and end their journeys: *a bus station* **3** a building for some special work: *a police station* ○ *a fire station* **4** a television or radio company

stationery /'steɪʃənri/ *noun* (no plural) paper, pens and other things that you use for writing

statistics /stə'tɪstɪks/ *noun* (plural) numbers that give information about something: *Statistics show that women live longer than men.*

statue /'stætʃuː/ *noun* the shape of a person or an animal that is made of stone or metal: *They erected a statue of Nelson Mandela in the square.*

stay[1] /steɪ/ *verb* (**stays**, **staying**, **stayed** /steɪd/) **1** be in the same place and not go away: *Stay here until I come back.* ○ *I stayed in the house all morning.* **2** continue in the same way and not change: *I tried to stay awake.* **3** live somewhere for a short time: *I stayed with my friend in Kisumu.* ○ *Which hotel are you staying at?* **stay behind** be somewhere after other people have gone: *The teacher asked me to stay behind after the lesson.* **stay in** be at home and not go out: *I'm staying in this evening because I am tired.* **stay up** not go to bed: *We stayed up until after midnight.*

stay[2] /steɪ/ *noun* (*plural* **stays**) a short time when you live somewhere: *Did you enjoy your stay in London?*

steady /'stedi/ *adjective* (**steadier**,

steadiest) 1 If something is steady, it does not move or shake: *Hold the ladder steady while I stand on it.* ✪ opposite: **unsteady 2** If something is steady, it stays the same: *We drove at a steady speed.* ○ **steadily** /ˈstedɪli/ *adverb*: *Prices are falling steadily.*

steak /steɪk/ *noun* a thick flat piece of meat or fish

> ✪ You **steal** things, but you **rob** people and places (you steal things from them). A person who steals is called a **thief**.
> *They **stole** my camera.*
> *I've been **robbed**.*
> *They **robbed** a bank.*

steal /stiːl/ *verb* (**steals, stealing, stole** /stəʊl/, **has stolen** /ˈstəʊlən/) secretly take something that is not yours: *Her money has been stolen.*

steam /stiːm/ *noun* (no plural) the gas that water becomes when it gets very hot: *There was steam coming from my cup of coffee.*

steam *verb* (**steams, steaming, steamed** /stiːmd/) **1** send out steam: *a steaming bowl of soup* **2** cook something in steam: *steamed vegetables*

steel /stiːl/ *noun* (no plural) very strong metal that is used for making things like knives, tools or machines

steep /stiːp/ *adjective* (**steeper, steepest**) A steep hill, mountain or road goes up quickly from a low place to a high place: *I can't cycle up the hill – it's too steep.* ○ **steeply** *adverb*: *The path climbed steeply up the side of the mountain.*

steer /stɪə(r)/ *verb* (**steers, steering, steered** /stɪəd/) make a car, boat, bicycle, etc go the way that you want by turning a wheel or handle

steering-wheel /ˈstɪərɪŋ wiːl/ *noun* the wheel that you turn to make a car go left or right ☛ picture at **car**

stem /stem/ *noun* the long thin part of a plant that the flowers and leaves grow on ☛ picture at **plant**

step[1] /step/ *noun* **1** a movement when you move your foot up and then put it down in another place to walk, run or dance: *She took a step forward and then stopped.* **2** a place to put your foot when you go up or down: *These steps go down to the garden.* **3** one thing in a list of things that you must do: *What is the first step in starting a company?* **step by step** doing one thing after another; slowly: *This book shows you how to play the guitar, step by step.*

step[2] /step/ *verb* (**steps, stepping, stepped** /stept/) move your foot up and put it down in another place when you walk: *You stepped on my foot!*

stepfather /ˈstepfɑːðə(r)/ *noun* a man who has married your mother but who is not your father

stepladder /ˈsteplædə(r)/ *noun* a short ladder

stepmother /ˈstepmʌðə(r)/ *noun* a woman who has married your father but who is not your mother ✪ The child of your stepmother or stepfather is your **stepbrother** or **stepsister**.

stereo /ˈsteriəʊ/ *noun* (*plural* **stereos**) a machine for playing records, cassettes or compact discs, with two parts (called **speakers**) that the sound comes from

stereo *adjective* with the sound coming from two speakers: *a stereo cassette player*

stern /stɜːn/ *adjective* (**sterner, sternest**) serious and strict with people; not smiling: *Our teacher is very stern.*

stew /stjuː/ *noun* food that you make by cooking meat or vegetables in liquid for a long time: *beef stew*

stew *verb* (**stews, stewing, stewed** /stjuːd/) cook something slowly in liquid: *stewed fruit*

steward /ˈstjuːəd/ *noun* a man whose job is to look after people on an aeroplane or a ship

stewardess /ˌstjuːəˈdes/ *noun* (*plural* **stewardesses**) a woman whose job is to look after people on an aeroplane or a ship

stick[1] /stɪk/ *noun* **1** a long thin piece of wood: *We found some sticks and made a fire.* ○ *The old man walked with a stick.* **2** a long thin piece of something: *a stick of chalk*

stick[2] /stɪk/ *verb* (**sticks**, **sticking**, **stuck** /stʌk/, **has stuck**) **1** push a pointed thing into something: *Stick a fork into the meat to see if it's cooked.* **2** join something to another thing with glue, for example; become joined in this way: *I stuck a stamp on the envelope.* **3** be fixed in one place so that it cannot move: *This door always sticks* (= it won't open). **4** put something somewhere: *Stick that box on the floor.* ✪ This is an informal use. **stick out** come out of the side or top of something so you can see it easily: *The boy's head was sticking out of the window.* **stick something out** push something out: *Don't stick your tongue out!* **stick to something** continue with something and not change it: *We're sticking to Peter's plan.* **stick up for somebody** or **something** say that somebody or something is right: *Everyone else said I was wrong, but Kim stuck up for me.*

sticker /'stɪkə(r)/ *noun* a small piece of paper with a picture or words on it, that you can stick onto things: *She has a sticker on the window of her car.*

sticky /'stɪki/ *adjective* (**stickier**, **stickiest**) Something that is sticky can stick to things or is covered with something that can stick to things: *Glue is sticky.* ○ *sticky fingers*

stiff /stɪf/ *adjective* (**stiffer**, **stiffest**) hard and not easy to bend or move: *stiff cardboard*

still[1] /stɪl/ *adverb* **1** a word that you use to show that something has not changed: *Do you still live in Nakuru?* ○ *Is it still raining?* **2** although that is true: *She felt ill, but she still went to the party.* **3** a word that you use to make another word stronger: *It was cold yesterday, but today it's colder still.*

still[2] /stɪl/ *adjective*, *adverb* without moving: *Please stand still while I take a photo.*

stillness /'stɪlnəs/ *noun* (no plural) *the stillness of the night*

sting /stɪŋ/ *verb* (**stings**, **stinging**, **stung** /stʌŋ/, **has stung**) **1** If an insect or a plant stings you, it hurts you by pushing a small sharp part into your skin: *I've been stung by a bee!* **2** feel

a sudden sharp pain: *The smoke made my eyes sting.*

sting *noun* **1** the sharp part of some insects that can hurt you: *A wasp's sting is in its tail.* **2** a hurt place on your skin where an insect or plant has stung you: *a bee sting*

stink /stɪŋk/ *verb* (**stinks**, **stinking**, **stank** /stæŋk/, **has stunk** /stʌŋk/) have a very bad smell: *That fish stinks!*

stink *noun* a very bad smell: *What a horrible stink!*

stir /stɜː(r)/ *verb* (**stirs**, **stirring**, **stirred** /stɜːd/) **1** move a spoon or another thing round and round to mix something: *He put sugar in his coffee and stirred it.* **2** move a little or make something move a little: *The wind stirred the leaves.*

stitch /stɪtʃ/ *noun* (*plural* **stitches**) **1** one movement in and out of a piece of material with a needle and thread when you are sewing **2** one of the small circles of wool that you put round a needle when you are knitting

stitch *verb* (**stitches**, **stitching**, **stitched** /stɪtʃt/) make stitches in something; sew something: *I stitched a button on my skirt.*

stock /stɒk/ *noun* things that a shop keeps ready to sell: *That bookshop has a big stock of dictionaries.* **in stock** ready to sell **out of stock** not there to sell: *I'm sorry, that book is out of stock at the moment.*

stock *verb* (**stocks**, **stocking**, **stocked** /stɒkt/) keep something ready to sell: *We don't stock umbrellas.*

stocking /'stɒkɪŋ/ *noun* a long thin thing that a woman wears over her leg and foot: *a pair of stockings*

stole, **stolen** *forms of* **steal**

stomach /'stʌmək/ *noun* **1** the part inside your body where food goes after you eat it **2** the front part of your body below your chest and above your legs ☞ picture on page A4

stomach-ache /'stʌmək eɪk/ *noun* (no plural) a pain in your stomach: *I've got stomach-ache.*

stone /stəʊn/ *noun* **1** (no plural) the

stone

very hard stuff that is in the ground. Stone is sometimes used for building: *a stone wall* **2** (*plural* **stones**) a small piece of stone: *The children were throwing stones into the river.* **3** (*plural* **stones**) the hard part in the middle of some fruits, for example avocados **4** (*plural* **stones**) a small piece of beautiful rock that is very valuable: *A diamond is a precious stone.* **5** (*plural* **stone**) a measure of weight (= 6·3 kilograms). There are 14 **pounds** in a stone: *I weigh ten stone.* ☞ Note at **pound**

stony /ˈstəʊni/ *adjective* (**stonier**, **stoniest**) with a lot of stones in or on it: *stony ground*

stood *form of* **stand**[1]

stool /stuːl/ *noun* a small seat with no back

stool

stoop /stuːp/ *verb* (**stoops**, **stooping**, **stooped** /stuːpt/) If you stoop, you bend your body forward and down: *She stooped to pick up the baby.*

stop[1] /stɒp/ *verb* (**stops**, **stopping**, **stopped** /stɒpt/) **1** finish moving or working; become still: *The train stopped at every station.* ○ *The clock has stopped.* ○ *I stopped to post a letter.* **2** not do something any more; finish: *Stop making that noise!* **3** make somebody or something finish moving or doing something: *Squeeze both brakes to stop the bike.* **stop somebody (from) doing something** not let somebody do something: *My dad stopped me from going out.*

stop[2] /stɒp/ *noun* **1** the moment when somebody or something finishes moving: *The train came to a stop.* **2** a place where buses or trains stop so that people can get on and off: *I'm getting off at the next stop.* **put a stop to something** make something finish: *A teacher put a stop to the fight.*

store[1] /stɔː(r)/ *noun* **1** a big shop **2** things that you are keeping to use later: *a store of food*

store[2] /stɔː(r)/ *verb* (**stores**, **storing**, **stored** /stɔːd/) keep something to use later: *The information is stored on a computer.*

storey /ˈstɔːri/ *noun* (*plural* **storeys**) one level in a building: *The building has four storeys.*

storm[1] /stɔːm/ *noun* very bad weather with strong winds and rain: *a thunderstorm*

storm[2] /stɔːm/ *verb* (**storms**, **storming**, **stormed** /stɔːmd/) move in a way that shows you are angry: *He stormed out of the room.*

stormy /ˈstɔːmi/ *adjective* (**stormier**, **stormiest**) If the weather is stormy, there is strong wind and rain: *a stormy night*

story /ˈstɔːri/ *noun* (*plural* **stories**) **1** words that tell you about people and things that are not real: *I write stories for children as a hobby.* ○ *a ghost story* **2** words that tell you about things that really happened: *My grandmother told me stories about when she was a child.*

stove /stəʊv/ *noun* a cooker or heater

straight[1] /streɪt/ *adjective* (**straighter**, **straightest**) **1** with no curve or bend: *Use a ruler to draw a straight line.* **2** with one side as high as the other:

straight line

straight   not straight

This picture isn't straight. **get something straight** make sure that you understand something completely: *Let's get this straight. Are you sure you left your bike by the school?*

straight[2] /streɪt/ *adverb* **1** in a straight line: *Look straight in front of you.* **2** without stopping or doing anything else; directly: *Come straight home.* ○ *She walked straight past me.* **straight away** immediately; now: *I'll do it straight away.* **straight on** without turning: *Go straight on until you come to the bank, then turn left.*

straighten /ˈstreɪtn/ *verb* (**straight-**

ens, straightening, straightened /'streɪtnd/) become or make something straight

straightforward /ˌstreɪt'fɔːwəd/ adjective easy to understand or do: The question was straightforward.

strain /streɪn/ verb (strains, straining, strained /streɪnd/) 1 pour a liquid through something with small holes in it, to take away any other things in the liquid: You haven't strained the tea – there are tea leaves in it. 2 try very hard: Her voice was so quiet that I had to strain to hear her. 3 hurt a part of your body by making it work too hard: Don't read in the dark. You'll strain your eyes.

strain noun 1 being pulled or made to work too hard: The rope broke under (= because of) the strain. 2 hurting a part of your body by making it work too hard: back strain

strand /strænd/ noun one piece of thread or hair

stranded /'strændɪd/ adjective left in a place that you cannot get away from: The car broke down and I was stranded on a lonely road.

strange /streɪndʒ/ adjective (stranger, strangest) 1 unusual or surprising: Did you hear that strange noise? 2 that you do not know: We were lost in a strange town. ✪ Be careful! We use foreign, not strange, to talk about a person or thing that comes from another country.

strangely adverb in a surprising or unusual way: She usually talks a lot, but today she was strangely quiet.

stranger /'streɪndʒə(r)/ noun 1 a person who you do not know 2 a person who is in a place that he/she does not know: I'm a stranger to this city. ✪ Be careful! We use the word foreigner for a person who comes from another country.

strangle /'stræŋgl/ verb (strangles, strangling, strangled /'stræŋgld/) kill somebody by pressing their neck very tightly

strap /stræp/ noun a long flat piece of material that you use for carrying something or for keeping something

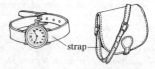
strap

in place: a leather watch strap

strap verb (straps, strapping, strapped /stræpt/) hold something in place with a strap: I strapped the bag onto the back of my bike.

straw /strɔː/ noun 1 (no plural) the dry stems of plants like wheat: The cows sleep on a bed of straw. ○ a straw hat 2 (plural straws) a thin paper or plastic tube that you can drink through the last straw a bad thing that happens after many other bad things so that you lose hope

stray /streɪ/ adjective lost and away from home: a stray dog

stray noun (plural strays) an animal that has no home

streak /striːk/ noun a long thin line: She's got streaks of grey in her hair. ○ a streak of lightning

stream /striːm/ noun 1 a small river 2 moving liquid, or moving things or people: a stream of blood ○ a stream of cars

stream verb (streams, streaming, streamed /striːmd/) move like water: Tears were streaming down his face.

streamline /'striːmlaɪn/ verb (streamlines, streamlining, streamlined /'striːmlaɪnd/) give something like a car or boat a long smooth shape so that it can go fast through air or water

street /striːt/ noun a road in a city, town or village with buildings along the sides: I saw Anna walking down the street. ○ I live in Nyeri Street. ✪ The short way of writing 'Street' in addresses is St: 17 Mfangano St

strength /streŋθ/ noun (no plural) being strong: I don't have the strength to lift this box – it's too heavy.

strengthen /'streŋθn/ verb (strengthens, strengthening, strengthened /'streŋθnd/) make something stronger

stress /stres/ noun (plural stresses)

1 saying one word or part of a word more strongly than another: *In the word 'dictionary', the stress is on the first part of the word.* **2** a feeling of worry because of problems in your life: *She's suffering from stress because she's got too much work to do.*

stressful /ˈstresfl/ *adjective*: *a stressful job*

stress *verb* (**stresses**, **stressing**, **stressed** /strest/) **1** say something strongly to show that it is important: *I must stress how important this meeting is.* **2** say one word or part of a word more strongly than another: *You should stress the first part of the word 'happy'.*

stretch[1] /stretʃ/ *verb* (**stretches**, **stretching**, **stretched** /stretʃt/) **1** pull something to make it longer or wider; become longer or wider: *The T-shirt stretched when I washed it.* **2** push your arms and legs out as far as you can: *Ali got out of bed and stretched.* **3** continue: *The beach stretches for miles.* **stretch out** lie down with all your body flat: *The cat stretched out and went to sleep.*

stretch[2] /stretʃ/ *noun* (*plural* **stretches**) a piece of land or water: *This is a dangerous stretch of road.*

stretcher /ˈstretʃə(r)/ *noun* a kind of bed for carrying somebody who is ill or hurt: *They carried him to the ambulance on a stretcher.*

strict /strɪkt/ *adjective* (**stricter**, **strictest**) If you are strict, you make people do what you want and do not allow them to behave badly: *Her parents are very strict – she always has to be home before ten o'clock.* ○ *strict rules*

strictly *adverb* **1** definitely; in a strict way: *Smoking is strictly forbidden.* **2** exactly: *That is not strictly true.*

stride /straɪd/ *verb* (**strides**, **striding**, **strode** /strəʊd/, **has** **stridden** /ˈstrɪdn/) walk with long steps: *The police officer strode across the road.*

stride *noun* a long step

strike[1] /straɪk/ *noun* a time when people are not working because they want more money or are angry about something: *There are no trains today be-* *cause the drivers are on strike.*

strike[2] /straɪk/ *verb* (**strikes**, **striking**, **struck** /strʌk/, **has** **struck**) **1** hit somebody or something: *A stone struck me on the back of the head.* **○ Hit** is the more usual word, but when you talk about **lightning**, you always use **strike**: *The tree was struck by lightning.* **2** stop working because you want more money or are angry about something: *The nurses are going to strike for better pay.* **3** ring a bell so that people know what time it is: *The clock struck nine.* **4** come suddenly into your mind: *It suddenly struck me that she looked like my sister.* **strike a match** make fire with a match

striking /ˈstraɪkɪŋ/ *adjective* If something is striking, you notice it because it is very unusual or interesting: *That's a very striking hat.*

string /strɪŋ/ *noun* **1** very thin rope that you use for tying things: *I tied up the parcel with string.* ○ *The little boy held a balloon on the end of a string.* **2** a line of things on a piece of thread: *She was wearing a string of blue beads.* ☛ picture on page A15 **3** a piece of thin wire, etc on a musical instrument: *guitar strings*

strip[1] /strɪp/ *noun* a long thin piece of something: *a strip of paper*

strip[2] /strɪp/ *verb* (**strips**, **stripping**, **stripped** /strɪpt/) **1** take off what is covering something: *I stripped the paint off the walls.* **2** (*also* **strip off**) take off your clothes: *She stripped off and ran into the sea.*

stripe /straɪp/ *noun* a long thin line of colour: *Zebras have black and white stripes.*

striped /straɪpt/ *adjective* with stripes: *He wore a blue-and-white striped shirt.*

strode *form of* **stride**

stroke[1] /strəʊk/ *verb* (**strokes**, **stroking**, **stroked** /strəʊkt/) move your hand gently over somebody or something to show love: *She stroked his hair.*

stroke[2] /strəʊk/ *noun* **1** a movement that you make with your arms when you are swimming, playing tennis, etc **2** a sudden serious illness when the brain stops working properly: *He had a stroke.*

stroll /strəʊl/ *verb* (**strolls**, **strolling**, **strolled** /strəʊld/) walk slowly: *We strolled along the beach.*

stroll *noun*: *We went for a stroll by the river.*

strong /strɒŋ/ *adjective* (**stronger**, **strongest**) **1** with a powerful body, so that you can carry heavy things: *I need somebody strong to help me move this desk.* ☛ picture on page A11 **2** that you cannot break easily: *Don't stand on that chair – it's not very strong.* ○ *a strong belief* **3** that you can see, taste, smell, hear or feel very clearly: *A cup of strong coffee will wake you up!* ○ *a strong smell of oranges* ○ *strong winds*

strongly *adverb*: *I strongly believe that he is wrong.*

struck *form of* **strike**²

structure /ˈstrʌktʃə(r)/ *noun* **1** (no plural) the way that something is made: *We are studying the structure of a bird's wing.* **2** (*plural* **structures**) a building or another thing that people have made with many parts: *The new hotel is a tall glass and brick structure.*

struggle /ˈstrʌgl/ *verb* (**struggles**, **struggling**, **struggled** /ˈstrʌgld/) **1** try very hard to do something that is not easy: *We struggled to lift the heavy box.* **2** move your arms and legs a lot when you are fighting or trying to get free: *She struggled to get away from her attacker.*

struggle *noun*: *In 1862 the American slaves won their struggle for freedom.*

stubborn /ˈstʌbən/ *adjective* A stubborn person does not change his/her ideas easily or do what other people want him/her to do: *She's too stubborn to say sorry.*

stuck¹ *form of* **stick**²

stuck² /stʌk/ *adjective* **1** not able to move: *This drawer is stuck – I can't open it.* ○ *I was stuck miles from home with no money.* **2** not able to do something because it is difficult: *If you get stuck, ask your teacher for help.*

student /ˈstjuːdnt/ *noun* a person who is studying at a university or college: *Tim is a student of history.*

studio /ˈstjuːdiəʊ/ *noun* (*plural* **studios**) **1** a room where an artist works **2** a room where people make films, radio and television programmes, or records: *a television studio*

study¹ /ˈstʌdi/ *verb* (**studies**, **studying**, **studied** /ˈstʌdid/, **has studied**) **1** spend time learning about something: *He studied Economics at university.* **2** look at something carefully: *We must study the map before we leave.*

study² /ˈstʌdi/ *noun* (*plural* **studies**) **1** learning: *He's doing a course in Business Studies.* **2** a room in a house where you go to study, read or write

stuff¹ /stʌf/ *noun* (no plural) any material, substance or group of things: *What's this blue stuff on the wall?* ○ *Put your stuff in this bag.*

stuff² /stʌf/ *verb* (**stuffs**, **stuffing**, **stuffed** /stʌft/) **1** fill something with something: *The pillow was stuffed with feathers.* **2** push something quickly into another thing: *He took the money quickly and stuffed it into his pocket.*

stuffy /ˈstʌfi/ *adjective* (**stuffier**, **stuffiest**) If a room is stuffy, it has no fresh air in it: *Open the window – it's very stuffy in here.*

stumble /ˈstʌmbl/ *verb* (**stumbles**, **stumbling**, **stumbled** /ˈstʌmbld/) hit your foot against something when you are walking or running, and almost fall: *The old lady stumbled and fell as she was going upstairs.*

stump /stʌmp/ *noun* the small part that is left when something is cut off or broken: *a tree stump*

stun /stʌn/ *verb* (**stuns**, **stunning**, **stunned** /stʌnd/) **1** hit a person or animal on the head so hard that they cannot see, think or make a sound for a short time **2** make somebody very surprised: *His sudden death stunned his family and friends.*

stung *form of* **sting**

stunk *form of* **stink**

stunning /ˈstʌnɪŋ/ *adjective* very beautiful; wonderful: *a stunning dress*

stunt /stʌnt/ *noun* something dangerous or difficult that you do to make people look at you: *Action films have a lot of exciting stunts.*

stupid /ˈstjuːpɪd/ *adjective* not intelligent; silly: *Don't be so stupid!* ○ *What a stupid question!*

stupidity /stjuːˈpɪdəti/ *noun* (no plural) being stupid

stupidly *adverb*: *I stupidly forgot to close the door.*

stutter /ˈstʌtə(r)/ *verb* (**stutters**, **stuttering**, **stuttered** /ˈstʌtəd/) say the same sound many times when you are trying to say a word: *'I d-d-don't understand,' he stuttered.*

style /staɪl/ *noun* **1** a way of doing, making or saying something: *I don't like his style of writing.* **2** the shape or kind of something: *This shop sells shirts in lots of different colours and styles.* ○ *a hairstyle*

subject /ˈsʌbdʒɪkt/ *noun* **1** the person or thing that you are talking or writing about: *What is the subject of the talk?* **2** something you study at school, university or college: *I'm studying three subjects: Maths, Physics and Chemistry.* **3** the word in a sentence that does the action of the verb: *In the sentence 'Sue ate the bread', 'Sue' is the subject.* ☞ Look at **object**. **4** a person who belongs to a certain country: *Kenyan subjects*

submarine /ˌsʌbməˈriːn/ *noun* a boat that can travel under the sea

subscription /səbˈskrɪpʃn/ *noun* money that you pay, for example to get the same magazine each month or to join a club: *I've got a subscription to 'Parents' magazine.*

subsistence /səbˈsɪstəns/ *adjective* producing only enough food for the farmer to use, not enough to sell: *a subsistence crop*

substance /ˈsʌbstəns/ *noun* anything that you can see, touch or use for making things; a material: *Stone is a hard substance.* ○ *chemical substances*

substitute /ˈsʌbstɪtjuːt/ *noun* a person or thing that you put in the place of another: *Our goalkeeper was ill, so we found a substitute.*

substitute *verb* (**substitutes**, **substituting**, **substituted**) put somebody or something in the place of another: *You can substitute butter for oil if you prefer.*

subtitles /ˈsʌbtaɪtlz/ *noun* (plural) words at the bottom of a film that help you to understand it: *It was a French film with English subtitles.*

subtract /səbˈtrækt/ *verb* (**subtracts**, **subtracting**, **subtracted**) take a number away from another number: *If you subtract 6 from 9, you get 3.* ☻ opposite: **add**

subtraction /səbˈtrækʃn/ *noun* (no plural) taking a number away from another number ☞ Look at **addition**.

suburb /ˈsʌbɜːb/ *noun* one of the parts of a town or city outside the centre: *We live in the suburbs of Nairobi.*

subway /ˈsʌbweɪ/ *noun* (plural **subways**) a path that goes under a busy road, so that people can cross safely

succeed /səkˈsiːd/ *verb* (**succeeds**, **succeeding**, **succeeded**) do or get what you wanted to do or get: *She finally succeeded in getting a job.* ○ *I tried to get a ticket for the concert but I didn't succeed.* ☞ Look at **fail**.

success /səkˈses/ *noun* **1** (no plural) doing or getting what you wanted; doing well: *I wish you success with your studies.* **2** (plural **successes**) somebody or something that does well or that people like a lot: *The film 'Titanic' was a great success.* ☻ opposite: **failure**

successful /səkˈsesfl/ *adjective*: *a successful actor* ○ *The party was very successful.* ☻ opposite: **unsuccessful**

successfully /səkˈsesfəli/ *adverb*: *He completed his studies successfully.*

such /sʌtʃ/ *adjective* **1** a word that you use when you say how much, how big, etc something is: *It was such a nice day that we decided to go to the beach.* ☞ Look at **so**. **2** a word that makes another word stronger: *He wears such strange clothes.* **3** like this or that: *'Can I speak to Mrs Wambui?' 'I'm sorry. There's no such person here.'* **such as** like something; for example: *You can see animals such as lions, elephants and crocodiles.*

suck /sʌk/ *verb* (**sucks**, **sucking**, **sucked** /sʌkt/) **1** pull something into your mouth, using your lips: *The baby sucked milk from its bottle.* **2** hold something in your mouth and touch it a lot with your tongue: *She was sucking a sweet.*

sudden /ˈsʌdn/ *adjective* If something is sudden, it happens quickly when you do not expect it: *His death was very sudden.* **all of a sudden** suddenly: *We were all sleeping when all of a sudden the door opened.*

suddenly *adverb*: *He left very suddenly.* ○ *Suddenly there was a loud noise.*

suffer /ˈsʌfə(r)/ *verb* (**suffers**, **suffering**, **suffered** /ˈsʌfəd/) feel pain, sadness or something else that is not pleasant: *I'm suffering from toothache.*

sufficient /səˈfɪʃnt/ *adjective* as much or as many as you need or want; enough: *There was sufficient food to last two weeks.* ✪ **Enough** is the word that we usually use. ✪ opposite: **insufficient**

suffix /ˈsʌfɪks/ *noun* (*plural* **suffixes**) letters that you add to the end of a word to make another word: *If you add the suffix '-ly' to the adjective 'quick', you make the adverb 'quickly'.* ☞ Look at **prefix**.

suffocate /ˈsʌfəkeɪt/ *verb* (**suffocates**, **suffocating**, **suffocated**) die or make somebody die because there is no air to breathe

sufuria /suːˈfuːriə/ *noun* (an East African word) a metal cooking pot

sugar /ˈʃʊɡə(r)/ *noun* **1** (no plural) sweet stuff that comes from some sorts of plant: *Do you take sugar in your coffee?* **2** (*plural* **sugars**) a spoonful of sugar: *Two sugars, please.*

sugarcane /ˈʃʊɡəkeɪn/ *noun* (no plural) a very tall, thick grass from which we get sugar

suggest /səˈdʒest/ *verb* (**suggests**, **suggesting**, **suggested**) say what you think somebody should do or what should happen: *I suggest that you stay here tonight.* ○ *Simon suggested going for a walk.* ○ *What do you suggest I say to John?*

suggestion /səˈdʒestʃən/ *noun*: *I don't know what to give her for her birthday. Have you got any suggestions?* ○ *I would like to make a suggestion.*

suicide /ˈsuːɪsaɪd/ *noun* killing yourself **commit suicide** kill yourself

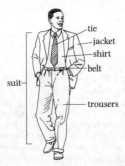

tie
jacket
shirt
belt
suit
trousers

suit[1] /suːt/ *noun* a jacket and trousers, or a jacket and skirt, that you wear together and that are made from the same material

suit[2] /suːt/ *verb* (**suits**, **suiting**, **suited**) **1** If something suits you, it looks good on you: *Does this hat suit me?* **2** be right for you; be what you want or need: *Would it suit you if I came at five o'clock?*

suitable /ˈsuːtəbl/ *adjective* right for somebody or something: *This film isn't suitable for children.* ✪ opposite: **unsuitable**

suitably /ˈsuːtəbli/ *adverb*: *Tony wasn't suitably dressed for a long walk in the sun.*

suitcase /ˈsuːtkeɪs/ *noun* a large bag with flat sides that you carry your clothes in when you travel

suitcase

sulk /sʌlk/ *verb* (**sulks**, **sulking**, **sulked** /sʌlkt/) not speak because you are angry about something: *She's been sulking all day because the teacher shouted at her.*

sum /sʌm/ *noun* **1** a simple piece of work with numbers, for example adding or dividing: *Children learn how to do sums.* **2** an amount of money: *the club paid a large sum of money for the player.* **3** the answer that you have when you add numbers together: *The sum of two and five is seven.*

summary /ˈsʌməri/ *noun* (*plural* **summaries**) a short way of telling something by giving only the most important facts: *Here is a summary of the news ...*

summer /ˈsʌmə(r)/ *noun* in cool countries, the warmest time of the year: *Many people in Europe go on their summer holidays in August.*

summit /ˈsʌmɪt/ *noun* the top of a mountain

sun /sʌn/ *noun* (no plural) **1** the sun the big round thing in the sky that gives us light in the day, and heat: *The sun is shining.* **2** light and heat from the sun: *We sat in the sun all morning.*

sunbathe /ˈsʌnbeɪð/ *verb* (**sunbathes**, **sunbathing**, **sunbathed** /ˈsʌnbeɪðd/) lie in the sun: *We sunbathed on the beach.*

Sunday /ˈsʌndeɪ/ *noun* the first day of the week; the day before Monday

sunflower /ˈsʌnflaʊə(r)/ *noun* a tall plant with big yellow flowers and brown seeds. We use sunflower seeds for food and oil.

sung *form of* **sing**

sunglasses /ˈsʌnglɑːsɪz/ *noun* (plural) glasses with dark glass in them that you wear in strong light: *a pair of sunglasses*

sunk *form of* **sink**[2]

sunlight /ˈsʌnlaɪt/ *noun* (no plural) the light from the sun

sunny /ˈsʌni/ *adjective* (**sunnier**, **sunniest**) bright with light from the sun: *a sunny day*

sunrise /ˈsʌnraɪz/ *noun* (no plural) the time in the morning when the sun comes up

sunset /ˈsʌnset/ *noun* the time in the evening when the sun goes down: *The park closes at sunset.*

sunshine /ˈsʌnʃaɪn/ *noun* (no plural) the light and heat from the sun: *We sat outside in the sunshine.*

super /ˈsuːpə(r)/ *adjective* very good; wonderful: *That was a super meal.* ○ *His new car is super.*

superb /suːˈpɜːb/ *adjective* very good or beautiful: *a superb holiday* ○ *The view from the window is superb.*

superior /suːˈpɪəriə(r)/ *adjective* better or more important than another person or thing: *This brand of coffee is su-*

perior to cheaper brands. ✪ opposite: **inferior**

superlative /suːˈpɜːlətɪv/ *noun* the form of an adjective or adverb that shows the most of something: *'Most intelligent', 'best' and 'fastest' are all superlatives.*
superlative *adjective: 'Youngest' is the superlative form of 'young'.*

supermarket /ˈsuːpəmɑːkɪt/ *noun* a big shop where you can buy food and other things. You choose what you want and then pay for everything when you leave.

supersonic /ˌsuːpəˈsɒnɪk/ *adjective* faster than the speed of sound: *Concorde is a supersonic aeroplane.*

superstition /ˌsuːpəˈstɪʃn/ *noun* a belief in good and bad luck and other things that cannot be explained: *People say that walking under a ladder brings bad luck, but it's just a superstition.*
superstitious /ˌsuːpəˈstɪʃəs/ *adjective* If you are superstitious, you believe in good and bad luck and other things that cannot be explained.

supervise /ˈsuːpəvaɪz/ *verb* (**supervises**, **supervising**, **supervised** /ˈsuːpəvaɪzd/) watch to see that people are working correctly: *I supervised the builders.*

supervision /ˌsuːpəˈvɪʒn/ *noun* (no plural) supervising or being supervised: *Children must not play here without supervision.*

supervisor /ˈsuːpəvaɪzə(r)/ *noun* a person who supervises

supper /ˈsʌpə(r)/ *noun* the last meal of the day: *We had supper and then went to bed.*

supply /səˈplaɪ/ *verb* (**supplies**, **supplying**, **supplied** /səˈplaɪd/, **has supplied**) give or sell something that somebody needs: *The school supplies us with books.* ○ *The lake supplies water to thousands of people.*
supply *noun* (plural **supplies**) an amount of something that you need: *supplies of food*

support /səˈpɔːt/ *verb* (**supports**, **supporting**, **supported**) **1** hold somebody or something up, so that they do not fall: *The bridge isn't strong enough to support heavy lorries.* **2** help somebody to live by giving things like money, a home or food: *She has three children to support.* **3** say that you think that somebody or something is right or the best: *Everybody else said I was wrong but Paul supported me.* ○ *Which football team do you support?*

support *noun* **1** (no plural) help: *Thank you for all your support.* **2** (*plural* **supports**) something that holds up another thing: *a roof support*

supporter /sə'pɔːtə(r)/ *noun* a person who helps somebody or something by giving money, or by showing interest, for example: *football supporters*

suppose /sə'pəʊz/ *verb* (**supposes**, **supposing**, **supposed** /sə'pəʊzd/) **1** think that something is true or will happen but not be sure: *'Where's Jenny?' 'I don't know – I suppose she's still at work.'* **2** a word that you use when you agree with something but are not happy about it: *'Can I borrow your pen?' 'Yes, I suppose so – but don't lose it.'*

supposed /sə'pəʊzd/ *adjective* **be supposed to 1** If you are supposed to do something, you should do it: *They were supposed to meet us here.* ○ *You're not supposed to smoke in this room.* **2** If something is supposed to be true, people say it is true: *This is supposed to be a good restaurant.*

supposing /sə'pəʊzɪŋ/ *conjunction* if: *Supposing we miss the bus, how will we get to the school on time?*

supreme /suː'priːm/ *adjective* highest or most important: *the Supreme Court*

sure /ʃɔː(r)/ *adjective* (**surer**, **surest**) *adverb* If you are sure, you know that something is true or right: *I'm sure I've seen that man before.* ○ *If you're not sure how to do it, ask your teacher.* **be sure to** If you are sure to do something, you will certainly do it: *If you work hard, you're sure to pass the exam.* **for sure** without any doubt: *I think he's coming to the meeting but I don't know for sure.* **make sure** check something so that you are certain about it: *I think they are arriving about eight, but I'll phone to make sure.* ○ *Make sure you don't leave your bag on the bus.* **sure enough** as I thought: *I*

said they would be late, and sure enough they were.

surely /'ʃɔːli/ *adverb* a word that you use when you think that something must be true, or when you are surprised: *Surely you know where your brother works!*

surf /sɜːf/ *noun* (no plural) the white part on the top of waves in the sea

surfing *noun* (no plural) the sport of riding over waves on a long piece of wood or plastic (called a **surfboard**) ✪ You can say **go surfing**: *We went surfing.*

surfer *noun* a person who surfs

surface /'sɜːfɪs/ *noun* **1** the outside part of something: *A tomato has a shiny red surface.* **2** the top of water: *She dived below the surface.*

surgeon /'sɜːdʒən/ *noun* a doctor who does **operations**. A surgeon cuts your body to take out or mend a part inside: *a brain surgeon*

surgery /'sɜːdʒəri/ *noun* **1** (no plural) cutting somebody's body to take out or mend a part inside: *He needed surgery after the accident.* **2** (*plural* **surgeries**) a place where you go to see a doctor or dentist

surname /'sɜːneɪm/ *noun* the name that a family has. Your surname is usually your last name: *Her name is Grace Ondieki. Ondieki is her surname.* ☛ Note at **name**

surprise[1] /sə'praɪz/ *noun* **1** (no plural) the feeling that you have when something happens suddenly that you did not expect: *She looked at me in surprise when I told her the news.* **2** (*plural* **surprises**) something that happens when you do not expect it: *Don't tell him about the birthday party – it's a surprise!* **take somebody by surprise** happen when somebody does not expect it: *Your phone call took me by surprise – I thought you were on holiday.* **to my surprise** I was surprised that: *I thought she would be angry but, to my surprise, she smiled.*

surprise[2] /sə'praɪz/ *verb* (**surprises**, **surprising**, **surprised** /sə'praɪzd/) do something that somebody does not expect: *I arrived early to surprise her.*

surprised *adjective* If you are surprised, you feel or show surprise: *I was surprised to see Thomas yesterday – I thought he was in hospital.*

surprising *adjective* If something is surprising, it makes you feel surprise: *The news was surprising.*

surprisingly *adverb*: *The exam was surprisingly easy.*

surrender /sə'rendə(r)/ *verb* (**surrenders**, **surrendering**, **surrendered** /sə'rendəd/) stop fighting because you cannot win: *After six hours on the roof, the man surrendered to the police.*

surround /sə'raʊnd/ *verb* (**surrounds**, **surrounding**, **surrounded**) be or go all around something: *The lake is surrounded by trees.*

surroundings /sə'raʊndɪŋz/ *noun* (plural) everything around you, or the place where you live: *The farm is in beautiful surroundings.* ○ *I don't like seeing animals in a zoo – I prefer to see them in their natural surroundings.*

survey /'sɜːveɪ/ *noun* (plural **surveys**) asking questions about what people think or do, or what is happening: *We did a survey of people's favourite TV programmes.*

survive /sə'vaɪv/ *verb* (**survives**, **surviving**, **survived** /sə'vaɪvd/) continue to live after a difficult or dangerous time: *Camels can survive for many days without water.* ○ *Only one person survived the plane crash.*

survival /sə'vaɪvl/ *noun* (no plural) surviving: *Food and water are necessary for survival.*

survivor /sə'vaɪvə(r)/ *noun* a person who survives: *The government sent help to the survivors of the earthquake.*

suspect /sə'spekt/ *verb* (**suspects**, **suspecting**, **suspected**) **1** think that something is true, but not be certain: *John wasn't at college today – I suspect that he's ill.* **2** think that somebody has done something wrong but not be certain: *They suspect Daniel of stealing the money.*

suspect /'sʌspekt/ *noun* a person who you think has done something wrong: *The police have arrested two suspects.*

suspicion /sə'spɪʃn/ *noun* **1** an idea that is not totally certain: *We have a suspicion that he is unhappy.* **2** a feeling that somebody has done something wrong: *When she saw all the money in his wallet she was filled with suspicion.*

suspicious /sə'spɪʃəs/ *adjective* **1** If you are suspicious, you do not believe somebody or something, or you feel that something is wrong: *The police are suspicious of her story.* **2** A person or thing that is suspicious makes you feel that something is wrong: *There was a man waiting outside the school. He looked very suspicious.*

suspiciously *adverb*: *'What are you doing here?' the woman asked suspiciously.*

Swahili /swə'hiːli/, **Kiswahili** /ˌkiːswə'hiːli/ *noun* (no plural) a language that many of the people of East Africa speak: *Do you understand any Swahili?*

swallow[1] /'swɒləʊ/ *verb* (**swallows**, **swallowing**, **swallowed** /'swɒləʊd/) make food or drink move down your throat from your mouth: *I can't swallow these tablets without water.*

swallow[2] /'swɒləʊ/ *noun* a small bird

swam *form of* swim

swamp /swɒmp/ *noun* soft wet ground

swap /swɒp/ *verb* (**swaps**, **swapping**, **swapped** /swɒpt/) change one thing for another thing; give one thing and get another thing for it: *Do you want to swap chairs with me?* (= you have my chair and I'll have yours) ○ *I swapped my T-shirt for Tom's cassette.*

swarm /swɔːm/ *noun* a big group of flying insects: *a swarm of bees*

swarm *verb* (**swarms**, **swarming**, **swarmed** /swɔːmd/) fly or move quickly in a big group: *The fans swarmed into the stadium.*

sway /sweɪ/ *verb* (**sways**, **swaying**, **swayed** /sweɪd/) move slowly from side to side: *The trees were swaying in the wind.*

swear /sweə(r)/ *verb* (**swears**, **swearing**, **swore** /swɔː(r)/, **has sworn** /swɔːn/) **1** say bad words: *Don't swear at your mother!* **2** make a serious promise: *He swears that he is telling the truth.*

swear word /ˈsweə wɜːd/ *noun* a bad word

sweat /swet/ *noun* (no plural) water that comes out of your skin when you are hot or afraid

sweat *verb* (**sweats**, **sweating**, **sweated**) have sweat coming out of your skin: *The room was so hot that everyone was sweating.*

sweaty *adjective* (**sweatier**, **sweatiest**) covered with sweat: *sweaty socks*

sweater /ˈswetə(r)/ *noun* a warm piece of clothing with sleeves, that you wear on the top part of your body. Sweaters are often made of wool.

sweatshirt /ˈswetʃɜːt/ *noun* a piece of clothing like a sweater, made of thick cotton

sweep /swiːp/ *verb* (**sweeps**, **sweeping**, **swept** /swept/, **has swept**) **1** clean something by moving dirt or other things away with a brush: *I swept the floor.* **2** push something along or away quickly and strongly: *The bridge was swept away by the floods.*
sweep up move something away with a brush: *I swept up the broken glass.*

sweet[1] /swiːt/ *adjective* (**sweeter**, **sweetest**) **1** with the taste of sugar: *Honey is sweet.* **2** pretty: *What a sweet little girl!* **3** kind and gentle: *It was sweet of you to help me.* **4** with a good smell: *the sweet smell of roses*

sweetly *adverb* in a pretty, kind or nice way: *She smiled sweetly.*

sweet[2] /swiːt/ *noun* **1** a small piece of sweet food, made of boiled sugar, chocolate, etc: *He bought a packet of sweets for the children.* **2** sweet food that you eat at the end of a meal: *Do you want a sweet?*

swell /swel/ *verb* (**swells**, **swelling**, **swelled** /sweld/, **has swollen** /ˈswəʊlən/ or **has swelled**) **swell up** become bigger or thicker than it usually is: *After he hurt his ankle it began to swell up.*

swelling /ˈswelɪŋ/ *noun* a place on the body that is bigger or fatter than it usually is: *She has got a swelling on her head where she fell and hit it.*

swept *form of* **sweep**

swerve /swɜːv/ *verb* (**swerves**, **swerving**, **swerved** /swɜːvd/) turn suddenly so that you do not hit something: *The driver swerved when she saw the child in the road.*

swift /swɪft/ *adjective* (**swifter**, **swiftest**) quick or fast: *We made a swift decision.*

swiftly *adverb*: *She ran swiftly up the stairs.*

swim /swɪm/ *verb* (**swims**, **swimming**, **swam** /swæm/, **has swum** /swʌm/) move your body through water: *Can you swim?* ○ *I swam across the lake.* ✪ When you talk about spending time swimming as a sport, you usually say **go swimming**: *I go swimming every day.*

swim *noun* (no plural) *Let's go for a swim.*

swimmer *noun* a person who swims: *He's a good swimmer.*

swimming *noun* (no plural) *Swimming is my favourite sport.*

swimming costume /ˈswɪmɪŋ kɒstjuːm/, **swimsuit** /ˈswɪmsuːt/ *noun* a piece of clothing that a woman or girl wears for swimming

swimming pool /ˈswɪmɪŋ puːl/ *noun* a special place where you can swim

swimming trunks /ˈswɪmɪŋ trʌŋks/ *noun* (plural) short trousers that a man or boy wears for swimming

swing[1] /swɪŋ/ *verb* (**swings**, **swinging**, **swung** /swʌŋ/, **has swung**) **1** hang from something and move backwards and forwards or from side to side through the air: *The monkey was swinging from a tree.* **2** make somebody or something move in this way: *He swung his arms as he walked.* **3** move in a curve: *The door swung open.*

swing

swing[2] /swɪŋ/ *noun* a seat that hangs down. Children sit on it to move backwards and forwards through the air.

switch[1] /swɪtʃ/ **switch**
noun (plural **switches**) a small thing that you press to stop or start electricity: *Where is the light switch?*

switch[2] /swɪtʃ/ verb (**switches**, **switching**, **switched** /swɪtʃt/) change to something different: *I switched to another seat because I couldn't see the film.* **switch off** press something to stop electricity: *I switched the TV off.* ○ *Don't forget to switch off the lights!* **switch on** press something to start electricity: *Switch the radio on.*

switchboard /'swɪtʃbɔːd/ noun the place in a large office where somebody answers telephone calls and sends them to the right people

swollen form of **swell**

swollen /'swəʊlən/ adjective thicker or fatter than it usually is: *a swollen ankle*

swoop /swuːp/ verb (**swoops**, **swooping**, **swooped** /swuːpt/) fly down quickly: *The bird swooped down to catch a fish.*

swop /swɒp/ = **swap**

sword /sɔːd/ noun a long sharp knife for fighting

swore, **sworn** forms of **swear**

swot /swɒt/ verb (**swots**, **swotting**, **swotted**) study hard before an exam: *Debbie is swotting for her test next week.*

swum form of **swim**

swung form of **swing**[1]

syllable /'sɪləbl/ noun a part of a word that has one **vowel** sound when you say it. 'Swim' has one syllable and 'system' has two syllables.

syllabus /'sɪləbəs/ noun (plural **syllabuses**) a list of all the things that you must study on a course

symbol /'sɪmbl/ noun a mark, sign or picture that shows something: *+ and - are symbols for plus and minus in mathematics.* ○ *A dove is the symbol of peace.*

sympathetic /ˌsɪmpə'θetɪk/ adjective If you are sympathetic, you show that you understand other people's feelings when they have problems: *Everyone was very sympathetic when I was ill.* ✪ opposite: **unsympathetic**

sympathetically /ˌsɪmpə'θetɪkli/ adverb: *He smiled sympathetically.*

sympathize /'sɪmpəθaɪz/ verb (**sympathizes**, **sympathizing**, **sympathized** /'sɪmpəθaɪzd/) **sympathize with somebody** show that you understand somebody's feelings when they have problems: *I sympathize with you – I've got a lot of work too.*

sympathy /'sɪmpəθi/ noun (no plural) understanding another person's feelings and problems: *She wrote me a letter of sympathy when my father died.*

symphony /'sɪmfəni/ noun (plural **symphonies**) a long piece of music for a large orchestra: *Beethoven's fifth symphony*

symptom /'sɪmptəm/ noun something that shows that you have an illness: *The main symptom of malaria is a high fever.*

synagogue /'sɪnəgɒg/ noun a building where Jewish people go to pray

synthetic /sɪn'θetɪk/ adjective made by people, not natural: *Nylon is a synthetic material, but wool is natural.*

syrup /'sɪrəp/ noun (no plural) thick sweet liquid made with sugar and water or fruit juice: *ginger in syrup*

system /'sɪstəm/ noun **1** a group of things or parts that work together: *the railway system* ○ *We have a new computer system at work.* **2** a group of ideas or ways of doing something: *What system of government do you have in your country?*

table /'teɪbl/ noun **1** a piece of furniture with a flat top on legs **2** a list of facts or numbers: *There is a table of irregular verbs at the back of this dictionary.* **set** or **lay the table** put knives, forks, plates and other things on the table before you eat

tablecloth — — table

tablecloth /'teɪblklɒθ/ noun a cloth that you put over a table when you have a meal

tablespoon /'teɪblspu:n/ noun a big spoon that you use for putting food on plates

tablet /'tæblət/ noun a small hard piece of medicine that you swallow: *Take two of these tablets before every meal.*

table tennis /'teɪbl tenɪs/ noun (no plural) a game where players use a round **bat** to hit a small light ball over a net on a big table

tackle /'tækl/ verb (**tackles**, **tackling**, **tackled** /'tækld/) **1** start to do a difficult job: *I'm going to tackle my homework now.* ○ *How shall we tackle this problem?* **2** try to take the ball from somebody in a game like football **3** try to catch and hold somebody: *I tackled the thief but he ran away.*

tact /tækt/ noun (no plural) knowing how and when to say things so that you do not hurt people: *She told him the meal was horrible – she's got no tact.*

tactful /'tæktfl/ adjective careful not to say or do things that may make people unhappy or angry: *He wrote me a tactful letter about the money I owe him.*

tactfully /'tæktfəli/ adverb in a tactful way

tactless /'tæktləs/ adjective not careful about people's feelings: *It was tact-less of you to ask how old she was.*

tag /tæg/ noun a small piece of paper or material fixed to something, that tells you about it; a label: *I looked at the price tag to see how much the dress cost.*

tail /teɪl/ noun **1** the long thin part at the end of an animal's body: *The dog wagged its tail.* ✪ pictures at **cat** and **fish**. **2** the part at the back of something: *the tail of an aeroplane* **3** **tails** (plural) the side of a coin that does not have the head of a person on it ☛ Note at **heads**.

tailor /'teɪlə(r)/ noun a person whose job is to make clothes for men

take /teɪk/ verb (**takes**, **taking**, **took** /tʊk/, **has taken** /'teɪkn/) **1** move something or go with somebody to another place: *Take your coat with you – it's cold.* ○ *She took her son to the hospital.* ☛ picture at **bring**. **2** put your hand round something and hold it: *She took the baby in her arms.* ○ *Take this money – it's yours.* **3** steal something: *Somebody has taken my bike.* **4** need an amount of time: *The journey took four hours.* **5** travel in a bus, train, etc: *I took a taxi to the hospital.* **6** eat or drink something: *I took the medicine.* **7** agree to have something: *We'll have to pay cash because they don't take cheques.* **it takes** you need something: *It takes a long time to learn a language.* **take after somebody** be or look like somebody in your family: *She takes after her mother.* **take away** remove something: *I took the knife away from the child.* **take down** write something that somebody says: *He took down my address.* **take off** When an aeroplane takes off, it leaves the ground. **take something off 1** remove clothes: *Take your shoes off.* ✪ opposite: **put on**. **2** have time as a holiday, not working: *I am taking a week off in June.* **take over** look after a business, etc when another person stops: *Robert took over the farm when his father died.* **take up** use or fill time or space: *The bed takes* *up half the room.* ○ *The new baby takes up all her time.*

take-off /ˈteɪk ɒf/ *noun* the time when an aeroplane leaves the ground

talc /tælk/ **1** a kind of soft, white rock **2** (*also* **talcum powder**) /ˈtælkm paʊdə/ a soft powder that is used to make the body smell good

tale /teɪl/ *noun* a story: *My mother used to tell us tales about giants and witches.*

talent /ˈtælənt/ *noun* the natural ability to do something very well: *Agatha has a talent for drawing.*

  talented *adjective* with a talent: *a talented musician*

talk¹ /tɔːk/ *verb* (**talks**, **talking**, **talked** /tɔːkt/) speak to somebody; say words: *She is talking to her boyfriend on the telephone.* ○ *We talked about our holiday.*

talk² /tɔːk/ *noun* **1** when two or more people talk about something: *David and I had a long talk about the problem.* ○ *The two countries are holding talks to try and end the war.* **2** when a person speaks to a group of people: *Professor Olumbe gave an interesting talk on Chinese art.*

  talkative /ˈtɔːkətɪv/ *adjective* A person who is talkative talks a lot.

tall /tɔːl/ *adjective* (**taller**, **tallest**) **1** A person or thing that is tall goes up a long way: *a tall tree* ○ *Richard is taller than his brother.* ✪ opposite: **short** ➥ picture on page A10. **2** You use 'tall' to say or ask how far it is from the bottom to the top of somebody or something: *How tall are you?* ○ *She's 1·62 metres tall.* ➥ Note at **high**.

tame /teɪm/ *adjective* (**tamer**, **tamest**) A tame animal is not wild and is not afraid of people: *a tame parrot*

  tame *verb* (**tames**, **taming**, **tamed** /teɪmd/) make a wild animal tame

tangerine /ˌtændʒəˈriːn/ *noun* a fruit like a small sweet orange, with a skin that is easy to take off

tangle /ˈtæŋgl/ *verb* (**tangles**, **tangling**, **tangled** /ˈtæŋgld/) mix or twist something like string or hair so that it is difficult to separate ✪ opposite: **untangle**

  tangle *noun*: *This string is in a tangle.*

tangled *adjective*: *If you don't comb your hair it will get all tangled.*

tank /tæŋk/ *noun* **1** a container for liquids or gas: *a petrol tank* (in a car) **2** a strong heavy vehicle with big guns. Tanks are used by armies in wars.

tanker /ˈtæŋkə(r)/ *noun* a ship that carries petrol or oil: *an oil-tanker*

tanning /ˈtænɪŋ/ *noun* (no plural) making leather from animal skins

tap¹ /tæp/ *noun* a thing that you turn to make something like water or gas come out of a pipe: *Turn the tap off.*

tap² /tæp/ *verb* (**taps**, **tapping**, **tapped** /tæpt/) hit or touch somebody or something quickly and lightly: *She tapped me on the shoulder.* ○ *I tapped on the window.*

  tap *noun*: *They heard a tap at the door.*

tape /teɪp/ *noun* **1** a long thin piece of special plastic in a plastic box, that stores (**records**) sound, music or moving pictures so that you can listen to or watch it later. You use it in a **tape recorder** or a **video recorder**: *We recorded the interview on tape.* ○ *I'm going to put on my new reggae tape.* **2** a long thin piece of material or paper

  tape *verb* (**tapes**, **taping**, **taped** /teɪpt/) put (**record**) sound, music or moving pictures on tape so that you can listen to or watch it later: *He taped the football match and watched it the next day.*

tape-measure /ˈteɪp meʒə(r)/ *noun* a long thin piece of metal, plastic or cloth for measuring things

tape recorder /ˈteɪp rɪˌkɔːdə(r)/ *noun* a machine that can put (**record**) sound or music on tape and play it again later

tapestry /ˈtæpəstri/ *noun* (*plural* **tapestries**) a piece of cloth with pictures on it made from coloured thread

tar /tɑː(r)/ *noun* (no plural) black stuff that is thick and sticky when it is hot, and hard when it is cold. Tar is used for making roads.

target /ˈtɑːgɪt/ *noun* a thing that you try to hit with a bullet or an arrow, for example: *The bomb hit its target.*

task /tɑːsk/ *noun* a piece of work that you must do; a job: *I had the task of cleaning the floors.*

taste[1] /teɪst/ *noun* **1** (no plural) the power to know about food and drink with your mouth: *Simon has a good sense of taste.* **2** (*plural* **tastes**) the feeling that a certain food or drink gives in your mouth: *Sugar has a sweet taste and lemons have a sour taste.* ○ *I don't like the taste of this fruit.* **3** (*plural* **tastes**) a little bit of food or drink: *Have a taste of the stew to see if you like it.* **4** (no plural) being able to choose nice things: *She has good taste in clothes.*

taste[2] /teɪst/ *verb* (**tastes**, **tasting**, **tasted**) **1** feel or know a certain food or drink in your mouth: *Can you taste onions in this stew?* **2** eat or drink a little of something: *Taste this meat to see if you like it.* **3** give a certain feeling when you put it in your mouth: *Honey tastes sweet.*

tasty /'teɪsti/ *adjective* (**tastier**, **tastiest**) good to eat: *The soup was very tasty.*

tattoo /tə'tuː/ *noun* (*plural* **tattoos**) a picture on somebody's skin, made with a needle and coloured liquid: *He had a tattoo of a snake on his arm.*

taught *form of* **teach**

tax /tæks/ *noun* (*plural* **taxes**) money that you have to pay to the government. You pay tax from the money you earn or when you buy things: *There is a tax on cigarettes in this country.*

tax (**taxes**, **taxing**, **taxed** /tækst/) make somebody pay tax

taxi /'tæksi/ *noun* a car that you can travel in if you pay the driver: *I took a taxi to the airport.* ○ *I came by taxi.*

tea /tiː/ *noun* **1** (no plural) a brown drink that you make with hot water and the dry leaves of a special plant: *Would you like a cup of tea?* **2** (*plural* **teas**) a cup of this drink: *Two teas, please.* **3** (no plural) the dry leaves that you use to make tea

tea bag /'tiː bæg/ *noun* a small paper bag with tea leaves inside. You use it to make tea.

teapot /'tiːpɒt/ *noun* a special pot for making and pouring tea

teach /tiːtʃ/ *verb* (**teaches**, **teaching**, **taught** /tɔːt/, **has taught**) give somebody lessons; tell or show somebody how to do something: *Mr Nassir taught us some French.* ○ *My mother taught me to knit.* ☛ Look at **learn**.

teaching *noun* (no plural) the job of a teacher

teacher /'tiːtʃə(r)/ *noun* a person whose job is to teach: *He's my English teacher.*

team /tiːm/ *noun* **1** a group of people who play a sport or a game together against another group: *Which team do you play for?* ○ *a football team* **2** a group of people who work together: *a team of doctors*

tear[1] /tɪə(r)/ *noun* a drop of water that comes from your eye when you cry   **be in tears** be crying: *I was in tears at the end of the film.*   **burst into tears** suddenly start to cry: *He read the letter and burst into tears.*

'Oh, no! I've **torn** my shirt!'   She **tore** the letter in half.

tear[2] /teə(r)/ *verb* (**tears**, **tearing**, **tore** /tɔː(r)/, **has torn** /tɔːn/) **1** pull something apart or make an untidy hole in something: *She tore her dress on a nail.* ○ *I tore the piece of paper in half.* ○ *I can't use this bag – it's torn.* **2** pull something roughly and quickly away from somebody or something: *I tore a page out of the book.* **3** come apart; break: *Paper tears easily.* **4** move very fast: *He tore down the street.*   **tear up** pull something into small pieces: *I tore the letter up and threw it away.*

tear[3] /teə(r)/ *noun* an untidy hole in something like paper or material: *You've got a tear in your shirt.*

tease /tiːz/ *verb* (**teases**, **teasing**, **teased** /tiːzd/) say unkind things to somebody because you think it is funny: *People often tease me because I'm short.*

teaspoon /'tiːspuːn/ *noun* a small spoon that you use for putting sugar into tea or coffee

tea towel /'tiː taʊəl/ *noun* a small cloth that you use for drying things like plates and cups after you wash them

technical /'teknɪkl/ *adjective* of or about the machines and materials used in science and in making things: *technical knowledge*

technician /tek'nɪʃn/ *noun* a person who works with machines or instruments: *a laboratory technician*

technique /tek'ni:k/ *noun* a special way of doing something: *new techniques for learning languages*

technology /tek'nɒlədʒi/ *noun* (no plural) studying science and ideas about how things work, and using this to build and make things: *Technology is very important for the future.* ○ *computer technology*

teddy bear
/'tedi beə(r)/ **teddy**
(*plural* **teddies**)
noun a toy for
children that looks
like a bear

teddy bear

tedious /'ti:dɪəs/ *adjective* very long and not interesting: *a tedious journey*

teenager /'ti:neɪdʒə(r)/ *noun* a person who is between the ages of 13 and 19
teenage /'ti:neɪdʒ/ *adjective*: *a teenage boy*

teens /ti:nz/ *noun* (plural) the time when you are between the ages of 13 and 19: *She is in her teens.*

teeth *plural of* **tooth**

telegram /'telɪɡræm/ *noun* a message that you send very quickly by radio or by electric wires

telephone[1] /'telɪfəʊn/ *noun* an instrument that you use for talking to somebody who is in another place: *What's your telephone number?* ○ *Can I make a telephone call?* ○ *The telephone's ringing – can you answer it?* **on the telephone** using a telephone to speak to somebody: *He's on the telephone to a customer.* ✪ **Phone** is the more usual word.

telephone[2] /'telɪfəʊn/ *verb* (**telephones**, **telephoning**, **telephoned** /'telɪfəʊnd/) use a telephone to speak to somebody: *I must telephone my boss.* ✪ **Phone** is the more usual word.

telephone box /'telɪfəʊn bɒks/ (*plural* **telephone boxes**), **telephone kiosk** *noun* a kind of small building in the street or in a public place that has a telephone in it

telephone directory /'telɪfəʊn dɪrek-təri/ *noun* (*plural* **telephone directories**) a book of people's names, addresses and telephone numbers

telescope /'telɪskəʊp/ *noun* a long round instrument with special glass inside it. You use it to look at things that are a long way from you.

television /'telɪvɪʒn/ *noun* **1** (*plural* **televisions**), **television set** a machine like a box that shows moving pictures with sound **2** (no plural) things that you watch on a television: *I watched television last night.* ○ *What's on television?* ○ *a television programme* **3** a way of sending pictures and sounds so that people can watch them on television: *satellite television* ✪ The short forms are **TV** and **telly**.

telex /'teleks/ *noun* **1** (no plural) a way of sending messages. You type the message on a special machine that sends it very quickly to another place by telephone. **2** (*plural* **telexes**) a message that you send or receive in this way

tell /tel/ *verb* (**tells**, **telling**, **told** /təʊld/, **has told**) **1** give information to somebody by speaking or writing: *I told her my new address.* ○ *This book tells you how to make bread.* ○ *He told me that he was tired.* **2** say what somebody must do: *Our teacher told us to read this book.* ☛ Note at **say**. **can tell** know, guess or understand something: *I can tell that he's been crying because his eyes are red.* ○ *I can't tell the difference between James and his brother. They look exactly the same!* **tell somebody off** speak to somebody in an angry way because they have done something wrong: *I told the children off for making so much noise.*

telly /'teli/ *short for* **television**

temper /'tempə(r)/ *noun* how you feel: *She's in a bad temper this morning.* **have a temper** If you have a temper, you often get angry and cannot control what you do or say: *He has a terrible temper.* **in a temper** angry:

She's in a temper because she's tired. **lose your temper** suddenly become angry

temperature /'temprətʃə(r)/ *noun* how hot or cold somebody or something is: *Some days, the temperature reaches over 40° C.* ○ *a high/low temperature* **have a temperature** feel very hot because you are ill **take somebody's temperature** see how hot somebody is, using a special instrument called a **thermometer**

temple /'templ/ *noun* a building where people go to pray and worship God or a god

temporary /'temprəri/ *adjective* Something that is temporary lasts for a short time: *I had a temporary job in an office.* ✪ opposite: **permanent**

temporarily /'temprərəli/ *adverb*: *The road is temporarily closed for repairs.*

tempt /tempt/ *verb* (**tempts**, **tempting**, **tempted**) make somebody want to do something, especially something that is wrong: *He saw the money on the table, and he was tempted to steal it.*

temptation /temp'teɪʃn/ *noun* **1** (*plural* **temptations**) a thing that makes you want to do something wrong: *Don't leave the money on your desk – it's a temptation to thieves.* **2** (no plural) a feeling that you want to do something that you know is wrong: *the temptation to eat another chocolate*

tempting *adjective* Something that is tempting makes you want to do or have it: *That food looks very tempting!*

ten /ten/ *number* 10

tenant /'tenənt/ *noun* a person who pays money to live in or use a place

tend /tend/ *verb* (**tends**, **tending**, **tended**) usually do or be something: *Men tend to be taller than women.*

tendency /'tendənsi/ *noun* (*plural* **tendencies**) something that a person or thing often does: *He has a tendency to be late.*

tender /'tendə(r)/ *adjective* **1** kind and gentle: *a tender look* **2** Tender meat is soft and easy to cut or bite. ✪ opposite: **tough 3** If a part of your body is tender, it hurts when you touch it.

tenderly *adverb* in a kind and gentle

way: *He touched her arm tenderly.*

tenderness /'tendənəs/ *noun* (no plural) *a feeling of tenderness*

tennis /'tenɪs/ *noun* (no plural) a game for two or four players who hold **rackets** and hit a small ball over a net: *Let's play tennis.*

tennis court /'tenɪs kɔːt/ *noun* a special place where you play tennis

tense¹ /tens/ *adjective* (**tenser**, **tensest**) **1** worried because you are waiting for something to happen: *I always feel very tense before exams.* **2** pulled tightly: *tense muscles*

tension /'tenʃn/ *noun* being tense: *Tension can give you headaches.*

tense² /tens/ *noun* the form of a verb that shows if something happens in the past, present or future

tent

tent /tent/ *noun* a kind of house made of cloth. You sleep in a tent when you go camping: *We put up our tent.*

tenth /tenθ/ *adjective, adverb, noun* **1** 10th **2** one of ten equal parts of something; $\frac{1}{10}$

term /tɜːm/ *noun* **1** the time between holidays when schools and colleges are open: *We have important exams next term.* **2** a word or group of words connected with a special subject: *a computing term*

terminal /'tɜːmɪnl/ *noun* a building where people begin and end their journeys by bus, train, aeroplane or ship: *Passengers for Nairobi should go to Terminal 2.*

termite /'tɜːmaɪt/ (*also* **white ant**) *noun* a small insect that eats wood

terrible /'terəbl/ *adjective* very bad: *She had a terrible accident.* ○ *Her spelling is terrible!*

terribly /'terəbli/ *adverb* **1** very: *I'm terribly sorry!* **2** very badly: *He played terribly.*

terrific /tə'rɪfɪk/ *adjective* **1** very good; wonderful: *What a terrific idea!* **2** very great: *a terrific storm*

terrify /'terɪfaɪ/ *verb* (**terrifies, terrifying, terrified** /'terɪfaɪd/, **has terrified**) make somebody very frightened: *Spiders terrify me!*

terrified *adjective* very frightened: *Di is terrified of dogs.*

territory /'terətri/ *noun* (*plural* **territories**) the land that belongs to one country: *This island was once French territory.*

terror /'terə(r)/ *noun* (no plural) very great fear: *He screamed in terror.*

terrorist /'terərɪst/ *noun* a person who frightens, hurts or kills people so that the government, etc will do what he/she wants: *The terrorists put a bomb in the station.*

terrorism /'terərɪzəm/ *noun* (no plural) *an act of terrorism*

test /test/ *verb* (**tests, testing, tested**) **1** use or look at something carefully to find out how good it is or if it works well: *The doctor tested my eyes.* ○ *These drugs are tested on monkeys before being sold.* **2** ask somebody questions to find out what they know or what they can do: *The teacher tested us on our spelling.*

test *noun*: *a blood test* ○ *a maths test* ○ *Did you pass your driving test?*

test-tube /'test
tju:b/ *noun* a long
thin glass tube
that you use in
chemistry

test-tube

text /tekst/ *noun*
1 (no plural) the
words in a book, newspaper or magazine: *This book has a lot of pictures but not much text.* **2** (*plural* **texts**) a book or a short piece of writing that you study: *Read the text and answer the questions.*

textbook /'tekstbʊk/ *noun* a book that teaches you about something: *a biology textbook*

textile /'tekstaɪl/ *noun* cloth or material: *Joseph works in the textile industry, making and exporting cloth.*

texture /'tekstʃə(r)/ *noun* the way that something feels when you touch it: *Silk has a smooth texture.*

than /ðən/, /ðæn/ *conjunction, preposition* You use 'than' when you compare people or things: *I'm older than him.* ○ *You cook much better than she does.* ○ *We live less than a kilometre from the beach.*

thank /θæŋk/ *verb* (**thanks, thanking, thanked** /θæŋkt/) tell somebody that you are pleased because they gave you something or helped you: *I thanked Tina for the present.* **no, thank you** You use 'no, thank you' to say that you do not want something: *'Would you like some more tea?' 'No, thank you.'* ✪ You can also say **no, thanks**. **thank you, thanks** You use 'thank you' or 'thanks' to tell somebody that you are pleased because they gave you something or helped you: *Thank you very much for your help.* ○ *'How are you?' 'I'm fine, thanks.'*

thanks *noun* (plural) words that show you are pleased because somebody gave you something or helped you: *Please give my thanks to your sister for her help.* **thanks to somebody** or **something** because of somebody or something: *We're late, thanks to you!*

thankful /'θæŋkfl/ *adjective* happy that something good has happened: *I was thankful for a rest after the long walk.*

thankfully /'θæŋkfəli/ *adverb* You say 'thankfully' when you are pleased about something: *There was an accident, but thankfully nobody was hurt.*

that[1] /ðæt/ *adjective, pronoun* (*plural* **those**) a word that you use to talk about a person or thing that is there or then: *'Who is that boy over there?' 'That's my brother.'* ○ *She got married in 1989. At that time, she was a teacher.* ☛ picture at **this**

that[2] /ðæt/ *adverb* so: *The next village is ten kilometres from here. I can't walk that far.*

that[3] /ðət/ *pronoun* which, who or whom: *An ostrich is a bird that can't fly.* ○ *The people (that) I met were very nice.* ○ *I'm reading the book (that) you gave me.*

that[4] /ðət/, /ðæt/ *conjunction* a word that you use to join two parts of a sentence: *Nelly said (that) she was unhappy.* ○ *I'm sure (that) he will come.* ○ *I was so hungry (that) I ate all the food.*

thatch /θætʃ/ *noun* (no plural) a roof covering that is made of dried grass or branches

thaw /θɔː/ *verb* (**thaws, thawing** /ˈθɔːɪŋ/, **thawed** /θɔːd/) warm something that is frozen so that it becomes soft or liquid; get warmer so that it becomes soft or liquid: *The ice is thawing.*

the[1] /ðə/, /ði/, /ðiː/ *article* **1** a word that you use before the name of somebody or something when it is clear what person or thing you mean: *I bought a shirt and some trousers. The shirt is blue.* ○ *The sun is shining.* **2** a word that you use before numbers and dates: *Monday the sixth of May* **3** a word that you use to talk about a group of people or things of the same kind: *the French* (= all French people) ○ *Do you play the piano?* **4** a word that you use before the names of rivers, seas, etc and some countries: *the Nile* ○ *the Atlantic* ○ *the United States of America* ✪ Before the names of most countries, we do not use 'the ': *I went to France.* (NOT: *I went to the France.*)

the[2] /ðə/, /ði/ *adverb* a word that you use to talk about two things happening together: *The more you eat, the fatter you get.*

theatre /ˈθɪətə(r)/ *noun* a building where you go to see plays: *I'm going to the theatre this evening.*

theft /θeft/ *noun* taking something that is not yours; stealing: *She was sent to prison for theft.* ○ *I told the police about the theft of my car.*

their /ðeə(r)/ *adjective* of them: *What is their address?*

theirs /ðeəz/ *pronoun* something that belongs to them: *Our flat is smaller than theirs.*

them /ðəm/, /ðem/ *pronoun* (plural) **1** a word that shows more than one person, animal or thing: *I wrote them a letter and then I visited them.* ○ *I'm looking for my keys. Have you seen them?* **2** him or her: *If anybody calls, tell them I'm busy.*

theme /θiːm/ *noun* something that you talk or write about: *The theme of his speech was 'The future of Africa'.*

themselves /ðəmˈselvz/ *pronoun* (plural) **1** a word that shows the same people, animals or things that you have just talked about: *They bought themselves a new car.* **2** a word that makes 'they' stronger: *Did they build the house themselves?* **by themselves 1** alone; without other people: *The children went out by themselves.* **2** without help: *They cooked dinner by themselves.*

then /ðen/ *adverb* **1** at that time: *I became a teacher in 1989. I was single then, but now I'm married.* ○ *I can't come next week. I will be on holiday then.* **2** next; after that: *We had dinner and then did the washing-up.* **3** if that is true: *'I don't feel well.' 'Then why don't you go to the doctor's?'*

theory /ˈθɪəri/ *noun* (plural **theories**) an idea that tries to explain something: *There are a lot of different theories about how life began.*

therapy /ˈθerəpi/ *noun* (no plural) a way of helping people who are ill in their body or mind, usually without drugs: *speech therapy*

there[1] /ðeə(r)/ *adverb* in, at or to that place: *Don't put the box there – put it here.* ○ *Have you been to Lamu? I'm going there next week.* **there you are** words that you say when you give something to somebody: *'There you are,' she said, giving me a plate.*

there[2] /ðeə(r)/ *pronoun* **1** a word that you use with verbs like 'be', 'seem' and 'appear' to show that something is true or that something is happening: *There is a man at the door.* ○ *Is there any more coffee?* ○ *There aren't any shops in this village.* **2** a word that makes people look or listen: *There's the bell for my class! I must go.*

therefore /ˈðeəfɔː(r)/ *adverb* for that reason: *Simon was busy and therefore could not come to the meeting.*

thermometer /θəˈmɒmɪtə(r)/ *noun* an instrument that shows how hot or cold something is

thermometer

these /ðiːz/ *adjective, pronoun* (plural) a word that you use to talk about people or things that are here or now: *These books are mine.* ○ *Do you want these?* ☞ picture at **this**

they /ðeɪ/ *pronoun* (plural) **1** the people, animals or things that the sentence is about: *Josephine and David came at two o'clock and they left at six o'clock.* ○ *'Where are my keys?' 'They're* (= they are) *on the table.'* **2** a word that you use instead of 'he' or 'she': *Someone phoned for you – they said they would phone again later.* **3** people: *They say that this area is dangerous.*

they'd /ðeɪd/ **1** = **they had 2** = **they would**

they'll /ðeɪl/ = **they will**

they're /ðeə(r)/ = **they are**

they've /ðeɪv/ = **they have**

thick /θɪk/ *adjective* (**thicker, thickest**) **1** far from one side to the other: *The walls are very thick.* ✪ opposite: **thin.** ☞ picture on page A10. **2** You use 'thick' to say or ask how far something is from one side to the other: *The wall is ten centimetres thick.* **3** with a lot of people or things close together: *a thick forest* **4** If a liquid is thick, it does not flow easily: *This paint is too thick.* ✪ opposite: **thin. 5** difficult to see through: *thick smoke*

thickness /'θɪknəs/ *noun* (no plural) *The wood is 3 cm in thickness.*

thief /θiːf/ *noun* (plural **thieves** /θiːvz/) a person who steals something: *Most of the class had money stolen but we didn't know who the thief was.*

thigh /θaɪ/ *noun* the part of your leg above your knee ☞ picture on page A4

thin /θɪn/ *adjective* (**thinner, thinnest**) **1** not far from one side to the other; not thick: *The walls in this house are very thin.* ☞ picture on page A10. **2** not fat: *He's tall and thin.* ☞ picture on page A10. **3** If a liquid is thin, it flows easily like water: *The soup was very thin.* ✪ opposite: **thick. 4** not close together: *My father's hair is getting thin.*

thing /θɪŋ/ *noun* **1** an object: *What's that red thing?* **2** what happens or what you do: *A strange thing happened to me*

yesterday. ○ *That was a difficult thing to do.* **3** an idea or subject: *We talked about a lot of things.* **4 things** (plural) what you own: *Have you packed your things for the journey?*

think /θɪŋk/ *verb* (**thinks, thinking, thought** /θɔːt/, **has thought**) **1** use your mind: *Think before you answer the question.* **2** believe something: *I think it's going to rain.* ○ *'Do you think Sara will come tomorrow?' 'Yes, I think so.'* (= I think that she will come) ○ *I think they live in Nakuru but I'm not sure.* **think about somebody** or **something 1** have somebody or something in your mind: *I often think about that day.* **2** try to decide whether to do something: *Paul is thinking about leaving his job.* **think of somebody** or **something 1** have something in your mind: *I can't think of her name.* **2** have an opinion about somebody or something: *What do you think of this music?* **3** try to decide whether to do something: *We're thinking of moving to the city.*

third /θɜːd/ *adjective, adverb, noun* **1** 3rd **2** one of three equal parts of something; $\frac{1}{3}$

thirst /θɜːst/ *noun* (no plural) the feeling you have when you want to drink something

thirsty /'θɜːsti/ *adjective* (**thirstier, thirstiest**) If you are thirsty, you want to drink something: *Salty food makes you thirsty.*

thirteen /ˌθɜː'tiːn/ *number* 13

thirteenth /ˌθɜː'tiːnθ/ *adjective, adverb, noun* 13th

thirty /'θɜːti/ *number* **1** 30 **2 the thirties** (plural) the numbers, years or temperature between 30 and 39 **in your thirties** between the ages of 30 and 39

thirtieth /'θɜːtiəθ/ *adjective, adverb, noun* 30th

this[1] /ðɪs/ *adjective, pronoun* (plural **these**) a word that you use to talk about a person or thing that is here or now: *Come and look at this photo.* ○ *This is my sister.* ○ *I am on holiday this week.* ○ *How much does this cost?* ☞ picture on next page

this, these, that and **those**

He caught **this** fish.

He didnt catch **that** fish.

this² /ðɪs/ *adverb* so: *The other film was not this good* (= not as good as this film).

thorn /θɔːn/ *noun* **1** a sharp point that grows on a plant: *Be careful, that bush has thorns.* **2** a tree or large plant that has thorns

thorough /ˈθʌrə/ *adjective* careful and complete: *We gave the room a thorough clean.*

thoroughly /ˈθʌrəli/ *adverb* **1** carefully and completely: *He cleaned the room thoroughly.* **2** completely; very or very much: *I thoroughly enjoyed the lesson.*

those /ðəʊz/ *adjective, pronoun* (plural) a word that you use to talk about people or things that are there or then: *I don't know those boys.* ○ *Her grandfather was born in 1850. In those days, there were no cars.* ○ *Can I have those?*
☛ picture above

though¹ /ðəʊ/ *conjunction* **1** in spite of

something; although: *Though she was in a hurry, she stopped to talk.* **2** but: *I thought it was right though I wasn't sure.* **as though** in a way that makes you think something: *The house looks as though nobody lives there.* ○ *I'm so hungry – I feel as though I haven't eaten for days!*

though² /ðəʊ/ *adverb* however: *I like him very much. I don't like his wife, though.*

thought¹ *form of* **think**

thought² /θɔːt/ *noun* **1** (no plural) thinking: *After a lot of thought, I decided not to take the job.* **2** (plural **thoughts**) an idea: *Have you had any thoughts about what you want to do when you leave school?*

thoughtful /ˈθɔːtfl/ *adjective* **1** If you are thoughtful, you are thinking carefully: *She listened with a thoughtful look on her face.* **2** A person who is thoughtful is kind, and thinks and cares about other people: *It was very thoughtful of you to come and help us.*

thousand /ˈθaʊznd/ *number* 1000: *a thousand people* ○ *two thousand and fifteen* ○ *There were thousands of birds on the lake.*

thousandth /ˈθaʊznθ/ *adjective, adverb, noun* 1000th

thread /θred/ *noun* a long thin piece of cotton, wool, etc that you use with a **needle** for sewing

thread *verb* (**threads**, **threading**, **threaded**) put thread through the hole in a needle

threat /θret/ *noun* **1** a promise that you will hurt somebody if they do not do what you want **2** a person or thing that may damage or hurt somebody or something: *Pollution is a threat to the lives of animals and people.*

threaten /ˈθretn/ *verb* (**threatens**, **threatening**, **threatened** /ˈθretnd/) **1** say that you will hurt somebody if they do not do what you want: *They threatened to kill everyone on the plane.* ○ *She threatened him with a knife.* **2** seem ready to do something bad: *The dark clouds threatened a storm.*

three /θriː/ *number* 3

threw *form of* **throw**

thrill /θrɪl/ *noun* a sudden strong feeling of excitement

thrill *verb* (**thrills**, **thrilling**, **thrilled** /θrɪld/) make somebody feel strong excitement

thrilled *adjective* very happy and excited: *We are all thrilled that you have won the prize.*

thrilling *adjective* very exciting: *a thrilling adventure*

thriller /ˈθrɪlə(r)/ *noun* an exciting book, film or play about a crime

throat /θrəʊt/ *noun* **1** the front part of your neck ➡ picture on page A4. **2** the part inside your neck that takes food and air down from your mouth into your body: *I've got a sore throat* (= my throat hurts).

throb /θrɒb/ *verb* (**throbs**, **throbbing**, **throbbed** /θrɒbd/) beat quickly and strongly: *His thumb throbbed with pain when he hit it.*

throne /θrəʊn/ *noun* a special chair where a king or queen sits

through /θruː/ *preposition, adverb* **1** from one side or end of something to the other side or end: *We drove through the tunnel.* ○ *What can you see through the window?* ○ *She opened the gate and we walked through.* ➡ picture on page A2. **2** from the beginning to the end of something: *We travelled through the night.* **3** connected by telephone: *Can you put me through to Mrs Tuiyot, please?* ○ *I tried to phone you but I couldn't get through.* **4** because of somebody or something: *She got the job through her father.*

throughout /θruːˈaʊt/ *preposition, adverb* **1** in every part of something: *We painted the house throughout.* ○ *She is famous throughout the world.* **2** from the beginning to the end of something: *They talked throughout the lesson.*

throw /θrəʊ/ *verb* (**throws**, **throwing**, **threw** /θruː/, **has thrown** /θrəʊn/) **1** move your arm quickly to send something through the air: *Throw the ball to Alex.* ○ *The boys were throwing stones at people.* **2** do something quickly and without care: *She threw on her coat* (= put it on quickly) *and ran out of the house.* **3** move your body or part of it quickly: *He threw his arms up.* **throw something away** or **out** put something in the dustbin because you do not want it: *Don't throw that box away.*

throw *noun*: *What a good throw!*

thrust /θrʌst/ *verb* (**thrusts**, **thrusting**, **thrust**, **has thrust**) push somebody or something suddenly and strongly: *She thrust the money into my hand.*

thrust *noun* a strong push

thud /θʌd/ *noun* the sound that a heavy thing makes when it hits something: *The book hit the floor with a thud.*

thumb /θʌm/ *noun* the short thick finger at the side of your hand ➡ picture on page A4

thump /θʌmp/ *verb* (**thumps**, **thumping**, **thumped** /θʌmpt/) **1** hit something hard with your hand or a heavy thing: *He thumped on the door.* **2** make a loud sound by hitting or beating hard: *Her heart was thumping with fear.*

thunder /'θʌndə(r)/ *noun* (no plural) a loud noise in the sky when there is a storm ✪ The light that you see in the sky in a storm is called **lightning**.

thunder *verb* (**thunders**, **thundering**, **thundered** /'θʌndəd/) **1** make the sound of thunder: *It thundered all night.* **2** make a sound like thunder: *The lorries thundered along the road.*

thunderstorm /'θʌndəstɔːm/ *noun* a storm with a lot of rain, thunder and lightning

Thursday /'θɜːzdeɪ/ *noun* the fifth day of the week, next after Wednesday

thus /ðʌs/ *adverb* **1** in this way: *Hold the wheel in both hands, thus.* **2** because of this: *He was very busy and was thus unable to come to the meeting.*

tick[1] /tɪk/ *noun* the sound that a clock or watch makes

tick *verb* (**ticks**, **ticking**, **ticked** /tɪkt/) make this sound: *I could hear a clock ticking.*

tick[2] /tɪk/ *noun* **1** a small mark like this ✓ that shows that something is correct, for example: *Put a tick by the correct answer.* **2** a small animal that lives on the skin of sheep, cattle, etc and drinks their blood

tick *verb* (**ticks**, **ticking**, **ticked** /tɪkt/) make a mark like this ✓ by something: *Tick the right answer.*

ticket /'tɪkɪt/ *noun* a small piece of paper or card that you must buy to travel or to go into a cinema, theatre or museum, for example: *How much is a ticket to Mombasa?* ○ *a theatre ticket* ○ *a ticket collector* (= a person who takes tickets from people on a train or at a station)

ticket office /'tɪkɪt ɒfɪs/ *noun* a place where you buy tickets

tickle /'tɪkl/ *verb* (**tickles**, **tickling**, **tickled** /'tɪkld/) **1** touch somebody lightly with your fingers to make them laugh: *She tickled the baby's feet.* **2** have the feeling that something is touching you lightly: *My nose tickles.*

tide /taɪd/ *noun* the movement of the sea towards the land and away from the land: *The tide is coming in.* ○ *The tide is going out.* ✪ **High tide** is when

the sea is nearest the land, and **low tide** is when the sea is furthest from the land.

tidy /'taɪdi/ *adjective* (**tidier**, **tidiest**) **1** with everything in the right place: *Her room is very tidy.* **2** If you are tidy, you like to have everything in the right place: *a tidy boy* ✪ opposite: **untidy**

tidily /'taɪdɪli/ *adverb*: *Put the books back tidily when you've finished with them.*

tidiness /'taɪdinəs/ *noun* (no plural) being tidy

tidy, **tidy up** *verb* (**tidies**, **tidying**, **tidied** /'taɪdid/, **has tidied**) make something tidy: *I tidied the house before my parents arrived.* ○ *Can you help me to tidy up?*

tie[1] /taɪ/ *noun* **1** a long thin piece of cloth that you wear round your neck with a shirt ☞ picture at **suit**. **2** when two teams or players have the same number of points at the end of a game or competition: *The match ended in a tie.* **3** something that holds people together: *Our country has close ties with Britain.*

tie[2] /taɪ/ *verb* (**ties**, **tying**, **tied** /taɪd/, **has tied**) **1** fasten two ends of string, rope, etc together to hold somebody or something in place: *The prisoner was tied to a chair.* ○ *I tied a scarf round my neck.* **2** end a game or competition with the same number of points for both teams or players: *France tied with Spain for second place.* **tie somebody up** put a piece of rope around somebody so that they cannot move: *The robbers tied up the owner of the shop.* **tie something up** put a piece of string or rope around something to hold it in place: *I tied up the parcel with string.*

tiger /'taɪɡə(r)/ *noun* a wild animal like a big cat, with yellow fur and black stripes. Tigers live in Asia.

tight /taɪt/ *adjective* (**tighter**, **tightest**) **1** fixed firmly so that you cannot move it easily: *a tight knot* ○ *I can't open this jar – the lid is too tight.* **2** small, so that there is no space between it and your body: *These shoes are too tight.* ○ *tight trousers* ✪ opposite: **loose**. ☞ picture on page A11

tight, **tightly** *adverb*: *Hold tight!* ○ *I*

tied the string tightly around the box.

tighten /'taɪtn/ *verb* (**tightens, tightening, tightened** /'taɪtnd/) become tighter or make something tighter: *Can you tighten this screw?* ✪ opposite: **loosen**

tightrope /'taɪtrəʊp/ *noun* a rope or wire high above the ground. **Acrobats** walk along tightropes in a **circus**.

tights /taɪts/ *noun* (plural) a thin piece of clothing that a woman or girl wears over her feet and legs: *a pair of tights*

tile /taɪl/ *noun* a flat square thing. We use tiles for covering roofs, walls and floors.

till[1] /tɪl/ *conjunction* up to the time when: *Let's wait till the rain stops.*

till *preposition* **1** up to a certain time: *I'll be here till Monday.* **2** before: *I didn't arrive till six o'clock.*

till[2] /tɪl/ *noun* a drawer or box for money in a shop: *She opened the till and gave me my change.*

tilt /tɪlt/ *verb* (**tilts, tilting, tilted**) have one side higher than the other; move something so that it has one side higher than the other: *She tilted the tray and all the glasses fell off.*

timber /'tɪmbə(r)/ *noun* (no plural) wood that we use for building and making things

time[1] /taɪm/ *noun* **1** (*plural* **times**) a certain point in the day or night, that you say in hours and minutes: *'What time is it?' 'It's twenty past six.'* ○ *What's the time?* ○ *Can you tell me the times of trains to Nairobi, please?* **2** (no plural) all the seconds, minutes, hours, days, weeks, months and years: *Time passes quickly when you're busy.* **3** (no plural) an amount of minutes, days, etc: *They have lived here for a long time.* ○ *I haven't got time to help you now – I'm late for school.* ○ *It takes a long time to write a book.* **4** (*plural* **times**) a certain moment or occasion: *I've been to Mombasa four times.* ○ *Come and visit us next time you're in Kenya.* **5** (*plural* **times**) experience; something that you do: *We had a great time at the party.* **6** (*plural* **times**) certain years in history: *In my great-grandfather's times, Nairobi was just a*

small town. **at a time** together; on one occasion: *The lift can carry six people at a time.* **at one time** in the past, but not now: *We were in the same class at one time.* **at the time** then: *My family moved to this town in 1990 – I was four at the time.* **at times** sometimes: *A teacher's job can be very difficult at times.* **by the time** when: *By the time we arrived they had eaten all the food.* **for the time being** now, but not for long: *You can stay here for the time being, until you find a flat.* **from time to time** sometimes; not often: *I see my cousin from time to time.* **have a good time** enjoy yourself: *Have a good time at the party!* **in a week's, etc time** after a week, etc: *I'll see you in a month's time.* **in good time** at the right time or early: *I want to get to the station in good time.* **in time 1** not late: *If you hurry, you'll arrive in time for the film.* **2** at some time in the future: *You will find speaking English easier in time.* **it's about time** words that you use to say that something should be done now: *It's about time you started studying if you want to pass the exam.* **it's time to** it is the right time to do something: *It's time to go home.* **on time** not late or early: *My train was on time.* **spend time** use time to do something: *I spend a lot of time studying.* **take your time** do something slowly **tell the time** read the time from a clock or watch: *Can your children tell the time?* **time after time, time and time again** many times

time[2] /taɪm/ *verb* (**times, timing, timed** /taɪmd/) **1** plan something so that it will happen when you want: *The bomb was timed to explode at six o'clock.* **2** measure how much time it takes to do something: *We timed the journey – it took half an hour.*

times /taɪmz/ *noun* (plural) a word that you use to show how much bigger, smaller, more expensive, etc one thing is than another thing: *Mount Kilimanjaro is three times bigger than Mount Kulai.*

times *preposition* multiplied by: *Three times four is twelve.*

timetable /'taɪmteɪbl/ *noun* a list of times when something happens: *A train timetable shows when trains arrive and leave.* ○ *A school timetable shows when lessons start.*

timid /'tɪmɪd/ *adjective* shy and easily frightened

timidly *adverb*: *She opened the door timidly and came in.*

tin /tɪn/ *noun* **1** (no plural) a soft white metal **2** (*plural* **tins**) a metal container for food and drink that keeps it fresh: *I opened a tin of beans.* ☞ picture at **container**

tinned /tɪnd/ *adjective* in a tin so that it will stay fresh: *tinned peaches*

tin-opener /'tɪn əʊpənə(r)/ *noun* a tool for opening tins

tiny /'taɪni/ *adjective* (**tinier**, **tiniest**) very small: *Ants are tiny insects.*

tip[1] /tɪp/ *noun* the pointed or thin end of something: *the tips of your fingers*

tip[2] /tɪp/ *verb* (**tips**, **tipping**, **tipped** /tɪpt/) give a small, extra amount of money to somebody who has done a job for you, for example a waiter or a taxi-driver: *He paid for the meal and tipped the waiter 10%.*

tip *noun*: *I left a tip on the table.*

tip[3] /tɪp/ *noun* a small piece of advice: *She gave me some useful tips on how to pass the exam.*

tip[4] /tɪp/ *verb* (**tips**, **tipping**, **tipped** /tɪpt/) **1** move so that one side goes up or down; move something so that one side goes up or down: *Don't tip your chair back.* **2** turn something so that the things inside fall out: *She opened a tin of beans and tipped them into a bowl.*

tip over turn over; make something turn over: *The boat tipped over and we all fell in the water.* ○ *Don't tip your drink over!*

tiptoe /'tɪptəʊ/ *verb* (**tiptoes**, **tiptoeing**, **tiptoed** /'tɪptəʊd/) walk quietly on your toes: *He tiptoed into the bedroom.* **on tiptoe** on your toes: *She walked on tiptoe.*

tired /'taɪəd/ *adjective* If you are tired, you need to rest or sleep: *I've been working all day and I'm really tired.* ○ *He's feeling tired.* **be tired of something** have had or done too much of

something, so that you do not want it any longer: *I'm tired of studying – let's go out.*

tiring /'taɪərɪŋ/ *adjective* If something is tiring, it makes you tired: *a tiring journey*

tissue /'tɪʃuː/ *noun* a thin piece of soft paper that you use as a handkerchief: *a box of tissues*

tissue-paper /'tɪʃuː peɪpə(r)/ *noun* (no plural) thin paper that you use for wrapping things

title /'taɪtl/ *noun* **1** the name of something, for example a book, film or picture: *What is the title of this poem?* **2** a word like 'Mr', 'Mrs' or 'Doctor' that you put in front of a person's name

to[1] /tə/, /tu/, /tuː/ *preposition* **1** a word that shows where somebody or something is going, etc: *She went to Italy.* ○ *James has gone to school.* ○ *I gave the book to Paul.* ○ *He sent a letter to his parents.* ○ *Be kind to animals.* **2** a word that shows how many minutes before the hour: *It's two minutes to six.* ☞ Look at page A8. **3** a word that shows the last or the highest time, price, etc: *The museum is open from 9.30 to 5.30.* ○ *Shoes cost from 2 000 to 5 000 shillings in this shop.* **4** on or against something: *He put his hands to his ears.* **5** a word that shows how something changes: *The sky changed from blue to grey.* **6** a word that shows why: *I came to help.* **7** a word that you use for comparing things: *I prefer football to athletics.*

to[2] /tə/, /tu/a word that you use before verbs to make the **infinitive**: *I want to go home.* ○ *Don't forget to write.* ○ *She asked me to go but I didn't want to* (= to go).

toad /təʊd/ *noun* an animal like a big frog, with rough skin

tobacco /tə'bækəʊ/ *noun* (no plural) special dried leaves that people smoke in cigarettes, cigars and pipes

today /tə'deɪ/ *adverb, noun* (no plural) **1** (on) this day: *What shall we do today?* ○ *Today is Friday.* **2** (at) the present time; now: *Most big companies today use computers.*

toe /təʊ/ *noun* **1** one of the five parts at the end of your foot ☞ picture on page A4. **2** the part of a shoe or sock that covers the end of your foot

toenail /ˈtəʊneɪl/ *noun* the hard part at the end of your toe ☞ picture on page A4

together /təˈɡeðə(r)/ *adverb* **1** with each other or close to each other: *John and Henry usually walk home together.* ○ *Stand with your feet together.* **2** so that they are joined to or mixed with each other: *Tie the ends of the rope together.* ○ *Add these numbers together.* ○ *Mix the eggs and sugar together.*

toilet /ˈtɔɪlət/ *noun* a large bowl with a seat, that you use when you need to empty waste from your body. The room that it is in is also called a **toilet**: *I'm going to the toilet.*

toilet paper /ˈtɔɪlət peɪpə(r)/ *noun* (no plural) paper that you use in the toilet

toilet roll /ˈtɔɪlət rəʊl/ *noun* a roll of paper that you use in the toilet

token /ˈtəʊkən/ *noun* **1** a small thing that you use to show something else: *This gift is a token of our friendship.* **2** a piece of paper, plastic or metal that you use instead of money to pay for something: *You can use these special tokens to buy books.*

told *form of* **tell**

tolerant /ˈtɒlərənt/ *adjective* If you are tolerant, you let people do things although you may not like or understand them: *You need to be very tolerant with young children.* ✪ opposite: **intolerant**

tolerance/ˈtɒlərəns/ *noun* (no plural) *tolerance of other religions* ✪ opposite: **intolerance**

tolerate /ˈtɒləreɪt/ *verb* (**tolerates**, **tolerating**, **tolerated**) let people do something that you may not like or understand: *He won't tolerate rudeness.*

tomato /təˈmɑːtəʊ/ *noun* (*plural* **tomatoes**) a soft red fruit that you cook or eat in salads

tomato

tomb /tuːm/ *noun* a thing made of stone where a dead person's body is buried

tomorrow /təˈmɒrəʊ/ *adverb, noun* (no plural) (on) the day after today: *Let's go swimming tomorrow.* ○ *I'll see you tomorrow morning.* ○ *We are going home the day after tomorrow.*

ton /tʌn/ *noun* **1** a measure of weight (= 1·016 kilograms). There are 2240 **pounds** in a ton. ✪ In the USA, a ton is 2000 pounds. **2 tons** (plural) a lot: *He's got tons of money.*

tone /təʊn/ *noun* how something sounds: *I knew he was angry by the tone of his voice.*

tongue /tʌŋ/ *noun* the soft part inside your mouth that moves when you talk or eat

tongue-twister /ˈtʌŋ ˌtwɪstə(r)/ *noun* words that are difficult to say together quickly: *'Red lorry, yellow lorry' is a tongue-twister.*

tonight /təˈnaɪt/ *adverb, noun* (no plural) (on) the evening or night of today: *I'm going to do my homework to-night.*

tonne /tʌn/ *noun* a measure of weight. There are 1000 **kilograms** in a tonne.

too /tuː/ *adverb* **1** also; as well: *Green is my favourite colour but I like blue too.* **2** more than you want or need: *These shoes are too big.* ○ *She put too much salt in the food.*

took *form of* **take**

tool /tuːl/ *noun* a thing that you hold in your hand and use to do a special job: *Hammers and saws are tools.*

tooth /tuːθ/ *noun* (*plural* **teeth** /tiːθ/) **1** one of the hard white things in your mouth that you use for eating: *I brush my teeth every day.*

> ✪ A **dentist** is a person whose job is to look after teeth. If a tooth is bad, the dentist may **fill** it or **take** it **out**. People who have lost their own teeth can wear **false teeth**.

2 one of the long sharp parts of a comb or saw

toothache /ˈtuːθeɪk/ *noun* (no plural) a pain in your tooth: *I've got toothache.*

toothbrush /ˈtuːθbrʌʃ/ *noun* (*plural* **toothbrushes**) a small brush for cleaning your teeth

toothpaste /ˈtuːθpeɪst/ *noun* (no plural) stuff that you put on your toothbrush and use for cleaning your teeth

top[1] /tɒp/ *noun* **1** the highest part of something: *There's a church at the top of the hill.* **2** a cover that you put on something to close it: *Where's the top of this jar?* **3** a piece of clothing that you wear on the top part of your body **on top** on its highest part: *The people got on the bus and their luggage went on top.* **on top of something** on or over something: *A tree fell on top of my car.*

top[2] /tɒp/ *adjective* highest: *Put this book on the top shelf.*

topic /'tɒpɪk/ *noun* something that you talk, learn or write about; a subject: *The topic of the discussion was war.*

torch /tɔːtʃ/ *noun* (*plural* **torches**) a small electric light that you can carry

torch

tore, **torn** *forms of* **tear**[2]

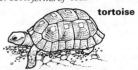
tortoise

tortoise /'tɔːtəs/ *noun* an animal with a hard shell on its back, that moves very slowly

torture /'tɔːtʃə(r)/ *verb* (**tortures**, **torturing**, **tortured** /'tɔːtʃəd/) make somebody feel great pain, often to make them give information: *They tortured her until she told them her name.*

torture *noun* (no plural) *the torture of prisoners*

toss /tɒs/ *verb* (**tosses**, **tossing**, **tossed** /tɒst/) **1** throw something quickly and without care: *I tossed the paper into the bin.* **2** move quickly up and down or from side to side; make something do this: *The boat tossed around on the big waves.* **3** decide something by throwing a coin in the air and seeing which side shows when it falls: *We tossed a coin to see who would play first.*

total[1] /'təʊtl/ *adjective* complete; if you count everything or everybody: *There was total silence in the classroom.* ○ *What was the total number of people at the meeting?*

totally /'təʊtəli/ *adverb* completely: *I totally agree.*

total[2] /'təʊtl/ *noun* the number you have when you add everything together

touch[1] /tʌtʃ/ *verb* (**touches**, **touching**, **touched** /tʌtʃt/) **1** put your hand or finger on somebody or something: *Don't touch the paint – it's still wet.* ○ *He touched me on the arm.* **2** be so close to another thing or person that there is no space in between: *The two wires were touching.* ○ *Her coat was so long that it touched the ground.*

touch[2] /tʌtʃ/ *noun* **1** (*plural* **touches**) when a hand or finger is put on somebody or something: *I felt the touch of his hand on my arm.* **2** (no plural) the feeling in your hands and skin that tells you about something: *He can't see, but he can read by touch.* **be** or **keep in touch with somebody** meet, telephone or write to somebody often: *Are you still in touch with Julius?* ○ *Let's keep in touch.* **get in touch with somebody** write to, or telephone somebody: *I'm trying to get in touch with my cousin.* **lose touch with somebody** stop meeting, telephoning or writing to somebody: *I've lost touch with all my old friends from school.*

tough /tʌf/ *adjective* (**tougher**, **toughest**) **1** difficult to tear or break; strong: *Leather is tougher than paper.* **2** difficult: *This is a tough job.* **3** If meat is tough, it is difficult to cut and eat. ✪ opposite: **tender**. **4** very strong in your body: *You need to be tough to run a marathon.* **5** strict or firm: *a tough leader*

tour /tʊə(r)/ *noun* **1** a short visit to see a building or city: *They gave us a tour of the neighbourhood.* **2** a journey to see a lot of different places: *We went on a tour of the whole country.*

tour *verb* (**tours**, **touring**, **toured** /tʊəd/) *We toured the country for three weeks.*

tourism /'tʊərɪzəm/ *noun* (no plural) arranging holidays for people: *This country earns a lot of money from tourism.*

tourist /'tʊərɪst/ *noun* a person who visits a place on holiday

tournament /'tɔːnəmənt/ *noun* a sports competition with a lot of players or teams: *The team has competed in tournaments all over the world.*

tow /təʊ/ *verb* (**tows**, **towing**, **towed** /təʊd/) pull a car, etc using a rope or chain: *My car was towed to a garage.*

towards /təˈwɔːdz/, **toward** /təˈwɔːd/ *preposition* **1** in the direction of somebody or something: *We walked towards the river.* ○ *I couldn't see her face – she had her back towards me.* ☛ picture on page A2. **2** to somebody or something: *The people in the village are always very friendly towards tourists.* **3** at a time near: *Let's meet towards the end of the week.* **4** to help pay for something: *Everyone in the class gave 10 shillings towards a present for the teacher.*

towel /ˈtaʊəl/ *noun* a piece of cloth that you use for drying yourself: *I washed my hands and dried them on a towel.*

tower /ˈtaʊə(r)/ *noun* a tall narrow building or a tall part of a building: *the Eiffel Tower* ○ *a church tower*

tower block /ˈtaʊə(r) blɒk/ *noun* a very tall building with a lot of flats or offices inside

town /taʊn/ *noun* a place where there are a lot of houses and other buildings: *Nyeri is a town near Nairobi.* ○ *I'm going into town to do some shopping.*

✪ A town is bigger than a **village** but smaller than a **city**.

town hall /ˌtaʊn ˈhɔːl/ *noun* a building with offices for people who control a town

toy /tɔɪ/ *noun* a thing for a child to play with

trace¹ /treɪs/ *noun* a mark or sign that shows that somebody or something has been in a place: *The police could not find any trace of the missing child.*

trace² /treɪs/ *verb* (**traces**, **tracing**, **traced** /treɪst/) **1** look for and find somebody or something: *The police have traced the stolen car.* **2** put thin paper over a picture and draw over the lines to make a copy

track¹ /træk/ *noun* **1** a rough path or road: *We walked along the track to the next village.* **2** **tracks** (plural) a line of marks that an animal, a person or a vehicle makes on the ground: *We saw his tracks in the mud.* **3** the metal lines

that a train runs on **4** a special road for races **5** one song or piece of music on a cassette, compact disc or record

track² /træk/ *verb* (**tracks**, **tracking**, **tracked** /trækt/) follow signs or marks to find somebody or something **track down** find somebody or something after looking: *I finally tracked her down.*

track suit /ˈtræk suːt/ *noun* a special jacket and trousers that you wear for sport

tractor

tractor /ˈtræktə(r)/ *noun* a big strong vehicle that people use on farms to pull heavy things

trade¹ /treɪd/ *noun* **1** (no plural) the buying and selling of things: *trade between Kenya and Britain* **2** (plural **trades**) a job: *David is a plumber by trade.*

trade² /treɪd/ *verb* (**trades**, **trading**, **traded**) buy and sell things: *Tanzania trades with many different countries.*

trade mark /ˈtreɪd mɑːk/ *noun* a special mark or name that a company puts on the things it makes and that other companies must not use

trade union /ˌtreɪd ˈjuːnɪən/ *noun* a group of workers who have joined together to talk to their managers about things like pay and the way they work

tradition /trəˈdɪʃn/ *noun* something that people in a certain place have done or believed for a long time: *In Britain it's a tradition to give chocolate eggs at Easter.*

traditional /trəˈdɪʃənl/ *adjective*: *traditional East African food*

traditionally /trəˈdɪʃənəli/ *adverb*: *Driving trains is traditionally a man's job.*

traffic /ˈtræfɪk/ *noun* (no plural) all the cars, etc that are on a road: *There was a lot of traffic on the way to work this morning.*

traffic jam /ˈtræfɪk dʒæm/ *noun* a long line of cars, etc that cannot move very fast

traffic-lights /ˈtræfɪk laɪts/ *noun* (plural) lights that change from red to orange to green to tell cars, etc when to stop and start

tragedy /ˈtrædʒədi/ *noun* (plural **tragedies**) **1** a very sad thing that happens: *The child's death was a tragedy.* **2** a serious and sad play: *John Ruganda's 'The Burdens' is a tragedy.*

tragic /ˈtrædʒɪk/ *adjective* very sad: *a tragic accident*

tragically /ˈtrædʒɪkli/ *adverb*: *He died tragically at the age of 25.*

trail¹ /treɪl/ *noun* **1** a line of marks that show which way a person or thing has gone: *There was a trail of blood from the cut in her leg.* **2** a path in the country: *We followed the trail through the forest.*

trail² /treɪl/ *verb* (**trails**, **trailing**, **trailed** /treɪld/) pull something along behind you; be pulled along behind somebody or something: *Her long hair trailed behind her in the wind.*

trailer /ˈtreɪlə(r)/ *noun* **1** a vehicle with no engine that a car or lorry pulls along **2** a short piece from a film that shows you what it is like

train

train¹ /treɪn/ *noun* carriages or wagons that are pulled by an engine along a railway line: *I'm going to Mombasa by train.* **catch a train** get on a train to go somewhere: *We caught the 7.15 train to Nairobi.* **change trains** go from one train to another: *You have to change trains at Kampala.*

> ✪ You get **on** and **off** trains at a **station**. A **goods train** or a **freight train** carries things and a **passenger train** carries people.

train² /treɪn/ *verb* (**trains**, **training**, **trained** /treɪnd/) **1** teach a person or an animal to do something: *He was trained as a pilot.* **2** make yourself ready for something by studying or doing something a lot: *Ann is training to be a doctor.* ○ *He goes running every morning – he's training for the race.*

trainer /ˈtreɪnə(r)/ *noun* **1** a person who teaches other people to do a sport **2** a person who teaches animals to do something **3** a soft shoe that you wear for running

trainers

training /ˈtreɪnɪŋ/ *noun* (no plural) getting ready for a sport or job: *She is in training for the Olympic Games.*

traitor /ˈtreɪtə(r)/ *noun* a person who harms his/her country or friends to help another person or country

tram /træm/ *noun* an electric bus that goes along rails in a town

trample /ˈtræmpl/ *verb* (**tramples**, **trampling**, **trampled** /ˈtræmpld/) walk on something and push it down with your feet: *Don't trample on the flowers!*

transfer /trænsˈfɜː(r)/ *verb* (**transfers**, **transferring**, **transferred** /trænsˈfɜːd/) move somebody or something to a different place: *John's company is transferring him to their USA office.*

transfer /ˈtrænsfɜː(r)/ *noun*: *Owen wants a transfer to another team.*

transform /trænsˈfɔːm/ *verb* (**transforms**, **transforming**, **transformed** /trænsˈfɔːmd/) change somebody or something so that they are or look completely different: *Electricity has transformed people's lives.*

transformation /ˌtrænsfəˈmeɪʃn/ *noun* a complete change

transistor /trænˈzɪstə(r)/ *noun* a small part inside something electrical, for example a radio or television

translate /trænsˈleɪt/ *verb* (**translates**, **translating**, **translated**) say or write in one language what somebody has said or written in another language: *This letter is in German – can you translate it into English for me?*

translation /trænsˈleɪʃn/ *noun* **1** (no plural) translating: *translation from English into French* **2** (plural **translations**) something that somebody has translated

translator /træns'leɪtə(r)/ *noun* a person who translates

transparent /træns'pærənt/ *adjective* If something is transparent, you can see through it: *Glass is transparent.*

transport /'trænspɔːt/ *noun* (no plural) a way of carrying people or things from one place to another: *road transport* ○ *The bus is the cheapest form of transport.*

transport /træn'spɔːt/ *verb* (**transports, transporting, transported**) carry people or things from one place to another: *The goods were transported by air.*

trap /træp/ *noun* **1** a thing that you use for catching animals: *The rabbit's leg was caught in a trap.* **2** a plan to trick somebody: *I knew the question was a trap, so I didn't answer it.*

trap *verb* (**traps, trapping, trapped** /træpt/) **1** keep somebody in a place that they cannot escape from: *They were trapped in the burning building.* **2** catch or trick somebody or something

travel /'trævl/ *verb* (**travels, travelling, travelled** /'trævld/) go from one place to another: *I would like to travel round the world.* ○ *I travel to school by bus.* ○ *She travelled 800 km in one day.*

travel *noun* (no plural) travelling: *Rail travel can be expensive.*

travel agency /'trævl eɪdʒənsi/ *noun* (plural **travel agencies**) a company that plans holidays and journeys for people

travel agent /'trævl eɪdʒənt/ *noun* a person who works in a travel agency

traveller /'trævələ(r)/ *noun* a person who is travelling

traveller's cheque /'trævələz tʃek/ *noun* a special cheque that you can use when you go to other countries

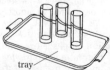

tray /treɪ/ *noun* a flat thing that you use for carrying food or drinks

tread /tred/ *verb* (**treads, treading, trod** /trɒd/, **has trodden** /'trɒdn/) put your foot down: *He trod on my foot.*

treasure /'treʒə(r)/ *noun* gold, silver, jewels or other things that are worth a lot of money

treasurer /'treʒərə(r)/ *noun* a person who looks after the money of a club or a group of people

treat[1] /triːt/ *verb* (**treats, treating, treated**) **1** behave towards somebody or something: *How does your boss treat you?* ○ *Treat these glasses with care.* **2** try to make a sick person well again: *The doctor is treating him for malaria.*

treat something as something think about something in a certain way: *They treated my idea as a joke.*

treat[2] /triːt/ *noun* something very special that makes somebody happy: *My father took me to a football match for a treat.*

treatment /'triːtmənt/ *noun* **1** (no plural) the way that you behave towards somebody or something: *Their treatment of the animals was very cruel.* **2** (plural **treatments**) the things that a doctor does to try to make a sick person well again: *a new treatment for cancer*

treaty /'triːti/ *noun* (plural **treaties**) an agreement between countries: *The two countries signed a peace treaty.*

tree

leaf

trunk — branch — twig

tree /triː/ *noun* a big tall plant with a trunk, branches and leaves: *an acacia tree* ○ *Mangoes grow on trees.*

tremble /'trembl/ *verb* (**trembles, trembling, trembled** /'trembld/) shake, for example because you are cold, afraid or ill: *She was trembling with fear.*

tremendous /trə'mendəs/ *adjective* **1** very big or very great: *The new trains travel at a tremendous speed.* **2** very good: *The match was tremendous.*

tremendously *adverb* very or very much: *The film was tremendously exciting.*

trench /trentʃ/ *noun* (*plural* **trenches**) a long narrow hole that you make in the ground

trend /trend/ *noun* a change to something different: *new trends in science*

trespass /ˈtrespəs/ *verb* (**trespasses**, **trespassing**, **trespassed** /ˈtrespəst/) go on somebody's land without asking them if you can: *A sign on the gate of the big house said 'No Trespassing'.*

trespasser *noun* a person who trespasses

trial /ˈtraɪəl/ *noun* **1** the time when a person is in a **court of law** so that people (the **judge** and **jury**) can decide if he/she has done something wrong and what the punishment will be **2** using something to see if it is good or bad: *trials of a new drug* **on trial 1** in a court of law so that people can decide if you have done something wrong: *She was on trial for murder.* **2** If you have something on trial, you are using it to decide if you like it, before you buy it: *We've got the car on trial for a week.*

triangle /ˈtraɪæŋgl/ *noun* a shape with three straight sides ☛ picture on page A5

triangular /traɪˈæŋgjələ(r)/ *adjective* with the shape of a triangle

tribe /traɪb/ *noun* a small group of people who have the same language and customs: *the Zulu tribes of Africa*

tribal /ˈtraɪbl/ *adjective*: *tribal dances*

tribute /ˈtrɪbjuːt/ *noun* something that you do, say or give to show that you respect or admire somebody: *They built a statue as a tribute to Nelson Mandela.*

trick[1] /trɪk/ *noun* **1** a clever plan that makes somebody believe something that is not true: *He used a clever trick to get money from me.* **2** something that you do to make somebody seem stupid: *The children hid their teacher's books to play a trick on her.* **3** something clever that you have learned to do: *He can do amazing tricks with a football.*

trick[2] /trɪk/ *verb* (**tricks**, **tricking**, **tricked** /trɪkt/) do something that is not honest to get what you want from somebody: *He tricked the old lady so that she gave him all her money.*

trickle /ˈtrɪkl/ *verb* (**trickles**, **trickling**, **trickled** /ˈtrɪkld/) move slowly like a thin line of water: *Tears trickled down her cheeks.*

trickle *noun*: *a trickle of blood*

tricky /ˈtrɪki/ *adjective* (**trickier**, **trickiest**) difficult; hard to do: *a tricky question*

tried *form of* **try**

tries 1 *form of* **try 2** *plural of* **try**

trigger /ˈtrɪgə(r)/ *noun* the part of a gun that you pull with your finger to fire it

trim /trɪm/ *verb* (**trims**, **trimming**, **trimmed** /trɪmd/) cut something to make it tidy: *He trimmed my hair.*

trim *noun*: *My hair needs a trim.*

trip[1] /trɪp/ *noun* a short journey to a place and back again: *We went on a trip to the mountains.*

trip[2] /trɪp/ *verb* (**trips**, **tripping**, **tripped** /trɪpt/) hit your foot against something so that you fall or nearly fall: *She tripped over the step.* **trip up** make somebody fall or nearly fall: *Alex put out his foot and tripped me up.*

triple /ˈtrɪpl/ *adjective* with three parts: *the triple jump*

triple *verb* (**triples**, **tripling**, **tripled** /ˈtrɪpld/) become or make something three times bigger: *Sales have tripled this year.*

triumph /ˈtraɪʌmf/ *noun* great success; winning: *The race ended in triumph for the German team.*

trivial /ˈtrɪviəl/ *adjective* not important: *She gets angry about trivial things.*

trod, **trodden** *forms of* **tread**

trolley /ˈtrɒli/ *noun* (*plural* **trolleys**) a thing on small wheels that you use for carrying things: *The man was pulling a trolley loaded up with boxes.*

trombone /trɒmˈbəʊn/ *noun* a large musical instrument. You play it by blowing and moving a long tube up and down.

troops /truːps/ *noun* (plural) soldiers

trophy /ˈtrəʊfi/ *noun* (*plural* **trophies**) a thing, for example a silver cup, that you get when you win a competition: *a tennis trophy*

the tropics /ðə ˈtrɒpɪks/ *noun* (plural) the very hot part of the world

tropical /ˈtrɒpɪkl/ *adjective* of or from the tropics: *tropical fruit*

trot /trɒt/ *verb* (**trots**, **trotting**, **trotted**) run with short quick steps: *The horse trotted along the road.*

trouble¹ /ˈtrʌbl/ *noun* **1** (*plural* **troubles**) difficulty, problems or worry: *We had a lot of trouble finding the book you wanted.* ○ *She told me all her troubles.* **2** (no plural) extra work: *'Thanks for your help!' 'Oh, it was no trouble.'* **3** (*plural* **troubles**) when people are fighting or arguing: *He left his country to escape from the troubles during the civil war.* **4** (no plural) pain or illness: *He's got heart trouble.* **be in trouble** have problems, for example because you have done something wrong: *He's in trouble with the police.* **get into trouble** do something that brings problems because it is wrong: *You'll get into trouble if you don't do your homework.* **go to a lot of trouble** do extra work: *They went to a lot of trouble to help me.*

trouble² /ˈtrʌbl/ *verb* (**troubles**, **troubling**, **troubled** /ˈtrʌbld/) worry somebody; bring somebody problems or pain: *I was troubled by the news.* ○ *I'm sorry to trouble you, but you're sitting in my seat.*

trough /trɒf/ *noun* a long open box that holds food or water for animals

trousers /ˈtraʊzəz/ *noun* (plural) a piece of clothing for your legs and the lower part of your body: *I got some new trousers today.* ☛ picture at **suit** ✪ Be careful! You cannot say 'a trousers'. You can say **a pair of trousers**: *I bought a new pair of trousers.*

trout /traʊt/ *noun* (*plural* **trout**) a fish that lives in rivers in cool places and that you can eat

truant /ˈtruːənt/ *noun* a child who stays away from school when he/she should be there **play truant** stay away from school

truce /truːs/ *noun* when people or groups agree to stop fighting for a short time

truck /trʌk/ *noun* **1** a big vehicle for carrying heavy things: *a truck driver*

2 an open part of a train where heavy things are carried

true /truː/ *adjective* **1** right or correct: *Is it true that you are leaving?* ○ *Casablanca is in Tunisia: true or false?* **2** that really happened: *It's a true story.* **3** real: *A true friend will always help you.* ✪ The noun is **truth**. **come true** happen in the way that you hoped: *Her dream of going to university came true.*

truly /ˈtruːli/ *adverb* really: *I'm truly sorry.* **Yours truly** words that you can use at the end of a formal letter

trumpet

trumpet /ˈtrʌmpɪt/ *noun* a musical instrument that you blow

trunk /trʌŋk/ *noun* **1** the thick part of a tree, that grows up from the ground ☛ picture at **tree**. **2** an elephant's long nose ☛ picture at **elephant**. **3** a big strong box for carrying things when you travel

trunks /trʌŋks/ *noun* (plural) short trousers that a man or boy wears for swimming

trust¹ /trʌst/ *noun* (no plural) feeling sure that somebody or something will do what they should do; feeling that somebody is honest and good: *Put your trust in God.*

trust² /trʌst/ *verb* (**trusts**, **trusting**, **trusted**) feel sure that somebody or something will do what they should do; believe that somebody is honest and good: *You can't trust him with money.* ○ *You can trust Haika to do the job well.*

trustworthy /ˈtrʌstwɜːði/ *adjective* A trustworthy person is somebody that you can trust.

truth /truːθ/ *noun* (no plural) being true; what is true: *There is no truth in what he says – he is lying.* ○ *We need to find out the truth about what happened.* **tell the truth** say what is true: *Are you telling me the truth?*

truthful /'truːθfl/ *adjective* **1** true: *a truthful answer* **2** A person who is truthful tells the truth.

truthfully /'truːθfəli/ *adverb*: *You must answer me truthfully.*

try /traɪ/ *verb* (**tries, trying, tried** /traɪd/, **has tried**) **1** work hard to do something: *I tried to remember her name but I couldn't.* ○ *I'm not sure if I can help you, but I'll try.* **2** use or do something to find out if you like it: *Have you ever tried Chinese food?* **3** ask somebody questions in a court of law to decide if they have done something wrong: *He was tried for murder.* **try and do something** try to do something: *I'll try and come early tomorrow.* **try on** put on a piece of clothing to see if you like it and if it is the correct size: *I tried the trousers on but they were too small.*

try *noun* (*plural* **tries**) *I can't open this door – will you have a try?*

tsetse /'tsetsi/ (*plural* **tsetse**), **tsetse fly** /'tsetsi flaɪ/ *noun* an insect that can fly and that drinks blood. You can get serious illnesses from tsetse flies.

T-shirt

T-shirt /'tiː ʃɜːt/ *noun* a kind of shirt with short sleeves and no collar

tub /tʌb/ *noun* a round container: *a tub of ice-cream* ☞ picture at **container**

tube /tjuːb/ *noun* **1** a long thin pipe for a liquid or a gas **2** a long thin soft container with a hole and a cap at one end: *a tube of toothpaste* ☞ picture at **container**

tuberculosis /tjuːˌbɜːkjəˈləʊsɪs/, **TB** /tiːˈbiː/ *noun* (no plural) a serious illness of the lungs

tuck /tʌk/ *verb* (**tucks, tucking, tucked** /tʌkt/) put or push the edges of something inside or under something else: *He tucked his shirt into his trousers.*

Tuesday /'tjuːzdeɪ/ *noun* the third day of the week, next after Monday

tuft /tʌft/ *noun* a group of hairs, grass, etc growing together

tug /tʌg/ *verb* (**tugs, tugging, tugged** /tʌgd/) pull something hard and quickly: *I tugged at the rope and it broke.*

tug *noun* **1** a sudden hard pull: *The little girl gave my hand a tug.* **2** a small strong boat that pulls big ships

tuition /tjuˈɪʃn/ *noun* (no plural) teaching: *A lot of students have extra tuition before their exams.*

tumble /'tʌmbl/ *verb* (**tumbles, tumbling, tumbled** /'tʌmbld/) fall suddenly: *He tumbled down the steps.*

tummy /'tʌmi/ *noun* (*plural* **tummies**) the part of your body between your chest and your legs; your stomach

tuna /'tjuːnə/ *noun* (*plural* **tuna**) a large fish that lives in the sea and that you can eat

tune /tjuːn/ *noun* a group of musical notes that make a nice sound when you play or sing them together: *I know the tune but I don't know the words.*

tune *verb* (**tunes, tuning, tuned** /tjuːnd/) do something to a musical instrument so that it makes the right sounds: *She tuned the guitar before playing.*

tunnel

tunnel /'tʌnl/ *noun* a long hole under the ground or sea for a road or railway

turban /'tɜːbən/ *noun* a long piece of material that you put round and round your head

turbine /'tɜːbaɪn/ *noun* an engine or motor that uses moving water or gas to work

turkey /'tɜːki/ *noun* (*plural* **turkeys**) a big bird that people keep on farms and that you can eat

turn[1] /tɜːn/ *verb* (**turns, turning, turned** /tɜːnd/) **1** move round, or move something round: *The wheels are turning.* ○ *Turn the key.* ○ *She turned round and walked towards the door.*

2 move in a different direction: *Turn left at the traffic-lights.* **3** become different: *The weather has turned cold.* **4** make somebody or something change: *The sun turned the paper yellow.* **5** find a certain page in a book: *Turn to page 97.* **turn down 1** say no to what somebody wants to do or to give you: *They offered me the job but I turned it down.* **2** move the switch that controls something like a radio or a heater so that it makes less sound, heat, etc: *The music's too loud— can you turn it down?* **turn into something** become different; change somebody or something into something different: *Water turns into ice when it gets very cold.* **turn off** move the handle, switch, etc that controls something, so that it stops: *Turn the tap off.* ○ *Turn off the engine.* **turn on** move the handle, switch, etc that controls something, so that it starts: *Could you turn the light on?* **turn out** be something in the end: *Michael was a small child, but he has turned out to be a very big man.* **turn out a light** switch off a light **turn over** move so that the other side is on top: *If you turn over the page you'll find the answers on the other side.* **turn up 1** arrive: *Has David turned up yet?* **2** move the switch that controls something like a radio or a heater so that it makes more sound, heat, etc: *Turn up the television— I can't hear it properly.*

turn² /tɜːn/ *noun* **1** turning something round: *Give the screw a few turns.* **2** a change of direction: *Take a left turn at the end of this road.* **3** the time when you can or should do something: *It's your turn to do the washing-up.* **in turn** one after the other: *I spoke to each of the students in turn.* **take turns at something, take it in turns to do something** do something one after the other: *The two boys took it in turns to be goalkeeper.*

turning /'tɜːnɪŋ/ *noun* a place where one road joins another road: *Take the first turning on the right.*

turquoise /'tɜːkwɔɪz/ *adjective* with a colour between blue and green

turtle /'tɜːtl/ *noun* an animal that lives in the sea and has a hard shell on its back

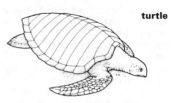
turtle

tusk /tʌsk/ *noun* a long pointed tooth that grows next to the mouth of an elephant ☞ picture at **elephant**

tutor /'tjuːtə(r)/ *noun* a teacher who teaches one person or a small group

TV /ˌtiː 'viː/ *short for* **television**

tweezers /'twiːzəz/ *noun* (plural) a small tool made of two pieces of metal that are joined at one end. You use tweezers for holding or pulling out very small things: *She pulled the splinter out of her finger with a pair of tweezers.*

twelve /twelv/ *number* 12

twelfth /twelfθ/ *adjective, adverb, noun* 12th

twenty /'twenti/ *number* **1** 20 **2 the twenties** (plural) the numbers, years or temperature between 20 and 29 **in your twenties** between the ages of 20 and 29

twentieth /'twentiəθ/ *adjective, adverb, noun* 20th

twice /twaɪs/ *adverb* two times: *I have been to Mombasa twice.* ○ *He ate twice as much as I did.*

twig /twɪɡ/ *noun* a small thin branch of a tree ☞ picture at **tree**

twilight /'twaɪlaɪt/ *noun* (no plural) the time after the sun has gone down and before it gets completely dark

twin /twɪn/ *noun* **1** Twins are two people who have the same mother and who were born on the same day: *David and John are twins.* ○ *I have got a twin sister.* **2** one of two things that are the same: *twin beds*

twinkle /'twɪŋkl/ *verb* (**twinkles, twinkling, twinkled** /'twɪŋkld/) shine with a small bright light that comes and goes. Stars twinkle.

twist /twɪst/ *verb* (**twists, twisting, twisted**) **1** turn strongly: *Twist the lid off the jar.* **2** change the shape of something by turning it in different directions; turn in many directions: *She twisted the metal into strange shapes.* ○ *The path twists and turns through the forest.* **3** wind threads, etc round and round each other: *This machine twists the sisal to make rope.*

twitch /twɪtʃ/ *verb* (**twitches**, **twitching**, **twitched** /twɪtʃt/) make a sudden quick movement with a part of your body: *Rabbits twitch their noses.*

two /tuː/ *number* 2 **in two** into two pieces: *The cup fell on the floor and broke in two.*

type¹ /taɪp/ *noun* a group of things that are the same in some way; a sort or kind: *A cashew is a type of nut.* ○ *What type of music do you like?*

type² /taɪp/ *verb* (**types**, **typing**, **typed** /taɪpt/) make words on paper with a **typewriter** or **word processor**: *Her secretary types all her letters.* ○ *Can you type?*

type *noun* (no plural) the letters that a machine makes on paper: *The type is too small – I can't read it.*

typewriter /ˈtaɪpraɪtə(r)/ *noun* a machine with keys that you use to make words on paper: *an electric typewriter*

typical /ˈtɪpɪkl/ *adjective* Something that is typical is a good example of its kind: *We had a typical Ugandan meal – matoke and meat stew.*

typically /ˈtɪpɪkli/ *adverb* in a typical way: *East African athletes are typically strong at distance events.*

tyrant /ˈtaɪrənt/ *noun* a person with a lot of power who rules a country in a cruel way

tyrannical /tɪˈrænɪkl/ *adjective*: *a tyrannical ruler*

tyre /ˈtaɪə(r)/ *noun* a circle of rubber around the outside of a wheel, for example on a car or bicycle: *I think we've got a flat tyre* (= a tyre without enough air inside). ☛ picture at **car** and **bicycle**

Uu

UFO /ˌjuː ef ˈəʊ/ *noun* (*plural* **UFOs**) a strange object that some people think they have seen in the sky and that may come from another planet. 'UFO' is short for **unidentified flying object**.

ugali /uːˈɡæli/ *noun* (no plural) (an East African word) soft food that we make from maize or millet flour and hot water

ugly /ˈʌɡli/ *adjective* (**uglier**, **ugliest**) not beautiful to look at: *an ugly face*

umbrella /ʌmˈbrelə/ *noun* a thing that you hold over your head to keep you dry when it rains: *It started to rain, so I put my umbrella up.*

umpire /ˈʌmpaɪə(r)/ *noun* a person who controls a baseball, tennis or cricket match

unable /ʌnˈeɪbl/ *adjective* not able to do something: *John is unable to come to the meeting because he is ill.*

unanimous /juˈnænɪməs/ *adjective* with the agreement of every person: *The decision was unanimous.*

unarmed /ˌʌnˈɑːmd/ *adjective* If you are unarmed, you do not have a gun or any weapon: *an unarmed police officer*

unavoidable /ˌʌnəˈvɔɪdəbl/ *adjective* If something is unavoidable, you cannot stop it or get away from it: *He had no money, so selling his car was unavoidable.*

unaware /ˌʌnəˈweə(r)/ *adjective* If you are unaware of something, you do not know about it: *I was unaware of the danger.*

unbearable /ʌnˈbeərəbl/ *adjective* If

un- *prefix*
You can add **un-** to the beginning of some words to give them the opposite meaning, for example:
unhappy = not happy
untrue = not true
undress = take clothes off (the opposite of **dress**)

something is unbearable, you cannot accept it because it is so bad: *Everyone left the room because the noise was unbearable.*

unbearably /ʌnˈbeərəbli/ *adverb*: It was unbearably hot.

unbelievable /ˌʌnbɪˈliːvəbl/ *adjective* very surprising or difficult to believe

unborn /ˌʌnˈbɔːn/ *adjective* not yet born: *an unborn child*

uncertain /ʌnˈsɜːtn/ *adjective* not sure; not decided: *I'm uncertain about what to do.*

uncertainty /ʌnˈsɜːtnti/ *noun* (*plural* **uncertainties**) not being sure: *There is uncertainty about who will be the next prime minister.*

uncle /ˈʌŋkl/ *noun* the brother of your mother or father, or the husband of your aunt: *Uncle Paul*

uncomfortable /ʌnˈkʌmftəbl/ *adjective* not comfortable: *The chair was hard and uncomfortable.*

uncomfortably /ʌnˈkʌmftəbli/ *adverb*: *The room was uncomfortably hot.*

uncommon /ʌnˈkɒmən/ *adjective* not common; that you do not see, hear, etc often: *That disease is very uncommon nowadays.*

unconscious /ʌnˈkɒnʃəs/ *adjective* **1** If you are unconscious, you are in a kind of sleep and you do not know what is happening: *She fell and hit her head and she was unconscious for three hours.* **2** If you are unconscious of something, you do not know about it: *Mike seemed unconscious that I was watching him.*

unconsciousness /ʌnˈkɒnʃəsnəs/ *noun* (no plural) being unconscious

uncover /ʌnˈkʌvə(r)/ *verb* (**uncovers**, **uncovering**, **uncovered** /ʌnˈkʌvəd/) take something from on top of another thing: *Uncover the pan and cook the soup for 30 minutes.*

under /ˈʌndə(r)/ *preposition, adverb* **1** in or to a place that is lower than or below something: *We sat down under a tree.* ○ *The cat ran under the table.* ○ *The boat filled with water, then went under.* ☛ picture on page A1 **2** less than something: *If you are under 18*

you are not allowed to vote. **3** covered by something: *I'm wearing a vest under my shirt.* **4** controlled by somebody or something: *The team are playing well under their new captain.*

undergo /ˌʌndəˈɡəʊ/ *verb* (**undergoes**, **undergoing**, **underwent** /ˌʌndəˈwent/, **has undergone** /ˌʌndəˈɡɒn/) If you undergo something, it happens to you: *Laura is in hospital undergoing an operation.*

undergraduate /ˌʌndəˈɡrædʒuət/ *noun* a student at a university

underground[1] /ˈʌndəɡraʊnd/ *adjective, adverb* under the ground: *an underground car park*

underground[2] /ˈʌndəɡraʊnd/ *noun* (no plural) an underground railway

undergrowth /ˈʌndəɡrəʊθ/ *noun* (no plural) bushes and other plants that grow under trees: *There was a path through the undergrowth.*

underline /ˌʌndəˈlaɪn/ *verb* (**underlines**, **underlining**, **underlined** /ˌʌndəˈlaɪnd/) draw a line under a word or words. <u>This sentence is under-lined.</u>

underneath /ˌʌndəˈniːθ/ *preposition, adverb* under or below something: *The dog sat underneath the table.* ○ *I was wearing a shirt with a vest underneath.*

underpants /ˈʌndəpænts/ *noun* (plural) a piece of clothing that a man or boy wears under his trousers: *a pair of underpants*

understand /ˌʌndəˈstænd/ *verb* (**understands**, **understanding**, **understood** /ˌʌndəˈstʊd/, **has understood**) **1** know what something means or why something happens: *I didn't understand what the teacher said.* ○ *He doesn't understand Swahili.* ○ *I don't understand why you're so angry.* **2** know something because somebody has told you about it: *I understand that you're leaving your job.* **make yourself understood** make people understand you: *My French isn't very good but I can usually make myself understood.*

understanding[1] /ˌʌndəˈstændɪŋ/ *adjective* If you are understanding, you listen to other people's problems and you try to understand them: *My parents are very understanding.*

understanding[2] /ˌʌndəˈstændɪŋ/ *noun* (no plural) knowing about something, or knowing how somebody feels: *He's got a good understanding of computers.*

understood *form of* **understand**

undertaker /ˈʌndəteɪkə(r)/ *noun* a person whose job is to organize **funerals** (the time when dead people are buried or burned)

underwater /ˌʌndəˈwɔːtə(r)/ *adjective*, *adverb* below the top of water: *Can you swim underwater?*

underwear /ˈʌndəweə(r)/ *noun* (no plural) clothes that you wear next to your body, under your other clothes

underwent *form of* **undergo**

undo /ʌnˈduː/ *verb* (**undoes** /ʌnˈdʌz/, **undoing**, **undid** /ʌnˈdɪd/, **has undone** /ʌnˈdʌn/) open something that was tied or fixed: *I undid the string and opened the parcel.* ○ *I can't undo these buttons.*

undone *adjective* not tied or fixed: *Your shoelaces are undone.*

undoubtedly /ʌnˈdaʊtɪdli/ *adverb* certainly; without doubt: *She is undoubtedly very intelligent.*

undress /ˌʌnˈdres/ *verb* (**undresses**, **undressing**, **undressed** /ˌʌnˈdrest/) take clothes off yourself or another person: *He undressed and got into bed.* ○ *She undressed her baby.* **get undressed** take off your clothes: *I got undressed and had a shower.*

uneasy /ʌnˈiːzi/ *adjective* worried that something is wrong: *I started to feel uneasy when the children didn't come home.*

uneasily /ʌnˈiːzɪli/ *adverb*: *She looked uneasily around the room.*

unemployed /ˌʌnɪmˈplɔɪd/ *adjective* If you are unemployed, you want a job but you do not have one.

unemployment /ˌʌnɪmˈplɔɪmənt/ *noun* (no plural) when there are not enough jobs for the people who want to work: *If the factory closes, unemployment in the town will increase.*

uneven /ˌʌnˈiːvn/ *adjective* not smooth or flat: *We had to drive slowly because the road was so uneven.*

unexpected /ˌʌnɪkˈspektɪd/ *adjective* surprising because you did not expect it: *an unexpected visit*

unexpectedly *adverb*: *She arrived unexpectedly.*

unfair /ˌʌnˈfeə(r)/ *adjective* Something that is unfair does not treat people in the same way or in the right way: *It was unfair to give homework to some of the children and not to the others.*

unfairly *adverb*: *He left his job because the boss was treating him unfairly.*

unfamiliar /ˌʌnfəˈmɪliə(r)/ *adjective* that you do not know; strange: *I woke up in an unfamiliar room.*

unfashionable /ʌnˈfæʃnəbl/ *adjective* not fashionable: *unfashionable clothes*

unfit /ˌʌnˈfɪt/ *adjective* **1** not healthy or strong: *She never takes any exercise – that's why she's so unfit.* **2** not good enough for something: *This house is unfit for people to live in.*

unfold /ʌnˈfəʊld/ *verb* (**unfolds**, **unfolding**, **unfolded**) open something to make it flat; open out and become flat: *Maria unfolded the newspaper and started to read.* ○ *The sofa unfolds to make a bed.*

unfortunate /ʌnˈfɔːtʃənət/ *adjective* not lucky: *It's unfortunate that you were ill on the day of your exam.*

unfortunately *adverb* it is unfortunate that: *I would like to give you some money, but unfortunately I haven't got any.*

unfriendly /ˌʌnˈfrendli/ *adjective* not friendly; not kind or helpful to other people

ungrateful /ʌnˈɡreɪtfl/ *adjective* If you are ungrateful, you do not show thanks when somebody helps you or gives you something: *Don't be so ungrateful! I spent all morning helping you!*

unhappy /ʌnˈhæpi/ *adjective* (**unhappier**, **unhappiest**) not happy; sad: *He was very unhappy when he lost the race.*

unhappily /ʌnˈhæpɪli/ *adverb*: *'I failed the exam,' she said unhappily.*

unhappiness /ʌnˈhæpɪnəs/ *noun* (no plural) *John has had a lot of unhappiness in his life.*

unhealthy /ʌnˈhelθi/ *adjective* (**unhealthier**, **unhealthiest**) **1** not well; often ill: *an unhealthy child* **2** that can make you ill: *unhealthy food*

uniform /'juːnɪfɔːm/ *noun* the special clothes that everybody in the same job, school, etc wears: *What colour is your school uniform?*

uninhabited /ˌʌnɪn'hæbɪtɪd/ *adjective* where nobody lives: *an uninhabited island*

union /'juːniən/ *noun* **1** (*plural* **unions**) a group of workers who have joined together to talk to their managers about things like pay and the way they work: *the National Union of Teachers* **2** (*plural* **unions**) a group of people or countries that have joined together **3** (no plural) coming together: *The President hopes to establish a closer union between the two countries.*

unique /juː'niːk/ *adjective* not like anybody or anything else: *Everybody in the world is unique.*

unit /'juːnɪt/ *noun* **1** one complete thing or group that may be part of something larger: *The book has twelve units.* **2** a measurement: *A metre is a unit of length and a kilogram is a unit of weight.*

unite /juː'naɪt/ *verb* (**unites**, **uniting**, **united**) join together to become one; put two things together: *East and West Germany united in 1990.*

united *adjective* joined together: *the United States of America*

universal /ˌjuːnɪ'vɜːsl/ *adjective* of, by or for everybody: *This subject is of universal interest.*

the universe /ðə 'juːnɪvɜːs/ *noun* (no plural) the earth and all the stars, planets and everything else in space

university /ˌjuːnɪ'vɜːsəti/ *noun* (*plural* **universities**) a place where people go to study more difficult subjects after they have left school: *I'm hoping to go to university next year.* ○ *My sister is at university studying Chemistry.* ✪ If you pass special courses at a university, you get a **degree**.

unjust /ˌʌn'dʒʌst/ *adjective* not just; not fair or right: *This tax is unjust because poor people pay as much as rich people.*

unkind /ˌʌn'kaɪnd/ *adjective* not kind; cruel: *It was unkind of you to laugh at her hat.*

unknown /ˌʌn'nəʊn/ *adjective* **1** that you do not know: *an unknown face* **2** not famous: *an unknown actor*

unless /ən'les/ *conjunction* if not; except if: *You will be late unless you leave now.* ○ *Unless you work harder you'll fail the exam.*

unlike /ˌʌn'laɪk/ *preposition* not like; different from: *She is thin, unlike her sister who is quite fat.*

unlikely /ʌn'laɪkli/ *adjective* (**unlikelier**, **unlikeliest**) If something is unlikely, it will probably not happen: *It is unlikely that it will rain today.* ○ *He is unlikely to pass the exam.*

unload /ˌʌn'ləʊd/ *verb* (**unloads**, **unloading**, **unloaded**) take off or out the things that a car, lorry, ship or plane is carrying: *I unloaded the sacks from the pick-up.* ○ *They unloaded the ship at the dock.*

unlock /ˌʌn'lɒk/ *verb* (**unlocks**, **unlocking**, **unlocked** /ˌʌn'lɒkt/) open something with a key: *I unlocked the door and went in.*

unlucky /ʌn'lʌki/ *adjective* (**unluckier**, **unluckiest**) **1** If you are unlucky, good things do not happen to you: *The team were unlucky – they played very well but they still lost the game.* **2** Something that is unlucky brings bad luck: *Some people think that the number 13 is unlucky.*

unluckily /ʌn'lʌkɪli/ *adverb* it is unlucky that: *Unluckily, I missed the bus.*

unmarried /ˌʌn'mærɪd/ *adjective* not married; without a husband or wife

unnecessary /ʌn'nesəsri/ *adjective* not necessary; not needed

unpack /ˌʌn'pæk/ *verb* (**unpacks**, **unpacking**, **unpacked** /ˌʌn'pækt/) take all the things out of a bag, suitcase, etc: *Have you unpacked your suitcase?* ○ *When I got home I unpacked and washed all my clothes.*

unpaid /ˌʌn'peɪd/ *adjective* not paid: *an unpaid bill*

unpleasant /ʌn'pleznt/ *adjective* not pleasant; not nice: *There was an unpleasant smell of bad fish.*

unpleasantly *adverb*: *It was unpleasantly hot in that room.*

unplug /ˌʌnˈplʌg/ *verb* (**unplugs, unplugging, unplugged** /ˌʌnˈplʌgd/) take the electric plug of a machine out of a place in a wall (called a **socket**) where there is electricity: *Could you unplug the TV?*

unpopular /ˌʌnˈpɒpjələ(r)/ *adjective* not popular; not liked by many people: *He's unpopular at work because he's lazy.*

unreliable /ˌʌnrɪˈlaɪəbl/ *adjective* not reliable; that you cannot trust: *Don't lend her any money – she's very unreliable.* ○ *an unreliable car*

unsafe /ˌʌnˈseɪf/ *adjective* not safe; dangerous: *Don't climb on that wall – it's unsafe.*

unsatisfactory /ˌʌnsætɪsˈfæktri/ *adjective* not satisfactory; not good enough: *Tina's work was unsatisfactory so I asked her to do it again.*

unstable /ˌʌnˈsteɪbl/ *adjective* Something that is unstable may fall, move or change: *This bridge is unstable.* ○ *unstable government*

unsuccessful /ˌʌnsəkˈsesfl/ *adjective* If you are unsuccessful, you have not done what you wanted and tried to do: *I tried to repair the bike but I was unsuccessful.*

unsuccessfully /ˌʌnsəkˈsesfəli/ *adverb*: *Gary tried unsuccessfully to lift the box.*

unsuitable /ˌʌnˈsuːtəbl/ *adjective* not suitable; not right for somebody or something: *This film is unsuitable for children.*

unsure /ˌʌnˈʃʊə(r)/ *adjective* not sure: *We were unsure what to do.*

untidy /ʌnˈtaɪdi/ *adjective* (**untidier, untidiest**) not tidy; not with everything in the right place: *Your room is always so untidy!*

untidiness /ʌnˈtaɪdinəs/ *noun* (no plural) *I hate untidiness!*

untie /ʌnˈtaɪ/ *verb* (**unties, untying, untied** /ʌnˈtaɪd/, **has untied**) **1** take off the string or rope that is holding something or somebody: *I untied the parcel.* **2** make a knot or bow loose: *Can you untie this knot?*

until /ənˈtɪl/ *conjunction* up to the time when: *Stay in bed until you feel better.*

until *preposition* **1** up to a certain time: *The shop is open until 6.30.* **2** before: *I can't come until tomorrow.*

untrue /ˌʌnˈtruː/ *adjective* not true or correct: *What you said was completely untrue.*

unusual /ʌnˈjuːʒuəl/ *adjective* If something is unusual, it does not often happen or you do not often see it: *It's unusual to see a cat without a tail.* ○ *What an unusual name!*

unusually /ʌnˈjuːʒuəli/ *adverb*: *She's unusually tall for her age.*

unwanted /ˌʌnˈwɒntɪd/ *adjective* not wanted: *unwanted children*

unwelcome /ˌʌnˈwelkəm/ *adjective* If somebody or something is unwelcome, you are not happy to have or see them: *an unwelcome visitor*

unwell /ʌnˈwel/ *adjective* not well; ill

unwilling /ˌʌnˈwɪlɪŋ/ *adjective* If you are unwilling to do something, you are not ready or happy to do it: *He was unwilling to lend me any money.*

unwrap /ˌʌnˈræp/ *verb* (**unwraps, unwrapping, unwrapped** /ˌʌnˈræpt/) take off the paper or cloth that is around something: *I unwrapped the parcel.*

up /ʌp/ *preposition, adverb* **1** in or to a higher place: *We climbed up the mountain.* ○ *Put your hand up if you know the answer.* ☛ picture on page A2 **2** from sitting or lying to standing: *Stand up, please.* ○ *What time do you get up?* (= out of bed) **3** in a way that is bigger, stronger, etc: *The price of petrol is going up.* ○ *Please turn the radio up – I can't hear it.* **4** so that it is finished: *Who used all the coffee up?* **5** along: *We walked up the road.* **6** towards and near somebody or something: *She came up to me and asked me the time.* **7** into pieces: *Cut the meat up.* **be up** be out of bed: *'Is Joseph up?' 'No, he's still asleep.'* **it's up to you** you are the person who should or should decide something: *'What shall we do this evening?' 'I don't mind. It's up to you.'* **up to 1** as far as; until: *Up to now, she has worked very hard.* **2** as much or as many as: *Up*

to 300 people came to the meeting.
3 doing something: *What is that man up to?*

update /ˌʌpˈdeɪt/ *verb* (**updates**, **updating**, **updated**) make something more modern or add new things to it: *The information on the computer is updated every week.*

uphill /ˌʌpˈhɪl/ *adverb* up, towards the top of a hill: *It's difficult to ride a bicycle uphill.*

upon /əˈpɒn/ *preposition* on ✪ **On** is the word that we usually use. **once upon a time** a long time ago (words that sometimes begin children's stories): *Once upon a time there was a beautiful princess ...*

upper /ˈʌpə(r)/ *adjective* higher than another; top: *the upper lip* ✪ opposite: **lower**

upright /ˈʌpraɪt/ *adjective, adverb* standing straight up, not lying down: *Put the ladder upright against the wall.*

upset /ˌʌpˈset/ *verb* (**upsets**, **upsetting**, **upset**, **has upset**) **1** make somebody feel unhappy or worried: *You upset Tom when you said he was ugly.* **2** make something go wrong: *The injury to the goalkeeper upset our chances of winning the match.* **3** knock something so that it turns over and things fall out: *I upset a bucket of water all over the floor.*

upset /ˈʌpset/ *noun* an illness in your stomach: *Sara has got a stomach upset.*

upset /ˌʌpˈset/ *adjective* **1** unhappy or worried: *The children were very upset when their dog died.* **2** ill: *I've got an upset stomach.*

upside down /ˌʌpsaɪd ˈdaʊn/ *adverb* with the top part at the bottom: *The picture is upside down.*

upstairs /ˌʌpˈsteəz/ *adverb* to or on a higher floor of a building: *I went upstairs to the second floor.*

upstairs *adjective: An upstairs window was open.* ✪ opposite: **downstairs**

upwards /ˈʌpwədz/, **upward** /ˈʌpwəd/ *adverb* up; towards a higher place: *We climbed upwards, towards the top of the mountain.* ✪ opposite: **downwards**

urban /ˈɜːbən/ *adjective* of a town or

city: *urban areas*

urge /ɜːdʒ/ *verb* (**urges**, **urging**, **urged** /ɜːdʒd/) try to make somebody do something: *I urged him to stay for dinner.*

urge *noun* a strong feeling that you want to do something: *I had a sudden urge to laugh.*

urgency /ˈɜːdʒənsi/ *noun* (no plural) the need to do something quickly because it is very important

urgent /ˈɜːdʒənt/ *adjective* so important that you must do it or answer it quickly: *The doctor received an urgent telephone call.*

urgently *adverb: I must see you urgently.*

us /əs/, /ʌs/ *pronoun* (plural) me and another person or other people; me and you: *The teacher asked us a lot of questions.* ○ *John wrote to us.*

use[1] /juːz/ *verb* (**uses**, **using**, **used** /juːzd/) **1** do a job with something: *Could I use your telephone?* ○ *Do you know how to use this machine?* ○ *Wood is used to make paper.* **2** take something: *Don't use all the milk.* **use up** use something until you have no more: *I've used up all the coffee, so I need to buy some more.*

use[2] /juːs/ *noun* **1** (no plural) using: *This library is for the use of students only.* **2** (*plural* **uses**) what you can do with something: *This tool has many uses.* **have the use of something** have the right to use something: *The school let us have use of a classroom for our meeting.* **it's no use** it will not help to do something: *It's no use telling her anything — she never listens.* **make use of something** find a way of using something: *If you don't want that box, I can make use of it.*

used[1] /juːzd/ *adjective* not new: *The garage sells used cars.*

used[2] /juːst/ *adjective* **be used to something** know something well because you have seen, heard, tasted, done, etc it a lot: *I'm used to walking because I haven't got a bicycle.* **get used to something** begin to know something well after a time: *I'm getting used to my new job.*

used[3] /ju:st/ verb **used to** words that tell us about something that happened often or that was true in the past: *She used to smoke when she was young.* ○ *I used to be afraid of dogs, but now I like them.* ○ *I didn't use to like fish, but I do now.*

useful /'ju:sfl/ adjective good and helpful for doing something: *This bag will be useful for carrying my books.*

useless /'ju:sləs/ adjective **1** not good for anything: *A car is useless without petrol.* **2** that does not do what you hoped: *It was useless asking my brother for money – he didn't have any.*

user /'ju:zə(r)/ noun a person who uses something: *computer users*

usual /'ju:ʒuəl/ adjective that happens most often: *It's not usual for such a young baby to be able to walk.* **as usual** as happens most often: *Julie was late, as usual.*

usually /'ju:ʒuəli/ adverb: *I usually ride my bike to school, but today I'm walking.*

utter[1] /'ʌtə(r)/ adjective complete: *The room was in utter darkness and I couldn't see anything.*

utterly adverb completely or very: *That's utterly impossible!*

utter[2] /'ʌtə(r)/ verb (**utters, uttering, uttered** /'ʌtəd/) say something or make a sound with your mouth: *He uttered a cry of pain.*

Vv

V short way of writing **volt**

v /vi:/ short for **versus**: *The final of the world cup was Brazil v France.*

vacancy /'veɪkənsi/ noun (plural **vacancies**) **1** a job that nobody is doing: *We have a vacancy for a secretary in our office.* **2** a room in a hotel that nobody is using: *The sign outside the hotel said 'no vacancies'* (= the hotel is full).

vacant /'veɪkənt/ adjective empty; with nobody in it: *an vacant room*

vacation /və'keɪʃn/ noun a holiday time when a university is not open: *the summer vacation*

vacuum /'vækjuəm/ noun a space with no air, gas or anything else in it

vacuum cleaner /'vækjuəm ˌkli:nə(r)/ noun a machine that cleans carpets by sucking up dirt

vague /veɪg/ adjective (**vaguer, vaguest**) not clear or not exact: *I couldn't find the house because he gave me very vague directions.*

vaguely adverb: *I vaguely remember what happened.*

vain /veɪn/ adjective (**vainer, vainest**) **1** too proud of what you can do or how you look ✪ The noun is **vanity**. **2** with no success; useless: *They made a vain attempt to save his life.* **in vain** with no success: *I tried in vain to sleep.*

valid /'vælɪd/ adjective If something like a ticket or a cheque is valid, you can use it and other people will accept it: *Your bus ticket is valid for one week.*

valley /'væli/ noun (plural **valleys**) low land, usually with a river, between hills or mountains: *Rift Valley Province*

valuable /'væljuəbl/ adjective **1** worth a lot of money: *Is this ring valuable?* **2** very useful: *valuable information*

value[1] /'vælju:/ noun **1** (plural **values**) how much money you can sell something for: *What is the value of this property?* **2** (no plural) how useful or important something is: *Their help was of great value.* **3** (no plural) how much something is worth compared with its price: *The book was good value at only 50 shillings.*

value[2] /'vælju:/ verb (**values, valuing, valued** /'vælju:d/) **1** think that something is very important: *I value my freedom.* **2** say how much money something is worth: *The property was valued at one million shillings.*

vampire /'væmpaɪə(r)/ noun a dead person in stories who comes to life at night and drinks people's blood

van

van /væn/ *noun* a kind of big car or small lorry for carrying things

vandal /'vændl/ *noun* a person who damages and breaks things that belong to other people: *Vandals have damaged our classroom.*

vandalism /'vændəlızəm/ *noun* (no plural) damage by vandals: *Vandalism is a problem in this part of the city.*

vanilla /və'nılə/ *noun* (no plural) a plant that gives a taste to some sweet foods, for example white ice-cream

vanish /'vænıʃ/ *verb* (**vanishes**, **vanishing**, **vanished** /'vænıʃt/) go away suddenly; disappear: *The thief ran into the crowd and vanished.*

vanity /'vænəti/ *noun* (no plural) being too proud of what you can do or how you look ✪ The adjective is **vain**.

varied, **varies** *forms of* vary

variety /və'raıəti/ *noun* **1** (no plural) If something has variety, it is full of different things and changes often: *There's a lot of variety in my new job.* **2** (no plural) a lot of different things: *There's a large variety of dishes on the menu.* **3** (*plural* **varieties**) a kind of something: *This variety of apple is very sweet.*

various /'veəriəs/ *adjective* many different: *We sell this shirt in various colours and sizes.*

varnish /'vɑːnıʃ/ *noun* (no plural) a clear paint with no colour, that you put on something to make it shine

vary /'veəri/ *verb* (**varies**, **varying**, **varied** /'veərid/, **has varied**) be or become different from each other: *These shoes vary in price from 1 000 to 5 000 shillings.*

vase

vase /vɑːz/ *noun* a pot that you put cut flowers in

vast /vɑːst/ *adjective* very big: *Australia is a vast country.*

veal /viːl/ *noun* (no plural) meat from a young cow (a **calf**) ☛ Note at **cow**

vegetable /'vedʒtəbl/ *noun* a plant that we eat. Potatoes, carrots and beans are vegetables: *vegetable soup*

vegetarian /ˌvedʒɪ'teəriən/ *noun* a person who does not eat meat

vegetation /vedʒɪ'teɪʃn/ *noun* (no plural) the trees and plants that grow in a place: *There is little or no vegetation in desert regions.*

vehicle /'viːəkl/ *noun* any thing that carries people or things from one place to another. Cars, buses and bicycles are all vehicles.

veil /veɪl/ *noun* a piece of thin material that a woman puts over her head and face: *Women wear veils in a lot of Muslim countries.*

vein /veɪn/ *noun* one of the small tubes in your body that carry blood to the heart

verandah, **veranda** /və'rændə/ *noun* an area like a room at the side of a house, with a roof and wooden floor but no walls: *We sat on the verandah.*

verb /vɜːb/ *noun* a word that tells you what somebody or something is or does. 'Go', 'sing', 'happen' and 'be' are all verbs.

verdict /'vɜːdɪkt/ *noun* what the **jury** in a court of law decides at the end of a **trial**

verse /vɜːs/ *noun* **1** (no plural) poetry; writing in lines that has a **rhythm**: *The play is written in verse.* **2** (*plural* **verses**) a group of lines in a song or poem: *This song has five verses.*

version /'vɜːʃn/ *noun* **1** a form of something that is different in some way: *a new version of a Beatles song* **2** what one person says or writes about something that happened: *His version of the accident is different from mine.*

versus /'vɜːsəs/ *preposition* on the other side in a sport; against: *There's a good football match on TV tonight – England versus Brazil.* ✪ The short way of writing 'versus' is **v** or **vs**.

vertical /'vɜːtɪkl/ *adjective* Something

that is vertical goes straight up, not from side to side: *a vertical line* ☛ picture on page A5

very[1] /'veri/ *adverb* You use 'very' before another word to make it stronger: *The Nile is a very long river.* ○ *She speaks very quietly.* ○ *I like athletics very much.* ○ *I'm not very hungry.*

very[2] /'veri/ *adjective* same; exact: *You are the very person I wanted to see!* ○ *We climbed to the very top of the mountain.*

vest /vest/ *noun* a piece of clothing that you wear under your other clothes on the top part of your body

vet /vet/, **veterinary surgeon** /ˌvetrənri 'sɜːdʒən/ *noun* a doctor for animals

via /'vaɪə/ *preposition* going through a place: *We went from Nairobi to Sydney via Bangkok.*

vibrate /vaɪ'breɪt/ *verb* (**vibrates, vibrating, vibrated**) move very quickly from side to side or up and down: *The house vibrates every time a train goes past.*

   vibration /vaɪ'breɪʃn/ *noun*: *You can feel the vibrations from the engine when you are in the car.*

vice- /vaɪs/ *prefix* a word that you use before another word, to show somebody who is next to the leader in importance: *The vice-captain leads the team when the captain is ill.* ○ *the Vice-President*

vicious /'vɪʃəs/ *adjective* cruel; wanting to hurt somebody or something: *a vicious attack*

victim /'vɪktɪm/ *noun* a person or animal that is hurt or killed by somebody or something: *The victims of the car accident were taken to hospital.*

victory /'vɪktəri/ *noun* (*plural* **victories**) winning a fight, game or war

video /'vɪdiəʊ/ *noun* (*plural* **videos**) **1** (*also* **video recorder**) a machine that puts television programmes on tape, so that you can watch them later **2** tape in a box (called a **cassette**) that you put into a video recorder to show films, for example: *We stayed at home and watched a video.* ○ *Can you get this film on video?*

view /vjuː/ *noun* **1** what you can see

from a certain place: *There is a beautiful view of the mountains from our window.* **2** what you believe or think about something: *What are your views on marriage?* **in view of something** because of something: *In view of the heavy rain we decided to cancel the match.* **on view** in a place for people to see: *Her paintings are on view at the museum.*

viewer /'vjuːə(r)/ *noun* a person who watches television

vigorous /'vɪgərəs/ *adjective* strong and active: *vigorous exercise*

   vigorously *adverb*: *She shook my hand vigorously.*

vile /vaɪl/ *adjective* (**viler, vilest**) very bad; horrible: *What a vile smell!*

village /'vɪlɪdʒ/ *noun* a small place where people live. A village is smaller than a town: *a village in the mountains*

   villager *noun* a person who lives in a village

villain /'vɪlən/ *noun* a bad person, usually in a book, play or film

vine /vaɪn/ *noun* a plant that grapes grow on

vinegar /'vɪnɪgə(r)/ *noun* (no plural) a liquid with a strong sharp taste. You put it on food and use it for cooking: *I mixed some oil and vinegar to put on the salad.*

vineyard /'vɪnjəd/ *noun* a piece of land where vines grow

violent /'vaɪələnt/ *adjective* a person or thing that is violent is very strong and dangerous and hurts people: *a violent man* ○ *a violent storm*

   violence /'vaɪələns/ *noun* (no plural) being violent: *Do you think there's too much violence on TV?*

   violently *adverb*: *Did she behave violently towards you?*

violet /'vaɪələt/ *noun* a small purple flower

   violet *adjective* with a purple colour

violin /ˌvaɪə'lɪn/ *noun* a musical instrument made of wood, with strings across it. You play a violin with a **bow**: *I play the violin.*

VIP /ˌviː aɪ 'piː/ *noun* a person who is famous or important. 'VIP' is short for

very important person: *The Prime Minister is a VIP.*

virtually /ˈvɜːtʃuəli/ *adverb* almost: *The two boys look virtually the same.*

virus /ˈvaɪrəs/ *noun* (*plural* **viruses**) a very small living thing that can make you ill: *a flu virus*

visa /ˈviːzə/ *noun* a special piece of paper or mark in your passport to show that you can go into a country

visible /ˈvɪzəbl/ *adjective* If something is visible, you can see it: *Stars are only visible at night.* ✪ opposite: **invisible**

vision /ˈvɪʒn/ *noun* **1** (no plural) the power to see; sight: *He wears glasses because he has poor vision.* **2** (*plural* **visions**) a picture in your mind; a dream: *They have a vision of a world without war.*

visit /ˈvɪzɪt/ *verb* (**visits, visiting, visited**) go to see a person or place for a short time: *Have you ever visited the National Museum?* ○ *She visited me in hospital.*

visit *noun*: *This is my first visit to Nairobi.* **pay somebody a visit** go to see somebody

visitor /ˈvɪzɪtə(r)/ *noun* a person who goes to see another person or a place for a short time: *The old lady never has any visitors.* ○ *Millions of visitors come to East Africa every year.*

visual /ˈvɪʒuəl/ *adjective* of or about seeing: *Painting and cinema are visual arts.*

vital /ˈvaɪtl/ *adjective* very important; that you must do or have: *It's vital that she sees a doctor – she's very ill.*

vitamin /ˈvɪtəmɪn/ *noun* one of the things in food that you need to be healthy: *Oranges are full of vitamin C.*

vivid /ˈvɪvɪd/ *adjective* **1** with a strong bright colour: *vivid yellow* **2** that makes a very clear picture in your mind: *I had a very vivid dream last night.*

vividly *adverb*: *I remember my first day at school vividly.*

vocabulary /vəˈkæbjələri/ *noun* (*plural* **vocabularies**) **1** all the words in a language **2** a list of words in a lesson or book: *We have to learn this new vocabulary for homework.* **3** all the words that somebody knows

voice /vɔɪs/ *noun* the sounds that you make when you speak or sing: *Steve has a very deep voice.* **at the top of your voice** very loudly: *'Come here!' she shouted at the top of her voice.* **raise your voice** speak very loudly

volcano /vɒlˈkeɪnəʊ/ *noun* (*plural* **volcanoes**) a mountain with a hole in the top where fire, gas and hot liquid rock (called **lava**) sometimes come out

volcanic /vɒlˈkænɪk/ *adjective*: *volcanic rocks*

volleyball /ˈvɒlibɔːl/ *noun* (no plural) a game where two teams try to hit a ball over a high net with their hands

volt /vəʊlt/ *noun* a measure of electricity ✪ The short way of writing 'volt' is **V**.

volume /ˈvɒljuːm/ *noun* **1** (no plural) the amount of space that something fills, or the amount of space inside something: *What is the volume of this box?* **2** (no plural) the

volume

3m

3m 3m

volume = 27m³
27 cubic metres

amount of sound that something makes: *I can't hear the radio. Can you turn the volume up?* **3** (*plural* **volumes**) a book, especially one of a set: *The dictionary is in two volumes.*

voluntary /ˈvɒləntri/ *adjective* **1** If something is voluntary, you do it because you want to, not because you must: *She made a voluntary decision to leave the job.* **2** If work is voluntary, you are not paid to do it: *He does voluntary work at a children's hospital.*

voluntarily /ˈvɒləntrəli/ *adverb* because you want to, not because you must: *She left the job voluntarily.*

volunteer /ˌvɒlənˈtɪə(r)/ *verb* (**volunteers, volunteering, volunteered** /ˌvɒlənˈtɪəd/) say that you will do something that you do not have to do: *I volunteered to do the washing-up.*

volunteer *noun* a person who volunteers to do a job: *They're asking for volunteers to help repair the road.*

vomit /ˈvɒmɪt/ *verb* (**vomits, vomiting, vomited**) When you vomit, food comes up from your stomach and out of your mouth. **۞** It is more usual to say **be sick**.

vote /vəʊt/ *verb* (**votes**, **voting**, **voted**) choose somebody or something by putting up your hand or writing on a piece of paper: *Who did you vote for in the election?*

vote *noun*: *There were 96 votes for the plan, and 25 against.*

voter *noun* a person who votes in a political election

voucher /ˈvaʊtʃə(r)/ *noun* a piece of paper that you can use instead of money to pay for something

vowel /ˈvaʊəl/ *noun* one of the letters *a, e, i, o* or *u* , or the sound that you make when you say it ☛ Look at **consonant**.

voyage /ˈvɔɪdʒ/ *noun* a long journey by boat or in space: *a voyage from London to New York*

vs *short way of writing* **versus**

vulture /ˈvʌltʃə(r)/ *noun* a large bird that eats dead animals. Vultures have no feathers on their head and neck.

Ww

wade /weɪd/ *verb* (**wades**, **wading**, **waded**) walk through water: *Can we wade across the river, or is it too deep?*

wag /wæg/ *verb* (**wags**, **wagging**, **wagged** /wægd/) move or make something move from side to side or up and down: *She wagged her finger at me.* ○ *My dog's tail wags when he's happy.*

wages /ˈweɪdʒɪz/ *noun* (plural) the money that you receive every week for the work that you do: *Our wages are paid every Friday.* ○ *low wages*

wagon /ˈwægən/ *noun* **1** a vehicle with four wheels that a horse pulls **2** a part of a train where things like coal are carried

wail /weɪl/ *verb* (**wails**, **wailing**, **wailed** /weɪld/) make a long sad cry or noise: *The little boy started wailing for his mother.*

waist /weɪst/ *noun* the part around the middle of your body ☛ picture on page A4

waistcoat /ˈweɪskəʊt/ *noun* a piece of clothing like a jacket with no sleeves

wait¹ /weɪt/ *verb* (**waits**, **waiting**, **waited**) stay in one place until something happens or until somebody or something comes: *If I'm late, please wait for me.* ○ *We've been waiting a long time.* **I can't wait** words that you use when you are very excited about something that is going to happen: *I can't wait to see you again!* **keep somebody waiting** make somebody wait because you are late or busy: *I'm sorry to have kept you waiting – my bus was late.* **wait and see** wait and find out later: *'What have you got in the box?' 'Wait and see!'* **wait up** not go to bed until somebody comes home: *I will be home late tonight so don't wait up for me.*

wait² /weɪt/ *noun* a time when you wait: *We had a long wait for the bus.*

waiter /ˈweɪtə(r)/ *noun* a man who brings food and drink to your table in a restaurant

waiting room /ˈweɪtɪŋ ruːm/ *noun* a room where people can sit and wait, for example to see a doctor or to catch a train

waitress /ˈweɪtrəs/ *noun* (plural **waitresses**) a woman who brings food and drink to your table in a restaurant

wake /weɪk/, **wake up** *verb* (**wakes**, **waking**, **woke** /wəʊk/, **has woken** /ˈwəʊkən/) **1** stop sleeping: *What time did you wake up this morning?* **2** make somebody stop sleeping: *The noise woke me up.* ○ *Don't wake the baby.* **۞** It is more usual to say **wake up** than **wake**.

walk¹ /wɔːk/ *verb* (**walks**, **walking**, **walked** /wɔːkt/) move on your legs, but not run: *I usually walk to work.* ○ *We walked 20 kilometres today.*

walk out leave suddenly because you are angry: *He walked out of the meeting.*

walk² /wɔːk/ *noun* a journey on foot: *The beach is a short walk from our house.* ○ *I went for a walk.* **go for a walk** walk somewhere because you enjoy it: *It was a lovely day so we went for a walk in the park.*

walker /ˈwɔːkə(r)/ *noun* a person who is walking

wall /wɔːl/ *noun* **1** a side of a building or room: *There's a picture on the wall.* **2** a thing made of stones or bricks around a garden, field or town, for example: *There's a high wall around the prison.*

wallet

wallet /ˈwɒlɪt/ *noun* a small flat case for paper money, that you can carry in your pocket

wallpaper /ˈwɔːlpeɪpə(r)/ *noun* (no plural) special paper that you use for covering the walls of a room

wander /ˈwɒndə(r)/ *verb* (**wanders**, **wandering**, **wandered** /ˈwɒndəd/) walk slowly with no special plan: *We wandered around the town until the shops opened.*

want /wɒnt/ *verb* (**wants**, **wanting**, **wanted**) **1** wish to have or do something: *Do you want a drink?* ○ *I want to go to Italy.* ○ *She wanted me to give her some money.* ✪ **Would like** is more polite than **want**: *Would you like something to eat?* **2** need something: *The roof wants fixing.*

war /wɔː(r)/ *noun* fighting between countries or between groups of people: *the First World War* **at war** fighting: *The two countries have been at war for five years.* **declare war** start a war: *In 1812 Napoleon declared war on Russia.*

ward /wɔːd/ *noun* a big room in a hospital that has beds for the patients

warden /ˈwɔːdn/ *noun* a person whose job is to look after a place and the people in it: *the warden of a youth hostel*

wardrobe /ˈwɔːdrəʊb/ *noun* a cupboard where you hang your clothes

warehouse /ˈweəhaʊs/ *noun* (*plural* **warehouses** /ˈweəhaʊzɪz/) a big building where people keep things before they sell them: *a furniture warehouse*

warm¹ /wɔːm/ *adjective* (**warmer**, **warmest**) **1** a little hot: *It's warm in the sunshine.* ○ *We went near the stove to keep warm.* **2** Warm clothes are clothes that stop you feeling cold: *It's cold in the mountains, so take some warm clothes with you.* **3** friendly and kind: *Martha is a very warm person.* ✪ opposite: **cold**

warmly *adverb*: *The children were warmly dressed.* ○ *He thanked me warmly.*

warm² /wɔːm/ *verb* (**warms**, **warming**, **warmed** /wɔːmd/) **warm up** become warmer, or make somebody or something warmer: *I warmed up some soup for lunch.* ○ *It was cold this morning, but it's warming up now.* ○ *It's important to warm up before a race, or you might pull a muscle.*

warmth /wɔːmθ/ *noun* (no plural) **1** heat: *the warmth of the sun* **2** friendliness and kindness: *the warmth of his smile*

warn /wɔːn/ *verb* (**warns**, **warning**, **warned** /wɔːnd/) tell somebody about danger or about something bad that may happen: *I warned him not to go too close to the fire.*

warning *noun* something that warns you: *There is a warning on every packet of cigarettes.*

was *form of* **be**

wash¹ /wɒʃ/ *verb* (**washes**, **washing**, **washed** /wɒʃt/) **1** clean somebody, something or yourself with water: *Have you washed the floor?* ○ *Wash your hands before you eat.* ○ *I washed and dressed quickly.* **2** flow somewhere many times: *The sea washed over my feet.* **3** move something with water: *The house was washed away by the river.* **wash up** clean the plates, knives, forks, etc after a meal: *I washed up after dinner.*

wash[2] /wɒʃ/ *noun* (no plural) cleaning something with water: *I gave my hands a quick wash.* **have a wash** wash yourself: *I had a quick wash.* **in the wash** being washed: *All my socks are in the wash!*

washbasin /'wɒʃbeɪsn/ *noun* the place in a bathroom where you wash your hands and face

washing /'wɒʃɪŋ/ *noun* (no plural) clothes that you need to wash or that you have washed: *Shall I hang the washing outside to dry?* ○ *I've done the washing.*

washing machine /'wɒʃɪŋ məʃiːn/ *noun* a machine that washes clothes

washing powder /'wɒʃɪŋ paʊdə(r)/ *noun* (no plural) soap powder for washing clothes

washing-up /ˌwɒʃɪŋ 'ʌp/ *noun* (no plural) cleaning the plates, knives, forks, etc after a meal: *I'll do the washing-up.*

washing-up liquid /ˌwɒʃɪŋ 'ʌp lɪkwɪd/ *noun* (no plural) a liquid that you use for washing plates, etc

wasn't /'wɒznt/ = was not

wasp /wɒsp/ *noun* yellow and black insect that flies and can sting people

waste[1] /weɪst/ *verb* (**wastes**, **wasting**, **wasted**) use too much of something or not use something in a good way: *She wastes a lot of money on cigarettes.* ○ *He wasted his time at university – he didn't do any work.* ○ *Try not to waste water.*

waste[2] /weɪst/ *noun* (no plural) **1** not using something in a useful way: *It's a waste to throw away all this food!* ○ *This watch was a waste of money – it's broken already!* **2** things that people throw away because they are not useful: *A lot of waste from the factories goes into this river.*

waste[3] /weɪst/ *adjective* that you do not want because it is not good

waste-paper basket /ˌweɪst 'peɪpə bɑːskɪt/ *noun* a container where you put things like paper that you do not want

watch[1] /wɒtʃ/ *noun* (plural **watches**) a thing that shows what time it is. You wear a watch on your wrist. ☞ Note at **clock**.

watch

watch[2] /wɒtʃ/ *verb* (**watches**, **watching**, **watched** /wɒtʃt/) **1** look at somebody or something for some time: *We watched television all evening.* ○ *Watch how I do this.* **2** look after something or somebody: *Could you watch my bag while I buy the tickets?* **watch out** be careful because of somebody or something dangerous: *Watch out! There's a car coming.* **watch out for somebody** or **something** look carefully and be ready for somebody or something dangerous: *Watch out for animals on the road.*

watch[3] /wɒtʃ/ *noun* (no plural) **keep watch** look out for danger: *The soldier kept watch at the gate.*

water[1] /'wɔːtə(r)/ *noun* (no plural) the liquid in rivers, lakes and seas that people and animals drink

water[2] /'wɔːtə(r)/ *verb* (**waters**, **watering**, **watered** /'wɔːtəd/) **1** give water to plants: *Have you watered the plants?* **2** When your eyes water, they fill with tears: *The smoke made my eyes water.*

watering can /'wɔːtərɪŋ kæn/ *noun* a container that you use for watering plants

watercolour /'wɔːtəkʌlə(r)/ *noun* a picture that you make with paint and water

waterfall /'wɔːtəfɔːl/ *noun* a place where water falls from a high place to a low place

water melon /'wɔːtə melən/ *noun* a big round fruit with a thick green skin. It is pink inside with a lot of black seeds.

waterproof /'wɔːtəpruːf/ *adjective* If something is waterproof, it does not let water go through it: *a waterproof watch*

water-skiing /'wɔːtə skiːɪŋ/ *noun* (no plural) the sport of moving fast over water on long boards (called **water-skis**), pulled by a boat

wave[1] /weɪv/ *verb* (**waves**, **waving**, **waved** /weɪvd/) **1** move your hand from side to side in the air to say hello or goodbye or to make a sign to somebody: *She waved to me as the train left the station.* ○ *Who are you waving at?* **2** move something quickly from side to side in the air: *The children were waving flags as the President's car drove past.* **3** move up and down or from side to side: *The flags were waving in the wind.*

wave[2] /weɪv/ *noun* **1** one of the lines of water that moves across the top of the sea **2** moving your hand from side to side in the air, to say hello or goodbye or to make a sign to somebody **3** a gentle curve in hair **4** a movement like a wave on the sea, that carries heat, light, sound, etc: *radio waves*

wavy /'weɪvi/ *adjective* (**wavier**, **waviest**) Something that is wavy has gentle curves in it: *She has wavy black hair.*

wavy line

wax /wæks/ *noun* (no plural) the stuff that is used for making candles

way /weɪ/ *noun* **1** (*plural* **ways**) a road or path that you must follow to go to a place: *Can you tell me the way to the station, please?* ○ *I lost my way and I had to look at the map.* **2** (*plural* **ways**) a direction; where somebody or something is going or looking: *Come this way.* ○ *She was looking the other way.* **3** (no plural) distance: *It's a long way from Mombasa to Kitale.* **4** (*plural* **ways**) how you do something: *What is the best way to learn a language?* ○ *He smiled in a friendly way.* **by the way** words that you say when you are going to talk about something different: *By the way, I had a letter from Ann yesterday.* **give way 1** stop and let somebody or something go before you: *You must give way to traffic coming from the right.* **2** agree with somebody when you did not agree before: *After a long argument, my parents finally gave way and said I could go and play with my friends.* **3** break: *The ladder gave way and Ben fell to the ground.* **in the way** in front of somebody so that you stop them from seeing something or moving: *I couldn't see the blackboard because the teacher was in the way.* **no way** a way of saying 'no' more strongly: *'Can I borrow your bike?' 'No way!'* **on the way** when you are going somewhere: *I stopped to have a drink on the way to school.* **out of the way** not in a place where you stop somebody from moving or doing something: *Get out of the way! There's a car coming!* **the right way up** or **round** with the correct part at the top or at the front: *Is this picture the right way up?* **the wrong way up** or **round** with the wrong part at the top or at the front: *Those two words are the wrong way round.* **way in** where you go into a building: *Here's the museum. Where's the way in?* **way of life** how people live: *Is the way of life in Europe different from America?* **way out** where you go out of a place: *I can't find the way out.*

WC /ˌdʌbljuː 'siː/ *noun* a toilet

we /wiː/ *pronoun* (plural) I and another person or other people; you and I: *John and I quarrelled yesterday – we're friends again now, though.* ○ *Are we late?*

weak /wiːk/ *adjective* (**weaker**, **weakest**) **1** not powerful or strong: *She felt very weak after her long illness.* ○ *a weak government* ➡ picture on page A11 **2** that can break easily: *The bridge was too weak to carry the heavy lorry.* **2** that you cannot see, taste, smell, hear or feel clearly: *weak tea* ✪ opposite: **strong**

weaken /'wiːkən/ *verb* (**weakens**, **weakening**, **weakened** /'wiːkənd/) become less strong or make somebody or something less strong: *He was weakened by the illness.*

weakness /'wiːknəs/ *noun* **1** (no plural) not being strong: *I have a feeling of weakness in my legs.* **2** (*plural* **weaknesses**) something that is wrong or bad in a person or thing

wealth /welθ/ *noun* (no plural) having a lot of money, land, etc: *He is a man of great wealth.*

wealthy *adjective* (**wealthier**, **wealthiest**) rich: *a wealthy family*

weapon /'wepən/ *noun* a thing that you use for fighting. Guns and bombs are weapons.

wear[1] /weə(r)/ *verb* (**wears**, **wearing**, **wore** /wɔː(r)/, **has worn** /wɔːn/) have clothes, etc on your body: *She was wearing a red dress.* ○ *I wear glasses.*
wear off become less strong: *The pain is wearing off.* **wear out** become thin or damaged because you have used it a lot; make something do this: *Children's shoes usually wear out very quickly.* **wear somebody out** make somebody very tired: *She wore herself out by working too hard.*

wear[2] /weə(r)/ *noun* (no plural) **1** clothes: *sportswear* **2** using something and making it old: *These are showing signs of wear – I will need to buy new ones soon.*

weather /'weðə(r)/ *noun* (no plural) how much sunshine, rain, wind, etc there is at a certain time, or how hot or cold it is: *What's the weather going to be like tomorrow?* ○ *bad weather*

weather forecast /'weðə fɔːkɑːst/ *noun* words on television, radio or in a newspaper that tell you what the weather will be like: *The weather forecast says it will be stormy tomorrow.*

weave /wiːv/ *verb* (**weaves**, **weaving**, **wove** /wəʊv/, **has woven** /'wəʊvn/) make cloth by putting threads over and under one other: *This cloth is woven by hand.*

weaver bird /'wiːvə bɜːd/ *noun* a small bird that builds a round nest, like a ball, with a small hole in it where the bird goes in and out

web /web/ *noun* a thin net that a spider makes to catch flies ☛ picture at **spider**

we'd /wiːd/ **1** = **we had 2** = **we would**

wedding /'wedɪŋ/ *noun* a time when a man and a woman get married: *Jane and Philip invited me to their wedding.* ○ *wedding guests*

Wednesday /'wenzdeɪ/ *noun* the fourth day of the week, next after Tuesday

weed /wiːd/ *noun* a wild plant that grows where you do not want it: *The garden is full of weeds.*

weed *verb* (**weeds**, **weeding**, **weeded**) pull weeds out of the ground

week /wiːk/ *noun* **1** a time of seven days, usually from Sunday to the next Saturday: *I'm taking the exam next week.* ○ *I have English homework twice a week.* ○ *I saw him two weeks ago.* ✪ A **fortnight** is the same as two weeks. **2** Monday to Friday or Monday to Saturday: *I work during the week but not at weekends.*

weekday /'wiːkdeɪ/ *noun* any day except Saturday or Sunday: *I only work on weekdays.*

weekend /ˌwiːk'end/ *noun* Saturday and Sunday: *What are you doing at the weekend?*

weekly /'wiːkli/ *adjective*, *adverb* that happens or comes every week or once a week: *a weekly magazine* ○ *I am paid weekly.*

weep /wiːp/ *verb* (**weeps**, **weeping**, **wept** /wept/, **has wept**) cry ✪ **Cry** is the word that we usually use.

weevil /'wiːvl/ *noun* an insect that has a very hard body and can destroy crops.

weigh /weɪ/ *verb* (**weighs**, **weighing**, **weighed** /weɪd/) **1** measure how heavy somebody or something is using a machine called **scales**: *The shop assistant weighed the tomatoes.* **2** have a certain number of kilos, etc: *'How much do you weigh?' 'I weigh 55 kilos.'*

weight /weɪt/ *noun* **1** (no plural) how heavy somebody or something is: *Do you know the weight of the parcel?* **2** (*plural* **weights**) a piece of metal that you use on **scales** for measuring how heavy something is. **lose weight** become thinner and less heavy: *Winnie lost a lot of weight when she was ill.* **put on weight** become fatter and heavier

weird /wɪəd/ *adjective* (**weirder**, **weirdest**) very strange: *a weird dream*

welcome[1] /'welkəm/ *adjective* If somebody or something is welcome, you are happy to have or see them: *The cool drink was welcome on such a hot day.* ○ *Welcome to Africa!* **be welcome to** be allowed to do or have something: *If you come to Kenya again, you're welcome to stay with us.* **make somebody welcome** show a visitor that you are happy to see him/her **you're welcome** polite words that you say when somebody has said 'thank you': *'Thank you.' 'You're welcome.'*

welcome[2] /'welkəm/ *verb* (**welcome**, **welcoming**, **welcomed** /'welkəmd/) show that you are happy to have or see somebody or something: *He came to the door to welcome us.*

welcome *noun*: *They gave us a great welcome when we arrived.*

weld /weld/ *verb* join pieces of metal together using heat

welfare /'welfeə(r)/ *noun* (no plural) the health and happiness of a person: *The school looks after the welfare of its students.*

we'll /wi:l/ **1** = we will **2** = we shall

well[1] /wel/ *adjective* (**better**, **best**) healthy; not ill: *'How are you?' 'I'm very well, thanks.'*

well[2] /wel/ *adverb* (**better**, **best**) **1** in a good or right way: *You speak English very well.* ○ *These shoes are very well-made.* ✪ opposite: **badly 2** completely or very much: *I don't know Catherine very well.* ○ *Shake the bottle well before you open it.* **as well** also: *'I'm going out.' 'Can I come as well?'* **as well as something** and also: *She has a flat in Nairobi as well as a house in Mombasa.* **do well** be successful: *He did well in his exams.* **may** or **might as well** words that you use to say that you will do something, often because there is nothing else to do: *If you've finished the work, you may as well go home.* **well done!** words that you say to somebody who has done something good: *'I got the job!' 'Well done!'*

well[3] /wel/ **1** a word that you often say when you are starting to speak: *'Do you like it?' 'Well, I'm not really sure.'* **2** a word that you use to show surprise: *Well, that's strange!*

well[4] /wel/ *noun* a deep hole for getting water or oil from under the ground: *an oil well*

well-known /ˌwel 'nəʊn/ *adjective* famous: *a well-known writer*

well off /ˌwel 'ɒf/ *adjective* rich: *They are very well off and they live in a big house.*

went *form of* **go**[1]

wept *form of* **weep**

we're /wɪə(r)/ = we are

were *form of* **be**

weren't /wɜ:nt/ = were not

west /west/ *noun* (no plural) where the sun goes down in the evening: *Which way is west?* ○ *They live in the west of the country.*

west *adjective, adverb*: *West Africa* ○ *The town is five miles west of here.*

western /'westən/ *adjective* in or of the west of a place: *There will be storms in the western part of the country.*

wet /wet/ *adjective* (**wetter**, **wettest**) **1** covered in water or another liquid; not dry: *This towel is wet – can I have a dry one?* ○ *wet paint* ☛ picture on page A11 **2** with a lot of rain: *a wet day* ✪ opposite: **dry**

we've /wiv/ = we have

whale

whale /weɪl/ *noun* a very big animal that lives in the sea and looks like a fish

what /wɒt/ *pronoun, adjective* **1** a word that you use when you ask about somebody or something: *What's your name?* ○ *What are you reading?* ○ *What time is it?* ○ *What kind of music do you like?* **2** the thing that: *I don't know what this word means.* ○ *Tell me what to do.* **3** a word that you use to show surprise or other strong feelings: *What a terrible day!* ○ *What a beautiful picture!* **what about ...?** words that you use when you suggest something: *What about going to the cinema tonight?* **what ... for?** why?; for what use?: *What did you say that for?* ○ *What's this machine for?* **what is ... like?** words that you use when you want to know more about somebody or something: *'What's her brother like?' 'He's very nice.'* **what's on?** what television programme, film, etc is being shown?: *What's on TV tonight?*

what's up? what is wrong?: *You look sad. What's up?*

whatever /wɒtˈevə(r)/ *adjective* of any kind; any or every: *These animals eat whatever food they can find.*

whatever *pronoun* **1** anything or everything: *I'll do whatever I can to help you.* **2** it does not matter what: *Whatever you do, don't be late.*

what's /wɒts/ **1** = what is **2** = what has

wheat /wiːt/ *noun* (no plural) a plant with seeds (called **grain**) that we can make into flour

wheat

ear

wheel /wiːl/ *noun* a thing like a circle that turns round to move something. Cars and bicycles have wheels. ☛ picture at **car**

wheel *verb* (**wheels**, **wheeling**, **wheeled** /wiːld/) push along something that has wheels: *I wheeled my bicycle up the hill.*

wheelchair /ˈwiːltʃeə(r)/ *noun* a chair with wheels for somebody who cannot walk

when /wen/ *adverb* **1** at what time: *When did she arrive?* ○ *I don't know when his birthday is.* **2** at the time that: *I saw her in May, when she visited us.*

when *conjunction* at the time that: *It was raining when we left school.* ○ *He came when I called him.*

whenever /wenˈevə(r)/ *conjunction* **1** at any time: *Come and see us whenever you want.* **2** every time that: *Whenever I see her, she talks about her boyfriend.*

where /weə(r)/ *adverb, conjunction* **1** in or to what place: *Where do you live?* ○ *I asked her where she lived.* ○ *Where is she going?* **2** in which; at which: *This is the street where I live.*

whereas /ˌweərˈæz/ *conjunction* a word that you use between two different ideas: *John likes football, whereas I don't.*

wherever /weərˈevə(r)/ *adverb, conjunction* **1** at, in or to any place: *Sit wherever you like.* **2** a way of saying 'where' more strongly: *Wherever did I put my keys?*

whether /ˈweðə(r)/ *conjunction* if: *She asked me whether I spoke French.* ○ *I don't know whether to go or not.*

which /wɪtʃ/ *adjective, pronoun* **1** what person or thing: *Which colour do you like best – blue or green?* ○ *Which flat do you live in?* **2** a word that shows what person or thing: *Did you read the poem (which) Louise wrote?* **3** a word that you use before you say more about something: *He hasn't telephoned or written, which means that he isn't going to come.*

whichever /wɪtʃˈevə(r)/ *adjective, pronoun* any person or thing: *Here are two books – take whichever you want.*

while[1] /waɪl/ *conjunction* **1** during the time that; when: *While I was coming home from school I started to feel ill.* **2** at the same time as: *I listen to the radio while I'm eating my breakfast.*

while[2] /waɪl/ *noun* (no plural) some time: *Let's sit here for a while.* ○ *I'm going home in a while.*

whilst /waɪlst/ *conjunction* while: *He waited whilst I looked for my keys.*

whine /waɪn/ *verb* (**whines**, **whining**, **whined** /waɪnd/) make a long high sad sound: *The dog was whining outside the door.*

whip /wɪp/ *noun* a long piece of leather or rope with a handle, for hitting animals or people

whip *verb* (**whips**, **whipping**, **whipped** /wɪpt/) **1** hit an animal or a person with a whip: *The farmer whipped the horse to make it go faster.* **2** mix food very quickly with a fork, for example, until it is light and thick: *Whip the whites of two eggs.*

whirl /wɜːl/ *verb* (**whirls**, **whirling**, **whirled** /wɜːld/) move round and round very quickly: *The dancers whirled round the room.*

whisk /wɪsk/ *verb* (**whisks**, **whisking**, **whisked** /wɪskt/) **1** mix eggs or cream very quickly **2** move somebody or something very quickly: *The President was whisked away in a helicopter.*

whisk *noun* a tool that you use for

mixing eggs or cream

whisker /'wɪskə(r)/ *noun* one of the long hairs that grow near the mouth of cats, mice and other animals ☞ picture at **cat**

whisper /'wɪspə(r)/ *verb* (**whispers, whispering, whispered** /'wɪspəd/) speak very quietly: *He whispered so that he would not wake the baby up.*
whisper *noun*: *She spoke in a whisper.*

whistle /'wɪsl/ *noun* **1** a small musical instrument that makes a long high sound when you blow it: *The referee blew his whistle to end the match.* **2** the long high sound that you make when you blow air out between your lips
whistle *verb* (**whistles, whistling, whistled** /'wɪsld/) make a long high sound by blowing air out between your lips or through a whistle: *I saw Daniel and whistled to attract his attention.*

white /waɪt/ *adjective* (**whiter, whitest**) **1** with the colour of snow or milk **2** with a pale colour: *white people* ○ *white grapes*
white *noun* **1** (no plural) the colour of snow or milk: *She was dressed in white.* **2** (*plural* **whites**) a person with white skin **3** (*plural* **whites**) the part inside an egg that is round the yellow middle part

whiz /wɪz/ *verb* (**whizzes, whizzing, whizzed** /wɪzd/) move very quickly: *The bullet whizzed past his head.*

who /hu:/ *pronoun* **1** what person or people: *Who is that girl?* ○ *I don't know who did it.* **2** a word that shows what person or people: *He's the boy who sits next to me in school.* ○ *The people (who) I work with are very nice.*

who'd /hu:d/ **1** = who had **2** = who would

whoever /hu:'evə(r)/ *pronoun* **1** the person who; any person who: *Whoever broke the window must pay for it.* **2** a way of saying 'who' more strongly: *Whoever gave you those flowers?*

whole /həʊl/ *adjective* complete; with no parts missing: *I'm so hungry I could eat a whole cow!* ○ *We are going camping for a whole week.*
whole *noun* (no plural) **1** all of something: *I spent the whole of the weekend*

working. **2** a thing that is complete: *Two halves make a whole.* **on the whole** in general: *On the whole, I think it's a good idea.*

who'll /hu:l/ = who will

whom /hu:m/ *pronoun* **1** what person or people: *To whom did you give the money?* **2** a word that you use to say what person or people: *She's the woman (whom) I met on the train.* ✪ **Who** is the word that we usually use.

whooping cough /'hu:pɪŋ kɒf/ *noun* (no plural) a serious illness, especially of children. If you have whooping cough, you make a loud noise when you breathe in after every cough.

who're /'hu:ə(r)/ = who are

who's /hu:z/ **1** = who is **2** = who has

whose /hu:z/ *adjective, pronoun* of which person: *Whose key is this?* ○ *That's the boy whose sister is a singer.*

who've /hu:v/ = who have

why /waɪ/ *adverb* for what reason: *Why are you late?* ○ *I don't know why she's angry.* **why not** words that you use to say that something is a good idea: *Why not ask Kate to go with you?*

wicked /'wɪkɪd/ *adjective* very bad: *Stealing is a wicked thing to do.*

wide /waɪd/ *adjective* (**wider, widest**) **1** far from one side to the other: *a wide road* ✪ opposite: **narrow** ☞ picture on page A10 **2** You use 'wide' to say or ask how far something is from one side to the other: *The table was 2m wide.* ○ *How wide is the river?* ☞ picture on page A5 **3** completely open: *wide eyes*
wide *adverb* completely; as far or as much as possible: *Open your mouth wide.* ○ *I'm wide awake!* **wide apart** a long way from each other: *She stood with her feet wide apart.*

widen /'waɪdn/ *verb* (**widens, widening, widened** /'waɪdnd/) become wider; make something wider: *They are widening the road.*

widespread /'waɪdspred/ *adjective* If something is widespread, it is happening in many places: *The disease is becoming more widespread.*

widow /'wɪdəʊ/ *noun* a woman whose husband is dead

widower /ˈwɪdəʊə(r)/ *noun* a man whose wife is dead

width /wɪdθ/ *noun* how far it is from one side of something to the other; how wide something is: *The room is five metres in width.* ☞ picture on page A5

wife /waɪf/ *noun* (*plural* **wives** /waɪvz/) the woman that a man is married to

wig /wɪg/ *noun* a covering for your head made of hair that is not your own

wild /waɪld/ *adjective* (**wilder**, **wildest**) **1** Wild plants and animals live or grow in nature, not with people: *wild pigs* **2** excited; not controlled: *She was wild with anger.*

wildlife /ˈwaɪldlaɪf/ *noun* (no plural) animals and plants in nature

will[1] /wɪl/ *modal verb* **1** a word that shows the future: *Do you think she will come tomorrow?* **2** a word that you use when you agree or promise to do something: *I'll* (= I will) *carry your bag.* **3** a word that you use when you ask somebody to do something: *Will you open the window, please?*

○ The negative form of 'will' is **will not** or the short form **won't** /wəʊnt/:
They won't be there.
The short form of 'will' is **'ll**. We often use this:
You'll (=you will) *be late.*
He'll (=he will) *drive you to the station.*
☞ Look at the Note on page 195 to find out more about **modal verbs**.

will[2] /wɪl/ *noun* **1** (no plural) the power of your mind that makes you choose, decide and do things: *She has a very strong will and nobody can stop her doing what she wants to do.* **2** (no plural) what somebody wants: *The man made him get into the car against his will* (= when he did not want to). **3** (*plural* **wills**) a piece of paper that says who will have your money, house, etc when you die: *My grandmother left me some money in her will.*

willing /ˈwɪlɪŋ/ *adjective* ready and happy to do something: *I'm willing to lend you some money.*

willingly *adverb*: *I'll willingly help you.*

willingness /ˈwɪlɪŋnəs/ *noun* (no plural) *willingness to help*

win /wɪn/ *verb* (**wins**, **winning**, **won** /wʌn/, **has won**) **1** be the best or the first in a game, race or competition: *Who won the race?* ○ *Henry won and I was second.* ☻ opposite: **lose 2** receive something because you did well or tried hard: *I won a prize in the competition.* ○ *Who won the gold medal?* ☻ Be careful! You **earn** (not **win**) money by working.

win *noun*: *Our team has had five wins this year.*

wind[1] /wɪnd/ *noun* air that moves: *The wind blew his hat off.* ○ *strong winds*

windy *adjective* (**windier**, **windiest**) with a lot of wind: *It's very windy today!*

wind[2] /waɪnd/ *verb* (**winds**, **winding**, **wound** /waʊnd/, **has wound**) **1** make something long go round and round another thing: *The nurse wound the bandage around my arm.* **2** turn a key or handle to make something work or move: *The clock will stop if you don't wind it up.* ○ *The driver wound his car window down.* **3** A road or river that winds has a lot of bends and turns: *The path winds through the forest.*

window /ˈwɪndəʊ/ *noun* an opening in a wall or in a car, for example, with glass in it: *It was cold, so I closed the window.* ○ *She looked out of the window.*

window-pane /ˈwɪndəʊ peɪn/ *noun* a piece of glass in a window

windowsill /ˈwɪndəʊsɪl/, **window ledge**/ˈwɪndəʊ ledʒ/ *noun* a shelf under a window

windscreen /ˈwɪndskriːn/ *noun* the big window at the front of a car ☞ picture at **car**

windscreen wiper /ˈwɪndskriːn ˌwaɪpə(r)/ *noun* a thing that cleans rain and dirt off the windscreen while you are driving

windsurfing /ˈwɪndsɜːfɪŋ/ *noun* (no plural) the sport of moving over water on a special board with a sail ☻ You can say **go windsurfing**.

windsurfer *noun* **1** a special board

with a sail. You stand on it as it moves over the water. **2** a person who rides on a board like this

wine /waɪn/ *noun* an alcoholic drink. Wine is made from grapes: *red wine* ○ *white wine*

wing /wɪŋ/ *noun* the part of a bird, an insect or an aeroplane that helps it to fly ☞ picture at **bird**

wink /wɪŋk/ *verb* (**winks, winking, winked** /wɪŋkt/) close and open one eye quickly to make a friendly or secret sign: *She winked at me.*

wink *noun*: *He gave me a wink.*

winner /ˈwɪnə(r)/ *noun* a person or animal that wins a game, race or competition: *The winner was given a prize.* ✪ opposite: **loser**

winning /ˈwɪnɪŋ/ *adjective* that wins a game, race or competition: *the winning team*

winter /ˈwɪntə(r)/ *noun* in cool countries, the coldest part of the year: *It often snows in winter in the mountains.*

wipe /waɪp/ *verb* (**wipes, wiping, wiped** /waɪpt/) make something clean or dry with a cloth: *The waitress wiped the table.* ○ *I washed my hands and wiped them on a towel.* **wipe off** take away something by wiping: *She wiped the writing off the blackboard.* **wipe out** destroy a place completely, or kill a lot of people: *The bombs wiped out many villages.* **wipe up** take away liquid by wiping with a cloth: *I wiped up the milk on the floor.*

wipe *noun*: *He gave the table a quick wipe.*

wire /ˈwaɪə(r)/ *noun* a long piece of very thin metal: *electrical wires* ○ *a piece of wire.*

wisdom /ˈwɪzdəm/ *noun* (no plural) knowing and understanding a lot about many things; being wise: *Some people think that old age brings wisdom.*

wise /waɪz/ *adjective* (**wiser, wisest**) A person who is wise knows and understands a lot about many things: *a wise old man* ○ *You made a wise choice.*

wisely *adverb*: *Many people wisely stayed at home in the bad weather.*

wish¹ /wɪʃ/ *verb* (**wishes, wishing,**

wished /wɪʃt/) **1** want something that is not possible or that probably will not happen: *I wish I could fly!* ○ *I wish I had passed the exam!* ○ *I wish I were rich.* **2** say that you hope somebody will have something: *I wished her a happy birthday.* **3** want to do or have something: *I wish to see the manager.* ✪ It is more usual to say **want** or **would like. wish for something** say to yourself that you want something and hope that it will happen: *You can't have everything you wish for.*

wish² /wɪʃ/ *noun* (*plural* **wishes**) a feeling that you want something: *I have no wish to go.* **best wishes** words that you write at the end of a letter, before your name, to show that you hope somebody is well and happy: *See you soon. Best wishes, Lucy.* **make a wish** say to yourself that you want something and hope that it will happen: *Close your eyes and make a wish!*

wit /wɪt/ *noun* (no plural) speaking or writing in a clever and funny way

with /wɪð/ *preposition* **1** having or carrying: *a man with grey hair* ○ *a house with a garden* ○ *a woman with a suitcase* **2** a word that shows people or things are together: *I live with my parents.* ○ *Mix the flour with milk.* ○ *I agree with you.* **3** using: *I cut it with a knife.* ○ *Fill the bottle with water.* **4** against: *I played draughts with my sister.* **5** because of: *Her hands were shaking with nerves.*

withdraw /wɪðˈdrɔː/ *verb* (**withdraws, withdrawing, withdrew** /wɪðˈdruː/, has **withdrawn** /wɪðˈdrɔːn/) **1** take something out or away: *I withdrew some money from my bank account.* **2** move back or away: *The army withdrew from the town.* **3** say that you will not take part in something: *Robert has withdrawn from the race.*

wither /ˈwɪðə(r)/ *verb* (**withers, withering, withered** /ˈwɪðəd/) If a plant withers, it becomes dry and dies: *The plants withered in the hot sun.*

within /wɪˈðɪn/ *preposition* **1** inside: *There are 400 prisoners within the prison walls.* **2** before the end of: *I will be back within an hour.* **3** not further than: *We live within a mile of the station.*

without /wɪ'ðaʊt/ *preposition* **1** not having, showing or using something: *I went out without any money so I couldn't buy anything to eat.* ○ *coffee without milk* **2** not being with somebody or something: *He left without me.* **do without** manage when something is not there: *There isn't any tea so we will have to do without.* **without doing something** not doing something: *They left without saying goodbye.*

witness /'wɪtnəs/ *noun* (*plural* **witnesses**) **1** a person who sees something happen and can tell other people about it later: *There were two witnesses to the accident.* **2** a person in a court of law who tells what he/she saw

witness *verb* (**witnesses**, **witnessing**, **witnessed** /'wɪtnəst/) see something happen: *She witnessed a murder.*

witty /'wɪti/ *adjective* (**wittier**, **wittiest**) clever and funny: *a witty answer*

wives *plural of* **wife**

wobble /'wɒbl/ *verb* (**wobbles**, **wobbling**, **wobbled** /'wɒbld/) move a little from side to side: *That chair wobbles when you sit on it.*

wobbly *adjective* If something is wobbly, it moves a little from side to side: *My legs feel wobbly.*

woke, **woken** *forms of* **wake**

woman /'wʊmən/ *noun* (*plural* **women** /'wɪmɪn/) a grown-up female person: *men, women and children*

womb /wu:m/ *noun* the part inside a woman or a female animal where a baby grows before it is born

won *form of* **win**

wonder[1] /'wʌndə(r)/ *verb* (**wonders**, **wondering**, **wondered** /'wʌndəd/) ask yourself something; want to know something: *I wonder what that noise is.* ○ *I wonder why he didn't come.* **I wonder if** words that you use to ask a question politely: *I wonder if you could help me.*

wonder[2] /'wʌndə(r)/ *noun* **1** (no plural) a feeling that you have when you see or hear something very strange, surprising or beautiful: *The children looked up in wonder at the big*

elephant. **2** (*plural* **wonders**) something that gives you this feeling: *the wonders of modern medicine* **it's a wonder** it is surprising that: *It's a wonder you weren't killed in the accident.* **no wonder** it is not surprising: *She didn't sleep last night, so no wonder she's tired.*

wonderful /'wʌndəfl/ *adjective* very good; excellent: *What a wonderful present!* ○ *This food is wonderful.*

won't /wəʊnt/ = **will not**

wood /wʊd/ *noun* **1** (no plural) the hard part of a tree: *Put some more wood on the fire.* ○ *The table is made of wood.* **2** (*also* **woods**) a big group of trees, smaller than a forest.

wooden /'wʊdn/ *adjective* made of wood: *a wooden box*

wool /wʊl/ *noun* (no plural) **1** the soft thick hair of sheep **2** thread or cloth that is made from the hair of sheep: *a ball of wool* ○ *This blanket is made of wool.* ☞ picture at **knit**

woollen /'wʊlən/ *adjective* made of wool: *woollen socks*

woolly *adjective* made of wool, or like wool: *a woolly hat*

word /wɜːd/ *noun* **1** (*plural* **words**) a sound that you make or a letter or group of letters that you write, that has a meaning: *What's the French word for 'dog'?* ○ *Do you know the words of this song?* **2** (no plural) a promise: *She gave me her word that she wouldn't tell anyone.* **have a word with somebody** speak to somebody: *Can I have a word with you?* **in other words** saying the same thing in a different way: *Joseph doesn't like hard work – in other words, he's lazy!* **keep your word** do what you promised: *Winnie said she would come, and she kept her word.* **take somebody's word for it** believe what somebody says **word for word** using exactly the same words: *Julius repeated word for word what you told him.*

wore *form of* **wear**[1]

work[1] /wɜːk/ *noun* **1** (no plural) doing or making something: *Digging is hard work.* ○ *She's lazy – she never does any work.* **2** (no plural) what you do to earn money; a job: *I'm looking for work.* ○ *What time do you start work?* **3** (no plural) the place where you have a job: *I phoned him at work.* ○ *I'm not going to work today.* **4** (no plural) something that you make or do: *The teacher marked our work.* ○ *The artist only sells her work to friends.* **5** (*plural* **works**) a book, painting or piece of music: *the works of Shakespeare* ○ *a work of art* **6 works** (plural) a place where people make things with machines: *the steelworks* **at work** doing some work: *The group are at work on* (= making) *a new album.* **get to work** start doing something: *Let's get to work on this washing-up.* **out of work** If you are out of work, you do not have a job that you are paid to do: *How long have you been out of work?*

work[2] /wɜːk/ *verb* (**works**, **working**, **worked** /wɜːkt/) **1** do or make something; be busy: *You will need to work harder if you want to pass the exam.* **2** do something as a job and get money for it: *Susan works for a national newspaper.* ○ *I work at the car factory.* **3** go correctly or do something correctly: *We can't listen to the radio – it isn't working.* ○ *How does this computer work?* **4** make something do something: *Can you show me how to work this machine?* **5** have the result you wanted: *I don't think your plan will work.* **work out** have the result you wanted: *I hope your plans work out.* **work something out** find the answer to something: *We worked out the cost of the new equipment.* ○ *Why did she do it? I can't work it out.*

workbook /ˈwɜːkbʊk/ *noun* a book where you write answers to questions, that you use when you are studying something

worker /ˈwɜːkə(r)/ *noun* a person who works: *factory workers* ○ *an office worker*

workman /ˈwɜːkmən/ *noun* (*plural* **workmen** /ˈwɜːkmən/) a man who works with his hands to build or repair something

worksheet /ˈwɜːkʃiːt/ *noun* a piece of paper where you write answers to questions, that you use when you are studying something

workshop /ˈwɜːkʃɒp/ *noun* **1** a place where people make or repair things **2** a time when people meet and work together to learn about something

world /wɜːld/ *noun* **1** (no plural) the earth with all its countries and people: *a map of the world* ○ *Which is the biggest city in the world?* **2** (*plural* **worlds**) all the people who do the same kind of thing: *the world of politics* **think the world of somebody** or **something** like somebody or something very much: *She thinks the world of her grandchildren.*

world-famous /ˌwɜːld ˈfeɪməs/ *adjective* known everywhere in the world: *a world-famous writer*

worldwide /ˌwɜːldˈwaɪd/ *adjective* that you find everywhere in the world: *Pollution is a worldwide problem.*

worm /wɜːm/ *noun* a small animal with a long thin body and no legs. Worms live in the ground or in other animals.

worn *form of* **wear**[1]

worn out /ˌwɔːn ˈaʊt/ *adjective* **1** old and completely finished because you have used it a lot: *I threw the shoes away because they were worn out.* **2** very tired: *He's worn out after his long journey.*

worried /ˈwʌrid/ *adjective* unhappy because you think that something bad will happen or has happened: *Agnes is worried that she's going to fail the exam.* ○ *I'm worried about my brother – he looks ill.*

worry[1] /ˈwʌri/ *verb* (**worries**, **worrying**, **worried** /ˈwʌrid/, **has worried**) **1** feel that something bad will happen or has happened: *I worried when Mark didn't come home at the usual time.* ○ *Don't worry if you don't know the answer.* ○ *There's nothing to worry about.* **2** make somebody feel that something bad will happen or has happened: *Philip's illness is worrying his parents.*

worry[2] /ˈwʌri/ *noun* **1** (no plural) a feeling that something bad will happen or has happened: *Her face showed signs of worry.* **2** (*plural* **worries**) a problem; something that makes you feel worried: *I have a lot of worries.*

worse /wɜːs/ *adjective* (**bad**, **worse**,

worst) 1 more bad; less good: *The weather today is worse than yesterday.* ○ *His singing is bad but his dancing is even worse.* **2** more ill: *If you get worse, you must go to the doctor's.*

worse *adverb* more badly

worship /ˈwɜːʃɪp/ *verb* (**worships**, **worshipping**, **worshipped** /ˈwɜːʃɪpt/) **1** show that you believe in God or a god by praying: *Christians worship in a church.* **2** love somebody very much or think that somebody is wonderful: *She worships her grandchildren.*

worship *noun* (no plural) *A mosque is a place of worship.*

worst /wɜːst/ *adjective* (**bad**, **worse**, **worst**) most bad: *He's the worst player in the team!* ○ *the worst day of my life*

worst *adverb* most badly: *Jane played badly, but I played worst of all.*

worst *noun* (no plural) the most bad thing or person: *I'm the worst in the class at grammar.* **if the worst comes to the worst** if something very bad happens: *If the worst comes to the worst and I fail the exam, I'll take it again next year.*

worth[1] /wɜːθ/ *adjective* **1** with a value of: *That house is worth a lot of money.* **2** good or useful enough to do or have: *Is this film worth seeing?* ○ *It's not worth asking Marion for money – she never has any.*

worth[2] /wɜːθ/ *noun* (no plural) value: *This painting is of little worth.* **worth of** how much of something an amount of money will buy: *I'd like 500 shillings' worth of petrol, please.*

worthless /ˈwɜːθləs/ *adjective* with no value or use: *A cheque is worthless if you don't sign it.*

worthwhile /ˌwɜːθˈwaɪl/ *adjective* good or useful enough for the time that you spend or the work that you do: *The hard work was worthwhile because I passed the exam.*

would /wʊd/ *modal verb* **1** the word for 'will' in the past: *He said he would come.* **2** a word that you use to talk about a situation that is not real: *If I had as much money as I wanted, I would buy a big house.* **3** a word that you use

to ask something in a polite way: *Would you close the door, please?* **4** a word that you use to talk about something that happened many times in the past: *When I was young, I would go to the river every day.* **would like** want; words that you use when you ask or say something in a polite way: *Would you like a cup of tea?* ○ *I would like to go to America.*

○ The negative form of 'would' is **would not** or the short form **wouldn't** /ˈwʊdnt/:

He wouldn't help me.

The short form of 'would' is **'d**. We often use this:

I'd (=I would) *like to meet her.*

They'd (=they would) *help if they had the time.*

Look at the note on page 195 to find out more about **modal verbs**.

would've /ˈwʊdəv/ = would have

wound[1] *form of* wind[2]

wound[2] /wuːnd/ *verb* (**wounds**, **wounding**, **wounded**) hurt somebody: *The bullet wounded him in the leg.*

wound *noun* a hurt place in your body made by something like a gun or a knife: *a knife wound*

wove, **woven** *forms of* **weave**

wow /waʊ/ a word that shows surprise and pleasure: *Wow! What a lovely car!*

wrap /ræp/ *verb* (**wraps**, **wrapping**, **wrapped** /ræpt/) put paper or cloth around somebody or something: *The baby was wrapped in a blanket.* ○ *She wrapped the glass up in paper.* ○ opposite: **unwrap**

wrapper /ˈræpə(r)/ *noun* a piece of paper or plastic that covers something like a sweet or a packet of cigarettes: *Don't throw your wrappers on the floor!*

wrapping /ˈræpɪŋ/ *noun* a piece of paper or plastic that covers a present or something that you buy: *I took the new shirt out of its wrapping.*

wrapping paper /ˈræpɪŋ peɪpə(r)/ *noun* (no plural) special paper that you use to wrap presents

wreath /riːθ/ *noun* (*plural* **wreaths**) a circle of flowers or leaves: *She put a* *wreath on the grave.*

wreck /rek/ *noun* a ship, car or plane that has been very badly damaged in an accident: *a shipwreck at sea*

wreck *verb* (**wrecks**, **wrecking**, **wrecked** /rekt/) break or destroy something completely: *The fire wrecked the hotel.*

wreckage /'rekɪdʒ/ *noun* (no plural) the broken parts of something that has been badly damaged: *They found a child in the wreckage of the plane.*

wrestle /'resl/ *verb* (**wrestles**, **wrestling**, **wrestled** /'resld/) fight by trying to throw somebody to the ground. People often wrestle as a sport.

wrestler *noun* a person who wrestles as a sport

wrestling *noun* (no plural) the sport where two people fight and try to throw each other to the ground: *a wrestling match*

wriggle /'rɪgl/ *verb* (**wriggles**, **wriggling**, **wriggled** /'rɪgld/) turn your body quickly from side to side, like a worm: *The teacher told the children to stop wriggling.*

wring /rɪŋ/ *verb* (**wrings**, **wringing**, **wrung** /rʌŋ/, **has wrung**) press and twist something with your hands to make water come out: *He wrung the towel out and put it outside to dry.*

wrinkle /'rɪŋkl/ *noun* a small line in something, for example in the skin of your face: *My grandmother has a lot of wrinkles.*

wrinkled /'rɪŋkld/ *adjective* with a lot of wrinkles: *His face is very wrinkled.*

wrist /rɪst/ *noun* the part of your body where your arm joins your hand ➥ picture on page A4

write /raɪt/ *verb* (**writes**, **writing**, **wrote** /rəʊt/, **has written** /'rɪtn/) **1** make letters or words on paper using a pen or pencil: *Write your name at the top of the page.* ○ *He can't read or write.* **2** write and send a letter to somebody:

My mother writes to me every week. ○ *I wrote her a postcard.* **3** make a story, book, etc: *Meja Mwangi writes books.*

write down write something on paper, so that you can remember it: *I wrote down his telephone number.*

writer /'raɪtə(r)/ *noun* a person who writes books, stories, etc: *Charles Dickens was a famous writer.*

writing /'raɪtɪŋ/ *noun* (no plural) **1** words that somebody puts on paper: *I can't read your writing – it's so small.* **2** putting words on paper: *Writing is slower than telephoning.* **in writing** written on paper: *They have offered me the job on the telephone but not in writing.*

writing paper /'raɪtɪŋ peɪpə(r)/ *noun* (no plural) paper for writing letters on

written *form of* **write**

wrong[1] /rɒŋ/ *adjective* **1** not true or not correct: *She gave me the wrong key, so I couldn't open the door.* ○ *This clock is wrong.* ✪ opposite: **right 2** bad, or not what the law allows: *Stealing is wrong.* ○ *I haven't done anything wrong.* ✪ opposite: **right 3** not the best: *We're late because we took the wrong road.* ✪ opposite: **right 4** not as it should be, or not working well: *There's something wrong with my bike – it's making a strange noise.* ○ *'What's wrong with Mrs Rono?' 'She's got a bad headache.'*

wrong *adverb* not correctly; not right: *You've spelt my name wrong.* **go wrong 1** stop working well: *The television has gone wrong – can you mend it?* **2** not happen as you hoped or wanted: *All our plans went wrong.*

wrong[2] /rɒŋ/ *noun* (no plural) what is bad or not right: *Babies don't know the difference between right and wrong.*

wrongly /'rɒŋli/ *adverb* not correctly: *The letter didn't arrive because it was wrongly addressed.*

wrote *form of* **write**

wrung *form of* **wring**

Xmas /ˈeksməs/ *short for* **Christmas** ✪ Xmas is used mainly in writing.

X-ray /ˈeksreɪ/ *noun* a photograph of the inside of your body that is made by using a special light that you cannot see: *The doctor took an X-ray of my arm to see if it was broken.*

X-ray *verb* (**X-rays, X-raying, X-rayed** /ˈeksreɪd/) take a photograph using an X-ray machine: *She had her leg X-rayed.*

yacht /jɒt/ *noun* **1** a boat with **sails** that is used for racing **2** a big boat with a motor: *a millionaire's yacht*

yam /jæm/ *noun* a sweet vegetable that grows under the ground

yard[1] /jɑːd/ *noun* a measure of length (= 91 centimetres). There are three **feet** or thirty-six **inches** in a yard. ✪ The short way of writing 'yard' is **yd.** ☞ Note at **foot**

yard[2] /jɑːd/ *noun* a piece of hard ground next to a building, with a fence or wall around it: *The children were playing in the school yard.* ○ *a farmyard*

yawn /jɔːn/ *verb* (**yawns, yawning, yawned** /jɔːnd/) open your mouth wide because you are tired

yawn *noun*: *'I'm going to bed now,' she said with a yawn.*

yaws /jɔːz/ *noun* (no plural) a serious illness that makes you get large red lumps on your skin. You can get yaws if you touch a person who has got it.

yeah /jeə/ *yes* ✪ This is an informal word.

year /jɪə(r)/ *noun* **1** a time of 365 or 366 days from 1 January to 31 December. A year has twelve **months**: *'In which year were you born?' 'In 1976.'* ○ *I left school last year.* **2** any time of twelve months: *I have known Chris for three years.* ○ *My son is five years old.* ○ *I have a five-year-old son.* ○ *a two-year-old* ✪ Be careful! You can say: *She's ten.* or: *She's ten years old.* (BUT NOT : *She's ten years.*) **all year round** through all the year: *The swimming pool is open all year round.*

yearly /ˈjɪəli/ *adjective, adverb* that happens or comes every year or once a year: *a yearly visit* ○ *We meet twice yearly.*

yeast /jiːst/ *noun* (no plural) stuff that you use for making bread rise

yell /jel/ *verb* (**yells, yelling, yelled** /jeld/) shout loudly: *'Look out!' she yelled as the car came towards them.*

yell *noun*: *He gave a yell of pain.*

yellow /ˈjeləʊ/ *adjective* with the colour of a lemon or of butter: *She was wearing a yellow shirt.*

yellow *noun*: *Yellow is my favourite colour*

yellow fever *noun* /ˈjeləʊ fiːvə/ (no plural) an illness that makes your eyes yellow and makes you feel very hot. You get yellow fever from mosquitoes.

yes /jes/ a word that you use for answering a question. You use 'yes' to agree, to say that something is true, or to say that you would like something: *'Have you got the key?' 'Yes, here it is.'* ○ *'Would you like some coffee?' 'Yes, please.'*

yesterday /ˈjestədeɪ/ *adverb, noun* (no plural) (on) the day before today: *I saw Tom yesterday.* ○ *I phoned you yesterday afternoon but you were out.* ○ *I sent the letter the day before yesterday.*

yet[1] /jet/ *adverb* **1** until now: *I haven't finished the book yet.* ○ *Have you seen that film yet?* ☞ Note at **already** **2** now; as early as this: *You don't need to go yet – it's only seven o'clock.* **3** in the future: *They may win yet.* **as yet** until now: *As yet, I haven't met her.* **yet again** once more: *John is late yet again!*

yet[2] /jet/ *conjunction* but; however: *We arrived home tired yet happy.*

yoghurt /ˈjɒɡət/ *noun* thick liquid food made from milk: *strawberry yoghurt* ○ *Do you want a yoghurt?*

yolk /jəʊk/ *noun* the yellow part in an egg

you /juː, ju/ *pronoun* **1** the person or people that I am speaking to: *You are late.* ○ *I saw you yesterday.* **2** any person; a person: *You can buy stamps at a post office.*

you'd /juːd/ **1** = you had **2** = you would

you'll /juːl/ = you will

young[1] /jʌŋ/ *adjective* (**younger** /ˈjʌŋɡə(r)/, **youngest** /ˈjʌŋɡɪst/) in the early part of life; not old: *They have two young children.* ○ *You're younger than me.* ☞ picture on page A10

young[2] /jʌŋ/ *noun* (plural) **1** baby animals: *Birds build nests for their young.* **2 the young** (plural) children and young people: *school books for the young*

your /jɔː(r)/ *adjective* of you: *Where is your car?* ○ *Do you all have your books?* ○ *Show me your hands.*

you're /jɔː(r)/ = you are

yours /jɔːz/ *pronoun* **1** something that belongs to you: *Is this pen yours or mine?* **2 Yours** a word that you write at the end of a letter: *Yours sincerely …* ○ *Yours faithfully …*

yourself /jɔːˈself/ *pronoun* (plural **yourselves** /jɔːˈselvz/) **1** a word that shows 'you' when I have just talked about you: *Did you hurt yourself?* ○ *Buy yourselves a drink.* **2** a word that makes 'you' stronger: *Did you make this cake yourself?* ○ '*Who told you?*' '*You told me yourself!*' **by yourself**, **by yourselves 1** alone; without other people: *Do you live by yourself?* **2** without help: *You can't carry all those bags by yourself.*

youth /juːθ/ *noun* **1** (no plural) the part of your life when you are young: *He spent his youth in Tanzania and came to Kenya when he was eighteen.* ○ *She was very poor in her youth.* **2** (plural **youths** /juːðz/) a boy or young man **3 the youth** (plural) young people: *the youth of this country*

you've /juːv/ = you have

Zz

zebra /ˈzebrə/ *noun* an African wild animal like a horse, with black and white lines on its body

zebra crossing /ˌzebrə ˈkrɒsɪŋ/ *noun* a black and white path across a road. Cars must stop there to let people cross the road safely.

zebu /ˈziːbuː/ *noun* a kind of cattle. A zebu has long horns and a high part (called a **hump**) on its back.

zero /ˈzɪərəʊ/ *noun* **1** the number 0 **2** the point between + and - on a thermometer: *The temperature is five degrees below zero.*

zigzag /ˈzɪɡzæɡ/ *noun* a line that goes sharply up and down

zip /zɪp/ *noun* a long metal or plastic thing with a small part that you pull to close and open things like clothes and bags

zip *verb* (**zips**, **zipping**, **zipped** /zɪpt/)
zip up close something with a zip: *She zipped up her dress.*

zone /zəʊn/ *noun* a place where something special happens: *Do not enter the danger zone!*

zoo /zuː/ *noun* (*plural* **zoos**) a place where you can see wild animals in cages or behind fences

zoom /zuːm/ *verb* (**zooms**, **zooming**, **zoomed** /zuːmd/) move very fast: *Mark zoomed past in his car.*

Irregular verbs

Infinitive	Past tense	Past participle
be	was, were	been
bear	bore	borne
beat	beat	beaten
become	became	become
begin	began	begun
bend	bent	bent
bet	bet, betted	bet, betted
bind	bound	bound
bite	bit	bitten
bleed	bled	bled
blow	blew	blown
break	broke	broken
breed	bred	bred
bring	brought	brought
broadcast	broadcast	broadcast
build	built	built
burn	burnt, burned	burnt, burned
burst	burst	burst
buy	bought	bought
catch	caught	caught
choose	chose	chosen
cling	clung	clung
come	came	come
cost	cost	cost
creep	crept	crept
cut	cut	cut
deal	dealt	dealt
dig	dug	dug
do	did	done
draw	drew	drawn
dream	dreamt, dreamed	dreamt, dreamed
drink	drank	drunk
drive	drove	driven
eat	ate	eaten
fall	fell	fallen
feed	fed	fed
feel	felt	felt
fight	fought	fought
find	found	found
flee	fled	fled
fling	flung	flung
fly	flew	flown
forbid	forbade	forbidden
forget	forgot	forgotten
forgive	forgave	forgiven
freeze	froze	frozen
get	got	got
give	gave	given
go	went	gone

Infinitive	Past tense	Past participle
grind	ground	ground
grow	grew	grown
hang	hung, hanged	hung, hanged
have	had	had
hear	heard	heard
hide	hid	hidden
hit	hit	hit
hold	held	held
hurt	hurt	hurt
keep	kept	kept
kneel	knelt, kneeled	knelt, kneeled
know	knew	known
lay	laid	laid
lead	led	led
lean	leant, leaned	leant, leaned
leap	leapt, leaped	leapt, leaped
learn	learnt, learned	learnt, learned
leave	left	left
lend	lent	lent
let	let	let
lie	lay	lain
light	lit, lighted	lit, lighted
lose	lost	lost
make	made	made
mean	meant	meant
meet	met	met
mislead	misled	misled
mistake	mistook	mistaken
misunderstand	misunderstood	misunderstood
mow	mowed	mown
overhear	overheard	overheard
oversleep	overslept	overslept
overtake	overtook	overtaken
pay	paid	paid
prove	proved	proved, proven
put	put	put
read	read	read
repay	repaid	repaid
ride	rode	ridden
ring	rang	rung
rise	rose	risen
run	ran	run
saw	sawed	sawn
say	said	said
see	saw	seen
seek	sought	sought
sell	sold	sold
send	sent	sent
set	set	set
sew	sewed	sewed, sewn
shake	shook	shaken
shed	shed	shed
shine	shone	shone
shoot	shot	shot

Infinitive	Past tense	Past participle
show	showed	shown, showed
shrink	shrank	shrunk
shut	shut	shut
sing	sang	sung
sink	sank	sunk
sit	sat	sat
sleep	slept	slept
slide	slid	slid
sling	slung	slung
slit	slit	slit
smell	smelt, smelled	smelt, smelled
sow	sowed	sown, sowed
speak	spoke	spoken
speed	sped, speeded	sped, speeded
spell	spelt, spelled	spelt, spelled
spend	spent	spent
spill	spilt, spilled	spilt, spilled
spin	spun	spun
spit	spat	spat
split	split	split
spoil	spoilt, spoiled	spoilt, spoiled
spread	spread	spread
spring	sprang	sprung
stand	stood	stood
steal	stole	stolen
stick	stuck	stuck
sting	stung	stung
stink	stank	stunk
stride	strode	stridden
strike	struck	struck
swear	swore	sworn
sweep	swept	swept
swell	swelled	swollen, swelled
swim	swam	swum
swing	swung	swung
take	took	taken
teach	taught	taught
tear	tore	torn
tell	told	told
think	thought	thought
throw	threw	thrown
thrust	thrust	thrust
tread	trod	trodden
understand	understood	understood
undo	undid	undone
upset	upset	upset
wake	woke	woken
wear	wore	worn
weave	wove	woven
weep	wept	wept
win	won	won
wind	wound	wound
wring	wrung	wrung
write	wrote	written

Notes

Notes

Notes

Notes

Notes

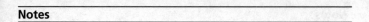

Notes

Notes

Notes

Notes